D1446324

Italian Foreign Policy 1870–1940

FOREIGN POLICIES OF THE GREAT POWERS
Edited by C. J. Lowe

The Reluctant Imperialists   C. J. Lowe

Vol. I British Foreign Policy 1879–1902

Vol. II The Documents

The Mirage of Power   C. J. Lowe and M. L. Dockrill

Vol. I British Foreign Policy 1902–14

Vol. II British Foreign Policy 1914–22

Vol. III The Documents

From Sadowa to Sarajevo: The Foreign Policy
of Austria–Hungary, 1866–1914   F. R. Bridge

The Foreign Policy of France from 1915 to 1945   J. Néré

Italian
Foreign Policy
1870–1940

C. J. Lowe

Professor of History,
University of Alberta

and

F. Marzari

Late Professor of Strategic Studies,
University of British Columbia

Routledge & Kegan Paul
London and Boston

First published in 1975
by Routledge & Kegan Paul Ltd
Broadway House, 68–74 Carter Lane,
London EC4V 5EL and
9 Park Street,
Boston, Mass. 02108, USA
Set in 'Monotype' Garamond
and printed in Great Britain by
W & J Mackay Limited, Chatham
© Cedric Lowe and the estate of Frank Marzari 1975

ISBN 0 7100 7987 7

Contents

Contents

Contents

Acknowledgments

The authors wish to acknowledge the kind permission of the officials of the Public Record Office, London, the Ministero degli Affari Esteri, Rome, and the Haus-, Hof-, und Staatsarchiv, Vienna, to make use of archives within their care.

Material from other sources is reproduced by kind permission of the following: Oxford University Press for *Documents on International Affairs 1928, 1933, 1934, 1935* and *1936*, published under the auspices of the Royal Institute of International Affairs; the Hamlyn Publishing Group for *Ciano's Diplomatic Papers* edited by Malcolm Muggeridge; Associated Book Publishers and Casa Editrice Licinio Cappelli for *Ciano's Diary 1937–8*; the *Chicago Daily News* for *Ciano's Diary 1939–43*; Arnoldo Mondadori Editore for *La guerra diplomatica* by Luigi Aldrovandi-Marescotti and *Diario 1914–18* by Fernando Martini; Giuseppe Laterza e Figli for *Storia della politica estera italiana dal 1870 al 1896* by F. Chabod and for Sidney Sonnino, *Diary*, edited by Benjamin Brown.

Transcripts of Crown Copyright material in the Public Record Office, London, and extracts from *Documents on German Foreign Policy Series C and D* appear by permission of the Controller of Her Majesty's Stationery Office. Quotations from the Sonnino Papers appear by permission of Xerox University Microfilms.

Abbreviations

AHR   *American Historical Review*
AMEI Ministero degli Affari Esteri, Rome
ASC   Archivio di Stato Centrale, Rome
BD   British Documents on the Origins of the War
BM   British Museum
Cab.   Cabinet Papers, Public Record Office
DBFP Documents on British Foreign Policy
DDF   Documents Diplomatiques Français
DDI   Documenti Diplomatici Italiani
DGFP Documents on German Foreign Policy
EHR   *English Historical Review*
FO   Foreign Office
FRUS Papers relating to the Foreign Relations of the United States
GP   Die Grosse Politik der europaischen Kabinette, 1870–1914
HJ   *Historical Journal*
HZ   *Historische Zeitschrift*
JCEA *Journal of Central European Affairs*
JCH   *Journal of Contemporary History*
JMH   *Journal of Modern History*
MRR   Museo del Risorgimento, Rome
NA   *Nuova Antologia*
NRS   *Nuova Rivista Storica*
RIIA   Royal Institute of International Affairs
RSPI *Rivista di Studi Politici Internazionali*
RSI   *Rivista Storica Italiana*
RSR   *Rassegna Storica del Risorgimento*
SAW   Haus Hof und Staatsarchiv, Vienna
SP   Sonnino Papers
SR   *Slavonic Review*

I do not believe that history provides many examples of a country which has been ruined so completely and so shockingly as ours. And how can we recover from this folly? How can we persuade a people to return to reason when its ideas have been so distorted that now it cannot tell right from wrong nor distinguish between victory and defeat?

Count Giuseppe Tornielli,
February 1896

Part I

Chapter 1

The Sixth Wheel

> Peace is an absolute necessity for our country. It is
> essential that it should last as long as possible until the
> time comes when, in an European crisis, Italy can act
> as a Great Power instead of being the prey of the strong.
>
> *Visconti Venosta*, 1875

> Nationalism must be pushed to its furthest possible
> limits in every question and towards everybody: this is
> an absolute necessity for us after so many years of
> foreign domination. This is the only way we can re-
> acquire a complete sense of national consciousness and
> demonstrate to the world that Italy is and must be only
> for the Italians.
>
> *Crispi*, 1870

These contrasting programmes provide the key to the dialogue in
Italian foreign policy from 1870 to 1919. To men of the Right such
as Emilio Visconti Venosta, Constantino Nigra, Edward de
Launay, Carlo di Robilant, Alberto Blanc, Italy had never really
become a great power. Born and bred in the Piedmontese tradition
of sitting on the fence, waiting for France, Austria or Prussia to
make up their minds and then adroitly choosing the right side, they
regarded Italy simply as a bigger Piedmont. To their way of
thinking the new state had been made by a combination of luck and
finesse in exploiting the European situation after the Crimean War.
If this was so she could equally be unmade by adverse circumstances or poor diplomacy, unless and until she had the power to
stand on her own feet. This is a constant refrain in the letters,
speeches and writing of the realist school in the 1870s and 1880s:
Blanc even went so far as to tell an Austrian diplomat that Italy did
not want to be a great power. Nor was this humble view confined
to Italy. The Russian Ambassador at Rome once explained in all
seriousness to Pasquale Mancini (Foreign Minister 1881–5) that
the powers only invited Italy to their conferences as a matter of

courtesy. It was a commonplace in European diplomacy until Mussolini's time to regard Italy as 'of no account as a Great Power'; the 'sixth wheel on the chariot': Bismarck, in particular, said so whenever his nerves were bad.[1]

Power was, of necessity, slow in coming. Italy was very much the sixth great power, both in population and resources of every kind except ingenuity. In 1870 she had 28 million inhabitants, rising to 37 million in 1914 and 43 million in 1939. Her industrial power measured by the yardsticks of the nineteenth century – coal, iron and steel – was slight, as the following figures show.[2] Even after 1914 progress was still slow: production of coal was up three times by 1939, iron and steel doubled, but these are still not the figures of a great industrial power. In fact it has been calculated that total Italian industrial production in 1901 was equal only to that of Belgium and Luxembourg.

Nor is the rate of increase, though steady, particularly startling. If Italy is compared with the leading industrial states of Western Europe – to say nothing of the USA, Japan or Russia – in the period 1861–1901 the rate of increase in her industrial production was slow: 94 per cent for Italy, 123 per cent for Great Britain, 146 per cent for France and 328 per cent for Germany. It is only in the twentieth century, beginning in the Giolitti era but mostly after 1945, that the *rate of increase* in Italian industrial strength has passed that of her competitors in Western Europe. Needless to say, in *overall levels* of industrial production she is still far behind.[3]

The effects of this situation upon the national wealth were severe. Italy until 1945 remained basically an agrarian state with the problems associated with an agrarian economy. It was not until 1930 that the contribution of agriculture to the private sector of the national economy was surpassed by industry or by tertiary activities.[4] In consequence, annual income *per capita* was low: it only doubled from 1870 to 1939 and progress in this respect was greater in the decade 1950–60 than in the previous ninety years. In 1861 national wealth was one third that of Germany or France, one quarter that of Great Britain. In 1893 it was calculated that *per capita* income in Italy after deducting the cost of armaments was roughly a quarter that of England, a third that of France, a half that of Germany.[5] Italy, in other words, had neither the resources nor the wealth to pay for her industrial development. In the period

of the great railway boom, 1866–87, not only were the greater part
of the materials imported through lack of a native metallurgical
industry, but the expansion was paid for by foreign loans, mostly
French. What money there was in Italy had little confidence in her
economic future and preferred to invest abroad: one fifth of the
French loan of 1872 was subscribed in Italy.[6]

The outcome was chronic budget deficiencies. Marco Minghetti
(Premier 1873–6) proudly announced the balancing of the budget
in 1876, the first time since 1861, as the major achievement of his
government, but this was achieved only by the expedient of
ignoring the costs of railway construction. If this is taken into
account then no budget balanced until 1898.[7] After 1881, when
Agostino Magliani (Finance Minister 1877–88) embarked on the
expensive – if popular – abolition of the flour tax (*macinato*),
introduced the convertibility of the lira, large scale public works
and railway expansion, deficits grew like weeds. When Francesco
Crispi (Premier 1887–91, 1893–6) added military expansion and
African empire, annual borrowing by the state doubled.[8] Hence
the Italian reputation until 1900 as 'the country of the deficit'.
Quintino Sella, the acknowledged financial expert of the Right,
once said that the reason he took up the subject was the proposal
in 1864 to set up a European commission for the Italian debt – the
fate that later overtook Turkey and Egypt.[9]

Slight industrial resources and little wealth meant that the
money available for armaments in Italy was limited. Bent on
putting finances straight, successive governments from 1870 to
1887 concentrated on internal reform and kept defence expenditure
to a minimum: in the 1870s it was actually cut. Though rising
slowly in the 1880s it was still only 21·95 per cent of total state
expenditure (as against 18·66 per cent, the all time low, 1871–5)
until the advent of Crispi.[10] Then it jumped rapidly, doubling in
two years, fell back again in the 1890s and remained static until
1904. From 1904 to 1914 it soared again to Crispi's levels, in
company with the general trend in Europe.[11]

In general from 1862 to 1914 a quarter of defence expenditure
went on the navy, though at times it did better than this, benefiting
from its relative popularity with the Left – battleships could not
suppress demonstrations.[12] Ministers of Marine (as of War) were
not subject to the usual rules of musical chairs and from 1876 there
were, really, only two: Admirals Benedetto Brin (1876–99) and

Carlo Mirabello (1903–9). Brin, a brilliant naval architect, succeeded in building a technically advanced fleet, which in the 1880s doubled the Italian tonnage and was the equal, ship for ship, of anything afloat. Its major disadvantage was its size – ten battleships in 1889 as against nineteen French and thirty British – but at least it established Italy in third place and gave some semblance to her claim to be a Mediterranean power. In the 1890s, however, she fell hopelessly behind, unable to keep pace with the vast naval expansion of the period, and turned instead to attempting to dominate the Adriatic. Here too she was thwarted by a new Austrian determination to become a naval power, so that despite a large increase in expenditure – 42 per cent higher in 1906–7 than in 1893–4 – Italy could only achieve a 3 : 2 superiority in dreadnoughts over her nominal ally.[13] This was insufficient to provide security even against the Austrian fleet, given Italy's long coastline, let alone against France or England.

The money available for the army permitted a peace strength of 234,000 in the 1870s, rising to 267,550 in 1888, a figure which remained more or less static until 1914.[14] These numbers could only be maintained by practising the most rigorous economy: in 1894 the only alternatives to abolishing two army corps were to cut out the annual manoeuvres and postpone the draft. Italian politicians had their own sense of priorities. Giovanni Giolitti, in power almost without a break in the decade before 1914,[15] resisted any increase in military expenditure as long as he possibly could and even when defence expenditure doubled from 1908 to 1914 it is far from clear that this had any appreciable effect on the army. In 1908 a parliamentary commission discovered that there was only one modern fort on Italy's 700 km of frontier with Austria: in 1914 Sonnino discovered with horror that the army possessed no mortars or heavy artillery capable of dealing with either the French or Austrian forts, despite the vast sums voted by parliament for this purpose.[16] There was widespread suspicion that Giolitti had, in fact, spent the money on fixing elections, an attitude he later justified by the fact that he never dreamt the army was to be used in a European war. In 1914 it was short of everything, including even overcoats. The Marquis Di San Giuliano (Foreign Minister 1910–14) said openly that it was 'wise and patriotic' to doubt the ability of the army to fight Austria, an attitude clearly shared by Antonio Salandra (Premier 1914–16).

In the circumstances it is not surprising that in Italy the professional soldier never acquired the mystique or position of his counterpart in Germany, Austria or even France. Though King Umberto (1878–1900) tended to judge politicians by their soundness on the 'military question' (whether to abolish two army corps), which was why he accepted Crispi so readily, he was in fact a bourgeois monarch. Bismarck once complained that Umberto never wore uniform, a contrast with his father, Victor Emmanuel II (1848–78), who longed to end his reign with 'a nice little war'.[17] Foreign diplomats frequently commented on the civilian atmosphere of Umberto's court, especially when William II paid a visit to Rome. It may well have been true, as Umberto, Domenico Farini and Francesco Crispi all believed, that the army was 'the only cement holding Italy together': in 1894 Crispi told parliament that he would cheerfully sacrifice all other public expenditure to preserve the army intact.[18] But this did not mean that Italy was a military state in the sense that Germany, Austria and Russia were. Crispi, easily the most bellicose of Italian politicians until Mussolini, said bluntly in 1887 that Italy might need their alliance but did not want the system of government of Germany or Austria: her ideal was England or the France of the July Monarchy.[19]

The main use of the army from 1870 to 1914 was in colonial campaigns and the maintenance of order at home. The Adowa campaign was a disaster and that in Tripoli little better: even the official history of the latter admits that the planning was 'excessively optimistic',[20] whilst Giolitti maintained that he was reduced to inventing victories to keep up morale. Two years after the province was supposedly pacified the army suffered a major defeat, despite the 70,000 troops stationed there. Bandit suppression in the 1860s and 1870s; putting down peasant revolts in Sicily and supposedly anarchist riots in Milan in the 1890s; containing the socialists in 1914; these were all serious distractions from the army's primary role as a defence force: 75,000 reservists had to be called out during 'Red Week' (7–14 June) and 10,000 were used in Emilia alone. In the circumstances it is not surprising that Italy was the least bellicose of all the European powers and that most of her politicians up to 1914 shared Visconti Venosta's view: Italy needed peace more than anyone.

To this were added considerations of a more general European nature. Although there was some sense of gratitude to France in

Victor Emmanuel's rejection of Bismarck's proposals that he should attack her in 1870, there were more practical considerations.[21] Italy, as the weakest state, depended for her existence upon some sort of balance of power, and, curiously enough, in 1870 Italian statesmen like Visconti Venosta began to talk in Metternichian terms of the European body politic, regretting its disappearance almost as much as Beust. To the Italian Right the new German colossus was frightening: France seemed to have disappeared, England sunk into oblivion, and the Russo–German alliance was astride Europe.[22] Hence their policy; to keep out of Bismarck's *Kulturkampf*, maintain good relations with Austria and France, and do nothing to further weaken these two survivors from the 'old regime'. Although they were out of office from 1876 to 1896 and from 1901 to 1922, the Right, as in most European countries, continued to dominate foreign policy through their stranglehold on Italian diplomatic posts and the key position of Secretary-General in the Foreign Ministry; so that men of the Left such as Benedetto Cairoli (Premier 1878, 1879–81), Agostino Depretis (Premier 1876–8, 1881–7), or Giolitti, carried out a foreign policy which was strongly coloured by these concepts.[23] By 1890 even Crispi, the only political leader on the Left with his own ideas on foreign policy, had become converted to the view that the Austrian Empire must be preserved, if only as a barrier against Russia. Sonnino and Salandra, the architects of the Treaty of London and Italy's entry into the war in 1915, had certainly no intention of destroying it.

In contrast to this almost eighteenth-century concept of European politics there was Crispi. To Crispi, 1870 represented Italy's opportunity to escape for ever from French political and cultural domination. Rejoicing in the demise of the 'old' Europe, he thought the future belonged to the 'new' nations. An ardent admirer of Prussia, he wanted a re-invigoration of Italy through state education, Swedish drill and general conscription. To Crispi, Italy was already a great nation, formed by her 'heroes', Mazzini and Garibaldi, who should now take the lead in re-forming Europe along Mazzinian lines of the principle of nationality. Bismarck, he assumed, would shortly take Austria: Italy must then absorb the 'unredeemed territory' and liberate the Balkan peoples from the Turkish yoke. But, significantly, this did not apply to Alsace-Lorraine. Crispi applauded the German annexation of these provinces because it fitted in with what was becoming his, in contrast to Mazzini's, doctrine of nationality. Nationality was not a personal choice, it was anterior to will: it existed as a right, a matter of race. Increasingly to Crispi, some races were more equal than others. As the exclusion of Russia from the Balkans came to replace his hatred of Austria in the 1880s as the major objective of Italian policy, so the rights of the Balkan peoples faded away, to be replaced by Italian claims to Albania.[24]

Naturally, to a man of his outlook, the pacific policy of the Right was anathema. The burden of his press campaigns and speeches throughout the 1870s and 1880s was that Italy should arm: only by so doing could she become a great power, 'an equal amongst equals'. Nor did he shrink from war: war would regenerate Italy, sunk into a slough of 'materialism' (Crispi's term for balancing the budget): 'Looking after material interests alone is too small minded. . . .'[25] Practically all D'Annunzio's nonsense about the joys of war can be found in Crispi's writing forty years before. These ideas, originally derived from a mixture of Mazzinian nationalism, the Piedmontese tradition of military defeat, and the general exaltation of things Prussian common to most European countries in 1870 – one thinks of Arnold, Renan – soon became bound up with Italy's own peculiar brand of nationalism: 'Mare Nostrum', the revival of the Empire of Ancient Rome.

The origins of this were simple enough. The Mazzinian tradition of the Risorgimento had laid enormous stress upon the importance of Rome as the birthplace of the new Italy: the Left generally in 1870 wanted to organise Victor Emmanuel's entry through Porta Pia into an imperial triumph. Vast hopes were built upon the recovery of the capital of the ancient world: by some mysterious alchemy it was going to transform all Italians into imperial legionaries and make Italy heir to the power and territories of their forbears. This immediately implied a conflict with France, the leading Mediterranean power, a conflict which certainly dominated Crispi's thinking and even Italian policy in general at times between 1880 and 1914. Tunis and Tripoli were a distraction from the preoccupation of most North Italians with the Austrian *terra irredenta*. Significantly it was Crispi who first raised the cry of Nice in 1870; Crispi and Mancini, both southerners, who launched Italy on the quest for that other resurrection of Roman grandeur, an African Empire:[26]

9

The people feel, without a doubt, that great moment when, quivering with inexpressible emotion, we salute the soldiers returning to Africa. Yes, returning to Africa, because the struggle between Italy and Africa has been going on for three thousand years, and Italy has already conquered Hannibal, subdued the Ptolemies, beaten the Saracens, and scattered the barbarians: because Italy, synthesising all Europe and presaging the future, fought against all the strength of the East and conquered.

This divergence between north and south was to become a particularly marked feature in the attitudes of the Left towards foreign policy.[27] Crispi always drew his parliamentary strength from the south, particularly Sicily and Naples, where politics were a question of personalities, especially after *trasformismo,* and his style of oratory had a marked appeal. Here the interest in expansion in the Mediterranean and Africa was natural, Sicily provided nearly all the Italian colonists in Tunis, whilst Naples was the centre of the Rubattino shipping concern with interests all over the Mediterranean. Southern politicians, faced with the agrarian crisis of the 1880s and pressure from the peasants, took up colonial expansion with alacrity as a means of exporting the poor and averting land reform. Hence the storm in the south when the French annexed Tunis, the appointment of a southerner – Pasquale Mancini – as Foreign Minister by Depretis in May 1881, and the support from the south both for Mancini's African adventure in 1885 and Crispi's anti-French crusade after 1887. Since, under Depretis, the south acquired ever increasing political importance – it has been said that *trasformismo* changed 'the social basis of the leadership of the state from the traditional dominant northern groups to those of the south' – this attitude was of considerable moment.[28] By contrast, the south showed almost no interest in irredentism: that it rallied to the national cause in 1915 seems to have been as much a demonstration of personal loyalty to their leader, Salandra – a southerner – as anything else.[29]

The north was much more sophisticated. Here, traditionally, liberalism meant an admiration for France, whether it was the France of Louis-Philippe or the France of 1793 was a matter of taste. Initially, in the 1870s, the clerical sympathies of the republic of dukes caused some difficulties, but once the victory of the Italian Left in 1876 was followed by that of Gambetta in 1877, *la sorella latina* became the main plank in their foreign policy,

relatively unshaken even by Tunis. As Benedetto Cairoli's newspaper, *Il Diritto,* repeated *ad nauseam*, 'Italy was the natural friend
of France', a sentiment widespread in moderate circles in the north
from Ruggiero Bonghi, editor of the conservative Milan newspaper *La Perseveranza,* to Felice Cavalotti, leader of the Lombard
radicals.[30]

Correspondingly, the north opposed colonial expansion; partly
because its initial focus on Tunis and Tripoli implied conflict with
France; partly because the costs seemed totally disproportionate to
the benefits. Giolitti, Sonnino and Silvio Spaventa, who had
supported Depretis until 1885, all went into opposition over the
Massowa expedition. Depretis himself disliked it as adding to the
budget deficit and showed signs of abandoning Massowa after
Mancini's resignation in May 1885. All the attacks on Crispi's
Abyssinian empire came from the north, resentful of the squander-
ing of their money to make a Roman holiday.[31] There were some
converts – particularly amongst the poets, Carducci, D'Annunzio –
and there was a general groundswell when the 'honour' of Italy
was affected; but these were exceptions to the rule, at least until the
Tripoli War of 1911 and a new wave of nationalism blurred the
lines of division. In 1896 not even the disgrace of Adowa could
stop the rioting in Milan, much to the disgust of Farini.

The dominant political passion in the north was irredentism, the
desire to obtain the Italian-speaking provinces of Austria that they
missed in 1861–6. It was based on a fierce hatred of *i tedeschi,* a
firmly established political tradition going back to the Middle
Ages. The irredentist riots which were such a sore trial to Cairoli
and Depretis from 1876 to 1882 (it didn't help that Cairoli was a
leading irredentist himself) started on the anniversary of the battle
of Legnano. This basic anti-Austrian feeling in the north was a
serious handicap to anyone trying to conduct Italian foreign
policy. Even at the best of times it made relations with Austria
difficult, as no one could predict when an outbreak would come.
Italian statesmen from Victor Emmanuel II and Umberto I down-
wards were generally well disposed towards Austria, as Vienna
recognised, and did their best to keep irredentism within reasonable bounds. Suppression was a marked feature of government
under Crispi and Giolitti. But nobody could alter the fact, as Di
San Giuliano pointed out in 1913, that in the long run Italy was
governed by 'the unanimous feeling of the Nation, which in Italy

is sovereign'. For this very reason Tornielli doubted from 1882 onwards whether the Triple Alliance could ever become effective: in Robilant's words, 'we only have parliamentary alchemy, not a foreign policy'.

There was one last basic consideration, which united Left and Right, the Roman Question. The refusal of the papacy to accept the decision of 20 September 1870 meant a permanent state of tension between the Vatican and the Quirinal. In internal politics this meant the complete abstention of practising Catholics from political life, a fact which was not unwelcome to the Left since it increased the ease of their political dominance. Only with the rise of the Italian socialist movement in the 1890s did they begin to have second thoughts about this: as Crispi put it in 1895, 'better the clericals than the socialists'. But until then, to anti-clericalists like Crispi, and even to Visconti Venosta, the Vatican was either a tolerated nuisance or a downright menace to the existence of the Italian state. It was fortunate, said Visconti in 1871, that the pope disdained democracy; it averted the necessity of open war between the Quirinal and the Vatican.[32]

Any quarrel between church and state in Italy threatened to become an international incident and, given the temper of the clericals in France and Austria, this could be dangerous for Italy. Visconti Venosta thought the Roman Question completely dominated her position on the international scene, a view certainly shared by Crispi in the 1880s. It was one of the principal considerations behind the approaches to Berlin and Vienna in 1882: it was the major cause of Crispi's war scare of 1889 and coloured his whole approach to relations with France. 'The Royal Government', he instructed the Italian ambassador in Paris, 'cannot abandon the educating of the children of 30,000 Italians [in Tunis] to Cardinal Lavigerie.'[33] It was only with the advent of Leo XIII and the *ralliement* in the 1890s that this preoccupation withered away, until Tornielli could state categorically in 1896 that the 'papal question in the hands of the French government is only something to annoy us: nobody in France thinks of unmaking Italy'. Only when this became a generally accepted fact was it possible to think in terms of a *modus vivendi* with France, as with the Vatican.[34]

Chapter 2

From Independence to Alliance

> We want only respect for treaties and the simple
> maintenance of peace, renouncing even any idea of an
> increase in our influence in the Mediterranean.
>
> *Launay*, 1882

The foreign policy of the Right from 1870 to 1876 might well be
summed up in the dictum of Visconti Venosta, 'independent
always, isolated never'. Liberated from her vassalage to Napoleon
III by Sedan, her prestige enhanced – at least in Italian eyes – by
the conquest of Rome, the new state yet managed to avoid the
alternative peril of becoming, in Visconti's words, 'Bismarck's
paid assassin'. There were those who urged this course. Launay,
Ambassador in Berlin, never tired of urging Rome to make a
German alliance whilst there was still time. 'It is distressing', he
wrote to Robilant on 1 April 1873, 'to see that there are still people
at home who preach that we should seek to hold the balance
between France and Germany.' At the other end of the political
spectrum, Crispi preached this gospel in and out of season. But
Visconti ignored them both. Good relations with the new
Jerusalem were of course essential but an alliance was very
different:[1]

> As for written agreements, treaties, we have not sought them and
> do not even want them, at least in present circumstances ... there
> are no immediate dangers.
>
> It seems to me, therefore, that the most practical policy is to keep
> the trust and sympathy of Germany ... so that when our interests
> require it and the moment arrives we can tie the knot.

The reasons for this attitude were a mixture of personal outlook
and political calculation. Visconti had none of the emotionalism of
Crispi and completely distrusted feeling as a basis for statecraft. He
was almost English in his preference for the empirical approach of

13

'wait and see'. What he saw of Bismarck he disliked, but this was not the reason why he avoided a German alliance. The price of this was bound to be an Italian commitment against France, yet it was not in Italy's interests to see France humbled further. 'Italy', he wrote to Robilant on 1 July 1875, shortly after the war scare, 'is one of those countries that can only fulfil its role and have a future in a Europe where there is a certain equilibrium of forces.' Not that he intended to support France; that would be 'to make common cause with disaster', but he did not wish to assist Bismarck either. What in fact he did during the war scare was, like Count Julius Andrássy, the Austrian Foreign Minister, to maintain a discreet silence, though he was distinctly pleased with the outcome of the Anglo–Russian pressure upon Berlin.[2]

In Visconti's view there was no danger to Italy from France great enough to justify seeking a German alliance. There was the Roman Question, the danger that the ultramontanes – especially if there were a Bourbon restoration – would launch a crusade to liberate Pius IX from his bondage in the Vatican. But apart from the summer of 1873 when Visconti, alarmed at the dismissal of President Thiers, gave way to the king's pressure and arranged a royal visit to Vienna and Berlin as a counter insurance, this danger never seemed very great. He thought, rightly, that given time the republicans under Gambetta would triumph in France and embark on an anti-clerical programme of their own.

The key to checking France on the papal issue lay in Vienna, because, Visconti thought, 'if the latter got nearer to France then the Roman question would provide the feast'. Moreover, much as the government in Paris preferred to avoid and ignore ultramontane pressures if it could, 'it would be almost impossible for her *not* to raise difficulties for us if France . . . could count on the help or example of Austria'. Hence the stress in these years on maintaining good Austro–Italian relations on the basis, both tacit and explicit, that in return for Austrian benevolence towards Italy in the Roman Question, Italy would acquiesce in Austrian policy in the east. This extended, in Visconti's view, even to welcoming the new understanding between Vienna and Berlin: certain of German support, Andrássy would have no temptation to seek French.[3]

This was a system which worked well enough until 1875. Remarkably, in view of 1859 and 1866, both the two governments and the two monarchs accepted the existing frontiers as final, a fact which was made clear by the Andrássy/Wimpffen letter of 24 May 1874 and Victor Emmanuel's frank acceptance of its implications. Andrássy, roused by what he called 'views which suggest a failure to recognise the inviolability of the new territorial order',[4] wrote a private letter to the ambassador at Rome – intended of course to be seen by the king and his ministers – stating bluntly that there was no possibility whatsoever of Austria ceding any territory to Italy. To do so would be to risk the dissolution of the empire. Any such pressure, he warned, would lead to Austria 'still following the system of nationalities, to incorporate in the monarchy the adjoining provinces': a delicate way of saying that she would retake Venetia. Visconti and Victor Emmanuel both then and in April 1875 at the Venice meeting with Francis Joseph accepted this reasoning absolutely, the king adding to Andrássy at the end of the Venice encounter that if there was ever any difficulty he was to contact him direct through his aide-de-camp, Natale Aghemo, avoiding his ministers.[5]

This happy state of affairs came to an end in 1875–6 with the outbreak of the revolts in Bosnia-Herzegovina and the victory of the Left at the Italian elections. The Bosnian revolts against the Turks and the near certainty that Austria, in agreement with Germany and Russia, would annex the two provinces, raised the hopes of all those in Italy who dreamt of completing her national unity by adding the Trentino and Trieste; the idea being that they could be acquired as compensation for Austrian expansion in the Balkans. This concept, the Italian dream until 1915, was not entirely confined to men like Giuseppe Garibaldi, Benedetto Cairoli and Renato Imbriani, the irredentist leaders in Italy.[6] Robilant, who had previously warned against listening to the 'more or less genuine "cries of grief" of the Triestines' as 'extremely dangerous', in August 1875 urged that the Bosnian revolt was 'our chance to improve our frontier in the Val d'Adige and on the Isonzo'. Even Visconti, who until 1875 had taken the simple view that Italy's interest was for the Balkans to remain quiet until she had the strength to exert some influence, showed momentary interest. In September he prompted a visit by Crown Prince Umberto to St Petersburg with, he said 'an *arrière pensée* which it is better not to discuss'. The hope was of course that the Three Emperors' League would break up under Balkan stresses, creating an opportunity for Italy to insert herself.[7]

On 16 March 1876 Minghetti's government resigned and was replaced by an administration of the Left headed by Depretis with Luigi Melegari as his Foreign Minister until his incapacity became too obvious in November 1877. Neither knew anything of foreign affairs. Depretis regarded them as a nuisance and diplomats as useless creatures, like professors: in fact the Consulta was run by the Secretary-General, Tornielli. Salisbury, who visited Rome in November 1876, thought he was 'the real foreign minister'; Haymerlé, the Austrian Ambassador, thought much the same.[8] Depretis' difficulty was that although he personally was quite content to leave well alone, others were not. Basically the official Left was split into three factions, the followers of Depretis, Cairoli, and Crispi. Cairoli was an irredentist who not only became a founder member of the National Association on 26 January but also stoked the fires by appearing as an official delegate at the Legnano ceremonies in Milan on 29 May 1876, ceremonies at which the banners of Trento and Trieste received the post of honour. Austria promptly dissolved the local so-called gymnastic societies at Riva and Rovereto which had sent delegations to Milan and protested to Rome at Cairoli's presence. Robilant, who never thought much of popular demonstrations as a way of obtaining the Trentino, urged that they be suppressed. Andrássy, he said, had confidence in the king's word and the government's sincerity, but the Legnano celebrations cast doubt on its ability to control the country: 'if the government believes it is an Italian interest to maintain relations with Austria, then it is absolutely essential to prevent repetitions of similar demonstrations'.[9]

In October Robilant went further. In July the three emperors had met at Reichstadt and agreed, amongst other things, that Austria should take Bosnia, news of which filtered through to Rome and led them to protest at Berlin and St Petersburg that they expected compensation. Andrássy, informed by his allies, was explicit: he told Robilant on 16 October that 'we will not even cede a village, and if we see ourselves menaced by aggression we will take action', a straight reference to the Wimpffen letter. Robilant, alarmed by the activities of Garibaldi, who was not only sending volunteers to Serbia but talking of a raid in the Trentino, now admitted that he had been wrong. There was no hope of getting the Trentino, even to ask for it was dangerous, and if Garibaldi was allowed another of his freebooting expeditions they must expect war. This was serious because the Austrian army was much stronger and, most important of all, it was clear that Austria had the support of both Germany and Russia. In February he sent yet more confirmation: General Ignatieff, the Russian pan-Slav leader, told him there was no hope whatsoever of the Trentino and, like Andrássy before him, suggested Tunis instead.[10]

It was, therefore, absolutely clear to Depretis that in allowing irredentist demonstrations and Garibaldi's activities to continue he was playing with fire. Unfortunately, however, he could not suppress them. The Left had been elected in 1876 on a platform of free speech and freedom of association: to clamp down this soon would in any case be difficult but, given the strength of the Cairoli faction, well nigh impossible for a government of the Left to undertake; a fact which Tornielli, loyal to Depretis, explained at some length to Robilant. The new government had, however, one advantage over the old: since February the Gambettists, if not in power, formed the government in France, a fact which made Depretis less dependent upon good relations with Austria than Visconti and Minghetti had been. Hence his despatch of Domenico Farini to Paris in August 1876 to consult the oracle and see if the *sorelle latine* could not collaborate on a common programme in the east. This fell flat because Gambetta, with understandable caution, insisted that any such joint programme must be approved by Bismarck.[11]

Everything came back to this: if Depretis were to do anything to content his associates on the Left he must get German support. Hence the great fiasco of 1877, Crispi's Grand Tour. Crispi, apart from being an essential cog in the majority in parliament, had strong ideas of his own. Since 1870 he had preached a German alliance and bitterly criticised the Right for their refusal to seek one. In his view it was to be obtained for the asking: that there was no alliance was due to the incompetence of the Right in general, with their slavish deference to France, and the lack of drive of diplomats like Launay, Robilant and Visconti in particular. The central point of Crispi's thinking was that Bismarck could be induced to dismember Austria, a continuation of his policy of 1866. Nor was he alone in his belief. Maffei, who succeeded Tornielli at the Consulta in March 1878, still thought that this was Bismarck's object even then. Moreover, Victor Emmanuel – obsessed with the idea of 'crowning his work with a victory to give our army power and prestige' – was quite willing in 1877 to forget his devotion to Francis Joseph. This despite the fact that as recently as February he had assured Haymerlé that he and his ministers wanted the best relations with Austria, 'and if they resist I will make them do as I want'.[12]

Crispi's official instructions following his interview with the king on 27 August leave no room for doubt that, even if the major idea was to remove one of the government's strongest critics, both the king and Depretis approved of his basic concept: in fact, as Chabod points out, they – not Crispi – initiated the project:

> His Majesty feels the need to make the friendly relations between Italy and Germany much closer and thinks that Y.E. should let Prince Bismarck know that it would be convenient to come to a complete agreement by means of an alliance treaty that, founded upon common interests, would provide for all eventualities ... not only the prevalence of the ultramontane party in France but also against the aggrandisement of Austria through the annexation of any Ottoman provinces. ...

It remained to put this into effect. At his first interview with Bismarck at Gastein on 17 September 1877 Crispi discovered his mistake: the prince, whilst perfectly willing to make an alliance against France, would not lift a finger against Austria.

By the time he met Andrássy at Pest on 2 October Crispi had learnt discretion, said nothing about the Trentino and dismissed any idea of taking Trieste: 'Trieste, ridiculous idea: ports are commercial outlets; who owns them has to have the territory from which the products come. What could we do with Trieste?' But this new-found moderation, largely instilled by Robilant who insisted that it was a *sine qua non* for Italy not to raise difficulties of any sort', was wasted: Bismarck had already informed Andrássy of the content of the Gastein conversations. Since Derby, the British Foreign Minister, had also told the Austrian Ambassador that Crispi was not to be trusted, Vienna was well aware of the new ideas in Rome and Melegari's disavowal of Crispi was ineffective. On 18 December, in a speech to the delegations, Andrássy revealed the Wimpffen letter, declared it to be his policy, and published it a few days later, much to the alarm of Robilant. He, fearing that it was but a prelude to action, urged Melegari on 4 January 1878 that the government sever all contact with the irredentists and avoid anything which might offer to Austria 'the chance to attack us on unfounded pretexts'.[13]

The result of Crispi's excursion into the world of diplomacy was then that Italo–Austrian relations were more tense than at any time since 1866 and Italy now faced the danger of an Austrian attack with no possible ally in sight. Worse was yet to come. On 9 January the king died, which, said Andrássy, was 'much to be deplored as he knew how to control the parties'. If by the end of 1877 there were some doubts in Vienna as to how far Victor Emmanuel could in fact influence events,[14] his constant professions of goodwill were still accepted at face value: the irredentists, he told Haymerlé, were 'dogs' (*chiens*). Certainly, all the evidence suggests that he completely controlled the Depretis government. Hence the shock when in quick succession Umberto I refused to continue the private means of communication with Vienna via Aghemo[15] and, on 24 March 1878, Haymerlé's worst fears came true with the appointment of Cairoli as Premier with Giuseppe Zanardelli, another leading irredentist, at the Ministry of the Interior. Whereas Crispi, Minister of the Interior under Depretis from December to March, had exercised some control, now irredentist meetings went completely unchecked, culminating in a great demonstration in Rome on 30 April which brought official protests from both Austrian and – for the first time – German diplomats. Cairoli, a good orator and a popular hero second only to Garibaldi but 'completely empty-headed', seemed destined to lead Italy into war. As Garibaldi put it, 'If a Cairoli–Zanardelli ministry cannot do good who the devil can?'[16]

Hence Cairoli's curious appointment of Corti to the Consulta. Count Luigi Corti (Foreign Minister March–December 1878) was a career diplomat (Minister/Ambassador at Constantinople, 1875–8, 1878–85, at London 1885–7), a close friend and confidant of Robilant, whose views on foreign policy he shared. He told Cairoli and Zanardelli bluntly on 25 March when they pressed him to take the post, that his concepts were the complete opposite of theirs; that, amongst other things, relations with Austria should be 'on a footing of frank and honest cordiality'; that he saw no reason to oppose an Austrian acquisition of Bosnia and Herzegovina; and that, anyway, since this had already been decided by the powers it would be 'useless and dangerous for Italy to contest it'. Since they still begged him to take the post, as did the king and Visconti Venosta, Corti put his head on the block.

It is quite clear that both in March and in June–July, when Corti led the Italian delegation to the Berlin congress to settle the fate of the Balkans, the leaders of the government accepted his policy of doing nothing. In the last days of the Depretis administration, London made approaches to Rome for an alliance against Russia: Corti, with the full consent of the cabinet, rejected it as too dangerous, a course thoroughly approved by Robilant. 'More than ever', he wrote on 2 April, 'I am of your opinion . . . an uncompromising neutrality is the only possible policy for Italy.' Cairoli needed Corti to give foreign powers, especially Vienna, some minimum confidence in his government in a period of a severe European crisis, the worst between 1870 and 1914. Hence his acceptance, with the rest of the Cabinet, of the instructions Corti drew up for himself for the congress: that Italian ambitions should be limited to securing that Austria merely *occupied* Bosnia and Herzegovina rather than *annexed* the provinces.[17]

Corti at Berlin was in fact eminently successful: his instructions were carried out to the letter and, more, he established friendly relations with Bismarck, Andrássy and Disraeli. Yet on his return he was stoned in Milan, reviled by Crispi in *La Riforma* on 18 August and remained ever after the symbol of all that was wrong with Italian foreign ministers in the eyes of the Left. 'Clean hands' (*mani netti*), Corti's policy at Berlin, became a term of abuse. And yet there is no doubt that Corti was right: as Robilant wrote him at this time, 'abroad Italy does not exist: we are falling into the state of Spain'. Bismarck, in 1880 – admittedly talking to the French ambassador – urged that 'Italy is not a serious state; she should make painters, musicians, singers and dancers, that is her real role.'[18] If Corti, as Crispi maintained, had insisted at Berlin on compensation for Italy the result could only have been a severe humiliation. 'The mind boggles', Corti wrote Cairoli on 1 July, 'at Italy's position if at this moment she had opposed all the Great Powers.'

This was, however, completely lost upon his detractors. The irredentist movement started up again seriously on his return from Berlin, reached peak proportions – again under Cairoli – in January 1880 at the funeral of its president, General Avezzana, and remained a serious irritant in Italo–Austrian relations until 1882. If Haymerlé, who succeeded Andrássy as Foreign Minister in

Vienna in 1879, was sufficiently aware of Italian realities to dis-
count the noisier element – it helped that in March 1880 both
Cairoli and Crispi announced to a packed Chamber their discovery
that Austria was a necessary element in the European stability – he
could still never be entirely sure of the outcome of the ministerial
snakes and ladders. Only when, from November 1879 to May 1881,
Cairoli and Depretis combined in one government did it possess
sufficient authority to check the more extreme irredentists.[19]

To the difficulties with Austria over irredentism were now
added a growing hostility towards France over Tunis. The axiom
of Visconti Venosta had always been that Italy could not afford the
enmity of both Austria and France at the same time, but from 1879
to 1881 this precaution was ignored. As Robilant observed to
Corti on 22 May 1879, 'we have lost every consideration in
Europe and yet we do not recognise this and behave, unfortunately, as if we were masters of the situation'. This was bound
to lead to disillusionment sooner or later: it came in May 1881
when the French occupied Tunis.

Italian interest in Tunis was long-standing but, until 1879,
limited to maintaining the commercial and cultural interests of the
Italian population – largely Sicilians – who resided there.[20] There
was certainly no thought of annexing what was nominally a
province of the Ottoman Empire, a view that Visconti constantly
repeated not only to the French but to his own diplomats. Italy
could not afford 'the luxury of an Algeria', all she wanted was the
status quo. This explains why frequent hints from Andrássy,
Bismarck and even London up to the Congress of Berlin that
Italy should seek her compensation in Tunis instead of in the
Trentino were ignored. Taking Tunis would cost money: as Corti
put it, 'Italy is not an old state, her finances, her administration,
her armed forces, all need to be developed and consolidated.' This
view was as much that of Depretis and Cairoli as it had been of
Visconti: Cairoli only became alarmed in July 1878 when, after the
British announcement of the acquisition of Cyprus, he suspected
that France had been offered Tunis. By then, of course, it was too
late to announce that Italy would like it after all; the most she
could have obtained was Tripoli which nobody in Rome wanted.[21]

Despite German and British 'offers' in 1878 the French were, in
fact, highly reluctant to take any positive steps in Tunis. The
French Left, like their Italian counterparts, were much more

interested in internal problems, had no enthusiasm for colonial adventures and – to the extent that they thought about foreign policy – were hypnotised by the German problem, the gap in the Vosges. Gambetta, like Depretis, was inclined to think in terms of *la sorella latina* and had little enthusiasm for a step which had few attractions and was certain to alienate Italy. Tunis, in the immortal words of President Grévy, was 'not worth a two sous cigar'. Jules Ferry, the Premier, told his Foreign Minister as late as February 1881 that they could not possibly risk a Tunis expedition in an election year.

The pressure for action came from a variety of sources; French diplomats preoccupied with questions of prestige and France's future as a Mediterranean power *vis-à-vis* England and Italy; the Algerian administration with all the usual obsessions of empire builders; last but not least Courcel, the extremely influential Directeur Politique at the Quai d'Orsay, who had much the same position in France as Tornielli and Maffei possessed in Italy. It was his decision to go for straight annexation (in the form of a protectorate) instead of a deal with Italy that determined the final outcome. Above all, it was he who converted Gambetta to the project on 23 March 1881.[22]

The real question in relation to Tunis, therefore, is what converted these two to a policy of annexation by France? The answer seems to be the inanities of Italian policy. This had two sources. The Ambassadors in Paris and London – Cialdini and Menabrea – were convinced until July 1880 that the French would not act and that Britain was at worst neutral, at best pro-Italian. There was some reason for their beliefs: Cialdini was told constantly by Gambetta, Grévy and Waddington that although France would not permit Italian annexation, France would do nothing without consulting Italy; Menabrea was told by Salisbury that he was 'absolutely impartial' between French and Italian claims and that, though he had no interest in Tunis himself, he was 'far from wishing to discourage the Italians'.[23]

This led Maffei to the idea that Italy should forestall France by annexing the province herself, the concept that lay behind the appointment of Maccio as Italian Consul-General in Tunis in 1878. Maccio, a man of considerable energy and an old rival of his French counterpart, Roustan, set about combating French influence wherever it could be found. This took the form of obtaining concessions for Italian firms throughout the bey's domains, the most important of which was the Tunis–La Goulette railway obtained for the Rubattino shipping company. On 12 July 1880 the Italian chamber voted a guarantee of 6 per cent on Rubattino's concession, a clear enough indication of the involvement of the state. Despite an explicit warning from Freycinet, the French Foreign Minister, that if this sort of thing continued France would be forced to intervene, Cairoli and Depretis took no heed. Apparently Cairoli thought, in his naïve fashion, that if Italian commercial interests were increased in Tunis – as they were – France could not annex the province. Cialdini was more realistic. He warned on 21 July 1880 that they should continue only 'if you are not alarmed by a clash with France, if you have secure alliances', but his advice was ignored. Maccio was allowed to continue as before and in January 1881 organised a deputation of settlers and a Tunisian prince, Hussein, to pay homage to King Umberto at Palermo.[24]

Italy of course had no alliances but Maffei at last set about rectifying this. His hopes raised slightly by an Anglo–French dispute (the *Enfida* case) which led to the despatch of a British ironclad to Tunisian waters in January 1881, Maffei now instructed a reluctant Robilant to approach Haymerlé for an Austro–Italian alliance. The basis was to be mutual neutrality in the event that the other was involved in war with a third power with diplomatic support for their respective interests in Tunis and the Balkans. Haymerlé was reasonably favourable, it offered some advantages to Austria, but Bismarck was violently opposed. Throughout 1880 he had been strongly anti-Italian, urging on the French to take Tunis and the Austrians to reconquer Venetia: he had no wish to see his plans for diverting France to North Africa thwarted at the last moment and on 19 March told Haymerlé flatly to reject Maffei's approaches.[25]

Since Italy could not hope to take on France alone this left Maffei with but one choice: in April he at last made a proposal to Paris that they partition Tunisia. If it had been suggested before it might have gained acceptance, on the pattern of the Anglo–French Dual Control in Egypt, but April 1881 was too late. Courcel had made up his mind that, secure in German support, he had no need to offer concessions to Italy – not even Tripoli – and had persuaded Gambetta to his view.[26] Action was swift to follow: in

April French troops from Algeria pursued the convenient Kroumirs until they entered Tunis and on 12 May imposed a French protectorate by the Treaty of Bardo. Maffei's last hope, action by England, wilted away under Gladstone's opposition,[27] Cairoli resigned and Maffei went with him, retiring to the honourable position of Ambassador at Madrid.

What Carocci calls the 'Tunisian bombshell' had a shattering effect in Italy precisely because it was totally unexpected: right up until the last moment Depretis's newspaper, *Il Popolo Romano*, assured its readers that France would not act. Hence the feeling of bewilderment, shock and isolation. It was not long before this turned against those mainly responsible and the government quickly lost the support of the extreme Left – Crispi and Cavallotti – Nicotera, and the small centre group around Sidney Sonnino. (Sonnino had pressed for the acquisition of Tunis since 1879.) The most likely result was a return to a government by the Right: Nicotera, 'king' of Naples, was known to be negotiating with Sella.

A crisis of this proportion brought out the best in Depretis. He dropped Cairoli – who as Foreign Minister could plausibly take the blame – brought in Zanardelli, ruler of Brescia and as important as Cairoli in the north, on the promise of electoral reform; and Pasquale Mancini – a Neapolitan – as Foreign Minister, with a promise of a strong foreign policy based on approaches to Germany and Austria. This not only won over Nicotera but even received the grudging approval of *La Riforma* on 27 May. To complete the system, Marco Minghetti, traditional leader of the Right, was induced to support the government on the basis that the 'ruling classes' needed to sink their differences and combine to defeat the Radical peril inherent in an extension of the suffrage. As Carocci says, Tunis was 'a fact of fundamental importance not only in foreign policy but also . . . in internal policy': *trasformismo* was born.[28]

Once Depretis was dependent upon men of a conservative outlook – Mancini, Sonnino and Minghetti – he had to take note of their views on foreign policy as well as internal problems: in fact in 1881 the two became almost indistinguishable. Tunis had little effect upon Depretis himself; he did not regard the Treaty of Bardo as final and expected to reach an understanding of sorts with Gambetta in time. The most likely means was Egypt.[29] In any case, an approach to Vienna or Berlin would not help Italy in Tunis: enquiries in July made this very clear. But since the Centre and Right press wanted a conservative alliance it was a pressure which could not be ignored, especially as Nicotera/Sella negotiations started up again in the autumn. To give force to the argument of the Right that radicalism was dangerous there were the vast disturbances in Rome on 12–13 July during the transport of the body of Pius IX to the Basilica of San Lorenzo, which gave rise to protests throughout the Catholic world. If, after the shock of Tunis, were now added a reactivation of the Roman Question not only would Depretis's new coalition collapse but, many thought, even the monarchy might be in danger: a second humiliation in such a short space of time would be too much.[30]

Depretis, always reluctant to take a decision, and Zanardelli, an unrepentant irredentist, were still opposed to approaches to Vienna, as were Robilant and Ruggiero Bonghi, editor of the right-wing *La Perseveranza*. But the ministers were won over by the insistence of King Umberto who, at an interview at Monza on 30 September, persuaded the Premier that he should go on a royal visit to Francis Joseph. This visit – so Blanc told the Austrian chargé on 8 October – could 'alone offer the necessary guarantee of good relations between the two countries as the policy of a minister did not bind his successors'. The royal pilgrimage, which took place on 27–31 October, in fact had little direct consequences in foreign policy – the Austrians were careful to keep it to pleasantries – but it resolved Depretis's internal problems. Minghetti, in two speeches at Legnano and Bologna in October and November, finally adhered openly to Depretis, carrying with him Luigi Luzzatti, Francesco Brioschi and Giuseppe Saracco. Sella was now so discouraged that he virtually abandoned politics and Depretis was secure. On 23 January 1882 he and Minghetti signed an alliance to combat 'the dangers which menace our institutions'.[31]

If Depretis was now largely satisfied, others were not. On 29 November Bismarck made a speech in the Reichstag commenting on the drift to republicanism in Italy and inviting the pope to take up residence in Germany if Rome became uncomfortable. Bismarck in fact was merely trying to get the support of the Centre party but this induced general panic in Rome: on 6 and 7 December, with the opening of parliament, both Sonnino and

Mancini spoke in favour of a German alliance. Blanc, impressed by warnings from Launay that Bismarck might well take up the Roman Question, rushed to tell the Austrian Ambassador, Wimpffen, that the monarchy was in danger and needed an Austrian alliance. At the end of the month instructions were sent to Robilant and Launay to announce that Italy intended to associate herself with the actions of the German powers, even if their existing obligations did not permit an alliance! According to Wimpffen this was the personal wish of the king, accepted by the entire cabinet.

Robilant, strongly against his wishes, was now instructed to open negotiations for an alliance, as was Launay at Berlin. The latter was totally unproductive – Launay reported on 31 January that Bismarck coldly observed that the path to Berlin lay via Vienna – the former, not much better. Kálnoky, now Austrian Foreign Minister, was friendly, but apparently uninterested and Robilant once more on 30 January advised Mancini against proceeding any further. It was, in his view, too undignified:

> It is obvious that the Vienna cabinet wants to maintain friendly relations with us, even cordial; but nothing more at present . . . they have no faith in the seriousness of our proposals. . . . If we really want an alliance with Austria and Germany . . . I would not seek any further contacts, which at present and for some time will be repulsed, with consequent harm to our dignity.

Since his advice was ignored, on 19 February he was instructed to propose to Kálnoky that they make a treaty guaranteeing the possessions of each monarch. This, as he had forecast, was rejected out of hand since it would have committed Vienna to supporting the Quirinal against the Vatican.

Here, in all probability, the negotiations would have ended but for a sudden change of front on Bismarck's part. Up to now he had poured cold water on the whole idea, but on 28 February, apparently impressed by the warmth of General Skobelev's reception in Paris and his bellicose speech on 17 February, Bismarck suddenly relented and sent a sketch of a treaty to Vienna. The basis of this was that Germany and Austria would support the existing social order in Italy and guarantee her against a French attack in return for an Italian promise of support for Austria and Germany if they were attacked by Russia and France. This, turned into proper form by Mancini and returned to Vienna on 22 March, became the first treaty of the Triple Alliance on 20 May 1882.[32]

What use was it to Italy? Its main importance was psychological, the sense of belonging to the European order, an end to the feeling of isolation and being the sixth wheel on the coach, the beggars at the feast. The guarantee against France was in fact useless since the French at no time dreamt of attacking Italy and, in fact, after Tunis and until the advent of Crispi, went out of their way to be pleasant. Nor, of course, was the alliance any use in getting back Tunis or in any other colonial friction that might arise: the Italians had to renounce any such ambitions as the price of alliance.[33] Mancini soon found that France, not Italy, enjoyed Bismarck's favour in colonial questions. The mutual guarantee of the 'social and political order in their respective states' probably meant something to Umberto, but on the whole the danger to the monarchy was exaggerated in 1881–2. It was a good rallying cry for the Right, a useful stick with which to beat the Left, and, of course, an appeal calculated to touch the hearts of Francis Joseph and William I. Kálnoky, admittedly writing for the pope's ears, told the Austrian Minister at the Vatican that the reason they signed the treaty was to conserve the monarchical principle against the 'destructive forces' emanating from France (and Russia). Nor did it, of course, offer any cast-iron guarantee on the Roman Question – the treaty was mute on this subject – but presumably it was thought unlikely that two powers who had just promised 'peace and friendship' would raise this issue.[34]

The result, therefore, was that the Left in 1882 had, under pressure from the Right, made the alliance which the Right could have made at any time from 1872 to 1876 but refused as too restrictive and repugnant to Italy as a liberal state. If one asks why, the answer lies in European events from 1876 to 1881 – the eastern crisis, the Berlin congress, the Tunis question – and the impact this had inside Italy – irredentism, powerlessness and a fear of isolation – with all its consequences for Italian politics. This may be summed up in one word: *trasformismo*. It was not without reason that Umberto told the Austrian Ambassador at the end of 1882 that what Italy hoped to derive from the alliance was security,[35]

> ... a period of internal tranquillity which she could use ... to develop her resources and raise herself to the rank of the great powers who are a solid guarantee of the maintenance of peace.

27

Chapter 3

Mancini, Robilant and the Mediterranean, 1882–7

> Italy in the Red Sea is not working for England or any other government: she has gone there to follow a policy which is essentially Italian.
>
> *Mancini*, 1885

The Egyptian Crisis

The limitations of the Triple Alliance for Italy became clear immediately in the Egyptian crisis of the summer of 1882. Since 1879 successive Italian governments, sporadically, had attempted to assert that, as a Mediterranean power with considerable interests in Egypt, Italy should be invited to join the Anglo–French Dual Control.[1] In September 1881, Pasquale Mancini went so far as to propose to London and Paris that in the face of the growing chaos in Egypt they should form 'an *accord à trois* for common action . . . since the recent outbreaks at Cairo appear most menacing, such as to require immediate and energetic preparations.'[2] What he hoped to get out of this, apparently, was to use participation in a triple control in Egypt as a means of pressure to induce France to install a similar regime in Tunis. The bey, like the khedive, would become subject to a collective European commission.[3] Since London and Paris had a secret agreement to keep all other powers out of Egypt, and Granville, the British Foreign Secretary, had no desire whatsoever to take energetic action, Mancini's proposal shared the fate of all similar Italian attempts in the past. Renewed advances by Menabrea, the Italian Ambassador at London, in November and December were simply evaded by Granville.

Mancini next tried an alternative tack. As the spring of 1882 brought the negotiations with Vienna and Berlin for an alliance to a successful conclusion, his idea became to enlist the support of his new partners to impose himself upon the Dual Control, Italy acting as the representative of the Austrian and German interests.

28

This again failed dismally. Kálnoky, the Austrian Foreign Minister, at first ignored Italian advances, then told Robilant that he refused to accept intervention in Egypt by any power except Turkey and insisted that a solution must be found within the concert of *all* the powers, a reply which the Italian Ambassador thought to have been formulated 'word by word' by Berlin. There was no chance of the Dual Control gaining acceptance:[4]

> At the cost even of moral sacrifices we must, it seems to me, stick closely to Austria and Germany: it is highly probable that their view will prevail over that of the ephemeral Franco–British front.

Blocked in both directions Mancini had little choice but to follow this advice and in May and June 1882 he became an enthusiastic protagonist of the 'concert of Europe' and Turkish intervention as the solution to the Egyptian question. At the Constantinople conference in June, however, as it became increasingly clear that the concert would achieve nothing – largely because Austria and Germany failed to support a solution of any sort – and that the 'ephemeral' Dual Control still survived, Mancini became increasingly uneasy.[5] As the premier, Depretis, urged upon him on 25 June,[6]

> We have interests in Egypt of the highest importance and if the friendship of Austria and Germany is to be taken seriously, as one cannot doubt, these powers must give us effective help, as their abstention puts us in a most difficult position. If England and France are given a free hand they will . . . deprive us of any influence . . . therefore I believe we must insist that Germany and Austria take heed of our interests and make common cause with us.

This was easier said than done.

Although Bismarck always preserved a sphinx-like countenance where Egypt was concerned, the general drift of his intentions was clear enough. The German and Austrian delegates at Constantinople were always 'without instructions', could neither approve nor disapprove proposals made at the conference, tactics which both left Italy to make all the running in opposition to Britain and France, and condemned her efforts to futility. In effect Bismarck was leaving the British a clear field[7] in the hope that an Anglo–French collision would follow: a concert solution (as Gladstone wanted) or Italy joining the Dual Control (as Mancini urged once more) might well drive Britain and France back together. Hence

the advice from Kálnoky via Robilant shortly after the bombardment of Alexandria on 11 July, that Italy 'had nothing to gain and
everything to lose in following those western powers from whose
irrational egoism she had already suffered so much . .' . .[8]

In late July Bismarck's tactics at last bore fruit: Gladstone
finally consented to British intervention; Freycinet, opposed by
the French chamber, was unable to follow suit and the first breach
in the Dual Control had been effected. It seems probable that this
was pure bonus as far as Bismarck was concerned – he made no
attempt to dissuade the French from acting – and that his main
hope had rested in Anglo–French disagreement *after* a joint
occupation. In some ways French inaction was positively undesirable, especially because it once more raised the possibility of
Italian intervention. On 27 July Gladstone and Granville, uneasy
at finding themselves isolated, invited Mancini to join them in
Egypt and assume the place Italy had sought since 1879. This time
the oracle, again via Kálnoky, was more explicit. The Austrian
foreign minister told Robilant point blank that[9]

> there was no point in opposing his [Bismarck's] wishes, it was useless
> to try and follow another path when he had clearly shown that which
> he preferred; we should therefore make a virtue of necessity, even
> though we did not agree with Prince Bismarck and had far greater
> interests at stake in Egypt than those of Germany.

Mancini now had a clear choice. On the one hand he could join
England, share in the occupation of Egypt and hope that from the
ensuing mêlée would follow some sort of Anglo–Italian understanding, and perhaps alliance, in the Mediterranean. But if he did
so it was absolutely clear that he would incur Bismarck's wrath as
well as French resentment. The outcome would be only too
obvious. Bismarck's policy since 1878 had been to appease and
distract France with colonial gains, as the fate of Tunis made
apparent. If Mancini were to cross him in Egypt then his support
of France would be redoubled and Tripoli would probably follow
Tunis. Consequently, Mancini told Depretis on 27 July, the British
offer must be refused: it would be 'a dangerous adventure,
entirely at our own risk, the profit uncertain, whilst it would
substantially alter the basis of our foreign policy'. By rejecting
Granville's advances, Italy could demonstrate her loyalty to her
alliance partners who, he added optimistically, 'will not fail to

value the service which we render to the cause of peace.'[10]

It has been suggested, notably by Morandi, that Mancini's hesitation derived partly from 'a moral obligation to respect the principle of nationality', in the person of Arabi Pasha, who was viewed by Italian public opinion as 'the Garibaldi of Egypt'.[11] There is no doubt as to Italian sentiment on the Left, since Paget had occasion to complain of *Il Diritto,* Cairoli's paper, and its anti-British tone after the bombardment of Alexandria. Nor is there any doubt that Italian elements in Egypt itself, including De Martino, the Italian Consul, from time to time advocated a policy of alliance with Arabi and the nationalists against the Dual Control.[12] However, this was far from being Mancini's policy. From start to finish he urged the suppression of the nationalist movement and supported the control, provided he were part of it: after Tel-el-Kebir he even disowned the press criticism of Britain. His motive appears to have been quite simple: he was convinced that Britain would not act alone, that the French and then the Italian refusal would force Granville back to the 'concert', from which would emerge the collective control in Egypt that he sought.[13] Supporting Arabi or persuading him to a *modus vivendi* with the British would have defeated this object. The error, of course, lay in the basic supposition, though since Gladstone shared this view until 22 July Mancini's mistake is excusable.

Mancini's critics, principally Crispi and Minghetti, maintained that this was another missed opportunity, a repetition of Corti's mistake at Berlin in 1878. The first had led to the loss of Tunis, the second to the loss of a share in Egypt and a British alliance. Pointing to German congratulation of Granville on the victory at Tel-el-Kebir, Crispi assumed far too readily that Germany would equally have congratulated Mancini if Italian forces had participated in the destruction of Arabi Pasha. In fact Mancini was congratulated by Berlin for *not* taking part.[14] Whilst it is true that Mancini got very little support from Berlin from 1882 to 1885, even after he had acquiesced in Bismarck's wishes in Egypt, if he had opposed them it seems all too probable that Mancini, in place of Gladstone, would have become Bismarck's whipping boy in his pursuit of a colonial *entente* with France over the next three years.

Moreover, would Mancini have obtained the British alliance that Crispi – and later critics – all too readily assumed was there for

the asking? Gladstone's major object from September 1882 onwards was to get out of Egypt – the opposite of Italy's interest –
and it is difficult to envisage his making an alliance with Italy to
achieve this. Certainly Robilant, not usually charitable where
Mancini was concerned, had no doubts that on this occasion the
Foreign Minister had shown good sense. In March 1883 the count
told his friend, Marco Minghetti, leading critic of the government's Egyptian policy, that 'despite the deep reverence I have for
you, I do not repent that I was – and always will be – of the
contrary opinion, in this special [Egyptian] question of course!'[15]
In retrospect it is apparent that Mancini was right to make *il gran
rifiuto*, and his critics, necessarily, unaware of the real issues at
stake.[16]

Via Tripoli to Massowa

Mancini's hopes of basking in the sunshine of Bismarck's favour
by acquiescence in his Egyptian policy were soon disappointed.
From 1882 to 1885 Bismarck consistently pursued an understanding with France and the tone of his utterances towards his nominal
ally became increasingly hostile as the years went by. Relations with
Vienna, enlivened by sporadic outbreaks of irredentism – such as
the Oberdan affair in September 1882 – were no better: Kálnoky
point blank refused to admit Italy to the *Dreikaiserbund* on its
renewal in 1884, lest it should give Rome some excuse for meddling
in Balkan politics.[17] Equally, in Rome, fear that the perennial
irredentist demonstrations might escalate into war with Vienna was
sufficient in 1884 that the general staff drew up mobilisation plans
for this contingency. The alliance was clearly at a low ebb. In fact,
as Salvemini points out in reference to these years,[18]

> it never was a pact of unconditional solidarity between the three
> allies . . . it functioned only when a question arose in which all three
> allies recognised a common interest. When this positive solidarity
> was lacking, mutual support was no longer obligatory . . . and in
> practice was always denied.

This state of affairs had dire implications for Italian interests in
the Mediterranean. Lack of support in the Egyptian crisis had been
bad enough but it became increasingly clear that this extended to
the whole of the Mediterranean littoral. In July 1882, Kálnoky

told Robilant that if France were to take Tripoli in recompense for the British occupation of Egypt, Austria would remain passive, an attitude which Launay thought to be shared in Berlin.[19] In May 1883, questioned on this point, Bismarck was evasive: his only comment was that he thought such a move on the part of France unlikely. In April 1884, when a series of incidents in Morocco pointed unmistakably to imminent French action and Mancini sought reassurance in Berlin, Bismarck was brutally frank. He would defend Italy if she were attacked by France:[20]

> But to seek quarrels with France and risk a large scale European war on account of vague preoccupations for Italian interests, which were at best potential, in Morocco, the Red Sea, Tunis, Egypt or any other part of the world, was a proposal which did not accord with our interests or indeed the interests of anyone except the Italians. . . .

For a conservative diplomat like Launay, who disliked intensely the unpleasant task of perpetually exposing himself to Bismarck's contempt for Italy, Mancini's agitation was positively dangerous. Italy, he thought, should rest content. Her major interest was peace, which was effectively provided by the tie with Berlin, and her major concern should be to maintain the alliance. The implication that Italy had little interest in renewal in the face of Bismarck's attitude, he thought totally unrealistic: in fact, it was the other way round. Berlin and Vienna had doubts whether it was worth renewing: 'the result of certain incidents which are held against us: to wit, the seditious cries, anarchist and anti-Austrian demonstrations, and red flags flying in the leading cities'. In his view, clearly enough, the government should forget about agitation abroad and concentrate on the suppression of agitation at home.[21]

Mancini, however, was forced to take a different view. Politics in the age of *trasformismo,* the art at which Prime Minister Depretis excelled, demanded that the major trends of public opinion – at least in parliament – should be appeased.[22] Of all external problems, that which found the most general consensus was the demand for Italian security in the Mediterranean. As Zaghi writes,[23]

> Opponents and supporters of a colonial policy were in agreement that the essential interests of Italy, her future even, lay in this sea. Even those who would never approve an undertaking in the Red Sea . . . and who affirmed that a policy of conquest abroad was a

contradiction of the principles of the *Risorgimento,* were prepared to back armed intervention that guaranteed the vital interests of the country in the Mediterranean.

This attitude cut across all party divisions, from Sonnino to Branca, 'the only question that had the unconditional support of Right and Left'. The fact that Italian commercial interests in Morocco were non-existent was beside the point: Italian strategic interests demanded that if France took Morocco then Italy must take Tripoli. 'Even if the coast of Tripoli were a desert', wrote Emilio Lupi in 1885, 'even if it would not support one peasant or one Italian business firm, we still need to take it to avoid being suffocated in *mare nostrum*.'[24]

'Our sea', of course, because it had been Rome's sea. The rising tide of 'Roman' feeling in the 1880s, the natural consequence of the heightened sense of nationalism after Sedan – as rampant in Italy as elsewhere in Europe[25] – had obvious application to Tripoli. Polemicists, even in their private correspondence, spoke of the *re*conquest of the former Roman province, of Italian 'rights', as if fifteen hundred years had been yesterday. 'I am convinced', wrote the explorer Rohlfs in 1879, 'that within a few years Tripolitania will be once more Italian. In saying "once more" I think I am completely accurate, since the present sons of the Appennine peninsula must be considered the successors of the Romans. . . .' Tripoli, clearly, could not be allowed to follow the fate of Tunis and, despite Bismarck's negative attitude, Mancini could not help but make a stand. 'M. Ferry should be under no illusion,' he telegraphed to Paris on 4 May 1884, 'anything which relates to the Mediterranean touches a sensitive point here.'[26]

These fears for Tripoli, coupled with the lack of support from Berlin – where the summer of 1884 saw the Bismarckian rapprochement with France at its height – brought Mancini to the only logical course, to seek an understanding with England. This trend, noticed by the French even in April,[27] became apparent at the London conference on Egyptian finance in July, where Italy voted against the Franco–German–Russian bloc and earned a personal letter of gratitude from Granville.[28] The events of the autumn only confirmed this. With France and Germany collaborating in an all-out attack on Britain at the Berlin West Africa conference – ignoring Italy to such an extent that Mancini had to protest even to get an invitation[29] – the popular demand that Italy should not once more return with 'clean hands' and the instinct for sheer self-preservation in the Mediterranean made an alliance with England essential. The perils now impressed even Launay.[30]

> Since we can place no reliance at all upon Germany for the security of our position in the Mediterranean, necessity imposes upon us that we seek support elsewhere so as to avoid a state of isolation that could be dangerous.

Convinced that France would take Morocco as her compensation from the West Africa conference, in November and December Mancini made serious preparation for an Italian counter-coup in Tripoli. An expeditionary force of 30,000 men was prepared and staff officers sent on reconnaissance.[31] That nothing in fact materialised was due to a multiplicity of factors – not least that Ferry decided against moving in Morocco – but, most important of all, that Mancini was diverted into the Massowa expedition. In the Red Sea, he thought, Italy could forge the alliance with England which was the essential precursor of any action in the Mediterranean. Massowa, as he told the Chamber of Deputies, would lead to Tripoli. It proved a very long way round.

Massowa

Italian involvement in the Red Sea started with the acquisition of the trading post of Assab in 1882. This had a dual origin. The Rubattino steamship company had run a government-subsidised monthly service from Genoa to Bombay since 1873, and was interested in Assab as a coaling station. Simultaneously, Cairoli was convinced by the explorer Matteucci (of the *Società d'esplorazione commerciale in Africa*) that Assab could make the best entrepôt for Italian trade with Abyssinia, particularly for the exports of Scioa. Since it was evident that the British Conservative government under Disraeli would oppose an official colony athwart its communications with India,[32] Cairoli conceived the idea that Rubattino should purchase Assab as a commercial undertaking from the Sultan of Raheita with a secret guarantee of reimbursement by the Italian government. This effected, in March 1880 Cairoli then blandly denied that Italy had 'any idea of conquest on the coasts of the Red Sea'.[33] In September 1881 Granville, perhaps due to a bad conscience over Tunis, reversed Salisbury's previous opposition. He now agreed to assist Rome in obtaining recognition of their acquisition from Cairo and Constantinople, provided that the base remained purely commercial and un-fortified; and in February 1882, after Turkish procrastination, Granville simply recognised Rubattino's acquisition. Almost immediately, on 10 March, the company ceded all its rights to the state. Granville, though clearly annoyed at the deception, was fully occupied in Egypt and made no protest.[34]

Having acquired Assab the next move was to make use of it. Count Pietro Antonelli, who had travelled extensively in Scioa on behalf of the *Società geografica italiana,* advocated the development of Assab by selling rifles to Menelik, King of Scioa. This, he thought, would create a 'moral and economic Italian preponder-ance' there. Mancini accepted his advice and on 21 May 1883 a treaty of commerce between Italy and Scioa was signed. The rifle trade boomed and for a while all looked well until it was dis-covered that Menelik had no means of paying for them: by 1884 he had paid only 20 per cent of the bill for rifles delivered during the previous two years, a fact which cast grave doubts upon the economic future of Assab. Clearly, it could prosper only upon the trade of the *whole* of Abyssinia.

At the same time the general Turco–Egyptian retirement from the Sudan and the Red Sea coast began. A British garrison replaced the Turks at Zeila in August 1884; in September the French moved in at Tagiura and Obock. Since it was announced that Egyptian withdrawal from Massowa, Suakin, and all points south was to follow, Mancini now feared that, unless he moved quickly, Italy would find her colony of Assab hemmed in north and south by French and British acquisitions who would take the lion's share of Abyssinian trade. More important from his point of view than the potential commercial gains – which did not appear to be excessive – was the use that the parliamentary opposition would make of his inaction at a time when all the European powers seemed bent on carving out colonies in Africa. The opening of the West Africa conference at Berlin in November 1884 suggested that the interior of Africa would follow the fate of the coastal provinces: Mancini had already been assailed by Crispi and others for missing the boat in Egypt in 1882; further abstention would almost certainly bring him down, as Italian feeling on Africa was particularly sensitive in 1884 after the murder of the explorer Bianchi in Abyssinia.[35]

It was the combination of these circumstances – the almost frantic search for a British alliance and the fear that his parliamentary opponents would exploit another repetition of *mani netti* – that led Mancini to Massowa. Until October 1884, Mancini had shown no interest whatsoever in Africa outside the Mediterranean littoral. Assab he had inherited from Cairoli and had done nothing with it. As recently as May 1884 he had made a speech in the Senate asserting his conviction that it was imprudent and downright dangerous for a young nation like Italy 'to launch out in expensive and perilous adventures in distant lands, to initiate what is called a colonial policy'. Italy needed peace, retrenchment and reform.[36] Yet, by January 1885, Mancini seemed a man transformed. The African fever generated by the Berlin Conference clearly had him in its grip. 'How could Italy refuse', he asked the Chamber of Deputies, 'to pay her contribution to the fight of civilisation against ignorance and barbarism?' Italy too must abandon prudence and embark on this historic mission, though, he hastened to add, the costs would be carefully watched.[37] The exhortation of a colonialist to Cairoli in 1880, 'Forget the flour tax, develop our trade,' had finally been heard.[38]

Two myths have long bedevilled the Massowa affair, both originating in Mancini's attempts to cover his mistakes by misleading his critics. Firstly, that Italy went to Massowa to help England: as Mancini put it, 'in response to a British invitation we consented to guard with our protection the coasts of the Red Sea'.[39] This simply was not true. Granville's enquiry of 20 October 1885 whether Italy would be interested in Massowa was consistently misread by Mancini. Granville, who had remarkably little guile for a Foreign Secretary, was simply making a friendly gesture. But, obsessed with the idea that 'England seeks that we do her a service',[40] Mancini saw visions of an Anglo–Italian alliance on terms favourable to Rome. This, he thought, would solve all Italy's Mediterranean problems, an idea he expressed in his speech in the Chamber of Deputies on 27 January 1885, in reply to criticism of his proposed Red Sea adventure:[41]

> But why do you not wish to accept that in the Red Sea, the neighbour of the Mediterranean, we can find the key to the latter, the road that will lead us to an effective security against every new disturbance of its equilibrium?

With this misconception governing his policy, Mancini waited hopefully for a formal offer from Granville which would, he told Nigra, 'be the moment for us to announce our conditions'. The least he would get, he thought, would be a defensive alliance. Unfortunately Granville had no such intentions. On 13 November he told Nigra brusquely, that there was 'no question of Italy doing England a service' and that the matter should be allowed to drop.[42]

Consequently, if Mancini was to obtain anything – and parliamentary considerations made it essential that he should[43] – he had to make the running himself, and on 23 December Nigra finally went to see Granville at Walmer. His reply was clear enough. All the Red Sea ports reverted to Turkey on Egyptian retirement and they were not in England's gift. If Mancini wanted them he should make his own arrangement with the Sultan. All Granville could say was that Britain would raise no objection if Italy were to occupy Zulla, Beilul or Massowa, provided that Abyssinian rights of access to Massowa under the recent Hewitt Treaty were observed. This, Nigra thought, was 'the most favourable reply that he could reasonably expect'.[44]

The occupation of Massowa followed on 5 February 1885. Giglio argues that this was largely because Mancini, having raised expectations in parliament by his veiled hints of important developments, had to show concrete results with which to appease national pride. By contrast, his biographer, Carlo Zaghi, insists that this action was but part of a great scheme for operations in the Sudan and – via Zeila – in the Abyssinian province of Harar.[45] This seems another of Mancini's myths.

The first suggestion that Italy should send a military expedition to the Sudan came, unofficially, from Lumley on 15 January 1885; whereas Mancini had announced his intention at London and Cairo of seizing Massowa on 29 December.[46] No doubt Mancini was attracted to the idea of a Sudanese expedition: it might well prove the key to Tripoli, if not the Mediterranean. But the point is that Nigra discovered that the suggestion had no official basis in London on 3 February yet Mancini made no attempt to stop the Massowa landing. This is not surprising when it is borne in mind that three days later, on 8 February, the Council of Ministers decided it was essential to promote the Sudan expedition to avoid a political crisis in Italy.

Mancini, in other words, had got himself in a fix by promising parliament a British alliance, which was considerably more than he could deliver. The announcement in London on 9 February that Britain had declined Italian offers of assistance in the Sudan only added to Mancini's embarrassment: he then had to work hard to persuade Granville to announce in the House of Lords that Italy never had made any such offer. As the Council of Ministers had feared, the result of this fiasco – which Nigra thought very un-dignified – was a parliamentary storm which played a considerable part in Mancini's overthrow in June 1885.[47]

Similarly in the case of Harar. It was only *after* 5 February, *not before,* that – prompted by the explorer, Commander Cecchi – Mancini began to see the possibilities of using Massowa as a springboard for the occupation of Zeila and Harar. Diverted in February by the mirage of the Sudan, it was not until late March that Mancini opened negotiations in London on this subject. Again, Granville took the same stance as in December: they were not in Britain's gift, but he would raise no objections if Mancini made his own arrangements with the Turks, as the Indian garrison at Zeila was shortly to be withdrawn.

Once more Mancini miscalculated. Since his critics, un-interested in Africa, were demanding evidence of his supposed understanding with England – in February he had staved them off with a premature announcement of joint operations in the Sudan – he tried desperately in May and June to obtain an open invitation from London to take Zeila and the Harar. This was not forth-coming. Granville had difficulties enough of his own in May 1885 without adding to them by gratuitously annoying the Turks – giving away their provinces – and on 11 June the Liberal govern-ment in London finally resigned. Mancini, in a hopeless position, unable to produce any evidence of his understanding with England, followed suit on 29 June. Once out of office, he tried to protect his reputation by blaming it all on the perfectly innocent Granville, whose sole crime was that he never had intended to seek Italian assistance against France in the Red Sea, or make an Italian alliance.[48]

Robilant's fortress

Carlo di Robilant became Foreign Minister on 6 October 1885 at the personal command of the king when the growing complexity

of the Bulgarian crisis persuaded Premier Depretis, who had held
the office *ad interim* since Mancini's resignation, that he needed the
guidance of an expert. He was, in Salvemini's phrase, 'the right
man in the right place'.[49] In the eighteen months that he held
office, Robilant's forceful diplomacy, aided by circumstances,
completely transformed Italy's diplomatic position. By the agreement with England signed on 12 February 1887 he obtained what
had eluded Mancini, a British guarantee of the *status quo* in the
Mediterranean. By the second treaty of the Triple Alliance, signed
one week later, Robilant obtained from Bismarck the commitment
he had consistently evaded from 1882 to 1885 – a guarantee that the
casus foederis should apply against France in the event of war
arising from an Italo–French quarrel in North Africa. Even
Kálnoky was induced to make concessions. By a separate Austro–
Italian agreement he accepted the principle of mutual consultation
before taking any action in the Balkans and reciprocal compensation for any territorial gains, the Article VII which was to form the
basis of Italian neutrality in 1914. As Robilant said on resignation
on 4 April 1887, he left his country 'in an iron cask'.

A Piedmontese aristocrat by birth, a soldier by inclination and
education, General di Robilant had taken to diplomacy in 1871 as
a second career when offered the Vienna Embassy, the post he held
until 1885. He always remained a man of action, given to blunt
speaking, whether giving advice or in discussion with Austro–
Hungarian ministers. 'With the Austrian government', he told
Nigra, in 1886, 'you gain nothing by letting things slide. Tolerance
is considered weakness at Vienna. . . .' Though generally considered a reactionary in Italy this was not in fact the case; he
belonged, if anywhere, to the Right Centre of Visconti Venosta
and Minghetti. Robilant was no admirer of strong men: Bismarck
he detested and regarded his illiberalism as a menace to European
peace; similarly Crispi, whom he regarded as *'un Bismarck minore'*,
and whose advent to power he thought 'the worst fate that could
overtake us':[50]

> Only Joshua was given the power to stop the sun, so Bismarck
> deludes himself if he thinks he can make the world go backwards: in
> my opinion he is sowing tremendous tempests which will be
> harvested by a future Emperor of Germany.

True, Robilant was a bitter critic of the Italian parliamentary system – on the grounds that ministerial instability completely effaced Italian influence abroad – and avoided as long as possible the call to ministerial office.[51] He only took it in October 1885 at the king's request, after turning down Depretis twice. Only too well aware of his own deficiencies for this post which, in Italy, demanded 'a man who was half-statesman . . . and half-clown',[52] Robilant's experiences in February 1887 confirmed what he had always thought: 'my complete inaptitude for parliamentary life'.[53] Understandably bitter, he absolutely refused to accept office again, which was Italy's loss. He was, after all, the only Italian Foreign Minister in this period who successfully stood up to Bismarck and got his own way. Crispi, by contrast, was a sycophant.

Robilant's abilities in this respect derived partly from his realism, partly from circumstances. He had no illusions where Bismarck was concerned. Whereas Launay was inclined to cling to Berlin at all costs as Italy's only salvation,[54] Robilant saw, rightly, that the alliance would last only as long as it suited German interests. Bismarck's solemn assurances about the 'natural alliance' between them meant nothing. He despised Italy and used her only to suit his convenience: 'Now his object is attained', Robilant wrote in December 1884, 'he treats us like a squeezed lemon.' Consequently, the Piedmontese aristocrat saw no point in humouring 'the temporary master of the world', resisted all invitations to take the train to Varzin *ad audiendum verbum*, and made no attempt to open negotiations for the renewal of the alliance.[55] The onus rested with Berlin: in this way Rome would obtain some clue as to Bismarck's intentions and could then insist on her own terms. 'The one course which I intend to exclude, for the present, is any initiative on our part.'[56]

Circumstances undoubtedly aided Robilant. Whereas Mancini, from 1882 to 1885, had to cope not only with Italian isolation but with Bismarck at the zenith of his power – secure in his Three Emperors' Alliance and colonial *entente* with France, bent on the destruction of Gladstone – in 1886–7 things were different. The *Dreikaiserbund* had broken down over Bulgaria, the French *entente* had collapsed with the rise of Boulanger and – with Salisbury in office – Bismarck actively wanted an understanding with England.[57] This situation gave Robilant much more room for manoeuvre. Whilst Bismarck in August 1885, in conversation with Kálnoky, treated Italy as an insignificant factor in European politics and stressed that 'there is no chance of Italy through her pranks involving us – perhaps deliberately – in a conflict with France', a year later his attitude was very different. By the end of October 1886 he thought it 'inexpedient for Germany to remain neutral in the event of a war between France and Italy, no matter what its cause may be'. Austria–Hungary, he urged, should look at Italian proposals in a spirit of accommodation and 'give further consideration to a possible Italian cooperation against Russia'.[58]

This change of heart was the direct result of Robilant's prompting. In August 1886, Keudell, the German ambassador at Rome, had still taken Bismarck's traditional line that Italian fears for Tripoli were mythical, that France had too much on her plate already. He was sharply rebutted by Robilant.[59]

> I could not admit this optimistic appreciation. The presence on the Tripolitanian frontier of General Allegro, who might well be termed a Boulanger No. 2, is sufficient to convince one that once the moment is opportune they will invent Kroumirs to carry them to Tripoli, repeating the result they attained in Tunis.

Italian apprehension was not confined to Tripoli. In the current Bulgarian crisis, Kálnoky's wish to avoid war with Russia and Bismarck's obvious intention to avoid taking sides if he could possibly help it, made it extremely difficult to predict German policy. The most likely result, Robilant thought, was a German-promoted Austro–Russian division of the Balkans. This, equally, it was essential to avert as the result would be Austrian control of the entire western Balkans and the Adriatic sea, leaving Italy powerless and hemmed in.[60]

The problem was how to prevent this, how to tie down Bismarck and Kálnoky in respect of both Tripoli and the Balkans. The means were presented by Freycinet, who, in search of an ally in the perennial Franco–British quarrel over Egypt, on 9 October 1886 suggested a Franco–Italian alliance in the Mediterranean.[61] The offer was immediately relayed to Berlin where it had the desired effect: Bismarck was now willing to discuss a renewal of the alliance on Robilant's terms.[62] It took another four months to bring about the new treaty, signed on 20 February 1887, largely because Kálnoky was extremely reluctant to accept Italian claims in the Balkans and rejected outright any Austrian involvement in Tripoli; but the final result was a complete victory for Robilant.

Germany guaranteed the *status quo* in North Africa, accepting that any Franco–Italian war arising from a quarrel in that region involved German military assistance to Italy. Austria–Hungary, equally, underwrote the *status quo* in the Balkans, the Adriatic and the Aegean and promised prior consultation and equivalent compensation for Italy in the event of any Austrian advance. The whole negotiations are an object lesson demonstrating what firm diplomacy can make of favourable circumstances, even for a weak power like Italy. The only snag, as Salvemini points out, was that the continued effectiveness of the treaty depended upon the perpetuation of the favourable circumstances that had brought it about.[63]

Part of the explanation of Austro–German willingness to extend their commitments to Italy in 1887 lay in Robilant's successful negotiations with England, culminating in the signature of an Anglo–Italian agreement on 12 February 1887. The origin of this lay in the peculiar combination of circumstances existing in the Balkans and the Mediterranean in the autumn of 1886. The return of the Conservative Unionist administration in Britain in August, under Salisbury, led to both a stiffening of resistance to Russian pretensions in Bulgaria and a determined attempt to negotiate a British withdrawal from Egypt. Unfortunately for Anglo–Italian understanding, on neither of these points did their mutual interests coincide.

Whereas Salisbury sought Austrian and Italian support over Bulgaria, it was Robilant's conviction that Italian interests were best served by keeping out of this question. He thought Russia had some rights in that country. The Berlin Congress, he wrote to Catalani, the Italian chargé d'affaires in London, 'whilst it intended to limit the consequences of the Russian victories, did not intend to exclude entirely Russian tutelage over Bulgaria, which owed its political existence to those victories'. The current attitude of public opinion 'in some countries' was wrong in claiming that Russia should disinterest herself from Bulgarian affairs, 'as if she were Spain or Portugal'.[64] Well aware of the current British policy of using others to bell the cat,[65] he strongly disapproved of any attempt to push the Bulgarian assembly into an anti-Russian stance by promising them the moral support of some of the powers. 'I told the British ambassador that I held it immoral to give moral support to a small state when you were not willing, if necessary, to give also material support.'[66] Behind this abstention lay of course the knowledge that Vienna would not move: as Kálnoky suggested, it was dangerous to force Bismarck to choose between Russia and Austria.

In Bulgaria then no Anglo–Italian co-operation was possible and Queen Victoria could justly complain at Berlin in December that British approaches to Rome had been rejected.[67] On Egypt Robilant sounded more hopeful. On 24 September Catalani approached Iddesleigh and offered, in return for temporary transit rights through the port of Zeila, 'to enter into almost any engagement with this country [Britain] to support us in Bulgaria, Egypt or elsewhere'. Though Bulgaria was promptly deleted three days later, the offer on Egypt still remained open.[68] What Robilant feared, of course, was an Anglo–French agreement: it was no secret that Salisbury contemplated a negotiated withdrawal from Egypt[69] and, if this were to occur, the whole basis of Italian policy in the Mediterranean would collapse. As he instructed Corti in December, negotiations between Britain and France over Egypt must be watched with the closest attention, 'as for us they are of the highest importance'.[70]

The September offer of support in Egypt failed to bear fruit, although Iddesleigh thought he would be 'very glad to get the hearty support of Italy in Egypt and the Mediterranean', largely because giving away Zeila – thus 'alarming the Sultan as to the limits of our vicarious generosity' – would render the whole exercise pointless. It was no use London obtaining the support of Rome if by doing so it alienated the Porte.[71] Nor did Robilant's attempts to swing the negotiations in the direction of an anti-French pact do him much good. On the advice of Berlin, on 22 October Robilant dropped heavy hints to Lumley that he was ready to 'talk on the Egyptian question'; on 28 November he made a set speech in the Chamber laying heavy emphasis on Italian solidarity with England, [72] but all to no avail; London was mute. As Robilant in his turn complained to Bruck, the Austrian Ambassador at Rome, Salisbury and Iddesleigh were completely unresponsive: 'It is an old piano which has lost its tone: we have struck the keys but nothing emerges.'[73]

Evidently against all his instincts as a diplomat, Robilant was driven, finally, to open negotiations himself – a step he had successfully avoided with Bismarck. On 11 January 1887 he sent for Lumley and stressed his anxiety for an interchange of ideas:[74]

> ... he did not ask Her Majesty's Government to enter into any engagement with Italy, but merely to agree as to the steps which each might take independently and simultaneously and which both countries might be prepared to put into action in two or three days.

This was, of course, merely an alliance under another name, the tactful phraseology reflecting the well-known British aversion to definite commitments: it is quite clear from the current Italo–German negotiations that what Robilant and Bismarck wanted was a naval alliance against France.[75] That, in the course of the negotiations that followed at London, the emphasis was switched from an alliance against France to a combination against Russia, was a reflection of Bismarck and Robilant's discovery of Salisbury's feelings. As the Chancellor told Launay,[76]

> not that we can expect to find a well prepared ground for armed action against France, but at London there is a sensitive point which can be more easily aroused, that of preparations against Russia.

This switch, together with the fact of German support, explains the comparative success of Robilant in January and February 1887 as opposed to his failure the previous autumn. German initiative was unimportant, Rome needed no prompting from Berlin to negotiate with London: what was crucial was German support. Bismarck's constant intervention made plain the importance that he attached to success. As Malet commented, 'The question is I think a much bigger one than it appeared when first innovated by Ct. Robilant.' These factors then induced Salisbury to an exchange of notes with Corti on 12 February.[77]

If one examines these notes it is clear that they amounted to little more than a declaration of intent, very different in character to the second treaty of the Triple Alliance signed at Berlin the following week. The question then arises as to why Robilant was so satisfied with them. It was, partly, that Salisbury said enough in the course of the negotiations to carry conviction as to his sincerity. He told Corti on 1 February that British and Italian interests in the Mediterranean coincided, that 'an understanding [*intesa*] would produce for England the same effects as if they were to sign a treaty'. Furthermore, 'if circumstances should so arise, Tripolitania should be occupied by Italy, not by France.' There was no point, in Corti's view, in pressing for more than Salisbury was willing to give: '. . . verbal declarations have more value than written documents obtained under pressure, which could raise difficulties, in view of the actual position of England.'[78] Since Corti was a close friend, whose judgment Robilant was inclined to trust, his views were important. Moreover, both Corti and Launay thought that the moral obligations would in fact lead to material co-operation. 'The door is open', wrote the latter, 'to more precise stipulations, the entente will soon develop in the way we desire.'[79] Depretis, Premier since 1882, was quite satisfied even with things as they were. He told the Cabinet on 18 February, 'As for England I must add that no Italian cabinet could have dared to hope to obtain that which our Count Robilant has achieved: our position is now secure by land and by sea.'[80]

Last but not least, Robilant's fall from office, initiated by the Dogali debate of 5 February, made any agreement better than none. If he had continued in office then the hopes of further development might have been fulfilled, but his determination after this debate to retire from political life led to his eventual replacement in July 1887 by Francesco Crispi, who was a very different proposition in Salisbury's eyes.

Chapter 4

The Crispi Era

France must forget the days of her influence beyond the
Alps and recognise that Italy is her equal.

Crispi, 1887

Francesco Crispi was sixty-eight years old when on 29 July 1887 he
finally became President of the Council, Minister of the Interior
and of Foreign Affairs, though he had in fact exercised these
functions since the end of April in an unofficial capacity. Except
for a brief period in 1878 this was the first time he had taken an
office under the crown, but it was not his first taste of political
responsibility. This had been gained as an assistant to Garibaldi in
1860 and his experiences then had left a lasting mark on Crispi's
approach to the problems of government. The discovery that the
majority of Italians had little understanding of the ideals of the
Risorgimento and would rather fight against their landlords than
for 'Italy', made him unsympathetic to the problems of the 'peasants'. Similarly, in his eyes, the major sin of the socialists was that
'their sense of internationalism makes them lose their sense of
patriotism, if they ever possessed one'.[1] The hero of the Risorgimento became, therefore, a lonely authoritarian figure with a
peculiar responsibility as custodian of 'his' Italy, a responsibility
which Crispi felt to the full. His whole life was a battle against the
'enemies' of the new state – Sicilian peasants, Emilian anarchists,
Roman cardinals, Lombard irredentists, French chauvinists: they
were all the same to him if they threatened the security of 'his' Italy.

For a man of Crispi's authoritarian views the tenure of the
Ministry of Foreign Affairs simply meant the imposition of his own
foreign policy. It was generally recognised in Rome that his
temperament made him an unsuitable candidate for that office. As
Kennedy, the British chargé d'affaires in Rome observed, 'It may
be admitted that Crispi is unfitted for the post of Foreign Minister
in which he delights. His friends recognise that his natural rashness

and impulsiveness have given rise to frequent misunderstandings and unpleasantness.'[2] But since neither Nigra nor Robilant, the two obvious candidates, would accept office under Crispi, he had perforce to continue and it soon became apparent that once in the saddle he would take a lot of shifting. For Crispi undoubtedly began to enjoy the power which his monopoly of the three most important offices brought him to formulate and execute foreign policy with little reference to anyone else. Apart from the advantages this brought for the maintenance of his internal position – the ability to distract criticism by a forceful policy – he had, undoubtedly, a strong interest in foreign affairs for their own sake.[3]

Crispi's ideas on foreign policy were largely those formed in the 1860s. He never entirely lost the habits of conspiracy, with a love for travelling incognito and dramatic personal interviews – particularly with Bismarck – which were to change the face of Europe.[4] This, the heritage of his Mazzinian past, was not without its effects on the execution of Italian policy in the 1880s, with much consequent confusion.

His debt to Mazzini came out quite clearly in his conception of the Italian position in Europe. Italy in his view was a great power by 'natural right', derived from the strength of her people in the struggles of the Risorgimento: struggles in which they had been led by Garibaldi, Mazzini and Crispi. In this view of the origins of Italy there was little room for Cavour. Italy had not been made by diplomacy or the accidents of European history: Italy had been made by awakening the Italian people – or the politically conscious amongst them – to their destiny as the heirs of ancient Rome. Hence the insistence in 1870 by Crispi and the majority of the Left that Rome must be seized at all costs: *Roma capitale* was to be the symbol of this reawakening.[5]

Crispi and France

Crispi's attitude towards France followed logically from this premise. He, in contrast to the Right, felt no gratitude for Magenta and Solferino, only annoyance at the persistence of French moral tutelage over Italy. To be independent Italy must break with France, and when the chance came in 1870 Crispi had been among the first to raise the cry of 'Nice and Savoy' and to demand a military alliance with Germany. This attitude he retained with remarkable persistence throughout the 1880s and 1890s: France was the natural enemy in the struggle for hegemony in the Mediterranean.[6] To add to this was his lasting anti-clericalism, for whereas most of the Italian Left gradually lost their fears of a French combination with the Vatican after 1878, Crispi – a free-mason and a deist – remained very suspicious. This fear of the 'Black International' and French intrigue contributed in no small measure to the war scares of the late 1880s.[7]

Italo–French relations were extremely bad during Crispi's first period of office from 1887 to 1891, degenerating at times to the verge of war, creating the suspicion in Paris that Crispi was Bismarck's *agent provocateur*. This suspicion, which derived from Crispi's mysterious trips to Varzin and Friedrichsruhe, knowledge of the Italo–German military convention[8] signed in Berlin on 28 January 1888, and Crispi's frequent storms, was in fact unfounded. To a large extent what seemed to successive French ambassadors as deliberate bellicosity on Crispi's part was simply his unfortunate manner, his normal method of doing business with anyone, including his cabinet colleagues. As Salvemini – no admirer of Crispi – wrote, 'He carried over into diplomacy the same instability of thought, the same intemperance of language, that one meets at every step in his parliamentary speeches whether in opposition or in power. . . .'[9]

Despite appearances, there is no reason to suppose that Crispi wanted war with France. The military convention,[10] a political blunder of the first magnitude on Crispi's part, derived less from aggressive intentions than from his need to impress Bismarck with Italian sincerity and worth as an ally. It is difficult to believe that Bismarck really wanted Italian assistance on the Rhine, but the opportunity served both to flatter Crispi[11] and to ensure his personal commitment to the alliance, a devotion which was far from certain in 1887. Crispi, after all, had a reputation as a wild man of the Left, and the German and Austrian Ambassadors at Rome were very cautious with him at first. Nor did this ever entirely wear off: their attitude, Kennedy reported at the end of a series of incidents in 1888, 'is one of alarm rather than confidence, but they believe he suits the purpose of the alliance better than any other statesman'.[12] Crispi's sincerity is always difficult to assess, but he was probably truthful when he told the republican Cavallotti in February 1888 that a Franco–Italian war 'would be an enormous and fearful disaster for both countries'. Certainly the French vision of Crispi as 'a sort of Cesare Borgia, methodically plotting to trap France into war' was erroneous: Crispi was far too spontaneous a character. There is the ring of truth in Salvemini's suggestion that whilst Robilant's motto was *'faire sans dire'* Crispi's should have been *'dire sans faire'*.[13]

However, if Crispi did not actively want a war with France, neither did he fear one. Secure – as none of his predecessors had been – in the knowledge of German support, confident that Britain could be induced to follow suit, Crispi saw no reason to perpetuate the deference towards France traditional in Italian foreign ministers. He would answer insult with insult and, in the process, assert Italian independence from *la sorella latina*. This attitude was at its clearest in the tariff war which dominated Italo–French relations during Crispi's first period of office, 1887–91.

In his exuberance following the first visit to Bismarck at Friedrichsruhe on 2–3 October 1887, Crispi 'indulged in arrogant and contemptuous language towards France, talking of bringing her to her knees in the commercial negotiations'.[14] This was a mistake. Crispi did not create the problem. He inherited an awkward situation due, basically, to the rising wave of protectionism in both the Italian and French parliaments. This had led in December 1886 to the Italian's chamber's denunciation of the 1881 Treaty of Commerce and Navigation with France, due to expire at the end of 1887, and stipulation that it should be replaced by a treaty more advantageous to Italian interests. Crispi made strenuous efforts to achieve this in the summer of 1887 but with no success since, with the French chamber similarly bent, the French government could make no concessions and even doubted if they could now renew the 1881 treaty. In these circumstances the standard Italian criticism of Crispi, that it was his Friedrichsruhe visit which ruined the negotiations,[15] is clearly misplaced: it is doubtful if anything could have been achieved in any case. All that can be said is that this visit and the policy of violent threats which followed finally killed any hope of negotiation as far as the French government were concerned. Rouvier told Ressmann on 21 October 1887 that the Chamber of Deputies was so excitable after the Friedrichsruhe visit that there was no hope of obtaining concessions until they calmed down.[16]

In consequence by the spring of 1888 Crispi was in a cleft stick. On the one hand his parliamentary supporters demanded improved commercial concessions; and in face of rising criticism in the Chamber Crispi, even if willing, could not ignore them. On the other hand the French would not or could not make concessions.[17] This problem, which was to dominate Crispi's foreign policy for the next two years, drove him into the series of incidents with France, on the apparent assumption that this would force Paris to negotiate in the commercial sphere.[18]

If this was Crispi's object it completely miscarried, since the French, instead of accepting Crispi's terms, gradually pushed up their own. As it became clear that the results of the tariff war, whilst disastrous for Italy, were of much less importance for France, Goblet and his successors demanded as their price first the settlement of all Tunisian difficulties, then Italy's withdrawal from the Triple Alliance.[19] Long before this stage had been reached Crispi's intransigence had melted. With the catastrophic decline of Italian exports in 1888–9 there rose a storm of criticism of Crispi's policy, particularly from the southern deputies normally his closest supporters. With his parliamentary position threatened once more, Crispi changed his tactics and began to feel his way towards a commercial *modus vivendi* based upon Italian concessions to France.[20]

Crispi, Austria and the Ottoman Empire

Crispi's original enthusiasm for the Mazzinian principle of national self-determination for all peoples underwent considerable modification in these years and by 1896, as Chabod points out, was indistinguishable from the demands of Italian nationalism. In 1877, when visiting Bismarck, Crispi had been all in favour of partitioning the Habsburg Empire between Germany and Italy but even by 1880 he had changed his mind. The disasters which befell the Cairoli government when allowing free rein to irredentism made a deep impression upon him: in March 1880 he marked his break with the traditional Left by announcing to the chamber that 'Austria is a necessity for us'. A constant admirer of all things Prussian he readily accepted the Triple Alliance and the Austrian corollary: he told Nigra in July 1889 that he did not even want Trieste. In October 1890 in an election speech at Florence he urged

his audience that '. . . the principle of nationality to which we owe
our existence may, if pushed too far, lead us to our ruin'.

This discovery was the direct outcome of his feud with France.
His constant fear of clerical conspiracies made him view irredentism as a liability since, he explained to Nigra in July 1890, 'if
Austria got away from us she would ally at once with France in
defence of the Pope'. Hence Crispi's rigid suppression of irredentist
societies like Imbriani's *Trento e Trieste,* an attitude which earned
him the undying hatred of the radical Left. Even his own friends
were not immune: Seismit-Doda, his Minister of Finance, was
dismissed by telegram for attending an irredentist banquet at
Udine. When the Austrian government dissolved the *Pro Patria*
society at Trento in 1890 – an action which raised a storm in North
Italy – Crispi made no protest. He half hinted to Nigra that Francis
Joseph should intervene with some concession to make it easier
for him to renew the alliance in 1892 but threw the principal blame
on the Jesuits! Nigra's reply, that the most liberal Viennese Jew
would have done the same and that if Italy failed to renew she
would face utter disaster, is conveniently omitted by Crispi's
biographer.

His ready acceptance of the Habsburg Empire as a necessary
evil and of Francis Joseph as the most able prince in Europe was
not confined to the papal issue. Increasingly in the 1880s and 1890s
Crispi brooded over the menace of Russia, 'the land of the knout',
and the threat which Panslavism posed to Italian interests. This led
him to view Balkan nationalism with a distinctly jaundiced eye.
Significantly, in contrast to Mazzini, the only Balkan people to
obtain much sympathy from Crispi were the Greeks – who were
not Slavs – and the Bulgars, who were distinctly anti-Russian. The
rest were a threat to Italian interests because they menaced
Austrian security: 'Austria should not disintegrate', he wrote to
Nigra in July 1890, 'since she is a barrier against our eventual and
more dangerous foes, whom we must keep away from our present
frontier.'[21]

If reconciled to Vienna, however, Crispi's attitude towards
Constantinople was curiously ambivalent: he could never entirely
accept that, as Sorel had pointed out in 1870, the Habsburg and
Ottoman empires were interdependent. On the one hand Crispi
personally instigated the schemes for the preservation of Turkey
which resulted in the Second Mediterranean Agreement of

December 1887:[22] on the other, he responded with naïve
enthusiasm to the movements for Bulgarian and Cretan independence from 1887 to 1889. Theoretically supporting the *status quo* in
the Ottoman Empire, he nevertheless embarked on a string of
quarrels with the sultan – actually recalling his ambassador, Blanc,
at one stage – and made no secret of the fact that he wanted to
obtain the Turkish province of Tripoli. Salisbury, more than once,
had to remind him that the object of the 1887 agreement was to
uphold Turkey, not divide her.

With Crispi this ambivalence was a question of tactics. As he
told Blanc in August 1887, the long-term aim of Italian policy was
the liberation of the suppressed nationalities, but for the present
Italy wanted to draw Turkey into the *Entente à trois* and preserve
the *status quo*. A straightforward pursuit of a policy of 'compensations' was too dangerous as Austria and Russia would gain the
lion's share. The result was that Italian policy towards Turkey
became a curious amalgamation of blandishments and threats in
which nobody was sure – possibly least of all Crispi – where Rome
stood.

Crispi's detestation of the Ottoman regime was of long standing
and based, primarily, on the familiar Mazzinian grounds that it was
an oppressor of the peoples. From the first moment he assumed
office in 1887 he launched a vast scheme for the reform of the
sultan's dominions under the aegis of the great powers, an idea
which was not without its effects in making the sultan extremely
hostile to both Crispi and his ambassador at Constantinople,
Blanc.[23] In 1888 the latter's energetic pursuit of this object,
amongst others, reached such a pitch that, after pressure from
Berlin and Vienna, he was temporarily recalled since it was feared
he would completely alienate the sultan from the Triple Alliance.
Re-appointed at the end of the year, within six months Italo–
Turkish relations were as bad as ever, with Crispi threatening to
bombard Benghazi if he were not given satisfaction for some
imagined slight. This highhanded treatment of the Porte led to
serious irritation at Constantinople, where, according to White, the
Franco–Russian bloc were urging that this was a prelude to an
attack upon Tripoli.[24]

Alarm in Berlin led to a direct rebuke which Salisbury supported, impressing upon Catalani 'the important issues which
depended upon the maintenance of a good understanding between

Turkey and Italy and that he should subordinate to these larger considerations any smaller matters'.[25] But Crispi, who seemed to be convinced that the sultan was inspired against Italy by the French, was unrepentant. When, in July 1889, the Cretan revolt broke out, he seized this opportunity of revenging himself by proposing that the powers should intervene by force with a military occupation of the island. This, in his view, was the only possible solution since, if the powers did nothing, Crete was liable to be the spark to set the east ablaze.

Crispi's attitude towards Turkey at this time was certainly coloured by his sympathies with the Cretans, but this was not the whole explanation of his violent antipathy to the Ottoman regime. Undoubtedly as a result of these incidents he conceived the idea, by no means without foundation, that the Turks regarded Italy as of no account. This obviously irritated him profoundly and, as Dering noted, he 'became very bitter respecting Turkey whom he considers as wishing to slight Italy on every possible occasion'.[26] This aspect came out again in an exchange with Nigra in January 1890 when the latter, under pressure from Kálnoky, suggested that it was not in Italy's best interests to further irritate the Porte. This Crispi rejected on the grounds that 'since the Sultan continued hostile to Italy he had little concern for Turkish feelings but only for Italian interests'.[27] This was to be the *leitmotiv* of his policy in 1890, since, as all reform projects had been abandoned, he thought the collapse of the Turkish Empire could not long now be delayed and intended to make certain in advance that Italy should acquire her share – Tripoli.

Crispi and Africa

Crispi was also responsible for the first serious attempt to found an Italian colonial empire in East Africa, the attempt that culminated in the disaster of Adowa in February 1896, and provided the basic incentive for Mussolini's more successful efforts in Abyssinia in 1935.

Crispi's involvement in Abyssinia was less a deliberate policy on his part than a series of reactions to events. On accession to office in July 1887 he inherited Mancini's folly, Massowa. On its own Massowa was an expensive liability, for Italian possession irritated the Negus Negusti, John, who evidently expected to inherit the port after the Anglo–Egyptian withdrawal from the Sudan and created immediate friction with the neighbouring Ras Alula. Mancini himself went to great pains to reassure the negus in April 1885 (the Ferrari–Nerazzini mission) and gave strict instructions to Massowa to avoid irritating the Abyssinians, who could easily make the Italian position untenable. His successor, Robilant, was similarly intent: the only way to make Massowa begin to pay its way was to encourage the negus to use it and develop closer Italo–Abyssinian relations.

Unfortunately, however, by 1886 the negus had other ideas. These varied from attacking and driving out the Italians to confining them strictly to the island of Massowa and himself developing the nearby port of Arafali. This latter scheme, General Genè, the commander at Massowa, acknowledged, 'will reduce [the] commercial opportunity of Massowa to zero'.[28]

Massowa itself proved so physically uncomfortable to live in that Italian troops quickly crossed to the mainland and sought the nearest range of hills. Ras Alula, long convinced that the Italians were about to attack him, engaged in local skirmishes. The negus, who feared that the Italian government held him responsible for Bianchi's death, and encouraged by Greek and French traders to believe that Italy was of no account, urged on the ras. Robilant, by training a soldier, increasingly convinced that the only language understood by the Abyssinians was force, equally urged Genè to teach them a sharp lesson if they raided towards Massowa.[29] The inevitable result was ambush and counter ambush culminating in the 'massacre' of an Italian force at Dogali in January 1887. This defeat raised a popular clamour in Italy against the government, brought down Robilant and eventually brought in Crispi.

Originally Crispi had been the most severe of Mancini's critics in 1885 on the grounds that his African adventure was a distraction from the Mediterranean.[30] Even after he assumed office under Depretis in April 1887 he was slow to change his mind. He accepted the cry for retribution after the Dogali defeat but, as he became increasingly responsible for policy making, showed no great enthusiasm for an expedition into the interior of Abyssinia. Certainly he put no pressure on the commander, San Marzano, a remarkable contrast with his behaviour towards Baldissera in 1889 and Baratieri in 1895–6. San Marzano's expedition was not to leave Massowa until December 1887 – after the autumn rains – and

Crispi in fact did his best to avoid any action at all by persuading Salisbury to mediate.[31]

All the evidence suggests that in 1887-8 Crispi's attitude towards East Africa was much nearer that of Depretis than that of Mancini. In January 1888 he offered to abandon Massowa to Britain in exchange for Zeila and made some attempt, when Salisbury refused his offer, to sell it to Bismarck. Even in 1889, Saracco urged him to abandon it as 'an incubus', a drain on Italian finances: his Minister of War, Bertolè-Viale, had no enthusiasm whatsoever for an Abyssinian campaign, an attitude fully shared by most Italian diplomats.[32] Hence the general enthusiasm for the idea, discussed with Bismarck at Friedrichsruhe, of using German pressure to persuade Salisbury to take up the thankless task of mediation. Salisbury in fact had little enthusiasm, but, under pressure from Berlin, did his best via Portal's mission to the negus to persuade him to accept Italian demands. Nor was this intervention unsuccessful. Portal's advice was rejected in December, but on 30 March 1888 – on the eve of battle – Negus John gave in and accepted Crispi's terms for compensation for Dogali. With the cession of Saati, Uuà and the Senahit valley to Italy, honour had been saved and, perhaps more important, by the accompanying treaty of commerce which made Massowa the entrepôt for the negus's dominions, the white elephant might at last pay its way.

So far then Crispi had been eminently successful in solving the problems bequeathed by Mancini and Robilant. The negus had been forced to accept Italian control of Massowa, whilst the outlay on what Launay termed 'this unfortunate enterprise which creates so much embarrassment for us' had been slight. Italy could once more concentrate her energies as her allies wished – in Europe. The fears, shared by both Salisbury and Bismarck, that Crispi would find himself dragged into an endless war in the interior, seemed baseless.[33]

If he had stopped at this point all would have been well, but in the course of 1888-9 two new developments occurred. In the first place, Crispi himself became convinced that Italy's East African empire could absorb the annual emigration that normally went to France or America and was lost to Italy. Instead, they should go to found a new Rome on the Red Sea and thus strengthen the homeland. As he told the chamber in May 1888,[34]

Italy needs colonies for her future and for her trade and this bourgeois habit of always counting the cost is unpatriotic: there is something greater than material interests, the dignity of our country and the interests of civilisation. You have always said that now we are in Rome we must create a new world ... assist the government, give it the means to succeed in its mission.

Second, Crispi fell under the persuasive charm of Count Pietro Antonelli, the former resident at the court of Menelik, King of Shoa, who convinced him that an African empire was there for the taking. The death of the Negus John in March 1889 created the opportunity for Italy to back Antonelli's client – Menelik – for the succession, the theory being that in return he would accept Italian protection and cede outright the Mareb frontier to the Italian colony.

It was of course a mirage. The obvious point, that Menelik would turn to a war of liberation against Italy as the only means of imposing himself upon the other ras, was lost on Antonelli. But, since he had Crispi's ear, and dominated the colonial section of the Consulta which dealt with Africa, the alternative and more sensible policy advocated by Massowa of playing off the ras against each other was excluded. As Count Augusto Salimbene, an experienced African explorer, noted in his diary in December 1889, 'When I entered the [foreign] ministry ... the Antonelli plan was already accepted ... there was nothing left to discuss: it was either "eat this or take a jump out of the window ... Antonelli is infallible".'

Bemused by his scrap of paper, the Treaty of Uccialli, by which Menelik on 2 May 1889 gave away the Mareb frontier and promised to allow Italy to conduct his relations with other powers in exchange for a loan of 3 million lire, Antonelli believed he had built an African empire. What is more, Crispi swallowed this whole and became impervious to any reasoned argument. 'Vast zones of colonisable land', he told his audience at Palermo on 14 October 1889, 'offer themselves in the not too distant future to the exuberant fecundity of Italy.' Throughout the summer and autumn of 1889 he belaboured Massowa and the Ministry of War to get Baldissera moving, in the hope of seizing more ground which he could then present to Menelik as 'the actual limit of Italian possessions'. The extent of his dream world can be seen in the instructions to Baldissera that he was actually to help Menelik establish his authority in Abyssinia, the last thing Massowa wished to do, and which led to Baldissera's resignation in disgust.[35]

The rising alarm in parliament as the extent of Crispi's African ambitions became apparent was partly based on the assumption that an Italian empire in East Africa would necessarily alienate England.[36] This in fact was not the case. As long as Crispi confined his attention to Abyssinia, Salisbury accepted Bismarck's theory that the Mediterranean alliance involved also supporting Italy in Africa. In 1887, apart from his mediation with the negus, Salisbury agreed to Italy controlling the Red Sea coast as far north as Ras Kasar in order to blockade Abyssinia – much against the wishes of Baring and Kitchener. In 1888 he rejected Crispi's bid for Zeila – despite German support – but explicitly told the India Office that Abyssinia was to be an Italian preserve because 'the alliance with Italy is a matter of Imperial policy'. In 1889 he accepted the Treaty of Uccialli without reservation.[37]

The concept of giving Italy a free hand in Abyssinia applied equally to the Somali and Benadir coasts of East Africa. Italian interest in these regions originated with Commander Cecchi's exploratory voyages in 1884–6, but there was little enthusiasm for annexation under Robilant as the coast was reported to be 'arid and deserted, of a rocky nature'. That interest quickened under Crispi was due partly to rumours of impending French annexation, but, more important, because the prospect opened up of obtaining the entire coast of the horn of Africa from east of Zeila to Kismayu. Taken in conjunction with the Antonelli schemes for Abyssinia, possession of the coast would offer considerable advantages, since it would put Menelik under complete Italian control. The means of obtaining this lay, once more, in exploiting German and British friendships. Bismarck waived prior German claims in the region; Mackinnon – Chairman of the Imperial British East Africa Company (IBEA) – was persuaded first to obtain a lease of the Benadir ports from the Sultan of Zanzibar, then in August 1888 to hand them over to Italy, though Kismayu, contrary to Salisbury's original offer, was now to be shared with the IBEA.[38]

That Italo–British relations deteriorated seriously in Africa in 1890 was due to Crispi's exorbitant appetite. Not content with the entire coastline to the Juba boundary, he wanted to push the IBEA out of Kismayu altogether. Moreover, exploiting an additional convention with Menelik of October 1889 giving Italy the right to protect all tribes dependent upon the negus, Crispi now claimed to control the Gallas south of the eighth parallel. (Since nobody knew where the Juba went once it left the coast the eighth parallel had been designated as the boundary between the Anglo–Italian spheres in the interior.) If 'Italy's just demands' (as he termed them) were rejected by Salisbury, he was to be threatened that Rome would contemplate handing over her protectorate to France or Russia. The Consulta, apparently, had assumed when making the final agreement on 3 August 1889 with Mackinnon that Germany would inherit the coast of Zanzibar and would assist Italy in squeezing out the British company: hence Salisbury's acquisition of the lion's share in the Heligoland–Zanzibar exchange of July 1890 came as a nasty shock.[39]

Salisbury side-stepped this particular issue by removing the Juba boundary from the agenda of the Anglo–Italian colonial conference at Naples in October 1890, but sufficient still remained to cause an explosion. This was due to Crispi's determination to expand into the Sudan. Following the death of the Negus John, in April 1889, General Baldissera was ordered by Crispi to occupy Keren and Asmara: in June 1890 his successor, Orero, pushed forward a column to Agordat. This put him within easy striking distance of Kassala and also provided the bulk of the official Italian case for its acquisition, the necessity of driving off the Dervishes from Kassala to prevent their raids on Keren. This was not, however, the real motive: Crispi ordered an advance to the Atbara – the river on which Kassala stands – on 14 October, three weeks before Massowa reported on 8 November that a Dervish raid was imminent. On 17 November, Gandolfi announced from Massowa that he had been mistaken but Crispi still went ahead: on 26 December he gave Gandolfi a free hand. As Colonel Slade, British military attaché in Rome reported after close contact with the Italian Ministry of War, 'The military necessities of the occupation of Kassala were all a myth. . . .'[40]

The real attractions of Kassala were threefold. In the first place it was the centre of the richest trade of the Sudan so that its capture would divert commerce from the Egyptian port of Suakin to the Italian port of Massowa. This was an aspect much stressed by General Dal Verme, an Africanist on the General Staff, and by Crispi himself. Probably more important to Crispi, however, was the hope that the capture of Kassala might help to rectify Mancini's error of 1882. Assuming, wrongly, that Salisbury wished to reconquer Khartoum, he thought that if Italy held an important part of the Sudan this would perhaps lead to a general Anglo–Italian partnership in the Nile Valley, with inestimable benefits to the general Italian position in Africa and the Mediterranean. Last, but not least, with Crispi's empire in Abyssinia fading before his eyes in 1890 as Menelik grew restive, a colonial agreement with England which brought Kassala to Italy was his only hope of winning the elections.

Unfortunately for Crispi, Salisbury had no wish to become entangled in co-partnership in Africa to underwrite what he regarded as 'Crispi's suicidal ambitions'. Confident that Italian resources were insufficient to support an expansionist policy in Africa, that her dependence upon Britain in the Mediterranean would prevent an advance into the Sudan without British consent, he was content to allow the Naples conference to collapse and to sit out Crispi and wait for his fall from power. Nor was there any pressure from Berlin to contend with over Kassala. The German attitude throughout was that by challenging England in the Sudan, Italy was sacrificing the substance for the shadow, a view which Tornielli, the Italian Ambassador in London, fully shared.[41]

In these circumstances Crispi's attempt to build an African empire on the cheap had not got very far by the time of his fall in January 1891. Menelik, whatever he promised in 1889, had no intention of accepting Italian suzerainty by 1890. In August 1890, Crispi sent a desperate instruction to Massowa to keep him quiet until negotiations with London were concluded, as the whole Italian case for Gallaland and Kassala rested on their position as protectors of Abyssinia. (Kassala, supposedly, had been ceded to Negus John by Granville in 1884.) On 17 November Salimbene announced from Massowa that it was all over, Menelik would not accept the Italian version of article 17. Crispi's last act before leaving office was to tell Massowa to leave the Dervishes alone after all,[42]

> as until we know the results of Antonelli's mission and whether this is favourable it is not in our interests to fight the enemies of Menelik. They might be useful to us if the Emperor fails to observe the agreement signed with us.

Moreover, by excessive demands on the Benadir coast and,

above all, the insistence on obtaining Kassala, Crispi all but completely alienated Salisbury. This was suicidal. Lacking the strength to pursue an independent policy in Africa, Italian expansion had been completely dependent on the goodwill of her allies. By attacking London on its most sensitive spot – the Nile Valley – Crispi put at risk not only his African empire, but also Italy's position in the Mediterranean. As Tornielli warned,[43]

If England should turn against us, France would lose no time in profiting by it. . . . If it were not for the millstone of Tunis certainly our 'liberty of action' in the Sudan would have more practical value. I beg you to take account of this situation. . . .'

This Crispi seemed incapable of doing. Attributing the breakdown of the Naples conference on 10 October to 'the caprices of Baring' he blithely announced that he reserved his freedom of action and that he would take Kassala 'if the exigencies of war obliged us to do so'. In other words, having exhausted his credit in London by his constant alarms over Tunis, Tripoli and Bizerta, he now intended to run up a deficit by seizing Kassala, without any regard for the consequences. Salisbury, he said, 'had treated us like enemies, not like the cordial friends that we are'.

Salisbury's view was different. As he put it to Tornielli as bluntly as diplomatic practice permitted, 'I can only regret that England . . . should have favoured the occupation of Massowa . . . the path you are treading leads only to the loss of treasure, blood and perhaps friendships too.'

Quite clearly the view propagated by Crispi – and perpetuated by Zaghi – that Salisbury 'was about to abandon his reserve on Kassala when Crispi's fall compromised the results obtained so far' is totally false. The truth is that Crispi's resignation in January 1891 averted a head-on collision.[44]

The road to Adowa

Crispi's administration from December 1893 to March 1896 was intended to be a government of order: it was to this purpose that Saracco and Sonnino, leaders of Piedmontese and Tuscan factions of the Right, were persuaded to join him. Peasant risings in Sicily, anarchist revolt in Massa Carrara and the republican movement in Milan were to be suppressed by martial law and proscription of the socialist parties. To this end Crispi was willing even to reach an understanding with the Vatican: as he now conceded, 'better the clericals than the socialists'. The Milan republicans were, in his view, 'Cisalpine Gauls', enemies of United Italy; a hatred which they fully reciprocated. Crispi, in their view, had to go before the corruption of Rome and the *Mezzogiorno* led the virtuous – and prosperous – Lombardy to ruin. In this condition of almost open warfare between Crispi and the enemies of the state, parliament became ungovernable and the Sicilian democrat, the arch exponent of the rule of parliament, had it prorogued. This action needed the support of the king but Umberto was increasingly restless, fearing that Crispi would bring about the revolution he had been brought in to prevent. Hence, especially in 1895–6, a growing urgency for Crispi to solve his internal and external problems before the king tired of supporting an authoritarian dictatorship.[45]

The connection between the two was that Crispi, as devoted as ever to the theme of French conspiracy as the origin of all Italian problems, blamed them for the trouble in Milan and even for the revolts in Sicily: these, he maintained, were but the prelude to a French invasion from North Africa. Consequently, his major idea from 1893 to 1896 was to resurrect the British alliance which, he said, had been lost owing to the equivocal policies of Rudinì.[46] In this he was aided by his Foreign Minister, Baron Alberto Blanc, a Savoyard who prided himself on his *Realpolitik* and his dislike of France, who since 1882 had preached the doctrine that Italy's policy must be 'with Germany on land, with England on the sea'. Blanc, a somewhat muddled thinker with a marked penchant for writing interminable memoranda, had been recalled from Constantinople by Rudinì in 1891 for not carrying out his instructions. Since he entertained hopes of obtaining the London Embassy from Crispi, he clung to his new master with a devotion that outran his sense of judgment – which, at least in Abyssinian affairs, was relatively sound.[47]

Blanc's major idea, therefore, once Salisbury returned to office in June 1895, was to resurrect the old *Entente à trois* of 1887 and push England into some form of positive action against the Turks. Otherwise, he feared, if Salisbury continued Rosebery's line of working with Russia and France over the reform of the Ottoman Empire, the all too likely result would be a tacit partition in which Italy would be deprived of her rightful inheritance of Tripoli.

Hence his enthusiasm in urging on Vienna to take an interest in the
Armenian problem and to open negotiations at London to renew
the Mediterranean agreement. Hence, too, the eagerness with
which Blanc supported action at the Straits, the instructions to
Vice Admiral Accini to lay the Italian squadron 'side by side' with
the British and support any action they took. If Salisbury wanted
them he could have 50,000 Italian troops to attack the forts at the
Dardanelles. This, Blanc told Bülow, was England's last chance to
win Italian confidence: if Salisbury were to adopt a 'clear and
decided policy' then Italy would follow him; if not, then she
would abandon her traditional alignment with England.[48]

Unfortunately for Blanc's hopes, Austrian interest in the
Armenian problem was slight. Moreover, with Berlin strongly
opposing any Austro–British initiative in the Near East, there was
no possibility of re-establishing the *Entente à trois* on the basis of a
policy of action. Salisbury himself, much as he wanted to do something, was prevented by his cabinet unless he could promise
Austrian support; which, plainly, he could not. Italian eagerness
was deemed insufficient, despite Blanc's offers of troops and
ships.[49]

By December Blanc and Crispi were in a state of despair. Convinced, by now, that the outcome of German policy would be the
resurrection of the old *Dreikaiserbund* and the cutting of the links
between the Central Powers and England, they thought the future
outlook for Italy hopeless. How could they, alone, combat France
and Russia both in the Mediterranean and in the Red Sea?
Desperately they tried once more to get an agreement with
Salisbury, though King Umberto, with long experience of failure
in this field, thought their chances unfavourable: 'He himself
would like it,' he told Pasetti, 'but did not believe they should rely
unconditionally on England or that the latter would allow herself
to be bound.' On 12 December, nevertheless, Ferrero – Tornielli's
successor at London – put Blanc's proposals for reactivating the
1887 agreements before Salisbury. He was told that the moment
was inopportune as it might alarm the Russians: neither Deym nor
Hatzfeldt - on instructions - gave him any support.[50]

The Kruger Telegram and Berlin's open espousal of a con-
tinental league against England in January 1896 seemed to justify
Crispi and Blanc's worst fears as it made their policy – with
Germany on land, with England on the sea – completely im-

possible. Blanc was particularly critical of German action: 'The Berlin Cabinet, which as soon as the Eastern Question is raised, says it is only secondarily concerned, chooses to treat as of first importance a colonial question which concerns Germany herself much less than the east and her allies not at all.' Austria and Italy, he urged Pasetti, must act together in this: as soon as Anglo–German relations calmed down they must try a joint approach at London in an effort to re-create the old understanding. Crispi was equally alarmed. The basis of his policy since 1887, he told Sonnino, had been that the *triplice marittima* complemented the *triplice territoriale* and secured the *status quo* in the Mediterranean and the Black Sea. In view of French hostility they would have to renew the alliance with Germany and Austria whatever happened, but if the maritime alliance were to collapse then the German powers would have to assume greater obligations. What he wanted in particular, he told Nigra, was an assurance that if Turkey broke up Italy could take Tripoli: '... since Bismarck's fall I have received no help from Germany against France: it is we who have born all the burden of the Triple Alliance.'[51]

As far as Rome was concerned they would have been content to renew the old agreement with London as it stood. Whilst welcoming 'improvements' in the sense of making it more positive – Blanc's 'clear and decided action' – they thought something was better than nothing, if only because it would prevent Salisbury from lining up with Russia and France. But Goluchowski thought otherwise. Pressed by Berlin, he would settle for nothing less than a military alliance with England; with the consequence that the Mediterranean agreements faded away.

Blocked in their hopes of assistance from that quarter, convinced that a Balkan uprising would set off a scramble for the Ottoman Empire in the spring, and increasingly desperate for support in Africa, Crispi turned once more to Berlin. Hohenlohe's reply, that Africa was outside the scope of the alliance, drove the Italian Premier to fury. If this was Berlin's idea of help, he wrote to Lanza, then Italy must have serious misgivings about renewing the *triplice*: 'the difficulties against which we have to fight derive in great part from the links which bind us to Germany.' Since Crispi had done more than anyone else to identify Rome with Berlin, this was – as Salvemini points out – outright condemnation of his own policy.[52]

Crispi's fatal mistake in 1895–6 was the decision, in the face of a hostile Menelik, to seek to impose the Treaty of Uccialli by force. By the summer of 1894 Antonelli was entirely discredited – he resigned from the Foreign Ministry in May – as it was clear that Menelik had no intention of accepting the Mareb frontier, and the way was now open for the policy that Massowa had advocated all along.[53] Unfortunately for Crispi it was too late. The semi-independent feudatories – Alula, Makonnen and Mangasha – were more impressed with Menelik's power than with Italian, whilst the general in command was no longer Baldissera but Baratieri. The former had the sagacity to proceed slowly and the status to stand up to Crispi's bullying; the latter, termed by Umberto 'a journalist', had neither. The result was that, despite the half-hearted opposition of Blanc, Saracco and Sonnino, Crispi was able to impose his will and his desperate need for a victory upon an increasingly reluctant general.

Initially Baratieri, instructed by Crispi that 'not even a handful of ground must be abandoned', was successful: by March 1895 he had defeated the Tigrean chiefs and advanced to Adigrat, a success which converted Crispi to the idea of an all-out offensive to conquer Menelik. As King Umberto commented to Farini at this time, 'Blanc has become reasonable [but] . . . Crispi would like to occupy everything, including China and Japan.' However, he came up against powerful opposition in the cabinet, since Sidney Sonnino, at the Treasury, was opposed to any further expansion in Africa. Sonnino was convinced that any further African expenditure, after the government's clear promises in December 1894 of retrenchment, would bring widespread opposition once parliament re-assembled in June. Temporarily Crispi was restrained: the army, he telegraphed to Baratieri on 13 April, must economise by living off the country. To parliamentary questions Crispi and Blanc replied with assurances that it was the government's intention to remain on the defensive.[54]

On 28 July Baratieri returned to Rome where, largely due to his irredentist affiliations, he received a great ovation from the Chamber. This, coupled with a vote of confidence on 2 July after a victorious general election in May, seems to have convinced Crispi that there was now little danger in a resumption of the offensive. Despite Baratieri's insistence that 'he had no intention of provoking the enemy or of expanding' and assurances to Sonnino that the funds allocated 'would suffice only for operations against Mangasha', he was in fact ordered by Crispi to risk an encounter with Menelik. Crispi needed a success. It was in this frame of mind, based on a complete underestimation of Menelik's strength, that the campaign was initiated which led to the defeats of Amba-Alagi and Adowa.[55]

After a minor reverse at Amba-Alagi in December more troops were sent out, but Baratieri found it almost impossible to use all of them as they had to be supplied by mule train from Massowa. Consequently, faced now with a confident and much strengthened Menelik to the front of him, and an increasingly hostile Makonnen on his flank, he proposed that they should stage a diversion in the Harar. At first this would have to be a demonstration, since the necessary troops to make an effective penetration could not reach Zeila until 10 February, but in the meanwhile even a token force might suffice to draw off Makonnen.[56]

This proposal to stage a diversion in the Harar brought to a head the whole dilemma of Italian colonial policy. Italian expansion in Africa was dependent upon the alliance system in Europe: as Crispi frequently put it, Italy was fighting the Franco–Russian alliance in the Red Sea. The French in fact had not much interest in Abyssinia, but they saw, rightly, that it provided an excellent lever to obtain what they wanted from Italy. In 1891 they had all but recognised the Italian position there, including rights in the Harar province, when the news leaked of the Italian re-renewal of the Triple Alliance. Promptly all negotiation was broken off. In succeeding years no attempt was made to check the arms traffic through Jibuti whilst some French support was given to an unofficial Russian military mission to Menelik.

Similarly, when in 1895 Crispi took up the question of fighting Menelik via the Harar again, the French supplied the main stumbling block. First they wanted Italian concessions in Tunis. Crispi, if grudgingly, was prepared to deal on this basis by 8 January but Berthelot, under pressure from his colleagues, called it off. Apparently the French agreement with England and Austria over Tunis removed most of the incentive for a further settlement with Italy, whilst the violent attacks on France in the Italian press for sending arms to Menelik made negotiations pointless.[57]

French opposition would not have mattered so much if Crispi could have got the support of his allies, but in the circumstances of

1895–6 this was not forthcoming. Hohenlohe told him bluntly that the alliance was a defensive pact, not a commercial undertaking for the exploitation of Africa.[58] Salisbury, whilst sympathetic, would not risk endangering the success of his negotiations with France over Siam. This situation put Crispi and Blanc in a cleft stick. However much they resented British indifference – 'all the English give us is kicks' – and talked of insisting on rewriting the Triple Alliance to cover the Red Sea on its renewal in 1896, nothing would give them any immediate help.

But if parliament reassembled with still no results and the prospect of a long-drawn-out campaign in East Africa, Crispi would be brought down. He had already, on 5 January, instructed Baratieri that 'the country expects another victory': now he made the fatal decision, the telegram of 25 February to Baratieri complaining that his campaign was 'a military disease, not a war': in effect urging him to seek a decision at all costs. Baratieri himself was highly dubious, now well aware of the optimism of his previous forecasts of Menelik's strength; but Crispi's telegrams, added to the urging of the brigade commanders newly arrived from Italy – whose verbal instructions from the War Ministry had been to get the African campaign over and the Italian troops back to Europe – decided him to order an attack on Menelik's forces at Adowa on 28 February. By the end of 1 March it was all over, and the Italian army destroyed.[59]

This defeat in itself need not have been decisive – after all only some 16,500 Italian troops were engaged – but it was exploited by Crispi's opponents to bring him down. The northerners among his own Cabinet – Sonnino, Blanc and Saracco – were more than uneasy at the prospect of endless campaigning in Abyssinia and relieved when the chance came to stop. The Opposition – on the Left the Milan republicans and on the Right Rudinì and Visconti Venosta – were at one in wanting an end to African adventure. Of popular feeling there was no doubt; vast demonstrations and blocking of railway lines to prevent the departure of further troop trains were reported all over Italy, particularly in the north. Crispi at first tried to stick it out – on 2 March he talked of proroguing the Chamber once more – but no politicians of note would risk their future by joining him. On 5 March 1896 he resigned.

Crispi's defeat at Adowa had considerable consequences. In Europe it led directly to the Franco–Italian *Entente*: in Africa it

produced the British advance to Dongola and the re-conquest of
the Sudan. Last, but not least, in Italy it produced a popular
aversion to colonial adventure which lasted for fifteen years and
enabled Giolitti in the early years of the twentieth century to
repeat the economic miracle of balancing the budget. Moreover, it
ensured that in so far as Crispi's successors thought of expansion
they turned their thoughts back nearer home, to the province
which had started Mancini on the road to Massowa, Tripoli.

Chapter 5

Back from Africa

Our task of serving as the link between London and
Berlin looks like wearing us out in seeking the
impossible.

Tornielli, 1896

The parliamentary crisis that followed the news of the defeat at
Adowa was of some magnitude, since all the old problems which
had induced King Umberto to send for Crispi in the first place now
reappeared. With republican demonstrations throughout the north
his throne seemed less than secure. As Farini noted gloomily on 3
March: 'The Crimean expedition was the vital seed of the new
Italy: may the African expedition not prove its death blow!' The
king's first instinct was to send for a reliable general, 'not a
journalist like the one they sent to Africa': he would even have
kept Crispi and given him another prorogation of parliament but
for the fact that this proved politically impossible. Crispi himself
wanted to stay, apparently oblivious of the storm he had raised, but
his colleagues' refusal forced his resignation. Farini explained to
him quite clearly why he had to go.

> When a government which rules without parliament can claim the
> credit for restoring order and improving the financial situation then
> the country – even if it disapproves – says nothing: but when,
> ruling without parliament, you give it – as now – defeat, then it
> rebels.

The outcome was inevitable, the return of Rudinì, Riccotti and a
ministry bent on their programme of 1891: economy at the
expense of Africa and the military establishment; reconciliation
with France. Since his first choice for Foreign Minister – Visconti
Venosta – was vetoed by Berlin, instead Rudinì appointed
Caetani, Duke of Sermoneta, a close friend and supporter, 'who
shared his opinions entirely in matters of foreign policy'; so that to

69

all intents and purposes the aims pursued from March to July were those of the Premier.[1]

Rudinì's first task was, in Cavallotti's words, to 'clean up the African mess'. By March Baldissera, sent out to replace Baratieri just before Adowa, had sufficient troops to risk a confrontation with Menelik but in Italy this was politically unthinkable. Rudinì, personally, as in 1891, would have liked to clear out of East Africa altogether and in March asked Stillman to write an article in the London *Times* advocating such a course. But, as in 1891, the opposition of the court, the military and the *Africanisti* was too strong for such a radical course. Instead he had to settle for peace with Menelik – signed in November 1896 – on the basis of renouncing the Treaty of Uccialli, leaving Italy with Eritrea to the river Mareb and the Somali coast protectorates. After several changes of mind, in April Rudinì decided to retain even Kassala – which Blanc had thought of abandoning – for another year.[2]

Rudinì and the settlement with France

Reconciliation with France, however, did not mean that the new regime had any intention of dropping the Triple Alliance. Rudinì gave the king the most formal assurances on this point in March. His remarks to Farini on 18 April that the alliance 'would be extinct in six years' and that 'it would be necessary to create a new situation' were a straight reflection of Tornielli's gloom rather than an expression of Rudinì's intentions. Tornielli, in March 1896, was more pessimistic than ever: he foresaw the complete estrangement of Britain and Germany and an alignment of London with Paris and St Petersburg, which would put Italy in a hopeless position. But his solution was equally impossible. He advocated giving Germany notice of one year (the alliance ran out in 1897) that unless she brought in England as a fourth partner within this time Italy would not renew. Rudinì knew better than this: 'the English will never sign anything' he told Farini on 27 March ,'they never make stipulations'. He had found this out in 1891 and the furthest he went in 1896 was to attempt to incorporate a clause making the alliance inoperable against England. When Berlin refused on the grounds that this would point it too much towards Russia and that 'war with England was beyond any reasonable thought,' Rudinì rested content: he had made his point. The object of this corre-

spondence and of his statements in the chamber on 25 May –
Caetani told Nigra and Lanza – was to make it clear to the allies
that, as in 1882, Italy could not contemplate a war against England.
Having said this, they renewed.[3]

One reason why Rudinì's attitude towards renewal was so
straightforward in 1896 compared with 1891 was the lack of any
internal pressures upon him to drop the alliance. His administration was essentially a Left-Right coalition, dependent upon the
votes of Cavallotti and Zanardelli to sustain it against Crispi. But
in 1896, in contrast to 1891, neither of these two leaders showed
any antagonism towards the *triplice*. Zanardelli's newspaper,
Provincia di Brescia, announced on 17 April that 'foreign policy was
above parliamentary mutations', a welcome discovery. Imbriani
still raved about a 'natural foreign policy, not the same old
dynastic one' but he got no support: Cavallotti announced that he
voted against all tyrannies, including that of Imbriani. To the
republican leader what mattered was to 'clean up the African mess'
and keep out Crispi, an attitude which gave the Premier almost a
free hand. He used it to good effect. On 25 May he appeared in the
Chamber in the guise of Metternich and announced that 'if the
Triple Alliance did not exist it would be necessary to invent it'.
Malvano, restored to the post of Secretary General at the Consulta
by Rudinì, had complete faith in the honesty of his master. The
programme to be pursued, he told his friend Pansa, was one of
'scrupulous faithfulness to the Triple Alliance, cordial friendship
with England and the avoidance of any dispute with France'. This
was to be effected 'without equivocation or second thoughts'.[4]

There is nothing that Rudinì – or Visconti Venosta – did in the
next four years to contradict this, a point which is emphasised
because there is a strong tendency to depict Italian foreign policy
from 1896 to 1915 in terms of a straight line. There was no
supposition in 1896 outside Tornielli's mind that Italy should seek
to change camps, try to substitute an alliance with France and
Britain – as occurred in 1915 – for the *triplice*. What Rudinì and
Visconti, after his appointment in July, sought was merely greater
flexibility. In their view Crispi had distorted the Italian position in
Europe by his crusade against France and his obsession with
Africa, neither of which could bring any result without the close
support of Britain, which was clearly not forthcoming. The only
result had been to make Italy completely dependent upon Berlin.

As Visconti Venosta wrote on 26 April 1895, 'I do not believe it good policy for a country to put itself in a position where its security depends entirely upon the goodwill of an ally and its fate decided by the assistance proffered or withdrawn.' This being so, the only sound policy was to revert to the position before Crispi: maintain the alliance as a safeguard (particularly against Austria); resume the dialogue with France to escape total dependence upon Berlin. There was of course no thought of seeking a French alliance; this would be to exchange one master for another. Billot, the French Ambassador in Rome, had no illusions on this score. After a year of negotiating with the new regime he concluded in a letter to Hanotaux in June 1897,[5]

> the ideal of M. de Rudinì and those who follow him is only to establish that Italian policy is not dependent on that of the German powers. . . . They want to add the benefits of a reconciliation with France to the advantages guaranteed by the Triple Alliance.

The means of effecting a reconciliation with France lay in a settlement of the Tunis dispute and the tariff war which had bedevilled relations for the past ten years. From the Italian point of view it was essential to tie the two together since in Tunis they could hope for very little: if, however, they were to concede the French position in Tunis without counter-concessions on French tariffs, then their hopes of obtaining these later were relatively slender. The question was of some urgency since the commercial treaty of 1868 between Italy and Tunis had been denounced by Paris on 15 August 1895, which meant that it expired in August 1896. If nothing was done, Italian trade with Tunis would be faced with a 30 per cent tariff and the privileges enjoyed by Italian schools abolished.

The main problem was public opinion. In France the Meline administration was dominated by protectionists and the Foreign Minister, Hanotaux, far too cautious to risk his parliamentary position. Consequently he rejected any idea of a tariff agreement and insisted that Caetani first settle the Tunis issue. Caetani's difficulty was precisely the same. Francophobia was still strong in the south of Italy and Crispi certain to attack any settlement over Tunis that did not include a *quid pro quo* for Italy. As Rudinì commented to Caetani on 4 April, they had to proceed carefully: 'There is a strong revival of patriotic sentiment, of megalomania.

We must stand firm but without offending this feeling, which affects many of our friends. It is the Italian vice. We are weak and wish to be strong.' The foreign policy debates in the Chamber at the end of June showed how right he was: Di San Giuliano, a government supporter but a Sicilian, whilst approving of better relations with France bitterly condemned any truckling to her. It was not, in his view, a question of making concessions to France but of the latter 'recognising the consequences of Italian Unity in the Mediterranean and North Africa'. In the circumstances, Caetani – against the advice of Tornielli – held firm and insisted that Hanotaux link the two issues.[6]

The result was deadlock, broken only by the resignation of Caetani with Riccotti on 18 July over the military budget and the appointment of Visconti Venosta.[7] The change was critical for, whereas Caetani seemed to resign himself to the impasse, the more experienced statesman saw the necessity of resolving it. If Paris would not budge then Rome must. In his view the Tunis affair had to be looked at in its European context. Trained in the Piedmontese school and sympathetic to the ideals of Cavour, he had never had much sympathy with the *furor consularis* or the way Crispi had played to the gallery over Tunis. To Visconti Venosta there were more serious issues at stake. With long experience of international affairs – he had been Foreign Minister for most of the 1860s and had a solid run from 1869 to 1876 – he saw this as the turning point in Italo–French relations, the chance to restore them to normalcy.

Not that he was particularly pro-French, like Zanardelli or Luzzatti. Of course he, like most conservative Italian foreign ministers up to 1914 including even Di San Giuliano, were more at home in Paris than in Berlin. This was the natural effect of their upbringing and education. Moreover, what he saw of Germany he did not like: 'Bismarck', he once said, 'is a travelling companion whom I do not want to have forever.' The German style of *Machtpolitik* had little appeal. But much more important was the way in which the Piedmontese looked at European affairs and Italy's place in them.

To Crispi the way to make Italy a great power was to behave like one, rather in the same way as Mussolini later made Italy run in order to teach her to walk. To Visconti, Italy was not a great power and never would be: she lacked the industrial strength to behave like Germany. It had been necessary to shatter the old

Metternichian equilibrium to create a united Italy: now it must be rebuilt to protect her. Italy, in other words, needed a strong France as a counterpoise to Germany, alliance or no alliance; needed good relations with France to give her the independence to bargain with her allies instead of meekly accepting whatever bones they threw her way. Otherwise, what would happen if Germany changed her mind? These ideas, though formulated in the 1870s, were equally applicable to the Europe of the 1890s and were certainly the motivating force behind 'changing the helm' (*il colpo di timone*) as Visconti Venosta later described his stewardship.[8]

Visconti Venosta's determination to settle the Tunis question once and for all was assisted by the discovery that all other interested parties were settling with France. Vienna actually signed an agreement on 20 July without bothering to consult Rome; London was known to be negotiating. An attempt was made in August to create a common front when Caetani was sent to see Salisbury but the latter was extremely non-committal: the most he would promise was 'to take things slowly', which he would probably have done in any case. Tornielli, with past experience of relying on England, advised strongly against such a course: they would trade off their rights in Tunis against a French concession elsewhere. In his view the only Italian interests that mattered in Tunis were school autonomy and fishing rights, which France would probably concede, so why delay?[9]

Moreover Hanotaux, though refusing another six months extension when approached on 18 August, did throw out the bait that a 'friendly solution [of the Tunis issue] would probably contribute to a quick settlement of the commercial question'. Luzzatti, again at the Treasury, promptly pointed out the scale of the issues involved: Italian exports to Tunis were 8 million lire, to France 150 million lire. Italian government bonds were again falling on the Paris Bourse: an Italo–French agreement would bring a rise, especially if the commercial treaty were to follow. Though Hanotaux refused to make a firm promise on this, it seemed a reasonable speculation. This decided the government's action: negotiations were opened on 30 September and by the end of the month agreement was reached. In effect Italy at last accepted the Treaty of Bardo against which Crispi had struggled for fifteen years, though she retained her fishing rights, school autonomy and most of her trade: the one real concession was that Italians in Tunis were now subject to French tribunals as the capitulations were abolished. As Tornielli rightly said, it was a compromise, proof of which lay in the savage attacks on the agreements by Doumer in *Le Matin*: these should be placarded throughout Italy, he suggested, to offset the government's critics.[10]

Despite Hanotaux's hints, a commercial agreement was slow in materialising. The protectionists were well entrenched in Paris and from the start it was obvious, Leon Bourgeois warned Rudinì, that there was no hope of getting back to the favoured position obtaining before 1886. From Hanotaux's viewpoint there was no urgency, an agreement would only complicate his own position, and the longer negotiations were dragged out the greater the hope of obtaining further concessions from Rome. What he wanted, ultimately, was for Italy to drop the Triple Alliance, but even if this were unattainable there were minor advantages to be picked up *en route,* for example the reversion of the Italian colonies on the Red Sea if Rome were to abandon them.[11] Given this attitude it is not surprising that negotiations were desultory, opening only in April 1897 and not concluded until November 1898.

All the pressure came from Rome, particularly from Luzzatti. His insistence, added to that of Visconti Venosta, had forced through the Tunis settlement and he was equally persistent in seeking a commercial and financial agreement. More than half of the interest payments abroad on Italian state bonds went to France and his only hope of converting them lay in the assistance of the Paris Rothschilds. Similar considerations applied to Italian agriculture: Austria was at best a very limited market for southern wine and vegetables, the only hope for expansion lay in France; a view also strongly held by Piedmontese silk producers and supported by the Turin paper, *La Stampa.* There was some opposition from Milan industrialists, particularly the wool sector which had done well out of protection from French competition since 1886, but Milan was far from unanimous. The Chamber of Commerce actually favoured a French agreement and thought Italian industry would benefit.[12]

Over the winter of 1897–8 Luzzatti busied himself in Paris cultivating his financial and political contacts, but the real breakthrough came in 1898 with the appointment of Barrère to the Rome Embassy in February and the arrival of Delcassé at the Quai d'Orsay in June. It was not that Billot was unsympathetic to

Rudinì, rather that after a decade in Rome he had few illusions. He had rightly grasped Visconti Venosta's intentions and knew there was little chance of Italy deserting her allies; more serious, he thought there was a good chance that Crispi might return to office, in which case commercial concessions would have been completely thrown away. Barrère, by contrast, was a new broom, eager to found a reputation upon a spectacular success, determined – like Delcassé, his close friend – on a Franco–Italian political under- standing in Europe whatever the cost. Delcassé himself visited Rome in the spring of 1898, before his appointment, and sketched out the main outline of an agreement with Visconti Venosta and Luzzatti, so that by the time the Rudinì administration fell in June there was already a fairly clear understanding.[13]

Continuity was provided by Luzzatti. The new Premier, General Pelloux, gave him charge of the negotiations so that, although out of office, he, Barrère and Delcassé continued as before. During the Fashoda crisis of the summer of 1898 Pelloux and his Foreign Minister, Admiral Canevaro, were careful to stress to Barrère that Italy had no alliance of any sort with England – a complete con- trast with Crispi's conduct. Canevaro immediately repudiated an anti-French speech made by one minister, Nasi, in October and, although the ministry contained several *Crispini* (Fortis, Nasi, Aprile), the Premier – fully supported by the king – pushed the negotiations on. At last, on 21 November 1898, Luzzatti and Delcassé signed an agreement in Paris, the basis of which was the application of the minimum French and Italian tariffs generally, the major exceptions being the import of Italian silk and French woollen goods.[14]

Barrère, naturally, set great store by this agreement and attri- buted to it a first-rate political importance. Now, he thought, the return of the followers of Crispi to power would make no dif- ference. It had, he claimed in a letter to Delcassé on 23 November, 'made it impossible for Italy to participate in a maritime war. The francophobes will find no public support with which to force the government's hand. The Italians will become genuinely interested in peace because they need us.' The ratification by the Italian parliament on 25 January 1899 by an overwhelming majority seemed to confirm his view: with a vote of 236 to 34 in the chamber it seemed clear that the French agreement was popular.

But whether, as Barzilai claimed, it was 'a new orientation of our foreign policy', is a different matter. Government speakers – Canevaro, Fortis – were careful to stress that this was an economic agreement, devoid of any political content. Di San Giuliano, who supported the government and joined it in May 1899, was quite specific. The Anglo–German agreement of August 1898 and the Anglo–French tension over Fashoda from September onwards showed that Crispi had been right all along: the European alignment of the twentieth century was going to be the Anglo–Saxon powers against the rest and in this contest it was clear where Italy's interests lay: with Germany and England. Whilst it could be argued that all this public speaking was mere window dressing for the benefit of Italy's allies, in fact Canevaro repeated this as an instruction to De Renzis, Ambassador at London, in February 1899:[15]

> ... in dissipating the traces of past strains between Italy and France the Royal Government has certainly worked advantageously for the two countries and for universal peace, but it has no intention whatsoever of departing from the policy dictated to it alike by treaties, interests and common tendencies. ...

Nor can it be argued that, whatever the government's intentions, the effect of the commercial treaty was to create such a volume of Italian exports to France and French investment in Italy that there grew up a vested interest in Italy in peace with France. Barrère himself provided evidence to the contrary. Writing to Delcassé in April 1900, a year after the commercial *détente,* he was still pursuing the same old line. If only, he argued, Italy could manage to export wine to France in any quantity, we could gain solid political advantages: 'the people, finding their material interests bound up with France, would tend to detach themselves from the Central Powers'. But this still lay in the future; up to then 'the commercial agreement has had very little appreciable effect'. The reasons were not difficult to find. France, despite the minimum tariff, remained a highly protectionist market, extremely difficult to penetrate.

Nor had the other expected benefit, the import of French capital into Italy, shown any signs of materialising. All Luzzatti's schemes for the Crédit Lyonnais and the Banque de Paris et des Pays Bas to open up in Italy remained on paper: the only projects actually operating by 1900 were Le Creusot's exploitation of Elban iron ore and a Franco–Italian company making artificial ice. True, Italian securities had risen on the Paris Bourse, but this was one of the few visible results, more than counterbalanced by the Dreyfus affair. This created the impression in Italy that the France of Boulanger, of militarism and clericalism, was once more in the saddle. As *La Tribuna,* a paper which had never supported Crispi, announced on 4 October 1899: 'Events now indicate whether Crispi or his adversaries were the more short-sighted: Crispi, who foresaw the decomposition of the new France . . . or his opponents who always saw the France of 1789.'[16]

It is apparent, therefore, that by January 1900 the amount of progress that Barrère and Delcassé had made towards their aim of detaching Italy from the Triple Alliance was minimal. The basic sources of tension since the 1880s – Tunis and the tariff war – had been removed, but Italy displayed no signs of undue gratitude towards *la sorella latina.* Indeed, suspicion of French intentions seemed as marked as ever. In March 1899 when France and England signed a convention settling the Fashoda crisis by partitioning the deserts of the Sudan, there was an outcry in Italy. The *Giornale di Sicilia* published an interview with Di San Giuliano on 28 March in which he declared that the convention[17]

> . . . threw serious doubts on the duration and solidity of the Italo–French rapprochement. . . . Whilst in Italy many hoped that it would lead to an equal division of their respective spheres in the Mediterranean, in France it is understood as signifying the acquiescence of Italy in the entire French programme of expansion or hegemony in North Africa and in the Mediterranean.

The fear that France was once more nibbling at Italy's heritage in the Tripolitanian hinterland was widespread. In 1896 similar fears had led Rudinì to seek assurances of British support and, when these were not forthcoming, direct agreement with Paris. In 1897, when Tornielli signalled an imminent *coup de main* in Tripoli, Visconti Venosta had first sought support in Berlin and, when this failed to materialise, tried to negotiate an agreement with Hanotaux. In neither case had it proved possible to obtain any concrete assurances from Paris, for the simple reason that French ministers saw no reason to make free gifts. Hanotaux, in 1897, made it plain that he expected Italian concessions in return.[18]

A similar fate befell Canevaro in April 1899. Delcassé was

perfectly willing to assure him that the March agreement with England did not affect what could reasonably be called the Tripolitanian hinterland, but was unwilling to go further. Canevaro's attempts to persuade Paris and London to make a joint declaration that they would not expand in Africa north of Fezzan or east and west of Tunis and Egypt respectively, drew a blank: neither Delcassé nor Salisbury would consent without a *quid pro quo*. Both feared, to some extent, that any overt recognition of Italy's rights would inspire her to seize Tripoli and spark off a scramble for the Ottoman Empire.[19]

Canevaro's failure to obtain reassurances on Tripoli with which to pacify the *Crispini,* combined with the complete fiasco of his China policy,[20] brought him down and the ensuing Cabinet crisis led to the departure of Crispi's followers and the return of Visconti Venosta to the Consulta on 14 May 1899, where he remained until February 1901. This period was crucial for the settlement of the Tripoli question. Visconti was quite clear in his own mind that 'after Tunis Italy could not tolerate a French occupation of Tripoli'. Such an act would certainly raise a storm and probably bring down the monarchy since, by 1899, even Zanardelli's followers regarded it as the promised land. That Italy would need to take the province eventually was agreed: it was, Visconti said, the only way 'to break through the ring of French, Spanish and British fortresses around Italy'. But he saw no immediate hurry; all he wanted for the present was a written agreement with Paris that Italy could take the province when she wanted. After all, the whole point of the Cabinet reshuffle which had led to the exit of the *Crispini* and Visconti's appointment was to return to the policy of no adventures.[21]

In July he initiated negotiations with Paris, as he explained in a private letter to Tornielli, under the impression that Delcassé no longer insisted – as Hanotaux had done – on Italian abandonment of the Triple Alliance as the price of agreement on Tripoli and its hinterland. In that case an understanding with France 'will in no way be incompatible with the duties of our alliances'. This proved a complete misconception. Delcassé, worked on by Barrère over the summer, finally offered in October a written agreement to respect the *status quo* in Tripoli – but wanted in return an exchange of views over Morocco. This, Tornielli pointed out, was a good deal less than Italy was seeking.[22]

Visconti had assumed since 1896 that the Crispi policy of working closely with England and Spain to check France in Morocco was no longer viable in view of their lack of concern and that 'our interest is now only secondary and indirect'. But there were his allies to be considered. The maintenance of the existing order in Morocco was covered by Article IX of the Triple Alliance and he felt some qualms at giving France a free hand there – which was obviously Delcassé's intention – without first consulting Berlin. From January to May 1900 he attempted to obtain some clear answer from Bülow but, as all he got amounted to a *fin de non recevoir*, concluded that they were not concerned and that there was no obstacle to an agreement with Delcassé.[23]

A deal on the basis of mutual disinterest in Tripoli and Morocco seemed, therefore, quite possible in May 1900 and Barrère thought it could be accomplished. But Visconti wanted more: French agreement that Italy could actually take the province. This brought considerable difficulties because Delcassé would only consent if Visconti Venosta could assure him that Italy had no commitments against France in Europe – the old idea of denouncing the Triple Alliance. This the Italian statesman rejected. He thought that in time – so he told Barrère – an improvement in Italo–French relations might effectively cancel out the anti-French clauses of the Triple Alliance: but he was not prepared to abandon it. Barrère's assumption that Italian concern for Tunis and Tripoli was the principal cause of the alliance with Berlin was mistaken. As Visconti told him in October, when pressed, 'there is also the question of guarding and defending ourselves against one of our allies'. No French agreement was any use against Austria.

Consequently the negotiations reverted to the idea of mutual disinterest in Tripoli and Morocco and became rather long-drawn-out – principally because Visconti began to doubt whether it was worth concluding on this basis, but also because Barrère liked a long summer leave. Finally, assisted by a concession from Delcassé, he made up his mind in January 1901 and the agreement was signed. It took the form of an exchange of notes, backdated to 14 and 16 December 1900, by which the French announced that they had no intention of encroaching upon Tripolitania or Cyrenaica or its caravan routes and Visconti professed disinterest in Morocco. The Italian note also contained Delcassé's concession: 'We are equally agreed that if political or territorial conditions change in Morocco, Italy reserves the right through reciprocity to develop her influence in respect to Tripolitania and Cyrenaica.'[24]

In effect Visconti obtained what he had been after since May – French recognition of the Italian right to take Tripoli – but conditional upon a prior French occupation of Morocco. Since he was in no hurry to take the province from the Turks this satisfied his requirements. Nor had he been jockeyed out of the Triple Alliance. Visconti's firmness on this point was as marked in 1900 as it had been in 1896–8. He had consulted with Berlin over Morocco and only gone ahead after their lack of interest was clear. There was certainly nothing in the eventual agreement with France that was contrary to Italy's existing alliance. Barrère must have been conscious of this. Writing to Delcassé in January 1901 he hailed the agreement as destroying 'all possibility of an *Anglo*–Italian coalition or alliance', a crucial consideration with Delcassé at this stage of development of his Moroccan policy, but not their original objective.[25]

Barrère also claimed that he had eliminated 'one of the principal bases' of the alliance with Berlin, but this was more dubious. True, he had removed another of the basic disputes between Italy and France; but Italian leaning towards Berlin was only partly based on specific fears for Tripoli; as Visconti had indicated in October there were other causes. One he didn't mention, no doubt from a sense of tact, was the basic anti-French feeling of the younger generation in Italy, marked – according to the French consul at Livorno – among the professional classes.[26] This was to be demonstrated abundantly from 1911 to 1914 at a time when, if Barrère had been right, it should have disappeared completely. It is in this sense that Salvatorelli's assessment of Visconti's agreement, that it 'emptied the Triple Alliance of a large part of its content', must now be treated with caution. It presumes that Visconti would have followed the same course as that pursued by his incompetent successor, Prinetti, of which there is no guarantee. What Visconti had achieved was an understanding with France which lessened the probability of an Italo–French conflict and, consequently, Italian dependence upon London and Berlin; a restoration of the position of 1886. It was Prinetti who contracted out of fighting France under any circumstances and virtually abandoned the treaty of 1882.[27]

The Prinetti–Barrère agreement

Visconti Venosta's successor at the Consulta from February 1901 until his resignation through illness in March 1903 was Giulio Prinetti, a bicycle manufacturer from Milan whose only claim to fame is as author of the Prinetti-Barrère agreement of 30 June 1902. This agreement, which in effect promised Italian neutrality in the event of a Franco–German war, was in complete contradiction to the spirit – if not the actual terms – of the Triple Alliance, renewed by Prinetti two days beforehand. It was the product of two factors, his ambition and his ineptitude: as Barrère himself commented, '. . . ses defauts m'ont servi à mener à bien affaires qui n'eussent peut-être pas about avec un ministre plus rompu aux prudentes tactiques de la diplomatie'.[28]

Prinetti was the only right-wing member of a Radical cabinet presided over by the veteran Zanardelli. Generally regarded as incompetent, depicted by cartoonists as a bull in a china shop, Prinetti was chosen as a political lightweight who could cause no problems to Zanardelli. As the Premier replied to critics who questioned his choice, 'I only gave him the Consulta.' Here Prinetti's critical attitude towards the Triple Alliance, which he had never troubled to conceal, was an asset which blended well with the sentiments of the arch-irredentist President of the Council.[29]

Moreover, it is clear that their views were supported by the young king, Victor Emmanuel III. Though his choice of Zanardelli as Premier owed more to internal politics than to foreign affairs – a desire to break with the reactionary reputation of the court in the last years of his father's reign and start the twentieth century with a new image – Victor Emmanuel certainly had strong opinions on foreign policy. He fully shared the almost universal dislike of the crowned heads of Europe for William II, resented Francis Joseph's refusal to visit Rome and showed a marked preference for a more independent line; if only to demonstrate to his allies and his mother that he was king. He seemed to resent the patronage of Berlin: Italy was no longer the Cinderella of Europe. The response of *Il Secolo* to Bülow's *tour de valser* speech – that Italy was old enough to choose her own dancing partners – was equally representative of the attitude of the king.[30]

The assumption on the Left was that the appointment of Zanardelli signified a 'democratic' foreign policy or, as *Il Secolo* put it in April 1901, 'a new policy with a latin slant' in place of Crispi's 'policy with a teutonic leaning'. They were given powerful encouragement by Zanardelli. In an interview with the *New York Herald* on 25 March he declared his lack of enthusiasm for the Triple Alliance and his determination that, if it were renewed, it would be conditional on an improved commercial treaty and the maintenance of the new cordial relations with France. Moreover, in April, the Duke of Genoa took the Italian fleet to Toulon for the first time in twenty years, an overt expression of the new relationship. But any hope that this would be the prelude to momentous changes in foreign policy were quickly dashed by Prinetti. In June he told the Chamber that he had been wrong about the Triple Alliance when he condemned it in 1891; he had since discovered that it was not a burden upon Italy: 'facts have clearly demonstrated that the closest relations with France are perfectly compatible with the *triplice*'.[31]

This did not of course satisfy the Left but, despite the 1900 elections, they were still a minority in parliament, divided among themselves, and no more able than Cavallotti had been in the past to impose their foreign policy upon an unwilling government. The unfortunate truth was, as one of their leaders, Ernesto Moneta, a former editor of *Il Secolo*, recognised, that foreign policy had little appeal to the electorate unless they were threatened with disaster.

In effect, therefore, the government had a free hand and there is no reason to suppose that Prinetti's actions were in any way dictated by the democratic pressures for Italy to abandon her alliances and become 'the friend of all nations, the slave of none'. His policy was as much that of the establishment as that of Rudinì and Visconti had been; the difference lay in their relative capacity to conduct foreign affairs. It was Prinetti's burning ambition that had led him to desert his natural alignment with Rudinì and Luzzatti for Zanardelli; his desire to escape from the shadow of the great Visconti and do something different, that made him such an easy victim for Barrère.[32]

The essence of Visconti's policy had been to restore normal relations with France, secure the Italian heritage in Tripoli and wait upon events. Prinetti decided to go further. Badgered by the constant solicitations of Barrère, who claimed he had a secret understanding with Visconti, Prinetti promised in June 1901 to ensure that if the alliance with Berlin were renewed it would contain nothing to which France could object. In return he was to get a French loan and a free hand to take Tripoli whenever he wanted. Not content with this, Prinetti decided to publicise the Visconti–Barrère agreement of the previous January. Visconti had kept this secret precisely because his object was limited to safeguarding Tripoli, no more and no less. Prinetti published it because he wanted to inform the world of the fact that there was 'a complete concordance of views' between Rome and Paris, as he announced to the chamber on 14 December. Why? Partly, no doubt, to please his critics in Italy; partly, perhaps, to bind the French; but mainly to set up a squeeze on Berlin and London. It was certainly not intended as a prelude to a French alliance: as Decleva points out, 'it is a very strange francophile who places first priority on improving . . . the links with the central empires'.[33]

In Berlin the trick did not work. Bülow's response to Prinetti's opening gambit was his *tour de valser* speech to the Reichstag on 8 January 1902: in a well-ordered marriage the husband does not object if his wife has a second dance with another man, an expression of patronising indifference. The Triple Alliance was not a necessity for Germany, as it was to her allies. All Prinetti's attempts to 'improve' the alliance met a similar fate. Bülow and Holstein would renew the alliance as it stood but would not change a word: would neither rewrite the preamble stressing the defensive purpose of the agreement, pledge the allies to oppose any change in the Balkans, or promise better terms in the expiring commercial treaty. They did, eventually, offer one concession: a declaration of disinterest in the fate of Tripoli *after* the alliance had been renewed for twelve years.[34]

This was a serious blow to Prinetti. The commercial agreement with France had failed to bring much benefit to Italy and he had hoped to make up for this by further concessions from her allies, particularly for wine, fruit and oil. Moreover, his object in rewriting the preamble was to make it publishable, so that this could be given to Barrère to obtain the free hand in Tripoli and a French loan. But he could not afford to allow the treaty to lapse. This would, so he later told Francesco Rota, have led to 'war with Austria in a very short time'. The mere suspicion that this was his object had already brought general criticism of his 'commercial machiavellianism' from Rudinì and Sonnino. At the end of March

1902 *La Perseveranza,* in an article inspired – if not written – by
Visconti and Luzzatti, warned him against any radical change of
policy. In May the *Corriere della Sera,* the leading Milan daily, stated
bluntly that, 'In the Triplice we have had peace and esteem and
positive commercial advantages. . . . In changing direction we see
nothing but dangers.' Consequently, Prinetti bowed to the inevitable and on 28 June renewed the alliance as it stood.[35]

With England he had rather better luck. Italo–British relations
had been at a low ebb since 1896, principally because London had
lost interest in the traditional Eastern Question and preferred to
settle her differences with France alone. The idea that Italy should
serve as a bridge between England and Berlin was dead: Salisbury
had little enthusiasm for close relations with Berlin after 1896 and
Chamberlain preferred to deal direct with Bülow, at least until he
burnt his fingers. British naval supremacy in the Mediterranean,
absolute in 1898, only reinforced this position. They had no need
of Italian support and regarded a commitment to Italy as a needless
embarrassment: 'It might be of less importance to us to save
Italian ships and ports', Lansdowne wrote Currie in December
1900, 'than to concentrate our ships at those points where we were
most threatened.' A year later, after Prinetti's revelations, Currie
thought the Franco–Italian *rapprochement* 'a distinct gain for us',
precisely because it lessened the chances of having to support Italy
in a war against France. As Visconti Venosta told Rodd, rather
sourly, when the latter took over the Rome Embassy in 1902, 'as
far as England is concerned there are no difficulties but you may
say there are also no relations'.[36]

Salisbury's indifference towards Italy had been made painfully
obvious by the San Mun affair. In the face of what appeared to be
the imminent partition of China by the European powers in 1898,
Canevaro made an attempt to maintain Italian prestige as a great
power by obtaining a share. Completely misled by his Minister in
Peking, De Martino, who thought there would be no opposition,
he put in a claim in January 1899 for the islands and part of the
hinterland of the Bay of San Mun. It was obvious from the start
that De Martino had miscalculated and that Peking would make no
concession unless Italy received strong British support. This
Salisbury, for reasons of his own, was reluctant to give, but De
Martino – instead of waiting until this was clarified – went ahead.
On 28 February his demand was rejected outright, the Chinese

explained, because Italy had no real political or economic interests in China. This was true enough, the demand had been based on considerations of prestige; but as the *Corriere della Sera* pointed out on 1 April, the result was that Italy 'was made to appear a third or fourth-rate power'.

The Left promptly denounced the China affair as 'another Africa'; Rudinì and most of the Right were hostile; and in the ensuing uproar De Martino was recalled and Canevaro forced to resign. As Barrère said, he was 'an honest sailor whom chance had made Foreign Minister'. Visconti Venosta was brought in to salvage the wreck of Italian prestige and fared no better. He reduced Italian demands to a settlement at the open port of Ningpo in the hope that this might be accepted: as he told the new minister at Peking, 'whether it is of any use is a matter of secondary importance'. Once more he was dependent upon Salisbury's support; again it was not forthcoming against Chinese resistance; so that in September 1899 Visconti quietly dropped the request as the only way to avoid the humiliation of another rejection.[37]

It is not surprising, therefore, that after years of studied indifference towards Italian interests in Tripoli – culminating in the Anglo–French agreement of March 1899 – and now the fiasco in China, Currie should discover that by 1900 Italian feeling towards England had 'sensibly cooled'. The last straw for Visconti was the Duke of Norfolk's pilgrimage to the papal jubilee in January 1901 when he made a speech calling for a restoration of the temporal power! Even making allowances for the political ineptitude of the noble duke, the Italian statesman thought this too much: in all the pilgrimages to Rome that year, he wrote Pansa shortly before his resignation, 'the only speech to offend national sentiment was that made by the Duke of Norfolk on the occasion of the English pilgrimage'.[38]

Both Visconti and his successor wrongly attributed this lack of consideration towards Italy to Currie, and Prinetti in 1901 made serious efforts to have him replaced by someone more sympathetic. The outcome of his manoeuvring was that the Ambassador was instructed by Lansdowne to apologise for Norfolk both to the king and to Prinetti, an opportunity which Prinetti exploited to the full on 31 December 1901 to open negotiations to obtain the British guarantee of Tripoli which had eluded Canevaro and Visconti.

By making great play of British neglect of her former ally, as evidenced by the Anglo–French convention of 1899, concluded 'without even consulting Italy, in open contrast to the spirit of the Italo–British agreement of 1887', and comparing this unfavourably with the so-called 'spontaneous' French action in giving Italy a free hand in Tripoli, Prinetti managed to create the conviction that something had to be done. Italy, he said, made no demands: 'she was too accustomed to refusals from the present British government to expose herself to another'; what she would like would be a 'spontaneous' declaration of disinterest from Britain, which would be no more than a 'confirmation in writing of what had often been said in the past'.[39]

Lansdowne and Salisbury showed no great sympathy for this obvious grab at Tripoli, the more so as there were indications that Prinetti intended immediate action: their initial response was limited to a declaration of self-denial. A draft note was sent to Rome on 14 January 1902 stating that they did not intend 'in any eventuality' to encroach west of the line of the 1899 convention. This was not enough for Prinetti. He replied on 21 January that he wanted a declaration of complete British disinterest in Tripoli, as France, Germany and Austria had already provided: a lie, but none the less effective.

Though he liked this even less since, he perceived, it was 'an entirely new question', Lansdowne was edged into further concessions. Salisbury, for once, was not inclined to quibble over words – perhaps because having swallowed the Japanese alliance Tripoli seemed a much lesser evil – and, provided that some form of lip service to the preservation of the Ottoman Empire could be included, was inclined to satisfy Rome. Assisted by a solemn assurance from Prinetti that he would *not* take Tripoli in the near future, Lansdowne now made up his mind. On 3 February he sent a revised draft to Rome which virtually conceded Prinetti's point: all that happened in the intervening month until the final note was handed over on 12 March was that his negatives were made a little more positive and his assurances made dependent upon Italy not making agreements with other powers concerning the coast of the Mediterranean 'of a nature inimical to British interests'.[40]

Once the agreement with London was in his pocket Prinetti turned again towards Paris. On 23 March he had an important interview with Barrère in which he told him that the military conventions concluded by Crispi had been denounced. Despite the forthcoming renewal of the Triple Alliance – announced to the Chamber on 23 May – it was therefore possible to satisfy the French demand for security and on 4 June Prinetti gave Barrère an official statement to this effect. Meanwhile Delcassé was persuaded that it was to France's advantage for Italy to remain in the Triple Alliance, provided that the offensive clauses were removed, as this would lessen the chance of an Austro–Italian war in which France would have to choose sides. Consequently, on 26 June Barrère told Prinetti that a new Italian 3 per cent loan would be floated on the Paris Bourse as soon as an agreement had been signed. Four days later Prinetti obliged.

By the agreement of 30 June (dated 2 November to conceal its proximity to the renewal of the alliance with Berlin and Vienna on 28 June) Prinetti obtained his loan and a free hand in Tripoli: Italian action was no longer dependent upon prior French occupation of Morocco. In return, however, he paid a heavy price. Italy bound herself to remain neutral in the event of any attack upon France or if France herself should be forced to go to war as the result of 'direct provocation'. On 20 July he defined this as events like the Ems Telegram, the insult to Benedetti, the Schnaebele affair or Fashoda: in short every international incident involving France in the previous thirty years! If Prinetti's engagement were honoured the French could now forget about their Alpine frontier and concentrate on England and Germany: both the Moroccan crises of 1905 and 1911 were reported to Rome as 'direct insults'.[41]

It is obvious, as Salvatorelli stresses, that Prinetti's agreement severely limited Italy's freedom of action – instead of increasing it – as it imposed a strict neutrality in the event of a Franco–German war, virtually whatever the cause. The major question is why he did this. It seems improbable that it was due to his French wife or to the hypnotic power of Barrère, strong though these influences may have been. Nor does the view that this was merely an extension of Visconti's agreement, a step in the direction towards the French alliance ardently desired by Italian liberals, bear close examination. There was no such wish outside the pages of *Il Secolo* or the imagination of Barrère. Rudinì, Visconti, Luzzatti and even Sonnino were at one in wanting to improve relations with France: but not at the expense of Italy's alliances. The *Giornale d'Italia,* Sonnino's mouthpiece, reproved Bülow for his *tour de valser* speech precisely on these grounds: Italy had the right 'to greater freedom of movement . . . wherever there was no direct contradiction with the major objectives of the alliance'. Prinetti, basically, belonged to this school of thought, not to that of Cavallotti.[42]

If one seeks Prinetti's object in making this agreement it is as well to look at what he obtained from it. First, a French loan. It seems evident that Prinetti was preoccupied with economic affairs throughout the winter of 1901–2; all the emphasis in his negotiations with Berlin and Vienna was in this direction. Having failed to obtain the trade concessions he sought from his allies he fell back on a French loan in the hope that this would stimulate Italian economic expansion: 'so that his eventual successor would have freedom of choice when it came to the next renewal of the alliance, and hence the possibility of improving it, if it were expedient to continue it.' In other words, he took the French loan to improve Italy's position in the Triple Alliance, not to get closer to France: the neutrality agreement was the unfortunate price, which Prinetti regretted almost as soon as he had signed it.[43]

Second, a free hand in Tripoli. Prinetti's obsession with Tripoli in 1901–2 was marked. Visconti had rejected Delcassé's price for a free hand in Tripoli because he did not think it was worth it: Prinetti, however, thought otherwise because he – in contrast to Visconti – intended to obtain the province immediately. This was why he put the pressure on London, pressure which Tornielli could not understand for the sake of 'an inhospitable region, without ports, an untamed race of people, that even when it is conquered – not without considerable sacrifices and dangers – will be a permanent source of enormous expense.'[44]

What Prinetti had in mind is quite clear. He told Currie and Wedel that he wanted Tripoli on the same terms as Britain held Cyprus and Egypt; that is, Turkey would retain the sovereign rights but Italy would be the administrative power. His method of obtaining this was simple. Once he had induced the European powers to declare their disinterest, he told Pansa, he would parade this at Constantinople and squeeze the Sultan, 'partly with love, partly with the threat of war'. In this way he could obtain control of Tripoli without a war.

What went wrong was that he reckoned without Giolitti and Zanardelli. As soon as rumours of Italian intention to take Tripoli appeared in the European press and produced official complaints from the German Foreign Office, Giolitti – the powerful Minister of the Interior – hastened to deny any such intentions publicly in *La Stampa* and the official *L'Italie*. Zanardelli, moreover, was 'absolutely opposed' to any such action, though Malvano thought he might accept 'a more or less friendly agreement with the Turks'. The Turks however were not inclined to be friendly. Prinetti's approaches to Constantinople in February and March to permit Italian emigrants to go to Tripoli and set up a self-governing colony were received with horror and immediate appeals sent to London and Berlin for protection. In northern Italy rumours in April that troops were to be sent to Tripoli produced riots. Since love had no effect and Giolitti and Zanardelli prevented the menace of drawing the sword, Prinetti's ambitions were frustrated. All that he achieved in Tripoli, as in his 'machiavellian mercantilism', was to ease the path for his successor: largely a waste of effort. Italy took the province only after the French had seized Morocco, as Visconti had agreed: there was no need to give away Italian neutrality to achieve this.[45]

Giolitti, Tittoni and the Entente Cordiale

In April 1904 the event predicted by Tornielli for the previous decade, the signature of the Anglo–French *Entente,* finally took place. On 1 May the London correspondent of *La Tribuna*, Malagodi, demanded its extension to Italy in an alliance of the three 'sisters in democracy and liberty', a demand echoed by Luigi Barzini in the *Corriere della Sera* on 30 October. Its significance for Italy was enormous since, if it *really* portended a British alignment with France, then in Rudinì's opinion, 'aucune force humaine ne saura retenir l'Italie dans ce qui reste de ses alliances; elle est fatalement amenée à chercher un point d'appui du côte de la France reconciliée avec l'Angleterre'. There was of course nothing new about this, Rudinì had told Berlin as much in 1896. The question was, however, the extent to which the *Entente Cordiale* actually ensured Anglo–German hostility; only when this was apparent would Italy finally come down on the side of France. Since right up to July 1914 Anglo–German relations were variable, so was Italian foreign policy. This was why, as Bertie reported in 1904, there was some uncertainty in Rome:[46]

Both the King and the Government would, I believe, be glad to substitute for the present Triplice another one viz: France, England and Italy, but they do not see their way to, or any pressing necessity for, it at the moment.

For this reason it is necessary to view Barrère's reports from Rome in 1903–4 with a little caution. According to the French embassy, what few hesitations remained in Rome after his agreements with Visconti and Prinetti were swept away in a tide of popular enthusiasm for *la sorella latina* after Victor Emmanuel's visit to Paris in October 1903 and President Loubet's banquet at the Quirinale in April 1904. Now France, he claimed, 'is once more in her [Italian] eyes the incarnation of modern ideas which lead to progress and the emancipation of the masses'. Admittedly, the supposedly pro-French Prinetti had left the Consulta in April 1903 to be replaced in November by Tommaso Tittoni, by reputation a triplicist;[47] but Barrère claimed that this was a matter of no importance. Giolitti, now Premier – an office he retained for nine of the next eleven years – had assured him that foreign affairs would be conducted by himself and Luzzati, 'the most influential man in the government'. True, Emperor William II had been given a state banquet at Naples in March 1904 and toasts drunk to the Triple Alliance; but this was mere flummery. Had not Tittoni sought Anglo-French support against Austria in the Balkans? Loubet's visit merely crowned the edifice. 'Decidedly', wrote Barrère on 21 June, 'Italy is lost for Germany. Nothing could make this country take up arms against us.'[48]

He was in part the victim of his own propaganda. The state visits had been engineered by Barrère, taking advantage of the king's love of travel and the fact that he had to go to London anyway to return Edward VII's visit. Victor Emmanuel had a strong desire that a Catholic sovereign should drink a toast to Italy in the Quirinale and, since Francis Joseph would not, a French president was the next best thing. There was certainly no intention by the Italian government to make this a pro-French demonstration. Tittoni told Monts – with some truth – that it was all part of a series of royal visits arranged by Zanardelli, which the present government regretted but could do nothing about. Equally, though Loubet's visit aroused popular sympathy for France in some quarters, he alienated it in others. The France of Combes and Waldeck-Rousseau had little appeal to Italian Catholics, who were beginning to participate in politics by 1904, and whose spokesman in the cabinet was Tittoni. After the Loubet visit these certainly became pro-German.[49]

Nor had Giolitti any desire to embark on a change of direction in foreign affairs. He certainly counted on French financial aid to bring about the economic *risorgimento* and was bent on a programme of democratic reform in alliance with the Left – 'war against illiteracy, ignorance and superstition' – but he had no wish that this should impinge upon foreign policy. The less said about this the better for all concerned was his view, which was no doubt why he appointed Tittoni – whom he could control – in preference to Visconti Venosta. Just because he wanted to remake Italy in the image of democratic France, Giolitti saw no reason to ally with her: after all, he pointed out to enthusiasts on the Left, France saw no need to harmonise internal with external policies; France was allied with Tsarist Russia. For all his assurances to Barrère – given after Tittoni's maiden and markedly triplicist speech on 15 December 1903 – there is no reason to suppose that Giolitti wished in any way to promote closer relations with France. His policy was that enunciated by Tittoni in instructions to Tornielli on 4 April 1904 on the eve of Loubet's visit:

> Alliance with the Central Powers and friendship with France are now the two essential rules of our foreign policy. The loyalty which Italy gives to her alliances must be the best guarantee of the loyalty we give to maintaining and reinforcing our friendship with France. . . .

Hence of course Giolitti's visit to Bülow at Homburg in September 1904 and revelation of the fact, though not the text, of Prinetti's agreement to Berlin on 25 February 1905. The object of this was not, as Luzzatti told Barrère, to reconcile the Germans to Italy's new relationship with France, but to assure Bülow that Giolitti did not intend it to go any further. Prinetti had made an agreement which Giolitti had inherited, that was the sum total of Italian commitments to France. Loubet's visit had no political significance: 'There was no agreement, either political or military, that diminished the value of the commitments assumed with the allied powers.'

Similarly in the case of Italo–Austrian relations. Barrère assumed from Tittoni's frequent complaints of Austrian proceedings in Macedonia and sporadic irredentist demonstrations that by

January 1905 Rome was prepared to desert her alliance for a new 'western *triplice*' in the Balkans. In fact Giolitti was determined to suppress irredentism and Tittoni announced in the Senate on 9 February 1905 that there was 'complete agreement and complete mutual trust' between the two governments. Almost immediately Barrère began to complain that neither the king nor Tittoni had either the resolution or the sense to perceive where Italian interests really lay, that Italy 'has stopped half way along her new route'; a complaint which speaks for itself. The Palazzo Farnese was always inclined to see Italian interests through French eyes.[50]

The Moroccan Crisis

The Italian policy of balancing delicately between alliance and friendships, Tittoni admitted, was based on the assumption that peace would be maintained: if it were not she would be in difficulties. This problem arose in acute form in 1905–6 with the Moroccan affair. It was not that Italy had conflicting obligations in Morocco: the *triplice* had protected only Italian interests there and, as Salvatorelli suggests, by making an agreement with France 'Italy had, if anything, relieved Germany of part of the burden of the alliance'. For twenty years since 1882 there had never been the slightest suggestion from Berlin to Rome of any German concern. The problem in 1905–6 lay elsewhere, principally in the danger that Germany would go to war against an Anglo–French coalition. This would raise enormous problems for Italy.[51]

Even if this danger were averted there still remained a basic difficulty, the fact that German insistence on a European conference would put Italy in a delicate position. She was bound not to oppose France, yet Bülow insisted on Italian support for Germany as a test of her good faith. Throughout the summer of 1905 Tittoni banked on the fact that Bülow and Rouvier would reach agreement after the dismissal of Delcassé and that the conference would be a rubber stamp, a view he repeated to Barrère as late as 16 November. This is why he chose Silvestrelli, his cousin, as the Italian delegate: as a protegé of Crispi his reputation was triplicist yet anything he said could be disavowed and put down to his incapacity, which was well known. Right up until his resignation in December Tittoni shrank from telling Berlin the unpleasant truth for fear of provoking German wrath.

As the possibility of an Anglo–German war loomed large in October and November Italian politicians grew increasingly uneasy. Fortis, temporary Premier by grace of Giolitti, an old associate of Crispi and a triplicist of long standing, gave out via the semi-official *Agenzia Italiana* that Italy would remain loyal to her alliances. This seemed the most obvious madness. Michele Torraca, a close friend of Sonnino and an equally long-standing supporter of the German alliance, urged publicly in the *Corriere della Sera* that this was impossible, that it must be made clear to Berlin – as Rudinì had done – that Italy could not fight against England. *La Stampa,* long critical of 'this new diplomatic venture of the restless Kaiser of Berlin', agreed and added waspishly on 6 January that if Tittoni had done this long ago there would have been no crisis.[52]

Tittoni's successor at the Consulta for the remaining two months of the Fortis administration, Di San Giuliano, immediately rectified this mistake. In an article in the *National Review* in November he had made his position abundantly clear: Italy's hopes of getting Tripoli depended upon her not opposing France in Morocco. In January he repeated this to Monts, the German Ambassador, adding that Italy could not accept that a war over this issue invoked the *casus foederis,* a statement in strict accordance with the facts. He sugared the pill, however, by emphasising that in all other respects the government still remained loyal to the alliance and that 'disinterest' in Morocco did not in any way imply support for France. Hence his appointment of Visconti Venosta in place of Silvestrelli as Italian delegate to the Algeciras conference. Since this was now to be a real affair, Italy would need the talents of her premier diplomatist.

By the time the conference actually convened Sonnino had become Premier with Guicciardini – 'the perfect example of incompetent mediocrity' (Barrère) – as Foreign Minister; but it made no difference to the policy pursued. Sonnino, long critical of Tittoni's *dolce far niente,* insisted that Italy could not face war, fully shared Di San Giuliano's views and allowed Visconti a free hand to mediate a settlement. His intention was clear:[53]

> Italy should emerge from the conference with her foreign relations in the same state as before she went in, without her allies having legitimate cause for complaint or the other side being able to accuse us of backing down on engagements, with the consequence that the

corollary [i.e. Tripoli] would fall to the ground through the non-fulfilment of the engagements.

In this he was over optimistic. Visconti did his best to mediate and avoid a confrontation between France and Germany: when he failed and it came to a vote on 3 March he abstained, a tactic which drew complaints from both sides. Certainly he failed to avert German wrath. Monts, in January, advocated dropping the Italian alliance as 'a dead weight': in May, William II talked angrily of war against his 'useless' ally. That in the end he relented and allowed the tacit renewal in 1907 was a calculation of pure self-interest rather than any faith in Italy.

Goluchowski, his 'brilliant second' at Vienna, thought it essential to maintain the connection with Rome as the only way to avert an Austro–Italian war, which he did not want. Aehrenthal, his successor in 1907, preferred Russia as a third partner but, accepting that this was not an immediate possibility, urged 'with great reluctance' that Italy was better than nothing. Bülow supported this view. German isolation after the Algeciras conference was painfully obvious and if they cut Italy adrift they might well lose Austria too. It was better to swallow their resentment, accept that Italy would never fight against France and England and renew the pact simply to prevent her making an open alliance with France. The Kaiser himself acknowledged this: 'If England succeeds in drawing Italy out of the Triple Alliance then everything will collapse and a general convulsion is inevitable.' Hence, under Austrian pressure, the joint telegram of the two emperors from Vienna on 7 June 1906 addressed to their 'troisième allié fidèle', though it was far from expressing William's true thoughts.

In fact Italy remained much more attached to the Triple Alliance than Berlin allowed. Her policy at Algeciras was inevitable, predictable since at least 1896, and in fact almost identical with that of Austria. Both had wanted to avoid the trial of strength over Morocco that Germany insisted on; both wished to avoid the polarisation of Europe into two hostile camps in which their interests were bound to suffer. There was in fact a good deal of sense in *La Stampa*'s criticism of Tittoni. Vienna had been highly critical of Germany's Moroccan adventure throughout 1905 and if Rome had also made its position clear before Germany was committed the confrontation might have been avoided.

Hence the Austrian eagerness to retain the Italian alliance in

1906. It was not only a means of repressing irredentism: Italy was also a useful check upon the wilder adventures of Berlin. Equally, in Rome the one thought after Algeciras was to strengthen the alliance, to which there was no alternative. On this all shades of opinion from Visconti to Giolitti were agreed, a stand supported even by much of the radical press in 1906. The alliance meant peace, all the more attractive after the recent exposure to the abyss of European war.[54]

By contrast any further moves in the direction of France had few attractions. Conservatives opposed it, not least on ideological grounds, as did the Catholics and many of Giolitti's followers: 'France governed by Clemenceau is a dangerous lover,' *La Stampa* announced in December 1906. It was hard to see what Italy would gain. For all her loyalty to her engagements towards France, there were few signs of French generosity. In the recent negotiations over Abyssinia the Quai d'Orsay had given nothing away. Even in the financial field French help was meagre: over the conversion of the Italian debt in July 1906 French banks had been very tight-fisted. Tittoni thought German banks had been at least as helpful and certainly felt no debt of gratitude to France. Since he returned to the Consulta in July this was a fact of some significance.[55]

Everything in the end came back to England: but had London definitely burnt its boats? Hardinge and Bülow both denied this. Hardinge told Tittoni in April 1907 that the fuss over a naval holiday was 'merely a matter of internal politics', which would soon blow over. Bülow, a year later, assured him that Italy 'would never have to choose between the German alliance and English friendship'. As late as February 1911 Grey told Imperiali that since 1906 'we had really no difficulties with Germany which strained our relations'. If this were so then why should Italy leave the Triple Alliance?[56]

Italy, Austria and the Balkans

Tittoni's encounter with Aehrenthal at Desio in July 1907 and their mutual agreement on Balkan problems saw Italo–Austrian relations at their highest point for ten years. It was always the case that they had more to gain by mutual co-operation than from aggression, but this simple fact was often obscured by the *furor consularis* in Albania or student riots in Milan or Innsbruck, until a major crisis – as in Morocco – and a mutual dislike of German recklessness forced them to forget their relatively minor squabbles and work together. The journalists and the military still remained as hostile as ever – in 1907 Conrad von Hotzendorff announced that Italy was the major enemy – but the diplomats and politicians resolved to make the alliance work. As Goluchowski observed in September 1906, 'between Italy and Austria there are only two possibilities, either alliance or war, and between the two the former is preferable'.[57]

The terms of the Desio agreement reflected the real anxieties in the complex relationship between Rome and Vienna. This was no longer the *terra irredenta*. Partly because irredentism was fiercely suppressed by Crispi as contrary to interests of state, partly because the intelligentsia were more attracted to the new religion of socialism, comparatively little was heard of the woes of the Italian population of the Trentino or Trieste – at least until the Hohenlohe decrees in 1912. There were riots from time to time, notably in 1902–3 under the patronage of the veteran irredentist Zanardelli and in November 1908 after Aehrenthal's annexation of Bosnia – which did nothing to improve relations between the allies. Goluchowski told Bülow in 1903 that he would not have renewed the Triple Alliance if he had anticipated these, which Austrian consuls regarded as serious. Monts reported that same December, with gloomy foreboding, that all the youth was irredentist: what was to happen when they came of age?[58]

This, however, was mere alarmism. It is quite clear that by the turn of the century the old republican Left around Cavallotti – killed in a duel in May 1898 – was a spent force. Barzilai lingered on, periodically advocating the virtues of alliance with France and a war against Austria, but nobody listened to him. The new Left, the PSI, approved of the Triple Alliance as the bulwark of peace, the prime requisite of the people. The alliance, claimed the socialist *Il Tempo* in 1903, was 'preparing under the feudal and monarchical stamp the basis of the future European democracy'. Irredentism, by contrast, was a regressive, bourgeois ideology. Leonida Bissolati, editor of *Avanti!* from 1896–1911, constantly harped on this theme and spent much of his time in forging closer links with the Austrian SPD. Gaetano Salvemini condemned irredentism as sterile, the work of 'mummified romantics', right down to July 1914 and thought the preservation of a reformed Austria essential

97

to the European equilibrium. As one socialist Deputy, Morgari, told his colleagues on 19 June 1909, '. . . we make a fuss because Austria refuses to establish an Italian university at Trieste; just think that from Rome southwards illiteracy runs from 60 per cent upwards, reaching 80 per cent in Calabria.'[59]

It is a mistake to assume – with the benefit of hindsight – that all Italians naturally wanted to acquire the Trentino and Trieste. Even the irredentists in the decade before 1914 would have been perfectly content with the concession of an Italian university at Trieste. General Ricciotti Garibaldi, considered by the Austrian Embassy as the leader of the movement, assured them in May 1905 that he was quite content with the territorial *status quo*. Guicciardini, formerly a supporter of Zanardelli and later Foreign Minister for brief periods in 1906 and 1910, announced in May 1904 that he did 'not believe in the irremedial contradiction of interests between Italy and Austria'. Lützow, the Austrian Ambassador, believed – rightly – that this was a general conviction amongst the political élite by 1906 and that the interest in Trieste was minimal.

This was certainly the attitude of Italian governments. Giolitti resigned in June 1903 because Zanardelli refused to suppress irredentist riots, but once he became Premier in October successive administrations from then until 1914 put them down with severity and with no apparent difficulty. This for the simple reason that outside the large towns the *paese* – the majority of the Italian people – were totally uninterested. Before 1913 this was never the major issue between Rome and Vienna: as the *Osservatore Romano* put it with slight delicacy in 1913, 'why should we compromise Italian interests in Albania and the Ionian Sea for the sake of half a dozen clerks in Trieste?' The histrionics of the press in general on this point, suggests Tommasini, were 'absolutely disproportionate to the real importance of the issue'. Even the nationalists, before July 1914, had other fish to fry.[60]

Much more important to Rome was the break-up of the Mediterranean agreements with Britain and Austria from 1896 onwards and the inclination of Goluchowski to solve Austria's Balkan problems by a separate agreement with Russia. As long as Austrian policy in the Balkans had been based upon opposing Russia in concert with Britain, then Italy had been a valuable ally, able to extract concessions – as Robilant had done – for her support. Once Goluchowski reached an understanding with Muraviev in May

1897, further extended at Murzteg in October 1903, the Triple Alliance was seriously devalued as far as Vienna was concerned: Rome was barely informed of his actions after the event. With Russian forces concentrated in the Far East, Austria could switch troops from Galicia to the Isonzo and from the end of 1896 onwards the military could afford to make contingency plans for war against their ally.

It was bad enough for Rome to be excluded from the Balkans by an Austro–Russian agreement to preserve the *status quo*, but what was to happen if this broke down and the two powers proceeded to an amicable division of Turkish territory including Macedonia? The major Italian concern – apart from prestige – lay in Albania. This for a variety of reasons but principally strategic. If Austria took Albania she would possess the entire eastern seaboard of the Adriatic and pose a constant menace to the long Italian coastline from Venice to Brindisi. As Rudinì told Pasetti in May 1897 – when the latter explained Goluchowski's defensive objective in making the agreement with Russia – Italy had no wish to take Albania or Tripolitania herself. These provinces[61]

> would be a source of weakness, not of strength. We should regret it however if these territories should pass into the hands of other powers. The reciprocal disinterest of the Great Powers reassured us and was quite sufficient. With that we are fully satisfied.

If, however, Italy were to succeed in obtaining Albania as her share of the break-up of Macedonia then she would control the Straits of Otranto on both sides and could close the Adriatic. This was as evident to Vienna as to Rome and explains why successive Austrian foreign ministers opposed any Italian claim to inherit Albania. In June 1914 Berchtold even advocated its union with Greece – a stance which had some influence upon Italy's decision in the July crisis.

Since neither side was prepared to give way the consequence was a local struggle for power, based upon controlling schools, the church, contracts for public works and bribing the various Albanian chieftains. These, if lacking in national consciousness, certainly had the wit to see that the road to fortune lay in playing off one side against the other. The Austrians had the advantage of being the official protector of the Catholics, perhaps one third of the population. The Italians scored in that they had an ethnic

Albanian community in southern Italy – Crispi supposedly belonged to it – organised as a pressure group by General Ricciotti
Garibaldi in 1904 with its own government-subsidised newspaper,
whose leaders were trained at the universities of Naples and
Palermo. These were so effective in developing Italian shipping
and commerce with Albania that by 1911 Italy had the lion's share
of the trade.[62]

Consequently, until 1914 Albania was the major point of dispute
in Austro–Italian relations. Every time one side gained a contract
there were complaints of unfair advantages – Berchtold said in
1914 that Italian malpractices would fill a 500-page book – with
constant fears that one side or the other was about to seize the
province whenever there was a Balkan crisis. It was in an attempt
to check this *furor consularis* that Visconti Venosta and Goluchowski
met at Monza in November 1897 at the height of the Cretan crisis
and made a self-denying agreement. The understanding, formal-
ised in an exchange of notes on 20 November 1900 and 9 February
1901, provided that both would respect the *status quo* 'as long as
circumstances permitted', would work towards autonomy for
Albania if this broke down, and would attempt 'to reconcile and to
safeguard our reciprocal interests'.[63]

On the spot the agreement had little effect but it did provide a
useful springboard from which Italy could advance. In August
1901 Prinetti appealed to Vienna for mutal restraint of the press
over Albania, assured Goluchowski that he would not support the
intrigues of Prince Nicholas of Montenegro, and suggested they
sponsor a reform programme in Albania similar to the Austro–
Russian scheme in Macedonia. In February 1902, with an eye to
obtaining German backing for the agreement, thus neutralising the
main danger of Austro–Russian action, Prinetti tried to have it
incorporated within the treaty of the Triple Alliance. Again he got
no response from Vienna.

In July Prinetti embarked on the alternative tack – the king's
visit to St Petersburg. Part of Prinetti's general scheme for making
Italy more independent of her allies – *La Tribuna* announced on 15
July 1902 that 'today our country acts for and by itself as an active
element in international politics' – the visit was a complete failure.
His immediate object, to circumvent Austro–Russian co-operation
in Macedonia by a separate understanding with St Petersburg, met
with no response. The official explanation of Russian coolness was

the threats of Italian socialists to arrange a hostile reception if Nicholas II were to pay a return visit – *fischi allo zar* – but this concealed the reality. Russia preferred to work with Austria. Prinetti in fact was reduced to instructing the embassy at Constantinople to associate themselves with any step that Austria and Russia took, thus creating the appearance of an *accord à trois*. As Albertini commented in his newspaper at the time, Prinetti 'had an exaggerated idea of the strength and importance of Italy'. It was not until Russian disillusionment with Austria reached its peak after Aehrenthal's annexation of Bosnia that the tsar signified his willingness to collaborate with Italy in the Balkans by his visit to Victor Emmanuel at Racconigi in October 1909.[64]

Prinetti's failure to make any impression on the Austro–Russian block and Zanardelli's encouragement of irredentism presented their successors – Tittoni and Giolitti – with a considerable problem. It was quite likely, Sonnino thought in August 1903, that 'Austria will seize a province and reward us with an Imperial visit'. Rattazzi, equally gloomy, warned his friend Giolitti in October that Prinetti and Zanardelli had succeeded only in pleasing the *piazza*: 'What clowns! With the fortyeighters and their idiocies we will finish up at the Treaty of Berlin and at Adua.' What was needed was a firm hand at the Consulta, for which he suggested Visconti Venosta, a sure enough indication that in Giolittian circles there was no desire for a 'democratic' foreign policy.[65]

What he got on 3 November was Tittoni, chosen apparently for the impression he made on Giolitti in suppressing riots as prefect of Naples, who for the next six years became the symbol in Italy of the Austrian alliance. As Giolitti told Monts, his very lack of experience or knowledge of foreign affairs was an asset in that he had no prejudices! A political nonentity with no great ability – both Bissolati and Barrère stressed his ignorance and idleness – he was the ideal man to carry out Giolitti's foreign policy, which in practice amounted to a passive acceptance of the Triple Alliance.[66]

Nevertheless, the basic hostility to Austrian exclusiveness still remained. After an attempt to use the Berlin lever upon Vienna failed, Tittoni in 1904–5 embarked upon a serious attempt to create a western *triplice* with France and England in Macedonia. What he feared was that Austrian forces – supposedly there to create some semblance of order – would remain permanently and, as Russia became absorbed in Asia, that Macedonia would pass by default to

Austria. In January and February 1904 he suggested to London and Paris that they co-operate 'to prevent or counteract isolated Austrian action and keep the Macedonian question entirely an European one'. His method was fairly drastic: an Anglo–Italian occupation of the ports, 'so as to hold guarantees for the withdrawal of Austrian forces in the interior'.[67]

Lansdowne, though he did not share Tittoni's suspicions of Austrian intentions, was reasonably interested in collaboration, especially if it entailed French support, but the whole concept broke down with Delcassé's refusal. He would do nothing to annoy Austria, despite Barrère's urging that this was the way to obtain the Italian alliance. Both England and France viewed the Macedonian question in a different light from Italy. Lansdowne was genuinely concerned with Macedonian reform and objected to the Austro–Russian monopoly because they seemed to do nothing. Delcassé regarded it as a question of power politics: Russia was his ally, Austria a potential ally. He had already obtained what he sought from Italy: an alliance in the Balkans would be an embarrassment since what Italy wanted was an anti-Austrian coalition or a share of the spoils.[68]

Since he could obtain no assistance elsewhere, Tittoni fell back upon direct agreement with Austria. On 9 April 1904 he met Goluchowski at Abbazia and reached a general understanding over the Balkans. He was assured that Austria had no expansionist intentions, that the agreement with Russia was solely to provide for the *status quo*, and that Austria would only occupy the Sanjak if it were absolutely necessary, and after due warning. In return he acknowledged that an eventual Austrian annexation of Bosnia – administered since 1878 – would entail no claim to compensation from Italy. In a general atmosphere of amicable understanding they renewed the Visconti Venosta agreement on Albania and Goluchowski, favourably impressed with Tittoni's pro-*triplice* sentiments, promised to try to expedite the commercial treaty that was still hanging fire from Prinetti's time.

All things considered, it was a satisfactory meeting. Goluchowski, in the summer, put the brake on the Austrian army's desire to carry out tours of inspection on the Italian frontier; Tittoni made very favourable references to Austria in his major foreign policy speech to the chamber in May. Downgrading the importance of the Loubet visit of the previous month he reiterated the government's loyalty to the *triplice*, distinguished carefully between Italy's allies and her friends and denied that he was juggling between the two sides: 'Such a policy would be unworthy of a great nation.' Even Monts, usually hostile, admitted it to be 'an able dance on the eggs'.[69]

How far both sides really trusted each other is, however, a moot point. Goluchowski on 15 October 1904 made a mutual neutrality agreement with Russia in the event that either were involved in war with a third power, which, though mainly intended to cover Russia in Asia, had obvious application to Italy.[70] In November he accepted the Austrian War Minister's desire to strengthen the Italian frontier on the grounds that Tittoni and Giolitti might not last for ever. In Italy the end of the Murzteg monopoly at the end of the year and the admission of six-power control of Macedonia was hailed with joy as a check upon Austria, Tittoni immediately instructing the Ambassador at Constantinople, Imperiali, on 11 December that 'he should maintain and increase in every way . . . contact with England, whose political aims in Macedonia are those closest to ours'. By the end of January 1905 he was once more suggesting a western *triplice* to Barrère, though again without result. According to Di San Giuliano, not the least of Italian worries in the Moroccan crisis – perhaps the reason why Tittoni never tried collaboration with Vienna – was the free hand this gave to Austria in the East: '. . . the continual worsening of Anglo–German relations seems bound to disorientate and embarrass our government, at the very moment when the temporary effacement of Russia removes the counterpoise which we need to Austrian influence in the Balkans'.[71]

For two years after the Moroccan crisis Italo–Austrian relations were relatively warm, a reflection of the comparative quiescence in the Balkans. Lutzow in March 1906 thought that what dislike of the Triple Alliance remained in Italy was now directed against Germany, a welcome change from the viewpoint of Austria. Bissolati seemed to confirm this: in July 1907, at the time of the Desio meeting, he suggested in *Il Tempo* that Rome and Vienna should work together to act as a brake on Berlin. Avarna, ambassador at Vienna, at this time even busied himself with founding Italo–Austrian friendship committees, until he was told nobody in Vienna would join.

Desio reflected this atmosphere. Aehrenthal and Tittoni agreed to share power in the Adriatic, to abstain from intervention if Macedonian politics produced a Balkan war and to support an independent Albania if Turkish power in Europe collapsed. To round off the picture of perfect harmony Aehrenthal agreed to support Italian claims to introduce reforms on the Macedonian pattern to that other Turkish province in decline, Tripoli. Even relations with Germany seemed to have improved: Tittoni noted that he was 'highly satisfied' with his meeting with Bülow at Venice in April 1908.[72]

This did not mean of course that all had been forgiven and forgotten. In Austria, Conrad, appointed in November 1906, went ahead with his war plans on the assumption that Italy was the major enemy and from this time onward until his dismissal in 1911 periodically urged a preventive strike. Aehrenthal himself, much as he wanted improved relations with Italy, thought her unreliable – especially when Tittoni supported the Russian alternative system from the Danube to the Adriatic in the Sanjak railway affair. As Di San Giuliano pointed out from the London Embassy in June 1908,[73]

> Austria and Germany ... are aiming at a political and economic hegemony in the Balkans and in the Ottoman Empire in general and at a position in the Mediterranean basin that is bound to make us uneasy ... we don't want them to build the Uvatz–Mitrovitza railway.

Nor was Tittoni as blindly trusting in Aehrenthal as Italian critics later made out. He too encouraged the Ministry of War to increase expenditure on the eastern frontier but, in 1908, tried to minimise the political consequences. It was not entirely possible to conceal the expenditure by fudging the figures because the Left would only vote money for the army if it were plainly directed against Austria. But he did his best: the ardent desire of the deputies to discuss the inadequacies of the strategic railway system in north Italy was squashed as 'beyond the natural competence of parliament'. In February he pulled off what had eluded his predecessors, an official visit of the Russian fleet to Naples, and asked Giolitti to order the absolute suppression of any demonstrations by the Naples socialists, 'those real idiots, who have no care of Italian interests'. On 28 September he even met Isvolski at Desio and, according to the semi-official hand-out, 'buried Murzteg'.[74]

The Bosnian Crisis

Tittoni's major error was not that he trusted Aehrenthal too much, but that he tried to be too clever. He kept quiet when the Austrian, at their meeting at Salzburg on 3 September 1908, discussed the forthcoming annexation of Bosnia and established that this would entail no Italian claim to compensation under Article VII. Even if it is true, as Tittoni later told Avarna, that Aehrenthal spoke about this as 'something that would happen in the next year or two', Tittoni completely failed to probe his intentions. It is obviously true, as Torre observes, that he 'lacked the backbone of Di Robilant or Visconti Venosta' but it must be borne in mind that at this stage Tittoni thought the annexation would go through by Austro–Russian agreement, with which Italy was proud to be associated. He had buried Murzteg. Hence his speech at Carate Brianza on 6 October: 'Italy could serenely await events since, whatever happens, she will not be surprised, unprepared or isolated.' Hence, too, his careless hints at benefits for Italy: now that he had finally inserted himself in the Austro–Russian agreement surely Aehrenthal would reward his efforts to promote Austro–Italian understanding?[75]

When the storm broke in Italy – as in Russia and Britain – Tittoni was reduced to proclaiming his innocence and joining in the demand for a conference. As it became patently obvious that Italian public opinion did not regard Austrian renunciation of her rights in the Sanjak as any compensation, he changed his tune on this as well: now he wanted an Italian university at Trieste, he told Aehrenthal on 16 December, as the only way of preserving 'the work to which I was dedicated . . . in favour of good Austro–Italian relations'. As Torre puts it, 'Tittoni had lost his head.' At the same time that he launched this demand he begged Aehrenthal not to reveal that he had been consulted over Bosnia! Even Tommasini admits that his hero 'did not appreciate completely various elements of his situation'.

Tittoni was in no position to make any demands. Bülow told him bluntly that if it came to war Austria could crush Italy with ease; Aehrenthal thought Tittoni overrated his own importance and wrote to Bülow that 'though we wish to keep Italy in the Triple Alliance we are not prepared to pay for it'. On 11 January 1909 he instructed Lützow that the question of an Italian university at Trieste was closed: the most he could offer – and even this was rejected by the Austrian Reichsrat – was an Italian faculty at the university of Vienna. To Tittoni's complaints, via Monts, that 'Aehrenthal has been my ruin' he replied that Tittoni was the victim of his own vacillation.[76]

The attack upon Tittoni inside Italy came on all sides. In the debates in parliament from 1–4 December the radical Left assailed him as the betrayer of the Turkish people and for his failure to obtain the Italian university at Trieste. Not the least of their objectives was to get him out and push Giolitti into a more radical foreign policy, as Barrère put it, 'more in conformity with the interests and traditions of his country'. On the Right he was attacked both on the grounds of abandoning the Young Turks – Di San Giuliano and Sonnino had cherished hopes that these would provide a barrier against Austrian expansion – and for his vacillation. If he had stuck to Aehrenthal he might at least have earned the gratitude of his allies: by his 'constant incoherence of action' all he had achieved was general contempt. Privately, Sonnino admitted to Guicciardini, the *triplice* had received a mortal blow in this affair: their idea had always been to use Austro–Italian collaboration to 'smooth down the rough edges between England and Germany'. Now what? But it was better to say nothing, especially as the army was in 'a deplorable condition' – the result of Giolitti's playing to the gallery, 'trying to keep the extreme Left friendly to the government'.[77]

That Tittoni survived for another twelve months until Giolitti himself resigned in December 1909 was only because he received the Premier's full support. *La Stampa* suggested on 8 October that Giolitti should himself take over the direction of foreign policy, but the Piedmontese would have none of it and made it a question of confidence in the government. Bosnia, he told the editor of the socialist *Il Secolo*, was unimportant: 'it belonged to Austria for thirty years . . . neither Turkey nor Russia will sacrifice a man or a lira to take it away'. Dismissing Tittoni would be fatal: since the attack upon him came from the irredentists, it would signify that Italy 'proposed to abandon the *triplice*'. Moreover, this would only be the start: 'the overthrow of the European equilibrium would provoke a war in a very short time'.

A circular to the prefects on 11 October instructed them to see that the provincial press supported the government, with a reminder that irredentism would lead to large armaments and less public works. In the debates in December he made the same point. When Fortis, an ex-Premier and prominent member of the government coalition, demanded large armaments 'to put our military power in a condition to guarantee peace', Giolitti first congratulated the speaker then went on to explain that: 'We are in a period of construction, we have great problems to resolve that are closely linked to economic, social and political life . . . and all this is impossible if we do not follow a policy of peace.' Peace was provided by the Triple Alliance, an attack on the alliance was an attack on Giolitti.[78]

There was no sign, despite the severity of the attacks, that Giolitti intended to make any concession to his critics. The budget of March 1909 made no provision for any increased military expenditure, most of the defence spending still going to the navy to counteract the Austrian dreadnought programme. Even so, Admiral Mirabello, the Minister of Marine, told the *Corriere della Sera* in April, Italian naval superiority in the Adriatic would be reduced to 1·3: 1·0 by 1912. The king fully supported this choice. According to Rodd, he 'shares the views held by many Italians that the menace of the Austrian Dreadnoughts . . . must be countered at all costs'. The army was in a much worse condition, so much so that the Minister of War resigned in protest against Giolitti's refusal to increase expenditure. His successor, the unfortunate General Spingardi, was given a supplementary grant in June and announced on the strength of it that 'our army and our defences would gain such efficiency that Italy could sit with tranquillity amongst the Great Powers, not only respected but feared'. Even so Giolitti was extremely careful to avoid giving offence to Vienna: in December he made the king dismiss a general who made an anti-Austrian speech.[79]

Obviously enough, the Bosnian crisis led to no radical departure in Italian foreign policy; even Albertini, otherwise highly critical, admitted that they must stay with the alliance until they could find something better: 'We entered the Triple Alliance to guarantee our territorial integrity. We will not renounce this guarantee until we can find one which is more suitable.' Lützow thought, obviously rightly, that whereas the press was still anti-Austrian in 1909, the politicians would stick to the Triple Alliance. Even Fortis, the sensation of the December debates, assured him in February that he did not want war. Tittoni at first talked airily of reducing his contacts with Aehrenthal to a minimum and instructed Avarna accordingly, but was soon dissuaded. What was the point, enquired the Ambassador at Vienna on 17 February, 'of subordinating interests of state to pure sentiment'? The central powers were all powerful, Russia a broken reed and France hastening to seek agreement with Berlin over Morocco. Hostility to Austria would only lead to isolation: why not take advantage of the breach between Aehrenthal and Isvolski to take the place of Russia in the Murzteg programme?[80]

Tittoni in fact adopted this idea with a difference. Obsessed, like all other European statesmen, with the belief that the annexation of Bosnia was but the prelude to a determined plan of Austrian expansion to Salonika, he wanted both to block this and to make sure that – if the worst happened – then Italy would obtain compensation. To make sure he opened negotiations with both Austria and Russia; in this way, he later explained to the king and Giolitti, he would make certain that Murzteg was not revived without Italian participation. He made a series of approaches to Aehrenthal from June to October hoping to obtain a favourable reply before the tsar and Isvolski – coming on a royal visit at last – reached Italy; which could then be put to them as the basis of an *accord à trois*. In the end he issued a sort of ultimatum: it was up to Vienna, he instructed Avarna on 18 October; 'the methods employed by Aehrenthal have created a painful sense of distrust'; either he gave cast iron assurances of future good behaviour or Italy would seek support from Russia.

Whilst Aehrenthal was still pondering a reply the Russian guests arrived at the royal hunting lodge at Racconigi. The trouble with Tittoni's whole scheme was now apparent. Throughout 1909 Isvolski had not been on speaking terms with Aehrenthal and *en route* to Italy he and the tsar had taken great pains to avoid Hapsburg territory. 'Isvolski's major idea at the moment', wrote Melegari from St Petersburg on 14 October, 'is animosity and distrust towards Austria, in contrast to your idea of a tripartite agreement.' In consequence Tittoni found himself in a slightly awkward situation.[81]

Having initiated negotiations with both, he now found Isvolski pressing him to conclude the sort of agreement with Russia that Italian foreign ministers since Rudinì had pursued with ardour.

Yet Aehrenthal had still to give a reply, whilst neither could be communicated to the other. Tittoni did not allow this to bother him unduly. He explained the facts to the king and Giolitti at Racconigi and received their authority to go ahead with both. As he excused himself *ex post facto* in a memorandum written after his resignation, once Aehrenthal and Isvolski were off the scene the separate agreements could be made into the basis of an *accord à trois*, 'which would guarantee the peace of Europe'.[82]

At Racconigi on 24 October Tittoni and Isvolski, after the latter had revealed the Austrian 'treachery' of October 1904, reached agreement to contain any further Austrian expansion. It was made in extreme secrecy, written by the two foreign ministers personally, and in Italy communicated only to Giolitti and the king. Isvolski promised to inform only the tsar and not to reveal it to either France or England. It provided for the maintenance of the *status quo* in the Balkans, for supporting the principle of nationality and no 'foreign domination' if this were disturbed; with a promise of diplomatic support to achieve this end. Neither would make an agreement with a third party without the other's consent. Lastly, each would 'consider with benevolence' the other's interests in Tripoli and the Straits respectively.

The next day Avarna simultaneously presented Aehrenthal with a discreet version of the Racconigi visit and the draft text of an Italo–Austrian agreement. The Austrian, rightly suspicious, first demanded a promise that no written agreement of any sort had been made with Russia. Reassured on this point, after a month of haggling on the exact terms as to what constituted the existing order in the Balkans – Tittoni said he didn't want any more surprises – an agreement was ready for signature. It was to last for the lifetime of the Triple Alliance and provided for mutual support of the Balkan *status quo*. If, unfortunately, Austria found it necessary to reoccupy the Sanjak then Italy was to be entitled to compensation under Article VII of the alliance. Neither would make agreements with third parties concerning the Balkans without the knowledge of the other and all proposals received from third parties on this subject would be communicated to the other. Absolute secrecy was to be maintained except in respect of Germany.[83]

At this stage, on 2 December, Giolitti resigned. The new Foreign Minister in Sonnino's cabinet, Guicciardini, did not share

Tittoni's airy assurance that if Russia and Austria were both sincere in their devotion to the *status quo* then the two agreements 'contained nothing that was contradictory'. An honest man – Lützow commented in 1906 that he was the most honest politician in Italy, a real gentleman – he had serious doubts that this was in fact the case:

> It could produce a situation in which we found ourselves in the fatal necessity of ratting on one or another of the agreements concluded, with damage to our loyalty and grave harm to Italian interests.

In the end he was converted by the argument that the negotiations were too far advanced, that if he refused to sign then Vienna would conclude that he and Sonnino were bent on a 'radical change of that political system which, also in my opinion, is the only one which serves the supreme interests of our country'. This would produce even worse consequences, so on 19 December he signed the agreement.[84]

The net result therefore of Tittoni's Balkan policy was that he had indeed officiated at the burial of Murzteg but at the cost of contradictory agreements with both Russia and Austria. This would not matter too much if the peninsula remained quiet and the two northern powers remained on good terms, but the aftermath of the Bosnian crisis made both of these assumptions unlikely: Austro–Russian collaboration was unthinkable whilst Aehrenthal and Isvolski remained in office. This could have awkward consequences for Italy if it came to an open contest.

As far as the Triple Alliance was concerned it had weathered the storm. Irredentism was no stronger when Tittoni resigned than when he first took office, despite the Bosnian affair. For this the primary credit must go to Giolitti, his determination to concentrate on social reform and refusal to be diverted into an anti-Austrian crusade. But one should not take this too far; most other leading politicians, as Lützow concluded, shared his determination to keep the alliance intact. It was much too dangerous for Italy to do otherwise, however much they might have liked a change.[85] The alliance may not have meant much to Vienna by the end of 1909 – Aehrenthal plainly regarded Tittoni as a weathercock – but it still had its supporters in Rome. As *La Stampa* put it on 12 April 1909, 'To denounce the treaty of alliance with the eastern frontier not strongly fortified and with the fleet inferior to that of Austria would bring our irreparable ruin.'[86] Italy, in other words, must arm. This was to become the major theme of the nationalists in the next two years.

Chapter 6

The Revival of Italian Nationalism

> Italian feeling towards Austria had become more
> friendly by last summer than it had ever been. . . .
> *Di San Giuliano*, 1914

The working assumption of successive Italian foreign ministers
since the fall of Crispi in 1896 had been that parliament and people
were opposed to foreign adventures. The one attempt to do something, Canevaro's San Mun affair, had been such a fiasco as to warn
off all others. Visconti Venosta and Prinetti had concentrated on
settling disputes with France with an eye to using French money
to rebuild the Italian economy. Under Tittoni the accent had been
on maintaining relations with Austria and deflating irredentism, so
that Giolitti could embark on a coalition with the Left in a programme of retrenchment and social reform. This programme had
proved politically feasible because the old militant republican Left
was in decline and the new Left, the PSI, approved of the Triple
Alliance. As Di San Giuliano told Aehrenthal in September 1910,
socialism had killed irredentism.[1]

The new nationalist movement, the *literati* led by Enrico
Corradini, equally supported the Triple Alliance. Like Gabriele
D'Annunzio, Corradini admired the strength of Germany and
despised the weakness of France. What was the point, enquired his
paper, *Il Regno*, in January 1905 shortly after the celebrated visit by
President Loubet, in resurrecting the old *fratellanza latina*? 'We
prefer the friendship of a first-class military power like Germany to
that with a nation whose army, weakened by freemasonry,
socialism and humanitarianism, offers so much less security.' This
tone, reminiscent of that of Crispi, dominated nationalist utterances
until August 1914: all of them were 'convinced triplicists, fervent
colonialists and virulent francophobes'. At the first Nationalist
Congress held at Florence in December 1910, proposals put
forward to revive Mazzini's old idea, an alliance with the Slavs in

an anti-Austrian crusade, were quickly squashed. Luigi Federzoni, a journalist on the *Giornale d'Italia,* asserted the incompatibility of Italian and Slav interests – the battle cry of D'Annunzio in 1919. Nationalism defended the interests of oppressed Italy everywhere, he proclaimed; but his efforts were mainly directed towards Italy's colonising mission 'on shores far from those bathed in the waters of the Adriatic'. His attack upon the government was limited to its failure to arm Italy up to the standard of the other powers: foreign policy since 1896 had been governed by 'timidity, weakness and lack of foresight on the part of the government; ignorance and impulsiveness on the part of public opinion'. Corradini confined himself to the theme of bourgeois decadence.[2]

The nationalist lack of interest in irredentism did not necessarily imply that they would not be a nuisance elsewhere: in fact, however, up to the Bosnian crisis, Corradini, Prezzolini and their following were of but slight political importance. As a lunatic fringe to the literary *avant garde,* their demands – that since Italy lacked the economic strength for growth she should expand by military force – were treated with the ridicule they deserved. Their attacks upon the 'decadence' of bourgeois life under Giolitti, *il ministro della malavita,* brought slightly more response, largely because Giuseppe Prezzolini's journal *La Voce* drew the support of respectable intellectuals like Benedetto Croce and Gaetano Salvemini. But even *La Voce* failed to dent Giolitti's parliamentary majorities.

That the nationalists wished to destroy Giolitti and parliament itself in favour of some mystical union between the 'true' forces in Italy – northern industry and southern peasants – was evident enough, but too laughable to be taken seriously. Corradini himself destroyed his only possible political base, syndicalism, when in September 1904 he attacked the revolutionary wing of the socialists and urged Giolitti to suppress their general strike with troops. As an apostle of reaction at home and violent, revolutionary nationalism abroad directed at no one in particular, Corradini seemed to carry irrationalism to the point of absurdity. The break between the two leaders on exactly this point, the collapse of *Il Regno* in 1907 and Prezzolini's concentration on the real problem of Italian politics – the *Mezzogiorno* – heralded the end of the neo-Romantic orgy of literary violence. It marked, in Thayer's words, the intellectuals' 'turning away from rhetoric and precocity ... a hopeful indication of greater political responsibility'.[3]

This prospect was wrecked by Aehrenthal's annexation of Bosnia in October 1908. The effect in Italy was out of all proportion to the issue involved largely because Tittoni, the apologist of the Austrian alliance, was made to look a fool. The sense of injured national pride was such that, for the first time since Adowa, the respectable bourgeois parties of the Centre now urged a policy of armaments and expansion: Corradini, almost overnight, achieved national recognition as a true prophet. The attack upon Tittoni once parliament assembled in December 1908 developed into a general onslaught upon Giolitti's administration in 1909 for its failure to arm adequately. Even Francesco Nitti, a supporter of the government and usually a sober economist, was carried away by this obsession with compensation, somewhere, somehow, at almost any cost: 'Only warlike peoples', he told the Chamber on 12 June 1909, 'have the ability to make sacrifices.'[4]

In the course of 1910–11 the constant chant for action from the nationalists became the major theme of the more influential newspapers, even before the Agadir crisis added fuel to the flame. As Barrère noted, 'nationalism has come out of its limbo'. By July 1911, when it seemed that France and Germany were carving up Morocco, *La Perseveranza* (the mirror of moderate Lombard opinion which had bitterly opposed Crispi's colonial expansion) backed the nationalist stance. 'Why', it asked, 'should the shame of being excluded [from Africa] be reserved for Italy?' *La Stampa*, which had formerly supported Giolitti's programme of concentration upon economic growth, now argued that his task had been accomplished: Italy was prosperous and could afford the luxury of overseas expansion. The *Corriere della Sera,* Albertini's paper, took up the old Crispi stance: the policy of 'clean hands' pursued in the crisis of 1878 had been disastrous for Italy; if it were repeated in that of 1911 she would cease to be a great power and become 'a maritime Switzerland'. 'The comforting phenomenon of the hour is the present change in public attitudes towards colonial expansion. The anti-expansionists are now in a minority. . . .'

It was this general insistence upon the need for action, plus Italy's obvious inability to risk a confrontation with Austria in the Balkans at this juncture that determined the conquest of Tripoli. Until 1911 successive governments in Rome had been quite content to play a waiting game and, for all their concern that it should not fall into French or British hands, from 1896 to 1909 Rome had shown remarkably little sign of actually wanting to take possession themselves. Prinetti had considered doing so but had dropped the idea when opposed by Zanardelli. Tittoni had confined himself to peaceful penetration – post offices and concessions for the Banco di Roma obtained by the diplomatic pressure of his allies upon the Turks. It was obvious that – in the days before oil had assumed any significance – the economic attractions of Tripoli were slight, and even the nationalists, full of Italy's imperial mission, were hard put to find convincing reasons for seizing it. Corradini in 1911 was reduced to citing Herodotus as evidence of its intrinsic worth and devoted most of his despatches to *L'Idea Nazionale* (the new weekly launched in March 1911) to lyrical descriptions of Roman ruins. Clearly, as Thayer argues, the motivation behind the *public* demand for the Tripoli venture was more psychological than material: the need for some outlet for a demonstration of Italy's status as a great power of more critical importance than the province itself.[5]

This was certainly the view of the leading political figures of the day. Sonnino, who as Finance Minister under Crispi had opposed the African adventure in 1895–6 and rejected any Tripoli move by Prinetti in 1902, now favoured it. On 13 September 1911, though a political opponent, he offered Di San Giuliano his parliamentary support on the grounds that he was 'profoundly convinced that if Italy did not take Tripoli now she never would, and instead someone else would take her place'. The thought was not absent, of course, from Sonnino's mind that if Giolitti went to Tripoli it would wreck his coalition with the radicals and socialists, thus averting the threat of universal suffrage and its attendant evils. Such an attitude on the part of the government's opponents on the Right was to be anticipated.

However, even most of Giolitti's supporters were acquiescent. Luzzati, though not eager and aware that the Tripoli expedition might set off a Balkan war, passively assumed that Giolitti knew what he was about. Barzilai, one of the old guard of the Cavallotti republicans and a staunch opponent of Crispi, strongly favoured the new venture on the grounds – ironic in restrospect – that Italy would be strengthened by a Tripoli war and be more capable of tackling Austria. Though they suspected Sonnino's motives, the

Lombard democrats in general thought it hopeless to oppose the war in the face of the fact that youth in general had gone over to Corradini; a view which Bissolati shared. Though personally opposed he would not urge this course upon the PSI lest he bring down Giolitti. Though Prezzolini, Salvemini and the *Il Voce* group still opposed war, it was only too obvious that the popular aversion to Africa which, in the 1890s, had offered a sound political base for opposing Crispi, no longer existed. As Guglielmo Ferrero observed, a new spirit of recklessness was abroad, not only in Italy: 'Soon, throughout Europe, they will be unable to govern public opinion any more . . . discontent will be constant and permanent in the public spirit.'[6]

This change in the temper of public opinion, added to their concept of the national interest, determined Di San Giuliano and Giolitti to take Tripoli. Di San Giuliano, who moved from the London Embassy to the Consulta in March 1910 and remained there until his death in October 1914, detested the wave of hysteria sweeping Italy. An autocrat, he thought like Robilant that foreign policy should be decided by interests of state, not the twists and turns of popular sentiment. 'We used not to be like this, we used to be a sensible people,' he wrote to Tittoni in February 1911; but he thought this 'general vague desire to do something' would have to be appeased.[7] The only alternative, to ignore it and employ diplomatic means to make Tripoli impregnable, was too expensive even in terms of interests of state, let alone the government's political position.

Despite all previous agreements with France and England it would be dangerous to rely on these indefinitely to keep France out of Tripoli. Tittoni, for one, was convinced that sooner or later, once Morocco were absorbed, she would turn eastwards again and what reliance could be placed on London, mesmerised by the German menace, to oppose her only ally? Di San Giuliano had discovered already that Grey had little enthusiasm for adventures with Italy as travelling companion. The only way to block France permanently would be to obtain the support of Berlin and Vienna, but he had already learnt the prohibitive cost of this in December 1910. Berlin was indifferent and Aehrenthal had no wish to disturb his relations with France or the Turks: Austrian support over Tripoli would have to be paid for. This, Di San Giuliano told the king on 7 September 1911, would have to be via 'greater benevolence towards Austrian policy in the Balkans'. It was cheaper to take Tripoli than, for example, to give up Italian claims to parity with Austria in Albania, since the Adriatic was a matter of life and death to Italy.[8]

These arguments based upon interests of state finally won over Giolitti. Though his exact motivation is hazy, it would seem that he was not impressed by the agitation of the nationalists whom, rightly, he regarded as politically intransigent. He was much more concerned with international pressures and the drift of his own supporters.[9] With a shrewd instinct for self-preservation, no sooner was the war launched than he made a major policy speech at Turin on 7 October blaming it on others: '. . . foreign policy cannot depend entirely on the will of the government and parliament, but has to take into consideration events and situations which it is not in our power to modify, nor sometimes even to accelerate or retard.' In other words, France, Germany and the growth of Italian nationalism were the villains of the piece. Despite his caution, however, the attempt by Giolitti to obtain the best of both worlds failed. The nationalists, naturally, castigated him for his lack of warlike spirit and cautious conduct of operations; his supporters, for going to war at all. During and after the Tripoli campaign the socialist, republican and radical parties all split over the issue, the majority in each case opposing both the war and the government. Although he managed to cling to office until March 1914, Giolitti's coalition system fragmented under the pressures of the Tripoli war.[10] This was to be important because if Giolitti had been in power in August 1914 it seems improbable that he would have been so convinced as his successor, Salandra, that Italy should intervene.

Once decided upon action in Tripoli, Giolitti and Di San Giuliano acted quickly. Parliament was not in session and not consulted. The king's consent was obtained on 17 September; eleven days later a twenty-four-hour ultimatum was presented to the Turks and war declared on the 29th. This haste effectively prevented any mediation. Until 4 September Grey was led to believe that it was only a question of diplomatic pressure on the Turks for more concessions. Berlin was not told until 22 September that Italy would take action in Tripoli once the Moroccan dispute was settled, information not given to London until the 27th. Any hopes that remained of a compromise were dispelled by Giolitti's action on 5 November declaring Tripoli and Cyrenaica annexed to the Italian crown under the new name of Libya. The expectation that this would induce the Turks to give in gracefully proved illusory and in fact the war dragged on for another year, posing increasingly difficult problems for the rest of Europe. It was obvious to all concerned that the longer the war lasted, the greater the danger of Balkan complications; yet it was equally clear that anyone who intervened would get their fingers burnt. Either the Turks or the Italians would be alienated, a serious consideration in view of the delicate balance of European power politics. The only solution was joint mediation by the powers as a whole but, although half-hearted attempts at this were made from time to time, mutual suspicion brought them to nothing.[11]

These considerations applied just as much to Italy's allies as to everyone else. In Berlin, where much effort had gone into cultivating the Young Turks, Italian action was greatly resented both by William II and by the Foreign Office. Yet fear of driving Italy into French arms prevented them doing anything and throughout the war the German official attitude varied only between a prudent neutrality and – especially towards the end – open support for her ally. In Vienna, Aehrenthal actually welcomed the war on the practical ground that the more Italy was embroiled in Africa the better for Austrian interests. Africa was a powerful distraction from the Balkans and, even if she succeeded in taking Tripoli, Italy would then become more, not less, dependent upon the Triple Alliance. She would need their support to defend it against France in Tunis and Britain in Egypt. For this reason he rejected Conrad's idea of utilising the occasion to recover Lombardy and Venetia as dangerous and unnecessary: interest alone would keep Italy faithful to the alliance.

Austria's only concern was to keep the war from spreading to the Balkans and the few signs of any tension in Italo–Austrian relations during 1911–12 were occasioned by Italian operations in this area. On 29 September, the day war was declared, when Turkish destroyers were attacked off Albania, Aehrenthal protested sharply and Di San Giuliano had to agree to the neutralisation of the Adriatic. In April and May 1912 an Italian fleet attacked the Dardanelles and occupied the Dodecanese, 'temporarily': Berchtold, who succeeded Aehrenthal on the latter's death in February 1912, warned Rome that if these islands were retained he would demand compensation under Article VII. But these were minor irritations. The salient facts in Italo–Austrian relations during the Tripoli war were Aehrenthal's friendly attitude, the dismissal of Italy's arch-enemy Conrad on 30 November 1911 and Di San Giuliano's own triplicist leanings.[12]

Italy's cordial relations with her alliance partners during 1911–12 were an ever increasing contrast to her relations to the *Entente*. Despite Grey's realisation in September that it was 'most important that neither we nor France should side against Italy', it became increasingly difficult to maintain this stance. As a result of the character of the war, the impossibility of identifying and pinning down the enemy, it rapidly became a punitive action against the Arab population. This not only aroused public support in Britain for the 'gallant little Arabs', including the bulk of the Liberal party, but induced apprehension in the imperial satrapies in Cairo and Delhi. As Churchill pointed out, 'we must not forget that we are the greatest Mahomedan power in the world. . . . Have we not more to gain from Turkish friendship than from Italian?' Italy's extension of the war to the eastern Mediterranean in the spring of 1912 which forced the Turks to close the Dardanelles only increased this feeling: British shipowners were losing £9,000 a day and were not slow to voice their objections. Mensdorff, kept well informed by his cousin George V, had no doubts that by March 1912 British feeling was strongly pro-Turk.[13]

This growing hostility towards Italy in London made it impossible to consider the scheme put forward by Rodd and Barrère at various times from October 1911 to use the war to bring Italy over to the *Entente*. Based on the expectation, noted by Aehrenthal, that the possession of Tripoli would increase Italian vulnerability in the Mediterranean, Rodd proposed that the three powers concerned should mutually guarantee their North African territories, as this 'would take all the sting out of the Triple Alliance, as far as Italy is concerned'. Grey rejected it on two grounds, one avowed and one silent. In the first place, he told Rodd, public opinion in Britain was hostile 'and the feeling being what it is, I should not be justified in making overtures to Italy for any political understanding'. Second, and this he kept to himself, the idea noted by Cambon in 1908 that British interests were better served by keeping Italy in the Triple Alliance, was still strongly held. If Italy were induced to change sides, an Austro–Italian war was a certainty.

Moreover, she would need British support. Given this choice Grey's course was clear and in December he concluded, 'It seems to me to be preferable that she should continue as a somewhat doubtful factor in the alliance than that she should be in open opposition to Austria and Germany.'[14]

The Quai d'Orsay was divided. The trouble with Barrère's schemes for pulling Italy out of the Triple Alliance was the effect upon the position of Austria. Since the long-standing French ambition was to weaken the ties between Vienna and Berlin, the last thing they wanted was to present Austria with the threat of a Russo–Italian coalition. With the Italian occupation of the Dodecanese, however, some French diplomats – in particular Paul Cambon – had second thoughts and supported Barrère: the danger of Italy offering her German ally a naval base in that area was thought too great to ignore. Cambon now became an advocate of some version of a triple *entente* to guard against this.

Whatever chance such a project possessed was ruined by the fact that its revival coincided with the *Carthage* and *Manouba* incidents on 16 and 18 January 1912. Riding the wave of nationalism which swept France during the Moroccan crisis, Poincaré took charge of foreign affairs himself in his new government formed on 14 January and chose to exploit these incidents to enhance his parliamentary position. Within a week of taking office he had managed to push relations with Italy to the verge of war. The immediate issues – Italian interception, search and removal of some Turkish passengers from two French ships – were trifling, yet Poincaré chose to issue a public ultimatum to Italy in a speech to the Chamber on 22 January. The seriousness of the situation was emphasised by Tittoni from the Paris embassy four days later:[15]

> Politicians here talk of nothing but naval demonstrations and corps of observation on the Alps . . . Poincaré himself said today that if our response had been delayed beyond midday tomorrow, Barrère would have been recalled. It seems as if a wave of hysteria is passing over France. . . .

The Italian reaction to Poincaré's arrogance was predictable. The nationalist organ, *L'Idea Nazionale,* announced on 1 February that they had 'no intention of extracting Italy from vassalage to Vienna in order to subject her to the republic next door'. Irredentists like Barzilai were 'blind francophils'; Tunis, Nice and

Corsica were equally *terra irredenta*. Significantly, in contrast to the popular enthusiasm for President Loubet in 1904–5, Poincaré was now jeered whenever he appeared on newsreels in Italy. Nor did this bitter resentment against France die down with the submission of the *Manouba* and *Carthage* affair to the Hague Court. In June 1912 it was Rodd's considered opinion that France 'now commands no confidence in that public opinion which here directs the orientation of politicians'. In fact it was only strong government pressure on the major newspapers which kept this resentment within reasonable bounds, as even Barrère recognised.

Nor was the reaction confined to the public. Tittoni, apparently under the erroneous impression that they lapsed with the existing treaty, urged his master not to repeat 'the most imprudent declarations of Prinetti of 1902' when he renewed the Triple Alliance. Di San Giuliano, further irritated by an absurd claim by Poincaré for compensation before he would recognise the Italian annexation of Libya, expressed his exasperation quite clearly to Tittoni in October 1912. France was the only power still withholding recognition: 'She should have been the first because of the 1902 agreements, our conduct at Algeciras and the fact that we were the first to recognise the Franco–German agreement on Morocco. . . .' Not surprisingly, by November, Rodd thought the minister had 'fallen under the charm of Berlin'. Even the king, normally more attached to a French alignment, told the British ambassador in January 1913 that a French alliance was impossible: 'The average man in Italy has not yet got over his resentment at the attitude of France. . . . France could never accept Italy as one of the great powers and always treated her as an inferior.'[16]

Consequently, when Grey and Poincaré at last made a half-hearted effort in October 1912 to explore the possibility of some understanding with Italy, they met with complete failure. Grey's objection in 1911 was largely that negotiation would infringe upon British neutrality and that Italy's exit from the Triple Alliance was undesirable on general grounds. The end of the war by the Treaty of Ouchy on 18 October removed one obstacle, whilst Admiralty obsession with the danger that Italy would hand over part of the Dodecanese Islands to Germany made Grey much more willing to contemplate a limited agreement if it would avert this. From the start, however, he excluded a mutual guarantee of North African territory, the only offer likely to attract Italy to a neutrality agree-

ment with the *Entente*. Poincaré, apart from the Dodecanese issue –
he wanted to give them to Greece to increase French influence
there – also wanted to ensure Italian non-interference with the
transport of French troops from Algeria in the event of a European
war. To this end, in contrast to Grey, he sought a form of general
agreement for the preservation of the Mediterranean *status quo*, in
effect the exclusion of warlike operations from this area.[17]

Di San Giuliano poured cold water on these ideas from the start.
On 31 October, though he was careful not to close the door completely in case of later need, he told Barrère casually that 'Italy
wanted to be loyal with all and for this reason could not make
agreements that were incompatible with her duties under the
Triple Alliance'. The only consolation that Di San Giuliano would
offer Barrère was that, though the Triple Alliance would shortly be
renewed, it would be renewed 'without modification' – which
meant that the 1902 agreements were still valid. Italian diplomats
generally were even more opposed to an agreement with the
Entente. As Avarna and Imperiali stressed, there was bound to be
another repetition of the embarrassments which had followed
Prinetti's *giri di valzer*. Tittoni thought there was no point whatsoever in continuing negotiation in view of Grey's super cautious-
ness, '. . . unless you want to impress the public with the announcement of the signature of an agreement which in substance would
signify nothing'. On 20 November he asserted to Poincaré that in
the event of an Austro–Russian confrontation in the Balkans,
Italy would support her ally; a statement that was well justified by
Italian policy at the London conference over the next six months.[18]

After this fiasco Poincaré abandoned the Barrère line – in which
he never had much faith – and settled instead for transferring
the entire French fleet to the Mediterranean. In 1913, from the
presidency, he reverted to his former practice of kicking the
Italians to persuade them to love France. The effect was continual
bickering over the Dodecanese and the Libyan frontier until
Italo–French relations were worse than at any time since 1900.
Giolitti and Di San Giuliano were equally indifferent to France.
They made friendly noises from time to time when they wanted
something from Paris or London, but this was almost entirely
window dressing:[19] for all practical purposes they returned to a
purely triplicist stance.

British and French diplomats at Rome professed to detect a

difference between Di San Giuliano and the Premier; the former (and his entire office) being dyed in the wool triplicists, the latter more open-minded. Giolitti, according to Rodd in November 1912, 'has evidently realised that the opinion of the country is not convinced by the arguments which the Foreign Office [i.e. the Consulta] has inspired in the semi-official press'.[20] But there was precious little evidence of this. In the Chamber of Deputies the only speaker to oppose the renewal of the alliance in December 1912 was Barzilai, who had been doing so for thirty years. The 'parties of order' – the nationalists, the liberals and the Catholics – all favoured the connection with the central powers. Amongst the newspapers the independents were just as favourable as the semi-official press, except for articles by Bissolati in *Il Secolo*. Most local papers, the real independents with too small a circulation to be worth bribing, approved: in Ancona, according to the prefect, the news of renewal had made 'the best impression'. The only criticism from *La Stampa* and the *Corriere della Sera* – the latter no friend of Giolitti – was that the government had not obtained further concessions for Italy from her allies.

As for Giolitti's open-mindedness, this was merely innate caution: he never liked to burn his boats. But he was certainly not pro-French in any way. In 1913 Frassati, editor of *La Stampa* – generally supposed a Giolittian paper – conducted a regular press war against France which brought frequent protests from Barrère: Frassati was made a Senator. Since there was no doubt that Giolitti controlled the government, a fact emphasised by all foreign diplomats in Rome, then one must conclude that Giolitti too favoured the renewal of the alliance.[21]

All the evidence in fact suggests that there was a general consensus of support for the Triple Alliance amongst Italian statesmen and diplomats and that its renewal was never in question. Tittoni, Sonnino, Avarna and Di San Giuliano all agreed on this, if for different reasons. For Sonnino and Tittoni it was a case of *pis aller*; non-renewal would make Italy a French satellite, especially now that the British had withdrawn from the Mediterranean. For Avarna it was a question of necessity, the only way to avert the flail of Conrad; though there was the added attraction that – in the late Aehrenthal's words – if Italy would 'finish with the policy of indecision, of making eyes at everyone which provokes mistrust in us' then the alliance could bring positive benefits.

The Foreign Minister fully shared this distrust of France and fear of Austria. Salvemini was wrong in attributing Di San Giuliano's triplicist outlook to his distrust of democracy: for him it was a question of power. As he told the king,

> joining the Triple Entente . . . even if it were desired by those three powers, which it is not, would not be enough to overthrow the military preponderance of the Austro–German bloc, and would not bring sufficient compensation for our interests from our new allies.

His view, in 1912, was that Russia was 'una grande impotenza' and that England would not intervene in a continental war. That being so, Italy should stay on the winning side and cover herself against French naval preponderance through a new naval convention with Vienna and Berlin. (Negotiations for this were opened by the chief of staff in December and completed in June 1913.) The reason he stalled during the summer of 1912 was simply to obtain recognition of Italian sovereignty in Libya from the *Entente*. Once this was in his pocket he met Berchtold at Pisa on 22–23 October and expressed his willingness to renew the alliance more or less as it stood. All Di San Giuliano wanted were minor amendments in the drafting so as to insert Italian sovereignty in Libya in the protocol and include the Austro–Italian agreements of 1901 and 1909 on Albania and Novibazar in the treaty, since Giolitti insisted. Most of the delay until signature on 5 December was due to Berchtold's vain hopes of a solution to his Balkan problems through a last-minute agreement with Russia.[22]

The shift in focus of European diplomacy to the Balkans and Asiatic Turkey from October 1912 until July 1914 gave additional emphasis to the Italian drift back to Austria and Germany. It had never formed part of Di San Giuliano's intentions to encourage the Balkan states to attack the Turks and repeated overtures from Sofia in 1912 had been pointedly ignored. The Serbs and Greeks were Italy's main rivals for the Albanian inheritance: far better, with Turkish power collapsing, to collaborate with Austria to establish a large, nominally independent, Albania along the lines of the Visconti Venosta/Goluchowski agreement of 1901. This did not mean, of course, that all was sweetness and light in Italo–Austrian dealings in Albania. In fact there was a running battle for two years, until Vienna was distracted elsewhere, for primacy of influence amongst the robber chieftains and the clergy, for control of schools, post offices and public works. Di San Giuliano threw himself into this with considerable energy, expending large funds obtained from Giolitti. Significantly, Carlo Galli – at this time Consul at Scutari – later wrote of his chief that 'there had not been a statesman like him since Cavour for high intelligence, lively spirit and far-sightedness'. He certainly possessed Camillo's nerve: though prevented from acting by Giolitti's caution, Di San Giuliano, in March 1913, even wanted to go to the lengths of joining Austria in a naval demonstration off Montenegro! As he told the Premier, if they left Vienna to act alone they risked 'a situation analogous to that created by England towards France in Egypt when the latter abstained in 1882'. In May Rodd thought them so close that it was 'difficult to tell which is the Italian Minister for Foreign Affairs and which is the Austrian Ambassador'.[23]

The concept that Italy and Austria must work together as the only means of preventing them falling apart was not new: in fact it was the *raison d'être* of the alliance. But in 1913 San Giuliano gave it a new extension. Influenced by the development of the Austrian fleet – stronger than the Italian in 1913 – the French naval concentration in the Mediterranean and open backing for Greece, he conceived the idea that Austria and Italy should extend their working alliance in the Balkans to the whole of the Mediterranean. The king had doubts about this. He accepted the alliance with Vienna as a necessary evil in view of the military predominance of the Central Powers, but thought *Entente* naval power equally dictated an understanding with them by sea. However, he could make little impression upon his Foreign Minister. Confident of popular support, Di San Giuliano announced to the Chamber on 22 February that French and British domination of the Mediterranean was at an end:

> In the Mediterranean sea, that the French used to call a Latin lake, and that England controlled ... a new competitor has arrived, to be dreaded for the valour of her people and the vastness of her new dominion. ... Never again can anyone call it 'Mare Nostrum'. ...

Henceforth, 'in partnership with Austria–Hungary, whose interests were identical', Italy would retain her position there as a leading power.

This prophecy was greeted with rapture by the chamber and the press, *La Stampa* adding that in view of the rate of growth of her population Italy would soon become *the* leading power. The speech and subsequent press comment naturally produced considerable French protest, but Di San Giuliano brushed this aside, almost with contempt. Culturally speaking, he told Tittoni on 28 February, he – like most Italians – used to be francophile: 'it depended upon France whether these sentiments grew again'. Poincaré, by his conduct during the Tripoli war, his efforts to replace Italy in the Dodecanese with Greece, and his open pursuit of Mediterranean predominance for France, had completely alienated Italian feeling: 'In other words, insufficient acceptance of the consequence of the fact that Italy is a Great Power. . . . It is evident that Italy, Austria–Hungary and Germany cannot allow the Mediterranean to be transformed into an Anglo–French lake. . . .'

Convinced that the Ottoman Empire was on its last legs even in Asia, from January 1913 onwards Di San Giuliano embarked on an attempt to ensure Italy her share through a partnership with Austria. Not that he wanted the 'Sick Man' to take to his deathbed, in fact he preferred a pause to give Italy time to digest her new conquests before embarking on fresh fields. His first thought was that a chunk of the Asian mainland would be 'dangerous and onerous': much better, in his view, was to stake out a claim to the Dodecanese as Italy's share. Here he had the advantage of possession, strong Italian garrisons, and sufficient of a case to bamboozle contenders. Gradually, however, influenced by Tittoni's conviction that since Briand denied any intention of taking Syria its seizure must be imminent, he changed his mind. On 23 January Di San Giuliano instructed Garroni, Ambassador at Constantinople, to seek a suitable sphere of interest in Asia Minor bordering on the Mediterranean and by March they had settled on the Gulf of Adalia. The primary purpose of this, he informed Avarna on 17 August, was to provide 'naval bases, so that Italy does not find herself in a position of too great inferiority when confronting France, who controls Morocco, Algeria, Tunis and in time Syria'.[24]

The idea of a counterpoise to France in Syria was coupled with Di San Giuliano's scheme for creating a basis of common action for the Triple Alliance in the Mediterranean; but this began to go wrong almost as soon as it was initiated. On 23 May Flotow delivered a sharp protest in Rome against Italian negotiations for a railway concession in Adalia: this was German territory. Worse was to follow. By July Di San Giuliano had negotiated a compromise with Berlin, based on limiting the Italian sphere from Mersina to the Gulf of Cos, only to find that Vienna had claims in this area too. This was disastrous because Italy had no desire to thwart Austria. On the contrary, he told Avarna, it was essential from the Italian viewpoint to encourage the Austrian interest in Asia Minor; it would draw her fleet out of the Adriatic and destroy her supremacy there; it would bolster up the Italian position *vis-à-vis* France: '. . . she always shows herself more friendly towards us when she knows us to be strong and is instinctively driven to suppress us when she believes us to be weak.'[25]

Faced with the Austrian counter-claim, Di San Giuliano's idea was to solve the problem by sharing the Italian zone with her, a proposal which met with less than enthusiasm in Vienna since Berchtold conceived he had the prior right. They might have reached some compromise but for the Hohenlohe decrees. These edicts of the Austrian governor of Trieste in August 1913 – aimed at appeasing Slovene sentiment by dismissing all Italians from public office – brought an almost complete breakdown in Austro–Italian relations. Berchtold affected to regard these decrees (as similar edicts in the Tyrol) as an internal matter in which neither he nor Italy should interfere. Even Avarna thought it was a waste of time pressing him. But the Consulta could not afford to ignore them. In Italy the press – with the exception of the *Osservatore Romano* – went wild. Feeling against Austria, Di San Giuliano told Avarna and Bollati, was 'fortissimo e generale': it was essential to obtain some concession from Vienna.[26]

> I agree that for the sake of our enormous common interests in the Adriatic and the Mediterranean it suits Italy and Austria–Hungary to remain united and the Royal Government will make every effort in this sense [but] . . . the Trieste decree cannot remain without consequence for the relations between Italy and Austria. This does not depend on the will of the government but on the unanimous feeling of the Nation, which in Italy is sovereign. . . . If you think that I am exaggerating try spending a few days in Rome or in other big cities instead of in remote country towns: then see if I am not right.

Though Di San Giuliano broke off negotiations on Adalia with Vienna at the end of August there was no possible chance of a permanent breach. As Sonnino instructed Bergamini, editor of the

Giornale d'Italia, on 23 September, 'the alliance is for the present a necessity for Italy': the press, in consequence, must not go too far. Up to a point the government could restrain the press for limited periods and suppress irredentist demonstrations, as it did in Venice in September. The real problem was how long Italy could remain an Austrian ally unless the latter withdrew the decrees. It was one thing to pass the word to newspaper editors in peacetime, quite another to persuade the urban Italian to fight for Austria in the event of war. The usual method of overcoming Austrian awkwardness – pressure via Berlin – was not available in this case since Jagow, when approached, declined the honour: Austro–German relations were already strained quite enough by their differing attitudes towards Romania and the Treaty of Bucharest.

Hence Rome's reversal to another old tactic when relations with her allies were bad, overtures to France. The object was very simple, as Di San Giuliano explained to the Ambassador in Berlin on 1 October.[27]

> The link, therefore, between the Trieste and now the Innsbruck decrees and the necessity of agreements between Italy and France – compatible, naturally, with the Triple Alliance – does not depend upon personalities but is in the nature of things. If they [Berlin and Vienna] persist in believing that our triplicist policy can remain unaltered without Austria doing anything to influence the state of feeling in Italy, then they are suffering under a dangerous illusion which will give rise to grave consequences.

The opportunity was provided by a series of approaches from Paris, both unofficial and official, in September and October 1913 for an understanding on the eastern Mediterranean. Though it is not entirely clear where these originated – Barrère seems the most likely candidate – Di San Giuliano's response was so welcoming that on 22 October Paleologue, on Pichon's authority, informed Rome that the Quai d'Orsai was preparing a concrete proposal. What he had in mind, it seems, was the old French idea of a neutrality agreement for the Mediterranean.[28]

At this point the negotiations once more collapsed. Originally Di San Giuliano had never meant to go beyond frightening Austria and had insisted time and again to Avarna and Bollati that there was nothing incompatible with the Triple Alliance in Italy negotiating an agreement on Asia Minor with France: Germany had similar negotiations with Russia and England whenever she pleased. All the same, Italian diplomats were uneasy, fearing lest the Consulta was to embark on new *giri di valzer,* an uneasiness evidently shared by Giolitti. On 28 October Di San Giuliano assured him that he had no such intentions, that he had every intention of consulting the allies, and that he viewed a repetition of Prinetti's tactics as 'a grave mistake'.

Despite Italian frankness, however, Zimmerman, when officially informed of the French approaches, exploded. On 30 October he told the Italian chargé d'affaires that 'any sort of agreement between Italy and France would have unpleasant repercussions upon German public opinion' and would give rise to all the old suspicions as to Italy's reliability, since France was Germany's inveterate enemy. However, agreements with Russia or England were in a different category and if Rome wanted to insure her position in the Mediterranean with the *Entente* then she should negotiate with London. Moreover, he added pointedly, neutralising the Mediterranean was contrary to Italian interests in the event of war, which the Triple Alliance would certainly win: 'Tunis . . . would be one of our spoils of victory.'[29]

After this outburst Di San Giuliano hastened to withdraw. On 1 November he assured Zimmerman, with a fair degree of truth, that he never had been thinking of a general neutrality agreement and that he, too, preferred to negotiate with London: France he would put off with fair words. In the meantime, perhaps Berlin would put pressure on Vienna to 'cancel the impression produced on Italian public opinion by the Hohenlohe decrees'. What he intended, he told Giolitti, was 'as you observed, to temporise and avoid taking initiatives', see what the French had in mind and try to stir Grey into taking the lead. There could be no harm in an agreement with London on Asia Minor to which France later adhered. At the very least, he hoped, the embarrassment the French had caused by their advances would pay off in German pressure on Vienna.[30]

Just what Di San Giuliano expected to get out of all this is debatable. Evidently his starting point had been to put pressure on Vienna but his reluctance to give up the possibility of an agreement with France suggests that he had changed his stance. Certainly the reason an agreement failed to materialise was due less to Italian reluctance than to a change of heart in Paris. Breaking the Italian diplomatic cipher at the end of 1913, the French discovered the existence of the new naval convention, concluded that negotiation with Rome was a waste of time and put pressure on London to follow their lead. In this they were successful. Grey himself was inclined to view Di San Giuliano as unreliable – largely the result of his twists and turns over the Dodecanese islands – and had little enthusiasm for negotiations with Rome. All that emerged from fitful talks in London over the next six months was a technical agreement in March 1914 between the rival British and Italian concessionaries for the construction of a railway line from Smyrna to Aidin. This never got beyond the drawing board. In effect Di San Giuliano achieved nothing from his approaches to London, possibly because – as Crowe suggested – his problem was insoluble:[31]

> Italy wants to square the circle: without exposing herself to a change of faith she wants to remain in the Triple Alliance and yet not go to war with France in accordance with its stipulations. No Anglo–Italian 'formula' can solve this ethical problem.

On the eve of the European conflict the position of Italy was thus still ambiguous. On the one hand her formal commitment to the Triple Alliance was clear. The treaty had been renewed in 1912; an additional naval convention added in June 1913 which committed the Italian fleet, under Austrian direction, to offensive action against France; and finally, in March 1914, the military convention of 1888 revised and renewed to provide for the deployment of three Italian army corps in Alsace within four weeks of mobilisation.

Yet in fact little reliance could be placed on these commitments. Italo–Austrian collaboration in the Balkans was at best fitful, their differences over Albania at times serious despite their common interests. In July and October 1913, when Berchtold showed determination to force the procrastinating Serbs to accept the decisions of the London conference over Albania, Giolitti and Di San Giuliano tried to remain neutral. By contrast, in April and July 1914, Rome threatened to fight Austria if she took Mount Lovcen. Neither move should be taken too seriously. In December 1914, Giolitti posed as a valiant restrainer of Austria in previous 'crises', but this owed more to hindsight than to fact. There was no 'crisis' in July 1913 and Di San Giuliano's 'restraint' upon Vienna at the time was no different from his 'restraint' on 9 April and 10 July

1914: what he wanted in all cases was compensation in return for acquiescence in Austrian action. His tactics on 24 July 1914 were similar: he told Vienna he would support the Serbs if he did not obtain compensation for Italy. There was nothing that was unexpected in Italian conduct in July 1914: Conrad had insisted since March, despite the military convention, that Italy would not fight.[32]

Similarly with the naval convention. This was more a move in Di San Giuliano's diplomatic campaign to use Austrian support to break the pretensions of Paris to make the Mediterranean a French lake than an indication that he intended to attack France. Italian naval construction in 1913–14 was aimed as much against her ally as her nominal opponent. Italy's relations with both France and Austria in 1914 were much the same as they had been in 1882. The Italian and French press still indulged in mutual vituperation and, according to General Pollio's sources, this reflected a growing dislike among the two peoples. But equally, as the Hohenlohe affair had indicated, irredentist feeling against Austria was still strong. Albertini in May 1914 had to restrain his diplomatic correspondent, Torre – a Triestino – from an all-out attack on both Di San Giuliano and Austria on the grounds that it was too dangerous:[33]

> We have always been a triplicist paper, repeatedly accused of Austrophilia, and if we were now to lose all restraint and let fly at Austria we might create an extremely serious situation which no Minister of Foreign Affairs could put right.

The difficulty for those inclined to criticise Di San Giuliano's supposed over-zealous attachment to the Triple Alliance was that, as Albertini indicated to Torre, there seemed to be no substitute. The only effect of Prinetti's ballroom flirtations had been to increase distrust among Italy's allies without any corresponding gains in the shape of love and friendship from France. Even the much vaunted commercial gains supposed to flow from Prinetti's policy had largely failed to materialise.[34] Any objective assessment of the balance of advantages in 1914 suggested that Di San Giuliano was right in supposing that Italy's interests lay in maintaining the alliance with Vienna and Berlin, especially as he interpreted it.

To him it was not a question of ideology but of expediency. Bollati, on 8 July, wrote to congratulate the ailing statesman – he died in October – on his achievements in the sisyphean task of 'imposing a harmony between the supreme necessities of our international position and popular sentiment in Italy'. Di San Giuliano's reply was interesting. In his view the difficulty lay in assessing where the long-term balance of power lay since Italy, a weak power, had to join the stronger group. In the long run he thought the *Entente* possessed the advantage and for that reason, ultimately, Italy would leave the Triple Alliance, '. . . but for the present, certainly, we should stay in it. At present the Triple Alliance is stronger than the Triple Entente by land and it is by land that the fortunes of war will be decided.'[35]

Chapter 7

Neutrality and War, 1914–15

> Serbia is more dangerous than Austria because she is not decadent. . . .
>
> *Salandra,* 1915

The outbreak of war in August 1914 between the five most powerful states in Europe inevitably created severe problems for the sixth. Should Italy participate, and thus assert her status as a great power? Or should she abstain, become another Switzerland and reap the benefits of neutrality? There were advantages and disadvantages to both courses of action. Since it was almost universally believed in Italy in July 1914 that Germany and Austria would win, at least on land, then supporting her alliance partners would bring all the benefits of being on the winning side. Conversely, abstention would be regarded in Berlin and Vienna as betrayal, would probably infuriate them and create severe post-war problems for Italy. This reasoning led Sidney Sonnino, who later became Foreign Minister and prime instigator of Italian intervention on the side of the *Entente*, to urge his friend, Premier Antonio Salandra, in August 1914 to honour the Triple Alliance. 'I am very doubtful of the wisdom of the decision for neutrality . . . what will become of us and the alliance in the future? I am afraid that *haute politique* will be beyond us from now on. . . .'[1]

The Foreign Minister in July 1914, Antonio di San Giuliano, personally favoured the same course which, he thought, honour and interest alike suggested.[2] Although he had pressed his allies since 24 July for compensation for Italy under Article VII of the alliance in the event of Austrian expansion in the Balkans and insisted that, in view of Austrian aggression and lack of prior consultation, the *casus foederis* did not arise for Italy, he had not refused to join them. 'I do not say', he told the German ambassador, Flotow, on 30 July, 'that in the end Italy will not take part in the war, only that she is not obliged to do so.'[3] A diplomat to his fingertips, with a 'scheming, contriving, subtle personality',[4] he saw clearly enough that Italy's only hope of obtaining the Trentino from her ally lay in extracting it *before* she supported her. The chances of getting it as a token of Austro–German gratitude after the war were slim. Hence his advice to Salandra on 26 July to stay away from Rome and create as much confusion as possible as to Italy's course of action. In the meantime he would continue to press for compensation:[5]

> As to the demonstrations against fighting for Austria, it seems to me that they are a help rather than a hindrance to our current negotiations. Anyway, we cannot re-assure public opinion and tell them that we will not go to war at any price because in that case we should obtain nothing. . . .

Di San Giuliano, obviously enough, expected a long-drawn-out crisis during which he could negotiate and obtain for Italy his maximum terms. There was nothing unethical in this, a point which needs stressing, since all the powers were inclined to view Italy as the jackal of the battlefield. The Triple Alliance, as Crispi had often been informed in the past, was a defensive alliance not a conspiracy for aggression. There was little point in Italy helping to establish Austrian supremacy in the Balkans unless it were made worth her while, which, Di San Giuliano insisted, meant the Trentino: offers of French territory were unacceptable.[6]

However, the speed of events at the end of July 1914 made his plan unworkable and on 31 July the Italian Cabinet had to take an immediate decision whether to honour the alliance, without any immediate prospect of compensation to act as an incentive. At this Cabinet the Foreign Minister was absolutely explicit: by acting without consulting her ally, he told his colleagues, Austria had broken Article VII of the agreement: 'Fortunately the *casus foederis* does not arise: neither the spirit nor the letter of the treaty of the Triple Alliance binds us to unite in this case with Germany and Austria.'[7] The result was a foregone conclusion: at a further Cabinet on 2 August the decision was made to declare Italian neutrality.

Premier Salandra insisted that Italian military unpreparedness made it impossible to go to war. His major object, he wrote to Sonnino on 7 August, was to gain time: 'To put the state, weakened by ten years of political mismanagement, back on its feet again. Every day gained helps to lessen the disparity between our actual strength . . . and the tasks expected of it.'[8] Whilst it is clear that Salandra, perhaps with good reason, had little faith in the ability of the Italian army to count for much in the European struggle,[9] his attempts to attribute its shortcomings – and hence Italian neutrality – to the mismanagement of his predecessor, Giolitti, was misleading. Salandra had no more faith nine months later at the time he decided to go to war, whilst most accounts agree that there was little substantive difference in the condition of the army. Di San Giuliano was nearer the mark when he told the Premier on 16 August 1914 that Italy could not risk war 'unless certain of victory', a certainty which he later defined as 99 per cent.[10]

General Luigi Cadorna, who became Chief of Staff only in June 1914 – and hence had no vested interest in proclaiming Italian preparedness – wanted to fight either with or against Austria in August. He had already sent the fortress artillery to the French frontier. In accordance with the military convention with the Central Powers, dating back to 1888 but revised as recently as March 1914, he urged the despatch of three army corps to the Rhine to join the invasion of France. A month later he urged an immediate attack on Austria and had ideas of marching on Vienna via Ljubliana![11] With Cadorna spoiling for a fight it is a little difficult to accept Salandra's contention that in 1914 he had to remain neutral because the army was unprepared. The army never was prepared for the actual war it had to fight, even in 1915. It was common ground amongst most Italian politicians – a tribute to their realism – to doubt their army's offensive abilities. As Di San Giuliano put it, this attitude might not be heroic 'but it is wise and patriotic'.[12]

Another excuse offered by Salandra at the time was the fear of internal disorder if Italy marched with the hated, if feared, *tedeschi*. There was perhaps more in this. The recent chaos of 'Red Week' (7–14 June) had required ten thousand troops in Emilia to maintain public order. The prefects of Forli and Verona forecast a repetition of this – 'strikes likely to assume revolutionary character' – if the government went to war in support of Austria. In Milan and Turin the prospects were even worse: *Avanti!*, the leading socialist newspaper, announced on 29 July that the king had the choice, either neutrality or a republic. There was *some* reassurance to be derived from the fact that the south had remained quiet during the June disturbances and was comparatively unaffected either by irredentism or by socialism, but the state of public opinion certainly urged caution.[13]

Again, however, this should not be taken too far as an explanation of Italian neutrality. In July the Right urged mobilisation and joining the Central Powers as the means of restoring order and preserving the monarchy: almost the entire liberal press supported them. As with the military argument, the weakness of Salandra's case is that public opinion was as much in favour of action in 1914 as in 1915. There never was a popular majority for war. As one critic has pointed out, 'Salandra, when signing the Pact of London, was fully aware that he was acting against the great majority of the Italian people.'[14] Clearly, once the Premier had decided to act, the state of public opinion was no deterrent; and Mussolini was probably right in claiming that the reason Italy chose neutrality in August 1914 was not so much pressure from the socialists as the sheer indecision and cowardice of the bourgeoisie. Mussolini's statement in 1943 that in 1915 Italy was 'dragged into war by a minority which succeeded in winning over three cities' seems a reasonably accurate reflection of contemporary reality.[15]

If there was any single factor which determined Italian neutrality on 2 August it was the attitude of Britain. Conscious of her naval power, successive Italian Foreign Ministers since 1882 had made it clear that no provision of the alliance could apply against Britain, as it was impossible for Italy to fight against her. 'Apart from other things', Di San Giuliano told Malagodi on 3 August, 'it is a question of power and Bismarck knew this. Our decision depended necessarily on that of England.'[16] The policy of preference for the Italian Foreign Minister was that Britain should stay out: in this way Italy would not be isolated and the two could operate as a neutral pressure group. If England were to join in, however, the pressure upon Italy to do so was that much the greater, if only to avoid the invidious position of being the only European power to remain neutral. As Senator Luigi Albertini wrote to his wife on 30 July, 'Heaven help us if we stay out of this conflict, unless England stays out too. In other words, if England comes in then we must march either with Austria or against her.'[17] On 31 July and 2 August when the vital decisions were taken in Rome the British course of action was still uncertain, but it was a safe assumption that she would not join the Central Powers. If she supported France then not only was it impossible for Italy to support her allies but, as Admiral Thaon di Revel, Chief of the Naval Staff, warned Salandra on 31 July, 'the probabilities of victory by our Triple Alliance become extremely slight. . . .'[18]

The news of British participation on the afternoon of 4 August removed any lingering doubts in the minds of Salandra and Di San Giuliano. Italian neutrality, they decided, must be maintained at least until the results of the great encounter battles, expected at the end of August, were clear: until then they would keep in with both sides. Martini, the Colonial Minister, an out-and-out austrophobe, assumed the Triple Alliance was now a dead letter and pressed the Premier to open negotiations with the *Entente*. But Salandra, though encouraging Martini to cultivate his contacts with the British Embassy, would not go that far. Personally he wanted an *Entente* success: an Austro–German victory, he told Malagodi, would mean servitude for Italy. 'Their ambassadors, powerful enough in the past, would then rule us like imperial proconsuls.' However, to want an *Entente* success was one thing, to risk contributing towards it quite another: Di San Giuliano, Salandra said, 'doesn't hear with that ear'.[19]

This attitude explains the failure of the approaches from Petrograd and London on 7 and 9 August. Di San Giuliano had no intention of risking serious negotiations until the military situation was a good deal clearer: the massive list of requirements that he sent to Imperiali on 12 August for Grey's inspection was pure contingency planning, aimed at keeping *Entente* interest alive but without compromising Italy in the slightest. The same sort of vague discussions were held with the German Embassy. On 10 August he suggested to Flotow that the Triple Alliance might be renewed after the war – which he, like everyone else, thought would end soon – and suggested Italian compensation in the Trentino and Gorizia for the expected Austrian annexation of Serbia. In contrast to Salandra, the Foreign Minister did not even want an *Entente* victory: what would suit Italy best, he thought, was a stalemate, a Russian defeat of Austria and a German success in France. The news of just such a success in northern France and the German march on Paris seemed to justify Di San Giuliano's caution: on 29 August the Council of Ministers in Rome hastily reaffirmed Italian neutrality. Even the most fervent supporters of the *Entente*, Martini told Rodd, had now moderated their ardour.[20]

During the week 5–12 September the German reverse on the Marne and the Russian success against the Austrians in Poland cast the first serious doubts upon the assumption that victory would go to the Central Powers and Salandra claimed in his memoirs that from this date he decided to bring Italy in on the side of the *Entente*. However, to judge by his actions at the time, this statement ignores considerable hesitations. On 12 September he told Malagodi that 'geographical reasons' made it unlikely that Italian intervention would have much effect. His Foreign Minister, the same day, complained bitterly to Martini of the Italian Ambassador in London, Imperiali, that 'he is a war-monger who exhorts us every day to go to war'.[21] In September, as in August, the pressure for war came from Cadorna: the resistance – however valid – from Salandra and Di San Giuliano. At the conference between the three on 22 September Cadorna still wanted war, despite his admission of deficiencies of equipment. His argument that Italy should intervene immediately apparently made some impression on Di San Giuliano, who at the last minute urged this course on the Premier on 29 September; but Salandra had decided to wait until the spring, a decision announced on 30 September.[22]

Di San Giuliano's interest in intervention was occasioned by the dead end which his diplomacy had reached by the end of September. On the news of the Marne he had initiated negotiations at Bucharest and at London, with the object of obtaining a clear offer from the *Entente* in the event that Italy decided to intervene. On 23 September he signed a convention with Romania which provided that each participant would give the other a week's notice of their intention to attack Austria, an obvious common interest in view of their geographical positions. This agreement – though not the exact terms – were immediately communicated to London, the point being that Italy could now claim to hold the key to Balkan politics: the attitude of Romania controlled that of Greece; acting jointly they would determine Bulgarian policy.[23]

Negotiations with Grey had been renewed on 16 September with the object, Di San Giuliano claimed, of checking the westward sweep of Slavdom. This was genuine. With the Russian armies nearing the Carpathians it seemed entirely possible that Austria would shortly collapse and Italy would have to move quickly, 'to peg out claims for the future'. Even so Di San Giuliano was cautious, risking practically nothing. His scheme involved first an Anglo–French naval attack in the northern Adriatic, preferably at Trieste, which would both destroy Austrian naval power and rouse public fervour in Italy. Then he would sign a pact, the terms of which were to follow the outline he had given on 12 August. Finally he would go to war, a programme which would provide the short war with a 99 per cent certainty of victory that he thought the Italian army capable of winning. It should be little more than a triumphal procession.[24]

As a scheme it was brilliant and offered a solution to the basic problems that Di San Giuliano had repeated *ad nauseam* since August, that Italy could not expect to gain another province by losing a war and that defeat would bring down the monarchy. It failed for two reasons. First, in importance if not in time, the Russian offensive ground to a halt in the Carpathians. Second, Grey, under some Russian pressure, showed no inclination to offer Italy territory in Dalmatia, which was predominantly Slav, and refused to consider hypothetical arguments. Rome, he said, should first make up its mind to fight, then he would negotiate; though he did urge the French on 20 September to attack the Austrian fleet on the grounds that 'this would produce a most favourable and possibly decisive effect upon the attitude of Italy'. Clearly he did not put much trust in the Italian Foreign Minister. Imperiali told Martini, after Di San Giuliano's death, that Grey 'complained to him of the constant changes in San Giuliano's proposals, which led to the conclusion that no faith could be placed in his words'.[25] Since Grey was the medium Rome had chosen for negotiations with the *Entente,* this meant that there was little prospect of success whilst the Sicilian remained in office, or until Italy decided to intervene.

Salandra's decision on 30 September to postpone consideration of intervention until the spring was then based upon a multiplicity of factors. One was undoubtedly the lack of proper equipment, the sheer difficulties of fighting a winter campaign in the mountains and the improbability that such a war would bring any tangible results. As Sonnino suggested to him on 24 September, 'since we must remain substantially inactive for five months it is better to pass the time in active neutrality than inactive belligerency'.[26] The stress in Salandra's memoirs upon the impreparation of the army is, however, misleading: it was a political decision. It should be borne in mind that Cadorna, despite the list of deficiencies he produced at Salandra's request, advocated war, and that there is good reason to suppose that he was right. The additional pressure upon Austria at this moment might well have been effective, certainly far more so than it was in the summer of 1915. If Salandra had wanted to go to war at the end of September the army was prepared to fight: but, having decided against war, he covered himself against his nationalist critics by putting the blame on the maladministration of the army by his predecessor, Giolitti.[27]

By September nationalist rhetoric was in full swing. 'The moral regeneration of Italy', announced Professor Alfredo Rocco on 5 September, 'can come about only through our participation in the great war.' Such action alone would provide the purge (*pulizia completa*) necessary to rid the country of Giolittian corruption and the permissiveness responsible for Red Week. The war, moreover, must be an Italian war; not a war for humanity or liberalism or similar rubbish: '. . . we want war, but war for Italy's sake, not war for the radical syndicalist French democracy which is both decadent and imperialist.' The war should, in nationalist eyes, serve two purposes: to finish off both the Habsburg empire and Italian social democracy.[28]

Salandra's constant insinuations that he was only prevented from launching the war that nationalist opinion demanded by the maladministration of the military budget under Giolitti, added fuel to these flames. 'Spingardi and Giolitti', Sonnino told the admiring Martini on 16 September, 'should be strung up by the head and feet.'[29] The nationalist organ, the *Giornale d'Italia,* on the basis of information supplied by Salandra, launched a violent series of articles in October on Giolittian corruption. The reason why there was no heavy artillery – and hence no war – Vilfredo Pareto told its readers on 15 October, was that Giolitti had diverted funds intended for the army into fixing elections.[30]

These tactics recoiled upon Salandra's own head. Since he had decided upon neutrality he wanted public opinion to remain quiet, and in fact gave instructions to this effect to the prefects at the end of September. Yet the natural effect of the press polemics was the precise opposite. To add to his difficulties, in September interventionism spread right across the political canvas. Democrats such as Gaetano Salvemini had urged war since August, on the grounds that Italy had a common interest with Britain and France in a war between feudalism and liberalism.[31] In September these ideas were taken up by the liberal press generally and liberal party associations deluged Salandra with telegrams calling for war. By the middle of the month Martini noted that all liberal newspapers were now interventionist, except *La Stampa*.[32]

Amongst socialists such sentiments, rare in August – though both Claudio Treves and Cesare Longobardi expressed some sympathy for France[33] – gained such a hold in September that the socialist party (PSI) became hopelessly split. On 20 September, to the amazement of the civic authorities, the 'Trento e Trieste' society held a public celebration in Ancona – the centre of 'Red Week' – without interruption. On 21 September the PSI congress adopted an extremely weak resolution against war which, Mussolini and other leaders recognised, meant they would do nothing to prevent it: 'no revolts, no strikes'. Even *Avanti!*, though opposed to war, publicly acknowledged on 13 September that many Italian socialists were not. Amongst the syndicalist wing there was open sympathy with France. Filippo Corridoni, imprisoned for his part in Red Week, announced on his release that 'neutrality is for the castrated': those more privileged should fight. The German Social Democrat leaders, then visiting Italy, were in his view flat-footed imperialists: 'Marx was the Bismarck of the proletariat.'[34]

There is no doubt, therefore, that if Salandra had *wanted* to act in September it would have been easy to whip up at least the semblance of public support and, to the extent that popular feeling was ever behind him, it was then. The real trouble – and this, according to Sonnino, was what worried Salandra – was that the press were totally unrepresentative of the actual state of opinion. The prefects' reports discounted the interventionist character of the 20 September demonstrations, distinguishing sharply between patriotic fervour and desire for war. The nationalists, in their view, were mere surface froth. In Piedmont and Lombardy it was thought that 95 per cent of the population were against war: Martini, for all his personal commitment, sorrowfully observed that it had few supporters, 'not even in Tuscany'.[35] Salandra feared that if he went to war and it went badly the socialists would turn and rend him at the first reverse. All the more essential, therefore, that he should choose his time carefully and only involve Italy in a short successful war.[36]

The problem, therefore, once intervention had been put off until the spring, was to find something with which to distract the attention of the government's critics in the meantime. Part of the solution was of course to divert them on to Giolitti but an even better stop-gap was discovered in the occupation of Valona, in Albania. Salandra discussed this with Sonnino on 16 September, to whom the idea made an immediate appeal. The strategic value of the Bay of Valona and island of Saseno was considerable as its possession would enable Italy to block the Adriatic at its narrowest point. On 26 September Sonnino returned to the charge, urging his friend to overrule the 'doubts and hesitations of San Giuliano and your other colleagues'. Speed was of the essence in his view, since whilst the powers were fully absorbed in battle in France and Poland neither side could afford to take objection. The benefits were considerable. Apart from gaining control of the Adriatic without a serious breach with Austria, it had internal uses: 'it would distract the mind from other too dangerous questions', give Salandra a good political following and, best of all, would fully absorb the energies of the December session of parliament.[37]

At this time, in September 1914, there was no intention of Italy seizing the whole of Albania. Sonnino himself envisaged its partition between Greece and Serbia as a first step towards the creation of a Balkan *entente*: only later, after he became Foreign Minister, did he conclude that this was a hopeless prospect and that Italy should take Albania for herself. De Martino, the Secretary-General at the Foreign Ministry, was quite explicit in September: Albania was to be divided between those who wanted it, 'to content all of them'.[38] Similarly, Di San Giuliano, who was extremely cautious when it came to any Italian expansion in the Adriatic, had but slight enthusiasm for Albania. Far from presenting the powers with a *fait accompli*, as Sonnino wished, he insisted on consulting them before acting – all the more so when Berlin urged him to ignore London. Grey, though willing to accept an Italian occupation of Valona as a necessary evil, stressed the importance of Rome obtaining the agreement of Athens. This Di San Giuliano accomplished, on the basis that the Italian occupation would be limited to Valona and its hinterland, leaving most of Albania to Greece and Serbia.[39]

Nor was the Foreign Minister alone in disliking this move: in the Cabinet nobody wanted Valona. The General Staff were highly reluctant to become involved, considered the operation would require an army corps and prove a serious distraction from the build-up of forces against Austria. Salandra, who had thought in terms of a brigade, was very discouraged: 'Our military', he wrote Sonnino, 'seem highly prepared only to find reasons for *not* making war.'[40] Far from the lightning stroke to assert Italian independence that Sonnino had envisaged in early September, the occupation of Saseno and Valona was a long-drawn-out process. Saseno was occupied by a party of marines on 29 October, after Di San Giuliano's death, with the consent of all the interested parties great and small, Valona itself not until 25 December.

This sense of filling in time in the autumn of 1914 was emphasised by the growing illness of Di San Giuliano, which made foreign powers reluctant to negotiate with a dying man. Salandra, though aware of this, was equally reluctant to replace him before his death on 16 October since a change at the Consulta was bound to bring exaggerated press speculation of a change in foreign policy. Even after his death the choice of a successor was not easy. Fasciotti could not be moved from Budapest at this critical juncture; Tittoni, then at Paris, had no political following and was too Giolittian for comfort. Martini, the Colonial Minister, was the obvious choice but his Austrophobia was too well-known and, perhaps, too clear-cut even for Salandra's taste. The temporary solution adopted by the Premier of taking over the Consulta himself could not last long as the demands on his time and energy were too great. Since Salandra's major contribution to Italian foreign policy during the three weeks he had charge of the Consulta was the disastrous *sacro egoismo* speech, it was perhaps as well that he had not the leisure to continue.[41]

This left Sidney Sonnino. He was in many ways the ideal choice. A close friend and confidant of the Premier – far more so than Di San Giuliano – his public image was that of a convinced partisan of the Triple Alliance. Yet, in fact, by October he inclined more strongly than Salandra to support of the *Entente,* a swing which won him the complete confidence and admiration of Martini. He had a reputation for absolute integrity: 'A man of intellectual distinction, a strong sense of dignity and complete devotion to his country.'[42] If a little old-fashioned, Sonnino had at least one other great virtue. Whereas others talked of secret diplomacy he practised it, an invaluable quality in the head of a foreign ministry which had a reputation rivalling that of the Quai d'Orsay for leaking information. Prince Bülow was later to complain that in a country of compulsive talkers he had the misfortune to deal with the one man who said nothing.[43] Since Italy was about to embark on a venture which entailed the government concealing their real intentions for five months, Sonnino's taciturn nature was a decided asset.

The dissentions within the administration over neutrality or intervention had been held in check until the end of September, but Salandra's decision then that Italy must make serious preparation for war in the spring brought them to a head. Opportunity was taken on the death of the Foreign Minister for a general reshuffle in which the more decided Giolittian element were excluded and a government created, in Sonnino's words, 'which could take a decision for war without further modification'.[44] It had, as its first concern, obtaining a vote of confidence from parliament since, Sonnino thought, until this was accomplished no foreign power would believe in their power to commit Italy.[45] On 3 December parliament opened for its winter session and, thanks to the support of Giolitti, who pointedly and at great length approved the government's stand on neutrality, Salandra obtained an overwhelming majority. With this behind them, Sonnino could take up negotiations abroad on a surer footing.

Sonnino's appointment on 5 November introduced not so much a change of objectives in Italian policy as a change of style. Di San Giuliano, by the end of September, had certainly aimed at war: he told Malagodi that continued neutrality would bring upon them 'all the hatred of the Central Powers . . . and all the ingratitude of the other side. . . '. Typical of his fine calculations was the suggestion that Italy needed her former allies to be weakened since they were her most probable enemies of the future.[46] War, to him, was a move on the chessboard of international diplomacy, to be made only when checkmate was in sight, an attitude which explains the over-elaborate schemes which had earned him Grey's distrust. War involved simply preparing the army. Public opinion was largely a nuisance, something to be manipulated: as Vigezzi puts it, San Giuliano 'worked out policy in a vacuum'.[47]

Sonnino, of course, was no demagogue; he was at least as secretive as his predecessor: neither consulted the Cabinet if they could possibly help it. Di San Giuliano suggested to Salandra in

September 1914 that 'in general I think (like Giolitti) that it is best to discuss foreign policy in the Cabinet as little as possible'. Martini noted that from the end of August to the end of March 1915, 'the Council of Ministers has not heard one word on foreign policy', a state of affairs which even he thought went beyond the needs of secrecy. Policy was decided between the Premier and Foreign Secretary with occasional reference to the king or Cadorna, though there is no evidence that either actually influenced decisions. Needless to say, parliament was not consulted at all.[48]

The real difference between Sonnino and the Sicilian aristocrat who preceded him was that whereas Di San Giuliano ignored public opinion as irrelevant, Sonnino was only too well aware of its importance and framed his diplomacy in order to influence it in the right direction. Hence his pressure for the Albanian expedition, 'per fare una cosa popolare'. He made his views very clear to Malagodi on 12 December, after the vote of confidence in parliament. The government was well aware of the confused state of public feeling, that the bulk wanted peace but that the noisy minority might well attempt a revolution to end Italian neutrality: 'But if we decide war is necessary or useful to Italy, we shall have to, and we shall know how to, act above the opinions of the crowd.'[49]

Since operations on the Isonzo could not commence at the earliest until the end of February, this gave Sonnino and Salandra at least two months in which to make up their minds. The time was employed, largely, in negotiation with Vienna because Grey refused to bargain until Italy had decided to intervene, a decision which Rome wished to put off until the last possible moment. There was always, of course, the offchance that Vienna would make a sufficiently attractive offer for continued Italian neutrality as to make intervention unnecessary; but Sonnino thought this unlikely from the start. Italian demands even for neutrality would be high. As he told Bülow on 19 December:[50]

> The majority of the country are favourable to the maintenance of neutrality and support the Government for this reason, but on the supposition that neutrality will lead to the satisfaction of some national aspirations . . . our very institutions (the monarchy) depend on the solution of this task. . . .

It was not that either Sonnino or Salandra were themselves irredentists or impressed by irredentist arguments, but that Italy –

to remain an independent state – had to secure her future against either an Austrian or a Russian victory. Either case meant the demand for defensible frontiers in the north and naval control of the Adriatic. 'Trentino and Trieste', the battle cries of the ardent nationalists, meant little to Sonnino and Salandra: as the latter told Malagodi in January 1915, the real question was 'the situation Italy would find herself in as a Great Power if the war was concluded without her participation and without her obtaining anything'.[51]

Sonnino's technique in negotiating with Vienna was to put in a general claim for compensation for any Austrian expansion in the Balkans – insisting that this must come from Austrian territory – and leave it to Berchtold and his successor, Burián, to make an acceptable offer. This was bound to be a time-consuming process,[52] a state of affairs which suited Sonnino's purpose well enough, but this does not mean that he had no intention of negotiating seriously with Vienna. As he told Rodd in March, 'If in effect they (Vienna) offered freely everything we could desire, then no Government could refuse, given our actual situation.'[53] Where Sonnino differed with Giolitti was in the definition of what was acceptable. On 2 February, when Giolitti wrote his *parecchio* letter to *La Tribuna*,[54] there is every reason to suppose that Sonnino was correct and Giolitti wrong.

For, up until 22 February when Sonnino broke off negotiations with Vienna on the grounds that two months of negotiation had got nowhere, Berchtold and Burián had offered nothing. The substance of their attitude was that Italy was not entitled to any compensation and, if she was, she had already obtained it in the Dodecanese islands seized in 1912 – and in Albania. They would not admit any claim on Austrian territory itself. Even Avarna, who wanted an agreement and was averse to war, was extremely pessimistic of the chances of obtaining it. The emperor, he insisted, would never cede the 'Erbland' of Trentino. His impression, derived from the Hungarian Count Károlyi, who was similarly inclined, was that Vienna had no serious intention of ceding anything: they were just stalling:[55]

> Austria has no intention of yielding to Italy. If she has not declined to negotiate at all, it is only to gain time. According to Károlyi, neither Tisza nor the Imperial and Royal Government believe that Italy wants to go to war. . . .

Obviously Sonnino shared this view. Even on 26 January he told Salandra that it was 'highly unlikely . . . the negotiations would lead to anything of practical use',[56] but until late February he was careful not to burn his boats. Pressure from Bucharest in January to put teeth in the Italo–Romanian agreement of 23 September 1914 in preparation for action in the spring was rejected: 'Italy,' he telegraphed Fasciotti on 14 January, 'has taken no definite decision yet as her interests are not yet harmed.' When Bratianu, panic-stricken by reports of Austrian concentration against Romania, pressed for at least a defensive alliance, Sonnino reluctantly agreed on 29 January but was absolutely insistent on its non-aggressive character. If Bratianu were to take the plunge into war he did so at his own risk. It was not until 19 February that Sonnino suddenly changed his tune: then he asked point-blank if Rome could count on a 'vigorous' offensive from Bucharest if Italy went to war at the end of April and if Bratianu could persuade Sofia to attack the Turks.[57]

If one seeks the explanation of Sonnino's change of attitude in mid-February it seems obvious that it derived from the Balkans. The assembly of the Anglo–French fleets off the Dardanelles was no secret and the supposed *démarche* at Athens on 15 February announcing the imminence of an allied landing at Salonika seemed likely to precipitate a landslide towards the *Entente*. As he told Bülow on 8 March,[58]

> In the last three weeks public opinion, affected also by the news from the Dardanelles, had become more exigent and belligerent. . . . Vienna should decide quickly if she wanted to reach a conclusion, because every day risked some new incident in the war, such as the entry of some other Balkan state, which would give a new impulse to the warlike current [in Italy].

In these circumstances it was obvious that the last man in would gain the least. If Greece, Romania and, perhaps, Bulgaria should precede Italy, then her hopes of extravagant gains would not be fulfilled, whilst it seemed improbable that anything significant would be prised out of Austria. Moreover, there was always the possibility that oppressed Imperiali, that some 'unforeseen incident' would lead to a rupture with Austria before negotiations with the *Entente* had been concluded. If that happened, 'we should lose the privileged position we hold at present'.[59] Hence the rapid shift in Sonnino's position. On 16 February he sent his terms to

Imperiali, on the 22nd finally broke off negotiations with Vienna and four days later urged Salandra that Italy should open negotiations at London. On 3 March, Salandra and the king agreed and Imperiali was instructed to announce Italy's readiness to intervene, if her terms were granted.[60]

That these negotiations, launched in the general euphoria surrounding the initial bombardments of the Dardanelles and further Russian successes in Galicia – Przemysl fell on 22 March – dragged on until 26 April, was mainly due to Russian resistance. Grey, though showing some initial misgivings at Italy's 'very sweeping claims', welcomed the approach and generally acted as an Italian spokesman in the negotiations with Petrograd. His reasons for doing so were simple. Greek support faded into oblivion on 6 March: Italy was now essential to swing the Balkans and 'in a comparatively short time, effect the collapse of German and Austro–Hungarian resistance'. The more success at the Dardanelles proved elusive, the more Italian assistance was needed 'without delay'.[61]

Sonnino's initial demands were heavy. Apart from the Brenner frontier in the north, Trieste and Istria, he wanted Dalmatia to the Narenta river, all the offshore islands, and partition of Albania, giving the central portion as well as Saseno and Valona to Italy. Never particularly interested in the irredentism which gripped Italian democrats like Salvemini or Bissolati, his claim was based firmly on strategic arguments. The Brenner would provide a defensible frontier in the north, Istria and Dalmatia would give Italy control of the Adriatic: this, he told Rodd, was necessary for the future. The problem that had beset Italian statesmen since Crispi was still with them: how to hit Austria hard enough to obtain what they wanted, yet not shatter her so completely that a Russian-dominated Slav colossus should succeed her. Sonnino's solution left Fiume (Rjeka) to Hungary, an old Italian ally, whilst by confining the Serbs and Montenegrins to the stretch of coast between the Narenta and Voyusa rivers, hemmed in by Italian possession of Valona and the islands, he averted the menace of Russian naval power in the Adriatic. This was essential, he told Rodd, because if Russia obtained Constantinople, she might well become the leading naval power in the Mediterranean:[62]

Italy would enter into the struggle in practical alliance with peoples who had certain rival interests, and therefore it was necessary to reassure her that she would not be fighting for a cause which might eventually prove to her disadvantage.

Sazonov's reluctance to accept Italian claims sprang from similar considerations. Her military assistance, he argued, was not worth much, certainly not as much as in August 1914, a view strengthened by the capture of Przemysl. He had no objection to the sacrifice of Austrian, Slovene and Croat interests from the Brenner to Istria, but initially he refused to concede Dalmatia south of Spalato (Split). Not only were Serbia and Montenegro Russian client states but Grand Duke Nicholas thought Cattaro (Kotor) would make an excellent Russian naval base. It was not until 7 April, when Russian progress in Galicia came to a halt and the Grand Duke became concerned with German concentration further north, that he urged any concessions to Italy to bring her in immediately and thus distract the Austrians. Since Sonnino had also softened in the meantime – he was now willing to concede from Cape Planca to the Voyusa, including Spalato and its five nearest islands, provided this were neutralised whilst Italy obtained the remaining islands free of restriction – an agreement was ready for signature by 14 April.[63]

The twelve days' delay that followed was due to Sonnino's casual announcement that Italy needed one month from signature before she could act, a condition Sazonov at first refused to accept. This was partly genuine, partly an attempt to postpone a decision until the last minute, as the Balkan scene began to look more uncertain,[64] and Austria had come to her senses.

Under strong pressure from Berlin, Burián announced on 8 March that he would concede the southern Trentino. Sonnino countered that any territory offered must be handed over immediately, a demand which would reveal if Vienna were serious.[65] He thought that there was little chance of this – on 16 March he told Salandra that they must continue to treat with Vienna for the present, 'pretending to believe a pacific solution possible' – but the Premier was rather more hesitant, conscious as he was of the internal problems involved in going to war.[66] On 8 April Sonnino therefore presented Vienna with Italy's minimum terms for neutrality: the Napoleonic frontier in the Trentino, Gorizia, an independent Trieste, the Curzolari islands and a free hand in Albania. Burián's reply, an ethnic frontier in the Trentino, decided them: this, Salandra told Malagodi, gave Italy the valleys but left

Austria with the peaks and hence effective military domination. Nor was it a precipitate judgment on their part: Avarna was still as pessimistic as ever. Even if Austria were to yield on the Gorizian frontier – which he thought improbable – there was still the question of immediate occupation to resolve:[67]

> An agreement with Austria–Hungary on the bases proposed by your Excellency seems almost unrealisable in the actual condition of affairs. It is unbelievable, anyway, that the Imperial Government could have ever deluded itself that it was really possible to reach an agreement.

Unable to drag out negotiations with the *Entente* any longer, Salandra and Sonnino now made the final decision that discussions with Vienna would not lead anywhere and that they should close with Sazonov before he withdrew his concessions.[68] On 26 April the Treaty of London was signed.

The preoccupation with strategic frontiers and control of the Adriatic to the near exclusion of all else was the aspect of Sonnino's diplomacy which was most open to criticism. Whereas he took infinite pains to dispute uninhabited islands in the Adriatic and even the interior of Albania, he took slight interest in colonial gains for Italy in Africa and relatively little even in the Middle East. It is easy to see why. Africa was unpopular at the time. The original first flush of enthusiasm for Libya had worn very thin by 1914: Martini, the Minister for the Colonies, noted wearily in September that 'Cirenaica is still in arms, whilst Eritrea and Benadir are menaced by Ethiopia'. The Libyan expedition had proved a costly delusion in his view and 'Italy could not support the weight of the L.130 million that Libya cost', not to mention the 70,000 troops.[69] In 1915 the army was withdrawn to the coast and the interior abandoned. With this as a precedent it is not surprising that Sonnino contented himself with a vague declaration (Article XIII) that Italy would be compensated for any British and French gains in Africa, despite Tittoni's urging that he should be much more specific. To haggle over Tittoni's suggestions – rectification of the Libyan frontiers with Tunis to give Italy control of the caravan routes to the interior of the Sahara, British cession of Kismayu, and an Anglo–French agreement to support Italy against Abyssinia[70] – would have taken weeks.

Similarly with provision for Italian expansion in the Ottoman

Empire. This was discussed between Sonnino and Imperiali in January 1915 and it was settled that she should demand Rhodes, with additional compensation for any Allied gains. Where this should be was left uncertain. Imperiali, who had been at the Constantinople Embassy and knew Turkey well, pressed for Smyrna, but Sonnino declined. Such a claim would wreck his relations with Greece, with whom he was engaged in an amicable partition of Albania. He preferred, therefore, a stretch of territory from Adalia to Alexandretta, which would not conflict with Greek ambitions.[71] But when, on 21 March, Imperiali tried to take this up with Grey, he found it impossible to pursue. Grey pointed out that the question of partition of Asiatic Turkey had not yet been discussed between Britain, France and Russia: the most he would concede was a general assurance that '. . . if Italy becomes an ally then it is clear that she must participate in these discussions when they are initiated'. Sonnino, initially, stuck to his guns. On 24 March he insisted that Italian gains must be defined since the 'zone of Adalia' was insufficient if the whole of Turkey was broken up. But Grey was adamant. He thought his previous assurances quite sufficient and point-blank refused to go any further. To open this question with Paris and Petrograd would postpone the conclusion of an agreement 'until God knows when': rather than do this he preferred to drop the negotiations. Imperiali's conclusion, 'based on five years of continual relations with Grey', was that although he wanted an agreement with Italy, 'he will not go beyond the point of view manifested to me today on the specification of our share of Asia Minor. . . '. It is not surprising, in the circumstances, that Sonnino yielded on this question – given his success in what he considered the major point, Dalmatia – and contented himself with the vague wording of Article IX, 'equitable compensation' in the zone of Adalia, further definition of which was left until 1917.[72]

More serious, perhaps, is the criticism that Sonnino's blind pursuit of Italian hegemony in the Adriatic undermined his own object of a quick Italian victory, based on promoting a Balkan coalition. Both Tittoni, the former Foreign Minister, now Ambassador at Paris, and Fasciotti at Bucharest, urged a more moderate course. In Tittoni's view Sonnino's policy was short-sighted: 'It seems to me that on one side we seek too much, on the other too little.' The insistence on the Trentino to the Brenner and Istria to the Volosca meant the inclusion within Italy of 'two focal points of irredentism, one German and one Slovene, which may become the pretext of future wars and will oblige us to pursue a policy of large armaments'. Dalmatia, apart from a few cities, was entirely Slav, yet Sonnino was asking for effective dominion over the Slav inhabitants, a demand which both Russia and the *Entente* were bound to resist. 'It is true that Zara is Italian, but so is Fiume; yet we understand that we cannot claim Fiume.' Why, therefore, claim Zara? For strategic control of the Adriatic the islands of the Quarnero, Lissa, the Curzolari group and Sabbioncello would be quite sufficient. Nor, in Tittoni's view, did it matter that the nationalists in Italy would howl at the modesty of these demands: 'Whatever you obtain they will think insufficient.'

Similarly in Albania. From the original modest beginnings of the island of Saseno and the Bay of Valona, by March 1915 Sonnino was laying claim to control of the bulk of Albania. This threatened the whole basis of *Entente* diplomacy in the Balkans. The main hope of enticing Bulgaria lay in giving her Macedonia and compensating Serbia and Greece in Albania. It was, therefore, in Tittoni's view, excessive to demand more than control of the coast and the hinterland. With this central core in Italian hands – and the diplomatic representation of Albania which Sazonov was willing to concede – what did it matter to Italy if the rest was broken up amongst Greece, Serbia and Montenegro? 'To us it is much more important that the future Albanian state should be smaller but exclusively under our influence, than that it should be larger and internationalised – that is open to every possible influence.' By the summer, with the Serbs incensed by the Romanian demands for the Banat and the Bulgarian insistence on Macedonia – on top of Italy's gains in Dalmatia – Tittoni's plea that Rome should concede them a greater share of Albania, in particular the port of Durazzo, made more sense than ever. If they got nothing it was abundantly clear that they would stop fighting.[73]

Unfortunately pleas for concessions to Serbia made little impression on Sonnino. His entire object from the inception of negotiations with London had been the prevention of Serbian expansion: to this end he had left Fiume (Rjeka) with Croatia, intending that it should remain part of a Hungarian state, and blocked any suggestion of annexation by Serbia. The utmost Sonnino would concede was that – in return for Serb evacuation of Macedonia and Albania – the Serbs should be told they would get

Spalato (Split) and Ragusa (Dubrovnik), already conceded by Italy in the Pact of London. The object of hanging on to Fiume, he said, was to facilitate a separate peace with Hungary, a view that even Tittoni approved.[74]

To a considerable extent Sonnino was responsible for the débâcle that followed. The extortionate nature of his terms in the Adriatic not only made the Serbs less willing to make concessions in Macedonia and the Banat, but made it almost impossible for Grey and Delcassé to press Russia to acquiesce in Romanian demands. As Imperiali observed, 'England and France warmly desire Romanian intervention but not if they have to start pressing Sazonov again after the efforts made to persuade him to consent to our demands.'[75] The inability to attract Romania proved fatal to all Sonnino's plans for a quick victory, dependent as these were upon a Balkan landslide towards the *Entente*.

Whilst it is true that Bratianu's humours followed closely the advances and retreats of the Russians – and to that extent were completely independent of Sonnino's control – Rome's handling of Bucharest was particularly selfish and inept. Italian diplomats liked to think that Italy was somehow different from the Balkan states and had a natural role as a leader in that region. Italy did not bargain: she stated her terms.[76] But even Fasciotti, though imbued with this concept, urged on Sonnino that Bratianu would need careful handling. Rome, however, instead of collaborating with Bucharest as Bratianu evidently expected, simply exploited her. Once he had discovered on 24 February that Bratianu would follow Italy's lead and would be ready for war by the end of April,[77] Sonnino made no further communication until 22 April. Then he told Bratianu that Italy had reached agreement with London and would go to war on 20 May: 'We hope Romania will be able to make diplomatic and military preparation for the same time.' Unconscious of irony, he even urged Bratianu to moderate his demands lest he made it difficult to reach agreement with the *Entente*, demands which Sonnino had the gall to qualify as 'relatively minor and not entirely justified'.[78]

This was pure folly. If, as Fasciotti urged, Sonnino had taken Bratianu into his confidence so that they negotiated jointly with the *Entente* as an independent alliance, the probability is that both could have obtained their terms. By pre-empting the ground Sonnino certainly obtained Italy's maxima but, as Bratianu complained, left Romania out in the cold. This was the more painful in that he had subordinated his own negotiations with the *Entente* to prior agreement between them and Italy. Consequently, in the haggling that followed over Bratianu's demands in the Banat and the Bukovina, Romania operated at a double disadvantage. Sazonov was already irritated by the excessive concessions made by Slavdom to Italy, whilst Bratianu could not claim – as Sonnino had done – to offer joint Italo–Romanian intervention. This fact, combined with the Russian defeats in Poland in May, made Bratianu increasingly intransigent and reluctant to commit himself unless he in turn obtained his maximum terms, his philosophy plainly being that the further Russia retreated the more concessions she would make.[79]

Whilst it is obviously difficult to be specific as to what Romania would have done if she had been included in the negotiations at London in March, Fasciotti had no doubts that her deliberate *exclusion* had been a mistake. It was only in the latter half of April – coinciding with the Russian withdrawal from the Bukovina – that Bratianu put in a claim for the Theiss and the Pruth as Romania's natural frontiers; in February – when he wanted to go to war – his major concern had been to obtain guarantees from London and Paris over the Straits. By May, obviously intent on avoiding war, his demands now included the support of 100,000 British and 200,000 Russian troops, an escalation which led Fasciotti to advocate trying Bulgaria instead: 'If Bulgaria should declare herself for the Triple Entente that would drag in Romania.'[80]

This was a far cry from the easy confidence of January and February when Bratianu was eager for war and Italian policy based on the carefree assumption that he would follow them more or less whatever happened. Romanian neutrality, in fact, made Sonnino's Pact of London an empty triumph. As Tittoni criticised, none too helpfully, on 20 April, 'As I have already said many times, it seems to me that we should not initiate hostilities unless jointly with Romania.'[81] But once he had signed the London agreement, what could Sonnino do?

Once the Treaty of London had been signed the problem became to implement it. The fact that the government had obtained another massive vote of confidence in parliament on 22 March meant nothing: Giolitti had told his followers to support it on the basis that Salandra was pursuing negotiations with Austria.[82] Both

Salandra and Sonnino were only too well aware that both parliament and the country were still neutralist – the prefects' reports in April left no shadow of doubt on that score. Hence their anxiety to postpone denunciation of the Triple Alliance until after 1 May lest they should touch off a wave of socialist demonstrations.[83]

To add to their difficulties the Hofburg, persuaded that Italian intervention would prevent exploitation of the breakthrough at Gorlice on 2 May, and convinced at last that honour would permit them to regain concessions extracted by force after the war, came up with a realistic offer. On 10 May Sonnino was officially informed that, apart from the linguistic frontier in the Trentino offered a month before, Burián now promised the right bank of the Isonzo, autonomy for Trieste and total disinterest in Albania. Tracing of the territory to be transferred would begin at once, execution was guaranteed by Germany within a month of signature. This was so near to Sonnino's demands of 8 April that he was hard put to find an excuse for rejection: if the offer had been made a month before, Salandra, almost certainly, would have been inclined to accept. Since the offer was attended with a maximum of publicity, leaked to Giolitti beforehand and printed in his paper *La Stampa* the next day, a major crisis was now at hand.[84]

Giolitti arrived in Rome on 9 May and immediately became the focus of all the neutralist elements – 300 deputies and 100 senators left their cards. Martini, typically, dismissed them as 'sordid private interests without a trace of patriotism',[85] but Salandra was seriously alarmed. On discovering from Giolitti that he was still firmly opposed to war, Salandra held a Cabinet on 12 May. This revealed a gloomy prospect. The British landings at Gallipoli had made no progress, the Russians were in retreat. In Greece the interventionist Venizelos had been dismissed and even Romania, which as recently as 1 May Sonnino thought certain to follow Italy, was determined on neutrality. 'The moment', Salandra acknowledged, 'was clearly not propitious.' The next day, on discovering that no more than 150 deputies would follow him, he resigned.[86]

The logical course was for Giolitti, who controlled a parliamentary majority, to form a government and take up the offer from Burián that Sonnino had rejected. There is no doubt that Giolitti opposed war on all possible grounds, some more rational than others. Irredentism was a bad business proposition: it was not worthwhile, he argued, risking the fate of 35 million Italians for the sake of gaining a few hundred thousand more. Moreover, he had 'an invincible antipathy and distrust towards everything French': he thought France was bound to lose the war, largely because her consumption of alcohol per head was three and a half times greater than that of Italy![87] In the Italian army he had no faith whatsoever. The rank and file 'had no sense of civic virtue as in Germany, France and England'; the generals were of little use, since 'they date from the period when families sent their most stupid sons into the army'. The troops had fled from the Arabs in the Libyan campaign, 'forcing him to invent heroics by falsifying the telegrams': what would they do in front of the Germans? Last but not least, the Italian economy would not stand a war. Already the most highly taxed country in Europe, the financial burden of even a short war would be such as to prevent public works for twenty years. How would the south survive the winters without them?[88]

Despite his strong feelings, however, Giolitti refused to head an administration. His excuse, that his neutralist views were so well known that he would get nothing from Vienna, seems feeble since an official offer had already been made. More likely, as a former colleague – Federico Tedesco – suggested, is that Giolitti's whole world was parliament and its management; he assumed that the parliamentary crisis could go on indefinitely until one of his nominees succeeded in putting a government together; it had not occurred to him that parliament could simply be ignored and stampeded into voting for Salandra.[89] There was, also, a further consideration which seemed to weigh with him. It might well have been arguable, as Giolitti maintained, that Imperiali's signature bound only Salandra and that there was no question of the king's honour – and hence abdication – if the Treaty of London were repudiated. Even if this were so, however, the effect upon Italy's reputation abroad of first deserting the Triple Alliance, then signing up with the *Entente*, and finally repudiating the new alliance in favour of the old, would be disastrous. As Giolitti put it to Malagodi on 10 May, 'It would not be so bad if we had a good name, but we already enjoy the worst reputation. . .'.[90]

Salandra's return on 17 May, when the king refused to accept his resignation, was the product of the spontaneous popular demonstrations known variously as the 'radiant' or 'South American' days of May, depending upon whether or not one supported war. There is not the slightest reason to suppose that they were officially inspired. Salandra, deliberately, maintained throughout this period the traditional attitude of the state towards popular disorders: they were to be suppressed, whatever their political complexion. As has been said, 'the essential instruments for the preparation of war were, in his view, two only: diplomacy and the army'. Sonnino, equally, was averse to any appeal to the *piazza*, partly of course because the prefects' reports in April showed opinion to be strongly against war. He thought that Barrère, who was stirring the interventionist pot, was making a big mistake for exactly this reason: the most probable result would be popular counter-demonstrations against war.[91]

The analysis of the demonstrations of 13 May onwards shows that they had a varied origin. In the south, the meetings and telegrams of support were organised by the local notables of the professional classes and their interventionist zeal was completely mixed up with their support for the right-wing government of Salandra as opposed to the more permissive Giolitti. There was also the fact that Salandra was a southern politician, in contrast to the Piedmontese. It was this fact, apparently, which explains the complete contrast between the prefects' reports in April – which insisted that southern opinion was neutralist – and the outburst of 15 May: local patriotism, hatred of Giolitti and genuine idealist enthusiasm for war – at least amongst the students – all fused together into fulsome demonstrations of support for Salandra:[92]

> The people of Calabria, always ready for sacrifices for the greatness of Italy, protesting against the cynical brigandage of Giolitti, a slave of the foreigner, trust that your ministry will avoid civil war by leading the country with a robust heart to fulfil its destiny in the glory of its blood.

Tuscany, as Martini had noted the previous November, still remained neutralist, but in the north, especially in Milan and Genoa, there were violent interventionist demonstrations. These, though far from spontaneous, were equally devoid of any government inspiration, since they were largely the work of Mussolini and Corridoni. Mussolini, after his resignation from *Avanti!* in October, had started his own newspaper, *Il Popolo d'Italia*, with funds derived from northern industrialists, whose aims were less to promote war than to split the socialists. (There is nothing to suggest that Italian business circles wanted war.) By the spring of 1915 he was certainly obtaining French subsidies, despite Barrère's dislike of his revolutionary politics and preference for the nationalists of the Right. Between Mussolini and the nationalists there was a complete gulf, the parrot cries of 'Trento e Trieste' meant nothing to him or Corridoni. 'War on the frontier or war at home' was the syndicalist slogan, which can hardly have endeared them to Salandra and Sonnino. Their effectiveness in Milan, however, was undeniable in bringing out crowds of 30,000 people in interventionist demonstrations on 15 May, subduing completely the few hardy souls who tried to protest their support of the official socialist line.[93]

In Rome the large-scale rioting was the work of D'Annunzio and the university students. On 5 May he had launched a call to arms on the Quarto in Genoa in a speech commemorating Garibaldi's Sicilian expedition. On 12 May he arrived in Rome to bring about 'the reawakening of national consciousness'[94] by inciting students to riot. In this he was so successful that in a few days Giolitti's followers among the deputies were completely terrorised and their leader fled in fear of his life. On 20 May the leaderless flock voted Salandra full powers: four days later they were at war.

As it turned out Giolitti was right and Salandra was wrong. He could not have chosen a worse moment to join the *Entente*. The Russian retreat which started on 4 May continued without interruption throughout 1915; British operations at the Dardanelles went from bad to worse; Joffre's offensive in Champagne failed dismally; Romania, wisely, remained neutral; Bulgaria joined the Central Powers; Serbia ceased to exist. Far from Italian intervention providing the *coup de grâce* to a dying Austria as Sonnino had anticipated, Cadorna found himself committed to the same war of attrition that operated in France, with the added disadvantage of infinitely worse terrain. Italy, he told Malagodi in January 1916, did not possess the equipment for this type of war; bodies were a poor substitute for artillery. In his Champagne offensive in September 1915, Joffre had employed 1,100 medium and 3,000 field guns firing in all 7,000,000 rounds. In the first battle of the Isonzo, on a comparable length of front, Cadorna had only 300 medium and 800 field guns and the ammunication to fire only

1,000,000 rounds.[95] Far from making a rapid advance to the Semmering or the Hungarian plain, Cadorna had made no progress at all: the fact that his performance was no worse than that of his allies was little consolation to a country dependent upon a short war. This was, of course, precisely why Giolitti preferred neutrality.

Chapter 8

Italy at the Peace Conference

Resist, resist, resist. Italy won on the Piave, she will win at Paris.
Orlando, 1919

There is a general consensus among historians that the policies of
V. E. Orlando and Sidney Sonnino at the peace conference in 1919
were utterly misguided. As one critic writes, their actions 'wrecked
the understanding between the three European powers and created
a disastrous political climate in Italy'.[1] Their decision to claim the
full measure of the Treaty of London – despite the changed
circumstances since 1915 – plus Fiume (Rjeka) in addition, put
them in an untenable position. A case for the 1915 treaty could still
be made in 1919 on strategic grounds, although these were far
weaker with the collapse of tsarist Russia and her failure to obtain
Constantinople. Equally, a case could be made for Fiume on the
ground of national self-determination, as the people had requested
incorporation within Italy. But, if the ideals of 1919 were to mean
anything at all, it was patently impossible to give the 24,212
Italians control of the 15,687 Slavs in Fiume on the grounds of
nationality and the 18,928 Italians dominion over 610,669 Slavs in
Dalmatia on the grounds of treaty rights.[2] The juxtaposition of the
two outraged not only the idealist Wilson but also such realists as
Balfour and Hardinge.[3]

Since the Fiume controversy had such disastrous political consequences in Italy, giving rise to the cry of *la vittoria mutilata*,[4] so
ably exploited first by D'Annunzio and the nationalists, then by
Mussolini and the fascists, to discredit the bourgeois politicians –
Orlando, Nitti and Giolitti – it is worth considering in some detail.

Two points should be stressed. First, as Balfour noted at the
time, Italy 'has not done so badly in this war, even if it does not
get all that it had hoped for on the Eastern coast of the Adriatic'.[5]
The Brenner frontier was conceded by Wilson on strategic grounds
despite the fact that this was well to the north of the linguistic

division. The cession to Italy of Trieste, Gorizia and western Istria
defined by the so-called Wilson line was unopposed by the Anglo–
American experts, despite the fact that this left 370,000 Slavs in
Italy and was bitterly contested by Trumbić and Pašić, the leading
Yugoslav delegates.[6] Wilson's willingness to concede Pola – Lissa
– Valona would have given Italy complete naval control of the
Adriatic.[7] Although this was a good deal less than the Treaty of
London, it certainly provided what Sonnino had striven for since
1915, secure strategic frontiers.

Second, if Orlando and Sonnino had been content with the
Treaty of London they would have received the support of their
allies. Here Italy had a solid case which might, in time, have worn
down even Wilson. The treaty was, of course, in flagrant contradiction of the doctrine of national self-determination, but the
Allies had known this in 1915 when they signed it. The Americans
might think that the terms of the treaty were contrary to President
Wilson's Note of 5 November 1918 and 'were by that agreement
abrogated and are no longer in force',[8] but nobody else accepted
this view. During the discussions of the armistice terms in the
Supreme War Council between 30 October and 4 November,
Sonnino and Orlando expressed considerable reservations on
Wilson's Fourteen Points. The only reason these reservations were
not included in the official inter-allied exchanges was that Lloyd
George insisted that Wilson's negotiations concerned only the
armistice with Germany. In the terms of the Austrian armistice
signed at Villa Giusti the Fourteen Points were not even mentioned.[9] Although Lloyd George was inclined to be slippery over
the St Jean de Maurienne agreement of 1917,[10] there was no
thought in London or Paris of departing from the Treaty of
London. Both Balfour and Pichon were adamant on this point:
Britain and France would observe their commitments.[11]

Why then did Orlando compromise a perfectly good case by
insisting on Fiume as well as Dalmatia when, as Clemenceau
pointed out with some exasperation,[12] this had the ludicrous effect
that Italy was demanding national self-determination in one province but denying it in the next?

There is some suggestion that if left to his own devices Orlando
would have favoured an understanding with the Yugoslavs. In
March–April 1918 he had promoted the congress of Slav nationalities at Rome against the opposition both of the French, who at

this time wanted to preserve Austria–Hungary intact as a counter to German predominance in central Europe, and of Sonnino, who regarded them with contempt.[13] In the crucial Cabinet discussions of 26 December 1918, Orlando strongly supported Bissolati's line of giving up Dalmatia in order to obtain Fiume which, both thought, was of far greater importance to Italy. In this view they were supported by General Diaz the Commander-in-Chief, who regarded Dalmatia as a hopeless liability whose defence would lock up one third of the Italian army. The opposition came from Admiral Thaon de Revel, who insisted that the navy needed Dalmatia to control the Adriatic, and from Sonnino, who was adamant: he insisted on claiming the full Treaty of London. In Fiume he had little interest, though inclined to claim it as a matter of tactics at the outset of the Paris negotiations, but prepared to drop it later, if necessary.[14]

Faced with the choice of supporting either Bissolati or Sonnino, Orlando opted for the latter. Sonnino's policy was popular in Italy and to have insisted on dropping Dalmatia in December 1918 would have required, as Barrère observed, *beaucoup d'audace*. This was a quality which Orlando did not possess: he was essentially a weak, impressionable man, very much inclined to swim with the tide.[15] Besides, as he told Malagodi, it was against all his instincts as a lawyer to give up something without the certainty of obtaining what he wanted in exchange, a view which put him much closer to Sonnino than to the somewhat idealistic Bissolati.[16]

The clamour in Italy for Fiume was a very late starter. Sonnino had not even considered it in 1915 and was evidently not over impressed with its utility even in 1918. According to Salvemini, 'nine tenths of our most intransigent agitators only discovered Fiume after the battle of Vittorio Veneto'.[17] Orlando admitted as much to House at Paris when he told him that if a peace settlement had been arranged quickly in December 1918, Italy would not have demanded Fiume. But by the time that the Italian demands were formally presented in February 1919 the clamour had grown, with the result that the demand for Fiume occupied as much space in the Italian brief as all the rest of her claims combined.[18]

This development was in part the outcome of popular pressures in Italy, which ranged from the democrats to the nationalists. Salvemini and Bissolati, though ardent interventionists and supporters of the *unione sacra* of 1917 after the Caporetto disaster, were insistent that the war should be fought for democracy on Wilsonian principles. This meant that the Treaty of London should be discarded as a piece of out-dated imperialism but that Fiume, whose Italian character was unquestioned and whose citizens requested union with Italy, should be brought into the fold.[19] D'Annunzio, the nationalist leader, had a rather different standpoint. As far as he was concerned the victory of Vittorio Veneto was not the end of the war but the beginning of the next, which would be a war for the domination of the Mediterranean and a *pace romana*. Reverting to an old theme, he claimed in April 1919 that Italy should inherit the former territories of Venice – Istria, Fiume and Dalmatia as far as Ragusa (Dubrovnik) – a claim that went far beyond the Treaty of London and was probably intended to force a war with the Slavs.[20]

Similarly Mussolini. Although in 1915 he had shown not the slightest interest in Fiume or Dalmatia and wanted war largely for war's sake – Sonnino and the nationalists were at that time regarded as *la bestia nera* – by the time of Caporetto his views were indistinguishable from those of D'Annunzio.[21] In return for her heroic efforts Italy was to inherit the Adriatic. The 'wild' imperialism of the Slavs, who were, after all, 'the gendarmes and heirs of the Habsburgs', was to be contained by the 'harmless' imperialism of Italy.[22] The new Rome must be realistic, like Foch and Clemenceau. All her problems – demobilisation, unemployment etc. – could be solved by creating this new empire in the Adriatic. Why should Italy make the sacrifices for Wilson's new order?

All nations should be treated alike, there must be no 'bourgeois' nations (the USA, Britain and France) and 'proletarian' nations (Italy). Mussolini, the futurists (Marinetti especially) and Lenin were at one in 1919: Wilson's League of Nations was a sham, a neo-Holy Alliance, an international nanny.[23] Fascism, young Italy, Mussolini announced, would break with the past; the 'fourth Italy', would fight for her future; 'we are the young Italy that fights . . . the young Italy that issues a shrill challenge to the future. . . '.[24] On 11 January Mussolini broke up Bissolati's attempt to convert an audience at La Scala to a peace of self-determination and swung the interventionist groups in Milan, formerly pro-Wilson, into the nationalist camp.[25] Henceforward the democratic interventionists, men like Albertini or Salvemini, were between the hammer and the anvil.

With such heady stuff pouring from the press on all sides, when even reasonable men like Bissolati – who resigned in December in protest against the decision to promote Croat separatism – thought Fiume a just claim, it would have taken a stronger man than Orlando to ignore it. Instead, adopting the view *che Fiume è italianissima*, that without it Italy would not have achieved her war aims, he gave himself up to the mood of the moment. At the time of his popular stand against Wilson in April 1919, Orlando became a folk hero in Italy.[26]

At Paris Orlando and Sonnino naturally maintained that it was the democratic pressures in Italy that made it impossible to renounce Fiume, that the government, after all, was merely the instrument of the will of the people. However, it is significant that they made no attempt to use the usual apparatus of the state to suppress the activities of D'Annunzio, or of Mussolini and his *fasci* who provided them with this alibi. They were in fact natural allies of the government. Orlando's administration of 1918–19 was to all intents and purposes similar to Salandra's of 1915–16. It had eventually won the war. Having done so it had to win the peace, had to obtain more from the allies than the neutralist Giolitti would have obtained by not fighting Austria. Hence the mutual opposition of Orlando, Sonnino and Mussolini to a Wilsonian peace: it could only discredit the governing classes and the interventionists in general.[27] Although his allies had agreed only to the Italian occupation of the line of the Pact of London in the Adriatic, Orlando personally authorised the occupation of Fiume on 15 November 1918, *before* the agitation in Italy started. On 9 December the Council of Ministers accepted a scheme put forward by General Badoglio, deputy to Diaz, to promote a separate Croat state, independent of Belgrade.[28]

Throughout the peace conference Italy disputed recognition of Yugoslavia and supported Montenegrin separatism – in January Sonnino tried to exclude Serbs from the Allied occupation troops 'so as to put the country into a condition to decide its own fate freely'. He treated the Croats and Slovenes always as enemies, openly deriding their last-minute conversion to the Allied cause. (There was good reason for this. The Croat troops fought for the monarchy until the end.) Even Austria was preferable to Yugoslavia. The Italian experts in the boundary commission urged that Austria's southern frontiers be pushed to the Karawanken moun-

tains and opposed the plebiscite wanted by the Americans. Nor
was this mere spite. As Sonnino frequently pointed out to Vienna,
they had a common interest that the Trieste–Tarvisio–Villach–
Vienna railway should not pass through any Yugoslav territory, a
concern that dictated the severe local fighting between Italian and
Yugoslav troops in Carinthia in February and April.[29]

In control of Albania with more than 100,000 troops, Sonnino
showed every sign of staying there and fought off all contestants
whether Greek or Yugoslav. He organised his own Albanian
delegation to Paris, worked on Albanian groups in the USA to put
pressure on American senators and did everything possible to
preserve it as an independent state – under Italian protection –
protesting strongly at the French habit of encouraging the Yugoslavs to wipe out inconvenient Albanian pockets. It was an uphill
task – even Sonnino wearied of organising the volatile tribesmen,
complaining to Valona in April that 'the lack of political stability
and character of Albanian notables is notorious'.[30]

In the Council of Ten Sonnino announced that he would
support even Bulgaria against Yugoslavia, a threat which he put
into execution in the expert committees to decide the frontiers of
the new state. Here the Italian delegates espoused every opponent
of Yugoslavia. From February onwards Sonnino had close connections with Hungary and Romania; Károlyi told him that
Budapest much preferred Fiume and the Austro–Hungarian fleet
to go to Italy; Sonnino in his turn was prepared to offer Hungary
special terms at Fiume. In June he instructed Prince Borghese, at
Budapest, to support a Romanian–Hungarian alliance as this
would be 'in conformity with the views of the Royal Government,
who would make the basis of such an agreement a common understanding to weaken and isolate Yugoslavia'.[31]

In other words, the claim to Fiume was not simply a response
to internal pressures in Italy. Nor, though Orlando might waver
on Dalmatia and Sonnino show indifference to the popular
clamour for Fiume, was there any fundamental disagreement on
the aims to be pursued. These aims were straightforward, *ragione
di stato* at its clearest. There had always been two traditions in
Italian foreign policy dating from the Risorgimento. One, derived
from Mazzini and expressed by the Left, favoured the destruction
of Austria and fraternity between Italy and the Slav peoples of the
Balkans. This was the policy advocated by Bissolati and Salvemini

in 1919. The second, derived from Balbo, espoused by Cavour and the Right, wanted both to obtain the *terra irredenta* and to use Austria as a bulwark against Slavdom in the Balkans. This was Sonnino's object in 1915 and he still clung to it in April 1918, rejecting the concept of a united Slav state as mere propaganda. Croatia and Slovenia were to remain parts of a reduced Habsburg empire which would naturally retain Fiume as its only outlet to the sea now that Trieste was to go to Italy. By the Treaty of London, Serbia was to acquire only southern Dalmatia – from Split to Dubrovnik – hemmed in by Italian control of the offshore islands.

Hence the surprise, annoyance and alarm in Rome when the reality of 1918–19 proved very different. Instead there had emerged a vigorous unitary Slav state which claimed not only Dalmatia, the islands and Fiume, but also Istria, Gorizia and Trieste![32] If these claims were to be conceded, for what purpose had Italy fought for four years? The new state evidently intended to be the Habsburg heir, as Mussolini had forecast, and, if it could not be strangled at birth by promoting Croat and Montenegrin separatism, then it must be contained. Supporting Romanian and Austrian claims, controlling Albania, seeking an open alliance with Hungary and denying Fiume were but means to this end. Since Fiume was Croatia's only viable commercial port, denial would ensure Italian economic control of the new state.[33] This explains why Orlando, far from seeking to suppress the agitation within Italy for Fiume, sought only to exploit it for his own ends. It would, he thought, be an advantage to be able to claim at Paris that both the inhabitants of Fiume and the whole Italian people were convinced *che Fiume è Italianissima*.

Unfortunately for Orlando, President Wilson did not share this conviction. According to the Italian Premier their Ambassador in Washington, Macchi di Cellere, was not in touch with the president's thinking, with the consequence that Orlando and Sonnino were ill prepared for the stance that he took in support of Yugoslavia.[34] It is true that Wilson was both vague and contradictory at times. During his official visit to Italy in January he declined to discuss the territorial settlement on the grounds that he left this to his experts. As late as 30 January, Wilson thought of promoting three separate states – Croatia, Serbia and Montenegro – an attitude in complete conformity with Italian views. Yet on 6 February he suddenly decided that the entire Italian–Yugoslav dispute should be settled by his own personal arbitration, and the next day recognised Yugoslavia as a unitary state.

Yet, making due allowance for Wilson's vacillation, and di Cellere's lack of contact with the president, it is difficult to accept that Rome could have been as ignorant as Orlando implied. Why, otherwise, did Sonnino take such great care to prevent Wilson making public speeches in Italy during his visit? The fact that the president went out of his way to meet Bissolati and Albertini, whose views were unmistakable after 11 January, must have seemed ominous.[35] Besides, in Paris it was common knowledge by December that Wilson was 'very anti-Italian' and 'sick to death of Orlando and Sonnino'. Balfour concluded on 31 January that the difficulties involved with Italy were so enormous that the Allies must reach a German settlement *before* they tackled the Adriatic problem.[36]

The prior concentration on Germany undoubtedly made things more difficult for Orlando and Sonnino. By the time serious discussion of the Italian–Yugoslav disputes began in the Council of Four on 19 April 1919, their case had been prejudiced by a series of armed clashes in Fiume and Dalmatia which even the official Allied report blamed on Italy.[37] More serious, Wilson's principles had undergone such erosion in the German settlement – the Rhineland, the Saar, reparations and Shantung – that he was all the more determined to stand on his Fourteen Points when it came to the Adriatic.[38] This proved fatal to any compromise. For, by April, Orlando was certainly willing to compromise. He implied to House on 3 April that he would give up Dalmatia for Fiume and he offered in the Council of Four on 19 April to accept the Treaty of London for the present and 'reserve' Fiume for later. But Wilson would grant neither Fiume nor the Treaty of London.

Orlando's tactics at this stage were to give way in Dalmatia in the hope of squeezing counter concessions from Wilson on Fiume, an approach which was acceptable to Lloyd George and Clemenceau. But Wilson would not budge. His maximum concession was that Fiume was to be a free city and no sophistries about 'free ports' would move him. The attempt by Lloyd George to mediate by conveniently forgetting some of the points at issue failed dismally. Wilson, perhaps afraid that he might give way if the pressure of negotiation was kept up long enough, now nailed his colours to the mast by a public statement of his position in *Le*

Temps on 24 April. This, widely assumed to be an attempt to appeal to the Italian people over the heads of their negotiators at Paris, only made matters worse. Orlando and Sonnino, affronted, left for Rome the next day and became popular heroes. Even Salvemini and Bissolati, their chief critics in Italy, thought Wilson's appeal sheer hypocrisy.

This stand by Wilson has been termed 'a capital error of judgment'.[39] The result, certainly, was to make negotiation impossible, since, as Wilson himself told Orlando on 24 April, how could he publicly announce his principles one day and contradict them the next? This was, of course, one of the basic problems of open diplomacy. Clemenceau and Lloyd George who, according to the Italian delegation at Paris, were pressured by Wilson, now made their position equally clear. They stood by the Treaty of London and would admit no modification except at Italian request: however, the treaty assigned Fiume to Croatia and in their view there was no compelling reason to alter this. There might be an Italian majority in Fiume but this was only achieved by ignoring the suburb of Sušak, which was solidly Slav and divided from Fiume only by a narrow canal 'in the same manner as Paris is divided by the Seine and London by the Thames'. The hinterland was of course entirely Slav. It was not, in the view of Clemenceau and Lloyd George, in Italy's best interests to wreck the peace conference on an issue where their case was so poor.[40]

What they ignored in this rational argument was that Fiume was an irrational feeling, part of the whole complex of sentiments – Venetian grandeur, racial superiority, massive casualties, Caporetto – which demanded Italian assertion of her position as a great power. Consequently the appeal fell on deaf ears. On 30 April Sonnino simply re-asserted Italian claims and added that, now parliament had voted its support for Orlando, the government could make no concessions. Consequently, Clemenceau and Lloyd George issued an ultimatum: if Orlando and Sonnino had not returned to Paris in time for the opening conference with Germany on 9 May they would consider the 1915 treaty null and void – a threat which worked.[41] But even when Orlando returned the deadlock was still unresolved. He and Trumbić managed to agree on 16 May that Fiume was to be a free city, but the exact definition of its frontiers remained as difficult as ever. Tardieu, Clemenceau's confidant, attempted to introduce a certain amount of give and take between 27 May and 6 June by constructing a package deal – the essence of which was to enlarge the frontiers of Fiume to take in all disputed territory in Istria whilst leaving only Zara and Sebenico to Italy in Dalmatia. It was rejected. Wilson absolutely refused to accept that the Treaty of London formed any basis for negotiation. It was, he said, 'inconsistent with the new style of agreements, i.e. the ethnical principle'.[42] Orlando's bitter conclusion, that 'it was less a peace conference than an arbitration by President Wilson',[43] had considerable justification.

Failing to obtain a settlement which they could accept, and beset by their parliamentary critics, on 19 June Orlando and Sonnino resigned. On 28 June, Wilson, equally, washed his hands of the Adriatic problem and left for the USA.

Colonial diversions

If the cry of mutilated victory had any substance it lay in the settlement of the Near East and Africa. Here Italy was the victim of sharp practice on the part of Britain and France. By Article IX of the Treaty of London, Italy had been promised a 'just share' in the 'region adjacent to the province of Adalia'. By the St Jean de Maurienne agreement of August 1917 this share was defined as southern Turkey from Smyrna to Mersina, an area comparable to the British and French inheritances in the Ottoman Empire in size, if not in wealth. But in November 1918 the agreement of 1917 was denounced by Britain and France on the highly specious – if formally correct – grounds that it had not been ratified by Russia.[44]

Muddle and confusion followed. Balfour for one regretted this action almost as soon as it was taken[45] and took a much more conciliatory line at Paris. Sonnino, who had no intention of accepting Italian exclusion from Asia Minor, instructed the naval Chief of Staff on 9 January to postpone landings for the moment, merely to give himself breathing space. As he told Sforza on 26 January, open annexation was out of fashion: they must find 'notables' and tribes in Anatolia to request Italian protection. In the interval he negotiated with Balfour and Lloyd George and on 8 February reached agreement for a partition of Asia Minor, from which Italy would obtain a large region around Adalia whilst Smyrna – included in 1917 in the Italian sphere – was to go to Greece. Since in March he was actually requested in the Supreme War Council to

relieve British troops at Konia and Ankara, it is not surprising that
Sonnino now thought the way clear for action in Anatolia. Moreover, since Wilson at this time opposed any Greek presence in Asia
Minor, there seemed little reason to be tender of Venizelos's
feelings. On 30 March Italian marines landed at Adalia and a
month later – following rumours of impending Greek action – at
Scala Nova, just south of Smyrna.[46]

Sonnino has frequently been criticised for not seeking an understanding with Greece – as did his successor, Tittoni – against
Anglo–French exclusiveness. Venizelos certainly would have
welcomed such an agreement on the basis of Smyrna to Greece and
his support to Italy in the Dodecanese, Adalia and Epirus. Apart
from the fact that Sonnino scorned backstairs intrigues with minor
powers – Italy was a great power and had her 'rights' – Venizelos's
offer contained a serious drawback. Smyrna was the pearl of Asia
Minor. Bianchieri told Sonnino on 18 February that its natural
wealth and key position in the Turkish railway system were such
that he would keep Smyrna even at the cost of concessions to
Greece in the Dodecanese – actually under Italian control since
1912 – and Epirus.[47] It is not surprising, therefore, that Sonnino
showed little interest in a deal with Venizelos, at least until after 6
May when he was faced with the Greek *fait accompli* at Smyrna.
This – accomplished with Wilson's approval by Lloyd George
during the absence of the Italians from Paris over the Fiume affair
– made Anatolia a less attractive proposition to Italy and explains
Orlando's willingness in conversations with Lloyd George on 18
May to abandon it entirely in exchange for Fiume – if the latter
could be obtained.[48]

Similarly in Africa. By Article XIII of the Treaty of London
'equitable compensation' for Italy was promised if Britain or
France were to take any German colonies in Africa. Yet, on 7 May
1919, in the absence of the Italian delegates, the mandates for the
ex-German colonies in Africa were distributed to France and the
British Empire, and when it came to discussion of compensation
for Italy from 15 May onwards her gains were negligible. This was
not due to any lack of claims. The Minister of Colonies, Colosimo,
had considerable appetite: Ghadames and Ghat in the Algerian
hinterland, Giarabub in Cyrenaica, Kassala, Jibuti, British
Somaliland and Jubaland, the abolition of the 1906 tripartite convention on Abyssinia and the recognition of Italy's sole influence

in the country. Though Sonnino hastened to inform his allies on 5 January that this demand 'does not imply in any manner that Italy intends to re-establish her protectorate over Abyssinia' in practice this was what it meant. His assurances to Milner, the British Colonial Secretary, on 16 May that all they had in mind was to exploit the country economically and industrially, leaving her politically independent, made Italian intentions clear.[49]

In the May discussions De Martino and Sonnino found the British – and especially the French – extremely suspicious. The demands in Algeria and Cyrenaica were readily conceded but when it came to East Africa it was quite different: Jibuti and Somaliland were not available and Milner even became lyrical in praise of Jubaland, a 'little Nile' and the jewel of the British colonial empire. Sonnino, at successive conferences on 16 and 20 May, managed to prise loose Jubaland from Milner and a half promise of Somaliland if the French would part with Jibuti. They would not. It was their only means of access to Abyssinia and they insisted on keeping it. Since Milner saw no reason why Britain should make all the sacrifices Somaliland also fell to the ground. Instead Sonnino was diverted into a scheme for the Italian development of Angola – which never materialised – and all he could do on Africa, as on Asia Minor, was to reserve Italy's position. It took another five years to reach a minimal settlement.[50]

This was a major error on the part of France and Britain – it would have been politic to have associated Italy with the victory over Germany by giving her a share of the colonial spoils. As Toscano points out, Rome developed a legitimate sense of grievance in Africa and had every reason, in the 1930s to become a 'revisionist' power.[51]

Why were Italian colonial acquisitions so slight in 1919? In the first place because London and Paris took the view that the defeat of the Turks and the conquest of the German colonies had been achieved by their own exertions with no assistance from Italy. Milner was not impressed by the argument that the Italian campaign against the Senussi in Cyrenaica had assisted the British conquest of Palestine from Egypt. Secondly, the initial Italian claim to the whole of Somaliland and Jibuti made it obvious that the real object of policy was to control Ethiopia, which Britain and France were not prepared to accept. The Italian case was badly prepared, which didn't help, but fundamentally it was never pressed. Interest in Italy in 1919 in colonial acquisitions was minimal. As Orlando told Rodd in January, 'Italians generally did not care a bit about Asia Minor, nor about colonies in Africa'.[52] Time and again Orlando made it clear that the claim he put forward for Anatolia was negotiable; that if he were given Fiume 'it would be quite another thing'. Lloyd George on the whole grasped this point. It was, he told Wilson on 19 May, worth Fiume to get Italy out of Asia Minor: the president, however, did not agree.[53]

Only when it was clear, by June, that there was no hope of getting Fiume at Paris did Orlando and Sonnino revert to a search for compensation in Asia Minor. On 3 June Orlando took up with alacrity Lloyd George's suggestion that Italy should replace Britain as protector of the Transcaucasian republics and preparations were made to ship out 100,000 troops. Simultaneously, Sonnino opened negotiations with Greece to define their respective zones in Anatolia, which resulted, after his resignation, in the Tittoni–Venizelos convention of 19 July. How seriously Orlando envisaged this new Asiatic role for Italy is difficult to say: it seems probable that his major object was a paper empire for the benefit of the Chamber, a manoeuvre which failed when he went down to defeat by 259 votes to 78 on 19 June.

Nitti, his successor, had not the slightest enthusiasm for this new role. His first act was to cancel the military expedition to the Caucasus on the grounds of economy and switch all the emphasis in Italian policy back to the Adriatic.[54] By the Tittoni–Venizelos agreement the Dodecanese islands, occupied by Italy since 1911, were given to Greece, Smyrna recognised as Greek, and Italian influence confined to the coastal strip from Scala Nova to Mersina. In return Greece was to support an Italian mandate for Albania. It is true that Italian troops remained in Anatolia until their defeat by the Kemalists at Konia in May 1920, but no attempt was made to hold the province. In retrospect, in view of the eventual fate of the Transcaucasian republics at the hands of the Bolsheviks and of the Greeks at the hands of the Turks, it seems obvious that this lack of serious interest in Asia was a blessing in disguise, not a catastrophe, as nationalist critics later maintained.[55]

Nitti and D'Annunzio

Francesco Nitti, Premier from June 1919 until his overthrow in

May 1920, wanted above all to concentrate on Italian domestic problems. These were serious enough. The enormous military expenditure of the war years had produced serious price inflation, whilst concentration on the demands of the army had naturally cut production of goods for export. Note circulation increased four times during the war and whereas the cost of living index showed an increase over 1914 of approximately 60 per cent by 1918, salaries of state employees had risen by only 20 per cent. Thus the real wages of white-collar workers had declined and did not recover until 1921.[56] By 1918 only 20 per cent of Italian imports were covered by exports, as opposed to 75 per cent in 1915.[57] Shipping shortages had pushed up the price of coal to extraordinary heights, with the inevitable result that Italian industrial prices became uncompetitive and production declined throughout 1919. Unemployment consequently rose, reaching 2 million by November 1919, precisely at the time when demobilisation threw large numbers of men on the labour market and US immigration restriction clamped down on the traditional outlet.[58] The outcome was serious industrial unrest, large-scale strikes, and riots, as this situation was exploited by the opponents of the government both on the Right and on the Left. In June, Nitti had to use troops in Rome to block an attempted Rightist coup. In November a strong swing to the Left at the polls destroyed the liberal majority, produced a strong socialist party who rejected any parliamentary compromise, and made successive liberal administrations fatally dependent upon Luigi Sturzo's *Partito Popolare*.[59]

Nitti's attempted solution to these problems was to retrench, wield the economy axe and seek foreign loans. In six months he reduced the Italian officer corps by half, cancelled the Georgia expedition and began the withdrawal from Albania completed by Giolitti. In Asia, though he supported Lloyd George to produce the Treaty of Sèvres in May 1920,[60] in fact this settlement was an empty gesture which bore no relation to Nitti's Turkish policy. This was largely made by Sforza. Count Sforza, recalled from Constantinople to become Tittoni's Under-Secretary at the Foreign Ministry, continued the same policy of collaboration with Kemal Ataturk that he had initiated as Italian High Commissioner in Turkey. Assuming, correctly, that the Greeks could never win, Sforza's object was to drop claims to political sovereignty in favour of a more realistic concentration on furthering Italian commercial interests. Accordingly, when promoted to foreign minister in June 1920, Sforza denounced the secret Tittoni–Venizelos convention and dissociated Italy from any collaboration with Greece. This policy was carried through also in Albania, where partition with Greece was dropped in favour of complete Italian withdrawal, even from Valona, Italy retaining only the island of Saseno. Since, according to Nitti, Albania was costing 300 million lire a year, with no prospect of any return, this was a worthwhile achievement.[61]

Obtaining foreign loans, chiefly from the USA and Britain, was more difficult. In London the banks shied away from lending money to an apparently unstable Italy. Lloyd George was more sympathetic but was unable to satisfy Nitti's immediate needs – 500,000 tons of coal a month to keep the railways running – owing to the current miners' strike in Britain. Negotiations in the USA were fruitless: the Treasury and leading banks claimed credits were impossible until late September, delaying tactics which Nitti attributed to American annoyance over Fiume.[62]

Nitti, therefore, obsessed with the conviction that Italy would face starvation if she could not obtain credits, had to solve the Fiume question as a matter of urgency. His own views were similar to those of Bissolati and Salvemini; that is, Fiume–Yes, Dalmatia–No. He had, like Bissolati, resigned from Orlando's cabinet in January 1919. However, more politically astute, Nitti had refrained from adopting a clear position, an act of foresight which made him an acceptable premier in June 1919.[63] His first act, therefore, was to send his Foreign Minister, Tittoni, to Paris to negotiate a settlement based upon the renunciation of Dalmatia in favour of some recognition of the Italian character of Fiume.

Tittoni's task was made absolutely impossible by the course of events in Fiume from July to September. The lynching of nine French soldiers by local hooligans, abetted by Italian troops, created such an uproar that the Supreme War Council in Paris demanded the withdrawal of most of the Italian troops, the suppression of Host Venturi's Fiumean volunteers and the effective policing of the city by British constables. These were to arrive in Fiume on 12 September. On 11 September D'Annunzio, responding to an appeal from a group of Italian officers stationed at Ronchi, near Trieste, drove into Fiume at the head of 1,000 troops and proclaimed himself dictator. To avoid incidents the French and British troops were withdrawn, leaving D'Annunzio in control. However, this *de facto* solution to the Fiume problem only made matters worse as Paris, London and Washington – especially the latter – were now more irritated than ever. Tittoni, after two months of fruitless negotiations, gave up in November and resigned.[64]

Logically there were two possible courses for Nitti to follow. The first was to support D'Annunzio, ignore the Allies and ride the wave of nationalist fervour which was gripping the country. This he rejected for economic reasons, as it would fatally alienate Wilson. The second was to eject the dictator, brave the consequent unpopularity in Italy, and negotiate a settlement with the Yugoslavs. This course was equally impossible since the army refused to fire on D'Annunzio's troops and, Nitti believed, the nationalist groups would overthrow the government by a *coup d'état*. No doubt Nitti was timorous by nature, temperamentally incapable of forceful action,[65] but he did have good reason to suspect that D'Annunzio and his supporters aimed at something much more ambitious than the seizure of Fiume.

The nationalists were the natural leaders of the wave of patriotic fervour which swept Italy in April 1919. Progressively, as Orlando failed to deliver Fiume in May and June, he was discredited: now both the nationalist and fascist press advocated a revolution as the only means of obtaining Italy's 'just demands' abroad and suppressing the 'traitors' – the neutralists and the socialists – at home. Nitti, suspect both as a pupil of Giolitti and as an 'economist', was a natural target for attack since he represented everything that D'Annunzio most disliked. Nitti's bourgeois approach to political problems, his concentration on cutting expenditure and negotiation over Fiume, were anathema to the poet: in his view all problems should be solved by heroic gestures simply because this was more poetic, more Italian, more irrational. The mark of a great civilisation he said, lay in its readiness for battle, not in its ability to balance the budget.[66]

Nationalist rhetoric was important in its ability to produce a riot on demand,[67] but the elements which lay behind it were of more serious concern to Nitti. Demobilisation was an unattractive prospect to the senior elements in the Italian officer corps which had risen from 142 generals in 1915 to 1,246 in 1918. In complete control in the war zones – the whole of north-east Italy – they had built up a political machine of sorts through the *uffici propaganda* and become serious rivals to the prefects in civil administration.[68] Many thought of perpetuating this happy state of affairs by maintaining the army on a war footing, for which the agitation over Fiume and the possibility of war with Yugoslavia provided a perfect excuse. They were supported by the leaders of heavy industry for the same reasons: the wartime expansion of industrial production – and profits – could only be maintained by continuing the war; it was no accident that both the nationalist press and Mussolini's *Popolo d'Italia* were heavily subsidised by Ansaldo. In May and June 1919 there were evident signs of a conspiracy amongst the generals to prevent a Nitti ministry, but they were checked by the determination of the king to stick to the constitutional process. How long this would last, Nitti had no means of knowing. It was clear that both the Duke of Aosta, commander of the 3rd Army in Venezia Giulia, and Admiral Millo, at Zara, were supporting D'Annunzio, and Nitti was convinced at the end of July that there was a 'serious plot to impose a Constituent Assembly and install a militarist government'.[69]

In these circumstances it was clearly essential for him to treat D'Annunzio with extreme caution. The army would not act against him, General Caviglia explained, because Orlando's rhetoric in April had convinced the soldiers that the September march on Fiume was fully justified. The question for Nitti was whether the army would go one step further: if D'Annunzio were to march on Rome, would the soldiers think that justified too? Hence Nitti, though taking the precaution of breaking up the Third Army, with the support of Diaz, left D'Annunzio severely alone: time, he hoped, would solve the problem, an expectation that proved correct.

Attempts were made to expand the revolution from Fiume to Rome but they were unsuccessful. The socialists completely rejected approaches from Fiume for them to join in overthrowing their common enemy, the bourgeois Nitti, just as they rejected invitations to collaborate with Nitti against the adventurers of the Quarnero. Mussolini equally abstained. He had not been involved in the September *coup* and, though fond of theatrical gestures like flying to Fiume to greet the hero, kept his feet firmly on the ground otherwise. He was, rightly, dubious whether the army would support a march on Rome and preferred the safer course of violent diatribes against Nitti in the press, whilst in fact doing nothing.[70] Gradually D'Annunzio, though still a colourful figure, lost political importance, a process completed by the November elections. The virtual annihilation of the Right, the nationalists and the fascists, made it clear, as Nitti announced, that 'the country is absolutely opposed to any policy of adventure and will react to violence with further violence, which could lead to bolshevism.'[71]

The Treaty of Rapallo

The consequence of the elections of November 1919 for the Fiume question was that rational discussion through the normal channels of diplomacy could be resumed: it was no longer a question of life or death for the Italian government. The fact that any eventual settlement had to be acceptable to the new Chamber now meant very little as the 'neutralist' majority, though regarding the acquisition of Fiume as desirable, did not share the passionate feelings of the nationalists.[72]

The major obstacle to a settlement from December 1919 to February 1920 was President Wilson, who objected violently to any pressure upon Yugoslavia; objections which were upheld by Lansing, the US Secretary of State, even after Wilson's collapse. On 13 February Washington intervened to the extent of threatening to abandon the American guarantee of the French frontier if Britain and France persisted in trying to impose a settlement on Belgrade. This action led Lloyd George and Millerand, the new French Premier, to withdraw from the scheme drawn up with Nitti at a meeting in Paris from 10 to 20 January, which had offered the best prospect of a solution so far.[73] Direct negotiations now ensued between Nitti and Trumbić, which rambled on until Nitti's first resignation on 12 May. Some progress was made, largely because Belgrade realised that Wilson was now a spent force, but the Yugoslavs still insisted on the partition of Albania, which Nitti rejected.[74]

Nitti's final resignation on 9 June, after three attempts to form a government, had no real cause beyond the unstable condition of Italian politics after the November 1919 elections in which no one political group had a majority. It brought no changes in foreign policy, despite Mussolini's praise for the Giolitti–Sforza régime as putting an end to Nitti's *politica disastrosa* and his subservience to

Anglo–French hegemony.[75] Giolitti and Sforza pursued much the same line as their predecessor in the Adriatic and that they achieved the settlement which had eluded Nitti was due simply to the lapse of time.[76] Trumbić closed with Sforza in November whereas he had stalled with Nitti in May because he could afford to wait no longer. As long as there was no settlement, Italian troops occupied the Treaty of London line in the Adriatic and D'Annunzio remained in Fiume. Up to April 1920, Belgrade could hope that Wilson might bail them out: by November this was plainly impossible.

Sforza's tactics were to adopt an attitude of reasonableness, obtain the diplomatic support of Britain and France, and thus isolate Belgrade. In June he told Trumbić that he and Giolitti disapproved of the Treaty of London. In August, spurred on by the confinement of Italian troops to Valona by insurgent tribesmen and the mutiny of a regiment of Bersaglieri embarking for Albania, Giolitti ordered the complete evacuation of the country. He even urged her admission to the League of Nations, thus making Yugoslavia appear the imperialist power. All he wanted, he told Millerand in September, was Zara, an independent Fiume and the Treaty of London, as opposed to the Wilson line, in Istria.[77]

With Rome so accommodating, London and Paris behind them and Washington mute, the Yugoslav cabinet had no choice but to accept Italian terms. At a conference at Santa Margherita from 8–12 November 1920, Sforza and Trumbić produced the solution to the Adriatic problem known as the Treaty of Rapallo. It followed the scheme Giolitti had outlined to Millerand in September. Istria was partitioned according to the 1915 agreement, which left Monte Nevoso to Italy and gave her a contiguous frontier with Fiume, which became a free city. Zara and the islands of Cres, Losinj, Palagruza and Lastovo went to Italy; the rest of Dalmatia to Yugoslavia. This settlement was almost exactly that which Tittoni had proposed and Lloyd George and Clemenceau supported in August 1919, but which Wilson had rejected.[78]

Curiously enough, for all his denunciations of Nitti and Tittoni, Mussolini accepted the Treaty of Rapallo without a murmur. Sforza, who visited him at Milan shortly before the conference, found the fascist leader 'convinced of the advantage of my solution to the Adriatic problem'. *Il Fascio,* the official journal of the movement, announced afterwards that 'the people today feel the need for peace more than for territorial expansion',[79] which was what Nitti had said twelve months or more earlier. Never inclined to support a lost cause, Mussolini now severed his always tenuous connections with D'Annunzio and left the poet an isolated and increasingly discredited figure.[80] In December, consequently, Giolitti felt strong enough to attack him with Italian troops and after three days' fighting forced his withdrawal, enabling the free city-state to be established. It had, however, a short life as it was re-occupied by Italian forces in late 1923 after the success of Mussolini's march on Rome.

In retrospect the handling of the Adriatic question by Italian statesmen in 1918–19 was disastrous. The eventual settlement of November 1920 was no better, from the Italian viewpoint, than could have been achieved at Paris if Orlando and Sonnino had adopted a reasonable attitude before President Wilson nailed his colours to the mast. It was not as if Dalmatia was of any use to Italy: the general staff thought it a liability, the navy were content with Pola, Lissa and Valona, which Wilson accepted. The major concept of 1915 had been to deny the use of the Dalmatian coastline to Russia, which was reasonable enough, but by 1918 this was no longer an issue. By insisting on the Treaty of London plus Fiume and supporting all Yugoslavia's opponents in the Balkans, Sonnino and Orlando were sowing dragon's teeth. Collaboration between the successor states to Austria–Hungary was difficult in any case; they made it absolutely impossible. The dreams of Mazzini and his latter-day apostles – Salvemini, Bissolati – of Italian patronage of some sort of Balkan federation were probably chimerical in view of the differences amongst the Balkan states themselves, but they offered the only possibility that remained in 1919 after the break-up of the Austrian Empire. Without it, Central Europe simply disintegrated, and became easy victims of renascent Germany in the 1930s.

To make matters worse, Orlando and Sonnino pandered to the cry of *la vittoria mutilata*. In so doing, they obscured the fact that Italy *had* won the war, *had* destroyed her hereditary enemy, to a far greater degree than France had done. Italy, consequently, had a vested interest in the *status quo* of 1919; her territorial acquisitions were considerable; for the first time she had a strong, defensible, natural frontier. But in creating the myth that Italy was a defeated power they laid the basis for Italian alignment with revisionism in the 1930s, in which Italy had as much to lose as anyone else. It was not an Italian interest to have a greater Germany on the Brenner. D'Annunzio and Mussolini may have believed in 1919 that it was Italy's destiny to become mistress of the Mediterranean, but this was mere poetic licence. Sonnino and Orlando did not share this view, yet they allowed themselves to become its propagandists. As Orlando admitted in April 1919, he had not initiated this course nor did he sympathise with it; he could see that it was dangerous; but he had to go along with it as the government could not oppose it.[81]

The consequences in Italy were considerable. Although there were other factors contributing to the overthrow of classical liberalism at the elections of 1919 – it was, after all, a general experience in Europe in this period – the Fiume issue was a serious weakness, which provided the *fasci di combattimento* with their main reason for existence in 1919. Moreover, it was difficult to support liberal politicians who, by their own confession, had so mishandled Italian interests at the peace conference. The immediate result was a stalemate, certainly not a strengthening of the nationalists, but the long-term result was that the traditional basis of Italian politics – *trasformismo* – had disappeared. The refusal of the socialist and populist parties to collaborate in maintaining liberal democracy created the void which Mussolini was later to fill. If Orlando and Nitti had been strong enough to ignore the nationalist furore in 1919 and concentrate on the real issue – economic reconstruction – perhaps the trains would have run to time before the march on Rome.

Part II

Chapter 9

Mussolini and the New Diplomacy

> Gentlemen, not only must the Rhine frontier be
> guaranteed but that of the Brenner also.
>
> *Mussolini*, 1925

Mussolini's ideas

Mussolini's accession to the Presidency of the Council and the
Portfolio of Foreign Affairs provoked the immediate resignation of
the Ambassador in Paris, Count Sforza, who pleaded his personal
reluctance to take a hand in a foreign policy which promised to be
a 'collection of sentiments and resentments'.[1] Sforza's resignation
was more than a personal declaration of non-confidence in fascism:
from a senior Ambassador and a former Foreign Minister, the
resignation was tantamount to a warning to international society.
The warning made little impression. Most international reaction
ranged from cautious to favourable. Whitehall's attitude was
described as 'optimistic'; the Quai d'Orsay was rather more
reserved, owing to Mussolini's indiscreet remarks on the status of
the Italians in Tunisia, but not hostile. Only in Germany were
some fears expressed that the march on Rome might offer a model
to local extremists; in the other defeated countries, on the other
hand, the ongoing disputes between Italy and the other two
members of the wartime coalition were seen as a possible rallying
point. Altogether the new Italian government was received rather
well in conservative circles which made a point of stressing the
constitutionality of the change.[2] Those so inclined noted with
approval the haste with which Mussolini forsook the black shirt
for morning coat and spats and the diligence with which he applied
himself to learning diplomatic etiquette.

The new Foreign Minister's first action was to send telegrams of
greetings to the major allied capitals and to pay courtesy calls on
the larger embassies. He became in a short time 'an excellent civil
servant',[3] but he did not become, as had been confidently expected,

a pliable instrument in the hands of Salvatore Contarini, the powerful Secretary-General of the Consulta, who acted as his personal tutor. The first few years of Mussolini's tenure of the Italian Foreign Office, until the resignation of Contarini in 1926 and the 'fascistisation' of the Foreign Service, was not a period of traditional Italian policies punctuated occasionally by some head-strong ministerial initiative; rather, it was a period when a series of drastic ministerial initiatives were barely restrained by the permanent bureaucrats. Against the greetings to foreign dignitaries, a warning to the more rabid in Fiume and the punctilious observance of protocol one has to set the thrust of fascist policies – essentially an attempt to break away from dependence on one's allies – combined with a social Darwinian view of relations among states and a style which at times could not be distinguished from that of the blackmailer. Mussolini's first speech to the Chamber on 16 November 1922 was typical. After issuing a stern warning that the treaties of peace were neither eternal nor immutable and asking the *Entente* to proceed to a 'severe examination of conscience', he outlined his foreign policy in all its simplicity: *do ut des*, nothing for nothing.[4]

Yet, despite the appearance of mere opportunism, it would be a mistake to assume that Mussolini had no political creed. Tested in the crucible of war, the reality of the nation had proved to be much more refractory than international socialism, his previous object of loyalty. The transfer of allegiance from class to nation had the effect of fusing his two former political convictions into one synthesis. In his writings and politics the nation became at once the vehicle and the objective of social regeneration. In a sense this was a clean break with Marxist socialism and at once the source and justification for the struggles against Marxism internally and externally. The break was clean as well because Mussolini's early socialism had always been less concerned with the redistribution of economic wealth, the classic and paramount socialist concern, than with a renewal of social life through the instrument of the class. But in another sense a remarkable continuity persisted. The objective of social regeneration remained, although the instrumentality and the locus changed as loyalty shifted from class to nation. This shift Mussolini regarded as evidence not of inconsistency but of intellectual growth. To the examination of the nation as the fundamental unit of both theoretical analysis and practical action

Mussolini brought an academic luggage free from the now rejected influence of more disciplined and wiser minds than his. In consequence the theoretical and practical synthesis which he called fascism obtained by necessity whatever intellectual coherence it came to possess from ransacking the cruder aspects of the contemporary milieu.

From these antecedents it was but a short step to revisionism, gradually seen by Mussolini as the unifying theme of his foreign policy during the late 1920s and its *leit-motif* during the late 1930s when it became necessary to outdo a much more bloody-minded dictator. Yet even in this area the contradictions derived from Mussolini's most outstanding characteristic – opportunism – frustrated a thoroughgoing policy. Mussolini's insistence on revisionism should not obscure the fact that he was not interested in the revision of the peace treaties. He insisted on the formula, but in practice he eschewed religiously its application even in the case of Hungary, the first of the defeated states to enjoy Mussolini's patronage. What few revisions took place of the territorial dispositions of Versailles – notably the Pact of Rome with Yugoslavia, the settlement of the Jubaland question with Britain and of the Libyan question with France – were more the aberrational result of contingent circumstances. Mussolini's style continued to be subversion in preference to revision. The result was a foreign policy which was by turn ambivalent, futile and malignant. Ambivalent because when it came to the point he had more in common with those who would conserve the *status quo* than with those who would destroy it; futile, for Italy lacked the strength to fulfil any but the most primitive of her designs of hegemony; and malignant, for her policy served mostly to exacerbate existing conflicts and to promote new ones.

The Near East

Three issues were at stake for Italy: the question of the Dodecanese islands, nominally under Turkish sovereignty but in fact under Italian occupation for the past ten years; the distribution of mandates in Asia Minor, and the question of Jubaland. The three issues converged in the autumn of 1922 after the Turkish victories over Greece had altered drastically the original peace settlement in the Middle East agreed to at Sèvres in 1920. By that treaty and the

Tripartite Accord which accompanied it, the Ottoman Empire was broken up into a number of nominally independent Arab states and what was left of Turkey divided into French and Italian spheres of economic influence. The last blow to Turkey was delivered by Greece, which at British instigation invaded the Turkish mainland. As it happened, a revivified Turkey turned the tables on Greece and the Allies. By late 1922 the Treaty of Sèvres and the Tripartite Accord were a dead letter and the *Entente*'s hold on the Straits precarious. In the new situation, the Italian government felt that an essential pre-condition to conversations with Turkey for a new peace treaty was a prior settlement of *Entente* policy, not merely *vis-à-vis* the heirs of the Ottoman Empire but on the whole range of problems left dangling, or settled unsatisfactorily, at the peace conference. The veiled threats in Mussolini's speech referred to this proposed exchange of views and the harshness of the language may be explained partly by the fact that when the new Italian Ambassadors in Paris and London, Della Torretta and Romano Avezzana, had raised the question early in November they had found the other two *Entente* capitals not only more than unwilling to reopen an issue likely to lead to renewed Italian demands for a mandate, but also quite insistent that Italy none the less carry out its agreement of 1920 to cede the Dodecanese islands to Greece, irrespective of the fact that conditions were now so different as to require a new peace treaty to replace the 1920 agreements.

The twelve islands of the Dodecanese, ethnically Greek but part of the Ottoman Empire, had been first occupied by Italy during the Turco–Italian war of 1912. By Article II of the treaty of peace concluded with Turkey at Ouchy in October 1912, Italy undertook to evacuate the islands immediately after the withdrawal of Turkish troops from Cyrenaica and Tripoli. On the grounds that certain officers of the Turkish Army had remained in Tripoli, Italian forces were still in occupation of the Dodecanese at the outbreak of war in 1914. The temporary occupation was to turn into permanent sovereignty by Article VIII of the Treaty of London. The subsequent adhesion of Greece to the cause of the Allies, her friendship with London and the new attitude towards self-determination after America's entry into war made it very difficult for Italy to retain the islands inhabited overwhelmingly by Greeks. The Italian delegation at the peace conference, realising the need to effect a compromise, concluded a convention with the Greek Prime Minister, Venizelos, on 29 July 1919 to cede all the islands to Greece with the exception of Rhodes, which was to remain under Italian sovereignty with the proviso that it might be ceded to Greece if and when Great Britain surrendered Cyprus to Greece, but in any case not before five years had elapsed. On 10 August 1920, a Greek–Italian treaty, following substantially the main lines of this convention, was signed and scheduled to come into force at the same time as the Treaty of Sèvres between Turkey and the Allies, one of whose provisions was the formal transferral of the Dodecanese islands from Turkey to Italy. As it happened, because of the outbreak of war between Greece and Turkey neither the Treaty of Sèvres nor the Italo–Greek treaty came into force. Italy remained in occupation of the islands, arguing, rather plausibly, that in the absence of other international agreements, the provision of Article VIII of the Treaty of London was operative.

It was at this point that the Dodecanese became tied to the issue of the cession to Italy of Jubaland under the terms of Article VIII of the Treaty of London, which had provided that if Britain and France added to their colonial possessions in Africa, Italy would be entitled to equitable compensation. Jubaland was the compensation agreed to in April 1920 between Lord Milner and the Italian Foreign Minister, Scialoja. Apparently, however, even at this time it was London's intention not to fulfil this agreement unless the Italians could be brought round to cede the Dodecanese to Greece. As Milner put it to Scialoja at the time, 'It remains, of course understood that the whole of our agreement about African matters can only become effective as part of the general settlement of all the issues raised at the Peace Conference.' Later, when the Italo–Greek treaty proved abortive, London, while acknowledging that the settlement of 10 August 1920 was no longer juridically operative, still maintained that its terms must constitute the basis of the settlement of the Dodecanese Question. In Curzon's words to the Italian Ambassador, those terms represented 'a moral obligation' which, though Curzon was careful not to put it this way, justified Britain in holding up its part of the bargain in Jubaland.[5] Over the objections of its Ambassador in Rome, the British government then decided in April 1921 to use the question of Jubaland as a lever to force the Italians to cede the Dodecanese to

Greece, refusing themselves to cede the territory promised until the Dodecanese question was settled.[6]

An attempt to settle both questions was made in July 1922 when the next Italian Foreign Minister, Schanzer, visited London with the purpose of discussing with Lloyd George all outstanding questions, including particularly the anticipated loss of the zone of economic influence in the Eastern Mediterranean. Schanzer brought with him a draft agreement by which the Dodecanese would be returned to Greece, with the exception of Rhodes and Stampalia, subject to the neutralisation of the Corfu channel. Nothing came of this proposal, not because Lloyd George found it unacceptable (on the contrary he volunteered to approach Greece with it) but because connected with it was an Italian offer of an Anglo–Italian *Entente* judged by the Foreign Office eventually to be more advantageous to Italy than to Britain and therefore turned down. Schanzer had taken the first step in May 1922 when he had submitted to the British Prime Minister the following formula:[7]

> The two governments, being desirous of concurring in the establishment of a lasting peace and in the reconstruction of Europe, in harmony with the Powers, acknowledge that their views are identical in this regard and give expression to their mutual desire to act closely together in the reciprocal interests and in the general questions of European tranquillity. Consequently the two governments have decided that, in regard especially to economic questions connected with the re-establishment of a normal situation in the Eastern Mediterranean and the Black Sea, they will exchange, whenever occasion arises, their views and will lend reciprocal support to the realisation of the agreement between them and the other interested powers.

Essentially an *entente* of this nature promised to Britain that the co-operation of the Italian government would be available at future international meetings. For Italy such an understanding could have had a wider and more remunerative scope. In a general sense it was intended to revive the internal and external prestige of the Italian government. In addition to leading to a condominium in the Eastern Mediterranean, it would have strengthened Italy's hand against France and her clients in Eastern Europe. If Britain's influence in the Council of the League were secured for Italy in such an agreement, the Foreign Office reasoned that Italy would have felt less uneasy about applying pressure on Czechoslovakia, Albania and Greece and less circumspect in her commercial dealing with Germany and Russia. The Foreign Office's view that Britain's 'prestige would inevitably suffer from association with Italy, and this without compensating advantages' prevailed with the result that Schanzer's other specific proposals, those concerning Jubaland, also fell on stony ground.[8]

Mussolini inherited this indeterminate state of affairs. On 9 October 1922, after the defeat of the Greek armies in Anatolia, the Italian government had made a verbal communication to the Foreign Office that Italy now definitely regarded the Greek–Italian agreement of 10 August 1920 as having lapsed. Curzon's reply that such repudiation would 'logically and inevitably' entail 'the cancellation of the other engagements in which as part of the general settlement, His Majesty's Government had entered', fell to Mussolini to deal with.[9]

This was a blunt threat. It referred both to Jubaland and the Dodecanese, the sovereignty of which in the absence of a treaty of peace with Turkey was still, legally as least, vested in Turkey.[10] Mussolini's reply took the stand that Italy's claim to the Dodecanese rested much more on the treaties of Ouchy and London than on the now inoperative Treaty of Sèvres. He went on, however, to acknowledge that since the settlement drawn up in 1920 had been the result of agreement between the Allies, the problem as a whole might be re-examined by them to arrive at a fresh settlement.[11] It soon transpired that this last stipulation had different meanings for Mussolini and Curzon. For the Italian leader, examining the problem as a whole meant reaching a settlement within the *Entente,* on the compensation due to Italy as a result of the Treaty of London, specifically the cession of Jubaland and the Italian request for a mandate (or a share of one) in Iraq to recoup the losses incurred with the abrogation of the Tripartite Accord. On that basis he was willing to negotiate the cession of the Dodecanese to Greece. Accordingly, he insisted that the Italian Ambassador in Paris take part in the talks between Poincaré and Curzon to settle *Entente* policy prior to meeting the Turks at Lausanne. Curzon held another view. He chose to interpret Mussolini's acknowledgment that the 1920 agreement was a matter of *Entente* policy as an implicit admission of its continuing validity. Or at least, such was the interpretation he favoured after his meetings with Mussolini had secured a united *Entente* front against Turkey.

The deliberate ambiguity of Curzon's policy explains in part why he and Poincaré acceded to Mussolini's peremptory request to meet them at Territet for private discussions before the opening of the conference in Lausanne. The importance of that meeting where, as Mussolini told the press, he would speak to them in fascist style, rested not in the communiqué issued afterwards – which, not unexpectedly, reaffirmed the full equality of the three members of the *Entente* – but in the act of public deference (a minor Canossa, the Italian press called it) which Poincaré and Curzon paid to the new Italian leader. For, at that meeting, as at Lausanne, the fundamental differences persisted. The basic agreement that the question of the Dodecanese should be settled among the Allies continued to mean for Mussolini that the applicable treaty was that of London, while for Curzon the operative treaty was the 1920 Italo–Greek understanding. To this fundamental misunderstanding must be added another and more important one. According to Mussolini, Curzon in their private meetings on 20 and 21 November agreed to satisfy Italy's request for a mandate,[12] leaving with the new Italian leader the welcome impression that he had succeeded where his liberal predecessors had failed abjectly. In this, he was quickly disappointed. His version of the Lausanne conversation was categorically repudiated by Curzon upon the latter's return to London. A Foreign Office official, much to the surprise of the Italian Ambassador who had come to formalise what Mussolini thought had been an agreement between two Foreign Ministers, produced a telegram from Curzon in which the British Foreign Secretary merely acknowledged but did not accept the Italian request for a mandate. In subsequent conversations, some extremely heated, Curzon maintained his position: he had not reached an understanding with Mussolini on mandates, he regarded the Italian request as a veiled form of blackmail and, if Italy disagreed, Britain and France would proceed to sign the Treaty of Lausanne without her.[13] The British ultimatum was crude but effective. It gave Mussolini the option of either abandoning his request for a mandate or remaining isolated diplomatically alongside Turkey and Russia. For a moment he entertained the latter alternative. The Consulta had supported Russia's request for equal treatment at the conference and cordial contacts had been maintained throughout with the unofficial Russian delegation. Moreover, the Italian Navy pronounced in favour of the Russian and Turkish programme for the Straits, that they remain under Turkish control, and against the British programme that the transit be free and the region demilitarised. None the less, in its present state the Soviet Union was not of much help while even Turkey appeared disposed to compromise. In the circumstances it was probably more advantageous for Italy to shelve the question of the mandate and accept the new Treaty of Lausanne which reproduced the clause from the Treaty of Sèvres by which sovereignty over the Dodecanese was formally transferred from Turkey to Italy. And if Britain then chose to consider the question of the mandates closed, Italy would choose to so regard the issue of its sovereignty over the Dodecanese. 'The question of the Dodecanese does not exist,' Mussolini announced on his return from Switzerland. 'It is of exclusively Italian concern, and already settled by the denunciation of the Italo–Greek Treaty. This is now admitted and there will be no further discussion on the subject.'[14]

Thus the first fascist attempt to impose 'an examination of conscience' on the *Entente* had resulted in stand-off – a public success at Territet and a private setback at Lausanne. The question of a share in the mandate over Iraq – at best a dubious prize since it was reputed to drain the British treasury of £100 million a year – was postponed for the time. Sèvres and the Tripartite Accord were now formally defunct but something had been salvaged by Italy gaining access to the Anglo–French economic consortium for the exploitation of the Near East. Italy's sovereignty over the Dodecanese was now considered beyond legal dispute. The question of Jubaland remained in abeyance, Curzon still holding to the view that the cession of that portion of British Africa should be used as a lever to force Italy to cede at least some of the Dodecanese islands to Greece. The result was a deadlock, eventually to be settled by Ramsay MacDonald in 1924 when it became clear that Jubaland was an ineffective lever as Italy did not really care for it but was desperately interested in the Dodecanese.

Reparations

The next round of inter-allied rivalries played itself out at the reparations conference held in London in the second week of

December 1922. Here the Anglo–French front which had faced Mussolini at Lausanne promised to disintegrate before the much more contentious problem of Germany. At the conference Mussolini presented a comprehensive proposal, partly his own draft, stressing the connection between reparation and inter-allied debts.[15] The proposal was essentially sound and it led Mussolini to hope, at least initially, that he might be able to mediate between Britain and France. But clearly no such mediation was possible so long as Poincaré was determined to follow a policy in which reparations were to serve as a pretext to contain Germany politically and economically by occupying the Ruhr while Britain was feeling its way towards a solution intended, by re-incorporating Germany into Europe's economic revival, to reduce French power to manageable proportions. The intractability of the issue forced Mussolini, in effect, to choose sides. If indeed France proceeded to occupy the Ruhr, the Italian government could either follow Britain's lead in condemning France or else align itself with France in the hope of extracting whatever advantages the new situation might yield. Conceivably, in the latter instance, the occupation of the Ruhr might lead to a radically new Franco–German relationship to which Italy could become party. On the other hand, if Rome supported London the result could well be English preponderance in Central and Eastern Europe to the detriment, as like as not, of Italian influence in the area.[16]

Thus, initially Mussolini tended to support the French position. But the support evaporated immediately it became clear that the seven Franco–Belgian divisions in the Ruhr were engaged in a military operation far more extensive than the protection and control of the coal mines. Mussolini dissociated Italy from the invasion not only in notes to the German, British and American governments, but, more to the point, in a sober warning to the French government in which he expressed 'his doubts and his fears on the usefulness of military operations and . . . his conviction that the advance into the Ruhr did not resolve but would likely complicate and exacerbate the problem of reparations'.[17]

And yet precisely at the same time that he judiciously eschewed complicity in an adventure whose complication he had not foreseen, his fertile mind produced a proposal of even more far-reaching consequences. The instructions to the Ambassador in Paris just cited contained also a proposal for a 'continental bloc' of

France, Italy, Belgium and eventually Germany and the Soviet Union designed to foster economic development on the continent to their mutual advantage and, implicitly, to the detriment of Britain. The 'continental bloc' has generally been dismissed as a personal fantasy, the more so since Mussolini imperturbably disavowed it within days. None the less, the proposal had been made seriously. Mussolini had just concluded a satisfactory economic agreement with France relating to Eastern Europe aided, no doubt, by his initial support of the French thesis of reparations. It was not inconceivable that, however blameworthy, the French occupation of the Ruhr would result in substantial concessions by Germany to France to Italy's great disadvantage. Hence the necessity to lay the groundwork immediately for a continental solution. Thus at bottom the proposal was not really directed against Britain; it was made to safeguard Italian interests. If, additionally, it served to prod Britain into adopting a more receptive attitude towards the questions Mussolini had raised at Lausanne and which had been so crudely dismissed by Curzon, so much the better.

But the reaction from all quarters was not such to encourage him further along these lines. Within four days the Embassy in London was instructed to soothe the press and within another week the Ambassador himself instructed to ask whether the British government had received the rumour of an anti-British bloc 'with all the incredibility it deserved'.[18] Mussolini now edged himself towards a more equidistant position. A request was sent to London to join Italy in an appeal to France and Germany and a formal offer of mediation sent to Paris.[19] Bonar Law answered phlegmatically that 'in the circumstances it was best to let events ride their course till the French became convinced of their mistake', while Poincaré remained adamant: mediation was premature and France would not withdraw her troops from the Ruhr.[20] The French leader's answer was tantamount to saying that Italy's solidarity, while still desirable, was superfluous.

In Rome the failure of mediation rallied those elements within the Consulta who judged not only that Mussolini had strayed too far from Italy's traditional pro-British policy but also that his adventures with France were downright dangerous. Their efforts at improving relations with London, supported by the British Embassy in Rome which consistently adopted a more pro-Italian attitude than the Foreign Office, ran into Curzon's just-as-consistent italophobia. In March 1923, Curzon curtly turned down an Italian proposal for joint conversations on how best to approach the military occupation of the Ruhr; in May, on the eve of the British monarch's visit to Italy, he vetoed a rather anodyne though friendly ending to the message the British king would read in Rome and in June he put an end to requests emanating from the embassy in Rome to settle the Jubaland issue in rather uncompromising tones: 'I do not believe that whatever price we pay to Italy we shall in return get her loyal support in any single question. I wholly distrust their government, from whatever party chosen.'[21] Curzon's mistrust stemmed partly from his suspicions that Mussolini was intriguing with certain Indian revolutionaries to 'ultimately drive the British out of India' (though in retrospect it is difficult to see how he could have credited Mussolini with serious political designs on the stability of India), but more fundamentally from his failure to secure the Dodecanese for Greece.[22]

The Corfu Incident

Italy's continued possession of the Dodecanese played a prominent part in the next international incident of fascist inspiration, the seizure of the Greek island of Corfu. The incident began with the murder on Greek soil on 27 August 1923 of the Italian general and his staff engaged in the delimitation of the Greek–Albanian frontier on behalf of the Boundary Commission, an organ of the inter-allied Ambassadors' Conference of 1921, the body which continued the functions of the Allied Supreme War Council. It escalated rapidly when the Italian government sent its fleet to occupy the Greek island of Corfu. The occupation could have been interpreted as an attempt by Italy to strengthen her demands for compensation from Greece or else as an attempt to occupy permanently the strategic island guarding the south entrance of the Adriatic, thus turning that sea into an Italian lake.

The second interpretation appeared the more likely. It had been expected in Italian Navy circles that the formal transferral to Italy of the Dodecanese, which took place at the end of July 1923 upon ratification of the Treaty of Lausanne, would cause political difficulties with Greece. At that time Mussolini, who wanted to despatch a naval squadron to take possession of the islands, had been barely restrained and the formal transferral of authority carried out by more orthodox means.[23] None the less, contingency plans had been made by the Italian Navy at this time for the eventual occupation of Corfu (the plans to be ready before the end of August) as a coercive measure against the anticipated Greek protests or refusals. Three squadrons were assigned to the task, one to occupy the island, the other to seal off the area and the third to be stationed in the Aegean Sea to threaten Athens.[24] In effect, a month before the murder of an Italian general provided a convenient pretext, the Italian Navy was preparing for the occupation of Corfu. The navy's contingency plans explain the speed with which the occupation was mounted, the availability of a sizeable contingent of troops on the shortest of orders, the state of alert in the Italian bases opposite Corfu – in sum they confirm the expectation that the island would be occupied. They do not explain, however, the circumstances surrounding the murder nor do they support allegations that it was organised with the connivance of Rome.

Mussolini's reaction upon hearing of the murder, on 28 August, was to order the occupation of Corfu at once. He was held back for a few days by the hope that the British and French governments would associate themselves in a protest to Greece, since the murdered general, though an Italian national, was discharging an inter-allied function. And in fact the Conference of Ambassadors on 31 August duly registered a protest with the Greek government, demanding an enquiry and reserving all rights of sanctions and reparations. But Mussolini in the meantime had gone much further. On 29 August, an ultimatum was delivered to Athens which in the harshness of its demands raised memories of another ultimatum nine years earlier. The Italian government demanded a formal apology from the highest Greek military authorities, a solemn funeral to be attended by the entire Greek government, honours to the Italian flag on the part of the Greek fleet, an enquiry into the murder to be completed within five days, with the participation of the Italian military attaché, the death penalty for those responsible, an indemnity of 50 million lire to be paid within five days and military honours to the bodies at the point of embarkation for Italy.[25]

The Greek answer, received within the twenty-four hours stipulated by the ultimatum, accepted to pay the requisite military honours but disclaimed responsibility for the murder and hence for the indemnity. It did, however, promise to pay the families adequate compensation, the sum to be determined by the League.[26] This reply being deemed unsatisfactory, Mussolini ordered the military occupation of Corfu by a naval squadron which arrived on the island in the late afternoon of the 31st. When the island's prefect refused to hand over authority, the officer commanding, exceeding his instructions to use force only to put down armed resistance, opened fire on the island, killing a number of civilians.[27] The result was predictable – the murders which touched off the incident fell into the background while world opinion unanimously condemned the excessive violence of Italy's reprisals.

The incident now assumed larger proportions. Not only did it become a test case for the League, since Greece immediately took the matter to the Council, alleging an act of war encompassing sanctions under Articles XII and XV; but also, since Mussolini refused to evacuate the islands until the manifestly difficult condition was fulfilled that those responsible for the murder be caught and punished, the likelihood of a permanent occupation raised the question of the balance of power in the Mediterranean and as such affected all the major European states. Nor did Mussolini take any steps to allay suspicions that he was putting forth conditions to retain the island permanently. He let it be known that rather than admit the competence of the League in a matter of national honour, he would leave the 'Ango–French *diet*'. At the same time he appointed an Italian governor for Corfu, landed an army division to occupy the island, issued a special series of stamps, began construction of a military base and had the Italian fleet mass opposite Greece. The Italian press made pointed references to the 400 years of Venetian rule over Corfu and generally hailed the government's intransigence as the first exclusively fascist step in foreign policy.

Mussolini's stand was particularly firm over the issue of the competence of the League and this brought him into direct conflict with the British government, which on 1 September had decided to uphold the Covenant and was permitting to go unchallenged press reports that the British fleet might be put at the disposal of the League. Mussolini argued essentially that the murders on Greek territory, after a Greek press campaign exciting the populace against Italy, were an outrage which affected national honour and prestige, two matters outside the competence of the

League. Furthermore, though Greece was a member of the League, its government was not recognised by any League member. Nor had the League sought to intervene in the much more serious Greek–Turkish conflict. He was prepared at most to accept an inquiry under the auspices of the Conference of Ambassadors.

The confrontation between Italy and Britain was short-lived. Curzon, grumbling that he knew 'of no article in the Covenant which provided for such a refusal on the plea of honour',[28] was none the less forced to acknowledge within days that without French support not much could be done to persuade Italy to bring the dispute before the Council of the League. No French support was forthcoming, not because Paris approved of Italy's installation in Corfu, which tended to raise rather acutely the question of influence in the Balkans, but because admitting the jurisdiction of the League in this matter might well open the door to the League in the matter of occupation of the Ruhr. A compromise was worked out in Geneva to harmonise Italy's request that the incident be treated by the Conference of Ambassadors with Britain's request that the Council of the League deal with an alleged breach of the Covenant: the Council sent a note to the Conference of Ambassadors asking to be kept informed of the latter's deliberations and at the same time forwarded the minutes of the Council meeting where the majority (but excluding France and Italy) had made recommendations for the settlement of the dispute. The compromise was the result of adroit manoeuvring on the part of the Italian Ambassador in Paris and Poincaré. In effect the Italian demands for reparations and an enquiry were now to be extended and conducted on behalf of the Conference, whose officer the murdered general had been. The compromise was acceptable in so far as it saved Italy's and Greece's prestige, safeguarded French interests and warded off the possibility of a naval clash involving British units. But stubbornly Mussolini still refused to evacuate Corfu. Despite the grandiloquent emphasis on honour, reparations and an enquiry, there could be little doubt of his intention to attempt to retain the island permanently. Accordingly, while accepting the compromise formula, he insisted that evacuation would take place only after the apprehension and punishment of the murderers, by now a manifestly unfulfilled condition whose intent was the permanent occupation of Corfu. A half-hearted threat by the British Ambassador to return the matter to the League had no visible effect[29] so long as the Italian and French members of the Conference of Ambassadors were prodding the matter along towards a settlement favourable to Italy. What probably persuaded Mussolini finally to accept 27 September as the day of evacuation were two documents, submitted by the Italian Navy in mid-September, which looked upon the possibility of a war with Britain with distinct disfavour.[30]

The incident was over and not surprisingly it came to be seen by the fascist press as incontrovertible proof of fascist Italy's new strength: the reparations and honour were duly paid and the League successfully defied. But in Mussolini's eyes the incident must have appeared otherwise. If his intention had been to alter drastically the Adriatic balance of power as a preparation for further encroachment in the Balkans, the evacuation could only be at best a strategic retreat, at worst an humiliation. This is certainly the way he chose to look upon it in 1940, just before ordering the disastrous attack on Greece when he recalled the unsettled score of 1923. Nor could he have drawn much personal satisfaction from what was generally seen as an unequal contest between a great power and a small country which had barely survived a catastrophic war. True, he had defied the League, but this aspect of the incident always carried much less weight with him than those supporters of Geneva, contemporary and posthumous, who later came to look upon the invasion of Corfu as a dress rehearsal for the invasion of Abyssinia. Never having shared the Anglo–Saxon doctrine of the harmony of interests which underpinned the Covenant, he did not regard the League, as he told the British Ambassador at the time, either with much friendliness or exaggerated respect.[31] At best it was a new vehicle for carrying out the old-fashioned business of power politics and his attraction to it was directly commensurate with the share which Italy had in the running of it.

The Corfu incident had served to underline to Italy and Britain the importance of Italy's possession of the Dodecanese. Though both countries had presently shied away from a naval confrontation, they remained uneasy about the ultimate future of the Aegean islands – Italy because her possession of them, of dubious advantage in a military confrontation with a great power, at the same time stood in the way of a settlement of the Jubaland issue;

Britain because the Corfu incident had spotlighted the dangers of safeguarding her interests in the Mediterranean and Greece while dealing from a position of weakness. Thus the incident probably contributed to the eventual settlement of the Jubaland question in 1924 when the new Labour government in Britain decided to separate it from the question of the Dodecanese, though still holding that Italy was morally, if not legally, bound to restore the islands to Greece. Ramsay MacDonald's decision came as a boon to Mussolini, for the Italian leader, once his country's legal title to the islands had been confirmed, might have been disposed to bargain some way. In the last days of the Conservative government, Della Torretta, the Italian Ambassador in London, had explored with Curzon a procedure in three steps to settle both matters permanently. Britain would first admit that all twelve islands were Italian possessions *de jure* as well as *de facto* so that the cession of any of them to Greece could be represented to public opinion as an act of spontaneous generosity and the foundation of more amicable relations with Greece. Then an understanding would be struck with Britain that Italy would retain Rhodes, Leros and Cos and restore the other nine to Greece. Simultaneously, Curzon would offer a more convenient arrangement regarding watering wells and nomadic tribes in the area of Jubaland to be ceded to Italy. Mussolini, for his part, though ill disposed towards it, had not formally turned down some such arrangement and might have negotiated on the basis of it when the fall of the Conservative government ended these discussions.[32] When the issue was revived by MacDonald a few months later it was on terms much more favourable to Italy. Mussolini easily assented to MacDonald's proposal to separate the two issues,[33] and the Jubaland cession was settled substantially on the lines of the Milner–Scialoja agreements of 1919–20 on 7 June 1924. This much accomplished, Mussolini felt he could be generous on the Dodecanese and informal conversations began on the best way to cede some of the islands to Greece. But at this point the Greek government also changed its attitude. It decided that it would be preferable for Italy to annex all the islands provided local autonomy were granted to maintain their Greek character, rather than they should be split up and those annexed by Italy definitely Italianised. Negotiations with Greece along these lines continued sporadically for the next few years. They eventually came to naught when it proved impossible to compromise the Dodecanesians' request that their autonomy be guaranteed by the League of Nations with Italy's distaste for that organisation. The Dodecanese came to be administered like a recalcitrant colony by a series of more or less heavy-handed governors.

Towards Locarno

The failure to hold Corfu and the successes in the Jubaland and the Dodecanese were due, in the last resort, not to the merits of the local issues but to the attitudes adopted by France and Great Britain. The successful defiance of the League in September 1923 had depended in no small measure on French support. Conversely, Mussolini's declaration of opposition in November of that year to any further occupation of German territory had served to remove Britain's suspicions that Italy had committed herself to France permanently on the German question and had paved the way for the accommodation over Jubaland. Those incidents laid bare, on the one hand, the traditional quandary of Italian (fascist or other-wise) foreign policy – the limited degree to which Italy could deviate from the coalition of which it was a member – and, on the other, the degree to which this quandary had been exacerbated by the failure of the peace conference to separate the problem of the balance of power in Europe from the problem of the liquidation of the spoils. The kindest verdict possible on Mussolini's behaviour during this period was that his preoccupation with the liquidation of the spoils prevented Italy from paying closer attention to larger and more important problems. The way in which the issue posed itself in 1924-5 was how far an allegedly dynamic, nationalistic and essentially dissatisfied Italy could afford to ignore strictly Italian claims to follow the lead of the two satisfied members of the *Entente* in such attempts to stabilise the existing configuration of power as the Geneva protocol and the Locarno agreements.

The political and territorial stability of Europe after 1919 derived from the power relationship established with the defeat of the Central Powers. Their maintenance depended in turn on the stability of the winning coalition. In Italian eyes it was indispens-able to that stability that Italy's claims at a minimum take prece-dence over such abstract rights as self-determination. On this point there was no essential disagreement between pre- and post-fascist Italy, merely a question of which tactics could bring the *Entente* to this realisation. But France and Britain in their quest for an American guarantee had shown an exaggerated respect for Wilsonian principles and overlooked the need for greater comprehension of the Italian position despite the important contribution which a satisfied Italy could make to the stability of the peace settlement and the containment of Germany. The result was that in Italy the aftermath of the war, down to the voluntary acceptance of the verdict of Versailles by Germany in 1925 at Locarno, came to be seen as a series of undeserved frustrations made more noxious by sanctimonious references in Britain and, to a lesser degree, in France to principles such as self-determination which London and Paris did not fail to invoke against others but would not apply themselves. It was in this sense that the Locarno agreements to stabilise and guarantee the frontiers between Germany, France and Belgium were a turning-point in Italian policy. For those agreements were concluded almost in spite of Italy since they signified the end of the wartime *Entente* and hence, in a practical sense, shut the door on Italy's claims arising from the war. That the claims persisted while no longer subject to negotiations exclusively within the winning coalition serves to explain the exasperation with which they were pursued by a fascist government one of whose major pretensions to popular allegiance rested in its determination to achieve for Italy a rightful place among the great powers.

The tension between the essential thrust of fascist foreign policy and the requirements of the situation created an ambivalence which in turn was reinforced, first, by the domestic crisis in the second half of 1924 after the murder by fascist thugs of the socialist deputy Matteotti and second by an elementary prudence which took over after the excesses of Corfu. The latter produced in short order friendship pacts with Yugoslavia and Czechoslovakia, the recognition of the Soviet Union and some initial support of the Geneva Protocol. These steps could be seen either as a prelude to a policy of collaboration or else as an attempt to pre-empt French influence in the Balkans and undermine the Little *Entente*. If Mussolini in the circumstances accredited the first thesis it could not be denied that the second found a larger echo in the fascist press and corresponded more closely to the aspirations of the government. A case in point was the attitude towards the Geneva Protocol. It was not so much a question of Italy objecting to the formulae of arbitration, security and disarmament, as much as the fact that the protocol was seen in Rome as the device which, after healing the split between Britain and France, would lay the groundwork for an Anglo–French directorate in European affairs from which Italy would be excluded. Rome had had too much experience since the war with a united England and France not to fear for her freedom of action. Whatever successes Italian policy had achieved in the previous five years had been due in no small part to Rome's ability to obtain either French or British backing. The protocol raised once again the spectre of isolation and it was with some relief that Mussolini welcomed the return to power in Britain in October 1924 of a Conservative government under Baldwin – with Austen Chamberlain at the Foreign Office – which shared the Conservatives' traditional suspicions of French designs in Europe and looked to Italy as a reliable counter. Chamberlain's decision to visit Rome in early December 1924, aside from being a notable boost for Mussolini at the time of his greatest domestic danger (Lady Chamberlain prominently displayed a fascist pin), brought the end of the Protocol and laid the groundwork for a realignment of Italian policy in London. In the midst of his conversations with Mussolini, Chamberlain asked publicly for a postponement of the Protocol's ratification until March of the following year. Mussolini, by now certain of London's attitude, went farther; in a speech before the Senate he all but announced that Italy would not be a party. And when, on 12 March 1925, Chamberlain formally announced his government's opposition to the Protocol, Mussolini readily announced his satisfaction at its demise.[34]

By the spring of 1925, the internal crisis overcome and the spectre of external isolation reduced to a scarecrow, Mussolini assessed the implications of the previous year's events. On the one hand, Italian policy should not provoke exclusion from any action affecting the fundamental structure of Europe; on the other, Italy's participation should be subordinated to receiving satisfaction for claims arising out of the war. In the circumstances this meant reliance on Britain, the country which had lately shown greater understanding in Africa and had the least interest in Eastern Europe, an important consideration if Italy's policy in the Balkans was likely to lead to a collision with France. It was this order of thinking which led Mussolini to go along with Britain as a guarantor of the Rhine frontier, passing over, on the one hand, London's indiscretions over *Anschluss,* a union between Austria and Germany, and on the other, a generous French offer 'to regard the line running from the Rhine to the Adriatic as a single frontier'.[35]

The French offer had been occasioned by the discussions for the western security pact eventually concluded at Locarno in October 1925. In January of that year Berlin had offered Paris a treaty, to be guaranteed by Italy and Britain, covering the Rhine frontier. Two fundamental points had emerged in the initial discussions: Britain's strong reluctance to add Germany's frontier with Austria to the boundaries under guarantee and France's converse desire to include all German boundaries under an international agreement. Hence the offer to Italy.

It might have been expected that Mussolini, always very sensitive about the Brenner and often paranoid about the possibility of an *Anschluss,* would have welcomed the offer.[36] It was after all inescapable, once the Rhine frontier was pacified and Germany's eastern borders settled, at least on paper, by the arbitration and guarantee treaties concluded between Germany, France, Poland and Czechoslovakia, that the post-war frontier most exposed to German irredentism had to be the southern one with Austria. It raised the possibility that if Austria and Germany were united the bulk of German power would come to bear on Italy, negating the value of Austria as a buffer state between Italy and Germany and raising in acute form the question of German-speaking minorities in Italy. For strategic reasons the Austro–Italian border had been set at the Brenner, a decision which handed to Italy the fate of more than 200,000 German-speaking people in the Sud Tyrol, now called the Alto Adige. These people had been subject to a shameful campaign of denationalisation and whilst Austria was too weak to mitigate Italian harshness, it was taken for granted that a greater Germany on the Brenner after *Anschluss* with Austria would both pose a strategic threat to Italy, nullifying the major achievement of the war, and be far less lenient on the mistreatment of its own race. That Mussolini, despite these compelling reasons, did not openly and readily accept the French offer was probably a measure of his anti-French sentiments, since immediately it became clear in May 1925 that Germany had designs on Austria, he changed his mind. An official Italian protest in Berlin over a virulent press campaign in Germany against the forced Italianisation of the Alto Adige, had elicited the answer from Stresemann that since 'German public opinion was unanimous in its request for Union', it would behove Italy to get accustomed to the idea of either *Anschluss* or a Danubian federation. 'It was up to Italy to decide which solution it preferred', Stresemann suggested, 'and whether it was worth Italy's while to oppose the almost unanimous desire of the Germans in the Reich to join to their state seven million brothers.'[37] Stresemann's language, altogether too strong not to have been the result of prior consultation (if no more) with Britain, provoked Mussolini into denouncing publicly and in no uncertain terms German aspirations for an *Anschluss*, as much for London's benefit as for Berlin's. And then for the first time he coupled the negotiations for the western security pact with Italy's interest in the continued independence of Austria. 'Gentlemen', he declared before the Senate on 20 May, 'not only must the Rhine frontier be guaranteed but that of the Brenner also.'[38]

But his outburst had no consequences. With the exception of this short-lived incident, which pointedly underlined the co-incidence of Italian and French interests in the permanence of the existing German frontiers, Mussolini stubbornly refused to accede to French requests to bring all frontiers under a single guarantee. His refusal was probably also due (aside from a general reluctance to strengthen the position of France) to the fact that, as has been suggested, Stresemann and Mussolini thereafter reached a tacit stand-off over Austria – the German leader understanding that his pursuit of an *Anschluss* could instead result in a new international affirmation of Italy's Brenner frontier and of the inadmissibility of union; the Italian leader fearing that his pursuit of an international guarantee would necessarily have to be paid by weakening the existing international sanctions against *Anschluss*.[39]

After Mussolini's outburst, Stresemann appreciated also that raising the question of the *Anschluss* might compromise the entire negotiation for a security pact and therefore took steps to place that contentious issue in cold storage by assuring Rome in a formal manner that 'it was not Germany's intention to raise the question in connection with the guarantee pact'.[40]

Mussolini's decision to do likewise and ignore France's overtures was probably short-sighted. Stresemann's declaration, far from abjuring the *Anschluss*, merely deferred it to some future time. But Mussolini must have decided that the indefinite post-ponement of the issue would strengthen, not weaken, his position *vis-à-vis* France. So long as the Brenner frontier was adequately protected by existing international agreements, Mussolini must have reckoned that if France was willing to pay for Italian partici-pation in the Rhine pact, the price had to be found in Africa in the fulfilment on the part of France of the provisions of the Treaty of London. By adopting this stance, Mussolini unfortunately went a long way towards developing those attitudes which, on the one hand, gradually lessened the determination of the western powers to defend the independence of Austria and, on the other, fore-shadowed a later Italo–German deal by which a guarantee of the Brenner frontier was traded against the *Anschluss*. In the context of 1925, his shortsightedness meant that France's repeated offers[41] to give Italy all the guarantees she cared to ask for would be turned down with temporary impunity on the pretext that France was offering no real concession, inasmuch as it was more in her interest than in Italy's that Austria's frontiers be inviolate, since if they were breached the weight of Germany would be directed not south but westward 'in her historical and fundamental conflict with France'.[42] It must be noted, though, that Mussolini's opposition was not directed to the Brenner guarantee *per se* but to its extension by France unilaterally and, in Italian eyes, somewhat haughtily. On the Duce's instructions, the Italian delegate to the League enter-tained Chamberlain on the importance of guaranteeing all borders and only after the Foreign Secretary had made abundantly clear Britain's refusal to go beyond the Rhine – Chamberlain viewed the *Anschluss* as a remote possibility while he set store in a directorate of the four European great powers as the key to European peace – did Mussolini order his ambassadors to try to exact from France a price for the privilege of guaranteeing Italy's border with Austria.[43] Otherwise, their instructions were to adopt a cautious wait-and-see attitude.

In the meantime negotiations for the security pact were con-tinuing without the participation of Italy. Mussolini's refusal to take part in them alarmed the permanent officials at Palazzo Chigi. Admittedly the proposed security pact acknowledged implicitly that the wartime coalition had come to an end but it also promised important political prizes. The fact that Italy (alongside Britain) would become an arbiter between France and Germany on the

Rhine offered the important advantage that in practice the success of the new arrangement would depend on the attitude the Italian government would adopt in the case of violation. Their advice to Mussolini was against trying to bargain membership in the proposed pact in exchange for a multilateral guarantee of the Brenner but rather to accede to the present arrangements. Mussolini's ambitions were wider. 'How can we use France to solve the major problems which interest us in Europe and outside?' he inquired again of his Ambassador in Paris in September.[44] Briand's answer – that, in exchange for 'a declaration by which the two nations pledged not to permit any modification of the *status quo*', the French government 'would well understand the necessity of eliminating all causes of attrition . . . and would therefore review the question of Tunis . . . Tangiers . . . and the African colonial mandates'[45] – was probably instrumental in persuading Mussolini to accept the security pact and to attend, along with the British, French, German and Belgian leaders, its signature at Locarno on 16 October. Briand's communication must have appeared to Mussolini as a belated recognition by France of Italy's extra-European claims, an answer to the question which Mussolini had put to Paris as early as 30 April 1925. 'Before Italy could collaborate in the peaceful reconstruction of Europe,' Mussolini had stipulated at that time, 'she would have to be able to assure to her growing population convenient outlets and supplies of raw materials. . . . It is therefore indispensable to take into consideration our aspirations for a colonial dominion in Africa susceptible of demographic and economic development.'[46] But in fact, Briand's pliant answer was probably no more than a device to secure Italy's prompt signature on the Locarno agreements. France continued to ignore Italy's colonial aspirations just as Mussolini continued to ignore France's search for security. The Italian leader's pursuit of colonial satisfactions thus led him to negate the importance of France's offer of a guarantee on the Brenner in exchange for an Italian guarantee on the Rhine – an eminently sensible bargain (as he was to recognise in 1935) and one which a statesman of the pre-fascist period brought up on the need to subordinate Italy's colonial expansion to her security in Europe would have had no hesitation in accepting. In effect both countries persisted in denying their common interests, France insisting the Brenner was essentially an Italian problem to whose security she was willing to contribute only in exchange for a parallel Italian commitment on the Rhine, and Italy insisting the Rhine was a European problem which did not prejudice her claims to compensation elsewhere. The inevitable consequence of such mutual shortsightedness was that both parties, until too late, wilfully ignored the nature of their real interests *vis-à-vis* Germany. Both, above all, failed to understand that if Locarno was to have any meaning beyond the temporary and contingent jockeying for position, that meaning had to derive from co-operation between the guaranteed countries – France and Germany – rather than from the co-operation of the guarantors, Britain and Italy. French suspicions of German policy on the one hand and Italian suspicion of French policy on the other conspired instead to ensure that Locarno, both in the larger sense and in the narrower context of Italo–French relations, would amount to little more than a truce.

With Britain, as the logic of this interpretation of the Locarno pacts would have it, the security arrangements on the Rhine became the foundation for a bond which lasted practically until Italian and British interests clashed in Abyssinia in 1935. Mussolini's adhesion to Locarno was received with great satisfaction in London. Chamberlain's admiration for Mussolini was reciprocated and the two got along very well until the end of the Conservative administration in 1929. Chamberlain showed himself inordinately understanding over Italian ambitions in Albania and elsewhere and not a little impressed with the vigour with which Mussolini disposed equally of liberal democracy and left-wing agitation, an attitude shared with more or less condescension by the Foreign Office.[47] At the end of 1925, Chamberlain ceded to Italy the Jarabub on the border between Libya and Egypt and revived the Anglo–Franco–Italian agreement of 1906 on Abyssinia, generally thought no longer to apply after Abyssinia's entry into the League as a sovereign state in 1923. Since the 1906 treaty defined the spheres of influence of the three powers in Abyssinia, in particular recognising Italy's claim to influence over large parts of that country, its revival laid the basis for Italy's future pretensions there. The protests of the Abyssinian government to the League Council were airily dismissed in London and Rome on the grounds that Abyssinia was free to decide whether or not she would grant those concessions on her territory which Britain and Italy were free to grant one another. Chamberlain visited Mussolini three times in less than two years, each visit reinforcing the feeling that the two men could do business with one another – Chamberlain glad to accommodate Italy in a policy he believed would gradually lead to the normalisation of European relations in the spirit of Locarno, Mussolini glad to have his support to avoid the isolation implicit in a forward policy in the Balkans bound to conflict with French and, in the long run, with German interests.

The *Entente* with Britain, to be sure, was an important by-product of Locarno. But of greater relevance to future Italian policy was the fact that Locarno modified the framework within which Italy pursued the settlement of the claims still outstanding from the war. Before the signature of the security pact, the attempt to reach a settlement had been conducted, so to speak, *en famille,* within the winning coalition. Admittedly this necessitated from time to time the support of one *Entente* member against the other and the exploitation of a divergence of views in London and Paris. But essentially, the problem of winding up the settlement of the war had been perceived as a task which belonged properly to the members of the *Entente*. After Locarno, this was no longer the case. The *Entente* had reached a settlement with the major enemy without first granting satisfaction to one of its own. The result was to stimulate the resumption of Italy's traditional policy of equidistance, a policy suited to the weakest of the major powers and requiring Italy to make unpredictable alterations in allegiance within the concert of the great powers at the same time that it increased the scope for independent mischief in areas, such as Eastern Europe, still vulnerable to interference by the great powers. In practice, however, the attempt at equidistance became increasingly difficult to sustain because of a double polarisation which took place in European politics in the next few years. The first polarisation was political. Europe came to be divided between those countries which supported the territorial *status quo* decreed at Versailles and those which challenged it, leaving little room (or sympathy) for a country trying to balance between the two camps. And since Italy's claims were aimed at the satisfied, *status quo*, former allies, the country came to militate more and more in the camp of the revisionists. The second polarisation was ideological: Europe came to be divided between totalitarian régimes and liberal democratic régimes. Again Italy, the prototype of the right-wing dictatorships, found itself opposite its former allies. The overall result was that the traditional pursuance of claims, power and influence came to operate in a novel environment fraught with mutual misperceptions and daily less susceptible to traditional diplomatic adjustments.

The change was first marked in the structures of the Italian state. By 1926, Mussolini had consolidated his hold over internal and external policy. No longer in need of the co-operation of the old liberal elements, he moved quickly to remove the vestiges of democracy and turn Italy into a totalitarian state. In external policy, he had suffered the tutelage of Contarini and the career diplomats only so long as they smoothed his first steps in foreign policy. By the beginning of 1926 Contarini himself was looking for a way out. His resignation in March after the fiasco of the Danubian *Entente* and the resumption of a hard-line policy towards Yugoslavia marked the beginning of the 'fascistisation' of the old Italian Foreign Office. Dino Grandi, one of the leaders of the march on Rome, had already been appointed Under-Secretary for Foreign Affairs. Romano Avezzana, Della Toretta and De Bosdari, holders of the three major embassies, submitted their resignations early in 1927. In 1928 a number of fascists were admitted into the diplomatic service without the benefit of the customary examinations. These 'twenty-eighters', as they were called, were initially relegated to the consular corps, but as the influence of the party became all-pervasive in domestic life, so did their influence increase at Palazzo Chigi. Their takeover was aided by the suppression shortly after the resignation of Contarini of the position of Secretary-General – the office which had provided the element of stability and continuity between the permanent career diplomats and their political chiefs. Henceforth, power became concentrated in the political side of the Ministry of External Affairs.

Mussolini had suffered the tutelage of the career diplomats with bad grace and had often by-passed the formal machinery of the department. He was obviously impatient with traditional diplomacy, but this was not his major failing. The fault lay deeper. Unsophisticated in his attitude towards relations among states, he substituted a strategy for a policy. To define a policy is to define an end; to define a strategy is to define means. His emphasis on means, in fascist parlance on 'action', packed together ends and means in semantic imprecision until the means, the acquisition of strength, became an end in itself. The confusion was fostered by both Mussolini and the party organs. Hidden behind the façade of totalitarian solidarity, the complex of forces which had brought Mussolini to power continued to vie for position. After the Matteotti incident and after the inception of the dictatorship, Mussolini faced challenges both from the conservative-nationalist wing of his movement, which had eased him into power, and from the extremist wing, whose extra-legal *squadrismo* had created the context for the fascist revolution but now saw itself betrayed by its legality.[48] Mussolini's solution (in the tradition of Giolittian transformism and yet remarkably consistent with Mussolini's own intellectual premises) was first to attempt to dissolve the opposition within the party and second to attempt to dissolve the party within the state – to transform fascism into the fascist régime. Neither synthesis really worked. Both required from time to time outlandish affirmations and demonstrations of support for one or other of several currents. His declaration to the Chamber at the end of 1925 that he personally considered 'the Italian nation in a permanent state of war' and his affirmation at the beginning of the next year that 'the fascist revolution will have in 1926 its Napoleonic year' were of a piece with later boasts of 'eight million bayonets' and an air force which would darken the sky. They tended to cloud, in Italy as much as outside, the fact that the Italian nation had in the Mediterranean, in the Balkans and in Africa legitimate aspirations which were susceptible to diplomatic adjustments. At the moment the rhetoric of the régime became identified with a statement of ends, Italian policy became the prisoner of that rhetoric.

Chapter 10

Italo–French Relations after Locarno

I am a great friend and admirer of Italy.
Briand, 1932

All in all, no accommodation proved possible between Italy and France in the 1920s. In Italy this indeterminate state of affairs was seen more and more as a haughty and deliberate refusal to acknowledge Italy's great-power status, a refusal accentuated by the rather uninhibited French press and the traditional and, in some cases, excessive French hospitality to political refugees. In France attempts at closer relations were not made any easier by fascist boasts that Italy would rather draw closer to former adversaries than to the ungrateful ally nor by the use made by fascist publicists of France as the model of the decadent liberal bourgeois régime they were trying to eradicate in Italy; for their part, of course, French spokesmen delighted in extolling these very qualities and giving them practical application by welcoming political refugees from across the Alps and opening their newspapers and presses to them.

But it had not been fore-ordained that Italy and France should end up as rivals in the aftermath of the war. The identity of their interests should have made them allies. Both were partly dissatisfied with the peace settlement: France had been unable to dispose permanently of the German problem, Italy of her Adriatic and colonial problems; both none the less shared an interest in maintaining the configuration of power decided at Versailles since the prospect of change was bound to work to their disadvantages: a resurgent Germany would threaten France on the Rhine, Italy at the Brenner, both in Eastern Europe. And yet, even before the coming to power of Mussolini exacerbated relations, their long-range interests had given way before the particularism of immediate problems. France early won Italy's thorough dislike for her championship of Yugoslav claims in the Adriatic and her refusal

to honour Italy's claims under Article XIII of the Treaty of
London for a rectification of her Libyan frontier. Those two causes
of friction served effectively to hide the mutuality of their interest
against Germany. France had no obsession greater than security;
Mussolini none higher than grandeur and expansion. The French
system rested on the Locarno pact in the west and the alliances and
ententes with Poland, Czechoslovakia, Romania and Yugoslavia in
the east, a makeshift adaptation of France's traditional policy of
alliance with the power in Germany's rear. So long as Italy's
policy in Eastern Europe kept to the spirit of the 1924 treaty with
Yugoslavia, no incompatibility existed. But Mussolini's policy
after 1926 not only began to threaten the Yugoslav fulcrum
(though the Yugoslavs were not blameless). By its none-too-subtle
advances towards the extremists in Germany, Austria and Hungary
and by the obstacles it seemed to be putting in the way of a
Franco–German *rapprochement,* it had the further demerit of easing
the path of German resurgence. At the same time the electoral
victory of the French Left had brought to power those forces most
opposed to fascism on ideological grounds. The Matteotti murder,
the progression towards dictatorship and the ever growing number
of political refugees compounded the difficulties. Fascist *agents
provocateurs* did not hesitate to infiltrate the ranks of the legitimate
refugees and to compromise them in French eyes as well as discredit further the French government in Italian eyes.

This last issue was indeed a serious one, given the extreme
sensibility of the fascist régime to real or imagined slights, and
there were several instances when promising diplomatic initiatives
were brought to a sudden halt by imprudent remarks or untimely
demonstrations on either side of the border. But ultimately closer
control over the activities of the Italian political refugees in France
was well within the capacity of the French authorities, just as the
fascist mobs could be made and unmade on order from Rome. The
refugee problem was a symptom, albeit an increasingly unmanageable one, of the ideological gulf between fascism and French
democracy and of Italy's profound dissatisfaction, self-consciously
fanned by fascism, with the colonial settlement of Versailles.
Mussolini's stock-in-trade was that Italy had been denied the fruits
of victory; his style was to emphasise Italy's need for expansion,
her new virility, her growing power and her irrepressible will to
solve problems in 'fascist style'.

In themselves none of the problems separating the two countries were beyond solution; they added up to a formidable list only when legitimate diplomatic disputes susceptible to normal diplomatic adjustments became inextricably compounded with internal misperceptions susceptible only to the kind of domestic interference neither government could tolerate. The misperceptions manifested themselves in what came to be called a French 'superiority complex', an inability and a reluctance to take Italy seriously as a great power with aspirations and ambitions no less legitimate than France's own. On the Italian side, they manifested themselves in the form of crude attempts at gunboat diplomacy and sometimes in exaggerated advances towards Germany. Thus the arbitration treaty between Italy and Germany of 1926, a normal statement of mutual goodwill no different from a plethora of others, was deliberately misrepresented by the fascist press as the first step towards a political *entente*. After the arbitration treaty, *Gerarchia* exaggerated for the benefit of France that 'the brotherhood of arms between Italy and France is . . . now lost. . . . Italy has now returned to her traditional continental ties with Germany on the continent and with England in the Mediterranean.'[1] *Gerarchia's* silliness became the occasion for a violent public speech by the governor-general of Algeria, in which he stressed the importance of preventing an Italo–German *rapprochement*. The indignation caused in Italy by the speech was still further increased by the murder, almost immediately after, of the Italian vice-consul in Paris by an Italian political refugee. Virulent press attacks were launched against France for giving a free hand to political terrorists whose avowed object was to overthrow the fascist government. And on the occasion of the fifth anniversary of the march on Rome, Mussolini celebrated in a manner all too reminiscent of William II by dispatching a naval squadron to Tangiers as a symbol of Italy's power in the Mediterranean and her unfulfilled claims for a share in the administration of that city.[2]

None the less, despite these difficulties, attempts were made to put relations on a better footing. The really contentious issues were the compensation due to Italy in Libya under Article XIII of the Treaty of London, the question of mandates, and the anomalous position of about 100,000 Italians in Tunisia (more than twice the number of French settlers in the French colony), at least half of them born there, yet by virtue of the 1896 convention Italian citizens. On the last question Italy wanted the continuation of the convention (already denounced by France in 1918 and since then renewed regularly for three-month periods at Italian request) while France, in response to the demands of public opinion, was quite determined to terminate it by law and issued decrees in 1921 (though they were not applied in deference to the small British colony in Tunisia) for the imposition of French nationality on foreigners born on its territory. With regard to the mandates, the problem had lately been made more acute by the publicity attached to a statement by Austen Chamberlain to the German delegation at the time of the signature of the Locarno treaties that Germany, upon admission to the League of Nations, would be a candidate for colonial mandates like all other members of the League. If one were available, Mussolini asked, would the French government favour it being conferred on Italy? The French reply (concurred in by Britain) was not such as to stimulate friendship: France declined to admit the possibility of a redistribution of mandates; the best it could offer was some vague assurance that in the unlikely event of a new mandate becoming available the ex-Allies would give preference to one of their number rather than the ex-enemy.

Still, the major problem was the compensation due to Italy under the Treaty of London. A Franco–Italian agreement signed in 1919 and ratified by both parties in 1923 had provided for the cession to Italy of several oases on the frontier between Tunisia and Libya as well as the cession of a further region including certain caravan routes; but this settlement had never been regarded by Italy as final. Rome maintained that the Anglo–French agreement of 1899, which defined the boundaries of France's African possessions and which was recognised by Italy in 1902, did not apply to the regions formerly under Turkish occupation and that Italy, as the successor to Turkey in these regions, had the right to penetrate southward to the limits of the former Turkish occupation as far as Lake Chad. The question now was whether Italy's quest for compensation and a colonial empire could be squared with France's passionate search for stability and security in Europe. It was this kind of bargain which had been suggested in 1925 and had lured Mussolini into the Locarno negotiations, and it had been the unwillingness of the French to carry it through which had soured Italo–French relations immediately afterwards.

Perhaps more at ease after the signature of the Franco–Yugoslav

treaty of 11 November 1927, Briand had declared himself before
the French Chamber of Deputies on 30 November 'a great friend
and admirer of Italy ... ready to re-examine all proposals for a
pact of friendship and arbitration which would bring the two
countries closer together'. Mussolini replied in kind. His declarations to the press included fulsome references to the brotherhood
of Latin countries and their fundamental affinity, only temporarily
obscured by disputes 'neither serious nor insoluble but only
delicate' which the appropriate agents could now begin to unravel.[3]

The unravelling, however, turned up more difficulties. Whereas,
as the semi-official *Le Temps* indicated on 13 December 1927, the
French saw a pact of friendship as 'an excellent starting point for a
policy of active collaboration', Mussolini seemed to have in mind,
as the *Giornale d'Italia* put it on 16 December, a reversed order of
priorities – first agreement on Tangiers, Tunisia, Libya, the
Balkans, mandates and emigration and then a pact. Even allowing
for initial exuberance, it was a formidable list from which only the
question of Abyssinia and disarmament appeared missing. In
exchange Mussolini did not have a great deal to offer except
amiability and a greater comprehension of France's need for
security, expressed perhaps by some suitable military arrangement.

But in the last analysis, this was all France was hoping to get.
The bases for a bargain were there, though perhaps not on the
grand scale originally envisaged. By the time the French Ambassador, the Count de Beaumarchais, began formal negotiations with
Mussolini in March 1928, the respective positions had been defined
and understood. Fundamentally, France was being asked to view
sympathetically Italy's hopes for expansion in Africa while Italy
was required to renounce (and oppose in others) a policy inimical
to France's security in Europe – the pattern established at Locarno
and later repeated in 1935.

In 1928 it did not work. The bargain turned out to be an unequal one, for it was soon clear that France was prepared only to
nod in the direction of Italy's colonial aspirations, even though,
conversely, Mussolini was prepared to give France concrete undertakings against Germany beyond those envisaged at Locarno.

A preliminary conversation took place between Mussolini and
De Beaumarchais on 30 January 1928.[4] What distressed the Italian
leader was the nonchalance with which the French Ambassador
postponed the beginning of meaningful discussions for three

months until after Easter. Prodded by hints of Mussolini's disappointment, De Beaumarchais returned to Palazzo Venezia on 19
March with the news that Briand was now prepared to consider
either a friendship pact to be followed by the resolution of colonial
questions or, if it suited Italy, the reverse order. Mussolini opted
for the following procedure: the continuation of the 1896 convention on Tunis for another five years; the delineation of the
southern and western boundaries of Libya; recognition by France
that Italy had a prior claim on mandates; the conclusion of a pact of
friendship.[5] The crucial points were the second and third.
Mussolini was governed by a memorandum drawn up in the
Italian Foreign Office on how in the future Libya could be used as
a jumping-off point for further penetration into the Sahara with
the view eventually of reaching the Atlantic near the Gulf of
Guinea and taking possession of at least part of the ex-German
colony of Cameroon now under French mandate. The dream of an
Italian colonial empire stretching from the Mediterranean south-
west to the Atlantic could be accomplished in stages more or less
quickly according to whether the French government were prepared to grant Italy's maximum, median or minimum demands in
Libya, the natural springboard for this process, and on whether
they might share part of their mandate in the Cameroons.[6]
Mussolini rejected as impractical his advisors' maximum requests,
instructed his Ambassador in Paris to begin negotiations on the
basis of the median with a view to falling back on the minimum
proposals – but nothing else. He granted to the British Ambassador
that[7]

> the French could never allow us to reach Lake Chad or anywhere
> near it and I never dreamt of such a thing. All I am asking is that we
> should obtain Tummo which is already marked on several French
> maps as being ours, and a small oasis just south of it which contains a
> useful supply of water.

The Italian Ambassador was instructed to break off negotiations if
the French government were not prepared to go this far.[8]

As it happened on the two substantive issues the Quai d'Orsay
turned out to be essentially negative. This was partly because of the
intractability of its public opinion, partly because Manzoni had
exceeded his instructions and put forth the maximum demands in
Libya, and partly because little could be decided during the French

elections and Briand's illness.[9] In the meantime the draft treaty of friendship which the French government eventually produced in August gave the impression, Mussolini told the British Ambassador, of deliberately excluding any expression of friendship. With considerable difficulty the French government were eventually persuaded to draft new proposals including some concessions in Libya and Tunis and these were at length presented to the Italian government in December, their presentation having been delayed by a storm of anti-French protest in the Italian press after the murderer of the Italian vice-consul had been let off by the French courts with an extremely light sentence. These proposals, however, contained one crucial proviso, that the cession could only take place when Italian occupation became effective, a proviso which in fact meant the indefinite postponement of the cession since effective Italian occupation was confined to coastal areas.[10]

Not unexpectedly, these proposals, the more so since they asked Italy to abandon her whole position as regards her nationals in Tunis and to undertake to raise no objections whenever the French wished to convert the dependency into a colony, left Mussolini with the impression that the French were not sincere and were less anxious to come to terms than to place upon Italy the odium of rejecting the conditions suggested. In reply, in June 1929, Italy put forth fresh demands for tracts of territory so extensive that no French government could cede them. Reportedly, Mussolini indicated that progress on the treaty of arbitration and conciliation was dependent on French agreement to the continuance of the Franco–Italian convention of 1896 on Tunis for a minimum period of ten years without any modification. He then stated that the territorial concessions proposed by the French on the Libyan frontier were insufficient, demanding now ten times more than the 40,000 square kilometres offered by Paris.[11] Matters thus reached a complete deadlock and no further progress was possible. Mussolini was still keen to arrive at a pact with France, but only provided some major concessions were made by the other side. He took a pliant view of French stubbornness on the issue of colonial compensation, preferring to remain a creditor under Article XIII of the Treaty of London than to accept 'some kilometres of sandy desert'. In the quest for a *quid pro quo* he suggested first that agreement with France would be easier were it not for the latter's policy of supporting Yugoslavia and later that concessions in the general negotiations could be bartered for French concessions in the sphere of naval disarmament.[12] To these hints the French government turned a deaf ear.

It was difficult to avoid the conclusion that in the Franco–Italian conversations, Mussolini (even admitting a large dose of arrogance arising from his perception of Italy as a creditor of France) did desire a settlement – if only in Africa and if only to consolidate his recent gains in the Adriatic and Eastern Europe. The contrary explanation, that he wished to keep open his quarrel with France to induce her to abandon Yugoslavia or to divert domestic attention from internal difficulties, was not so much untrue as incomplete. It was a question of degrees. Certainly in 1927–8 Italian policy in Eastern Europe tended to try to supplant the influence of Paris. But this had given way, towards the end of the decade, to a somewhat more restrained attempt to consolidate the rather meagre gains which the Italian irruption into Eastern Europe had produced. During this interval it might have been possible for the two countries to go quite some way in the direction of ending their difference in North Africa and examining their differences in Eastern Europe. This, at any rate, was the import which Mussolini attached to the proposed pact of friendship which was to cap the settlement of France's ten-year-old debt.

It did not work out this way for several reasons. First, the differences in approach remained beyond composition. Mussolini's emphasis on dynamism and action was difficult to reconcile with France's interest in stability; the result was that the rhetoric of fascism effectively clouded the mutuality of their interest in resisting some change while the rhetoric of conservatism shut the door on practically any change. Second, there was no pressure in the late 1920s to cut through the impasse: the German danger, though manifest, appeared distant, while British admonitions carried little weight, especially in Paris. There was no urgency to make concessions even in fields such as naval disarmament, where they would have been more of form than of substance, but appreciated all the more because of it, since Mussolini's major objective was to have confirmed the theoretical equality at sea between France and Italy earned by his liberal predecessors. In turn this led to the third and, as time went on, most intractable reason – the use Mussolini chose to make of the revival of German power to cow France into yielding. This was a dangerous game.

Mussolini played it with varied skill throughout the 1930s, until in the end he succumbed to it. It was one of his fundamental errors: to think that he could control German irredentism or, at least, direct it towards the Rhine and keep it away from the Brenner while boiling up that of others and, at the same time, not become a pawn of the process. It was also the fundamental difference between him and the permanent officials of Palazzo Chigi. The electoral victories of the Nazis had led Grandi, promoted to Foreign Minister at the end of 1929, to press for agreement with France and for conciliation with the Yugoslav and Austrian governments. By 1932 opinion on this subject was practically unanimous within the higher echelons of the Ministry.[13] Mussolini thought differently, not because he was under any illusion on the manner in which a National Socialist Germany would exercise her power, but because he felt he could exploit the German card on the Rhine to wring concessions from France in Africa and, at the same time, by adroit manipulation – the Four Power Pact and the Rome Protocols – contain and compete with German revisionism on the Danube. This attitude was remarkably of a piece with the pose he had struck at Locarno, refusing the collaboration of France and seeking an exclusive power base in Eastern Europe. But the Germany of Hitler, as the Ministry saw more clearly – perhaps less impressed, in the words of a British official, by the common use of shirts as an instrument of government – was not the Germany of Stresemann, and if the Locarno system was to have any consequence it had to be found, even if at the lowest common denominator, in the refusal to exploit one country at the expense of another, especially in so sensitive a matter as the issue of security.

Grandi's efforts to deflect Mussolini from this course and contemporaneously to persuade him to entertain, and the French to make, some concessions, were his swan song. His preoccupation with the growth of pro-German feeling in Italy, especially in the ultra-fascists around Mussolini, had progressively alienated him from his chief. His policy was openly described as 'renunciatory'. Only some concessions from those countries he had befriended, he warned Graham on 15 June 1932, could reverse the trend in Italy towards Germany. He asked nothing of Britain. 'It was from France', Graham noted, 'that he hoped for some concession. So far the French had gone no further than empty expressions of amity.' Italy desperately needed a colony or a mandated territory from which she could draw raw materials and to which she could send her surplus population. The French had in the former German colony of the Cameroons a mandate which, if it could be transferred to Italy, 'would not only ensure friendly relations between Italy and France, but would obviously drive a wedge between Italy and Germany'.[14]

Within weeks of this conversation Grandi had been dismissed from the Portfolio of External Affairs and sent to the London Embassy. Mussolini later told his ambassador to Spain that Grandi[15]

> had made a mess of everything in the last three years; he had made himself a prisoner of the League of Nations . . . had gone to bed with the pacifists and made Italy pregnant with disarmament . . . and had taken Italy out of the groove of egoism and realism.

Mussolini himself took over the Portfolio of Foreign Affairs with, as his Under-Secretary, Fulvio Suvich, a competent young functionary elevated to the post largely because of his background and experience in Danubian and Balkan affairs. Baron Aloisi, a man of similar experience, became Mussolini's personal *chef du cabinet*. The changing of the guard was made complete by a wholesale redistribution of diplomatic posts. Altogether they suggested the simultaneous emergence of two contradictory strains in Italian foreign policy. On the one hand, the elevation of men like Suvich, a native of Trieste, and Aloisi, experts in Balkan affairs, seemed to confirm the pre-eminence of the Adriatic wing in the Italian Foreign Office and suggested a continued emphasis on East European affairs; on the other hand, the dismissal of Grandi, the impatience with the machinery of the League and the resurgence of fascist influence at Palazzo Chigi led one to anticipate a more bellicose mood in Italy. The contradiction lay in the fact that, despite the espousal of revisionism and subversion, the scope for mischief and meaningful change in Eastern Europe was severely limited by the preponderance of French power in the area and by the close co-ordination between France and her East European allies. It was Mussolini's expectation that the resurrection of German power by conjuring up the bogey of another Triple Alliance, would provide Italy with a lever with which to constrain France into loosening her hold over Eastern Europe. As it turned out, within less than two years it had become all too clear that

Italy's and Germany's interests in Central and Eastern Europe were not complementary but conflicting. By the time the contradiction had been revealed, the bellicose strain had gained the upper hand. The thirst for expansion would have to be slaked in Africa if not Europe, although still relying on the derangement in the distribution of power brought about by the resurgence of Germany. Up until 1932 a fundamental premise of Italian policy had been not to sacrifice the nation's security on the altar of territorial expansion. Given a static configuration, Italy's adventures had remained circumscribed. After Hitler's accession to power, the premise was not abandoned but a fluid balance increased the scope for overt adventurism. Once Mussolini realised that Hitler's revolution, if it would not facilitate his intrigues in Eastern Europe would also not jeopardise Italian security because the action was now on the Rhine, the stage was set for forcible colonial adventure.

Significant in this connection were the rumours circulating in Rome in the summer of 1932. These said that after the changing of the guard, Mussolini had entirely re-written the article on fascism in the *Enciclopedia Italiana* stressing in the new version the tonic effect of war and thereby necessitating the reprinting of the volume which had already issued from the press. Apparently the objectives of Italian policy – grandeur, economic reconstruction and an outlet for surplus population – had not changed but the tactics were now being revised. In the past, the hope had lingered that these objectives could be achieved through collaboration with the *Entente* and in the fields of disarmament, reparations and debts Italy had been ready to go perhaps further than any other power; she had preached economic co-operation and to a large extent had refrained from following other countries along the road of quotas and exchange restrictions. The results had been nil. Politically and economically France remained the jealous mistress of the situation and Italian proposals after being received with empty applause in Geneva had been quietly relegated to the wastepaper basket.

The nature of the coming change was indicated in the fascist press, now upholding the German thesis on rearmament and re-iterating the view that, since the limitations imposed by the peace treaties on Germany, Austria, Hungary, Bulgaria and Turkey constituted a clear and binding promise of a general reduction of armaments, the victorious powers' refusal to disarm down to Germany's level implied a violation of the peace treaties. That this view was becoming official policy was made evident by Mussolini in a series of public pronouncements during the course of October 1932, most forcefully in a speech in Turin on 23 October where he laid as much stress on Germany's claim for equality as on his own hopes for a four-power directorate to guide European affairs.[16] The conclusion was not far-fetched that the thrust of this policy was to weaken France as much as to strengthen Germany. With France sufficiently weakened and isolated, Italy would then be in a good position to advance her ambitions for expansion (or, in a kinder interpretation, solve the demographic and economic problems to which Grandi had alluded) in North Africa, or Abyssinia or Eastern Europe.

Chapter 11

The Watch on the Brenner

> It is essential to keep both Austria and Hungary under
> my influence. . . .
>
> *Mussolini,* 1934

Mussolini seemed to have drawn several conclusions from his
first encounter with thoroughgoing German revisionism. There
was no hope of harnessing German dynamism for his own purposes so long as the question of Austria stood between him and
Hitler. At the same time the events of the autumn had revealed all
too painfully that, whatever his hopes, he could not impose his will
on an Anglo–French combination – a lesson he treasured more and
more as it came time to prepare to strike in Africa. The conclusion
was clear: for some time the action would be on the Rhine; if, at
the same time, he could make the Brenner frontier secure, the way
would be open for a forward policy in East Africa. What, therefore,
was required was a limited *rapprochement* with France (and, by
extension, with Yugoslavia) and the stabilisation of Italian
influence in Vienna.

In a manner only dimly perceived at the time, a substantial
revolution in the thrust of Italian policy was now under way – the
transformation of Mussolini into a pillar of the *status quo* in Europe.
As it turned out, this was a passing phase lasting only from the end
of 1933 until the beginning of 1936 at the latest, but it was the time
when Mussolini was most alert to the dangers to European stability
presented by Hitler. As well it was probably the only time when
the policy suggested succinctly by one of the shrewdest of the
British officials – 'land Mussolini first and lecture him later' –
might have worked. Of course the price demanded by Mussolini
for his co-operation was high as always – practically a free hand
on the Danube and in East Africa. But it was a price in many ways
tolerable and one which France, at least, now seemed willing to
pay. The pre-eminence which Mussolini sought in Austria and

223

Hungary could easily be granted: neither of the western powers had much influence in Vienna or Budapest and so long as those capitals courted Italian patronage there was little point in opposing it, especially since the alternative was dependence on Germany. Furthermore, it was also becoming apparent that Mussolini would be content with this consolidation of Italian power and that he would consequently forswear what had previously been implicit in his East European policy, the pursuit of the break-up of the Yugoslav state and of the Little *Entente*. The quest for glory and colonies in East Africa was a different matter – it raised separate problems, though not unmanageable ones. But it was important that in the context of the major problem facing Europe at the time – the dangerous revival of German power – Mussolini, albeit with typical vacillation and not a little opportunism, was lining up on the side of European stability.

The Four Power Pact

This order of thinking was behind the impetus which changed the low-level exchanges with France – kept up mostly through the will of Grandi and Guariglia after the abortive official negotiations of 1928–30 – into something resembling a dialogue. Throughout 1931 and 1932 contacts had been maintained unofficially through the medium of conversations in Paris between the Italian chairman of the League's Mandate Commission, the Marquis Alberto Theodoli, and one of his French colleagues, Robert de Caix, and extended through contacts with such influential proponents of Italo–French collaboration as the President of the French Senate's Committee of Foreign Affairs. They had not borne immediate fruit.[1] In late 1932 when the major threat was Germany's pretensions in the armament field, Mussolini felt that more concessions could be extracted from a distraught France: 'France should allow us complete liberty on the Danube where, together with Austria and Hungary, we could form the rampart which could prevent the *Anschluss*.'[2] But by 1933, after the ominous tendencies in German politics had been consummated in the Nazi revolution, Mussolini was ready to entertain more sympathetically France's advances. Early in the year, Henri de Jouvenel, a newspaper editor and an avowed supporter of reconciliation with Italy, was appointed Special Ambassador to Rome for six months.[3]

It soon became clear, however, that De Jouvenel had not been equipped with the necessary material to transform his good intentions into something concrete. The proposals he brought to Rome were in fact inadequate. They hinted – as six years before – at the development of the Franco–Yugoslav treaty into a tripartite arrangement but they offered no satisfaction to Italy on the question of naval parity and on other points they appeared studiously vague. Amongst these vague suggestions was one for the encouragement of Italian colonisation in Syria.[4] Mussolini did not give the impression of being unduly bothered by such vagueness. In the spring he thought he had found in the Four Power Pact the instrument which would also smooth Italo–French relations. 'It must be loyally recognised', he told the Senate on presentation of the pact,

> that the French government have vigorously struggled against the stream, that is to say, against the interests, feelings and misgivings existing in the French mind. . . . In the improved situation brought about by the Four Power Pact, it is perfectly possible to proceed to that speedy settlement of certain definite questions dividing Italy and France.

But the opening created by this evidence of a new attitude in Rome was largely dissipated by France's ambiguous reaction to the Pact. Instead of seizing the opportunity for a settlement, Paris declared that questions concerning France and Italy alone could be settled at leisure; as regards the questions of common European interest raised by Mussolini, the French government, before committing itself to the Pact, would seek more assurances that Italy was ready to collaborate in the maintenance of the independence of Austria, the maintenance of political stability in Eastern Europe – by which was meant the alignment of Italy with France and the Little *Entente* – and to abjure any attempt to break up individual states – an undiplomatic reference to Italian policy in Yugoslavia.[5]

Raising the ante in such a way as to amount to a total Italian capitulation before French requirements in Central and Eastern Europe led Britain to remonstrate with France: it would encourage Germany to adopt a recalcitrant or bellicose attitude at the same time that it was unfair to Mussolini. Daladier in reply stated that France did not want to attach conditions to her signature of the Four Power Pact but merely wanted a few words from Mussolini to enable him to meet future parliamentary criticism that he had entered into the pact blindfolded. In the event De Jouvenel offered a compromise – closer relations between Austria, the Little *Entente* and their respective sponsors – and on this basis the last version of the Four Power Pact was signed.[6] Mussolini, who had by this time come to value the form of the Pact as much as if not more than its contents, showed no hesitation in concurring that neither France nor Italy should have any territorial ambitions in Central Europe, that the independence of Austria should be maintained and that nothing should be done to impede Austria and Hungary coming to an understanding with their Little *Entente* neighbours.[7] De Jouvenel then left Rome and was succeeded by De Chambrun.

Mussolini pronounced himself happy with those arrangements. The specific Franco–Italian questions which had formed the subject of controversy had sunk into the background and he felt that in the new atmosphere they could easily be settled. The first question he meant to broach was disarmament. Next in order of importance was a settlement in Central Europe and help to Austria and Hungary. A third area was economic relations between Italy and France and last was Daladier's suggestion of Italian expansion in Syria. Specifically, he thought that naval parity had ceased to have much importance. He hoped for some satisfaction in Libya and Tunis and, regarding disarmament, he thought some agreement had to be reached at the Disarmament Conference before driving Germany into complete intransigence.

That De Chambrun's task would be a challenging one was obvious from the start. Both countries were drawn together by their growing fear of Germany, but they were divided on how that danger should be met and both continued to be hampered by France's special relationship with the Little *Entente,* and by Italy's championship of Austria and Hungary. The French Ambassador opened his conversations with Italy late in the summer of 1933. The German menace to Austrian independence had begun to make itself felt in Italy and to incline Mussolini to a more favourable attitude towards French policy in Central Europe. But in August 1933 Italy refused to join France and Britain in a *démarche* at Berlin on the Austrian question, preferring to maintain what Mussolini fancied was a special relationship with Germany and to exercise his influence there independently of the other two powers. By the following month he was beginning to come round to the French point of view. Although he still liked to keep a foot in both camps and was shortly after to encourage Berlin to 'expose' France's fears of Germany's clandestine rearmament, in September 1933 he did promise De Chambrun that 'If you are attacked, we will be with you'[8] – a major reversal of the policy hitherto followed of supporting Germany at France's expense. By way of response France then began to encourage Rome to play a leading part in the economic restoration of Central Europe and to do what it could to calm the Little *Entente*'s fears of Italian policy in that area – an equally large reversal.

The event which served more effectively than any amount of negotiations to bring Italy and France together was Germany's withdrawal the following month from the Disarmament Conference and her resignation from the League of Nations. The step greatly angered Mussolini. Aside from the wound to his *amour propre,* for the withdrawal took place without either prior consultation or notification, it was a clear setback to his policy of mediation and it sounded the death knell of the Four Power Pact which had been concluded within the framework of the League. Germany having thus resumed her freedom of action in the matter of armaments and Nazi activities becoming more and more menacing, France and Italy continued for the remainder of the year to draw closer together. In the new year, Italy began to play a prominent part in measures designed to defend Austria, and on 17 February 1934 Italy associated herself with France and Great Britain in a declaration that the three governments took 'a common view as to the necessity of maintaining Austria's independence and integrity in accordance with the relevant treaties'. By the beginning of 1934 Italy and France were in fundamental agreement on the essentials of the Austrian question.

On disarmament, there was more ground to be made up. On 31 January 1934 Italy issued a memorandum the gist of which was that it would be necessary to recognise the fact of German rearmament and to legalise it up to a given point, a view decidedly opposed by the new French Foreign Minister, Louis Barthou. In May 1934 Suvich, referring to rumours of a projected visit to Rome by Barthou, indicated that such a visit, if it took place before the meeting of the General Commission of the Disarmament Conference at Geneva, might embarrass the Italian government since the latter were not certain they would be able to follow the French line in the Commission. The French were no less cautious, stating that Barthou would not visit Italy until the policies of France and Italy were sufficiently in agreement to ensure that the visit would result in accord.[9]

The murder by the Nazis on 25 July 1934 of Dollfuss, the Austrian Chancellor who had come to lean more and more on Italy for support in his internal and external policy, had the effect of making Italy abandon any semblance of mediation in Berlin. Mussolini immediately moved troops to the Brenner so that, if necessary, they might help the Austrian government put down the Nazi risings which had broken out in some parts of the country following the murder. This precautionary action, though applauded as the firmest evidence of Mussolini's determination to prevent an *Anschluss*, was at the same time a cause of serious concern in Paris, where it was known that if Italian troops entered Austria, Yugoslav troops would immediately do likewise – a situation pregnant with risk.[10]

The Tardieu Plan

As early as 1931 the German government had accompanied its announcement in Rome of a projected customs union with Austria with hints that comprehension of the exigencies of German irredentism would be recompensed with the kind of closer understanding both states had sought since the death of Stresemann. In effect the choice it presented to the Italian government was to accede to the principle of *Anschluss* or else lose support in the disputes with Paris. The choice had been avoided by temporising, by not opposing the project but not accepting it either, allowing the opposition of others to carry the day. In fact when the categorical opposition of France and the Little *Entente* was added to London's more cautious refusal, Rome, secure in the knowledge that the customs union was doomed, accepted it in principle on the transparent condition that Italy participate as an equal and that the German government renounce in writing any intentions of proceeding to an *Anschluss*.[11] For good measure when the International Court of Justice at the Hague proclaimed the union contrary to the existing international undertakings, the Italian judge showed copious appreciation of the economic imperatives which had motivated Germany by abstaining from the decision. As a result Italo–German relations did not suffer from the incident, although they did not prosper. Grandi was careful to avoid any commitments during the course of his visit to Berlin in late October 1931.[12] He satisfied himself that the time had not come to draw closer to a Germany which was still weak, isolated and furthermore not disposed to renounce an *Anschluss*. None the less, though the particular danger of a customs union had been averted, its underlying causes, the political and economic weakness of Central Europe, continued to provide ample scope for independent mischief, whether on the part of Italy, Germany or France. Austria and Hungary were more or less in a state of intermittent bankruptcy, despite financial assistance from the League. Hungary had already declared a moratorium on debts and Austria was getting ready to follow suit. In both cases the fundamental cause of their chronic insolvency was the lack of equilibrium in their economic life, Austria being burdened with a capital city and an administrative machinery out of all proportion in a small and comparatively poor country; Hungary having been reduced to a small agrarian state without an alternative source of wealth, without access to the sea and surrounded by hostile neighbours. Czechoslovakia, Yugoslavia and Romania, though not actually in a state of collapse, were also feeling in increasing measure the strains of the economic depression and all had seen their staple exports ruined by the fall in world prices of agricultural products.

The attractive solution, the elimination of tariff and other barriers among the five states by binding them into one economic unit, sensible though it might have been, had a tendency to weaken both French influence in the Little *Entente* and Italian influence in Austria and Hungary by accentuating common ties. The preferred Italian solution was for separate agreements between the different countries leading to a general agreement with negotiations taking place simultaneously between the representatives on the one hand of the five East European states and, on the other, of the four great powers. A simultaneous proposal by the French Foreign Minister, André Tardieu, modified the Italian suggestion just sufficiently to ensure the prevalence of French interests. Tardieu's plan called essentially for a conference between the Danubian states (where the Italian protégés would be outnumbered) without the participation of the great powers to work out a system of preferential tariffs, but with them declaring in advance their readiness to welcome such a system. France's ulterior motive was clearly to strengthen her political hold over the successor states to the detriment of Italian (and German) interests. This, of course, raised the fear in Italy that the former Austro–Hungarian territories would be reconstituted as a political unit and that the closer financial and economic links would eventually emerge into a full-blown political *entente*. Another ominous implication for Italy was that Austrian and Hungarian membership would probably have to be paid for by their acquiescence in the political *status quo* of the area – and by the consequent abandonment by Italy of her strongest suit in Austria and Hungary, her commitment to a policy of treaty revision.

Thus the negotiations over Tardieu's proposals which were to take place initially in London assumed from the start the appearance of a test of Italy's willingness to abandon her special position on the Danube and to co-operate in a larger European framework. This unpalatable choice was further complicated because Germany's opposition to the Tardieu plan was clear cut, at the same time that Tardieu let it be understood that on Italy's attitude depended his support for Rome's colonial aspirations. Essentially Italy was being asked to join a pro-French, anti-German political coalition, precisely the kind of request Rome had assiduously tried to avoid so as not to lose the leverage available in Berlin. In the circumstances, the Italian government's tactics consisted first of all in an attempt to enlarge the technical difficulties by pleading for the inclusion of Bulgaria, Albania, Greece, Poland, and Turkey, who could be counted on to make the negotiations more complicated and lengthy and, if they none the less succeeded, to counterbalance the influence of the Little *Entente*. The second tactic was to make common cause with Germany and conversations to this end opened at the end of March 1932, shortly after the Tardieu proposals had been made public. But immediately they came up against an even more astute German tactic. Berlin, in fact, suggested the alternative of a customs union amongst Italy, Germany, Austria and Hungary, a proposal of obvious effectiveness as it recalled the Triple Alliance, but one which would also have meant a formalisation of German preponderance on the Danube as well as a return through the back door of the customs union with Austria. The approach to Germany was quickly abandoned and the Italian government then went through the thoroughly unpleasant experience of seeing Germany make advances to Britain and France when the conference opened in London. The mirage of an agreement between Germany and France proved sufficiently attractive to sidetrack discussions on the Balkan question long enough for the constitutional revolution which brought the Nazis to power to take place. As usual Italy was partly relieved and partly disappointed by its own tactics – relieved that nothing was concluded, disappointed by the facility with which others could play the same game.

Negotiations with Austria

The fiasco of these negotiations and the ominous victory of the Nazis underlined the need to reaffirm the exclusiveness of Italian policy in Austria. There, the *Heimwehr,* a coalition of forces on the Right with a nationalist programme geared to the revival of Austrian prestige and influence, had been enjoying Italian support, subsidies and arms since 1927. Hitler, for his part, had encouraged Prince Ernst Starhemberg, the leader of the *Heimwehr*, to approach Mussolini and in April 1930 had advised him to sound out the Duce on his reaction to *Anschluss* in exchange for the Nazi's recognition of the Alto Adige as Italian – the trade always preferred by Hitler and ultimately implemented in the late 1930s. In July 1930 Mussolini had disabused Starhemberg of these notions – no *Anschluss* under any guise; rather, he renewed the invitation to espouse the cause of a nationalist, fascist and Catholic Austria on the Italian model and with Italian support.[13]

Mussolini's proposal matched rather closely the prince's own inclination and, though it took some time to make up his mind, by mid-1932 he had decided definitely to orient the *Heimwehr* towards a form of clerical fascism and against Pan-Germanism and an *Anschluss*. He and Mussolini agreed when they discussed German designs on Austria in June 1932 that the 'Prussians on the Brenner would mean war. But let war come rather than Austria should become part of greater Germany.'[14] Strengthened by further Italian promises of arms and money, Starhemberg in mid-September 1932 presented the Austrian Chancellor Dollfuss with Mussolini's programme – a sovereign Austria, anti-Socialist and anti-Nazi, politically and economically tied to Italy. In exchange Starhemberg promised the support of his group for Dollfuss's party. Dollfuss accepted the deal. The Austrian Chancellor shuffled his government to make room for Major Fey, the *Heimwehr*'s commandant in Vienna, as Minister of Public Security. Immediately afterwards Rome implemented a commercial agreement, previously held up, while the Austrian Minister in Rome communicated Dollfuss's readiness to discuss a customs union with Italy. In mid-February 1933 Starhemberg signed in Rome an agreement which renounced the *Anschluss*, paved the way for a corporative Austria and reaffirmed the inviolability of the Brenner frontier.[15] Italian diplomacy appeared to have scored a remarkable success over its competitor in the area.

None the less, that Mussolini had prevented Berlin from imposing its will on Vienna did not mean that henceforth he could manoeuvre Dollfuss like a puppet. A case in point was the conversation in Rome between 2 and 6 June 1933 during which the Austrian Chancellor complained loudly about Nazi interference in his country's internal affairs but also turned down unceremoniously the one course of action Mussolini suggested to counter this trend – an Italian military guarantee to Austria – as smacking too much of vassalage along Albanian lines and as likely to provoke a crisis with the Little *Entente*. A further check on Italy's freewheeling against the Austrian Nazis came from the necessity to keep in step with Hungary. Since the Nazis' accession to power, the Hungarian government had not been slow to see that the Germans' unreconstructed revisionism was more likely to produce results on their behalf than Italy's more timid efforts, a conclusion underlined by the metamorphosis the Four Power Pact had undergone from March to June.

The Nazis were clearly a considerably more determined lot than previous German governments. Hitler's policy was as dangerous to Italian interests as it was straightforward. His ultimate goal was *Anschluss*; in the interim he would settle for *Gleichschaltung,* a policy which, while formally respecting the independence of another state, aimed at its internal co-ordination. In the Austrian case this meant that Austrian institutions should be similar to Germany's, that is to say, ruled by the Nationalist Socialist party – hence the emphasis Hitler placed on new elections in Austria which 'would create clear-cut conditions and, in particular, give the Nationalist Socialist movement the place to which it is entitled'.[16] Conversations to this end in the spring of 1933 between Dollfuss and

Habicht, the Austrian Nazi leader, and between Mussolini and Göring and Papen, had proved abortive and in consequence Hitler had given his consent to stepped-up subversive activities against the Austrian government, ranging from the imposition of a staggering tax on Germans visiting Austria to depress the Austrian tourist industry, to vituperative press and radio outbursts and to the dropping of subversive leaflets from the air. Dollfuss's answer to this harassment, aside from seeking support in Italy, had been to plead with the major powers to remonstrate severely in Berlin by means of a joint note.

A diplomatic note, no matter how phrased, implied taking a formal open stand against Berlin and this was something Mussolini wished to avoid as it would undermine the special position between Germany and the Western Powers he was so laboriously trying to construct. He tried to avoid a firm stand in two ways – first by drawing Austria still more within his orbit so that Italy alone of the major powers could then play the role of protector and, second, by putting pressure on Berlin privately to ease the acts of political sabotage. On 1 July 1933 he put to Dollfuss the suggestion that Austria, Hungary and Italy should arrive at a closer political and economic *entente*. Eventually Austria could draw closer to the Little *Entente* and Hungary closer to Germany, but only after strengthening their position with Italy so as to avoid absorption by the Little *Entente* or Germany. In the meantime, he counselled Dollfuss to be somewhat more sympathetic and accommodating towards Berlin while strengthening his hold over Austria internally by transforming the country into a fascist, authoritarian state.[17]

Dollfuss had already gone part of the way in this direction. In addition to bringing the *Heimwehr* into the government with the help of Starhemberg, he had created the Fatherland Front, a super-patriotic organisation designed to stand above party politics and indeed to make them and parliamentary democracy superfluous. After receiving Mussolini's suggestion for closer relations with Hungary, Gömbos, the Hungarian Prime Minister, was invited to Vienna. The meeting did not produce the results desired by Mussolini owing to Gömbos's reluctance to take a stand against Germany, but it did result in a general affirmation of co-operation both political and economic in the Danubian basin.[18] Gömbos's reluctance, moreover, was more than matched by Dollfuss, not because of any fear of offending German sensibilities but because he did not wish to prejudice his request in London, Paris and Rome for a collective step against German propaganda in Austria. For this reason also, he replied to Mussolini on 22 July 1933, the time was not 'propitious' for the assumption of immediate and concrete undertakings with Hungary. And two days later he requested officially an Anglo–French–Italian intervention in Berlin – a strange reply to Mussolini's plea for an attenuation of the dispute with Germany.

Almost by coincidence Gömbos and his Foreign Minister, De Kanya, arrived in Rome on 25 July. It appears that at this point so exasperated were the Hungarians that they were talking of a break with Austria. Mussolini pulled out all the stops to persuade them otherwise. At the end of the three-day conversation he had succeeded in obtaining their consent not only to closer Austro–Hungarian relations but also on a programme including the early implementation of a tripartite customs union; opposition to any form of *Anschluss*; an offer of collaboration to Germany (extending to membership in the proposed customs union) if Berlin dropped its demands for *Gleichschaltung*; adamant opposition to any French or Little *Entente*-sponsored plans for the Danube, and measures to ease the Austro–German tension.[19]

Having thus, after a fashion, patched up some of the seams in his coat, Mussolini felt he could act more directly in Berlin. Cerrutti, the Italian ambassador, sought out Bülow to suggest to him that the only way to avoid the humiliation implied in Dollfuss's request for three-power intervention was for Germany 'to pull the rug from under the Austrian protest' by extending to Italy the assurances sought by Dollfuss and, second, by improving Austro–German relations by agreeing on a coalition government for Austria to include the Nazis alongside the *Heimwehr* and the Fatherland Front and by renouncing in advance any attempt at *Anschluss*.[20] These were stiff terms. Berlin's alternatives were either to keep a haughty silence on the ground that relations with Austria, by the logic of Nazi propaganda, were an internal matter for German-speaking peoples, or else extend generic assurances to Italy to obviate the proposed *démarche*. When it became apparent, on 5 August, that the Western Powers proposed to go ahead with the protest, the second alternative was accepted. Cerrutti was informed by Bülow that despite the patent inadmissibility of the proposed western *démarche*, the German government as a gesture of goodwill was willing to put a brake on radio broadcasts and clandestine flights. But the other Italian requests were not acceptable so long as Dollfuss remained Chancellor and elections were not called.[21] Berlin had thus complied with at least those aspects of the Italian request which related to the proposed *démarche* and might have thus hoped that Rome would take immediate steps to hold back the other powers. This Italy did but only in a formal way. Rome advised them of Bülow's concessions but certainly not so peremptorily as to prevent the joint *démarche*. Mussolini must have thought that, not having obtained satisfaction on matters crucial to Italy, it would do no harm to have Britain and France put Germany in her place if for no other reason than that it should then make the German government think twice before disregarding Italian wishes. The Anglo–French protest was presented on 7 August 1933 'in the spirit of the Four Power Pact'. Mussolini, still playing in both sides of the field, dissociated himself, but, of course, his dissociation was gratuitous since, had he wanted, he could have prevented the protest.[22] Hitler had no difficulty seeing through the Italian manoeuvre. He would not stand 'for that sort of tutelage' he told von Neurath.[23] Henceforth his policy towards Austria would become progressively more rigid until it touched its nadir with the *putsch* of July 1934 and the assassination of Dollfuss.

After the Anglo–French step in Berlin, Dollfuss, as if to underline his preference, visited Mussolini at Rimini on 19–20 August. It was one of their more important meetings. Dollfuss resisted and resented Mussolini's pressures for an accommodation with the Germans, not quite following the narrow path the Italian leader was treading but acquiescing in a great deal more than he had been willing to contemplate a few months earlier. He agreed to proceed to an early implementation of the triangular agreement with Hungary and, in deference to Mussolini's German policy, to leave room as well for Berlin on the condition that any idea of a *putsch* be abandoned. An approach would later be made to the Little *Entente* in accordance with the discussions then taking place with France. But by far the most important part of the conversation dealt with the steps Italy was now permitted to take in the event of overt German interference. An Italian expeditionary corps of 5,000 men now was empowered to enter the country and proceed towards the German frontier.[24] In effect Mussolini now had the right to intervene militarily in Austria, a right which placed Austria in the position much more of a vassal than an independent state, especially when this concession was coupled with the strengthening of the *Heimwehr* by a healthy infusion of small arms and the steps which Dollfuss took the next month to run the state along fascist lines. On 11 September the Chancellor announced, with a genuflection towards the encyclical letter *Quadragesimo Anno*, the formation of a 'social Christian German state with a corporative basis'. It was by now but a short step to violent suppression of Austrian socialism and the negation of all civil liberties.

The transformation was not unappreciated in foreign capitals. For its part London was grateful for Italy's new eminence in Austria. If an *Anschluss* took place before the West had obtained Mussolini's co-operation, Vansittart prophesied accurately, Mussolini, with Hitler on his border, would have to turn his back on Britain and France.[25] This assessment was shared only in part in Paris. The argument that unless Italy and France settled their disputes in a hurry, Italy, in all probability, would line up on the wrong side carried weight but not urgency in Paris. To speed up matters the British cabinet met on 5 September and issued to France an ultimatum of sorts: to compose differences and to grant Mussolini as much latitude as he wanted in Austria in the hope of setting him permanently against Germany or to give up all hopes of isolating Germany. The warning had its effect. On 10 September Paris produced a plan for the economic integration of the Danubian basin, which, by acknowledging Italy's special interests in Austria and Hungary, in effect offered Italy a condominium in the area with France only sponsoring the interests of the Little *Entente*.[26]

The incipient acknowledgment by the Western Powers of Italy's pre-eminence in Austria went a long way towards restoring Italy's influence after the fiasco of the Four Power Pact. The price was being paid by Dollfuss, who, though he might dislike Hitler more, was daily becoming more exasperated with Mussolini's none-too-subtle tutelage. His position was not eased by the fact that Mussolini (in pursuit of his role as honest broker and to pre-empt Hitler) was applying constant pressure on him to reach a *modus vivendi* with the Nazis as well as to implement two crucial aspects of the Rimini agreement which had not yet been fulfilled – the elimination of all socialists and the conclusion of an agreement with Hungary. Suvich was due in Vienna on 18 January 1934 and the day before he arrived Dollfuss turned to the international community. He addressed a note to Germany and the Western Powers to the effect that 'unless the illegal activities ceased, Austria would have to bring the question of Austro–German relations before the League'.[27] When Berlin rejected the note on 1 February, Dollfuss had to turn to the League.

Mussolini had to act quickly. Dollfuss's attempt to international-ise the problems of Austria could not but weaken his position in Vienna as well as cause an irreparable rift with Berlin. The Italian leader's decision to press Dollfuss for the immediate liquidation of the Austrian socialists probably derived from a desire to pre-empt the *démarche* towards Geneva by compromising the Austrian Chancellor before international public opinion and tying him closer to Italy. Certainly the brutal suppression of the socialists in February 1934 had the effect of killing Dollfuss's appeal to the League.[28]

Following the purge Rome stepped up its attempts to bring about a political and economic *rapprochement* between Austria and Hungary. This was no easy task. Hungary had already decided it could not place all its eggs in the Italian basket since after the accession to power of the Nazis, Italy was no longer the revisionist power *par excellence*. Out of deference to Rome, Hungary tried to remain completely neutral on the Austrian question although, clearly, an *Anschluss*, by destroying the Treaty of Trianon and enfeebling the Little *Entente*, would have been to Budapest's advantage. By the same token, Mussolini also had to steer a course between inordinate Hungarian revisionism,[29] strident Austrian pleas to keep a line open to the West and keeping a semblance of support for Berlin's aspirations in the field of equality of rights. In the circumstances, the Rome Protocols signed on 17 March 1934 between Italy, Austria and Hungary could be counted a success for Italian policy. Dollfuss, who had been striving not to tie himself too closely to Italy, and Gömbos, who had come to Rome deter-mined to circumvent any tripartite political agreement, ended by affixing their signatures to a document which required tripartite consultations at the bidding of any of the three signatories. And, as if to emphasise the two Danubian countries' dependence on Rome, Mussolini curtly ruled out a Hungarian suggestion to issue a public invitation to Germany to join the circle.[30] He equally dismissed the howl which came from the Little *Entente*. As he asked Drummond, the new British Ambassador:[31]

Why can't the French and the Little Entente understand that I am compelled to talk of revisionism, if I am to hold the Hungarians and prevent their passing into the German camp? It is essential to keep both Austria and Hungary under my influence and the French and the Little Entente ought to understand this. They cannot themselves provide any other method of obtaining the above ends.

The Rome Protocols which began as Mussolini's attempt to steal Hitler's thunder marked the beginning of Italy's conversion to the status of a satisfied power in Europe. They placed Italy on the defensive on the Danube largely as a reaction to Hitler's undiluted revisionism, although in part also they were the necessary prelude to a forward policy in Africa. At any rate Hitler seemed to go along. Determined to have Italy as an ally and Austria in his grip, he temporarily relaxed the pressure on Vienna while he explored the possibilities of an agreement with Mussolini. Their meeting in Venice on 15–16 June 1934 did not, however, produce the results Hitler hoped for and, while there was probably no direct causal relationship between the failure of this meeting and the Nazi *putsch* of July, it is fair to say that the inability to solve the problem at the diplomatic level removed its solution to the level of violence. Hitler, as he told Mussolini when they met for the first time, was willing to put the *Anschluss* into cold storage provided that Dollfuss was replaced by someone who would call an election as soon as possible and give the Austrian Nazis a share in the government proportionate to the votes they obtained. Afterwards, he promised Mussolini, all economic questions in Austria would be handled by Germany and Italy in closest consultation. But no matter how these proposals were dressed up, in Italy they appeared, if not like an *Anschluss,* very much like *Gleichschaltung.* Mussolini took cognizance of them but went no further.[32] The Nazi *putsch* in Vienna the following month ended the dialogue. Mussolini's anger was fuelled by the fact that Dollfuss, who lost his life in the *putsch,* was to have been his guest within a few days and that indeed his family were already in Italy. The Duce regarded the *putsch* and the murder as a personal affront. He quickly persuaded his *Heimwehr* friends to mobilise and occupy key points in Vienna at the same time that four Italian divisions were rushed to the Brenner. The abortive *coup* ended any likelihood of a *rapprochement* with Germany. Its major importance was that it confirmed Italy as a pillar of the *status quo,* in Europe at least, and formed the basis for the Franco–Italian

agreement of January 1935. France moved quickly to still Yugoslavia's fears – the Yugoslav government had made it clear even to
Germany that it too would enter Austria if Italy did.[33] At the end
of July, the French government proposed a standing committee to
watch over Austria, a suggestion turned down by Britain, loath as
always to enter into a formal commitment, as was an Italian suggestion of a guarantee for Austria between France, Britain and Italy.[34]
Eventually the three powers settled on a step least likely to involve
Britain in Central Europe – a reaffirmation on 27 September 1934 of
the declarations they had made in February of that year. The
important outcome, however, was the fact that, owing to Britain's
reluctance to accept commitments in Central Europe in support of
French policy and owing to Italy's inability to reach an accommodation with Germany, the two Latin countries came to appreciate their common interest in co-operating against Hitler. The
Laval–Mussolini pact of 7 January 1935 had at its core a con-
sultative pact with the object of maintaining the integrity and
independence of Austria. To this pact other countries might
accede, although this was not to be. The acknowledgment of
Italy's special position in Austria might have been the beginning of
a new phase in fascist foreign policy, a phase marked by a toning-
down of Mussolini's strident revisionism and the acceptance by
Italy of a role as custodian of the peace decreed at Versailles as well
as the acceptance by France principally, of great-power status for
Italy. As it was, it merely marked the end of a brief interlude. Italy's
designs on Abyssinia saw to it that what had been gained on the
Danube would be lost in the Red Sea.

Chapter 12

The Abyssinian War

Collective security should be confined to Europe, not
Africa.

Mussolini, 1935

Colonial expansion – imperialism – was implicit in fascism. In a
movement permeated by crude social Darwinism and intoxicated
by the discovery of the efficacy of violence, the notion took root
early that the conquest of 'inferior' peoples was as legitimate as it
was desirable and profitable. After the victory over the Central
Powers, the nostalgic exaltations of the works of Crispi and of the
grandeur of Rome and Venice acquired a new promise of fulfilment. 'The war', Grandi wrote in 1920, 'has appealed to the
nation's pride, to irredentism both territorial and economic and
these, violently brought forth, are nothing but the instrument of a
higher and all-embracing concept – the imperial idea.'[1]

The fascist imperial idea, it turned out, was substantially different from the imperialism practised between the wars by the
other major powers. If the latter could largely be described as
tending towards contemporary neo-colonialism, the former had
rather the marks of an anachronistic neo-mercantilism, modified to
suit the needs of fascist rhetoric. In the Italy of the 1920s and 1930s,
the competition for colonial spoils came to be perceived and
justified in quasi-Marxist terms as a new international struggle,
though one in which the nation replaced the class as the supreme
protagonist. Something along these lines had already been adum-
brated by Corradini before the war. His notion of Italy as a proletarian nation had made possible a *rapprochement* between his wing
in the nationalist movement and the revolutionary syndicalists on
the basis that Italy's imperial expansion would in fact be a form of
proletarian imperialism.[3] This notion provided the linch-pin between Mussolini the socialist and Mussolini the fascist. Earlier than
it became fashionable, Mussolini understood that as the war

240

coalesced whole populations into cohesive national units, traditional class distinctions would inevitably give way to distinctions
between nations. The transfer of loyalty from class to nation, his
rejection in effect of the cruder aspects of Marx and his discovery
of the cruder aspects of Mazzini, allowed his activist spirit to forge
a new synthesis – the conversion of the class struggle at home into
an imperialist struggle abroad on behalf of proletarian nationalism.
It did not go unnoticed that the synthesis was a perversion of both
Marx and Mazzini, but the combination was potent and the notion
all too agreeable that in a world divided into 'rich nations and
proletarian nations', the latter who were 'demanding a place in the
world to which they have a right' should, if the opportunity arose,
seize it.[4]

These considerations supplied whatever intellectual coherence
there was in such fascist organs as *Impero*. A demonstrative sample
appeared in 1923, when *Impero* theorised[5]

> ... the solution for an imperial nation such as Italy is and must be
> one alone, an extra-European Empire over people unable to govern
> themselves, over lands whose produce will give a nation such as ours
> not so much wealth as the raw materials which now rule out our
> commercial autonomy. The Empire will weld all Italians into a
> 'single class'. By possessing provinces ... those who are workers
> will become employers or owners or at any rate members of the
> dominant class. The class struggle will cease to be an internal
> problem and will become almost a problem of external policy
> between the Italians and the inhabitants of the Empire.

The force of such appeals as these cannot be underestimated. A
constant refrain in fascist writing from 1919 on, they indoctrinated
a whole generation to look to conquest as the solution to poverty,
misery and conflict at home. To this extent, the conventional
explanation of the conquest of Abyssinia as an exasperated
nationalism seeking to divert internal discontent into foreign
adventures is certainly correct. Ineluctably, the rhetoric of the
régime and the magnitude of its domestic problems served to
channel Italian policy into a colonial showdown soluble only,
given the Africans' reluctance to be colonised and the fascists'
penchant for the use of force, by war.[6] 'How else', *Impero* asked
rhetorically as early as 1925, 'can the idea of empire be cultivated in
the soul of a people without indicating at the same time the only,
the most realistic way of achieving it? To add to the territory of the

Fatherland we must conquer and to conquer we must fight.'[7]

It was not surprising that what had been confidently predicted should finally take place. But attractive and correct though it is, the explanation of the conquest of Abyssinia in terms of the ideological presumptions of the régime, its self-fulfilling rhetoric and its deliberate diversion of domestic discontent into colonial ventures, is incomplete. Conquests in Africa were not a fascist invention; mercantilism had a long pedigree; frustration with the Versailles colonial settlement was shared by practically all sectors of the Italian political spectrum; the myth of the mutilated victory predated the fascists' exploitation of it. Certainly the will to war in Italy was the catalytic agent, but an understanding of the context in which the attack on Abyssinia took place must, in addition to Italy's pre-disposition, take into account as well the extent to which Italy's opportunity was abetted and influenced by ambivalence and prevarication in the other major powers. None of them emerged from this sordid episode in imperialism with honour.

The rise of the Africanisti

Of the factors propelling Italy to expand her holdings in East Africa, one that must not be underrated was the availability, or so it appeared to Italy, of Abyssinia, the only tropical country not to have succumbed in the 'scramble' for Africa in the nineteenth century and one which, moreover, straddled the two Italian East African colonies, Eritrea and Somaliland. Gradual Italian expansion northward from Somaliland had already resulted in the occupation of substantial lands claimed by Addis Ababa and the fertile soil of the Abyssinian highlands was all the more tempting. Historical memories added their own impetus: under the Treaty of Uccialli, Abyssinia had become an Italian protectorate, a delusion ended by the defeat of Adowa. Given the temper of the present Italian rulers, the desire to avenge Adowa severely limited the prospects of a peaceful solution. Then there was the hope that any Italian aggression would not arouse the opposition of Britain and France. France's major interest, the Jibuti–Addis Ababa railway, would be safeguarded; as to Britain, Italy's hopes for acquiescence were largely strengthened by the knowledge that British interests in Abyssinia were not such as to make likely a policy of active opposition to the detriment of general Anglo–Italian relations, as well as by the recollection that in 1925 Britain had sought Italian support to obtain concessions which Abyssinia was not prepared to grant.

That particular deal was indicative of the lightheartedness with which all major powers had long treated Abyssinia, before and after that country had entered the League of Nations. Abyssinia had not been an original member of the League but had applied for and had been admitted to membership in 1923 after giving certain undertakings with regard to slavery and the traffic of arms, but without, it seems, thereby abrogating the rights over her territory claimed by the great powers by virtue of the 1906 treaty. The Italian government as early as November 1919 had asked that the whole of the western part of Abyssinia should be regarded as an exclusive sphere of Italian influence. The then head of the Italian Colonial Office, Baccari, had apprised his British counterpart of Italy's wish to construct a railway west of Lake Tsana to link eventually Eritrea and Italian Somaliland. The railway proposed by Italy cut right across the basin of the Blue Nile and the district in which Italy asked for exclusive influence included the whole of that basin. The relative positions of Italy and Britain were laid down in the 1906 agreement, since then the subject of conflicting interpretations – Britain maintaining that the agreement gave her territorial as well as 'hydraulic' rights in the Abyssinian part of the Nile basin; Italy claiming that the British rights were only 'hydraulic', that is, they referred only to the control of the Nile waters.[8] That particular Italian request had come to nothing but the roles were anxiously reversed in 1923 when the British government found its wish to construct a dam on Lake Tsana thwarted by the fact that the region in question, under the protocol of 15 April 1891, was in the Italian sphere of influence and that instrument was cited in the 1906 agreement. The advice of the British Minister in Addis Ababa at that time was curiously similar to advice later offered by the Italian representatives in Africa when faced by native opposition. 'I presume that His Majesty's Government will not be prepared to accept that a few dunderheads who happen to direct the affairs of the country should be allowed to veto a project calculated to be of benefit to millions,' he wrote to Curzon, advising him to ride over the Abyssinians and square the Italians later. 'I would next advise that Ras Hailu of Gojjam should be detached from his allegiance to the central government, his

independence recognized in a treaty and an agreement made with
him for the construction of the dam.'[9] By 1925 Italian and British
interests in Abyssinia were in harmony. In an exchange of notes
between Mussolini and Graham dated 14 and 15 December 1925,
the British government accepted Italian support for their efforts to
obtain the concessions to build the dam and water road between
Lake Tsana and the Sudan (in the Italian sphere of influence
according to the 1906 treaty), while Italy obtained British support
in her efforts to obtain from the Abyssinian government the concession to construct and operate a railway from the frontier of
Eritrea to the frontier of Italian Somaliland through Abyssinian
territory and an exclusive zone of economic influence in the area
crossed by the railway.[10] The substance of this agreement was
subsequently communicated to the French and Abyssinian governments. To the Abyssinian protests before the League of Nations
that the Anglo–Italian deal was hardly consistent with the sovereignty of a League member, Britain and Italy in effect replied that
just as they were free to grant these concessions to one another, so
was the Abyssinian government free to grant or not to grant these
concessions to them. The immediate result of the Italo–British
exchange of notes was that Britain proceeded to discourage British
enterprise throughout northern and western Abyssinia in favour
of Italy and that Italy embarked on a programme to acquire the
pre-eminent position occupied in Abyssinia by France.

The key to the French position was the Jibuti–Addis Ababa
railway, the only link between Abyssinia and the sea and thus at
once the symbol of Abyssinia's dependence on European techno-
logy as well as her only window on the outside world. It was a
cardinal point of Abyssinian policy, and in particular the policy of
Ras Taffari, the regent who in 1930 became the Emperor Haile
Selassie, to break that dependence by means of an independent
corridor to the sea either through Italian Eritrea or French or
British Somaliland. In 1924 Ras Taffari had visited Paris to try to
obtain independent access to the sea by acquiring or leasing an
enclave of land on Jibuti Bay in French Somaliland. The French
government was at first willing to entertain this request but on the
condition that the construction of the necessary quays, warehouses,
railway extensions, etc., was left to French industry, a condition
which, as expected, proved too onerous. Discouraged from applying to Britain for the cession of the port and hinterland of Zeila in

British Somaliland, in the same year the regent then asked for access to the sea through Italian territory at the Eritrean port of Beilul to be ceded for ninety-nine years, subject to granting a concession to an Italian firm to build a railway to the interior.

Nothing came of these proposals until 1927 when the deal with Italy was revived in another form. A visit to Addis Ababa by the Duke of Abruzzi and the return visit to Rome by Ras Taffari in July yielded a draft agreement according to which Italy would grant Abyssinia a free zone at Assab in Eritrea and would build a road from there to the Abyssinian frontier while Abyssinia would continue the road from the border to Dessie.[11] The draft agreement marked an important turning point in Italian foreign policy. It was in part the result of a struggle for power within the fascist administration between those who favoured a forward policy in the Balkans – the Adriatic wing – and those, dubbed the Africanists, who looked to expansion south of the Mediterranean. In 1927–8 the Adriatic wing got the upper hand and held it roughly until the early 1930s when it became apparent, on the one hand, that the friendly policy towards Abyssinia initiated by the 1928 agreement had not borne economic fruit and, on the other, that possession of an overseas empire with its attendant mercantilist economic policy might relieve the unemployment and stagnation of trade caused by the Depression. In the meantime the Africanists had been relegated to the Ministry of Colonies there to vent their impotence in some heavy-handed repression of recalcitrant natives or in hatching schemes of subversion across the borders of Eritrea and Somaliland. The Italo–Abyssinian Pact of Arbitration and Friendship signed on 2 August 1928 declared that neither government would take any action which might prejudice or damage the independence of the other and that disputes not susceptible to settlement by ordinary diplomatic means would be submitted to a procedure of conciliation or arbitration. The treaty also bound the two governments to develop and promote commerce between the two countries and in pursuit of this clause a supplementary convention providing access to the sea and the construction of a road were added to the treaty.[12]

As it happened, little effect was given to these arrangements. The Italians attributed this to the Abyssinians' procrastination and intransigence; the Abyssinians' answer was that the experts appointed to decide the technical problems connected with the construction of the road were at complete variance. Difficulties centred over the location of the road between Assab and Dessie, a southern route being preferred by Italy, a northern one being suggested by Taffari's French advisers who hoped thus to divert the road from the traffic routes served by the Jibuti–Addis Ababa railway and keep it away from the Abyssinian capital. The result was that work was constantly postponed to the double disappointment of the Italian government, on the one hand because the road was not getting built and on the other because it saw in the delays confirmation of Abyssinian and French ill will, an ill will readily emphasised by General Emilio de Bono, the future conqueror of Abyssinia and presently Under-Secretary of the Italian Colonial Office, himself as obstructionist as Taffari's French advisers.[13] The upshot was Mussolini's refusal of Taffari's request for two light tanks and two aeroplanes – the former to be landed at Assab and driven to the capital (over the route proposed by Italy) for the purpose of impressing on the rebel frontier chieftains the new might of the central government – in effect showing that Mussolini preferred not to strengthen the emperor's authority, even if the pay-off for Italy was the implementation of the road convention. A joint memorandum drafted by Grandi and de Bono in January 1930 argued that to accede to the emperor's request might give the unwanted impression that Italy was 'an active supporter and defender' of the negus and to risk[14]

> compromising definitely the present friendly relations with Ras Hailu . . . one of the most important feudal chiefs of the empire, destined to play an important role in the case of the death of the present Negus or of internal troubles which in that country one must always be ready for.

A thoroughgoing policy of internal subversion, though it had its proponents, probably did not begin at that point but it was clear as early as 1930 that the Treaty of Friendship was practically a dead letter. In July 1931, the Abyssinian government evidently also considered the friendship pact moribund for it began to put a check on what it saw as Italian encroachments on its territory. The frontier between Abyssinia and Italian Somaliland in the region of the Ogaden had never been demarcated and it was common knowledge that the Italians had been encroaching further and further inland. Ostensibly to collect taxes from the tribes in the region but really to show the flag, the Abyssinian government now sent a strong expedition into the Ogaden. The Italians retired to a post ten miles inside allegedly Abyssinian territory but they refused a request to discuss the location of the frontier and, after the expedition retired, their encroachment continued to the point where they were able to offer British nomadic tribes the use of wells at Wal-Wal and Wardair, alleged by the Abyssinians to be roughly sixty miles on the Abyssinian side of the frontier laid down by the treaty of 1897. The conclusion was difficult to avoid that Rome was in the process of adopting a deliberate policy of expansion at the expense of Abyssinia, a conclusion supported by the extensive encouragement which Italian colonial officials were extending to disgruntled elements in Abyssinia to hinder the emperor's policy of centralisation.

These activities revealed the strength of that current within Palazzo Chigi and the Ministry of Colonies, which saw the only independent territory remaining in Africa as the area foreordained for Italian expansion. A long, important memorandum by Guariglia, Political Director for Europe, the Near East and Africa, spelled out in August 1932 the steps the Italian government would eventually take. Guariglia's fundamental assumption was that the two Italian East African colonies were but beach-heads for the penetration 'under *whatever form*, of the Abyssinian hinterland'; this task had been rendered more difficult on the one hand because the emperor 'was arming . . . had destroyed the ancient feudal structure . . . and represented a much more formidable obstacle' and on the other because 'Italy could not confront the Ethiopian question' without prior agreement with France and Great Britain. A military conquest, Guariglia cautioned, could be contemplated only after prior agreement had been secured from Britain and France, the two powers upon whose good will Italy would have to depend to minimise repercussions in Europe and within the League. To do otherwise would be sheer folly on military as well as political grounds in view of the more than 3,000 miles of sea routes controlled by the British Navy separating Italy from East Africa. None the less, the time for preparing the ground diplomatically was at hand, Guariglia continued, citing hopeful signs that Paris, in an attempt to put Italo–French relations on a better footing, seemed inclined to grant Italy a free hand in Abyssinia. In the meantime, he recommended as a first step 'to use a heavy hand

and await results'. The dissident chiefs in the border regions had
to be shown 'that there was still a great country to which they
could look: Italy'; the emperor might be threatened with the
cancellation of the pact of friendship; Eritrea and Somaliland had
to be reinforced militarily and the emperor's offer to exchange
territory in the Ogaden for an outlet to the sea was to be treated in
a dilatory manner.[15]

Guariglia's recommendations fell on fertile ground. Admittedly
it was not until 1934 that the failure of the disarmament conference
and the wranglings over measures to cope with the Nazi threat
suggested to Mussolini that the major European powers were not
in a mood to take concerted action together: their inertia, regret-
table in the European context, was propitious for an extension of
the Italian empire in Africa. Yet as early as the summer of 1932
evidence could be seen of a more militant line at home and abroad.
By then the fascistisation of Italy was an accomplished fact. After
the dismissal of Grandi, power was again visibly concentrated in
Mussolini's hands. The second purge of the Italian Foreign Office
that summer sent abroad those career diplomats, Guariglia included, who, though their allegiance to the régime and its aims
was not in doubt, could be counted on to pursue them with some
moderation and skill. At the same time, the concentration of
internal and external power had not produced either material well-
being or the foreign policy successes so confidently predicted a few
years before. Measures taken to cope with the world economic
crises, ostentatiously successful in the area of grain production,
had led to the neglect of the more productive regions of Italian
agriculture. Trade was falling off, unemployment proving irre-
ducible and the real value of wages dropping drastically while the
government, even after the reforms establishing the corporate
state, continued to be incapable of sustaining social and economic
progress. At the same time the constant appeals to the Italians'
martial virtues were finding more receptive ears particularly among
the more rabid supporters of the régime. Official fascist doctrine
that 'war alone keeps all human energies to the maximum tension
and sets the seal of nobility on those people who have the courage
to face it' provided a ready and traditional form of escape from
frustration.[16]

In the East African colonies release from these frustrations took
the form of 'inflexible reciprocity' in dealings with Abyssinia. As a

first step the frontier police were reorganised and the natives trained for military service.[17] In September 1932 General de Bono visited the colonies to study their potential as bases of operations against Abyssinia.[18] In the spring of 1933 he was confirmed as military commander in the event of a colonial war. By the beginning of 1933 Mussolini had accepted at least the principle of the Africanists' schemes. The instructions he gave to the new Ambassador in Addis Ababa, Count Luigi Vinci Gigliucci, on 3 January 1933 were to pursue a policy of friendship designed to disguise Rome's real plans. He believed 'that a military operation in Abyssinia would succeed provided we were completely free in Europe'. Vinci's task was to eliminate all suspicion and to sidetrack any discussion for a settlement by an exchange of territory.[19] In mid-1934 the Chief of Staff, General Pietro Badoglio, was brought into the plans. Two stages were envisaged; the first involved strengthening the military potential of Eritrea, at the same time adopting a non-provocative attitude towards Addis Ababa as well as Britain and France; the second involved a study of how best Abyssinia could be provoked into taking action against Eritrea to provide Italy with an excuse for war.[20] Preparations proceeded apace for both stages. While Vinci Gigliucci kept relations with Abyssinia on a formally friendly level, the military attaché (and commander of the Royal Corps in Eritrea) Colonel Vittorio Ruggero was instructed to prepare the ground for an incident[21] and the Under-Secretary for War, General Federico Baistrocchi, ordered to provide a plan for a swift attack to be put into effect the moment the appropriate political groundwork had eliminated the danger of great-power interference.[22] Badoglio himself in July 1934 conducted an on-the-spot examination of the defensive and offensive preparations in Eritrea. His report, generally negative in view of the higher manpower priorities he assigned to the Brenner frontier after the Nazi *putsch*, was apparently overridden by Mussolini: the following month the American military attaché in Rome reported that the Italian General Staff had plans ready for 'the military conquest and occupation of Abyssinia ... to be undertaken whenever Abyssinia commits an "overt act".'[23] By the end of that summer the existence of plans for the invasion of Abyssinia were common knowledge among the upper echelons of the Italian Foreign Office and the party. The plans were still of a contingent nature until such time as Abyssinia provided the necessary provocation and the great powers the necessary acquiescence. But that some form of armed action was contemplated in the near future was beyond doubt.

Wal-Wal

It was in the nature of Abyssinian politics that as relations deteriorated with one signatory of the 1906 agreement, they improved correspondingly with the others. Just as it had always been the habit of the emperor to play off the interests of the three powers to preserve his own strength and obtain his major territorial ambition, an outlet to the sea, so it had also been policy in London, Paris and Rome to take advantage of another signatory's unpopularity in Abyssinia to improve one's position. Early in 1934, the British representative in Addis Ababa was authorised to start personal and confidential conversations with the emperor. In return for the cession to Abyssinia of the port Zeila in British Somaliland and a corridor connecting it to the Abyssinian hinterland, the emperor was invited to cede to British Somaliland an area embracing roughly the grazing grounds of the British Somali tribes, to agree to a rectification of the Kenya and Sudan frontiers and to enter into a treaty of friendship. At the appropriate moment, the emperor was told, the French and Italian governments would be informed as required by the tripartite agreement of 1906.

On the whole, the emperor accorded a favourable reception to these proposals, though he was clearly nervous of French and Italian reactions to them. His nervousness was privately shared in London – and with very good reasons. On the one hand there were reports in July 1934 that Louis Barthou, the new French Foreign Minister, might offer Italy a free hand in Abyssinia. 'We certainly don't want anything of the kind,' a Foreign Office official noted. 'It suits our book much better to endeavour to reach our own agreement with Ethiopia.'[24] On the other hand, even more to the point, the grazing territory which Britain sought in exchange for the port of Zeila included the watering spots of Wal-Wal and Wardair in the Ogaden both *de facto* if not *de jure* in Italian hands. With understandable overstatement, a minute on a Foreign Office memorandum of 25 August 1934, discussing the proposed exchange, predicted that 'If and when the Zeila concession comes to the stage . . . fur will fly'.[25]

It is still a moot point whether the Italian Secret Service was photographing the contents of the safe of the British Ambassador in Rome as early as 1934, but at any rate it must have been disingenuous of the British government to suppose that these kinds of negotiation could remain secret for long. The upshot was that the Italian government must have felt that Great Britain was poaching in its territories and in this light the incident which took place at Wal-Wal in the autumn of 1934 assumed a far larger scope than a mere frontier squabble.

As early as January 1934, a British boundary commission engaged in delineating the frontier between Abyssinia and British Somaliland had ascertained that Wal-Wal and Wardair were in Italian possession. After a good deal of British pressure, the emperor was persuaded in the summer of 1934 to have the area surveyed again, this time by a mixed British–Abyssinian Boundary Commission, the purpose being to settle the matter of possession in favour of Abyssinia so as to facilitate the transfer of territory to Britain. Shortly afterwards, an exchange of public *communiqués* between Rome and Addis Ababa which clearly acknowledged an increase in Italo–Abyssinian tension had the effect of provoking a second look at a step which would clearly appear provocative to Italy. The border region in question, between Abyssinia and the British and Italian Somalilands, had been a subject of dispute since the beginning of the century. Most maps showed Wal-Wal inside Abyssinian territory, but Italy had been in occupation since 1930 when an Italian garrison fort had been established in the area and, by custom if not by law, the occupation authorities exercised sovereign rights over the wells. On 9 October 1934 an interdepartmental meeting was held in London to decide whether the Anglo–Abyssinian Boundary Commission should persist in its plans to visit the Ogaden country 'admittedly within the Italian sphere of influence' and 'permanently occupied by Italy'.[26] The meeting decided that the Boundary Commission should proceed to visit Wal-Wal and Wardair but clearly in the company of Abyssinians. The leader of the expedition, Colonel Clifford, was enjoined from discussing the implications of the Italian occupation with either his Abyssinian colleagues or with the Italians. If the latter challenged him or refused him access to the wells, Clifford was to register a strong protest, citing the relevant treaties and report to the Colonial Office. 'It was desirable', he was told, 'to obtain more certain knowledge of the dispositions and intentions of the Italians at Wal-Wal and Wardair.'27

The expedition had all the markings of a carefully prepared political probe and after the emperor had been persuaded to provide an Abyssinian military escort for the mixed commission, the head of the African department in the Italian Ministry of Foreign Affairs was informed of the impending visit, though in an informal manner 'because it was feared that formal action might give the Italian government a pretext to claim that their military occupation of the wells had been recognized by His Majesty's Government'.28 Apparently, however, the Italian government took no steps to inform the local Italian authorities who were left, or maintained they were left, in entire ignorance of the commission's plans.

In the event, a force of about 600 Abyssinian soldiers provided by the Abyssinian government met on 20 November at Ado, eighteen miles from Wal-Wal, with the Anglo–Abyssinian Boundary Commission and, acting as an official escort, proceeded the following day towards the Italian garrison, where they arrived on 22 November. The arrival of 600 armed men could not but appear threatening to the Italian garrison, the more so since the Boundary Commission arrived only on the following day to explain its purpose and presumably also its need for such a disproportionately large escort force. The Italian garrison housed 160 native soldiers under a Somali non-commissioned officer but at the moment of the arrival no Italian nationals. Soon after the arrival something in the nature of a scrimmage apparently ensued in the course of which no shots were fired. Colonel Clifford reportedly made some gestures indicating British recognition of Abyssinian sovereignty over the area and at the end of the day the Abyssinian section invited the British section of the commission to hoist their flag, presumably to indicate that they were under British protection. The following day, after an Italian officer appeared at the scene, the commission held a meeting and addressed to the Italian commander a protest, an explanation of their presence in the region and an invitation to visit the commission the following day.29

On his arrival the Italian officer, Captain Cimmaruta, insisted that the commission's protest was a matter for the political authorities and not for him, but he was persuaded to write an acknowledgment of it. His suggestion that a provisional arrangement should be concluded to avoid incidents was found not acceptable, since it was based on the assumption that the wells were in Italian territory and that the Abyssinian escort was not entitled to camp on them.[30] At this point, according to instructions, Colonel Clifford withdrew the British section from the mixed Boundary Commission leaving the Abyssinian escort force, in the meantime reinforced substantially by levies drawn from the neighbourhood, to face the Italians.

The first confrontation at Wal-Wal had thus resulted in an embarrassment to all sides. The Abyssinians' attempt to assert their claim over territories they intended to cede to Britain had made no progress. The parallel British attempt to support Abyssinian sovereignty was at best crude and at worst ineffectual. The Italians, who in all likelihood intended to engineer a border clash in the future, probably judged this incident premature. Meanwhile more than 1,000 men stood facing one another at the wells.

The emperor was very nervous and had 'no idea what to do next'.[31] No help was forthcoming from Britain. The British Minister in Addis Ababa, Barton, was advised on 29 November to inform the negus that 'no advice can be given . . . until a decision can be taken here as to general policy'.[32] But obviously the British government had decided to withdraw from the probe as gracefully as it could. A note sent to Rome on 3 December stated that the Italian posts at Wal-Wal and Wardair were a matter for Italy and Abyssinia to sort out and London had no desire to intervene. The British government was now merely concerned that the traditional watering and grazing rights of the British Somali tribes should be safeguarded.[33] As to the demarcation of the frontier, the mixed Anglo–Abyssinian Commission had suspended its work but the Italian and Abyssinian authorities were urged to continue that work themselves. This latter suggestion did not appeal to the Italian government, which instead obligingly agreed to allow the British commissioner and his Abyssinian colleagues to enter Wal-Wal and Wardair to carry on their work, but before any steps could be taken in that direction serious fighting broke out on 5 December at Wal-Wal, where, after a clash in which about 150 men lost their lives, the Abyssinian force was put to flight.

This skirmish acted as the catalyst for both sides – Abyssinia saw in it the chance to challenge the legitimacy of Italian occupation before the League; Italy, to assert her claim and, if necessary, use it as justification for war. The emperor's first inclination, to fly at once to the League, was deterred by the personal advice of the British representative who thought such application premature until the emperor had negotiated with Italy. But as the notes exchanged between Italy and Abyssinia between 6 and 11 December made no progress towards solving the dispute, the emperor, with British encouragement, on 14 December drew the attention of the League to the incident, although he omitted to mention any article of the Covenant as applicable in the circumstances. As was expected, Rome denied the competence of the League as well as the allegations in the Abyssinian note but showed no qualms at all about renewing the work of demarcating the boundary. Though, as will be seen in a moment, Mussolini's mind was made up that the Abyssinian question was to be disposed by force of arms within the next two years, he appeared genuinely worried that this incident might force him into an uncompromising position before military preparations were ready. Accordingly, the good offices of Britain and France were sought and the disposition to compromise was reinforced by personal messages. Their gist was that the Italian government felt it right to regard the clash at Wal-Wal (for which Italy probably bore no immediate responsibility) and the demarcation of the boundary as two separate questions in the sense that the former had to be disposed before the latter could be tackled.

Essentially, however, Italy's good will at the end of December was a matter of tactics. Mussolini's decision to use force in Abyssinia was crystallised in a secret memorandum circulated on 30 December. The paper drafted by Mussolini described Italy as being in a race against time with Abyssinia:

> History, in modern times, marches fast, especially when aided by European missions.... This political development augments the Ethiopian Emperor's capabilities and warlike efficiency ... time works against us ... it is imperative that the problem be resolved as soon as possible, as soon as our military preparations will give us the certainty of victory....

'Having decided on this war,' he went on, 'the objective can be no other than the destruction of the Abyssinian armed forces and the total conquest of Ethiopia. The Empire cannot be made any other way.' The delicate question was the timing. In a few years the situation in Europe might not be so propitious. Italy was coming to an agreement with France which in turn would also improve Italo–Yugoslav relations; Germany would not be ready for some time for military adventures and Poland's drift back to France was slowing down the dynamism of the Third Reich. All in all, Mussolini could see peace lasting in Europe for at least another two years, long enough to despatch Abyssinia before that country improved its military strength. Italy's own preparations had to be ready by October 1935. 'No one will raise any difficulties in Europe if the conduct of military operations will result rapidly in a *fait accompli*,' he predicted confidently, and 'there will be no embarrassment from the League of Nations or at least not such to prevent us carrying out the operation to the end.' In the meantime, it was imperative to avoid all incidents which might anticipate the conflict. 'The Gordian knot of Italo–Abyssinian relations is going to become increasingly entangled,' Mussolini concluded. 'We must cut it before it is too late.'[34]

Diplomatic preparations

Cutting the Gordian knot, as Mussolini realised, would leave several loose strands. Italian diplomacy was charged with the task of gathering them together. First on the agenda was an agreement with France. Franco–Italian differences had paled recently in the face of a resurgent Germany. Their contrasting interests in Eastern Europe could always provide a source of friction, given the obstinacy of both governments, but they had never been beyond composition. Other disputes were of longer standing and hoarier with accumulated animosities. The status of the Italians in Tunisia had been in suspense for years and the compensation due to Italy according to the Pact of London never satisfactorily paid. In Tunisia, the French government had curtailed the rights of the Italian majority and in Libya, in contrast to Britain which had settled its bill in 1924 with the cession of Jubaland, successive French governments had frustratingly put off Italian claims.

France's unaccommodating attitude towards Italy's colonial aspirations had been under review in Paris for several years. There had always been a current in France willing to pay a price for, if not Italian friendship, certainly Italian disinterest in France's North African holdings, by far the French empire's most important resources. That price could be support of Italian ambitions either in Asia Minor or East Africa, with the latter the likelier candidate since Ataturk's Turkey had long passed the point where designs could be seriously entertained on its territorial integrity while, by contrast, Abyssinia was manifestly a semi-feudal state unable to exercise authority over its outlying territories. As early as 1931 Berthelot, the Secretary-General of the Quai d'Orsay, had encouraged Marquis Theodoli, the Italian chairman of the Mandates Commission of the League who had been sent to Paris to try to advance, in a semi-official way, the recently stalled Franco–Italian negotiations, to think that a bargain might be struck over Abyssinia. This impression was confirmed by subsequent conversations between Theodoli and his French colleague in Geneva, Robert de Caix.[35] By late 1932 the outlines of a deal were evident. The French government was considering offering some substantial concessions in its sphere of influence in Abyssinia, some territory in Libya, some shares in the Jibuti–Addis Ababa railroad and closer control over the traffic in arms into Abyssinia through Jibuti in return for an Italian pledge of support for France in Europe including the integral application of the sanctions machinery, Italy's membership in a Mediterranean naval agreement, an end to Rome's espousal of treaty revision and a lasting settlement of the Tunisian question in France's favour.[36] It was significant in this connection that in 1932 and early 1933 France had turned down two offers of alliance by the Abyssinian emperor 'the outcome of which would have been the conversion of his country into a virtual French protectorate'.[37]

This attitude, distinctly unfavourable to a country which until recently had enjoyed wide French patronage, had to be attributed to the exigencies of the European situation where the coming to power of Hitler made it much more pressing to square the Italians. By the same token, though the concessions which could be extracted were substantial, Mussolini felt that the French requirements in Europe were too constricting and designed to provoke a breach between him and Germany. They were turned down partly in the expectation that in the near future the German threat would be felt more pressingly in France.[38] By late 1934 that prediction had come true. With Germany rearming and Britain refraining from involvement in Eastern Europe, what had been implicit at Locarno – that French security depended on Italian co-operation so as to permit the concentration of French forces on the Rhine and the unimpeded passage of colonial reinforcements through the Mediterranean – had become painfully all too clear. Coincidentally, Mussolini's flirtations with Hitler had resolved themselves after the Nazi *putsch* in Austria into rage and fear.

When Pierre Laval succeeded Barthou at the Quai d'Orsay in October 1934 a draft agreement with Italy already existed. At the end of that month Laval confirmed to Mussolini his desire to continue Barthou's policy of *rapprochement* and suggested a visit to Rome as soon as the ground had been prepared.[39] At the same time the French Ambassador to Rome was summoned to Paris for consultation. He returned at the end of November 1934 with fresh instructions for negotiating a comprehensive settlement with Italy on the question of Austria, Yugoslavia, German rearmament and Africa, the settlement of purely Franco–Italian questions in Africa being dependent on that of European problems. Regarding Austria, De Chambrun was to take up the negotiations at the point where they had broken down in September, seeking, at a minimum, agreement on a declaration (to which members of the Little *Entente* might accede) of the signatories' interest in maintaining Austria's independence and in provisions for consultations should it be threatened. If Italy rejected this, De Chambrun was to fall back on the idea of a general European convention again open to all states binding the signatories not to interfere in one another's affairs. As to Yugoslavia, there was no hope of securing a tripartite agreement with that country and Italy but Rome was urged to conclude a treaty of arbitration with Belgrade, accompanied perhaps by declaration to the effect that the two countries were separated by no territorial ambitions. On the crucial question of German re-armament, De Chambrun was to persuade Italy not to acquiesce in it and if Germany denounced Part V of the Treaty of Versailles, to concert with France and others on how most effectively to meet the threat. Compensation for these Italian concessions was to be found in Africa. The French government expected Italy to ask for rectifications in the Libyan frontier and for the *modus vivendi* in Tunis (embodying the Italian settlers' privileges and renewable every three years) to be converted into an agreement for ten years. In Abyssinia, Italy was expected to ask for a share in the Jibuti–Addis Ababa railway and, more important, France's compliance in a policy of encroachment. Provided agreement was reached on European matters, France would propose a joint Franco–Italian declaration to the effect that all the outstanding questions (African ones included) had been settled and both countries had agreed to collaborate to maintain peace.[40]

The importance of these negotiations could not be under-estimated. If they bore fruit at a stroke they would eliminate Italy's and France's competition in Central Europe which had poisoned European relations for a decade; the fulfilment of Italy's pretensions in North and East Africa seemed an agreeable price to pay in view of the much more ominous developments in Germany. Negotiations reached a climax in December. On Austria, there was unity of aims but a divergence of method: the French wanted to internationalise the problem completely while the Italians desired to avoid bringing Czechoslovakia and Yugoslavia into consultations, or at any rate to relegate them to a second category of states to be consulted. Mussolini's great-power complex similarly precluded any mention of Yugoslavia in the text of any agreement with France, though he professed good will towards that country. During the Christmas holidays the tempo was accelerated with some help from Britain. Italy's need of French support after the Wal-Wal incident had gone to the League coincided with France's dependence on Italy as the Saar plebiscite approached. Agreement was reached on the Central European questions[41] and Laval left for Rome on the night of 3 January to resolve the African issues. On 7 January after a closed session with Mussolini, the two men put their signatures to a series of agreements, protocols and declarations covering armaments, central Europe and their interests in Africa. Four of these agreements were made public – a general declaration of amity; a treaty ceding to Italy a sizeable portion of Libyan hinterland and 13·5 miles of East African coastline; a protocol whereby Italy promised to relinquish the special rights of Italian citizens in Tunisia; and a proposal for a non-aggression pact open to all countries bordering on Austria, a device by which France through the Little *Entente* and Italy along with Hungary might take part in the protection of Austria against Germany. Four other agreements remained secret. The crucial one from the French point of view stipulated immediate consultations if Germany broke the restrictions imposed on her by Part V of the Treaty of Versailles; moreover, in the event discussions were resumed on the limitation of arms, Italy and France were to 'concert their efforts so that the figures on limitations inscribed in the agreement will ensure the two countries, in relation to Germany, the advantages which will be justified for each of them'. The others called for the maintenance of the *status quo* at the mouth of the Red Sea, the transferral to Italy of 2,500 of the 34,000 shares in the Jibuti–Addis Ababa railroad, and, the crucial provision for Italy, a pledge that 'the French government does not look in Abyssinia for the satisfaction of any interests other than those economic interests relating to the traffic of the Jibuti–Addis Ababa railway'.[42]

These agreements – the Mussolini–Laval Accords – could be and were justified by the relevance to the European situation of Franco–Italian co-operation. But it was most unlikely that Mussolini would liquidate the fate of his compatriots in Tunisia for less than a 7 per cent share in a railroad and any number of square miles of desert. What he received in addition, if not in writing certainly verbally, was French acquiescence not only in Italy's economic penetration of Abyssinia but also, if need be, political domination. Admittedly, Laval, as Mussolini later acknowledged, at no point gave the Italian dictator his formal approval for a war of aggression, but of course the approval was not sought in those terms. Neither man was endowed with the saving ingenuousness which might have excused a literal interpretation of the secret treaty.[43] No doubt, a political solution of the Abyssinian dispute favourable to Italy (perhaps after a suitable show of arms on the pattern employed previously by the French in Morocco) would have been preferable but no French or Italian statesman at the time suffered any illusions about the scope of the French *désistement* if no such solution appeared feasible, especially after the arrangements on Central Europe were translated into a military convention. On 25 January 1935 Badoglio wrote to his French counterpart, General Gamelin, suggesting the study of a plan for Franco–Italian military co-operation. The French Chief of General Staff's reply on 2 February broached the possibility of an exchange of units – French forces would be placed on the Yugoslav side facing Austria so as to relieve Belgrade's fears of an Italian diversionary thrust into Yugoslavia; Italian forces would be despatched to the Franco–German–Swiss frontier ostensibly to ensure Switzerland's neutrality. In April, Gamelin and General Denain travelled to Rome on the occasion of the Stresa conference to establish direct contact with Badoglio.[44] A radical revolution of inter-European affairs was in the making.

By the end of January 1935 not only had the *entente* with France been sealed, but Italy, with British and French support, had also persuaded Abyssinia to abandon her appeal to the League in favour of arbitration. It now became a question for Italy of associating Britain with the French *désistement*. Obtaining a free hand in Abyssinia from Britain proved a much more difficult task than Italian diplomacy anticipated, not necessarily because Great Britain had any vital interests to protect nor indeed because the British government was seized of the moral issue but rather because its secret negotiations with the negus had now become increasingly embarrassing. On 29 January Grandi informed the British Secretary of State of the agreements reached with France and invited the British government to conclude a similar arrangement.[45] He had been preceded the day before by the Italian counsellor Vitetti, also seeking an exchange of views with the United Kingdom concerning the 'mutual and harmonious' development of their interests in Abyssinia. There was no ambiguity in the Italian proposals. 'From the summary he gave me,' Thompson, the Foreign Office official on the African desk, noted after his conversation with Vitetti, 'it seems pretty clear that France has given Italy politically a free hand so far as Ethiopia is concerned, merely reserving her economic rights in the so-called railway zone.'[46] In effect, therefore, London was being asked to abandon its negotiations with the emperor and associate with France in also giving Italy a free hand. The first part was easy. When at the end of December, the emperor declared that Britain could now obtain all her requests in the Ogaden in exchange for the cession of Zeila, a Foreign Office official had noted that[47]

> ... the Emperor's acceptance can no longer be of any use to us. Perhaps His Majesty hoped that this acceptance would be sufficient bait to attract us to his side in his dispute with Italy. It is manifestly impossible for us to go to the Italians and suggest that we are negotiating with the Ethiopians for the cession of Wal-Wal and Wardair. I would advocate that we should merely put the whole project in cold storage.

To another Abyssinian request in the middle of January 'to negotiate ... a comprehensive settlement', Thompson, whose earlier fears appeared confirmed 'that Rome knew all about our "secret" talks about Zeila in Addis Ababa', proposed to reply that 'an Anglo–Ethiopian combination against a Franco–Italian one is hardly to be considered'.[48] The Cabinet evidently agreed that the secret negotiations to obtain from Abyssinia territory coveted and occupied by Italy were now an embarrassing liability. On 22 January the foreign secretary advised Addis Ababa that the 'present situation makes it inadvisable to pursue even informally possibility of all around settlement involving territorial adjustment'. And to the emperor's renewed plea for at least an agreement in principle, Simon answered stiffly on 31 January that 'no assurances of even the most general and personal nature' could be given.[49]

It still remained, however, to deal with the no less embarrassing Italian offer of 29 January. London, of course, had not given up all hope of securing the Ogaden for Abyssinia and so gaining the good will of the emperor eventually to build a dam on Lake Tsana: that ambition had merely been put into cold storage. This consideration alone suggested that, since Italy and Britain were after favours from the same quarters, no favourable answers would be returned to the Italian *démarche*. And in fact none ever was, although London's evasive tactics constituted some kind of an answer. Both Grandi and Vitetti had been told that the Italian proposal would be carefully considered and indeed a statement of Britain's interests in Abyssinia – the Maffey report – was produced by mid-1935. Long before that date, however, the question had become academic since the deterioration of Italo–Abyssinian relations had rendered any conversations with Italy on the lines proposed out of the question. But it was still difficult to translate disapproval into practical terms. Eventually the British government decided that its strongest ammunition lay in Geneva and in domestic public opinion – as it turned out, two ineffectual sources of pressure, the first because Italy had no respect for the League except as a vehicle for a great power directorate and the other because, having manipulated public opinion at home for thirteen years, Mussolini discounted its reactions in advance. The first British warning was occasioned by the mobilisation on 11 February 1935 of two Italian divisions for service in East Africa. On 21 February Simon spoke to Grandi of the increasing suspicion of Italian intentions in the British public and a somewhat stiffer warning was conveyed by Sir Robert Vansittart within the week and repeated in Rome. The British Permanent Secretary at the Foreign Office forecast that there would be justifiable attacks on Italy in the British press which it would be quite impossible for his government to prevent.[50] Drummond the following day left with Mussolini a memorandum calling attention to the dangers of a policy which would not be understood by British public opinion. The Italian reply – another request for collaboration in the sense first suggested by Grandi on 29 January – was left unanswered.

In the meantime, the two parties had been wrangling over the setting up of a neutral zone in the Ogaden to prevent further incidents. When at length it was set up in early March and Addis Ababa asked that a commission finally be nominated in accordance with the provisions of the 1928 treaty, the Italian government replied by reiterating its original demands for compensation and apologies as a precondition to any discussions of the Wal-Wal incident.[51] On 17 March, its patience exhausted, the Abyssinian government brought the entire dispute before the League. As a result of the Italian build-up of arms in East Africa, Addis Ababa claimed, there now existed 'a dispute likely to lead to a rupture'; appeal was therefore made not only to the League's arbitration machinery but also to Article X on the grounds that Abyssinia's territorial integrity and political independence were now threatened.

Abyssinia's timing was unfortunate. The previous day, 16 March, the German government had repudiated the disarmament provisions of the Versailles Treaty, thus creating an immediate bond of solidarity amongst the ex-*Entente* powers. As Italian co-operation became more crucial to Britain and France, their scruples over the situation in Abyssinia receded into the background. A conference was called to meet on 10 April in the Italian town of Stresa and deal with the German breach. At the same time, ostensibly as a reply to the German rearmament measures, Mussolini called to the colours another class of reservists and, confident of western support, persuaded the League council to disinterest itself in the Abyssinian *démarche* while arbitration, which in Italian eyes had not yet been exhausted, continued.

The success of Italy's plans to isolate Abyssinia depended on keeping the dispute out of the League and on securing British and French acquiescence. By the time the Stresa conference opened the first objective was still in sight – the fiction of arbitration had been allowed to continue. The second objective had been half fulfilled

by Laval's *désistement* in January; ascertaining where the British
government stood was proving more difficult than anticipated. In
London, the Cabinet and the Foreign Office, after the incon-
clusiveness of their first warning, were divided. The Foreign
Secretary, while aware of the dangers of war, thought the dispute
'must be handled in a way which will not adversely affect Anglo–
Italian relations';[52] on the other hand, Anthony Eden, the Minister
for League Affairs, looked to the Stresa conference as an opportunity to confront Mussolini; MacDonald, on the contrary, looked
to it as an opportunity to attach Mussolini permanently to the
western camp in the face of German resurgence. In the event, at
the Stresa conference the issue of Abyssinia was carefully relegated
to the back room. Both delegations had brought their African
experts, Thompson and Guarnaschelli. At Vansittart's direction,
Thompson raised the question of the dangers of a forward military
policy by Italy in Africa. Guarnaschelli's answer was not reassuring. He did not think the question would be settled by conciliation
commissions. Italy had been denied the opportunity for construc-
tive labour. 'Something would have to be done to remedy the
situation, and he could only see one way of doing it, either sooner
or later.' Vitetti who was also present at some of the talks ex-
patiated on the difficulties of Italy's colonial position:

> Thanks to Britain and France, she had been denied any of the
> colonial fruits of victory over Germany. Now Germany was once
> more becoming a threat and her demand for equal rights was under-
> stood to include the right to overseas possessions. . . . It was not
> suggested that she intended to take physical possession of the
> Ethiopian Empire but the policy of the old pre-War Germany *vis-à-
> vis* Turkey should not be forgotten; the Italian government was
> convinced that Germany was politically interested in Abyssinia, a
> country which, but for the tragedy of Adowa and the then existence
> of a weak and vacillating government in Rome, would today have
> been an Italian protectorate.

In reply, Thompson made it clear that it would be useless to hope,
as Guarnaschelli tentatively suggested, that Britain could in any
way actively assist Italy to obtain her Abyssinian objectives.[53]

The fundamental point, however, was not raised by the Foreign
Ministers themselves. Mussolini interpreted the silence to mean, if
not consent or co-operation, at least acquiescence. When the final
declaration was drawn up at the end of the conference registering

the three governments' opposition to 'any unilateral repudiation of treaties which may endanger the peace', Mussolini asked if it was not necessary to add the words 'in Europe'. No one moved. The words were added and there could have been no misunderstanding that the sanctity of treaties did not reach as far as Africa. Henceforth Mussolini could have been pardoned for his opinion that an implicit agreement similar to that reached with Laval in January had also been struck with the British. Simon and MacDonald reluctantly but probably thought so also, although of course, whatever they had in mind was not binding on Hoare and Baldwin who followed them. The conference wound up on 14 April having established a common front in the coming meeting of the League on German rearmament. Britain and Italy reaffirmed their pledge under the Locarno agreements and all three governments promised to consult if Austrian independence was threatened. London, however, was still sufficiently hopeful of an agreement with Berlin not to enter into a military commitment on the continent and especially not over Austria. Vansittart, who in vain had advised MacDonald to 'land Mussolini first and lecture him later', saw the British Prime Minister deliberately eschew the one course of action – a guarantee of the Brenner and a firm commitment against the *Anschluss* with or without a concomitant bargain over Abyssinia – which might have induced Mussolini to pay attention to London. When, later, the British government began to lecture Rome on the indivisibility of peace, their credit had long been exhausted, the more so since at the end of April, as will be seen later, neither Vansittart nor Simon formally declared their opposition after Grandi – on specific instructions from Mussolini, who deliberately wanted to leave no doubts – explained in detail to them Italy's plans in Abyssinia. Vansittart, reportedly, even saw merit in the Italian argument that London 'should collaborate with Italy to hasten as much as possible the Ethiopian affair instead of encouraging, by its vacillating policy in Geneva, the resistance of Ethiopia', but he adduced the intractability of public opinion as a reason for his country's behaviour while Simon could do no better than forecast the weakening of the Stresa front as a result of prolonged Italian operations in East Africa.[54] Not even after Mussolini had pressed Drummond on 4 May did the British government alter its stand. Altogether Mussolini must have concluded that if London would not close both eyes as Paris had done, it would close at

least one. Thus in May reasonably satisfied of London's unwillingness seriously to oppose Italy in Abyssinia, he accelerated his preparations. Three more divisions were mobilised, the militia placed
on a war footing and three classes called to the colours. In the
middle of the month de Bono's instructions were confirmed:
operations would begin in October.[55]

Britain's quandary was reinforced by Grandi's frank exposition
of Italian plans. 'We now have the clearest indication from the
Italian government', Simon said in a paper circulated to the British
Cabinet on 15 May, 'that they contemplate military operations on
an extended scale against Abyssinia as soon as climatic conditions
permit and Italian preparations are complete . . . it is probable that
the advance will take place in October. . . .' The choices facing the
British government were unpalatable. 'If they support against
Italy a practical application of League principles,' Simon wrote,
'their action is bound greatly to compromise Anglo–Italian relations and perhaps even to break the close association at present
existing between France, Italy and the United Kingdom,' a state of
affairs which, the Foreign Secretary noted, could hardly be more
welcome to Germany. 'On the other hand, if the UK acquiesces in
a misuse of League machinery, His Majesty's government will
undoubtedly lay themselves open to grave public criticism. . . .'
At the same time, Germany was rearming and if 'substantial Italian
forces would be locked up in North East Africa, Italy's strength in
Europe [would be] correspondingly weakened'. On the whole, if
it came to the point, Simon concluded, Italian co-operation in
Europe was more precious than Abyssinia's sovereignty. He
advised the Cabinet that Britain and France recommend to
Abyssinia 'to follow a policy more in accordance with modern
conditions by recognising Italy's claim to taking fuller part in
increasing the trade between Abyssinia and the outside world and
in assisting the development of the economic resources of the
Abyssinian Empire.'[56]

Behind this statement there was a small glimmer of hope that
Italy's appetite might be satiated by the achievement in Abyssinia
of a position comparable to Britain's position in Egypt, that is to
say the imposition of a virtual protectorate camouflaged by the
retention of nominal sovereignty and independence. This avenue,
the logical continuation of Simon's recommendation, was explored
by the British Ambassador in a lengthy conversation with Mussolini

on 24 May. 'What troubled, and troubled seriously, my Government,' Drummond told the Duce, 'was not any sympathy they had with Abyssinia or the question of British interests in that country (I did not think that either of these would weigh greatly against our old friendship with Italy) but solely the maintenance of the prestige and effective working for peace of the League.' Drummond begged Signor Mussolini to avoid . . . that His Majesty's Government should be placed in a position where they would have to choose between the old friendship with Italy and their support of the League' since 'public opinion might well feel bound to support the League as against Italy'. In reply Mussolini catalogued his by now familiar complaints against Abyssinia. The situation 'had become intolerable and must be ended', because 'if Italy was engaged in a conflict in Europe the Abyssinians would not hesitate to attack one or both of the colonies, particularly as the Emperor's desire was for an outlet to the sea which could most easily be obtained through Eritrea.' Moreover, 'the Abyssinians had never carried out their side of the Treaty of Friendship. The economic and commercial promises had remained practically unfulfilled. . . . If in order to clarify the situation and to obtain security, it was necessary for him to resort to arms, in short to "go to war", he would do so.' He was also impatient of the suggestion that such a war would destroy the League and the Locarno system. 'Collective security should be confined to Europe', not Africa, Mussolini remarked firmly. 'This had been specifically emphasized at Stresa.'

In reply to Drummond's query about a method 'of securing the results that he wanted short of war', Mussolini allowed that he would be pleased 'if he could obtain his aims by other means . . . but he did not think this would happen' although 'it was, of course, just possible that the Emperor might yield if he realised that the Italian forces were so great that resistance would be futile and if advised to do so by France and Great Britain'. At this point Drummond made mention of the Egyptian model. Mussolini

> found the analogy of Egypt interesting and worth pursuing. In Egypt there was a King who was more or less independent and the people were allowed to carry on their political affairs but they would not, in fact, be allowed to do anything which would endanger the interests of Great Britain in the country or in the vital spots like the Suez Canal.

Britain appointed in Egypt a High Commissioner, the head of the army, the Chief of Police and various advisers. 'He would not rule out such a solution or a solution along the lines of the French position in Morocco.'[57]

London had also not ruled out that kind of solution – at least not yet. But Italy's preparations for war, so manifestly thorough, were beginning to have the opposite impact. The options were as stark as ever – to support the League meant a rupture with Italy and, quite likely, vice versa. But the Cabinet and the Foreign Office, though still divided, were slowly moving towards a harder line. On 15 May, after reading Simon's memorandum, the British government took a small step suggestive of the line it would eventually follow: Eden was instructed to obstruct Italy's attempts to bypass the League.[58] On 19 May, the day before the Council was scheduled to discuss Abyssinia's plea for protection against aggression, representatives of the four most interested nations met in private session. In the meantime the dispute had been inscribed on the agenda after Italy's procrastination over arbitration had exhausted the Abyssinians' patience. After much delay, Italy had recently agreed to name its arbitrators in the hope of postponing the matter coming before the League until September when, if the decision went against her, she might leave the League of Nations. On 25 May, on British prompting, the League adopted two resolutions. Under the first, the Italo–Abyssinian conciliation commission was to settle the Wal-Wal incident within the next three months; by the terms of the second resolution, the Council decided to meet if agreement between the four arbitrators on the selection of the fifth had not been reached by 25 July. If, at the end of the three months, settlement by means of conciliation or arbitration had not proved fruitful, the Council agreed to take the dispute under its jurisdiction. The compromise was acceptable to Mussolini. It satisfied his minimum requirement that the League did not take an immediate hand in the matter. It equally satisfied British requirements that the League's competence be affirmed, if only for some future date; it satisfied as well the French requirement that London and Rome agree on something and the Abyssinian requirement that an armed solution be postponed. But it also revealed the shape the dispute would take in the future. It was becoming apparent to Italy, a month after it was thought the issue had been settled at Stresa, that the British government now had to be

The Abyssinian War

counted as an unreliable opponent. The dispute, the Italian representative in Geneva noted on 24 May, had become 'not Italo–Ethiopian but Anglo–Italian'.[59] France at the same time was slowly acquiring the characteristics of an unreliable friend: if the dispute produced a break between London and Rome there was no guarantee that Laval would side with Rome.

By the same token there was no guarantee Laval would side with London, either. At this stage he continued to register a persistent optimism for which little real basis existed. Yet the causes of his hesitations were perfectly understandable. His major accomplishment was the agreement of 7 January. He was under great pressure from the French General Staff to do nothing which might upset their military understanding with Italy which was about to be turned into a secret convention. Mussolini had recently not only agreed to support France's protests about German rearmament in Geneva; a private agreement had also been struck on Austria and Locarno: Mussolini had agreed to conversations between the general staffs presently taking place, with a view to sending into Italy one or two French divisions should Italy mobilise in the event of an *Anschluss*. In return Italy promised to send several air squadrons to France's eastern frontier if the Rhineland were under threat from Germany and to exchange technical information on air warfare.[60] No doubt this agreement, like the one in January, could influence Mussolini to take direct action in Africa secure in the knowledge that troops would be available if the Brenner frontier were threatened, but from the point of view of France's obsession with Germany both agreements made sense. Laval had to reckon with a public caring little for Abyssinia and not much more for the League (except as an instrument of French policy) and quite determined not to fight unless France were directly attacked. He was as cognizant as London of the naval, military and air weakness of the United Kingdom and therefore of Britain's inability to give France any definitive military undertaking to come to France's aid in Europe. Lastly, he was also aware that the logic inherent in the quadrille of power would draw Italy and Germany closer together as the Stresa front showed signs of weakening. And indeed something of that nature was already taking place. As always, whatever affinity existed between the two dictatorial régimes was troubled by the problem of Austria. Eventually Mussolini would have to face the incompatibility of Austrian independence with German friendship, though in his view the former could be sacrificed only after the latter had been secured. In the meantime both governments were taking steps to blunt their differences. Hitler in a speech of 21 May had abjured any designs over Austria and spoken warmly of Italo–German relations while in reply Mussolini had talked of a gradual *rapprochement*.[61] In these circumstances, the French remained understandably ambivalent but also loath to lose Italian friendship and military support.

While a reconciliation with Germany was still a gleam in the eyes of a coterie of germanophiles in the Italian Foreign Office and France continued to be obsessed with German power, it was Britain's attitude which continued to govern the development of Mussolini's plans for Abyssinia. By now the Duce's prestige, and by extension the fascist régime's, were at stake. However thoroughly rationalised for public consumption by appeals to the need for colonies in view of Italy's prolificity and to Italy's thousand-year-old civilising mission in Africa, the fact was that dictators did not easily back down. What strengthened Mussolini's stubbornness was the absence of any British interests in Abyssinia, none, at least, for which formal Abyssinian independence was necessary. The country had long been recognised as falling largely within Italy's sphere of influence and whether it remained independent or was absorbed by Italy was a matter of indifference. This, at any rate, was the burden of the report of the Maffey Committee, a report to which the Italians became privy thanks to their Military Information Service which obtained a copy from the British Ambassador's safe immediately it was deposited there in June.[62]

The Maffey Committee had been set up on 6 March in response to Grandi's *démarche* of 29 January. The hiatus had been taken up by the Foreign Office's efforts to make up its mind as to Italy's ultimate intentions. By the time the committee was struck, these had been defined as 'not a mere economic preponderance only, but the virtual absorption of as much Ethiopian territory as can be achieved without jeopardy to their interests and influence in other parts of the world'. The committee was asked by the Foreign Office to forecast the effect of such absorption on British interests, a job the committee declined to do on the grounds that it was 'not qualified to advise His Majesty's Government on the fundamental question of what British policy should be in regard to Italian aims in Ethiopia', preferring instead to attempt 'to determine and to set out what are the main British interests . . . and to say how these interests would be likely to be affected if Ethiopia passed under Italian control'. The committee's major conclusion, that 'No such vital British interest is concerned in and around Ethiopia as would make it essential for His Majesty's Government to resist an Italian conquest of Ethiopia', must have been a major influence on Mussolini's decision to persevere in his course of action and turn down the compromise proposal which Eden offered him at the end of June. British interests in the Nile Basin were more substantial, the report stated, but there was no suggestion that these might be threatened by Italy's aggression in East Africa; and only by stretching the chain of causality to the point of incredulity could it be suggested that an Italian war against Abyssinia would rebound to Britain's disadvantage in the Far East – 'the threat to British imperial interests is a remote one', the report had concluded. Indeed, as Vansittart in particular argued, only if London wilfully antagonised Italy would Britain's international position become precarious because at that point it could be expected that Italy and Germany would come together (perhaps drawing in Japan as well) in common opposition to the Versailles system, in which case Britain would have to face a war on the continent and in the Mediterranean possibly without French support.

This was the gist of the advice Samuel Hoare received when he replaced Simon at the Foreign Office in June. The repercussions of the signature of the Anglo–German Naval Treaty immediately afterwards confirmed at least the last part of Vansittart's analysis. Paris was understandably furious at a pact which made a mockery of the Stresa Accords by granting Germany the right to build a fleet equal to France's in firepower if not in tonnage. Shortly afterwards, General Gamelin initialled the secret military agreement with Italy for co-operation against Germany. As Churchill pointed out later when summoned to give counsel to the Foreign Secretary, the extent to which France could now be expected to extend even benign neutrality in a British war with Italy was severely circumscribed.[63]

Why Britain should contemplate sanctions against Italy at the same time that it was abetting Germany's breaches of the Versailles Treaty was a matter of some concern and perplexity in Rome. Partly, no doubt, British feelings of guilt towards the harsh treatment meted to Germany in 1919 reinforced the desire to uphold the more enlightened clause of the Covenant in an area where the guilty party could not only be more easily identified but also more easily brought to heel. And to lend sanction to a programme of sanctions, the British government had at hand the results of the Peace Ballot in which fully 94 per cent of the more than 10 million people polled approved the imposition of economic measures if the Covenant were breached. To be sure, that percentage dropped to 74 on the question of adding military sanctions, but the turn-out of voters and the proportions in favour of sanctions could not be easily ignored by a national government intent on finding a common denominator of support. Admittedly the Peace Ballot was framed in general terms and eventually the General Election of 1935 was decided mostly on domestic issues, but in the early summer of 1935 the British Prime Minister had no hesitation in proclaiming publicly that the League was 'the sheet anchor of British policy'.

Such forthrightness did not prevent the British government from attempting the kind of deal which would obviate the need to honour imprudent and uncomfortable commitments. At the end of June, Eden was sent to Rome to put before Mussolini a plan whereby Abyssinia would grant Italy substantial concessions in exchange for an outlet to the sea at Zeila in British Somaliland. It was a plan both generous and self-serving. Britain would give up territory in Zeila and receive nothing in return – the two chief beneficiaries being Italy and Abyssinia – save safeguards for the rights of British Somali tribes to graze in the Ogaden. The scheme had matured in the first half of June. Drummond, after his lengthy conversation with Mussolini at the end of May had suggested four alternative solutions to his government: (a) some form of Italian mandate over Abyssinia, (b) some scheme by which Italy played in Abyssinia the role which Britain played in Egypt, (c) some kind of Italian protectorate and (d) outright annexation. He ruled out the last two alternatives because of the risk of war and loss of face to the League and advised London to work out something along the lines of the first two and preferably the second.[64] On 17 June, after consultation with Hoare and Eden, Vansittart had replied that none of the four courses suggested would work and proposed instead the scheme whereby Britain would cede to Abyssinia the port of Zeila and a corridor to it in exchange for which Britain would be entitled to insist that Abyssinia should cede to Italy the Ogaden country and make some economic concessions elsewhere.[65] Addis Ababa was not informed or consulted at this stage but it was expected that the plan would prove acceptable to the emperor since an outlet at Zeila had practically been agreed upon at the end of the previous year and the Ogaden, which Abyssinia would now be expected formally to cede to Italy instead of Britain, had already passed under Italian control.

In Rome, where Drummond's view of the alternatives was probably known, expectations ran high. Suvich had made it clear to Drummond, when the latter announced Eden's visit, that for Italy it was no longer a question merely of the Ogaden or economic concessions, but, encouraged by Drummond, whose preference for a solution on the Egyptian model was scarcely disguised, he welcomed the visit of the English Minister for League Affairs. By the time Eden arrived in Rome on 25 June, ostensibly to discuss the Anglo–German Naval Pact, his scheme had already become public knowledge through the indiscretion of a parliamentary secretary. The following day Mussolini disabused Eden very quickly of any notion that the scheme might be accepted. The Zeila swap would add to Abyssinia's prestige by making it a maritime power and to its strength by allowing it to import arms free of international controls; it would make Britain appear Abyssinia's protector; it would be a blow to Italian prestige since the concessions would be granted through an intermediary. Even if these difficulties could be surmounted,

> the scheme had still more serious disadvantages. It would not enable Italy's two colonies to be connected and it would result in Abyssinia claiming a victory for herself. He regarded it not only as unsatisfactory but as positively dangerous. He would not accept it.

But because he appreciated the sincerity and good efforts of the British government, Mussolini said he would reciprocate by explaining his Abyssinian objectives which he hoped would still be obtained without war.

> He would be content with those parts of Abyssinia which had been conquered by Abyssinia in the last fifty years and which were not inhabited by Abyssinians . . . the central plateau could remain under Abyssinian sovereignty but only on condition that it was under Italian control. If, however, Abyssinia could not come to terms with Italy upon these lines, then, if Italy had to fight, her demands would

be proportionately greater . . . he had no desire to leave the League [but] he had not closed his eyes to the fact that he might have no choice but to leave it.

As for the suggestion that Laval's *carte blanche* in January extended only to economic matters, Mussolini continued,

> That might be so far as the written documents were concerned but since he had yielded to France the future of 100,000 Italians in Tunis and received in return half a dozen palm trees in one place and a strip of desert which did not even contain a sheep in another, it must be clear that he had understood that France had disinterested herself in Abyssinia.

Told that Laval insisted on the economic nature of the free hand, Mussolini 'flung himself back in his chair with a gesture of astonishment'.

Throughout this conversation, Mussolini appeared to Eden to speak quietly, even resignedly. There was no attempt at bluster of any kind. This gloomy fatality was even more marked in the second conversation the following day. Eden, Mussolini stressed, had to take back with him the clear impression that Italy was determined to settle the question once and for all. He did not rule out a peaceful solution but the only way to bring the Abyssinians to a settlement was to let them see with their own eyes the Italian divisions, the Italian aircraft and tanks.[66]

But lest Eden take back the impression that Italy wanted war for its own sake, other members of the fascist administration dwelled on possible peaceful solutions. While not inclined to accept concessions already under Italian domain, they laid stress on a settlement which would, first, greatly increase Italy's colonial holdings by adding to Eritrea and Somaliland those contiguous territories conquered by the Abyssinian empire in the last fifty years and, secondly, institute over the central nucleus of Abyssinia a protectorate similar to the British one over Egypt or the French one over Morocco. A settlement along these lines had been discussed with officials of the British Embassy in anticipation of Eden's visit to Buti, the political director at Palazzo Chigi, and by Quaroni, the head of the European department.[67] After the formal conversations, Aloisi reverted to it. He proposed to Strang, who had accompanied Eden, that Abyssinia should be a mandated territory. Further to ease Britain's misgivings over the role of the League, in fact to ascertain whether British opposition stemmed solely from concern for the League, Aloisi also offered to proffer documented charges in Geneva that Abyssinia had not fulfilled the conditions imposed on her for membership in 1923 – the suppression of slavery and the traffic in arms – and was thus unfit for further membership. The matter could then be referred to the jurisdiction of Britain and France for appropriate action.[68]

Reportedly the proposal was received by Eden with a great deal of interest. There were precedents for it in the Chaco dispute and Eden himself the previous year had attempted to expel Liberia from the League on precisely the same grounds. Moreover the proposal did not rule out continued membership in the League of a reconstructed Abyssinia with more defensible borders shorn of its outlying territories, then entrusted to the care of the Italian government which could be expected to eliminate the traffic in arms and slaves which had sullied the Abyssinian empire's reputation. Laval also appeared very much in favour of some such solution, as Eden found out when he stopped off in Paris on the way back.[69]

As it happened, it was not taken any further. Eden returned to London convinced of the unacceptability of a deal along the lines of the Zeila swap to face an unsympathetic public opinion and the House of Commons. Aloisi's compromise was not taken further despite the support for it from France and the Foreign Office. Vansittart, fearful of the consequences for Europe of alienating Italy, had come to regret that 'the League had even embarked on this disastrous policy of electing these grotesque members'. Eden's conviction that 'though Abyssinia may be grotesque, it is not she who is contemplating violating the Covenant' carried the day in the Cabinet.[70] The dispute now became essentially a test of the viability of the fundamental interests Italy and Britain assumed to be at stake: for Britain, the system of collective security which permitted the British Empire to sustain its international eminence with a minimum of formal commitments and a minimum of land forces; for Italy, the prize of imperial expansion in return for the containment of Germany and support for the European *status quo* decided at Stresa.

The psychological import of Mussolini's shift in his European policy from the arch-revisionist to one of the pillars of the *status quo* was never quite understood outside Italy. And yet it was a role he had profoundly craved as an avowal of Italy's great-power status and an acknowledgment by the other great powers of their need of Italy's support. Stresa had been the culmination of this radical shift, which had begun with the Four Power Pact. And now the action of Britain (especially after the Anglo–German naval agreement) was tantamount to down-grading Italy's international stature: if Hitler's Germany remained the major threat at the same time that Italy's availability to counter it was dismissed, no other conclusion appeared open to Mussolini.

A note setting out the views of the British government confirmed Mussolini's paranoia. The note, drafted on 6 July after the Cabinet had heard Eden's report, was not delivered until 24 July, the interim period being taken up by an attempt, seconded by France, to convene a meeting in Rome to examine the Abyssinian question under Articles I and III of the tripartite agreement of 1906. On 18 July Mussolini agreed to such a meeting, but as he did not give an assurance that peace would be maintained and that Italy would attend the Council meeting in Geneva on the 25th and state her case against Abyssinia, the note was delivered on the 24th. It made two major points, first, that 'the war generation and its successors believed firmly in the League as they considered that it was only by a system of collective security that peace would be preserved and only through the League that the United Kingdom could play its part in Europe', and second, that Italy's demands for the non-Amharic portion of Abyssinia contravened a host of international agreements from the Covenant to the Briand–Kellogg Pact. There followed a warning: 'Deliberate disregard of the Covenant of the League of Nations and of the Pact of Paris would strike at the root of public law and international security and would be so viewed by public opinion in the United Kingdom'.[71]

In reply, Mussolini stressed again that Italy had no intention of injuring the League, of lessening Italy's collaboration in pursuit of collective security in Europe or of disregarding her obligations towards Britain and France. He recalled the exclusion of African matters from the recent discussion of collective security at Stresa and, in a pointed reference to the Anglo–German Naval Treaty, underlined that 'it has certainly not been the Italian government that has taken initiatives or concluded agreements which were not in harmony with the results of collective decisions'. For good measure he then listed a number of recent instances in which

Britain in her imperial interests had specifically ruled out the applicability to countries outside Europe of the collective security provisions of the Covenant. He deplored a forced choice between a colonial conflict in Africa and the contribution which Italy could make to the tranquillity of Europe.

> To refuse to admit this standpoint [he concluded], would be tantamount to a readiness to sacrifice deliberately the interests of a state such as Italy to the application of principles which in the case of Abyssinia cannot be applied and ... of which Abyssinia avails herself to her own exclusive advantage, but to which she is unable to make any effective and responsible contribution in the comity of civilised nations in Europe.

Italy's contribution to European security on the other hand was dependent on a satisfactory solution of the Abyssinia dispute because her colonial insecurity[72]

> prevents Italy from attaining that degree of security to which she, in common with other states, is entitled in order to be in a position to bring to bear on European collective security the whole weight and force of her collaboration.

Mussolini's attitude looked rather like a thinly disguised form of blackmail – Italy was capitalising on the German danger to get her way in Abyssinia. This was true up to a point. By 1935 Mussolini was certainly alert to the general threat of a resurgent Germany, particularly of the threat to Italy's strategic position in the north. He realised the importance to Italy of a secure Brenner frontier as much as he desired a colonial empire at Abyssinia's expense. But it seemed possible to him to accomplish both goals within two years – to conquer Abyssinia and return to Europe to contain Germany – and it would be wrong to suggest that his pursuit of African glories blinded him to the realities of Europe. The race, as he indicated at the end of 1934, was against time and he very nearly pulled it off. What eventually drove him into Hitler's arms was not so much the incomprehension of Britain and France (though this was a factor among the more rabid elements of the party) but the unfortunate concatenation of his gratuitous involvement in Spain with the delusions of invincibility to which successful dictators are prone.

In Britain, on the other hand, the gamble was of a different nature. Here, too, it was a combination of domestic and external factors which determined the nature of the conflict. On the one hand Britain's security demanded a strong League; on the other, resort to war demanded a strong moral case to ensure public support. To what precise extent these two factors were played off against the other and exacerbated the conflict will remain a moot point. What is not in dispute is that by the end of July 1935 the British government had come to the conclusion that a military confrontation with Italy was an acceptable wager. That it was not pressed in the autumn of 1935 was the result only partly of divided counsels in London and rather more of Britain's failure to persuade France to take a share in the gamble.

The process of persuasion began in earnest in August 1935. Like Rome, Paris had also been too inclined to draw a distinction between European and non-European controversies. The political education of France, with a view to persuading her to make common cause with Britain against Italy, consisted of painting several outcomes to an Italo–Abyssinian war, all of which, it was pointed out, would rebound to France's disadvantage. Were Italy's war with Abyssinia short and successful, Italy's 'opportunistic and incalculable' policy would become more so, for it could then be expected that 'Mussolini's contempt for foreign opinion and confidence in his own judgement' would increase correspondingly. Were the war to be long and protracted, 'her political energy in Europe will decline . . . and the unstable equilibrium on which the independence of Austria is poised will be upset'. Were Italy to be defeated by Abyssinia, the results would be even more alarming, for Italy's foreign policy would then 'be pawned to those who could and would help her'. Regardless of the outcome, two other results would flow from an Italo–Abyssinian war: 'The financial strain of war . . . will diminish the power of the Italian government in the near future to play that part in European politics to which her size and resources prudently nourished would otherwise have entitled her'. Second, the effect of war upon the League of Nations would be wholly bad: 'There would have been destroyed one of those factors – and that a very important factor – which join the United Kingdom with France in the moral leadership of Europe.' Not only would the repercussions be very serious in the smaller European countries which look 'to the two great conservative democracies for support and guidance', but also it would be unlikely that the unanimous assent of the British people 'would be forthcoming unless it were clear that the cause for which Britain was engaging herself in war was in defence of international order under the authority of the League'. Lastly, any 'failure on the part of France and the UK to show their disapproval of the conduct of Italy must surely arouse the resentment of the coloured races', while conversely the defeat of Italy by a black nation would have repercussions in the neighbouring territories which 'consist largely of France's possessions or of countries under British and French influence'. In conclusion, France was invited to consider 'which of the three possible results on the League offers the fewest disadvantages from the point of view of French and British interests'.[73]

The effect of Britain's open invitation to France to threaten war on Italy to save the League may be judged by the fact that Laval immediately conveyed to Aloisi the text of it.[74] As Laval later explained to Eden, so long as Italy held to her policy of keeping troops on the Brenner, as Aloisi had just confirmed to him (as well as to the secret military arrangement of July), while Britain refused to enter into any commitment on the continent, the French government had little choice but to give tacit support to the power which was holding Germany in check. If London were willing to reverse these roles, if 'it could give him assurance that Britain would be as firm in upholding the Covenant, to the extent of sanctions, in the future in Europe as she appeared to be today in Abyssinia', Laval felt his government would take a less sanguine view of the impending aggression in Africa.[75] The question was first put to Eden in mid-August, informally at the beginning of September and formally in a communication to the Foreign Office on 10 September. What would Britain do in 'the eventuality of a resort to force in Europe on the part of some European state, whether or not that state might be a member of the League of Nations'?[76] Hoare's answer was not such as to stiffen French resistance. It drew a distinction between armed aggression on the one hand and repudiation of treaties – Locarno – on the other. In the latter case Hoare felt his government ought to have some 'flexibility'; in the former he intimated that, since aggression varied in the scope and 'degrees of culpability', London would not make an advance commitment. The effect of this attempt at elucidation could only be construed as a net loss of security for France, not so much because Britain would not make an advance pledge in the case of aggression (understandably in the absence of discussion on what might constitute the *casus belli*), but particularly because Britain now seemed to be interpreting away her obligations under the Locarno treaty.[77] At this stage, at least, it was an unequal contest for France's loyalty.

In the meantime, Italy's military preparations were proceeding at a frantic pace. Almost a quarter of a million men were on their way to Africa. The ports of Massowa and Mogadishu had been enlarged substantially to receive the endless streams of supplies and a campaign of subversion was being conducted among those chiefs in the outlying territories who had long opposed Haile Selassie's rule by, in some instances, armed rebellions. Furthermore the contemptuous references to Mussolini, his régime and the Italian people contained in the British memorandum forwarded by Laval had predictably infuriated the Italian dictator. His instructions to Aloisi in preparation for a conference of the three signatories of the 1906 agreement which had been finally scheduled for mid-August reflected a new harshness born out of wounded pride. The Italian representatives to the League were to concede nothing and play for time.[78] On 16 August Aloisi put forth a suggestion at the conference for a tripartite declaration in favour of Italian political and economic preponderance in Abyssinia. The Anglo–French counter-proposals granted Italy practically complete economic suzerainty over Abyssinia but no political preponderance. They suggested the extension to Abyssinia of collective assistance under the auspices of the League to enable her to carry out wide measures of internal reform. Territorial rectifications were not ruled out but the draft stipulated the continuation of Abyssinian independence and sovereignty. Mussolini's reply came the following day. He found the Anglo–French counter-proposals 'absolutely unacceptable from any point of view . . . the equivalent of trying to humiliate Italy in the worst possible fashion'.[79] The Paris conference ended fruitlessly on 18 August.

After the failure of the tripartite conference there could be no mistaking Italy's intentions. Her refusal of the Anglo–French proposals revealed to those who were still in doubt the speciousness of Mussolini's economic and demographic arguments. Italy would settle for nothing short of a political victory. An irrevocable decision had not been reached yet on whether it was to be accomplished entirely by force of arms, although by now some military action in the region of Adowa was deemed essential to redress the balance of prestige so rudely shaken at the end of the previous century. On 25 August de Bono was advised by Mussolini to be ready to assume the offensive at any time after 10 September. Whether and how after the initial show of force the offensive would resume 'awaited events on the international plane'.[80]

The event to be awaited with most trepidation was Britain's reaction. Badoglio and the Chiefs of Staff in particular were pessimistic about Italy's ability to withstand determined opposition from Britain.[81] But no such steps were being contemplated in London. By the end of August, the Board of Trade, the Treasury and the Foreign Office had reluctantly reached the unanimous conclusion that economic sanctions would be useless. The prohibition of Italian imports would have a minimal effect while acting as an irritant and a pretext for retaliation. Serious loss of face would result if the economic sanctions were withdrawn following pressure from Britain's trading partners. Estimates of Italy's capacity to pay for imports without counter-balancing exports ranged from a minimum of one and a half to an average of three years, suggesting that economic sanctions would be effective only if it were anticipated that the war would last at least two years.[82] Lastly, it seemed futile to impose economic sanctions if they conflicted with American commercial policy, and Roosevelt's legislation was widely interpreted to mean that the USA would not take part in a trade embargo against Italy. Thus Hoare and Laval had little choice but to agree during the course of their discussions in Geneva on 10 and 11 September before Hoare addressed the Assembly, that 'any economic pressure upon which the League collectively decided should be applied cautiously and in stages and with full account of the inescapable fact that the United States, Japan and Germany were not members of the League'.[83] The matter of military sanctions received even shorter shrift. As Laval later told the Chamber of Deputies, he and Hoare found themselves 'instantaneously in agreement upon ruling out military sanctions, not adopting any measures of naval blockade, never contemplating the closure of the Suez Canal – in a word, ruling out everything that might lead to war'.[84] This last statement was not entirely correct. The British Committee of Imperial Defence at the end of August had taken certain steps which implied, if nothing else, the risk of war. The Mediterranean Fleet had been grouped in the eastern part of that sea; the Home Fleet had been reinforced and was ready to proceed to Gibraltar; and anti-aircraft guns, submarines and fighter squadrons were on their way to Malta and Egypt. But before the CID could view the prospect of war with equanimity it desired to have France's naval co-operation in the western part of the Mediterranean, a promise that France and Yugoslavia would attack Italy from the air and the lease of a naval base in Greece.[85]

Meanwhile in Geneva discussions had reached a complete deadlock. On 31 July the League's Council had appointed a fifth independent arbitrator to the four previously selected by Italy and Abyssinia. On 3 September they returned the ingenious and unanimous verdict that neither Italy nor Abyssinia was to blame for the Wal-Wal incident. One of the implications of this decision was that Italy could no longer justify her military build-up on the grounds of Abyssinian armed provocation. The tactic now followed by the Italian government was to attempt formally to discredit Abyssinia along the lines proposed during Eden's visit to Rome. A lengthy memorandum was tabled in Geneva alleging Abyssinia's unfitness for membership in the League on the grounds that she had not fulfilled the conditions laid down for admission in 1923; detailing instances when she had threatened the security of Italy's colonies and arguing that the present Abyssinian empire was the result of unbridled aggression against neighbouring tribes. The Italian presentation reached the predictable conclusion that Abyssinia, not having fulfilled the obligations of a civilised state, was not entitled to its privileges, while Italy, far from pursuing an aggressive course, was in fact defending the League's civilised values against barbaric oppression. This presentation went beyond the more prudent course of action originally suggested by Aloisi in June. At that time Italy's goals were limited to the expulsion of Abyssinia. Now Italy weakened her argument by suggesting steps inconsistent with the second and third charges, for if it were indeed true that Abyssinia threatened Italy's colonies and had been guilty of aggression in past years, surely this was a matter for League, not unilateral Italian, action. In a sense, however, Italy's accusations were beside the point. What was crucial was the reaction of the Western Powers and both Britain and France decided to treat the Italian memorandum as irrelevant. Neither Laval nor Eden commented on it. Both instead supported a move to have the entire dispute referred to an *ad hoc* committee of five – Britain and France, Poland, Spain and Turkey – which with commendable speed produced a compromise solution on 18 September. There were those within the Italian government to whom the compromise commended itself as a sensible escape from a perilous international situation, the more so since Hoare's speech to the League on 11 September had been received with a rapturous approval which completely overlooked the qualifications and limitations on collective action deliberately emphasised by the British Foreign Secretary. With the mood in Geneva passionately in favour of collective action, Aloisi, Guariglia and Grandi argued for acceptance of the committee's compromise, which had set forth not only a comprehensive plan for the League's supervision and control of Abyssinia – a kind of 'international mandate' the committee's chairman had called it – but also included a specific Anglo–French promise 'to facilitate territorial adjustments between Italy and Abyssinia . . . and to recognize a special Italian interest in the economic development of Abyssinia'.[86]

Mussolini rejected the compromise outright. Indeed while the committee was still deliberating, the Fascist Grand Council had issued a communiqué confirming 'in the most explicit manner that the Italo–Ethiopian dispute does not admit of a compromise solution after the immense effort and sacrifices made by Italy and after the irrefutable documentation contained in the Italian memorandum'.[87] The rejection, however, was not enough to deter a further British attempt at compromise 'in view of the somewhat altered atmosphere produced in Rome', as Hoare cabled to Eden on 24 September, 'by the combination of pressure and friendly message'.[88] Hoare's optimism resulted from the impressive show of strength the Admiralty had mustered in the Mediterranean and the Red Sea – 144 ships of war were clustered around Gibraltar, Alexandria and Aden in the second half of September. If Mussolini was not particularly impressed by the concentration (he blithely ordered his generals to prepare plans for a land attack on Egypt and the Sudan from Libya and Eritrea), the Italian General Staff was. Badoglio rushed off a long letter to Mussolini pointing out how really weak Italy was *vis-à-vis* Britain: the British Fleet protected by destroyers could damage Italian coastal towns and installations at will; the Italian Air Force was 'in a state of crisis', the troops in East Africa cut off from supplies; the counterattacks on Egypt 'impossible'; the French undependable. Inescapably, Badoglio concluded, Italy had to avoid a war with Britain.[89] The letter had some effect since Mussolini moved immediately to stave off a confrontation by suggesting to Laval (who conveyed the message to Hoare) an Anglo–Italian *détente* in the Mediterranean: if the Western Powers promised not to apply military sanctions, Mussolini would recall the two divisions he had sent to Libya. Hoare answered quickly. Having already agreed with Laval not to impose military sanctions he assured Mussolini, 'speaking as an old friend of Italy', that the naval build-up was a purely precautionary measure since Britain had no intention of either imposing military sanctions or closing the Suez Canal.[90]

'The combination of pressure and friendly message' thus turned out to have an effect opposite to that intended, for Mussolini could now allay the misgivings of the General Staff by proffering evidence that Britain would not go to war for the sake of Abyssinia. On 3 October, after the customary justification had been deposited in Geneva, de Bono, without the benefit of a declaration of war, on Mussolini's orders crossed the Abyssinian frontier.

Sanctions

The invasion of Abyssinia faced the League with a *fait accompli*. On 7 November the Council found Italy guilty of violating Article XII of the Covenant; three days later the sixteenth League Assembly expressed its concurrence with only Italy, Austria, Hungary and Albania dissenting. The implementation of Article XVI was placed in the hands of a committee of eighteen which fixed the entry into effect of economic sanctions against Italy for 18 November. Aloisi pleaded in vain with Laval for a postponement of sanctions, pointing to the seventeen months it had taken to mount similar steps against Japan. The French politician took refuge in Eden's attitude and in the need to establish a firm precedent in the case of a future violation of the Covenant by Germany, but he did allow that in no event would France apply military sanctions while economic sanctions would be applied as gradually as possible. At the same time Laval affirmed his intentions of trying to obtain for Italy the non-Amharic portions of the Abyssinian empire as well as a mandate over the remainder of the country. He had already made a somewhat similar promise to the Italian Ambassador Cerruti, who had raised the issue on Mussolini's instructions on 14 October: the Tigré, Ogaden and Herar provinces should be ceded to Italy outright and the remainder of Abyssinia placed under an international mandate with Italian influence predominating, as proposed earlier by the committee of five. Abyssinia should receive an outlet to the sea and the whole settlement should be carried out under the aegis of the League. Mussolini's counter-proposals a few days later indicated a softening of the Italian position. No exception was taken to the League's participation, the Duce adding only that Abyssinia should be disarmed and her outlet to the sea be under Italian control in the Eritrean port of Assab.[91]

These proposals contained the essence of a possible settlement. It was fairly clear that Mussolini, having so to speak avenged Adowa, would have been content with a political solution leaving in existence a rump Abyssinia. Laval's penchant for a settlement which permitted the quick repatriation of Italian troops was also not in doubt. The stumbling block continued to be the position of the British government. London's attitude was now largely governed by the coming General Election in November where fidelity to the League, dexterously balanced with the search for an honourable settlement and with a display of force, was expected to bring about a handsome dividend of seats for the government. The balancing act was extremely difficult because counsels in London continued to be desperately divided between the armed services – which took an increasingly pessimistic view of the prospect of war with Italy – the Foreign Office, itself divided but in the main in favour of a compromise solution, and the Cabinet, the proponent, so long as Eden's influence remained strong, of an intransigent posture.

In the end a unified British position came to depend on Britain's ability to carry France along. As early as 24 September, at the height of Britain's naval concentration in the Mediterranean, Hoare had asked the French Ambassador for assurances that if Britain should be attacked by Italy, before other members of the League were expressly bound to mutual support against a Covenant-breaking state, France would help out. Laval's reply to what amounted to a plea for support in the event of an Italian pre-emptive strike was a conditional affirmative, the condition being that Britain show the same sensitivity to a possible German pre-emptive attack by committing herself to advance preparations for that eventuality. In the end Laval was brought round to abandon his demand for reciprocity. 'We have had to get it out of the French with forceps and biceps . . . we've got it and we mustn't wonder if the client burbles a bit,' Vansittart commented when France's formal pledge to assist Britain was received on 18 October.[92] But translating the commitment into military preparations was something else again. Here the reluctance of the British armed forces to be drawn into a war with Italy matched France's. It was the opinion of the Chiefs of Staff that the British Navy was too weak to confront Italy without reinforcements; while, for its part, the Naval Staff could see no reason why such a war should be undertaken.[93] On 3 October, the day the invasion began, the Admiralty had registered its opposition to sanctions on the grounds that, since they were bound to be ineffective, they would irritate without helping. If, on the other hand, they were effective, the results would be just as bad, for effective sanctions would drive Italy into war against Great Britain, necessitating in turn the withdrawal of the China fleet and thus encouraging Japan to become aggressive.[94]

Eventually discussions were begun to arrange naval, military and air co-operation with France. But if the military spirit was weak, the military flesh was weaker still. The French were willing only to provide repair facilities, but otherwise they were not ready for war. France's and the British Chiefs of Staffs' reluctance to take irrevocable steps reinforced one another. In November the British military leaders sounded a cautionary note.[95]

> We wish to emphasize the danger which would arise if political agreements on the application of fresh sanctions outran the arrangements for co-operation between the forces of the powers concerned. We submit that it is essential that this country alone should not be committed to risks for which other members of the League are militarily unprepared. Powers agreeing to sanctions should be ready to meet the situation which may arise therefrom. When, therefore, further discussions take place likely to lead to fresh pressure on Italy, we urge that steps be taken simultaneously to initiate military discussions with all the powers whose duty this is to co-operate in the Mediterranean in the event of Italian aggression.

The kinds of measures which the British Chiefs of Staff wanted to obtain from other countries were quite substantial. From France they wanted the assumption of naval responsibility for the western Mediterranean and docking and repair facilities for the British fleet; the conquest of the industrial quadrilateral Milan–Alexandria–Turin–Novara, military engagements on the Tunisian frontier with Tripolitania, as well as air attacks on northern Italy. Yugoslavia was expected to attack Istria by land, northern Italy by air and close the Straits of Otranto in the Adriatic. Greece was to provide free use of ports and docking facilities, airfields and assume responsibility for shipping in the eastern Mediterranean. From Turkey, the Chiefs of Staff expected air attacks on the Dodecanese islands. Romania and Spain were asked to provide respectively oil and troop transports while, lastly, Russia was to be asked what it wished to contribute.[96]

Though a tall order, it was at least partly filled. Greece, Yugoslavia and Turkey, between 6 and 13 December, expressed a readiness to fulfil, and in the case of Turkey more than fulfil, their obligations under the Covenant should there be an armed clash between Italy and the League. But the contribution of the Balkan powers, though useful, had always been regarded as peripheral to the central contribution to be made by France. And so long as London could not rely on the full and immediate support of Paris, steps had to be taken to avoid a military clash. On 17 October, Hoare called in Grandi to make two points, 'firstly, that the British government were in no way engaged in a conflict with fascism, secondly that war was in no way inevitable between Great Britain and Italy'. War could only come from a provocative act by either Britain or Italy, and for Britain's part Hoare promised that 'we had not the least intention of doing anything that might be provocative'. After this auspicious beginning the conversation turned to the removal of some of the provocative steps already taken, Grandi asking for a reciprocal and simultaneous withdrawal of British ships from the Mediterranean and Italian reinforcements in Libya. 'In the present atmosphere we could not consider any such proposition', Hoare replied, allowing only that Britain would 'refrain from sending a division to Egypt if the Libyan garrison was substantially reduced.' Grandi, not surprisingly, 'did not think it likely that Signor Mussolini could withdraw troops from Libya on the sole condition that [Britain] did not send further troops to Egypt'.[97] Britain was in fact disposed to reduce her strength in the Mediterranean only if France promised to allow the use of the ports of Toulon and Bizerta and satisfy the Admiralty of her willingness to engage Italy. In the end two battle cruisers were withdrawn in exchange for a reduction in the Libyan garrison, but this was as far as Britain would go. A proposal from Mussolini in November for a wider Mediterranean *détente* was ignored on the grounds that it might lead to a limitation of British naval forces in the area to a specific tonnage.[98]

The next development, the Hoare–Laval proposals for a settlement of the war put forth in December, were largely the result of the stalemate in the Mediterranean and, as the British Ambassador in France later noted, were 'conditioned throughout by our naval, military and air position and by the situation in France'.[99] In the second half of November, the British expert on East African affairs, Sir Maurice Peterson, had worked out with his French counterpart, René de Saint-Quentin, a draft settlement not much dissimilar from the ones proposed in June and October – essentially a plan to place all non-Amharic Abyssinia under *de facto* if not *de jure* Italian administration with an Italian delegate-general in Addis Ababa. The plan was given serious attention in Britain after the elections in November had returned a majority for the government coalition. The search for a compromise was spurred by the fact that Geneva was scheduled to discuss the imposition of oil sanctions on 11 December, and thus in a sense the discussions between Hoare and Laval were held under the shadow of a possible war with Italy, for Laval from the start maintained that if an embargo on oil was imposed he knew for certain that Mussolini would fight, an opinion corroborated by the British Embassy in Rome.[100] It was for this reason that Laval repeatedly asked London for a pledge not to impose an embargo on oil and why he feared that Addis Ababa would refuse a compromise offer precisely in the hope of bringing oil sanctions into play. For this reason too, Vansittart pleaded unsuccessfully with his government for a promise that, in the event of Abyssinia's refusal, oil sanctions would not be imposed. The British government maintained that in the event of Italy accepting and Abyssinia refusing a compromise, London would neither propose nor support the imposition of sanctions but would make no pledge to oppose further sanctions in the future.[101]

The Hoare–Laval settlement was agreed to in private conversation between the two statesmen in Paris on 7 December. It stipulated the cession to Italy of most of the Tigré and Ogaden regions in exchange for an Abyssinian corridor to the sea through

Eritrea at Assab and an arrangement for Italy to develop and exercise wide economic influence in a vast zone in southern Abyssinia under some form of League control.[102] It had been Laval's original intention to submit the compromise to Italy, obtain Mussolini's approval and only then put the proposals publicly to the League to forestall the scheduled discussion on oil sanctions. His plan was frustrated by the storm of disapproval following leaks in the Paris press on the morning of 9 December. The British Cabinet, meeting that evening amidst unprecedented public indignation and faced with the choice of either repudiating the plan or the foreign secretary, took shelter in a compromise. The plan had to be submitted simultaneously to Mussolini and the emperor and approved by both. To facilitate the emperor's choice the British and French governments were also now prepared privately to grant Abyssinia access to the sea through their own territory if access through Eritrea proved unacceptable, though at the price of an undertaking not to construct from that part any railway communicating with the interior and an undertaking to safeguard the interests of the port of Jibuti and the railway to Addis Ababa.[103]

The Hoare–Laval plan was communicated officially to the Italian government on the afternoon of 11 December, two days after it had become public property. Grandi was decidedly in favour of it, as was Guariglia, now the head of the East African section at Palazzo Chigi. Both suggested slight modifications which were communicated to the British and French governments. Aloisi, who since September had tried several stratagems to keep Italy within the Geneva framework, also was in favour. But in the last analysis the decision was Mussolini's. It will remain a matter of conjecture why the Italian dictator did not readily accept a compromise essentially so similar to those he had himself proposed earlier. His announcement on 16 December that a decision would be made after the Fascist Grand Council's meeting on the 18th was rather more an indication that he was temporising than an indication of respect for that body. As it turned out, Mussolini and the Grand Council on 18 December did decide to accept the plan 'as a possible basis for discussion', but before the announcement was released to the press, the public furore in London had persuaded Baldwin that both the plan and Hoare were to be sacrificed to save the British government. On hearing of Hoare's forced resignation,

Mussolini held up his acceptance temporarily. But by now his acceptance was irrelevant. Baldwin had announced on the 19th that the plan was 'completely and absolutely dead'. The emperor rejected it the same day; the League Council recognised it would not have any further consequence and wound up its deliberations for session. Laval put up a good front but he too resigned the next month. And Mussolini issued a completely different statement blaming Britain for the repudiation of the plan.[104]

In a sense he was right. The Hoare–Laval proposals were also in keeping with Britain's larger policy – an attempt to secure for France the grounds for war. 'Mr. Laval told us that the only condition on which he would eventually bring his public opinion to face war was that a reasonable offer should have been made to S. Mussolini and refused by him', Vansittart explained to Britain's Ambassador in Washington on 21 December. And in a paragraph which was omitted from the final draft of the despatch to Lindsay, Vansittart continued: 'The League could and can tighten up [the terms] to the degree that would render the proposals probably unacceptable to S. Mussolini'.[105]

Neither in Geneva nor in the western capitals were further attempts made towards a peaceful solution.[106] Sanctions continued to be imposed in a very haphazard manner but the crucial question of an oil embargo had been referred to an experts' committee which reported in February that only in the unlikelihood of the USA, which had trebled its oil exports to Italy, returning to the pre-1935 figures could the embargo be effective.[107] The other effective sanction, closure of the Suez Canal, had earlier been rejected by the British and French governments on the grounds that it was tantamount to a declaration of war. In the meantime, the Abyssinian counter-attack begun in late December had played itself out. The final Italian offensive in February led to the flight of the negus and the occupation of Addis Ababa on 5 May. Four days later Mussolini proclaimed the annexation of Abyssinia and the creation of the Italian Empire.

The Italian conquest of Abyssinia shocked those who had been living under the illusion that the world had turned over a new leaf in 1919. It did not, however, make Italy into a threat to world peace. Indeed, by pinning down substantial Italian forces in Africa and consuming inordinate proportions of the Italian budget, it made Italy less so. None the less, this anachronistic colonial enter-

prise played a not inconsiderable part in starting the holocaust of
1939. This was not so because the subjugation of Abyssinia showed
beyond all doubt that the League had not, and could not have,
ushered in a new era in international politics, for in fact that
realisation might have had salutary effects; nor was it because it
gave comfort to warmongers in Germany and Japan. But it was so
because for more than a year it hid the nature of the real threat to
European peace and by the time that threat was revealed, positions
were lost, power had corrupted and the split between Italy and the
Western Powers was practically beyond repair. This was Mussolini's fundamental political miscalculation. He gambled his prestige
and the future of his régime on a colonial enterprise at a time when
German rearmament and Nazi Germany's political philosophy represented the largest danger to European peace. When Mussolini
announced that no one could nail Italy to the Brenner, he overlooked that the Brenner was the fulcrum of Italian security and
independence. By treating the German danger publicly (if not
privately) as a scarecrow to induce the Western Powers to give him
carte blanche, he miscalculated profoundly. By the time the last conquest was over in the long cycle of Europe's subjugation of Africa,
the balance of power in Europe had been drastically deranged
by the German occupation of the Rhineland. Italy would be
among the first to succumb to the new order.

Chapter 13

The Brenner Abandoned

Tell Mussolini I will never forget this. . . .
Adolf Hitler, 1938

In August 1933, when it still seemed possible to contain Nazi Germany by a united front of the ex-*Entente* powers, the Permanent Under-Secretary at the Foreign Office, Vansittart, had surmised that if the Western Powers did not strike an agreement with Italy before Germany reached the Brenner, Italy would line up on the wrong side. Five years later, this forecast had been proved correct. The German absorption of Austria was the turning-point of post-Versailles Europe: Germany now had control of Central Europe; the subjugation of Czechoslovakia was a mere question of time. So was the Pact of Steel.

'It may be observed', Mussolini told the Chamber of Deputies on 16 March 1938, a few days after the *Anschluss,* 'that when an event is fated to take place, it's better it takes place with you rather than despite of, or worse still against you.' The rationalisation was in a sense quite correct. The inevitability of the *Anschluss* was one side of the coin on whose reverse one could see etched the impotence of the Western Powers and of Italy. But Mussolini's rationalisation wilfully ignored the extent to which Italy's impotence was due to conscious policy choices made after the outbreak of the Abyssinian war. Mussolini had subordinated his collaboration with the Western Powers to a free hand in pursuit of those aims of grandeur which had been the *leitmotif* of his political programme since 1922. So long as some doubt existed about the willingness of the West to risk war in Africa, Mussolini persisted. His rigidity found a match in the West. Mistakes and bluff piled upon one another. And when Germany afforded Italy an opportunity to weaken France, Mussolini seized it. His refusal to see in the German reoccupation of the Rhineland the *casus foederis* stipulated by Locarno was gratuitously matched by a relaxation of vigilance on the Brenner.

The growing solidarity with Germany was counterpoised against the West and those within Palazzo Chigi who had not appreciated the value of the 'German card' were ruthlessly replaced by more pliant men. The outbreak of the Spanish Civil War complicated a power struggle in the Mediterranean by the infusion of ideological and personal elements even less susceptible to composition. Germany, again *tertium gaudens* as in Abyssinia, profited from the war to sharpen the cleavage. Mussolini visited Germany, acceded to the Anti-Comintern Pact and withdrew from Geneva. The decision of 11 December 1937 marked the final abandonment by the Duce's Italy of the Europe of Versailles.

None the less, even after the *Anschluss* there remained in Italy a trace of the traditional policy of 'equidistance' fuelled from time to time by Teutonic arrogance. The crude attempts to wedge Italy between Britain and Germany or between Britain and France were testimony to this, as was the attempt to build around Yugoslavia a new sphere of influence in south-eastern Europe to replace the one just vacated to Germany. Still, Italy was daily succumbing to the pull from the north. In 1938, Mussolini loosened a barrage of ordinances ranging from the imitative to the idiotic which finally demolished the last saving grace of Italian fascism – the knowledge that Italians had neither the inclination nor the wherewithal to indulge in the totalitarian excesses cultivated in the Reich. At the same time, relations with Britain, despite the promising start of the Easter Accords, came to be governed by attempts to induce White-hall to abandon Paris; shortly even that pretence was abandoned and full scope was given to the resentment over Britain's pre-eminent position in the Mediterranean. Eventually, when war came, Italy took temporary refuge in 'non-belligerence,' but doubts about the wisdom of aligning Italy with Germany did not begin to bother Mussolini until his country was invaded by the Germans.

Belgrade

By the beginning of 1937 Italy had reinforced her position in the Mediterranean by means of agreements with Spain and Britain. Both agreements in a sense had been made viable by the diplomatic leverage resulting from alignment with Germany in the Axis. In its simplest formulation the Axis aimed at an apportionment of spheres of influence – to Italy, the Mediterranean, to Germany, the Baltic and the North Sea. In the Balkans, the obvious area in which German and Italian interests might collide, the Ciano–Neurath agreement called for consultation and collaboration without for the moment defining the modalities or assessing the political implications. From Neurath's words, however, Ciano had obtained the impression that Germany supported Italy's claims to pre-eminent interests in Yugoslavia, Albania and possibly Romania.[1] Thus while in Hungary, and especially in Austria, Italy now had to act with rather more circumspection, in Yugoslavia the field was wide open.

This is not to say that Ciano and Mussolini anticipated easy passage for the proposals they were about to put to the Yugoslavs. Relations with Belgrade had been consistently bad since the creation of the Yugoslav state, and the never-ending disputes had left fixed in the Yugoslav mind the conviction that fascist Italy had not renounced her ambition of, if not breaking up Yugoslavia, at least of obtaining possession of Dalmatia and turning the Adriatic into an Italian lake. The belief was strengthened, apart from fascism's strident rhetoric, by the less than subtle moral and financial encouragement extended to the Croats in their dispute with the Serbs and by the asylum given on Italian soil to the Croatian terrorists and their leader, Ante Pavelich. Moreover, there was no doubt in Yugoslavia's mind of Italy's responsibility if not complicity in the murder of King Alexander. Relations between the two countries were still suffering from its consequences when Yugoslavia joined in applying sanctions against Italy in 1935. Stoyadinović, the Yugoslav Prime Minister, though he was loath to lose overnight 25 per cent of his country's total trade, subscribed none the less to Geneva's decision in the hope of curtailing Italy's power for some time to come. The Italian victory and the League's failure to prevent it undermined the basis of his policy. By late 1938, the weakness of France, the inability of Britain to render effective aid and the powerlessness of the League all made it imperative to come to terms with an imperious neighbour.

Aided also by the less than vengeful treatment he had received from Rome during the period of sanctions,[2] Stoyadinović made the first public overture. Mussolini responded in his Milan speech of 1 November. In the same month Italy made a formal offer of a treaty of friendship or even of alliance. While proposing this treaty to the Yugoslav Minister in Rome, Ciano had remarked that if the proffered hand were refused, it would be war to the knife, a remark not conducive to the mutual trust normally preceding such treaties but likely none the less to increase Belgrade's anxiety to avoid a rupture.[3] If Italy's treaties proved to be ephemeral, Yugoslavia could at worst obtain a breathing spell; at best a treaty with Italy could undercut the support which the Croatian separatists were finding in Rome, obtain an improvement in the treatment of the Slovene minorities in Istria and perhaps even induce Italy to adopt a more obliging attitude on the ever-present issue of Albania. The problem, of course, was to obtain these advantages without alienating existing friendships – primarily with Britain and France but also with the Little *Entente*. This problem was not an easy one, although its solution appeared to be simplified by the announcement of the Anglo–Italian gentleman's agreement of 2 January 1937, which allayed Yugoslav fears as to how close relations with Italy would be received in London. This explained why Stoyadinović lost no opportunity of publicly welcoming the agreement and took the lead, during the course of the meetings of the Balkan *Entente* in Athens, in advocating that its members should follow the British example, unaware until later of how disturbed Eden was by the suggestion that the agreement was facilitating the Italo–Yugoslav negotiations. In February 1937, the British Foreign Secretary, who regarded the agreement as an unfortunate concession to the pusillanimity of the three services, let Belgrade know how premature in his view it would be to assume that Italian policy was no longer predatory and in particular counselled Belgrade emphatically against accepting an Italian offer of an alliance.[4] The British Minister in Belgrade, Campbell, who kept in close touch with Prince Paul, was instructed to use his special relationship to thwart Italian designs for an alliance described as fundamentally opposed to British interests.[5]

The fact none the less remained that the pact which Rome had just proposed promised advantages to both sides so important that some compromise would be struck. Despite the haughty pose, it was evident that the pact was a matter of high priority in Rome. Clearly the Italian government wanted to detach Yugoslavia from the French and British orbits it had followed so closely during the Abyssinian period; of more moment was the need to weaken Yugoslavia's relations with the Little *Entente,* an urgent task since the French government was angling at this time for a pact of mutual assistance of a comprehensive character with the Little *Entente*. But probably most important was the feeling in Italy that the *Anschluss* was only a matter of time. The inevitable had to be postponed as long as possible and certainly long enough to try to link together Rome, Belgrade, Bucharest and possibly Sofia in a bloc powerful enough to balance the expected increase in Germany's preponderance in Austria and Hungary. In this sense the draft produced by the Italian government in January 1937 – the effect of which would have been to deprive Yugoslavia of her freedom to conduct an independent foreign policy – was paradoxically an admission of weakness, an indication of retrenchment in the expectation of an onslaught from the north.

For his part, Prince Paul spent considerable time in consultation with the British Minister, trying to water down the offer of an exclusive alliance.[6] He eventually gave up and the task of framing a counterdraft was handed over to the experts at the Yugoslav Ministry of Foreign Affairs with instructions to produce an impressive document combining a maximum of words with a minimum of meaning. The results of their labours were submitted to London at the beginning of March. Britain found two clauses objectionable – one imposing consultation in the event of an agreed threat to the parties' common interests and another stipulating benevolent neutrality in the event of one party becoming the victim of unprovoked aggression. Prince Paul and Stoyadinović were at pains to emphasise to London that these obligations amounted in practice to nothing at all – an assurance which caused them a great deal of difficulty when the Italian Military Information Service (SIM) came to know of it.[7] None the less, in the end the Italian government relented its pressure to make the pact into an exclusive alliance; in part because, under the stress of seeking some diversion from the reverses in Spain, it was impatient to conclude matters at an early date and in part because some form of formal acknowledgment of its influence in south-eastern Europe was high on its list of priorities. Italy needed something which could be claimed a diplomatic success and was prepared to pay a price for it. The final terms of the Italo–Yugoslav Pact of 25 March 1937, in addition to a reiteration of the undertakings imposed by the Briand–Kellogg Pact, called for a guarantee of the common frontier, a pledge that Italy would keep her hands off

Dalmatia and a promise to desist from seeking to disintegrate
Yugoslavia by encouraging the Croat cause. In four secret annexes
Yugoslavia obtained the assurance that Italy, in exchange for the
recognition of the position conferred upon her by the decision of
the Ambassadors Conference of 1921, would not go beyond it in
her dealings with Albania; a promise that the Ustashe terrorists
would be kept under rigorous supervision; the prospect of
economic advantages in excess of those specified in the commercial
agreement signed simultaneously with the political treaty; and,
lastly, a promise that in exchange for the settlement of the claims
of the Italian optants in Dalmatia, the Slovene minority in Istria
would regain the right to have their own schools and to use their
language in their religious worship.[8]

These were very substantial benefits for Yugoslavia. They
settled disputes which had been simmering for almost twenty
years for a price – recognition of Italian pre-eminence in Albania –
which by now amounted merely to the recognition of the *status quo*
and on terms as favourable as Yugoslavia ever could hope to
extract from her fascist neighbour. The pay-off for Italy was that,
regardless of Prince Paul's personal reservations, it could not be
denied that the settlement implied a re-orientation of Yugoslavia's
foreign policy towards Italy and away from France and the Little
Entente.[9] This was precisely the way the treaty was interpreted not
only by Ciano but also by Stoyadinović in their conversation in
Belgrade on 26 March 1937.[10] Ciano's record makes it clear that
the agreements just concluded were merely the first step towards
the alliance 'which Stoyadinović considers natural and inevitable'.
The Italian Foreign Minister congratulated himself on having
circumvented the French offer of a military alliance to the Little
Entente. Stoyadinović for his part now described Yugoslavia's
relations with Czechoslovakia as an 'empty formality'. The Yugoslav Prime Minister also talked at length about how the Rome–
Belgrade Axis would 'oppose the German descent towards the
Adriatic or along the Danube valley', of his disgust with Geneva,
of the glowing economic prospects for Italy in his country, of
England's 'bluffs' – all statements which led Ciano to the conclusion that 'Stoyadinović is a Fascist' with 'the marks of a dictator
in Yugoslavia' as well as the sudden discovery that Yugoslavia
now had 'a profound knowledge of the Italian language and
culture'. Ciano promised himself to prepare a vast plan of action so

that 'Italy will shortly be able to take the place in Yugoslavia of France herself'.[11]

The Rome–Berlin Axis

Despite the success of the Italo–Yugoslav agreement, Italy's strenuous struggle to maintain the influence she exercised in Central Europe previous to her Abyssinian adventure was just beginning. Talk of the inevitability of an *Anschluss* was rampant in Rome's diplomatic circles and, even though Mussolini was said to be unconvinced, it was generally acknowledged that Ciano had made up his mind that there was no profit in attempting to oppose it. Ciano's feelings were reinforced by those within the fascist administration who, with the victory in Abyssinia as proof of Italy's virility, no longer feared the disparities in power between the dictatorships and were leaning towards the conclusion that Italy would be well worth Germany's consideration as an ally.

In the meantime it had been deemed wise to take precautions. The agreement with Yugoslavia was seen as the first step towards the formation of a bloc composed of Italy, Yugoslavia, Romania and Bulgaria, to balance and impose limits on German expansion. The idea of dividing central Europe into spheres of influence between Italy and Germany was, of course, not new. It had been raised in 1932 when discussions had taken place on the reapportionment of the Central European countries into two sets of confederations, one under Italian, the other under German tutelage, but there had been little reason to believe at the time that Mussolini, despite his penchant for supporting the German thesis of equality of rights, was bent on the idea of sharing quite so equally. By 1937 those conditions had changed. Italy was now alienated from her former associates and thrown into close touch with the power she had once attempted to tutor and now was proving to be the master in the realm of bellicosity. Hence the desire both to co-operate and reinsure by the formation of an exclusive Italian sphere of influence.

It was doubtful if that policy could prove successful. Yugoslavia, despite the protestation of Stoyadinović, had always, and with good reasons, been suspicious of Italian policy and would likely continue to be so. Bulgaria was beginning to realise that Italy was no help in her quest for the recovery of territory lost at the

peace treaty to Romania. Romania was increasing her trade with
Germany at a faster rate than with Italy and had shown no disposition to conciliate Bulgaria. Italy's aim to unite the four
countries as a counter-weight to Germany's influence in Central
Europe was, more than anything else, revealing the dangers of a
pro-German policy and laying bare the price Italy would ultimately
have to pay in the weakening of her European position in order to
found an empire. The creation of an empire simultaneously with
a sphere of influence in south-eastern Europe was presenting
Mussolini with the threat of failure in a sphere to which previously
Italy had attached the highest importance. This threat explained in
part why Mussolini was now so desperately anxious that his gamble
in Spain should succeed. In a similar vein the visit to Libya and the
flamboyant utterances which accompanied it also had the sub-
sidiary aim of diverting domestic attention from Italy's want of
success in Central European affairs.

Yet regardless of these diversions, the fulcrum of Italian policy
was still at the Brenner rather than in the Mediterranean. But
Mussolini's Austrian policy required more dexterity than he or
Ciano could muster after the birth of the Axis. It was a question of
reconciling two irreconcilable propositions – collaboration with
Germany and independence for Austria. Mussolini had allowed
himself to believe that the Austro–German July Accords of 1936
represented the maximum of German demands: consanguinity had
been affirmed and the Nazis admitted to public life. He thought he
could now proceed on the assumption of the continued existence
of a buffer state and the viability of the Rome Protocols. In
September 1936 Mussolini and Ciano assured the Austrian Foreign
Minister, Guido Schmidt, that there existed no political or military
agreements between Italy and Germany, and in November of that
year the Rome Protocols were further strengthened. But even as
the three Foreign Ministers met it was evident that Italy did not
possess the wherewithal to support Austria against renewed
German pressures. Schuschnigg, who told Ciano of Göring's open
advocacy of the *Anschluss,* was told that Italy could no longer
supply Austria with arms because of her involvement in Spain.[12]

Confirmation that the July Accords were for many in Germany
a starting rather than a terminal point, came during Göring's visit
to Rome in the middle of January 1937. His was partly a personal
visit, void of official sanction, but there was no mistaking the gist

of it: Nazi Germany could not give up its hopes of *Anschluss* with Austria. In exchange he held out the carrot of formal recognition of the Brenner frontier (the almost 200,000 German-speaking inhabitants of the Alto Adige could be resettled in Germany or Austria) and 'Germany's support at critical moments, such as might arise from Italy's Mediterranean policy'. When Mussolini indicated he did not appreciate this form of tutelage, Göring backed down and suggested that Germany would only act in Austria after consultation with Rome. But he would not put this promise in writing. In subsequent conversations he was careful not to mention again the inevitability of the *Anschluss,* lingering instead on the disruptive effects which the Austrian issue, unless settled, might have in the hands of the Western Powers – a veritable hand grenade with which to blow up the Axis.[13]

None the less, the message had been fairly clear. And in the following months Italian policy took cognisance of it by falling back on an exclusive zone of influence south of the area about to come under Berlin's sway and, more prudently, by trying to arrange matters in Austria in such a way that Hitler could not possibly have a pretext to intervene. The new Italian Press Officer in the Vienna Embassy, Tuninetti, appointed in early March 1937, was in fact a secret agent charged with bringing about an arrangement between Schuschnigg's Fatherland Front and the Austrian Nazis, whereby the latter would hopefully dissolve into the former. Working feverishly with the Austrian Minister of the Interior, Tuninetti evolved a plan by which, at the forthcoming meeting in April in Venice between Schuschnigg, Schmidt, Mussolini and Ciano, the Austrian Chancellor would present, and Mussolini would accept, a proposal to give former Nazis about six less sensitive Cabinet posts in return for the absorption of the Austrian Nazi party into the Fatherland Front and an end to their anti-government agitation. In the event of unfavourable repercussions in Berlin, Schuschnigg could claim that he had acted with the knowledge and sympathy of Rome while Mussolini, if queried about Italy's role, could claim that he had merely acknowledged the communication of a proposal from a friendly government.[14] In the event, things went according to plan until, at the last minute, Ciano overplayed his hand. Schuschnigg had made and Mussolini accepted the proposals when they were leaked by Ciano to the *Giornale d'Italia* in the hope, as he explained later, of binding

Schuschnigg publicly to the deal. The effect was the opposite. Schuschnigg, who had not yet informed the Fatherland Front of the proposed secret agreement with the Nazis, feared a ministerial crisis and immediately backed off.[15]

This gauchely mishandled attempt to forestall the inevitable was Italy's swan-song in Austria. Ciano and Mussolini had been sincere as they averred to Schuschnigg that Italy still desired Austria's independence, but essentially their meeting in Venice amounted to a confession of impotence. What could Italy do for Austria, Mussolini asked, when Italy and Germany 'find themselves confronted by the same enemies, since the democratic bloc, whose active existence is being revealed increasingly openly, is attempting to isolate the two Powers in order to be able to eliminate them'?[16] By necessity Italy and Germany had to co-operate with one another. Austria's independence would last only so long as Hitler could find no pretext to intervene. For this reason, he emphasised to Schuschnigg, it was important that the July Accords be applied scrupulously. But the writing was on the wall. The final communiqué made no mention of Austrian independence; at the same time it stressed that a final settlement in the Danubian basin could 'not be concerned and effected without the active participation of Germany'.[17]

The ensuing months revealed the narrowness of the field of manoeuvres Italy had left herself. Mussolini could no longer hope that the Nazis, if brought to political power, would be content to leave it at that. Faced with the choice of sacrificing the Axis for the sake of Austria or Austria for the Axis, he chose albeit reluctantly the latter. His visit to Germany in September 1937 confirmed the choice. Hitler had deliberately chosen not to discuss Austria at that time or indeed any subject likely to reveal a difference of opinion between the two régimes. Göring's instructions for his private conversation with Mussolini were to play down his previous assertions of the inevitability of union and to emphasise the assurances of consultation. A projected conference of the foreign ministers of the countries adhering to the Rome Protocols to take place in Berlin during the course of the visit was quietly side-tracked by the Wilhelmstrasse.[18] Mussolini went along more than willingly in this exercise in mutual deception. He saw the primary purpose of the visit to be an outlandish affirmation of Italo–German friendship unencumbered by the protestations of such minor allies as the Protocol countries. The Austrian and Hungarian ministers in Berlin who had been waiting anxiously for an audience with the Duce were told unceremoniously that his tight schedule did not permit it.[19]

Mussolini's visit to Berlin turned out to be one of the crucial events of the inter-war period, not necessarily because of any agreements reached then or the pageantry (which had its tragi-comic aspects in the competition of new uniforms on both sides and the downpour and faulty loud-speakers which dampened Mussolini's address to 800,000 people in the Maifield), but because of the lasting impression German military strength made on Mussolini. After September 1937 the Italian leader became unalterably convinced that whatever revision had to take place in the physiognomy of Europe would have to be accomplished with Hitler, not against him. Similarly, the esteem (if not reverence) in which Hitler held Mussolini, dating back to the 1920s when as the leader of an obscure party he had asked for (and not received) a signed photograph of the successful Italian dictator, was reinforced by the present conviction that only Mussolini, as an historical genius second only to himself, could inculcate in the Italian people those martial qualities he so revered.[20]

No formal pacts were signed during this visit and in particular the contentious subject of Austria was deliberately not permitted to interfere with the military displays and the vows of totalitarian solidarity. But both dictators appreciated that after September 1937 the ground rules had changed. Hitler's new confidence was reflected in the extraordinary meeting at the Reichskanzlei on 5 November, when he outlined plans of rearmament and hopes for conquest and in the stepped-up campaign of Nazi subversion in Austria. Mussolini's acquiescence in the *Anschluss* could be discounted in advance after he remarked abjectly to Ribbentrop on 6 November following the signature of the Anti-Comintern Pact that Italy's interest in Austria 'is no longer as lively as it was some years ago for one thing because of Italy's imperialist development which was now concentrating her interest in the Mediterranean and the Colonies'.[21] Austria was a German country by race, language and culture, he admitted, and in the next breath allowed that Italy's decreased interest was also due to the fact that the Austrians 'had not modified in the slightest their cold and negative attitude towards us'. The best thing to do, he went on, 'is to let events take their natural course. . . . France knows that if a crisis should arise in Austria, Italy would do nothing.'[22] He made a half-hearted attempt at the end of the conversation to elicit a promise from Ribbentrop that Germany would honour her previous promises of consultation, but with no apparent success. The most he could now hope for was a gradual solution which, if it did not blow up into a European crisis, would not force him to take a public stand. The new Italian Minister in Austria, Ghigi, was told to act 'like a doctor who administers oxygen to a moribund patient without the knowledge of the heir'. But if in doubt, Ghigi was advised, 'we are more interested in the heir than the patient.'[23]

The moribund patient took another three months to expire. In that time, far from administering oxygen, the Italian government appeared more intent on shutting off the valves. By December 1937, Ciano considered the Rome Protocols superseded.[24] At the last meeting of the Protocol countries in Budapest in January 1938, he refused, out of consideration for Germany, to make a public declaration about the independence of Austria. As to the economic aspects of the Protocol, the Hungarians noted bitterly that Rome's extension of preferential tariffs to Yugoslavia had voided them of any content.[25] It should have come as no surprise to the Italian government that Hitler finally called Schuschnigg to Berchtesgaden in February 1938 to lay down the ten-point ultimatum which within a month led to the incorporation of Austria into the German Reich. Nothing could have illustrated Italy's impotence better than the fact that neither Hitler nor the hapless Schuschnigg found it necessary to consult Mussolini. The first news of their meeting reached Rome through a journalist's report. On the 14th, Ribbentrop replied to the Italian Ambassador's question with vague generalities, and the Secretary-General of the Wilhelmstrasse four days later still maintained that nothing substantial had taken place.[26] The German explanation convinced no one. Ciano found it expedient immediately to accelerate the Anglo–Italian conversations which had been lagging for six months, primarily with a view to obtaining better terms so long as the British hoped that Italy might yet return to her 1934 policy, but also with the hope of pressuring Hitler into postponing the *Anschluss*. In the meantime, he unburdened himself to the Prince of Hesse. 'If one kept in mind the exemplary correctness of our policy towards Germany and considered the verbal agreements which exist on the subject of

Austria', he complained, 'the way in which things happened could not be considered by us to be altogether agreeable'. And then, referring to a speech Hitler was scheduled to make in a few days, he suggested 'it would be well to declare that Austria continues to exist as an independent state, since the threat of a final absorption of Austria would produce reactions in world opinion which are at present neither easy to forecast nor prudent to arouse.'[27] Some of the reactions alluded to by Ciano were already taking place in Italy. Inevitably, it was becoming brutally clear that the economic and political penetration of the Balkan–Danubian region, which had been one of the constant themes of Italian policy since the break-up of the Austro–Hungarian Empire and had recently been included in the protocol as the basis of the Axis, would be imperilled. Vienna, after 1918 as before, remained the hub of Danubian commercial traffic whether by road, river or rail. With Austria as part of the Reich, what hopes would Italy have of influencing Hungary and Yugoslavia, Romania and Bulgaria? What status other than junior partner remained? Even more serious, did the Germans at the Brenner not signify the complete bankruptcy of Italy's strategic policy? Would it not lead to an exasperation of the Alto Adige problem? To a recrudescence of the persecution of Catholics which could not sit well with the Lateran concordat?

Rome had no answers. Mussolini and Ciano had written off Austria but the reckoning had come too quickly. A special Italian envoy was hurriedly sent to Vienna where he appeared to the local Nazis to be attempting to sabotage the *Anschluss*.[28] But when it came to the point and Mussolini was asked to take a stand on the plebiscite Schuschnigg was planning to head off a German invasion, he backed off. Schuschnigg's desperate announcement of the plebiscite was followed by a German ultimatum that he call if off and resign. Mussolini refused to give counsel.[29] A similar answer was received from London while Paris was paralysed by a Cabinet crisis. The French chargé d'affaires in Rome was none the less instructed to ask Ciano for an interview to discuss the Austrian appeal. Ciano would not receive him and, as if to emphasise his loyalty to Germany, the Western Powers' entreaties were scrupulously reported to Berlin.[30] In the meantime, Hitler had again sent off his special messenger, still the Prince of Hesse, with a message for Mussolini. The Duce received him at nine in the evening of 12 March. 'Italy is following events with absolute calm,' he told him.

Hesse phoned Hitler at 10.25 p.m. The Führer was ecstatic.[31]

> Tell Mussolini I will never forget this. . . . Never, never, never, whatever happens. . . . If he should ever need any help or he is in any danger, he can be convinced that I shall stick to him, whatever may happen, even if the whole world be against him.

Mussolini's accommodating attitude meant that the tragi-comedy of conflicting orders and preparations could be resolved in favour of a peaceful occupation. The *Anschluss* was accomplished with no external resistance. The event left a profound mark on both men. Hitler had discovered that an adroit combination of pressure and threats had secured a goal for which he had been prepared to wait longer. Mussolini saw confirmed the German strength which had so impressed him in September 1937. This realisation brought home the full consequences of the policy he had followed since the invasion of Abyssinia. He had taken a gamble in 1935 and moved the centre of gravity of fascist foreign policy to the Mediterranean. The cost of his ambitions in Africa had been enmity with France and Great Britain, a cost barely made tolerable by the solidarity he found north of the Alps in Germany. In March 1938 Germany had exacted her price. With the Germans at the Brenner, there could be no going back.

There were some satisfactions. Hitler had tried to offset Mussolini's wounded pride by a firm reference to the inviolability of the Brenner frontier. 'Whatever the consequences to the next events', he promised Mussolini, 'I have traced a clear German frontier with France and now I am tracing one just as clear with Italy. It is the Brenner. This decision will never be placed in doubt or challenged.'[32] Hitler asserted that his resolution dated back to the end of the last war but its significance lay in the fact that for the first time it was made explicit from one head of government to another. The pledge was appreciated in Rome where Mussolini saw in it some compensation for his inaction as well as a justification of his policy before Italian public opinion.[33] This was the first time the irrevocability of the Brenner frontier had been announced so unambiguously and Mussolini quickly sought Berlin's approval for publication in Italy of Hitler's communication.[34] That request was readily granted (as was a request that Hitler include a reference to the Brenner in his forthcoming speech to the Reichstag) though, ominously, not a request that the Führer's pledge be published also in Germany. Yet nothing could modify the irritation and dissatisfaction felt throughout Italy after the *Anschluss*, inflamed by the now openly anti-Italian behaviour of the German minorities in the Alto Adige, by the prospect of the extension to Austria's Catholics of German legislation on elementary education, marriage and religious houses, and by the immediate abrogation of the economic benefits Italy had derived from the Rome Protocols. Not even a formal proposal by Göring that the problem be settled by a wholesale transferral of the German-speaking dissidents from the Alto Adige to the Reich mollified the Italian government. A transfer of population (a device eventually resorted to when Italian subservience was much more marked) was neither foreseen nor desired by Mussolini, who looked upon the scheme as a diminution of Italian sovereignty. 'If the Germans behave well and are respectful Italian subjects', the Duce telephoned to Ciano upon receipt of Göring's proposal, 'I might favour their language and culture. But if they are thinking of moving the frontier by a single meter they must know that the result would be the fiercest war in which I would coalesce the whole world against Germany.'[35] Such was the epitaph on Italy's fifty-year quest for a strategically secure frontier in the north.

Mussolini's exasperation revealed clearly the importance he attached to the Brenner. Similar outbursts would multiply in succeeding years, all of them evidence that Mussolini was aware of the danger of being dragged more and more at the wheels of the German chariot and not able to break away even sufficiently to safeguard what he used to consider his vital interests in Central Europe. And yet he had come to the conclusion that German expansionism was so inevitable, that there was no longer any hope of stemming it and that the more prudent course was a continuance of close friendship with a powerful and well armed Germany even if in Europe as a whole he had to play second string to the Führer. Here was the real genesis of the Pact of Steel – the craven admission of impotence married to the greed for aggrandisement. Much as the progression towards the formal signature of the Italo–German alliance reflected contingent events, this was the quintessential driving force behind it.

The first of the formal discussions to turn the loose bonds of the Axis into what eventually became the noose of the Pact of Steel took place during the course of Hitler's visit to Italy between 3 and 9 May 1938. The draft treaty of mutual respect prepared by

Palazzo Chigi before the Führer's arrival reflected Italy's apprehensions after the *Anschluss*.[36] It called on the two parties to
respect their mutual frontier and to settle all controversies peace-
fully. The second article asked the parties to pledge themselves not
to tolerate, or to help in any way, whatever activity which might
be directed against the territorial integrity or the order established
by the other party. Obviously the previous German declaration of
respect for the Brenner frontier had not sufficiently dissipated
Rome's apprehensions. The German-speaking population of the
Alto Adige thought of themselves as part of those three and a half
million Germans not yet 'freed' to which Hitler had made ample
allusion in his speech of 18 March 1938. The agitation in the Alto
Adige had recently erupted into armed skirmishes and had been
the subject of several official protests by the Italian Embassy in
Berlin. Admittedly the demonstrations might have been caused by
local hotheads, but the fact that Berlin had not yet intervened
forcibly to put an end to them was a further cause for suspicion.[37]
Thus before moving to more binding engagements, the Italian
government wanted precise and public guarantees of the Brenner
frontier and of Berlin's intention to keep its *irredenta* in check.

On the German side, on the other hand, the talk was of a
binding military alliance. The Germans submitted a project which
harked back to earlier discussions about a tripartite pact with Japan
and was not unrelated to the liquidation of the Sudeten problem
which in Hitler's mind could only be solved satisfactorily with a
friendly Italy refusing to make common cause with Britain and
France.[38] Of the various draft projects prepared in the Wilhelmstrasse, one, comprising a public pact and a secret protocol, was
presented to the Italians on 5 May. The pact, in addition to the
normal clauses calling for diplomatic support and consultation in
the event of an external threat, made reference also to the common ideologies and to the common 'inviolable' frontier, though
the permanence of inviolability was somewhat watered down by
the five-year time limit on the alliance. The secret protocol, on the
other hand, would have turned a more or less innocuous pact of
mutual support into a full-fledged military alliance. It called for all
military aid in the event of unprovoked attack from France or
Britain, immediate and continuous consultations to that end between the two high commands and a mutual pledge not to sign a
separate peace or armistice.[39]

Italy's reception was decidedly cool. There were several reasons. One was that Mussolini had not yet given up hope of a tripartite pact with Japan which would have been a much more useful instrument of pressure on Great Britain. As early as March 1936 Gayda, a close confidant of Mussolini and editor of the *Giornale d'Italia,* had raised the possibility of a tripartite agreement with the Japanese Ambassador in Rome.[40] The announcement on 18 November 1936 that Japan would recognise the Italian empire had been accompanied by an offer to tighten 'the bonds which unite the two nations in the economic, cultural, political, military fields',[41] but the conversation had not gone further owing to Japanese fears of repercussions in England and to the chronic inability of the Japanese government departments to keep in step with one another. The renewal of fighting in the Far East between China and Japan issued in another Japanese step towards Italy. On 31 July 1937, the new Ambassador, Hotta, delivered to Ciano a personal letter from the Japanese Foreign Minister proposing a bilateral anti-Communist *entente* to be completed by a secret agreement 'of technical collaboration in the military field . . . and very, very benevolent neutrality'.[42] Ciano was well disposed. Disregarding Grandi's advice that such a pact should follow the signature of an agreement with London, he proposed in October a public anti-Bolshevik agreement along the lines of the Anti-Comintern Pact between Japan and Germany, complete with a 'secret agreement of benevolent neutrality in all contingencies with a clause of consultations for eventually a more active solidarity in specific cases'.[43] But once again the contrast between the Japanese Army, Navy and Foreign Office caused the proposal to be dropped as too provocative to Britain and the USA. The Japanese government, Hotta told Ciano on 20 October 1937, could agree only to Italy's adhesion to the Anti-Comintern Pact between Germany and Japan with no secret or supplementary agreements.[44] The Italian Foreign Minister, though disappointed at losing a club with which to beat Britain, readily agreed, the more so since Hotta assured him that the earlier verbal promise of benevolent neutrality still stood. On 6 November, Ciano, Ribbentrop and Hotta signed instead the milder protocol making Italy a charter member of the Anti-Comintern Pact.[45]

Ostensibly, the pact sought to make a distinction between communist ideology and the Soviet Union. In fact, a secret protocol (to which Italy was not made a party) stipulated benevolent neutrality and consultation in the event of war between the Soviet Union and either Germany or Japan.[46] For Ciano, however, the main enemy remained Britain. The 'alliance of three military empires', he noted with some exaggeration, 'throws into the scales the weight of armed strength without precedent. London will have to review her position.' Seldom had he been so happy. 'It's no longer the situation of 1935. Italy has broken out of her isolation; she is now at the centre of the most formidable military-political combinations which ever existed.'[47] And within a month, secure in her diplomatic position, Italy had withdrawn from the League of Nations. There was no specific reason for the step, no special motion of censure. The withdrawal was merely Italy's announcement that she would pay not even lip service to the political philosophy enshrined in the Covenant or to the territorial arrangements sanctioned at Versailles. She had gone over to the camp of those powers which decried the Covenant and was showing her determination to create with them a new international order based on another political philosophy.

But despite Ciano's early optimism, no tripartite military alliance had yet been signed and the pact which Germany was presently offering, useful though it was on the continent, bore little relevance to the Mediterranean, where only a threat from the Far East could bring about a diminution of British forces. Moreover, the Easter Accords had just been signed with Britain and a similar agreement was under study with France. A formalisation of the loose Axis undertakings of 1936 in conjunction with closer relations with London and Paris, would have broken the diplomatic isolation Italy had suffered since the Abyssinian war as well as alleviated the psychological set-back of the *Anschluss*. This the Italian draft was intended to accomplish. But the military alliance offered by Hitler, on the other hand, could well have compromised Italy's delicate balancing act at a time when Chamberlain was bringing London around to recognising the Italian empire in Africa. Thus Ciano replied to the German offer by presenting his own draft treaty of mutual respect which now appeared not so much like a counter-proposal as a refusal and as a warning that unless those questions raised by the Italian draft were settled no basis existed for a military alliance. Implicitly, the Italian draft let it be known that two years of Axis collaboration had not entirely cleared the air and that therefore the public assumption of an antagonistic posture towards the Western powers was at best premature. Ribbentrop, reportedly, took the rebuff as a personal affront. His dislike for Ciano probably began at this point. Hitler on the other hand, concerned about the damage to his plans for Czechoslovakia which might result from a *rapprochement* between Italy and the West, took care to pour oil over the troubled waters. At a state dinner at Palazzo Venezia he announced his 'unshakeable will and also my political testament to the German people to consider intangible forever the frontier at the Alps erected by nature between us'.[48] Such a formal pledge on such a solemn occasion brought an immediate warmth to the political air and played a not inconsiderable role in the further progression to an alliance. The German leader left Italy on 9 May after a whirlwind tour of Florence, without a pact but with a reasonable expectation that the subject could be broached again. For his part, Mussolini agreed with Ciano that, contingent on other developments, a military alliance with Germany would be 'convenient'.[49]

An opening to the West?

The other developments Mussolini had in mind ranged from his intractable public opinion, only partly mollified by the Führer's assurances, to an even more intractable pope, who had pointedly closed the Vatican museums and returned to his summer residence whence he delivered fulminations about the other cross now flying over Rome, but in particular to Italy's relations with the Western Powers. Italy's refusal to entertain the military alliance proposed by Hitler was related to the prospects that the Easter Accords with Britain might come into force just as Hitler's ardour at this particular time could be ascribed to the contingent needs of his Czechoslovak policy. The two coalesced in the summer of 1938. On the one hand, London proved to be much less accommodating and the Duce much more demanding over a parallel Italo–French agreement and, on the other hand, Paris and London's firmness over the crisis in the Sudetenland in mid-May confirmed in Berlin the necessity to offset such tenacity by sedulously courting Italian support.

In the preliminary stages of the negotiations for the Easter Accords London had contemplated the accession of other

Mediterranean powers, principally France, but, as Ciano had been adamant on leaving France out, the ensuing negotiations had been strictly bilateral. This pointed exclusion underlined the deterioration leading eventually to the withdrawal of ambassadors which had taken place in Italo–French relations since their intimacy of early 1935. At the height of their mutual recriminations, the French cabinet had gone so far as to try to force Britain to make her negotiations with Italy conditional on French participation and requirements. In April 1938, a new French government, more inclined to accommodation, took another tack. On the morning of the day the Easter Accords were to be announced, the French chargé d'affaires, Blondel, announced to Ciano France's readiness to begin immediately bilateral discussions. The suggested agenda reproduced and amplified the subjects recently discussed and settled by Great Britain and Italy: an Italian pledge not to seek territorial advantages in Spain and to withdraw its volunteers on terms to be decided by the Non-Intervention Committee; a share in the Anglo–Italian agreement relating to the Red Sea; the continuation of the Mussolini–Laval agreement of 1935 on the status of the Italian nationals in Tunisia. Both Mussolini and Ciano, still suffering from the shock of the *Anschluss,* appeared very receptive. Although Ciano pledged to Mackensen, the German Ambassador, that no European subjects would be discussed,[50] he also let it be known in Paris that if a new ambassador were appointed quickly and some hint given that France was disposed to recognise the empire, a Franco–Italian agreement was within reach.[51]

In Paris the best way to proceed towards a settlement was discussed intensely all during April. There were those at the Quai d'Orsay, led by Leger, the italophobe Secretary-General, who looked upon Italy's terms as ill-disguised blackmail. Others, more favourably disposed towards Italy none the less felt that more concessions could be extracted from an Italy distraught by the *Anschluss.* On the whole, the general feeling was that unless Italy committed herself to some far-reaching agreement during Hitler's forthcoming visit, an agreement was likely.[52] This was also London's opinion. Hore-Belisha, the Minister of War, insisted with Daladier that France show more comprehension towards Italy and relayed the favourable reception of his suggestion to Rome. Daladier and Bonnet, after discussing the matter with Chamberlain and Halifax in London on 28 April, appeared confident of a successful conclusion, provided Italy's goodwill was demonstrated by observance of the statute relating to Tunisia.[53]

As it turned out, both London and Paris misjudged Mussolini's intentions. His overtures towards France had served to point out to Hitler that irons other than those of the Axis were in the fire. Probably he had also hoped to pressure the French government into a quick pledge to recognise the empire before Hitler came. After the visit this pretence was dropped. Ciano, on behalf of Mussolini, refused to enter into any discussions on Spain and ruled out French participation in the Red Sea agreement.[54] He did not close the door entirely since on 12 May the League Council was debating a British proposal that members of the League should be free, if they wished, to recognise the Italian conquest of Abyssinia, but once that issue was settled in Italy's favour, all further meetings with Blondel were cancelled.[55] A few days later came Mussolini's speech in Genoa. He extolled the *Anschluss,* reviled the democracies, harped on the sanctions and saved his harshest words for France. Referring to the conversations in progress, he despaired of their success[56]

> if for no other reason, because in an operation which is very much to the fore, that is the war in Spain, we are on opposite sides of the barricades. They desire the victory of Barcelona, we, on the other hand, desire the victory of Franco.

His words might have meant that if France abandoned the Republicans an agreement with Italy was possible. In fact, because of the absurdity of the demand, far in excess of the terms of the Easter Accords, the Genoa speech had to be construed as an uncouth but deliberate attempt, soon to be followed by the inevitable journalistic denigrations, to isolate France from Britain.

London was not unaware of this possibility and Chamberlain and Halifax had promised their French counterparts not to bring the Easter Accords into force until a similar Franco–Italian agreement had also been concluded.[57] But at the same time the Czechoslovak crisis was brewing and London was looking to Italy as a moderating influence on Hitler. Despite Mussolini's fulsome references to the strength of the Axis in the Genoa speech, London appreciated that no military alliance had been signed. Indeed Ciano had hastened to inform Perth and the American Ambassador that Germany's advances in that direction had been rejected. In reply

Ciano was advised that if France were compelled to go to the aid of Czechoslovakia, Britain could not stand idle. The Italian government should have no illusions, Perth emphasised, about the likelihood of localising a conflict. This warning was coupled with another one, that friendly relations with Britain in the future depended on an Italian change of heart towards France.[58]

There was no mistaking the implication of this last injunction. Italy had just announced her intention to withdraw some of her 'volunteers' from Spain, a step which, as Perth had to agree, called for Britain to bring the Easter Accords into effect regardless of Italy's relations with France.[59] The British government, on the other hand, faced with the unpleasant choice of continuing its *rapprochement* with Italy or standing by its pledge to Paris not to bring the Accords into force unless France were also included, was leaning towards the second course.

The final British decision on whether to accede to the Italian request to give immediate effect to the Accords was two weeks in the making, two weeks during which, as in the previous year, air attacks on British shipping and the bombing of population centres in Spain turned the weight of public opinion decidedly against co-operation with Italy. Perth presented himself at Palazzo Chigi on 20 June 1938 with two notes. In the first, the British government acknowledged the fulfilment of Italy's pledges, but felt that the coming into force of the Easter Accords depended on a general settlement of the Spanish War. Italy's adhesion to the plan for the evacuation of volunteers was a step in the right direction but not, by itself, sufficient. The British government proposed three alternatives: (a) the execution of the latest plans of the Non-Intervention Committee for the evacuation of volunteers, (b) the unilateral withdrawal of the Italian forces in Spain, and (c) an armistice in Spain. The British government strongly favoured the third alternative. It had sounded Paris and the French government was also said to be in favour of an armistice. Perth now hoped that Italy would equally agree. The second British note dealt with relations between Paris, London and Rome. The British government acknowledged that the entry into force of the Easter Accords had never been made dependent on the conclusion of a similar agreement with France, but since the Franco–Italian dispute over Spain was incompatible with the general abatement of European tension, the British government now felt that Italy should propose resumption of the negotiations with France for without a Franco–Italian settlement 'it is difficult to take into consideration that pacification of Europe which is the common purpose of our two governments to promote'.[60]

The Italian reply was no easier to draft. On the one hand, withdrawing the volunteers or proposing an armistice was out of the question. Even though a gradual withdrawal was planned in view of the generally favourable course of the war, at this juncture Franco's forces were engaged in a counter-attack from which Mussolini could not withdraw support without at the same time sabotaging their cause. On the other hand, Rome was aware of how really tenuous Chamberlain's position was, of the risks it ran of seeing Eden back in the Cabinet. Still, at the end of June, Mussolini decided the British proposals were unacceptable. A memorandum handed to Perth on 1 July explained that an armistice was inadmissible unless the Republicans first surrendered, in which case Italy could bring to bear some moderating influence on the Nationalists. As to France, there could be no connection between Italy's relations with that country and the Easter Accords.

> To establish today any connection of the kind – a connection which was never put forward either at the beginning of the Anglo–Italian negotiations or during their course, but was, on the contrary, formally excluded, would mean running the risk of wrecking the Anglo–Italian agreement.

Eventually, negotiations with France could be resumed after the Accords had come into force; meanwhile the Italian government requested London's permission to publish their diplomatic correspondence since 3 June and warned that, if the Accords were not brought into force, the Italian government reserved the right to resume its freedom of action.[61] On 11 July, London acknowledged formally that the negotiations to bring the Accords into force had reached an impasse. Mussolini's attitude amounted to 'an attempt to separate Paris and London', Perth told Ciano, and since 'nothing of *the kind is possible,* it is useless and harmful to lend support to a supposition of the kind'.[62]

In effect, Mussolini's attempt to split Britain from France had not merely failed but had also issued in a formal enunciation of solidarity between the two Western Powers. In view of the fact that the interpretation London was now giving to the settlement of the Spanish problem was indisputably more rigid than either party had permitted during their negotiation, while Mussolini had complied faithfully with his part of the bargain by withdrawing troops from Libya and curtailing the propaganda broadcasts, the Italian disappointment was at least understandable. But it was justified only as it related to the coming into force of the Easter Accords. Clearly these Accords were meant to be instruments in a wider appeasement. Yet the Italian government had chosen to use them as a stick with which to beat France. The Genoa speech had been interpreted correctly as an Italian attempt to humiliate and isolate France. It should not have been surprising to find London unable to accept the humiliation of its best friend on the continent. Faced with the stark choice of *rapprochement* with Italy or continued friendship with France, London inevitably chose, indeed was forced into choosing, the latter.

Chapter 14

Munich and After

We cannot change our policy, we are not whores.
Mussolini, March 1939

During the next twelve months the pattern tentatively set in the summer of 1938 – to keep France in perpetual fear of Germany on the continent so as to procure her pliability in the Mediterranean – hardened into the central feature of Italian foreign policy. It was not inevitable that it should work out this way, and in fact twice, after the Munich conference and after the final occupation of Czechoslovakia, it looked as if Italy's rush into the arms of Germany might be halted and the harmony promised by the Easter Accords be given a chance to provide some stability for Europe. In fact, partly in gratitude for Mussolini's mediation at Munich and partly because the arrangement was clearly to its advantage, the British government decided on 16 November to ratify the Accords. But the Accords were not allowed to develop their potential as an instrument of general pacification because Mussolini additionally continued to demand, in effect, the surrender of France, unaware until too late that his price for British friendship was impossibly high and that his chosen instrument of pressure – a relationship with Germany more binding and more threatening than the Axis – would inevitably ensnare him and deprive him of practically all freedom of action.

The loss of the initiative

This pattern, discernible in the summer of 1938, was practically set by the beginning of February 1939. Speaking to the Grand Council at that time, Mussolini would justify the policy he had followed in the last three years by specious references to the imprisonment of Italy in the Mediterranean:[1]

The premise from which I speak is the following: States are more or less independent according to their maritime position . . . Italy is bordered by an inland sea which communicates with the ocean through the Suez Canal, an artificial means of communication which is easily blocked, and through the Straits of Gibraltar, dominated by the guns of Great Britain.

Italy has in fact no free access to the oceans; Italy is really a prisoner in the Mediterranean and the more populous and powerful she becomes, the more she will suffer from her imprisonment.

The bars of the prison are Corsica, Tunisia, Malta and Cyprus: its sentinels Gibraltar and Suez. . . .

The tasks of Italian policy, which could not and does not have European territorial aims, save Albania, is in the first place to break the prison bars. . . .

We are faced with the opposition of Britain and France. To brave the solution of such problems without first having secured our rear on the continent would have been absurd. The Rome–Berlin Axis thus answers a fundamental historical necessity. The same applies to our conduct in the Spanish Civil War.

This justification had a sadly familiar ring: to pursue her aspirations in the Mediterranean and Africa, Italy by necessity had had to secure her rear through a treaty with the greatest land power in Europe and through the installation in Spain of a friendly régime. No mention was made, aside from the reference to Albania for which new plans were under way, of Italy's former pre-eminence in Central and Eastern Europe. The bulk of the speech was dedicated to recriminations against France and the prospects of a war against that country. These were said to be good owing to the support of Germany on the continent. By 1941–2, Mussolini anticipated, Italy's war potential while not 'ideal' would be a great deal better. By then also Italian artillery would be entirely re-equipped, eight battleships and twice the number of submarines would be ready, the empire would be pacified and in a position to supply a colonial army, the plans for self-sufficiency more than half completed, the foreign currency reserves repleted by the Universal Exposition in Rome in 1942 and the three-quarters of a million Italian emigrants in France repatriated.[2]

Mussolini envisaged a naval and air war in the Mediterranean. He made it clear he had no interest in a European or global land conflict. His explanations serve to place the negotiations from May 1938 for an alliance with Germany in the proper perspective. The alliance was seen, first, as a means to put pressure on France on the continent and in the Mediterranean and second, if it also included Japan, to weaken Britain's naval disposition in the Mediterranean – a combination designed to ensure Italy's superiority in that theatre. But also, although Mussolini lost sight of this aspect as his judgment was overcome by events and by his own cupidity, the alliance was intended to restrain Germany from pursuing aims likely to provoke the Western Powers into a premature land conflict.

Thus in June 1938 it was still possible for Mussolini to reject Ribbentrop's offer of a 'plain, open military alliance'[3] as distinct from the secret arrangement suggested in May. Though it flattered his self esteem in the wake of the recent Western rebuffs and though it would have provided also an opportunity to gauge more closely German intentions in Czechoslovakia and elsewhere, he judged it premature. The wisdom of holding aloof appeared confirmed by Germany's evasive behaviour in the following months during the course of the Sudeten crisis.[4] Berlin left a deliberate silence in Rome over the timing of the clash it intended to provoke in Czechoslovakia, and indeed ruled out the Sudeten crisis as a possible *casus foederis*. Hence whatever verbal support Mussolini extended to the German dictator before the end of September 1938 was doubly gratuitous, though perhaps justified in his own mind as part of the war of nerves. He must have been convinced he was not risking a great deal when he was blithely telling the Hungarians that if Germany attacked Czechoslovakia, Italy was ready to mobilise and indeed attack France if necessary. Of course, he made it clear he would not have to go to those extremes, for neither Britain or France would intervene.[5] There is no reason to suppose that at this time his nonchalance was in any sense feigned: the only direct interest Italy seemed to have had in the Czechoslovak crisis was the extent to which it could be used for the cheap aggrandisement of such client states as Hungary. Despite some alarming reports by the Italian Ambassador in Berlin, Bernardo Attolico, who had as good a nose for war preparations in 1938 as the following summer, Mussolini continued to be satisfied with Ribbentrop's assurances of 23 August that 'as soon as the Führer made his decision . . . the Italian government would be the first one to receive such notification', and with Hitler's personal message of 6 September (delivered ironically at the same time the German General Staff was setting the invasion date for 1 October) that the Führer was 'unable to state any definite time because he does not know himself'.[6]

Thus the speaking tour which Mussolini undertook through northern Italy in the second half of September when he trumpeted Henlein's claims, castigated Benes who had had the misfortune of chairing the League Assembly which had voted sanctions, and matched Hitler in vituperation and malevolence was probably undertaken in all innocence of Germany's real plans. Only on 25 September, when Hesse arrived with the inevitable message, did Mussolini understand that something was scheduled to happen in Czechoslovakia by 1 October.[7] His inclusion of that date in one of his speeches was, no doubt, deliberate – it was as much a warning to the Western Powers as to Germany. And when, at 2 a.m. on the 27th, he received Attolico's deduction that, if the occupation of the Sudetenland was to be completed by 1 October, German mobilisation would be announced sometime on the 28th, he lost no time in telephoning Hitler and in accepting the Western suggestion of a summit conference. By noon on the 28th he had obtained Hitler's acquiescence to delay all marching orders for twenty-four hours; by 3 p.m., after another telephone call from Mussolini, Attolico had persuaded the Führer to accept a four-power conference; by 4 p.m. Mussolini and Ciano were on the train to Munich.[8]

Before Mussolini left Rome, Attolico had furnished him with a set of 'moderate' demands on Czechoslovakia provided by the Wilhelmstrasse. As it turned out, by the time Mussolini boarded Hitler's train at the old German–Austrian frontier these demands had been superseded: the Nazi chiefs spent the time between the border and Munich detailing how they would liquidate Czechoslovakia by war.[9] It was in the light of this incident that Mussolini became the real architect of the Munich conference, for when the session began at noon he presented the 'moderate', though now superseded, German demands as his own personal compromise. Chamberlain, Daladier and, with less good grace, also Hitler, eventually accepted them and they became the basis of the agreement signed that night which provided for the cession of the Sudetenland in stages, for plebiscites under international control in other zones of mixed population, for the right of option for the inhabitants and for a four-power guarantee of the new rump Czechoslovakia.

Munich was a success for Mussolini not so much because he was universally heralded as the saviour of the peace, nor because his inglorious withdrawal from Austria tended to be forgotten or because London now deemed it wise to recognise the Italian empire and bring the Easter Accords into effect and Berlin to treat his opposition to a military alliance more respectfully. Essentially it was a success because the Italian leader had recognised and adroitly checked Hitler's will to war. Not that Mussolini was opposed to war. This was simply the wrong war at the wrong time in the wrong place for Italian interests. But it was also the last time the Italian leader was able to render such signal service to his nation and to Europe. With the advantage of hindsight, it might be said as well that Europe would have been served better by allowing the confrontation to run its course. Yet from the strictly Italian point of view, Munich, while a short-run tactical success, gave great cause for concern for the future. By recklessly sponsoring the German minorities in Czechoslovakia, Mussolini was unwittingly undercutting his hold over the German-speaking inhabitants of the Alto Adige; by backing Hitler, whose ends and methods he did not know, he was encouraging similar behaviour in the future. And finally, by permitting a German stranglehold over Czechoslovakia and her resources, he altered dramatically the balance of strategic and political power in Europe with results which could not but accentuate the growing imbalance within the Axis as well as within Europe.

But all this was in the future. For the moment Ciano and Mussolini had no difficulty in putting off another German draft for a still more binding and comprehensive alliance,[10] a move designed, at least in part, to circumvent the post-Munich isolation from which Germany suffered. But an alliance with Germany, by the same token, would have lost for Mussolini the credit he had earned in Munich. 'I am still inclined to put it into cold storage,' Ciano wrote of the latest German proposal, hand-delivered by Ribbentrop, 'particularly since Perth has secretly informed me of the British decision to implement the Easter Accords as from the middle of November. We must keep both doors open. An alliance would now close, perhaps forever, one of the two, and that not the less important. The Duce also seems to think so.'[11]

The new German draft derived its stronger military flavour from the stipulation to make no separate peace or armistice and to make the alliance operative for ten years immediately upon signature. In this context the consultation envisaged by the additional secret protocol could only be interpreted as joint planning for a common war. Mussolini and Ciano were decidedly negative. Privately, Ciano found Ribbentrop's warmongering particularly inappropriate and Mussolini, concerned to avoid mass resentment, agreed on the necessity of a postponement. As he and Ciano explained to Ribbentrop, several stumbling blocks stood in the way of an alliance. In the first place, it was not necessary. 'Why', asked Ciano, 'open the door to rumour by a pact the only consequence of which would be to draw upon us the odium of aggression?'[12] Second, large segments of the Italian population were not ready for it. It was Mussolini's wish to enter into an alliance after the idea has been allowed to mature for the necessary period among the great mass of the people. 'Today, this is not the case. The Italian people have reached the stage of the Axis; but not yet that of the military alliance.' Third, 'its objectives' had not been established, Mussolini emphasised, and, so as not to leave the impression of pusillanimity in Berlin, he explained how he, eventually, wished to contract not a defensive alliance but one 'to change the map of the world'. The Reich Foreign Minister was sent back to Berlin with an *aide-mémoire* listing these points for the benefit of his chief.[13]

But Mussolini's reservations in these matters could be discounted in advance. The masses, the opportunist in him explained, 'may, reach . . . very rapidly' the point of readiness. Other ratiocinations could be and were abandoned just as rapidly. In fact, within a month, the adumbration of a *rapprochement* between Paris and Berlin, and the visit of Chamberlain and Halifax to Paris, by raising the spectre of isolation, sent Mussolini scurrying to make repairs. 'Inform Von Ribbentrop immediately', he instructed his Ambassador in Berlin the moment the press began to talk of a full-fledged Anglo-French military alliance, 'that if this should be the outcome of the Paris colloquies, we will consider the observations made on the occasion of his recent journey to Rome no longer valid and that we will be ready to draft the military alliance with Germany without further delay.'[14]

Ironically enough, Mussolini's forecast was correct. The Paris meeting resulted in quite precise military undertakings between France and Great Britain. What he overlooked was the extent to which these Anglo-French conversations were due to his own anti-French campaign launched early in November with a view to pre-empting what appeared to him like an incipient *rapprochement* between Berlin and Paris. The vituperative campaign, culminating on 30 November 1938 in the march of fascist deputies to the square below Palazzo Venezia to rabid shouts of 'Tunis, Corsica, Nice and Savoy', led inevitably to the denunciation of the Mussolini–Laval agreements of January 1935 and the end of whatever prospects may have once existed for a normalisation of relations in the Mediterranean through France's accession to the Easter Accords. By the end of December, Mussolini, carried along by a crisis of his own making, had pretty well opted for the immediate transformation of the Axis into a full-fledged military alliance with Germany and with Japan as well, if the tergiversations to which the Japanese decision-making process was prone could be overcome.[15] 'The true reasons which have led the Duce to accept your proposals at this point,' Ciano wrote to Ribbentrop on 2 January 1939, 'are as follows: (1) The existence – now proved – of a military pact between France and Great Britain; (2) The acceptance of the possibility of war in responsible French circles; (3) The military preparations of the United States which are intended to furnish men and above all materials to the Western democracies in case of necessity.'[16]

No doubt Paris's warmongering could be explained by the events of 30 November while the 'proven existence' of an Anglo–French alliance had been deemed irrelevant as recently as the last conversation between Mussolini and Ribbentrop when the Duce had avowed that the democracies would never dare attack the totalitarian states. What, however, was of real consequence was the fact that Mussolini's decision at this juncture to accept an alliance with Germany contained within it the seeds of a fundamental misunderstanding. Because of the emphasis on France, one permissible deduction in Germany was that the Italian government intended to use the projected military alliance as a club with which to beat France. Such an interpretation certainly corresponded to the long-term intentions of Rome, yet it tended to obscure Italy's contingent reasons – the prevention of a Franco–German *rapprochement* and the pre-emption of hostile reactions to the planned occupation of Albania. Consequently, Germany tended to overly dramatise Italy's complaints against France and to suppose they might be a prelude to the kind of military confrontation which normally followed

similar German demonstrations. Germany had no more intention
than Italy of being dragged into a war by its partner's rashness.
Thus Berlin, whilst eager to conclude an alliance, readily and
repeatedly agreed in Rome on the need to maintain the peace for
several years – an agreement which came under the headings of
tactics in Berlin but of strategy in Rome, thus giving rise to crucial
misunderstanding at the bottom of the Pact of Steel.

The broad objectives of Italy's policy were spelled out by
Mussolini in a conversation with Ciano at the beginning of
1939:[17]

> Tripartite pact. Closer understanding with Yugoslavia, Hungary and
> possibly Poland with a view to ensuring supplies of raw materials.
> Alliance with Spain as soon as the war has been won. Claims against
> France. Neither Nice nor Savoy because outside the boundary of the
> Alps. Corsica: autonomy, independence, annexation. Tunisia:
> statute for the Italians, autonomy for the Bey, Italian protectorate.
> Jibuti: free port and railway, joint administration of the colony,
> cession. Suez Canal: substantial participation in its administration.
> Agreement with Belgrade to liquidate Albania, if necessary by
> supporting Serbian claims to Salonika.

Evidently, in Ciano's and Mussolini's eyes, the proposed pact
was an instrument of pressure more than an instrument of war, and
of gradual long-range pressure at that. The exception to the
general will to avoid military action was the decision, made final
after the fall of Stoyadinović on 4 February 1939, to occupy
Albania as soon as practicable. In those circumstances an immediate alliance with the most powerful country on the continent,
supplemented by well-publicised staff talks, would more than offset
the ground lost by the removal of a pliable Yugoslav prime
minister. Thus a few days later Mussolini took a position against
waiting on the Japanese to make up their minds and in favour of
concluding immediately a bilateral pact with Germany.[18] By the
beginning of March, Berlin was in agreement. Ribbentrop acknowledged that Tokyo's objectives to a tripartite pact were so fundamental that nothing could be done on that scale at the moment. At
the same time Berlin's own plans for the complete occupation of
Czechoslovakia within the next few days called for an immediate
reinforcement of the Axis front. Somewhat reluctantly, Ribbentrop
put aside the negotiations for a tripartite pact till more propitious
times and agreed to an Italian request for immediate general staff

talks as a prelude to turning the Axis into a full-fledged military alliance.[19]

Set in this context the entry of German troops into Prague on 15 March 1939 appeared to most to have been the result of careful Axis planning. It was not realised then to what extent the *coup* created acute incertitude, consternation and resentment in Rome to the point where Ciano, and to a degree Mussolini, contemplated seriously a change of policy.[20] 'The Axis functions in favour of only one of its pacts,' Ciano complained bitterly when he heard the news. Hitler, without so much as a nod in Rome's direction, had just destroyed a settlement in which Italy had been a principal party. 'What weight', he wondered pointedly 'can be given in the future to those [German] declarations which concern us more directly?'[21] A watershed obviously had been reached, although, ironically, it was Rome which was indignant while the Western Powers were acquiescent. Yet within a week these roles were reversed as Britain and France launched into a far-reaching attempt to build a 'containment' front, while Rome, less by calculation than misadventure, proceeded to bind herself more and more closely to the German Reich. The catalyst for both metamorphoses was the unsettled situation in the Balkan peninsula especially in Yugoslavia following this latest manifestation of German aggression.

The rationale behind the Italo–Yugoslav agreement of 1937 was that Rome had surrendered all territorial aspirations in Yugoslavia in exchange for a buffer against German expansion. The fall of Stoyadinović in February 1939, less than two years after the laborious construction of this line of retreat from the *Anschluss*, threatened positions claimed though not yet fortified. Two alternatives seemed attractive: either the patient rebuilding of the positions so devastated or the immediate satisfaction of long-standing territorial ambitions in Croatia. Personal inclination and the pressure of events had produced, by early March, a hybrid solution: a politically-dependent Croatia cast in the same role formerly assigned to Yugoslavia. To this end, the links with the Croatian separatists, recently allowed to wither, had been quickly revitalised.[22]

The Prague *coup*, coming as a bombshell in the midst of such delicate manoeuvres, appeared to present a direct threat to Italian interests in Croatia for it was immediately feared that the Croatian separatist movement might draw the (for Italy) wrong conclusions from the events of 15 March. The hasty departure for Prague of the Croatian peasant party's deputy leader looked like an unwelcome attempt to learn the technique of acquiring German sponsorship in the drive for independence. Mussolini spent a sleepless night before deciding to accept the obliteration of Czechoslovakia with outward good grace – but only if his sphere of influence in Yugoslavia was not in jeopardy. Ciano noted:[23]

> He now believes that Prussian hegemony in Europe is established. In his opinion a coalition of all other powers, ourselves included, could check German expansionism but could not hold it back. . . . I asked him, as things stand, whether it would not be better for us to retain our freedom of action . . . rather than bind ourselves in an alliance. Mussolini declared himself decidedly in favour of the alliance. I expressed some reservation because I fear Germany will use the alliance to put ahead her expansionist policies in central Europe.

As an antidote, Ciano had suggested advancing the date of the projected invasion of Albania. Significantly, Mussolini disagreed because, 'disturbing the unity of Yugoslavia, it might favour an independent Croatia under German rule'. His declaration – and Ciano's hesitant reservations – held the essence of Italy's future policy. The Duce's conviction that 'Prussian hegemony' was irreversible fuelled the headlong rush into the Pact of Steel and set the stage for the subsequent subservience and disregard for other options. Ciano's reservations, too, would reappear intermittently but always in the guise of tactical calculations. The crisis – as the one which would take place in August of that year – confronted the fascist government with the consequence of its own ineptitude. To change direction, abandon Germany and become the target of German ire before having secured the sympathy of Paris and London was, even if possible, too risky an enterprise for the fascist leaders. But if changing horses in mid-stream was out of the question so was giving up a position of influence in Yugoslavia, for that would have effectively shut off all access to the Balkans. Italy's big-power status was at stake and consequently Germany's disinterest in Croatia was made, temporarily, into the touchstone of the solidarity of the Axis. A telegram was dispatched to Belgrade to apprise Prince Paul that Italy 'had called a halt to the German actions' at the same time that troops were prudently rushed to the Yugoslav border. 'If a revolution breaks out we intervene; if the

Germans think they can stop us we will fire on them,' Ciano added impetuously:[24]

> The events of the last few days have reversed my opinion of the Führer and Germany . . . he is disloyal and untrustworthy. . . . From now on I am going to press Mussolini for an agreement with the Western Powers. But will Paris show a modicum of good sense. . . ?

Mussolini also allowed that it was now impossible to proceed to an alliance, but unlike Ciano he merely favoured postponing the impending negotiations. He had already crossed his Rubicon as far as relations with Britain and France were concerned. For Ciano's hope to have any prospects of success, there would have had to be not merely that modicum of good sense in Paris but also a super-human intuition in view of the dictator's past record. And lastly there would have had to be a great deal of insensitivity in Berlin. In fact the opposite happened.

The British Ambassador in Rome had tried to persuade his government that Italy had not been an accomplice in Germany's aggression against Czechoslovakia, but London was loath to send a message to Mussolini which did not include a warning lest it be interpreted as a sign of weakness.[25] The French Ambassador equally had tried to persuade Paris that the resentment in Rome over the Prague *coup* afforded a unique opportunity to conciliate Mussolini and split the Axis, but the French Council of Ministers rejected the suggestion, arguing that the dictators were acting in concert.[26] In Belgrade also, Italy's motives were viewed with cynicism. Prince Paul doubted that Germany was interested in Croatia. He marvelled at the sight of Italy 'which had always fomented trouble in Croatia now endeavouring to bring Serbs and Croats together'.[27] By contrast Berlin had lost no time in flattering Mussolini and easing his mind. Mackensen hurried to Palazzo Chigi and was followed by an unctuous letter from Ribbentrop reiterating that Germany had no interests in Croatia or the Mediterranean, both clearly in Italy's sphere of influence.[28] Ribbentrop acknowledged that Croatian spokesmen had approached German officials but he claimed they had been left in no doubt that Germany's attitude in that area depended on Italy. The cumulative effect was to remove Mussolini's principal preoccupation. 'We cannot change our policy,' he told Ciano after reading Ribbentrop's letter, 'we are not whores.'[29]

The brief trial of strength between Germany and Italy over Croatia had concluded with an Italian victory confirmed in a German circular dated 25 March in which Ribbentrop acknowledged that 'in political questions in the Mediterranean countries. ... Italy's intention should exercise a decisive influence on Germany's attitude'.[30] The next step ought to have been a clarification throughout the range of the Axis' common interests. It turned out to be of fundamental importance that such a clarification did not take place. The next series of Italo–German high-level exchanges – whether the staff talks between Generals Keitel and Pariani, the Göring–Mussolini conversations in mid-April or the Ciano–Ribbentrop meeting in early May which issued in the Pact of Steel – left the essential questions unanswered. The Axis rested ultimately on the solidarity of two totalitarian governments and on their common will to expand, but the goals of that expansion were bound to bring them inevitably to clash. By the time the cards were finally laid on the table at Salzburg in August, too much water had run under the bridge. The blame for this state of affairs rested as much in Rome as in Berlin for, while Hitler judged that too full a briefing might well lose him his reluctant partner, Mussolini, apart from occasional outbursts, never managed to overcome his fears. Thus Hitler was careful to minimise, and indeed suppress, his real intentions towards Poland after the end of March, while Mussolini did not find it convenient to press for a clarification until the balance of power had been redressed. And this is precisely what Italy hoped would take place on 7 April 1939, Easter Friday.

The seizure of Albania

'He who holds Bohemia holds the Danubian basin. He who holds Albania holds the Balkans,' Mussolini reportedly told the Fascist Grand Council on 9 April.[31] The remark was quite in character – short, bombastic, superficial. Yet there is no reason to suppose it was not widely believed. The outright occupation of Albania was reckoned to turn the Adriatic into an Italian lake and open the old Roman route to Macedonia. But, typically, no thought was given to the consideration that under the existing arrangements the Adriatic was already an Italian lake, that the old Via Ignatia was the most impracticable of routes and that there still was no decent road between Durazzo and Tirana. Nor was the strategic consideration that Albania could lend itself to operations against Greece and Yugoslavia a major factor, nor the country's meagre economic wealth, for the oil fields behind Valona were already in Italian hands and several years of virtual protectorate had not yielded an appreciable increase in either mineral or agricultural production. A more serious consideration was the fear that the Albanian king might seek support in Berlin. There had been an Albanian approach in that direction in February 1939.[32] Given Mussolini's pervasive fear of being outclassed by the other dictator, the alleged German designs on the Adriatic and the loss of prestige after the Prague *coup*, it was probably this consideration which finally led Mussolini and Ciano to seek with one stroke to redress the balance of power and prestige.

The thought of some modification in the status of Albania had come to Ciano early in his tenure at Palazzo Chigi. Although Albania had been written off since 1927 as an Italian fief by practically the entire international community, Italy perceived her status as independent, a state of affairs which implicitly allowed room for a show of force to bring theory in harmony with practice – raping one's own wife, an Italian diplomat called it. But it was not until after the *Anschluss* that the balance of advantage in the Foreign Minister's mind swung so clearly towards annexation. Here was an opportunity to pass it off as a precautionary step against the German *Drang* towards the Balkans. In Ciano's calculations, Albania (alongside a dependent Yugoslavia) would become the fulcrum of a new Italian sphere of influence, acceptable to the Balkan states because counterpoised to Germany's sphere to the north. After the *Anschluss*, Ciano had insistently talked with the Yugoslav minister of consolidating the Italo–Yugoslav agreement into a military alliance 'to tie the future of the two countries in the common defence of their worlds' and had agreed to frontier modification in Yugoslavia's favour should an alteration take place in the status of Albania.[33] Almost any excuse could be seized to that end. In the week before Hitler's visit to Rome in May 1938, Ciano had attended the marriage in Tirana of Zogu to an Hungarian countess, a match which, since Zogu had earlier coveted an Italian princess, appeared to Ciano as an attempt to remove Albania from Italy's tutelage. His report to Mussolini dilated on 'the danger that Germany, reinforced by the *Anschluss* ... might attempt to recapture and expand the political and economic

327

positions which Imperial Austria once held in that country'.[34] He
went on about the mineral resources, the sympathy of the people,
the mendacity of the royal house before coming to the conclusion
that the country was ripe for annexation. His own men, he added,
had been at work quietly for some time and the preparations
would be complete by May 1939.

The date was advanced after the Prague *coup*. The Germans were
informed of the solution planned for Albania only in the last few
days, although still with more of an advance than they had
extended before moving into Czechoslovakia. Their effusive and
immediate congratulations stood in curious juxtaposition with the
avowed anti-German ends of the occupation and as a poignant
comment on totalitarian solidarity. A most secret telegram from
Ciano to the embassies in London and Paris dispatched on 4 April
suggested that:[35]

> If our military occupation of Albania takes place, you are urged,
> through third parties, to spread the information that the Italian
> action is designed to block further German expansion in the Balkans.
> It would be useful if a newspaper made reference to this hypothesis.
> I repeat that this step must be taken with the utmost discretion in
> order to make it absolutely impossible to identify the origin of this
> interpretation of our eventual move.

The intention here was to court favour in London and Paris on
the strength of the occupation's anti-German bias. With this in
mind the attack had been planned not to come as a surprise to the
democracies. Hints had been dropped, and assiduously collected,
that some kind of radical alteration was afoot. Indeed, when the
Italian troops were landing in Tirana on the morning of 7 April,
the Italian chargé d'affairs in London, Crolla, was extending
Mussolini's assurances to Halifax that the occupation would not
provoke a crisis in Anglo–Italian relations, while Ciano made the
same reassuring remark in Rome. Halifax welcomed the assurances.
It was evident from the stress he laid on the Mediterranean that his
immediate concern was not the fate of Albania – long dismissed as
an Italian backyard – but the status of the Easter Accords. 'You
should not', he instructed his ministers in Belgrade and Athens,
'give the impression that His Majesty's Government are prepared
to take any active part in this Albanian development.'[36]

In Rome, Ciano had come to the same conclusion. He did not

seem worried by speculation in the foreign press – based on the juxtaposition of the Keitel–Pariani talks just finished, Spain's adherence to the Anti-Comintern Pact, reports of troop concentration on the Egyptian frontiers and the Dodecanese and, most of all, Germany's warm approval – that the invasion was but a further step in a concerted Axis plan to occupy the Balkans piecemeal. Chamberlain had been moved to interrupt his Easter vacation, but as the British Foreign Office saw it – and Corbin, the French Ambassador, concurred – the course of events could only be checked by a general European war which did not seem at the moment to be justified. The British cabinet had considered denouncing the Easter Accords but had dismissed the thought as 'premature', especially as the British 'judged ourselves to have been greater beneficiaries under the agreement than the Italian government'. Withdrawing the Ambassador seemed futile as Perth's appointment had only two more weeks to run. The best that could be got out of a difficult situation appeared to be a tightening of mutual obligation between the West and the Balkans.

Yugoslavia watched the attack unfold on Albania with knowing aloofness. The understanding under which Belgrade would agree to the occupation in return for territorial concessions, a demilitarised frontier, possibly an alliance and help in the eventual acquisition of Salonika had been of a personal nature with Stoyadinović and was now overtaken by events. Cristić, the Yugoslav Minister in Rome, who was given an inkling of what might happen on 29 March – the only diplomat favoured by so early an announcement – reportedly 'offered no objections'.[37] His attempts to persuade Ciano to give Albania at least a semblance of independence, or, alternatively, to let Yugoslavia occupy some border areas, fell on deaf ears.

The occupation did not cause a wave of panic in the other country most directly concerned. Greece had quietly taken the most elaborate precautions, but it was not until two days after the occupation that the Greek dictator, Metaxas, suddenly convinced that the Italians would take Corfu next, appealed dramatically to Britain. His appeal seemed to lend substance to what hitherto had been speculation about Italy's ultimate intentions. London could not have welcomed the appeal but none the less considered that an Italian threat – real or imaginary – might well chase Greece off the fence and into the Anglo–French camp. Accordingly Halifax and

Chamberlain started to draft an uncompromising warning to Mussolini only to drop it when Crolla again called with assurances of peaceful intentions which his government would also extend to Greece.[38] Thus no warning was issued but preparations were quickly made for the worst. Halifax had no difficulty in securing a promise of French support in case of war against Italy over Greece. The French Navy and Air Force were already on as much of a war footing as possible without calling for mobilisation. The greater part of the Atlantic Fleet had been ordered to the Mediterranean, the Air Force was deployed within range of the Turin–Genoa–Milan industrial triangle, reinforcements had been ordered to Africa and all leaves cancelled. 'Italy can and should be smashed in the early stages of the war,'[39] Daladier concluded after reviewing these steps to the British Ambassador. Similar precautions were taken in Britain: the Mediterranean Fleet was ordered to a mustering station off Malta and on 10 April, the Cabinet decided that within a few days it would issue a guarantee to Greece ('cover note' was the accepted phrase).

Paradoxically, at about the same time in Athens the Italian chargé d'affaires, Fornari, was declaring to Metaxas on behalf of Mussolini that 'all rumours . . . of an Italian action against Greece are false. . . . Fascist Italy reaffirms her intention to respect absolutely the integrity of the Greek mainland and islands'. Metaxas received the communication 'with the greatest possible satisfaction' and ordered the press to give it due prominence.[40] So far as the Greeks and the Italians were concerned, the crisis had passed. The rumours of an Italian attack were now publicly described in Athens as 'false and ascribable to malefactors'. In London, however, there was no going back on the decision to guarantee Greece unilaterally. Indeed the disappearance of the threat – along with France's willingness to join in the guarantee and then rally the Balkans into a containment front – was a large factor in the decision. At the last moment, due to French insistence, Romania was also included. On 13 April the announcement was made in London and Paris that Greece and Romania were now the recipients of a Western 'guarantee'.

Rome reacted unexpectedly mildly to the reinforcement of the Western position in areas it traditionally assumed were in its sphere of influence. Berlin, on the other hand, had considered asking Bucharest and Athens for an explanation and suitably stiff draft telegrams to the two Balkan capitals were submitted to Rome. Mussolini could not be bothered. He 'did not attach the slightest importance to the guarantee to Greece . . . Greece was dependent on the good grace of Rome'.[41] His lackadaisical attitude was strangely shortsighted. Mussolini may have feared pushing Greece and Romania further into Britain's arms or he may have resented Germany's initiative in what he liked to think of as his private reserve. It may well be, as he said, that he did not attach the slightest importance to the guarantees. Yet the aftermath of Easter Week 1939 changed the complexion of Italian policy probably much more than Ciano and Mussolini would admit to themselves. Unquestionably there had been an anti-German element in the occupation of Albania. Paradoxically its effect was the opposite. Germany had hastened to shower Rome with expressions of solidarity, while the democracies showed no appreciation of this finer point of Italian diplomacy. Rome could not help but reflect that Germany was her only reliable friend. If the choice facing Italy was either isolation (as appeared to be the case, especially so long as Paris and Rome continued to trade insults) or alliance with the Reich, the alliance always carried with it the possibility – or the illusion – of exercising restraint on Germany's dynamism.

The Pact of Steel

It was not long before this order of thinking was put to the test. Göring arrived in Rome in mid-April. Five general points of agreement emerged from his discussions with Ciano and Mussolini, each in its own way a step towards the formal alliance. The first, a general Italo–German unanimity of views, implied that further revisions of Axis policy might be superfluous. The second point, agreement on the inevitability of war against the democracies, betrayed a fatalistic acquiescence in war as the solution and the terminal point of Axis policy. The third, the advisability of waiting some years before starting hostilities, confirmed in Mussolini the illusion of being able to restrain his partner and paved the way to the signature of a military alliance which in his eyes was not intended to become operative until after 1942. The fourth point, Germany's determination to settle the Polish problem, was the one which alarmed Ciano and led to a further meeting with Ribbentrop in May where caution was thrown to the winds and the alliance concluded. The fifth point, Axis relations with Yugoslavia, suggested agreement in the most contentious area.[42]

It was ironic that it had to be the question of Poland which compelled Ciano to seek a further meeting with Ribbentrop, for at that meeting, as the Polish issue was minimised, the alliance was concluded only to be tested within three months over Germany's intentions towards Poland and be found wanting. Ribbentrop had agreed readily to meet Ciano in early May and had suggested they both bring drafts of a bilateral alliance. It was of crucial importance that Rome did not produce a draft of its own. On 6 and 7 May, Ciano met Ribbentrop in Milan equipped only with a lengthy handwritten memorandum from Mussolini, which, while it summarised ably Italy's interests in all areas, did not provide guidance as to how they might be protected or advanced in a final treaty of alliance. By far the lengthiest and most important portion of Mussolini's memorandum dealt with the military, economic and political reasons why the Axis needed a period of peace of not less than three years. These reasons occupied fully the first page of the memorandum and really amounted to the essential premise for the transformation of the Axis into a full-blown alliance. Relations with the Balkans, Britain and France, by contrast, merited only one paragraph each. Two further aspects of this signally important document were revealing: first, it contained nothing on Poland, an extraordinarily naïve omission in view of the reasons for the meeting; second, in referring to the alliance, Mussolini expressed a preference for military undertakings which 'would operate almost automatically'. This last point turned out to be crucial for, although Mussolini may have tossed it in as witness to his own bellicosity, Ribbentrop, who read the memorandum in its entirety, seized the opportunity it presented to make the treaty as binding as possible.[43]

Three additional factors, compounded equally of Italian stupidity and German cunning, combined to produce the compelling document signed formally on 22 May in Berlin. In the first place, Mussolini, irked by the news that the French press was having a field day with the lukewarm response of the Milanese masses to the distinguished German visitor, decided suddenly to announce while Ribbentrop was still in Milan that an alliance would be concluded. Second, this precipitate decision doubly aggravated Ciano's disregard of normal diplomatic practice and allowed Ribbentrop the privilege of drafting the final text upon his return to Germany unimpeded by an Italian draft. Third, the Italians' ineptitude permitted the Nazi leaders to settle upon their own policy and then fit into it an alliance with Italy on terms most advantageous to themselves. This third step took place at Hitler's hideaway in Berchtesgaden where Ribbentrop joined him directly from Milan. The Berchtesgaden meeting had been called to settle a new policy towards the Soviet Union with the view of isolating Poland. Into this policy was fitted an alliance which by binding Italy as closely to Germany as possible would demoralise the democracies with the prospect of a united Axis front.

Mussolini's sudden eagerness to enter into a military alliance – on almost any terms – came as an unexpected windfall for Germany. The fact was that Ribbentrop, keen though he also was on an alliance, was more preoccupied with the task of isolating Poland. Consequently he had two objectives as he began his conversations with Ciano: first, to undercut support for Poland by a show of Axis strength and unity; second, to allay Italian qualms about the implications of the policy Germany was pursuing towards Warsaw. He had gone to Milan with three documents drafted by the Wilhelmstrasse, one a memorandum to guide his discussions with his Italian counterpart, the other two draft treaties prepared by his legal consultants. The first document revealed a very critical assessment of Italian policies and capabilities while the other two, not unexpectedly, embodied terms for a very loose alliance: a pact with much more window dressing than substance.[44] On the subject of Poland, the ostensible reason for the meeting, Ribbentrop had come prepared to educate Ciano on the inevitability of a German–Polish war. He succeeded, but only to the extent that such war, while inevitable, did not immediately appear in the offing. Neither Ciano nor Mussolini, inured to what must have appeared to them as German rhetoric, were particularly concerned about this question and neither ventured nor were asked for an opinion on whether such a war, once started, could be localised.[45] Here was the fundamental misunderstanding. When Ciano talked (with Ribbentrop in agreement) of a period of peace of at least three years, he appeared to have in mind absolute peace and therefore assumed, in view of the West's guarantee to Poland, that the Danzig issue would be settled on the diplomatic plane. The question of whether a war with Warsaw could be localised was therefore irrelevant: there would be no war. Ribbentrop, for his part, granted that a major war would not be provoked for some time but did not specifically rule out a local conflict such as he imagined a war between Poland and Germany would be. Thus the German Foreign Minister returned home with no Italian instructions on the contents of the alliance he was now going to draft (save that it be operative almost automatically) and also with no precise Italian ultimatum on Germany's sparring with Poland. The crucial Italian qualification that nothing be done likely to lead to a major war in the next three years, he dismissed partly wilfully and partly because he felt that the new approach to Russia would reduce to vanishing point the likelihood of great-power intervention.

The draft treaty submitted to Italy on 12 May consequently bore not the slightest resemblance to the two limited and cautious drafts prepared earlier. The new document was as compelling as any produced since the 1870s. Its first article called for permanent consultation with a view to arriving at common agreement; the second, consultation on steps to take to protect common interests; the third, all military aid to the party involved in war; the fourth, military and economic co-operation; the fifth, no separate peace or armistice; the sixth, improved relations with friendly powers; and the seventh, entry into effect immediately upon signature. A secret protocol added details on how the co-operation envisaged in Article IV would be pursued.[46]

'It's real dynamite,' commented Ciano when he saw the draft.[47] And so it was but not for the reasons which immediately sprang to the mind of the Italian Foreign Minister. It was one thing to be elated by the compliment paid to Italy by the most powerful European nation. It was quite another to disregard the automaticity of Article III, which stipulated immediate help regardless of whether the conflict was provoked by the partner. In the light of that article, the obligations to consult and agree contained in the first two articles lost a great deal of their value. Yet no modification of substance was suggested in Italy. Mussolini approved the draft on 17 May, conferred Italy's highest decoration on Ribbentrop and dispatched his son-in-law to Berlin on 22 May to sign the treaty.

The Pact of Steel, as the alliance was immediately dubbed, represented for Rome the terminal point of a policy embarked upon with the announcement of the Axis in 1936. It provided Mussolini with what he reckoned to be two inestimable advantages – an alliance with the strongest country in Europe (thus eliminating the spectre of isolation which had chased him since the breakdown of the Stresa front) and, second, several years' time in which to exploit the political advantages of the alliance in the Mediterranean and in the Balkans. To be able once again to negotiate from a position of strength he had opted for a very binding pact with which to intimidate the democracies. So as not to lessen its effect, nothing was said publicly about a period of peace. But that such a war-free period was crucial to his policy cannot be doubted. It was stressed in a memorandum which Mussolini sent to Hitler by personal messenger within a week of the signing of the alliance. The Cavallero Memorandum made three points: that war with the democracies was inevitable for ideological reasons; that none the less the Axis needed at least three years of peace (here Mussolini repeated word for word the arguments he had given Ciano, which, in turn, had been submitted to Ribbentrop), and that, once war broke out, the Balkans had to be occupied.[48] Of the three points, the second was obviously the one to which Mussolini attached the highest importance: even though Hitler and Ribbentrop had repeatedly agreed to it (the last time on the occasion of the signature), Mussolini deemed it essential at this stage to restate it unequivocally. His insistence on it meant in effect that for him it continued to be the essential premise of the alliance. In Mussolini's mind, at least, the declaration of the inevitability of war, and indeed the whole Pact of Steel, assumed an essentially dilatory and contingent character.

Against this evaluation, one has to set Hitler's view of the alliance. Ciano had barely left Berlin when Hitler called in the régime's highest military figures for an exposition of his future policy. Three aspects stood out – war was inevitable, though not for ideological reasons but for expansion; Poland would be attacked at the first opportunity; Germany's objectives had to be kept secret from Italy. Wilfully now the fundamental misunderstanding would not be cleared up. In his own mind and with his closest collaborators Hitler drew the distinction between a general war which he wished to avoid for several years and a local war with Poland which would take place before the year was out. The preparations for a war with Poland would be kept from Italy on the grounds that Rome would dispute the evaluation that it would remain localised and might thus feel compelled to reject the alliance

on the grounds that the essential premise had gone unfulfilled.
This was precisely what happened in August when Mussolini,
forced to choose between the text of the alliance and its premise,
chose the premise. In the meantime, Hitler rejected several requests
for a meeting with Mussolini. He did express a general agreement
with the essence of the Cavallero Memorandum but refused to be
drawn into a formal commitment. Only when Rome's increasingly
worried and persistent requests for a clarification of Germany's
intentions towards Poland could no longer be sloughed off, did
Hitler agree to a further meeting between Ciano and Ribbentrop at
Salzburg. By then the attack on Poland was barely weeks away.

Chapter 15
War, 1940

To merely think of taking the offensive . . . is ingenuous.
Badoglio, 1940

August 1939 was destined to be the last month of peace in Europe for six years. It is true, of course, that the war which broke out at the end of that month was initially a local conflict which took almost a year to escalate into a European one and two more before it became global. But in early August, the only country to entertain eagerly the proposition that an attack on Poland would remain localised was Germany. No one else held such dangerous illusions. No European country really expected to ride out the storm un-scathed. The few which did owed their luck as much to a fortuitous geographical position as to their diplomatic skills.

There were some surprises when in September the major protagonists took sides. Italy, which for seventeen years had made a profession of warlike posturing, was unexpectedly, almost unaccountably, neutral. 'Non-belligerence', a new term in international jargon, was coined by Mussolini to avoid the opprobrium attached to 'neutrality'. But the underlying reality was the same. When the titanic struggle which Mussolini had extolled and prepared for since the march on Rome finally came, Italy stood half dejected, half relieved on the sidelines. And curiously, Italy's non-belligerence was due in no small part to the efforts of the Italian Foreign Minister, a last-minute convert to the senselessness of a catastrophe in whose build-up he had played a not inconsiderable part.

Avoiding the catastrophe

Ciano went to Salzburg, 'documents in hand', to prove to Hitler and Ribbentrop that to unleash a European war would be folly.[1] The Duce's son-in-law talked with Ribbentrop on 11 August and with Hitler on the 12th and 13th. From the very beginning of the conversations, in spite of his previous prevarications, Ribbentrop did not hide that a clash between Germany and Poland was inevitable and now imminent. He cited no new facts but dramatised the old ones. Germany's honour, and by inference that of the Axis, was at stake. Two premises he stolidly regarded as indisputable even if they were contradictory: on the one hand, the Western Powers would not intervene and Europe would watch impassively the obliteration of Poland; on the other, even if Britain and France intervened, they could not prevent the victory of the Axis. Ribbentrop's knowledge of Britain's 'psychology' assured him that London would stay out; the democracies were unprepared; the Soviet Union, with which Germany was engaged in 'fairly precise' negotiations, would not move; the USA was leaning more and more towards neutrality thanks to his clever press campaigns; for various reasons Germany could count on the neutrality of Belgium, Holland, Romania and Turkey. Admittedly, Yugoslavia was perfidious and unreliable but Italy could seize the occasion to settle matters in Croatia and Dalmatia.[2] The conversation went on in this vein most of the afternoon. At the end Ciano had not succeeded in obtaining any precise information on Germany's plan of attack but he had become fully convinced of Ribbentrop's determination to provoke a conflict and to thwart all attempts at a peaceful solution.

A more precise outline of Germany's plans, unobtainable from Ribbentrop, Ciano heard from Hitler the following day, 12 August. In their three-hour conversation (more exactly, a monologue) Hitler, with the now-customary maps at hand, took Ciano through an analysis of Germany's defensive and offensive position culminating in the decision 'to liquidate definitely the situation before 15 October', that is before the autumn rains made operations impracticable. As his reasons he alleged he could no longer tolerate the Poles' provocations, or the injuries to German honour, or the attacks on German minorities. Poland, he said, was preparing to attack Danzig, a situation he likened to a dagger in the back. Italy was similarly threatened by Yugoslavia and here his customarily calm voice became excited for the first time as he also urged Ciano to seize the opportunity to dispose of a bothersome neighbour. The international repercussions Hitler dismissed with the same ease and dogmatism shown earlier by Ribbentrop. The understanding to take no action likely to lead to war for at least three years he shrugged off with the assertion that the attack would not provoke a general conflict, and Germany would not therefore ask for Italy's help 'according to the existing agreement'. The following day Hitler was shorter and more decisive. He opposed issuing a communiqué after the talks and reaffirmed the need to act without delay, by the end of August at the latest.[3]

Hitler's curtness at the mention of a joint communiqué masked a gauche German attempt to persuade world public opinion that the articles of the Pact of Steel calling for consultation and agreement had been fulfilled. Ciano had brought to Salzburg a draft communiqué reaffirming the Axis' desire for peace and faith in a diplomatic solution. It was obviously not acceptable to the Germans and at Hitler's insistence it was decided to issue none. But two hours after Ciano had left Salzburg, the Germans issued a release to the foreign press which completely falsified the Italian positions. The release, displayed on the front pages by most newspapers, said that the meeting had been conducted within the framework of the two countries' formal obligations; that the foreign ministers had been in complete agreement on all issues, Danzig included; that the conversations had treated all subjects exhaustively and that therefore no further meetings were planned; and finally, for good measure, that the meeting had witnessed not only Italy's and Germany's totalitarian friendship but also 'their totalitarian readiness'. What was worse, the Italian press, without direction from Rome, similarly picked up and reprinted the release.[4]

Ciano's emotions after such transparent prevarication were given full vent in his Diary. He was[5]

> disgusted with Germany, her leaders and their behaviour. They have tricked us and lied to us. And today they are trying to draw us into an adventure which we do not want and which would compromise the country and the régime. The Italian people will shake with horror when they will know of the attack on Poland and might even take up arms against the Germans.

A radical change now took place in Ciano. Until Salzburg he had deluded himself into thinking he played a decisive role in European affairs. He probably did not realise even now how much of a sham his office had been, how little influence he could bring to bear on his putative allies. But to his credit, the gravity of the situation brought forth an unsuspected tenacity and he embarked on a stubborn fight to persuade Mussolini to stay out of the war.

It was not an easy task. Mussolini had equally good reasons not to go to war and he was just as vitriolic about the Germans. But he, more than Ciano, realised that a break with Germany at this point would have meant a denial of his whole political life. To make naked violence the centre-piece of international relations, to associate with the most rabidly revisionist states, to affirm unequivocally and repeatedly the ineluctability of conflict with the decadent democracies and then at the decisive moment to pull back, appeared to him not only as intolerable cowardice but also as political suicide.

And yet some kind of a break was utterly necessary, especially after the German press release had allowed the inference that, the first two articles of the Pact of Steel calling for consultation and agreement having been fulfilled, so would the third one calling for mutual support in case of war. Consultations had indeed taken place, but they had resulted in a complete divergence of views. They had also, unfortunately, resulted in a complete paralysis of will in Rome. Mussolini during the next two and a half weeks wavered from day to day, sometimes from hour to hour. Ciano, too, despite his conversion to peace, wavered momentarily when informed of the Nazi–Soviet Pact. Only the Italian Ambassador in Berlin, the career diplomat Attolico, pressed unhesitatingly for a clarification of views to cause the Germans formally to admit that the first two articles of the Pact of Steel had not been fulfilled, a task all the more essential since both Hitler and Ribbentrop, while permitting the inference, had scrupulously refrained from actually invoking the Pact of Steel. Attolico was called to Rome by Ciano on the afternoon of the 15th for two days of uninterrupted meetings. It was of paramount importance to persuade the Duce to inform Berlin clearly and unequivocally that Italy would not follow it in a war. But Mussolini would not go this far. Caught between 'the fear of war and the fear to reveal his fear of war',[6] the Italian dictator preferred to affirm his desire to fight while allowing that in the present circumstances he could be more helpful to Germany from the sidelines. He evolved a compromise: if Britain and France went to war he would disengage Italy from Germany; if the Western Powers remained neutral, he would profit from the occasion 'to settle accounts with Belgrade' – a parallel war.[7] He drafted several documents, a letter to Hitler, a memorandum, another letter, each more casuistic than the former, all unbelievably convoluted, all in the end dropped because they committed him to a certain course of action. Finally Attolico was sent to meet Ribbentrop on 18 August without a formal written document explicitly rejecting a German war but with oral instructions to say Italy did not think a conflict with Poland could remain localised and that the Italian government was in no position to engage in a long war. The meeting was a stormy one. The German Foreign Minister berated the Italian Ambassador, at one point inviting Magistrati (Attolico's Minister Counsellor who took notes at the meeting) to step outside while he challenged Attolico's political integrity.[8] There were no positive results. Ribbentrop maintained that in all probability the conflict would remain localised and when he allowed himself to think on the distant possibility of a general war he always referred to it as an 'Axis war'. Attolico returned to Rome with the distinct impression that when Germany attacked Poland, Ribbentrop and Hitler fully expected Italy to follow suit.

A week had thus gone by since Ciano had first heard Germany's plans to attack, a week during which Rome's hesitation had not been communicated formally and unequivocally to its ally and during which Berlin could blandly assume, if not agreement, certainly Italian acquiescence in its plans. Clearly the situation demanded less equivocation and more forthrightness. Of this even Mussolini now appeared convinced, especially after a particularly friendly British communication, delivered by the British Ambassador, Sir Percy Loraine, on the 20th, had left the door open to further negotiations on Danzig.[9] A meeting was called that evening at which all military leaders and ministers were present, including at the last minute the peripatetic Foreign Minister who had selected that particular day to absent himself from the capital and had flown to Albania. Ciano arrived in time to lend his weight to the peace faction inside the fascist hierarchy, barely in time, because during the afternoon Mussolini had had another change of heart and now was determined to enter the war alongside Germany. The discussion went into the night with Alfieri, Starace and Pariani, respectively the Minister of Popular Culture, the Party Secretary and the Under-Secretary for War, on the interventionist side, and Ciano, Attolico and Grandi conducting a dogged rear-guard action, trying to delay a decision, arguing

essentially that Italy was unprepared militarily and that the
Germans had broken faith with Rome – two arguments which
sounded as unwelcome as they appeared unchallengeable. The
meeting resulted in a stand-off: the anti-war party was successful
to the point of drafting a projected note to the German government to which it was proposed to attach the British note as proof
of the good prospects of a diplomatic solution. The war party
succeeded to the extent that Mussolini did not authorise the dis-
patch of the draft note. The indecision continued. The following
day Ciano 'burned all his powder' to persuade his father-in-law to
stay out:[10]

> You cannot and you must not do it. The faithfulness with which I
> served you in the politics of the Axis authorises me to speak clearly.
> I went to Salzburg to arrange a common line of agreement. I found
> myself faced with a German diktat. The Germans – not us – have
> betrayed the alliance in which we were associates not servants. Rip
> up the pact, throw it in Hitler's face and Europe will recognise you
> as the natural leader of the anti-German crusade. Do you want me to
> go to Salzburg? Alright I'll go and I'll speak to the Germans as is
> necessary.

This outburst obviously had some effect. Ciano obtained author-
isation to seek a further meeting with Ribbentrop (still in Salzburg)
and to hand him a document showing conclusively why Italy was
not bound to, and would not, follow Germany into war. The
remainder of the day was spent in drafting two remarkable documents, the first a compilation of all the events, declarations and
documents proving Italy's right not to be automatically involved
in a German war, the second a set of conclusions derived from it
pointing out that a diplomatic solution to the Danzig issue,
particularly in view of Loraine's note of 20 August, was still
within reach.[11]

At this point – in the late morning of 21 August – it appeared
possible that years of fascist foreign policy might be irresistibly
reversed. The career diplomatists who drafted the two document to be submitted to Ribbentrop started from the premise
that Italy and Germany had long agreed the two countries could
not expose themselves to war without an adequate period of preparation. They recorded that the point had been acknowledged
most explicitly by the Prince of Hesse in a personal communication
from Hitler to Mussolini after the fall of Czechoslovakia and by

General Keitel to General Pariani in the first week of April.[12] On the basis of an agreed period of peace the alliance had been concluded in Milan in May. Ribbentrop had not only acquiesced in a period of peace of at least three years but had also gone so far as to increase that period to no less than four years and to aver Germany's intention not to provoke a general conflict with Poland over Danzig. He had, moreover, declared himself 'entirely in agreement' with the gist of the Cavallero Memorandum.[13] Since no consultation as stipulated by the Pact of Steel had taken place before Salzburg, all that existed of a binding nature between the two countries was an understanding to avoid war for at least three years. This understanding, the Italian career officials argued, could not be set aside except by mutual consent. At Salzburg, Italy had been faced not with a proposal to set aside this understanding but with a unilateral decision to make war. Italy could not accept the decision and had let it be known explicitly first through Ciano and then through Attolico that a general war was neither in Italy's nor in Germany's interests. Hence the Italian government was now proposing an international conference to find a peaceful solution to the issue of Danzig.

While the two documents enlarging on these arguments were being prepared, Ciano was trying vainly to telephone Ribbentrop in Salzburg to arrange a meeting. After several hours of fruitless calls and awkward excuses he reached him at 4 p.m. and proposed a meeting at the Brenner. Ribbentrop promised an answer between six and seven that evening. Immediately Ciano returned to Mussolini who approved the two documents in preparation and added a personal letter for Hitler in which he defined Italy's posture as follows: first, if Germany attacked Poland and the conflict remained localised Italy would give Germany any help requested; second, if Poland and the Allies attacked Germany, Italy would intervene beside Germany; third, if Germany attacked Poland and Britain and France intervened, 'Italy will not undertake military operations in view of the present conditions of our military preparation already communicated to Hitler and Ribbentrop'; and fourth, if negotiations failed because of the opponents' intransigence, and Germany decided to solve the issue by force of arms, Italy would intervene beside Germany.[14]

Despite its chicanery, the letter represented a substantial victory for Ciano. Of the four eventualities, three were most unlikely while one, the third, was absolutely crucial. Clearly points one, two and four were designed to launch the third which amounted to a declaration of neutrality however clumsily veiled. To all intents and purposes Mussolini had disengaged Italy from the coming war. All that remained now was to hand the documents and the letter to Ribbentrop. But the elusive German Foreign Minister could not be reached. When he finally telephoned Ciano towards ten that evening it was to tell him he could not meet him at the Brenner because he was on his way to Moscow to sign a pact of non-aggression with the Soviet Union. Could Ciano meet him first at Innsbruck? The announcement of the Nazi–Soviet Pact caught the Italian Foreign Minister completely by surprise. He conferred immediately with Mussolini. Both agreed instantly to shy away from a 'precipitate decision' in the direction of neutrality. Might it not be best, Ciano wondered, 'to take our share of the booty in Croatia and Dalmatia'?[15] Opportunists to the marrow, both men felt that a meeting to present Hitler with an Italian declaration of neutrality would be inopportune. With the Russians on the side of Germany, surely the Western Powers would not dare to move. Accordingly, the meeting was postponed till Ribbentrop returned from Moscow. No mentioned was made of the content of Mussolini's letter. Ciano proceeded to closet himself for the rest of the evening with the two shrillest interventionists in the Italian Cabinet, Alfieri and Starace. Before going to bed he alerted 'the Croatian friends' in Italy and Yugoslavia. Mussolini called his chief of general staff, Badoglio, to prepare a plan of attack on Greece and Yugoslavia.[16] So far as Mussolini and Ciano were concerned, the last conversation with Ribbentrop had plainly solved all those irksome disputes about consultations and agreements. Sheer opportunism had swept the board of all other considerations. The Western Powers would not dare intervene, Germany would have her fight, Italy could share in the spoils.

The Western Powers, however, were not quite so accommodating. It became clear within the day that, the Nazi–Soviet Pact notwithstanding, Britain and France were not going to remain neutral and that a war could not be localised. So once again Ciano, not in the least bothered by inconsistency, reversed his course. He prevailed again upon Mussolini to entertain sympathetically the suggestions for an international conference coming from London and then left to visit the king vacationing outside Rome.[17] By the

morning of the 25th when he returned, Mussolini, no less inconsistent, was once again ready to follow Hitler into war. Not
without difficulty Ciano dissuaded him, the argument now being
that the king would not sign a declaration of war without further
consultations. Together with Mussolini he drafted yet another
letter for immediate despatch to Hitler. This one reiterated only
the first and the third eventualities first discussed five days earlier
for submission to Ribbentrop – the first one pledging all Italian
help short of military if the war remained localised; the third
pleading unpreparedness if the Western Powers intervened.[18] But
not even this letter was despatched. While it was being drafted
Mussolini had another change of heart. While in this condition,
Mackensen, the German Ambassador, arrived with a message from
Hitler, the first of a long list of personal letters which as the war
went on took the place more and more of normal diplomatic
negotiations. This particular letter was one of three steps Hitler
took that day to minimise the consequences of the war he was
about to launch. The others were a letter to Daladier on the use-
lessness of a Franco–German war and the renewal of conversations
with London through Henderson and Dahlerus. The letter to
Mussolini, in no sense a direct request for help, stressed the
tremendously strengthened Axis position as a result of the non-
aggression pact with Moscow. It assured Mussolini that both
Romania and Turkey would remain neutral and anticipated a
forcible solution to the Polish problem.[19] Mussolini was left to
draw his own conclusion.

By this time Mussolini was no longer in a position to say
honourably he would not go to war. Too many days had passed
since the first Salzburg meeting to resort now to legal arguments
about mutual obligation to consult and agree. His only way out
was to say that despite his inclinations he had not the wherewithal
to fight. Reluctantly, he drafted a reply in which, after approving
'completely' the Nazi–Soviet Pact, he allowed that in a European
war he 'would not begin military operations'. But even at this
point he succumbed to the temptation to hedge his bet. 'The
Italian intervention', he said, 'could be immediate if Germany provided the necessary war materials to withstand an Anglo–French
attack.'[20] Ciano hastened to telephone the letter to Attolico before
his chief changed his mind again. Hitler received the letter with
ill disguised disappointment. It arrived at roughly the same time as

the implication of the British pact of mutual defence with Poland were being assessed in the Reich Chancery. The attack scheduled for 28 August was postponed till the 31st.

Hitler's reply curtly asked what materials were needed and by when.[21] The list of materials required was concocted in Rome during the morning of the 26th, Mussolini himself intervening from time to time to increase the amounts suggested by the Chiefs of Staff by 50 to 100 per cent. It proved to be quite a task to keep this list, ostensibly of materials needed for the first twelve months of war, within the bounds of decency. Attolico received it at noon on the 26th. The Germans, who had been anxiously enquiring about it during the morning, at first thought it a joke. Attolico was asked when deliveries were expected. Immediately before the outbreak of hostilities, he replied with no hesitation. The Ambassador, as it turned out, had no instructions to set a deadline, but his answer settled the matter of Italy's intervention on the spot. Hitler dictated a reply saying he could probably furnish some of the requirements but certainly not all and not, in any case, before the outbreak of hostilities.[22] He appreciated Mussolini's position and asked only that Italy support his war with the appropriate postures and gestures. That message was received in Rome at four in the afternoon of the 26th, and by six that evening Hitler had a reply. There were apologies all around for Attolico's mistake. But, as Mussolini concluded, relieved that his ambassador had so neatly shifted the responsibility from his shoulders, 'even though the misunderstanding has been cleared it is obvious that you are not in a position to help me fill the large voids in the Italian armaments produced by the Ethiopian and Spanish wars. I will therefore adopt the posture you suggest.'[23] To all intents and purposes Italy was now out of the war Hitler was about to launch.

It had not been an edifying fortnight. It was merely fortuitous that two weeks of prevarications had resulted in another nine months of peace for the Italian people. Certainly there was never any appreciation that lives were at stake. Ciano, Mussolini and their cronies, with the solitary exception of Attolico, talked of war with the same contemptuous ease with which a spoiled child arranges his toy soldiers. Their cynicism was more than matched in Berlin, and it may be that one reason why Mussolini hastened to take advantage of Attolico's indiscretion was the fact that, as the day of the attack drew closer, Germany's deception grew apace in contrast with the solicitude displayed by London. During the second half of August the British Embassy in Rome took care to keep Palazzo Chigi informed of all steps taken in Berlin to avert war. Leaving aside the fact that London's frankness made the version of the same peace moves sent from Berlin to Rome appear doubly evasive, this inside information presented Mussolini with several chances to stage another Munich. Apprised of the contents of London's communications to Berlin well in advance of their delivery, and fully aware that Berlin was stalling for time while readying its defensive position in the West, Mussolini intervened twice with proposals for a general conference, once on the afternoon of 29 August and the second time on the last day of the month. Hitler declined the first offer; the second offer fell when the British government insisted on a prior withdrawal of German forces from Poland.

Italian diplomacy had thus failed to avert the war it had long extolled but had not expected quite so suddenly.[24] Still, Italy's non-involvement had to be counted at least a diplomatic success in so far as it left various options open. The declaration of non-belligerence announced on 1 September was, essentially, a temporary stratagem. The very phrase indicated that Mussolini intended to leave the door open for a further decision, either definitive neutrality or intervention. Indisputably he had decided on non-belligerence not because he considered it the ideal solution but because Italy's military unpreparedness had left him no alternative. But the compromise was essentially repugnant to a man who for years had proclaimed the necessity of war and had glorified it as the supreme act in life. The very word neutral offended Mussolini's ear, and neutrality, however masked, appeared to him unworthy of a great country, a specific renunciation of its role as a great power. Propelling him towards intervention at Hitler's side was the conviction, lodged in his mind since his visit to Germany in 1937, that the Reich was militarily and spiritually more powerful than the decadent democracies. There was little use arguing against this assessment before September 1939 and even less after the lightning Polish campaign. Hence the temptation to join the winner and share in the spoils. Lastly, there was the mortification Mussolini felt while Hitler, until not long before the diligent pupil, realised his programme by force. All this did not, however, preclude a long period of neutrality. But when compared with the factors making for intervention, the ones making for neutrality appeared not so much weak as irrelevant. There were above all the economic and political advantages to be gained from neutrality or from leading a bloc of neutral states, but these, in Mussolini's eyes, paled before the spoils of conquest and the glory to be gained from warring. Only one aspect of neutrality held any appeal – the chance to play once again the arbiter of Europe, to stage another Munich. Not only could he thus gain further gratitude from the Allies, demonstrably unprepared for war, but he could also render a favour to his German ally by saving it from a protracted war and sanctioning its victories in Poland.

None the less, as the German armies were conquering Poland, the Italian dictator had a limited choice of options ranging realistically from intervention on Germany's side to permanent neutrality, with, in between, the opportunity to create a third force in Europe by grouping under Italian leadership a bloc of smaller neutrals. Which of the options would be chosen depended ultimately on Italy's relations with Germany. These varied according to whether one focused attention on the masses or on the hierarchies, or on the two leaders themselves. At the popular level, despite the hyperactive propaganda machines, the German and Italian peoples were hardly enamoured of one another. There were long-standing causes for this state of affairs. At this juncture what exacerbated the German public's animosity towards Italy was, in Italian eyes, the deliberate non-publication in Germany, despite several Italian requests, of Hitler's letter to Mussolini of 1 September, explicitly exonerating Italy from the obligation of war. On the other hand, among high officials in both countries relations were rather better. Göring alone had refrained from the customary friendly references and appeared still piqued by the exorbitant list submitted on 26 August. But he too in private had hastened to make amends. Other officials had been careful to make no disparaging allusions to Italian neutrality, if for no other reason than that most were convinced a negotiated peace, following a timely Italian intervention, was still possible. At the summit relations were best of all. The respect and faith Mussolini and Hitler professed in one another was indeed genuine. The Italian dictator, despite the occasional anti-German outburst, showed more rather than less admiration for the Führer. Hitler, for his part, had long been convinced that the Axis and the Pact of Steel were absolutely dependent on

Mussolini's friendship and was not about to take steps which might cause that friendship to waver. While he no doubt would have preferred to have Mussolini alongside him in the crucial last days of August – either to intimidate the Western Powers into not opposing his aggression in Poland or, failing that, as a co-belligerent – he none the less appreciated that an Italian declaration of war could have been more of a liability than an asset. The war, which because of the Maginot and Siegfried lines had remained circumscribed, could not but have erupted along several fronts if Italian troops clashed with French, thus eliminating the possibility, on which Hitler was still intent, of splitting off Paris from London. By the same token, Mussolini also had no interest in defining his attitude more precisely, on the one hand because Italy's non-belligerence served the useful purpose of limiting the conflict and on the other because too precise a definition of his position would limit his freedom of action in the event of a peace conference.

Thus cordial generalities sufficed well enough in the first month of the war. But once Poland had been conquered, the deep-seated differences which had been buried in the enthusiasm of a successful war kept pointedly limited, resurfaced with a vengeance. At issue was the further direction of the alliance, the issue which had never been tackled satisfactorily. To this end Ciano was invited to Berlin on 1 October. The ensuing discussions marked first of all a subtle German attempt to capitalise on Italy's non-belligerence. The German peace terms which Hitler was to announce on 6 October had already gained the support of the Soviet Union. The present meeting was designed first to pre-empt any Italian move in the same direction and then to lodge the impression at the same time that Hitler's offers (credible only if Italy could be thought to exercise some effective restraint on Germany) had Italian backing. It was at this meeting that Hitler, for the first time, used rather peremptory language towards the Italian Foreign Minister. Aside from the malicious insinuation that Britain 'would never have signed a definitive treaty with Poland had it not known Italy's position beforehand', Hitler also referred ominously to Italy's ambitions in the Balkans and stated explicitly that Italy's neutrality could lead 'to the end of her imperial ambitions in the Mediterranean'.[25] These not-so-veiled threats had different effects on Ciano and Mussolini. The Italian Foreign Minister counted his trip a success in so far as he first publicly dispelled the impression that Hitler's quixotic peace plans had Italy's sanctions and, second, was not subjected to a firm demand for intervention. Mussolini, on the other hand, drew different conclusions. Aware now of the unacceptability of the German peace plans, he had to face the conclusion that his aspirations would not be satisfied by a general peace conference. The choice had now come down to giving up his aspirations or obtaining them by force. Neutrality was daily becoming a less viable alternative.

Ironically, at the same time that the failure of the German peace offers had brought Mussolini closer to the German side, it had also brought about a recrudescence of anti-Italian feelings within the Nazi leadership. Hitler's charge that Britain's guarantee to Poland had been due to prior knowledge of Italy's non-belligerence was now being made openly by Göring and Ribbentrop, despite insistent Italian denials. Italy's equivocal attitude towards the British blockade was an added irritant. The mutual bad feelings reached their height in December and early January. Ciano selected the occasion of a major speech before the Chamber of Fasci e Corporazioni on 16 December for a thoroughly self-conscious attempt to sabotage the alliance. Despite the usual fascist phraseology, the gist of the message was inescapable. Ciano accused the German government of not having fulfilled its obligations towards Italy at several points, but in particular in two instances which, Ciano argued, justified fully Italy's decision to remain outside the conflict. First he revealed the May agreement not to make war for at least three years. Second, he added for good measure that the German government had also explicitly promised at that time not to raise any contentious issues with Poland or any other country before the period of preparation had elapsed. Also remarkable was the Foreign Minister's tone as he related that the Nazi–Soviet pact had come as a complete surprise, in contravention, of course, of the obligation to keep mutually informed. His tone and the worsening of Italo–Russian relations following Moscow's invasion of Finland left the inference open that a serious split existed within the Axis on relations towards Russia as well.[26]

Even more momentous for the future of the Axis appeared to be a private letter which Mussolini addressed to Hitler on 5 January 1940. As if to confirm Ciano's malevolence, the letter began by describing Ciano's speech as Mussolini's thoughts 'from the first to the last word'. Then in a review of the international scene,

Mussolini appeared at pains to underline the deleterious aspects of Germany's recent policy, criticising particularly Berlin's Russian orientation and emphasising the need to recreate an independent rump Poland as the absolutely crucial foundation for a compromise peace. After castigating Hitler for forsaking 'the antisemitic and antibolshevik flag you have flown for twenty years', he went on:

> It is my precisive duty to add that any further step in your relations with Moscow would have catastrophic effects in Italy, where especially among the fascist masses, antibolshevism is absolute, solid as a rock, unshakeable . . . the solution to your *Lebensraum* is in Russia not elsewhere. . . . This development [the Nazi–Soviet pact] has profoundly troubled the fascists in Europe and perhaps also many national socialists in Germany. The day on which we demolish Bolshevism, we shall have kept faith with our Revolutions. Then shall come the time of the democracies.

On the subject of Poland, the tone was not reproachful, but exhortative:

> It is my conviction that the creation of a modest, disarmed Poland exclusively Polish – freed from the Jews with regard to whom I approve fully your plan to collect them all in a large ghetto in Lublin – can never again represent a danger for the great Reich. But the fact would be an element of great importance which would remove all justification for the democracies to continue the war. . . . Unless you have irrevocably decided to pursue the war until the end, I think that the creation of a new Polish state under German tutelage would be a crucial element to resolve the war and a sufficient condition for peace.

After some tactical advice on how to create a climate conducive to peace negotiations, Mussolini came to the nub of the matter:

> . . . it is not certain that it will be possible to force the British and French to their knees or even to divide them. To believe this is to delude oneself. The United States would never permit the total defeat of the democracies.

The letter then ended with the conclusion that Italy was Germany's 'reserve' ready to help bring about a diplomatic solution to the war, ready also to help circumvent the Allied blockade and eventually also prepared to help out militarily if the help was not, as at present, more burdensome than not. Italy's position, Mussolini took pains to assert, after so much veiled criticism, fell within, not outside, the framework of the alliance, a fact he desired brought to the attention of the German people.[27]

The message was extraordinary. It suggested not simply a disagreement but a fundamental divergence of views. While Hitler was preparing to attack the West, Mussolini was suggesting a compromise peace; while Hitler was staking his future on the superiority of German arms, Mussolini was describing the hopes of a Western defeat as illusory; while Hitler was moving even closer to the Soviet Union, publicly approving Soviet aims in Finland, Mussolini was emphasising anti-Bolshevism and providing military aid to the Finns. Such sentiments were indeed so extraordinary as to suggest either some temporary aberration or else, more likely, the pursuit of a goal even more substantial than a compromise peace. That goal appears to have been nothing less than a final attempt to persuade Hitler not to launch an invasion of the West. Only the pursuit of this goal can serve to explain such astounding assertions as the Axis' inability to defeat the democracies after years of contrary statements, or Mussolini's sudden respect for American might after he had studiously ignored the USA for years and had not received an American diplomat in almost two years. The conclusion seems inescapable that the letter represented Mussolini's last-ditch attempt to prevent the expansion of the war to the West, not for any sudden aversion to war or friendship for the democracies but for the more egotistical reason that enlargement of the conflict in that direction, regardless of the outcome, would relegate him and Italy to a permanent inferiority. Much better to persuade his partner to come to some accommodation with the West by recreating Poland, so as to launch a more profitable attack on Russia. Hence the attempt to divert Hitler's animosity from the West, first on the grounds adduced, and second by such steps as informing secretly the Belgian government of an impending German invasion.[28] The lightheartedness with which Mussolini would have invaded Russia (as in the end he did with disastrous results) was remarkable only in so far as it represented the conventional wisdom of European right-wing governments on Soviet Russia's capabilities. Equally important was the light the letter shed on Mussolini's overriding egoism. Twice now, when he had come face to face with the results of his own ineptitude, his egoism acted as a brake, as when the pitiful state of Italian arms caused him to pull back in August 1939 or, presently, to caution

Hitler against attacking the West. But such beneficial results were purely fortuitous. His egoism prevented him from seeing that after seventeen years in power, he led a nation diplomatically isolated, militarily unprepared and economically ruined. His major concern was to give substance to all those illusions of which fascist policy was made up, and if reality proved recalcitrant he would retreat into the specious casuistry of which his letter to Hitler was an example. Failing that (as this attempt failed, for Hitler did not answer him for more than two months), his egoism propelled him into the winner's camp. As much as Hitler he was the prisoner of his own vision.

A neutral bloc?

It was this vainglorious dogmatism which more than anything else determined the failure of the one project which might have kept Italy permanently out of the war – the formation of a bloc of neutrals, primarily Balkan, under Italian leadership.[29] Three such projects flourished during the last four months of 1939 all sharing the cement of Italian neutrality but otherwise independent of one another. The first germinated in Ciano's mind early in September and was all over by the middle of October; the second, concocted between Gafencu, the Romanian Foreign Minister and his Yugoslav counterpart, ran parallel and competed with the Italian project; and the third, the most ambitious, was put forth by Gafencu towards the end of October, and had proved unworkable by the end of November.

Of the three, only the Italian project had any objective chances of success. It owed its temporary vogue to the fact that, early in September, keeping the Balkans outside the conflict appeared not only a more useful enterprise than attacking them (the thought had crossed Mussolini's mind in the euphoria of the first German victories) but also the only practicable one, given the existing state of Italian arms. Moreover, it offered the advantage of being consistent with the policy of non-intervention just announced, as well as of being acceptable to both sets of belligerents and to the Balkans themselves. Having ascertained early in September that keeping the Balkans in 'absolute tranquillity' corresponded also to German wishes, Italian officials lost no occasion to underline the role played by Italy in guaranteeing the peace of the Balkans.

Ciano in particular seemed to appreciate instantly that leading a bloc of Balkan neutrals might not only satisfy Germany and his chief's *amour propre*, gravely wounded by the forced inactivity, but also recover some of those advantages Italy had lost after the *Anschluss* now that the Allies and Germany were marking time.

The Balkans, too, were more than favourably disposed. In south-eastern Europe, Italy's non-belligerence was quickly seen as a possible rallying point around which to consolidate a precarious neutrality. Divided, the states of south-eastern Europe were at the mercy of those among the belligerents who at any time might choose to over-run their neutrality in the name of a superior national interest. United, they might have earned respect for their collective neutrality. Led by a big power such as Italy, which could have co-ordinated their efforts and lent its prestige, the neutrals' desire for peace might even have been translated into a containment action for what was still in practice, if not in theory, a local war. Diffidently at first, more openly after it became clear that non-belligerence was not an Axis trick, the Balkans, including countries like Romania and Turkey which had not recently entertained particular sympathies for fascist Italy, addressed to Rome embarrassing protestations of fealty. The moving force behind these appeals was Romania, whose precarious position as one of the recipients of a Western 'guarantee' was compounded by territorial claims advanced by Bulgaria and Russia and veiled threats from Berlin. From Bucharest, therefore, came the strongest invitation. On 21 September Gafencu addressed a formal communication to Italy in which, after pointedly stressing the Bolshevik danger hanging over Eastern Europe, he appealed to Italy as the only hope of the neutrals. A week earlier Ciano, on Mussolini's instructions, had prepared a telegram charging Attolico to sound Berlin on a similar project, but the instructions had then been rescinded. Now, after the receipt of Gafencu's message, they were renewed. The Italian Ambassador was to point out to Germany that Italy's present attitude usefully prevented the expansion of the conflict to the countries from which Germany received her most important raw materials and to solicit German opinions on the formation of a neutral bloc similar to the Oslo grouping in the north.[30] Ciano in his instructions was very careful to present the project in the only form acceptable to Berlin – as an economic bloc – but privately he allowed that Italy's political interests were uppermost and the economic overtones essentially a formality.[31] In Berlin the proposal was received well enough. Ribbentrop had nothing against Italian leadership of a bloc to resist the effects of the Allied blockade 'but would be interested if the move assumed a political character'.[32] Evidently Berlin saw the political potential behind the economic façade, and was careful to point out the limits within which the Italian initiative would be welcomed. The cautioning did not in the least deter Ciano, who appeared satisfied with the result of the sounding and proceeded to solicit, as well, Spain's and Japan's adhesion to the projected bloc; it is not clear whether he intended to make it more palatable to Berlin by the inclusion of prospective allies or whether, on the contrary, to avoid his country's isolation implicit in the latest Russo–German agreement. Most likely the intention was to group as many larger powers as would be sympathetic so as to make the Italian-led group as prestigious as possible.[33] On 29 September Ciano began drafting a common declaration as a basis for the projected bloc, but before drafting could be completed he was called to Berlin to be briefed on the results of Ribbentrop's trip to Moscow. On the 30th, Mussolini confirmed to the king that the formation of a bloc including Spain and the Balkan countries was under active consideration.[34] The Hitler–Ciano conversation on 1 October was crucial for the future prospects of the bloc. Hitler mentioned his approval of a bloc of neutrals, but it was made absolutely clear that the German Chancellor and the Italian Foreign Minister viewed the project in contrasting fashion. For Ciano the bloc was a means of reinforcing Italy's non-belligerence and extending her influence in the neutral world, but primarily in the Balkans; for Hitler, it was a means of off-setting the effects of the Allied blockade and causing a severe rift between Britain and Italy, thus emphasising the latter's dependence on Germany. In context, Hitler's qualified approval sounded more like a rebuke to the vaster aspirations of the fascist government, and his repeated assertions that Germany's fight would also determine Italy's fate, a clear warning not to develop too close ties with the neutrals so as to make intervention on Germany's side more difficult.[35]

Germany's warnings had their effect on Mussolini. During the next two and a half weeks there was practically no mention of the bloc. The interval between 1 October and 17 October when Italy finally dismissed all thoughts of leading a bloc was filled by intense discussions amongst the Balkans themselves. But all these negotiations were henceforth destined to be conducted in a vacuum, because at that point the doubts Mussolini had always nurtured about permanent neutrality finally crystallised in an outright rejection of that option. On 17 October Ciano called in the German Ambassador and, after referring to a press despatch according to which Italy was about to lead a Balkan bloc as a prelude to abandoning the Axis, told him Mussolini had dropped the project:[36]

> In no circumstances did the Duce want to be made the spokesman of the neutrals. He simply detested that word because Italy belonged neither to the belligerents nor to the neutrals; her status, as before, remained that of maximum preparedness for which the Duce was working by every means in order to be ready at any given moment. . . . Leadership of a bloc of neutral Balkan states would only mean a tie for him that might prove embarrassing some day.

These remarks were not far off the mark. From the beginning, the irony of Mussolini, the leading exponent of the power of the sword, becoming the number one neutral had been a powerful deterrent. The Italian leader must have realised the restrictions that leadership of a neutral bloc would impose on his freedom of action. Given his sensitivity to the foreign press, he may also have resented its speculations. Whatever the reasons, his decision meant that any further negotiations were bound to fail. It was futile to try to group a number of buffer states, divided amongst themselves by the most pernicious territorial issues, unless they could both sublimate their particular differences in the interest of self-preservation and draw on the support and sympathy of a great power. Given the Balkans' rivalries and Italy's decision, neither condition existed after 17 October. Yet negotiations amongst the Balkans continued undeterred because the Italian government, probably for no better reason than dictatorial arrogance or internal inertia, did not communicate its decision to the Balkan governments.

These latter countries had been busy since early in September and discussions for an Italian-led bloc continued well into December, when Ciano finally made public the decision reached two months earlier. The discussions, now almost academic, were based on a much more ambitious plan put forward at the end of October and circulated amongst Balkan capitals by Gafencu, unaware, of course, of Italian opposition.[37] This plan, consisting of a number of interconnected agreements to place inter-Balkan rivalries into cold storage, to affirm neutrality and to promote closer political and economic relations under Italian leadership, elicited first the approval of London, and later more reluctantly that of Paris as well. London's approval followed a decision reached as early as the middle of September that the best policy to follow in the Balkans was indeed to promote the formation of a bloc of neutrals. Early in November, through semi-official contacts between the Political Intelligence Department and the Italian Embassy in London, it had been established that Britain viewed the role played by Italy in the Balkans with great appreciation, and the question was even raised whether Italy might like to be asked formally to lead a bloc of neutrals.[38] The French government, on the other hand, in keeping with its plans for the Balkans, was at first loath to see these countries form into a neutral bloc and in particular opposed granting Italy a position of pre-eminence in south-eastern Europe. Only after a strong Romanian *démarche* in Paris, did it grant its reluctant approval in mid-November.[39] At this time, the Russian government had also been informed by Turkey of the proposed bloc. Molotov's reception was anything but encouraging. The Soviet Union had no interest in furthering a project to strengthen Romania and Italy at a time when relations with Rome were worsening daily.[40] Directly upon receipt of the draft, Molotov communicated it to Berlin to ascertain whether the Romanian project, as claimed, had Axis support.

Moscow's communication caused no surprise in the Wilhelmstrasse, which had already had direct confirmation of Gafencu's plan, but it rekindled a strong suspicion that Rome might be manoeuvring in the Balkans behind Germany's back. If the projected bloc reached fruition, Italy's adhesion would have placed Germany in a very delicate position in the Balkans and would have reached critical proportion when the USSR, on the basis of the secret protocols of the Nazi–Soviet pact, asked Romania for the cession of Bessarabia. Accordingly, the German Ambassador in Rome was instructed to seek an explanation from Ciano at once. As it turned out, Germany's fears that Italy might be conducting secret negotiations with the Balkans in contravention of Ciano's statements of 17 October were totally unfounded. Naturally,

Palazzo Chigi had ample information and was reasonably certain that its participation was the cornerstone of the Romanian project, although it had not seen fit to inform the capitals of south-eastern Europe – with the exception, lately, of Budapest and Sofia – that Italy had no interest in the project. The misunderstanding, therefore, was only cleared up on 16 November when Mackensen ascertained that Mussolini's attitude had not changed since October.[41] A month later, on 16 December, Italy's attitude was finally made public through Ciano's speech. The Foreign Minister, after emphasising Italy's particular interests in the Balkan peninsula, finally announced that the formation of any kind of bloc was not deemed useful to the countries involved nor to the higher cause of peace.

The abortive bloc proposal had also been, potentially, the most powerful tool in the hands of Western diplomacy to encourage a permanent Italian neutrality. Regretfully it had not been exploited, primarily because London and Paris assessed the meaning and the implication of Italy's non-belligerence in irreconcilable fashion. Admittedly, both countries welcomed Rome's neutrality. But London, estimating that Italy would be forced to intervene if the Allies opened a Balkan front, decided to take no steps likely to bring about that intervention, while Paris discounted Italy's possible intervention and looked upon her present neutrality as a unique opportunity to open a front in south-eastern Europe, and thus to drain Germany's power in a series of long and indecisive campaigns. But the French failed to consider that in the existing circumstance a Balkan front could be opened only if Italy acquiesced, or if Italy were first defeated. This was well understood in the Balkan countries on whose participation the French were counting. They had made clear that they could only entertain belligerence if Italy were knocked out immediately. Yet France continued to press ahead with plans for a Balkan front without, however, including in them provisions for the elimination of Italy. Britain, on the other hand, had already decided that Italy could not be eliminated and that consequently the question of opening a Balkan front did not arise. In London's view, the French argument that the Balkans' participation in the war alongside the Allies would offset Italy's participation alongside Germany was not so much weak as irrelevant. The picture was further complicated because some members of the British and French governments also clung at the same time to the hope that Italy could be induced to join the Allies and therefore, presumably, acquiesce in the opening of a Balkan front. Consequently, during the period of Italian non-belligerence London and Paris followed a policy which placed them at cross purposes with one another, and with Rome. They were at odds because Paris insisted on putting forth plans dependent on Italy's attitude, while Italy's position was still equivocal; and they became at odds with Italy because, while appeasing Rome, they tried to extend their influence in the Balkans and impose blockade control measures which were bound to irritate the irascible Italian dictator.

The Allied 'serenade under the balcony', as Ciano called it, began immediately the war broke out. As early as 5 September the French Ambassador in Rome, François Poncet, had delivered a syrupy note expressing his country's appreciation for Italy's inaction and, encouraged by its reception, had returned to Paris to plead for a conciliatory policy towards Italy. Steps were taken in Paris to purchase Italian armaments and assurances extended that the French Army of the Levant under General Weygand would only be employed after Italy had received prior notice.[42] Halifax also had sent a fulsome message designed to flatter the young Foreign Minister's vanity, and on the Foreign Office's assumption, accepted by the War Cabinet, that there were prospects of bringing Italy into the war on the Allied side, instructions were sent to the Ambassador in Rome to inquire how best to proceed in that direction.[43]

It should be noted, however, that this Allied policy represented a change from their earlier position. At the end of March 1939, the policy evolved through conversations between the British and French military staffs had been based on the supposition that Italy and Germany would attack together. If, as anticipated, Germany attacked through Belgium and Holland, and Italy through Libya and Abyssinia, the plan had been to hold Germany while dealing Italy a decisive blow. After command of the sea was established, the defeat of Germany would follow. The plans presupposed Italian enmity from the very beginning of hostilities, but clearly by August this enmity was in no sense welcomed. Allied resources were already spread dangerously thin. After the breakdown of the Allied–Russian discussions for a mutual assistance pact, the fear of over-extension caused the British Chiefs of Staff to urge the

Cabinet that 'no attempt should be made to compel her [Italy] to declare her position if that was likely to bring her into a war against us'. This attitude was hastily approved by the British Cabinet, where Italian neutrality enjoyed a long-standing priority. On 30 August, therefore, when the Allied commanders received instructions to stand by for a possible state of war with the Axis, the instructions specifically ordered that precautions taken against Italy were to be as far as possible non-provocative.[44]

In retrospect, it is hard to dispute the contention that the Western Powers made a serious error in judgment in the summer of 1939. The Italian Mediterranean Fleet consisted of four battleships, of which only two were operational (four additional battleships were from one to three years away from launching), seven 8-inch and twelve 6-inch cruisers, about fifty destroyers and no aircraft carriers because it relied on shore-based aircraft for operations and tactical support. Against these ships the combined English and French fleets in the Mediterranean totalled ten battleships, seven 8-inch cruisers, sixteen 6-inch cruisers, sixty destroyers and one aircraft carrier.[45] The Italian fleet, though outnumbered, was faster and had an edge in seeking or breaking off action and, by virtue of its central position, could concentrate more quickly in the area of its choice and cause serious embarrassment through its superiority in submarines, 108 versus 50. But, its position could also be a liability if the Allies attacked from both sides with fleets whose combined strength was clearly superior and with orders to seek and destroy. Moreover, the French were in an excellent position to cut Italy's communication with Libya while the British could always contain the eight Italian submarines operating in the Red Sea with, if needs be, units from east of Suez. Thus the British Admiralty's reluctance to propose and to advocate strongly a knockout blow against the Italian navy could not be excused on strategic grounds. Nor could the admitted Italian manpower superiority in North and East Africa have been adduced as an excuse for the decision to seek Italian neutrality. The Italian colonial troops, if cut off from reinforcements and supplies from the mother country by Allied control of the Mediterranean, would have been in an indefensible position.

By November 1939 the policy of calculated niceties towards Italy had not materially altered the situation. The French attempts to buy Italian arms had been rebuffed; a British proposal to continue the exchange of military information and troop movements as stipulated in the Easter Accords had gone unanswered. The favoured treatment accorded to Italy in the matter of contraband control worked to the advantage of her military preparation, and it was obvious that, despite hopes to the contrary, Italy had still to be realistically ranked in the list of potential enemies. The British Ambassador in Rome continued to suggest extreme caution in applying blockade measures, but could hold out no prospects that the Italian dictator might reverse his course.[46] Clearly, the Italian government, despite its differences with Berlin, was loath to be drawn into closer relations with the democracies. Yet both London and Paris still felt optimistic about their chances so long as the negotiations to supply Italy with a large proportion of her coal needs were going reasonably well and, even more encouraging, Italy was obviously resisting German pressures to circumvent the blockade.

For its part, Germany had tolerated Italian neutrality in the hope that Italy might first act as a funnel for neutral goods, thus eluding the blockade and, second, might decide to oppose the blockade openly. Berlin had consequently insisted that its supplies of coal to Italy be sent not overland, but primarily by sea from the Dutch port of Rotterdam. Its hope was thereby to divert to the continent Italian ships loading in England and thus force Italy to take a position against the blockade and provoke a rift between London and Rome should the Allies try to intercept the German coal on the high seas. In this connection Chamberlain's announcement on 21 November, that the Allied governments were blockading German exports by sea, appeared in Berlin as a blessing in disguise. It was put to the Italian government that overland supplies of coal would be increased substantially if Italy publicly opposed the Allied blockade. The ruse did not work, primarily because Ciano already had reasonable assurances, immediately the new blockade measures were imposed, that they would not be applied to coal in transit to Italy. By the beginning of December, after a last unsuccessful attempt to persuade Mussolini to condemn publicly the Allied blockade, the German government resigned itself to the fact that Italy could not be pressured into a crisis with the Western Powers.[47]

By the same token the Western Powers could not pressure Italy either. The hope that Italy might still make common cause with the

Allies had not been ruled out. Chamberlain, speaking to the Allied Supreme War Council on 19 December admitted that Mussolini 'was as closely bound as ever to Germany', but privately he expressed his appreciation of the anti-German portions of Ciano's speech of 16 December.[48] That speech had momentarily rekindled Western hopes. Once more the Allied ambassadors were instructed to approach Palazzo Chigi. François Poncet's call on 24 December was inconclusive. Ciano recorded Loraine's visit on 29 December. The British Ambassador, deduced from his conversation that Mussolini still wished to retain his freedom of action, that he displayed no eagerness to join the fray, and that he looked to a negotiated peace with the balance tipped on the German side as the ideal solution. But he could offer no new guidance for future decisions on policy towards Italy.[49]

Intervention

The reasons for Italy's aloofness from both sides at the beginning of 1940 were to be found in Mussolini's letter to Hitler of 5 January. That message represented the Duce's last-ditch attempt to dissuade Hitler from continuing the war. Consequently, the reception the message received in Berlin was crucial for the future of Italian politics. It was such as to leave the Italian dictator with no illusions. The German government had no intention to postpone its plans of attack. The letter caused a momentary disorientation in the Wilhelmstrasse because of the suspicion that Mussolini's reference to an independent rump Poland might have been the result of prior consultations with the Allies. But once Ribbentrop had ascertained, in a conversation with Attolico on 10 January, that this was not the case, he made it clear that Mussolini's cautionings were unacceptable.[50] With some variations, this was the attitude also of Göring, Admiral Canaris and General Bodenshatz, who had also been entertained on the subject by the Italian Embassy. It was their unanimous view that operations in the West could no longer be put off. It was only a small consolation for the Italian diplomats to ascertain that Göring and Canaris at least had more limited goals in mind and had not ruled out, however unrealistic the prospect, a compromise peace in the future. But all agreed that a preventive attack against Holland and Belgium was justified on the grounds of protecting the Ruhr industries, circumventing the blockade, and getting within air reach of London.[51] Mussolini could draw no other conclusion than his failure to stay Germany's hand.

The Reich's decision to carry the war to the West eliminated Mussolini's second option – intervention on the Allied side. Admittedly, this option belonged much more to the realm of the possible than the probable especially so long as the memory of 1914 preyed on Mussolini's mind, but, like permanent neutrality, it had not been totally discounted. Certainly, Ciano, growing more Germanophobe by the day, had entertained the thought. But in February 1940 Mussolini intervened decisively twice; first to put an end to economic negotiations with the Western Powers, and secondly to revive similar negotiations with Germany which had run aground. The implications of these decisions were inescapable – the bridges with Paris and London were being burnt at the same time as those with Berlin were being repaired. The importance of these two decisions was underlined by the fact that they flatly contradicted the views of the economic experts charged with conducting the negotiations. It was the opinion of the Minister of Trade and Commerce, Raffaelo Riccardi, and the Director General of commercial affairs in the Foreign Ministry, Amadeo Giannini, that Britain's terms were more advantageous. Mussolini's intervention was thus determined by political reasons. On 7 February 1940, the Italian dictator ordered the exclusion of war materials from the Anglo–Italian economic negotiations, a move which was bound to determine their failure.[52] On 21 February he ordered Giannini and Riccardi to accept the less attractive German offer.[53] Italy's intervention alongside Germany now became merely a question of selecting the opportune moment.

The conclusion that Mussolini had opted for the Reich in February 1940 was borne out by his behaviour in the next few weeks when he met successively the Reich's Foreign Minister and Hitler himself. Ribbentrop was despatched to Rome on 10 March, ostensibly to deliver Hitler's belated reply to Mussolini's letter of 5 January, but more likely to stave off what looked to Berlin like the making of an *entente* between the world's three most prestigious neutrals – Italy, the Vatican and the USA.[54] The Führer's letter could not be properly construed as an answer to Mussolini's misgivings. More in an expository than in an argumentative mood, Hitler recapitulated the course of events in the previous seven months, letting it be understood that Mussolini's views had not had the slightest influence on his plans. But by this time, of course,

Mussolini had also reconciled himself to the fact that the attempt to ward off an attack on the West had failed. Significantly, in an *aide-mémoire* he had drafted for himself, listing several points to be taken up with Ribbentrop, two were subsequently crossed out – 'Is an attack necessary to defeat the Western powers?' and 'Your war aims have been reached'.[55] And, in fact, neither point was raised in the conversation with Ribbentrop or with Hitler later in the month. The two points summarised the gist of his January letter; by March, Mussolini had deemed it futile to raise them again.

It was not therefore altogether surprising to either Ciano or Mussolini to hear Ribbentrop reveal in the first conversation that Germany intended to attack in the West that summer, just as it should not have come as a surprise to Ribbentrop to hear Mussolini declare suddenly the following day that 'it was practically impossible for Italy to remain outside the conflict' and that 'at the right moment' she would intervene alongside Germany. Both conversations with Ribbentrop touched familiar chords but this time the key had changed. Mussolini, whose earlier anti-Bolshevism had been 'absolute', 'solid as a rock', 'unshakable', now developed a sudden comprehension for the tactical exigencies of the situation and suggested a parallel improvement of Italian relations with Moscow. Finland, which during the course of the winter war with Russia had enjoyed Italian sympathy and Italian help, was now dismissed in a sentence. The Western Powers, previously thought to be undefeatable, were now revealed as spineless relics of an anachronistic past; the USA, which in the January letter would never allow the democracies to be defeated, was by now a confirmed isolationist convinced of the hopelessness of the Allied cause. The turnabout was as complete as it was abject. Even the attempts to salvage Italian honour sounded offensive. The inevitable reference to 1914 was as untrue as it was unfair to the Italian people. Only on the subject of the Balkans did Mussolini sound a peaceful note, asking in particular that Russia be deterred from any action in Bessarabia – a request with which the Reich Foreign Minister imperturbably agreed. The focal point of the conversation was, of course, the Italian pledge to intervene. Not unexpectedly, Ribbentrop, who had hardly expected such a bonus, pressed for further details. Mussolini's details were murky – he posed several hypotheses all leading inevitably to intervention, and he stressed that Italy could contemplate only a short war in which her contribution would be 'decisive'. But his dilatoriness and reservations, which Ciano manfully tried to emphasise, in the last analysis were not nearly as important as the fact that a decision had been reached and announced to the German ally.[56]

The decision was confirmed at a meeting hastily arranged between Hitler and Mussolini at the Brenner on 18 March. 'Italy's entry into the war is inevitable,' Mussolini declared. Moreover, he was now convinced how impossible it would have been for Germany to postpone its attack on Poland in September. He only regretted that the voids caused by Italy's previous wars had not been filled so that he too could have entered the fray at the same time. Unfortunately, those voids were not entirely filled even now, and in particular Italy's financial situation could not permit a long war. None the less, Italy would intervene either to deal the democracies the decisive blow or to hold the Western Powers while Germany regrouped its forces. He only asked whether the offensive could be postponed for some months while Italy could get ready. On this point, however, Hitler was adamant: the weather did not permit delays. The Führer's tactics were particularly effective. On the one hand, he reinforced in Mussolini's mind the fear of going empty-handed unless he intervened, and on the other he took pains to impress on his colleague the certainty of complete victory. He assured him that an attack in the West was imminent, although he refrained from saying where and when it would take place.[57]

Such reticence might have led Mussolini to believe that the attack might not come for some months. He was now, of course, totally committed to intervention, though not on a very large scale, as the operational orders he issued to the Chiefs of Staff at the end of March revealed. Unlike his meeting with Hitler, when the German dictator had a tendency so to monopolise the conversation and Mussolini had a tendency, in his presence, so to strut, the orders to the Chiefs of Staff on the other hand show Mussolini in one of his more lucid, though not very prescient, moments. They began by assuming that a compromise peace was now impossible. Progressing then to the further development of war, Mussolini ruled out an Allied attack on Germany, primarily for demographic reasons (one of his pet dynamic determinants), and predicted instead that the Allies would concentrate on the blockade. Passing to an examination of probable German actions, he equally ruled out (in ignorance of German plans formulated in February) an attack on either the Maginot Line or through Belgium and Holland, first because in his view the Germans had now reached their war aims and could afford to wait and, second, because in the case of failure 'an internal crisis in Germany would be inevitable, given that the morale of the German people is on the whole mediocre and in some big cities such as Berlin or Munich less than mediocre'. He therefore forecast strong measures against the blockade and an attack only in desperation, or in the 'mathematical certainty' of an overwhelming victory. As to Italy – 'If the war continues, to believe that Italy can stay out of it till the end is absurd and impossible.' The possibility that Italy might join the Allies was ruled out on the ground that Italy would then have to fight Germany immediately, and *by herself*:[58]

> . . . it is only the alliance with Germany, that is, a state which does not yet need our military help and is happy with an economic contribution and moral solidarity, which permits our present state of non-belligerence. Having ruled out the hypothesis of a turnabout, which in any case even the Allies are not contemplating thus showing their appreciation for us, there remains the other hypothesis, that is a war parallel to Germany's to achieve our objectives summed up as follows: freedom on the seas, window on the ocean.
>
> Italy cannot be a truly independent nation so long as Corsica, Bizerta and Malta are the window bars of her prison and Suez and Gibraltar the walls. Having solved the problem of its land frontiers Italy, if she wants to be a world power, must resolve the problem of her maritime frontiers: the very security of the Empire is tied to the solution of this problem.
>
> Italy cannot remain *neutral* for the entire duration of the war without resigning from her role, without disqualifying herself, without reducing herself to the level of a Switzerland multiplied by ten.
>
> The problem is not therefore to know whether we will or will not enter the war; it's only a question of knowing when and how; it is a question of delaying our entry as long as is possible and consistent with our honour and dignity.

Italy's intervention was going to be the *coup de grâce*. Prudently, Mussolini ordered a defensive posture for all units with the exception of the navy and the army in Abyssinia, which were to engage in limited offensive actions. The timing of the intervention was left to future developments and to his discretion.[59]

Indubitably, it was the German victories in Norway, Holland,

Belgium and France which induced Mussolini to enter the war on 10 June 1940. Their decisive effect cannot be underrated, although other factors as well played an important part in shaping modern Italy's most important decision. Hitler's attitude, in particular, was critical. From April onwards, the German dictator became uncommonly effusive and communicative, showing an unrivalled understanding of his counterpart's psyche. Hitler's letters between the beginning of April and their meeting in June to decide armistice terms for France touched on Mussolini's pride, his presumption, his desire to make Italy great, and his envy (not least towards Hitler himself). Above all Hitler was clever enough to ask for nothing, to make none of the customary references to the common future of the Axis, to advance no contrary arguments but simply to reinforce whatever bellicose tendencies were always present in Mussolini. Such tactics played an important part in accelerating Mussolini's decision. In early April he had set the date of intervention for the spring of 1941.[60] After the German victories in Norway and Denmark he had moved it forward to the summer of 1940.[61] After the German attack on Holland and Belgium, on 10 May, he could hardly contain himself. 'Any delay is unthinkable,' he told Ciano on the 13th, 'we have no time to lose. Within the month I'll declare war. I will attack France and Britain in the air and on the sea. I am not thinking any longer of an attack on Yugoslavia; it would be a humiliating fallback.' Ciano commented,[62]

> Unfortunately there's nothing I can do to hold him back. He has decided to act and he will act. He believes the Germans will succeed and will succeed quickly. Only a new turn in the war could make him change his mind, but for the time being things are going so badly for the Allies that there is no hope.

Ciano had exerted a moderating influence on his father-in-law since August 1939 and, while as late as 13 May he still sounded a note of fear and caution, he too eventually succumbed to the lure of war. During the spring, as the Germans won victory after victory, the caution, moderation and Germanophobia which had characterised the previous eight months melted as quickly as the French divisions. He offered no opposition when, in April, Attolico was sacrificed to Ribbentrop and removed from the Embassy in Berlin; in mid-May he delivered a particularly bellicose speech drafted by Mussolini; at the end of May, after assuring a stupefied Mackensen that 'he was working with all his strength for an immediate Italian intervention', he admitted the fear of arriving too late, and complained of the delays put forth by the Italian military.[63]

Hitler's mellifluousness and Ciano's delusions made important, though not crucial, contributions to Mussolini's decision to intervene. The opposition of the king and of the armed services, on the other hand, might have been decisive. Neither took the risk. Only after considerable evasions did the Italian Chiefs of Staff finally spell out their inability to conduct a war even on the limited scale envisaged in the orders of 31 March.[64] By the time they had impressed their reluctance on Mussolini, the issue had practically been decided by the German victories in the West. All Mussolini required was a token war.

Badoglio, the Chief of General Staff, had replied to Mussolini's directives with assurances which in no way suggested that the Duce's orders were extravagant. When the Chiefs of Staff met on 9 April, reality proved more intractable. There were only 300 tanks, not enough uniforms, no supplies to build defensive positions on the Alps, while the empire was in a state of open insurrection. 'All our preparations are defective,' he had to admit. 'We are barely operating at 40 per cent capacity and in some sectors even less. To merely think of taking the offensive . . . is ingenuous.'[65] Days later the navy submitted a memorandum stating their inability to undertake any actions beyond submarine attacks.[66] Badoglio now took the line that an Italian intervention could be considered only 'if the enemy was so prostrated to justify such audacity' or 'when the state of prostration of the enemy was such to give us hope of success'.[67] He had thus narrowly discharged his duty – the head of government had been informed of the true state of Italian arms. But, at no point did he go beyond the narrow confines of duty to point out that no matter how prostrated an enemy might be, declaring war against a major power was a risky open-ended business. It may well be that Mussolini would not have been persuaded had the effort been made. After all, he had known since the end of 1939, when he had received the report of the Commission of War Production, that Italian industry would not begin to meet the requirements of the three services before 1944 at the earliest and could guarantee one year's supplies only by 1949.[68]

But the Duce had pushed aside such pusillanimity, as he chose to see it. On 29 May he found the condition of the army 'not ideal but satisfactory' and reconfirmed his directives on 31 March. 'If we wait two weeks or a month', he explained, 'we will not improve our situation while we might give Germany the impression of arriving when the game is over and the risks minimal. Moreover, it is not our moral habit to hit a man when he is about to fall. All this, in any case, could be very serious at the time of drawing up the peace treaties.' Any day after 5 June, he announced, was a 'good time' to enter the war. No voice was raised in opposition. On the last day of May, Mussolini announced the decision to Hitler who seemed to prefer either 6 or 8 June.[69] The date settled on was the 10th, enough time for Mussolini to prepare defensive positions in Libya and time enough also to reject several appeals from Roosevelt, one drafted in the first instance by the Allied ambassadors in Washington, which promised to entertain sympathetically all Italian grievances and include Italy as a belligerent in any peace conference.[70] Not even such inducements could work now. Mussolini had decided that, in spite of the armed forces' unpreparedness, he could safely intervene, and that if he did not he would be excluded from the spoils by the Germans themselves. The armed forces' condition was therefore dismissed as irrelevant, though to be on the safe side orders were issued that Italian troops while in a state of war should take only very limited initiatives on land.[71]

Clearly the decisive factor in the timing of the intervention was the opportunity presented by the German victories in France. The decision to enter the war was essentially a political decision, a risk, though not a well calculated one, that the opportunity should be seized now to take part in the redistribution of power in Europe expected to follow from the defeat of France. The possibility that Britain would continue the war single-handed was dismissed alternately as idiotic or irrelevant. Even as he was entering the war, Mussolini was thinking of a *rapprochement* with a weakened France and possibly the Soviet Union to counterbalance future German preponderance on the continent.[72] He was alternately piqued and relieved that the sudden capitulation of France a week after Italy's intervention did not give him the opportunity to earn his passage. The extravagant demands he made of France reflected his dismay, but they did not last beyond a meeting with Hitler and

Ribbentrop in Munich on 18 June to agree on armistice terms. The German leaders, in contrast with Mussolini's pretensions, put forth terms designed on the one hand to make it easier for France to break with England and end her resistance and on the other to suggest to Britain that she also should sue for peace. Hitler and Ribbentrop did not insist that Italy tone down her demands, but amongst the reasons which induced Mussolini on 21 June to suggest much more moderate terms must be included the practical impossibility of backing the war's real winner. Not to be discounted, however, was the role Mussolini foresaw for France in the post-war configuration of power. With an eye to balancing German power and avoiding a Franco–German *rapprochement* implicit in the mild German terms, Mussolini responded favourably to an appeal from the new French Foreign Minister, Baudoin, stressing France's desires for a lasting peace which would serve as foundation for the future collaboration of the two Latin countries.[73] The armistice with France, stipulating only a token Italian occupation of 50 kilometres of French territory, came into effect at 7.30 p.m. on 24 June.[74] As far as Mussolini was concerned, the war was over.

Documents

1. *Italy and Austria: Robilant to King Victor Emmanuel, 26 January 1877* (F. Chabod, *Storia della politica estera italiana dal 1870 al 1896*, pp. 690–1, extract)

The government of Y[our] M[ajesty] believes that it is contrary to the interests of Italy that Austria should augment her power in the Adriatic through the annexation of Bosnia and Herzegovina. The government of H[is] I[mperial] M[ajesty] in turn affirms that it does not want to annex Turkish provinces but declares solemnly, even threateningly, that if this should happen against its wishes it will not cede an inch of ground to Italy. In my view we are right but I believe firmly all the same that it is useless to be right without the strength to prevail. Austria, secure in her alliance with Germany, does not fear us and can defy us with impunity. I cannot see that Italy has allies who in case of necessity would support her with arms in her claims and what would happen to us would be the fate of France against Germany in 1870.

Of necessity therefore we must resign ourselves to seeing our neighbour eventually increasing her power, without compromising our prestige and even perhaps our existence by useless complaints ... avoiding not only inopportune discussions on the question but also all those public demonstrations. ... Our interest would be to try to establish and maintain the alliance between Germany, Austria and Italy. This would also be in the interests of Europe as a whole as it would no longer have to be afraid of war, the three powers united being strong enough to impose peace on the others.

2. *Mancini refuses to join Britain in Egypt: Mancini to Menabrea, 1 August 1882* (*Affari di Egitto del 1881–2*, pp. 27–8)

It would have been enough to clarify the intentions of the two powers [Germany and Austria] if, though avoiding an explicit mandate, they had given us the certainty – even in a private and friendly communication – of their assent to a special action by

Italy in Egypt. But, far from that, their warning soon assumed a different and no less explicit form, directed towards Italy as to any other power. Our conviction on this important question was confirmed by the impression made on me by the language of the ambassadors of Germany and Austria–Hungary, as soon as the two cabinets knew of the replies sent by us to the twice repeated invitation from England: their language testified to the satisfaction of the two governments at our loyalty.

3. *Renewal of the alliance: Robilant to Launay, 5 August 1886*
   (MRR, Carte Crispi 666/10/7)

[Keudell asked if we were going to renew the alliance] I said that we would always be in agreement with Germany and Austria–Hungary whether or not the alliance was renewed. To renew it was necessary to satisfy Italian public opinion which lamented the continual lack of support for our interests. The French occupation of Tunis had made it easy for the government [in 1882] to persuade public opinion to support the Triple Alliance, but if France takes Tripoli it will have the opposite effect since it will be plain that the alliance is useless. It seems quite likely that she [France] will do so despite her assurances.

He [Keudell] observed that there was no longer any danger of France wishing to take Tripoli as she already had too many colonial embarrassments on her hands.

I did not believe myself in this optimistic appreciation so I put forward the presence of General Allegro, who might well be termed a Boulanger No. 2, on the Tripolitanian frontier. This was sufficient to convince me that when the French thought it opportune they would invent the Kroumirs necessary to bring about in Tripoli the results they had obtained in Tunis. . . .

The important point to bear in mind, however, is to leave the initiative to Prince Bismarck. The one thing that I intend to exclude for the moment is an initiative on our part.

4. *Launay to Robilant, 26 August 1886* (MRR, Carte Crispi
   666/10/20, extract)

If at Berlin and Vienna they think themselves certain of Italy then they will not show themselves so eager to conclude new agreements with us in the manner we would like. At the worst, I think any alliance is preferable to none. It is true that there is France, but monarchical Italy could not be the ally of the Republic. And if the Italian people were so mad as to throw themselves into her arms in a moment of pique, hoping to force the hand of her allies, in that event we should make a very bad exchange. The evils that would result would be much worse than the consequences of a French occupation of Tripolitania.

Besides, it is not proven that if the French made such an attempt and we offered opposition Germany and even England would not give signs of life. The attitude of Germany would be very different without an agreement.

5. *Launay to Robilant, 30 December 1886* (AMEI, Archivio Gabinetto, 230, TA cassetta 1c, extract)
Baron Holstein told me that in the instructions from Friedrichsruhe which had formed the basis of our interview, the Chancellor suggested the idea that there was every advantage for Italy in contracting either an alliance or in establishing a common action with England. His Highness believes that the idea, long popular in England, has become more feasible following the exasperation resulting from the last incidents in the Egyptian question. It is a fact that the thought of a struggle against France has gained ground. . . . An alliance with England would eliminate at one stroke the danger of a French landing on the shores of Italy, and at the same time would make it easier – if the need arose – to turn the position of the Alps by disembarking our troops on the French coast under the protection of the Anglo–Italian fleet.

6. *Second Treaty of the Triple Alliance, 20 February 1887** (A. F. Pribram, *The Secret Treaties of Austria–Hungary,* I, pp. 107–15)
   (a) The Treaty of 1882 was renewed until 1892.
   (b) Separate Treaty between Austria–Hungary and Italy.

ARTICLE I

The High Contracting Parties, having in mind only the maintenance, so far as possible, of the territorial *status quo* in the Orient, engage to use their influence to forestall any territorial modification which might be injurious to one or the other of the Powers signatory to the present Treaty. They shall communicate to one

* For the first treaty of 1882 see F. R. Bridge, *From Sadowa to Sarajevo,* London, 1972, pp 406–7.

another all information of a nature to enlighten each other mutually concerning their own disposition, as well as those of other Powers.

However, if, in the course of events, the maintenance of the *status quo* in the regions of the Balkans or of the Ottoman coasts and islands in the Adriatic and in the Aegean Sea should become impossible, and if, whether in consequence of the action of a third Power or otherwise, Austria–Hungary or Italy should find themselves under the necessity of modifying it by a temporary or permanent occupation on their part, this occupation shall take place only after a previous agreement between the two Powers aforesaid, based on the principle of a reciprocal compensation for every advantage, territorial or other, which each of them might obtain beyond the present *status quo,* and giving satisfaction to the interests and well founded claims of the two Parties. [ARTICLES II and III omitted.]

(c) Separate Treaty between the German Empire and Italy.

ARTICLE I
Identical to para. 1 of Austro–Italian treaty, but for insertion after 'forestall' of the words 'on the Ottoman coasts and islands in the Adriatic and Aegean Seas'.

ARTICLE II
The stipulations of Article I apply in no way to the Egyptian question. . . .

ARTICLE III
If it were to happen that France should make a move to extend her occupation, or even her protectorate or her sovereignty, under any form whatsoever, in the North African territories, whether of the Vilayet of Tripoli or of the Moroccan Empire, and that in consequence thereof Italy, in order to safeguard her position in the Mediterranean, should feel that she must herself undertake action in the said North African territories, or even have recourse to extreme measures in French territory in Europe, the state of war which would thereby ensue between Italy and France would constitute *ipso facto,* on the demand of Italy and at the common charge of the two Allies, the *casus foederis* with all the effects foreseen by Articles II and V of the aforesaid Treaty of May 20 1882, as if such an eventuality were expressly contemplated therein.

Documents

ARTICLE IV

If the fortunes of war undertaken in common against France should lead Italy to seek for territorial guaranties with respect to France for the security of the frontiers of the Kingdom and of her maritime position, as well as with a view to the stability of peace, Germany will present no obstacle thereto; and if need be, and in a measure compatible with circumstances, will apply herself to facilitating the means of attaining such a purpose.
[ARTICLES V to VII omitted.]

7. *The Mediterranean agreements: Corti to Depretis, 7 April 1887*
    (MRR, Carte Crispi 666/11/21, extract)
England will not bind herself in positive terms or to military co-operation, because such an obligation was not permitted either by the English political tradition or by the state of public opinion at present. But the agreement reached has, none the less, the highest importance; both because it contains a clear indication of the side England would take in the event of a conflict; and because in this eventuality the moral obligations assumed . . . would lead to her co-operation in an active manner. From the words used by the Prime Minister it seems apparent that this support will more likely be at sea than by land. Your Excellency will easily understand how important the maritime co-operation of England will be.

8. *Crispi to Nigra, 11 September 1887* (DDI, ii, XXI, no. 130, extract)
To sum up, Austria wants a policy of nationalities in the Balkans, her interests being the *status quo* for the present and the formation of autonomous states in the future. This is the traditional policy of Italy and is certainly mine. All the same, to make sure this common programme is maintained against any return to the policy of compensations of 1876, it is not sufficient to watch out: this brought us very little success in 1876. Now we must have agreements guaranteeing reciprocal observation and the eventual armed co-operation of the three powers against Russia in the event of aggression. The Berlin cabinet is, from what we know, secretly favourable to these agreements. . . . Blanc believes that Kálnoky hopes to give a practical character to our *entente*. As you know, I am entirely in favour. There only remains to overcome the dislike of the London cabinet of engagements on a hypothetical basis . . . as for Turkey, I believe

for my part that from the day that the understanding between the three powers takes a concrete form, the Sultan will not be long in recognising that his interests demand that he march alongside us.

9. *Crispi and Abyssinia: Launay to Crispi, 8 October 1887* (MRR, 666/2/12)

Referring to one of the points touched on by Y[our] E[xcellency] in the Friedrichsruhe conversations with the Chancellor, Count Bismarck has just told me that he has spoken, as if on his own initiative and very confidentially, to the British Chargé d'Affaires on the Abyssinian business. 'The Berlin cabinet, without pressing the matter unduly, but in view of her friendship towards Italy and of the importance that the latter should preserve her forces intact to assist in the maintenance of peace in general, would be very grateful if England would intervene of her own initiative. What was needed was to obtain from the Negus a satisfaction of a nature to safeguard our dignity and our interests.' He thought that English good offices stood a good chance of success. If this were not so then the blockade would no doubt help or the moral support of England should be sufficient.

10. *Italian interests in the East: Blanc to Crispi, 12 February 1888* (DDI, ii, XXI, no. 573, extract)

. . . instead of following England on the road to special agreements with France, and Germany on the road to special agreements with Russia, we should strive incessantly to follow Italian interests. These are harmed by Anglo–French condominiums in Egypt and Austro–Russian partitions of the Balkans. We should seek to base our position not in reconstructing the Concert of Europe – which would mean the dissolution of our alliances and has always worked only for the interests of others, as experience showed at the Congress of Berlin and the Conference of Constantinople – but in the closest possible union of the alliances. To this end we should subordinate any co-operation with an Anglo–French agreement over Egypt – in which we could only play a secondary role – or an Austro–Russian agreement on the Orient, to our prior obligations. (The latter, which would give Salonika to Austria and Constantinople to Russia, would so prejudice Italian interests that not even the acquisition of Tripoli would be sufficient compensation.)

Instead we should inspire our allies with confidence in Italy so that they rely on us in Balkan and African questions. . . .

From 1882 until 1885 we tried to maintain a coherent policy of excluding solutions to the Egyptian problem . . . except in agreement with France, seeking to use the position given us by the alliance with the Central Powers (who claimed to be indifferent to Mediterranean and especially Egyptian questions) to associate Italy with France and England in tripartite action in Egypt and obtain guarantees from them for the *status quo* in the Mediterranean. . . .

In January 1884 we had an exchange of views with France from which it resulted that, since the continued British protectorate in Egypt seemed inevitable, we should occupy Massowa in order to re-enter Egypt as a tripartite condominium . . . Italian action in the Red Sea and her mediation between France and England was advised by Paris. Italy made it a condition that the *status quo* in Morocco and Tripoli should be maintained. In 1885 French congratulations on the Massowa expedition were accompanied by a new exchange of views for the condominium *à trois*. . . .

I must know whether I am to understand my instructions to co-operate fully with England in the above sense or whether they are to be understood in the sense that I have suggested to the Royal Ministry from my arrival here. . . .

Experience has shown that the weight of Italy in the European balance is such that every step she takes towards co-operation or agreements with France and England leads Germany to return to the alliance of the Three Emperors, with designs such as those demonstrated at Skiernewice: the abandonment of Constantinople to Russia, Salonika to Austria–Hungary, and Africa to France.

11. *Massowa and Tunis: Robilant to Crispi, 17 September 1888*
    (AMEI, seria politica 29/1448/70)
[Refers to Crispi's telegram of 15th.] I believe that I have no need to assure you that I shall try as hard as I can to see that, in so far as it is in my power, our relations with England are put back on that special level of trust and intimacy which the common interest of the two countries demands. In the past I worked towards this, not altogether without result.

There is not much I can do at present as Lord Salisbury is away and Lister is not very favourable towards us.

The motives for this change in British policy were listed in my report of 4 September* and amount to Lord Salisbury's attitude towards Massowa, as Catalani reported on 29 July [Tel. 1854]: 'He told me that the present state of relations between France and Italy kept him in a continual state of alarm and anxiety; that French irritation was extreme and if things went on like this they would end in a war. According to Salisbury France would have yielded already if the command at Massowa had used a little more finesse. ... He added that he had no wish to be dragged into a quarrel with France for a trifling issue such as the capitulations at Massowa.'

Catalani on 1 August thought the Kismayu affair was now settled. ... My impression is quite the contrary. The manner in which Lord Salisbury insisted on 28 July that our two disputes with the Sultan should be discussed, then without further transaction gave us a vague assurance that he would obtain Kismayu for us and at the same time advised us to accept Mackinnon's proposals – which would only give us half of Kismayu – is not reassuring.

It appears to me therefore as established that if there was a change in Lord Salisbury's attitude towards us this dates from the last days of July.

12. *Crispi to Launay, 19 September 1888 (repeated to Vienna and London)* (AMEI, Tels 131/1785, extract)

No other governments have colonies or associations in Tunis to speak of and in accepting the recent decrees other governments have nothing to lose. We have. ... For others the question is one of principle: for us it is one of principle and material facts. This and for no other reason is why we insist that the decrees should not apply to us. The occupation of Tunis was a misfortune for everyone but above all for Italy: for the moment we limit ourselves to asking that Italy should not suffer new and greater damage and all we ask for is respect for our rights. I would point out that the Italian nation is singularly sensitive to what happens in the Regency. The occupation of Tunis was the cause of the fall of the Cairoli ministry in May 1881. The present decrees will certainly arouse disputes and discussions once the parliamentary session

* No. 44. Not printed. It stressed Salisbury's coolness over Massowa and Kismayu and the absolute necessity of avoiding the appearance of provoking France.

resumes and it will not be easy for the government to resist the opposition if the schools question is decided in a manner contrary to our interests. For France this would be a victory as she would like nothing better than the fall of the present cabinet, which she would regard as good luck. I do not believe that one could say the same of this government [i.e. Berlin, Vienna, London].

13. *Crispi to Tornielli, 17 October 1890* (ASC, Carte Pisani Dossi, 18, extract)

It is true that at one time we thought of renouncing Kassala in exchange for Zeila and a study was made on this basis. But for various reasons we decided not to present the proposal to the English delegates. Above all, we were convinced of the utmost importance of Kassala for the commercial future of Eritrea. Moreover, since the English had instructions only for the Sudan [negotiations] we should not have obtained Zeila and would have lost the force of our arguments for Kassala, since these were based on the necessity of defending our territory and tribes against Dervish attacks. Besides, since affairs on the Juba [River] are complicated we thought it best to keep back Zeila for these negotiations. . . .

Any renewal of the negotiations must be left to the English. If they make any comment on our troop movements towards the Atbara [River] say it is simply military necessity and that it is not our fault if there is no agreement.

We now reserve freedom of action and the occupation of Kassala is simply a matter of choosing the right moment. . . .

But this must not spoil Italo–British relations, cemented so long by our common interests. . . .

14. *Tornielli to Crispi, 23 October 1890* (ASC, Carte Pisani Dossi, 18, extract)

[Refers to Crispi of 17 October.] The conclusions of the despatch to which I have to reply, Minister, are extremely grave. . . . You say that you do not want to compromise Italo–British relations. Well, if we really want this then we have to take account not only of Salisbury's repeated declarations on this subject but also of public opinion, which is almost unanimous. I must insist that I have no reason to believe that any expansion of ours in the Sudan would leave the English government and public opinion indifferent. I have repeatedly said so for some time past.

If, as I firmly believe, common interests of prime importance link our foreign policy to that of Great Britain; if we want our military and political position not to be compromised and the idea to grow here that Italy is her natural ally; then we must move extremely carefully lest we should create the least suspicion of challenging English supremacy in the Nile Valley. If England should turn against us France would lose no time in profiting by it and must already know that London is far less intransigeant in the Mediterranean than Rome. If it were not for the millstone of the Tunisian question certainly our 'liberty of action' in the Sudan would have more practical value. Please take this into account in choosing the 'opportune moment'.

15. *Crispi to Torniellì, 20 November 1890* (AMEI, Tels 154/289, extract)

The Foreign Office are badly informed. The Dervishes are preparing against us and we are not supplying them.

Kassala was abandoned by the Egyptians and ceded to the Abyssinians and we can prove it. Anyway, if it were accepted that a territory which had been conquered by our blood and our money had to be restored to Egypt because Egypt had possessed it once upon a time, this would be an entirely new theory in international law and not a sovereignty in Europe would be safe. . . .

The behaviour of Lord Salisbury in recent times has not been what it was formerly and I do not know why. I appeal to your prudence and experience to make him as helpful as he used to be.

16. *Gandolfi to Rudinì, 19 February 1891* (AMEI, Tels 155/1028, extract)

Crispi's policy of expansion in Abyssinia was reduced to maintaining Article XVII, abandoning the Mareb–Belesa frontier through lack of troops and money. . . . This same motive forced Crispi, despite his wish to extend our possessions to Kassala, to give up its occupation. . . .

Actually, the troop strength for Africa approved last year was dictated by the concept of limiting our effective occupation to the Massowa–Asmara–Keren triangle . . . their numbers do not make it possible to conserve our frontiers in the south, unless we reach a friendly agreement with Menelik, nor to profit from the present

British hostility towards the Dervishes by extending our possessions west of Keren.

17. *Third Treaty of the Triple Alliance, 6 May 1891* (A. F.
    Pribram, *Secret Treaties*, 1, pp. 151–63)
[ARTICLES I–V are identical with ARTICLES I–V of the 1882 Treaty.
ARTICLE VI is identical to ARTICLE I of the German–Italian Treaty
of 1887. ARTICLE VII is identical with ARTICLE I of the Austro–
Italian Treaty of 1887. ARTICLE VIII is identical with ARTICLE II of
the German–Italian Treaty of 1887.]

ARTICLE IX

Germany and Italy engage to exert themselves for the maintenance
of the territorial *status quo* in the North African regions on the
Mediterranean, to wit, Cyrenaica, Tripolitania, and Tunisia. . . .

If unfortunately, as a result of a mature examination of the
situation, Germany and Italy should both recognise that the
maintenance of the *status quo* has become impossible, Germany
engages, after a formal and previous agreement, to support Italy
in any action in the form of occupation or other taking of guaranty
which the latter should undertake in these regions with a view to
an interest of equilibrium and of legitimate compensation.

It is understood that in such an eventuality the two Powers
would seek to place themselves likewise in agreement with
England.
[ARTICLE X is identical with ARTICLE III of the German–Italian
Treaty of 1887. ARTICLE XI is identical with ARTICLE IV of the
German–Italian Treaty of 1887. ARTICLES XII and XIII omitted.]

ARTICLE XIV

The present treaty shall remain in force for the space of six years
. . . but if it has not been denounced one year in advance by one or
another of the High Contracting Parties, it shall remain in force
for the same duration of six more years.
[ARTICLE XV is omitted.]

PROTOCOL

1. . . . the High Contracting Parties promise each other, from this
moment, in economic matters (finances, customs, railroads), in
addition to most-favoured-nation treatment, all of the facilities and

special advantages which would be compatible with the requirements of each of the three States and with their respective engagements with third Powers.

2. The accession of England being already acquired, in principle,
to the stipulations of the Treaty of this day which concern the
Orient . . . the High Contracting Parties shall exert themselves at
the opportune moment, and to the extent that circumstances may
permit it, to bring about an analogous accession with regard to the
North African territories of the central and western parts of the
Mediterranean, including Morocco. This accession might be
realised by an acceptance, on the part of England, of the programme established by Articles IX and X of the Treaty of this
day. . . .

Note. The Fourth and Fifth Treaties of the Triple Alliance, of 28
June 1902 and 5 December 1912 respectively were identical with
that of the Third, except as follows:

1. The Fourth Treaty had an additional Protocol dated 30 June
1902, an exchange of notes between Austria and Italy concerning
Tripolitania, in which 'the Austro–Hungarian Government, having no special interest to safeguard in Tripolitania and Cyrenaica,
has decided to undertake nothing which might interfere with the
action of Italy'.

2. The Fifth Treaty had an additional Protocol recognising that
'the territorial *status quo* in the North African regions . . . implies
the sovereignty of Italy over Tripolitania and Cyrenaica', and that
'the special arrangements concerning Albania and the Sanjak of
Novi-Bazar agreed upon between Austria–Hungary and Italy on
December 20, 1900/February 9, 1901, and on November 20/
December 15, 1909* are not modified by the renewal of the
Treaty of Alliance. . . .'

18. *Crispi in 1896: Blanc to Tornielli, 19 January 1896* (AMEI,
   Tels 219/105)
The basis of negotiations remains the simultaneous delimitation in
the Gulf of Aden with the changes in Tunisia. . . .

Without going so far as to recognise Tunisia as a simple French
department, our concessions in the Regency could, given the
exchange, be considerable. . . .

* Printed by F. R. Bridge, op. cit., p. 439.

Since the French are contemplating the usefulness of a concrete understanding with Italy, in view of the questions that are pre-occupying Europe and the various positions that the governments may take up, I leave it to Y[our] E[xcellency] to make it understood that also in other points we could find a common ground.

19. *Blanc to Ferrero, 20 January 1896* (AMEI, Tels 219/109, extract)

I do not know if the Vienna Cabinet is proceeding with this [the approach to Salisbury concerning the Mediterranean Agreements] out of simple courtesy to us, as Nigra says that Goluchowski does not believe the moment favourable. Nigra persists in the belief that if Germany does not explicitly affirm her solidarity with the Mediterranean group in the Eastern Question, then we shall not really obtain the support of Austria–Hungary. . . . We are inclined to believe that . . . England intends to re-acquire her freedom of action, if necessary alone, in the east. In this case I think that we shall have to accompany her, even if Austria–Hungary – basing herself on the German attitude – adopts a hesitant position. Y[our] E[xcellency] should bear in mind this situation and associate yourself to the extent that you think useful with Count Deym's approach.

20. *Crispi to Sonnino, 27 January 1896* (MRR, Carte Crispi 668/1/5, extract)

These conventions [the Triple Alliance and the Mediterranean Agreements] are a guarantee of peace for Europe but we must not forget that they are a burden for our country.

The Triple Alliance was renewed by Rudinì in 1891 for twelve years . . . the time to renew it is very near . . . should we denounce the treaty or keep it? And if we keep it should we revise it? . . .

To renew the *Triplice* on the original terms would be damaging, we must improve the conditions. Through being allied to Germany we incur the enmity of France. They are waging war against us, which we have to bear alone without any assistance from our allies.

By denouncing the treaty of the *Triplice* we shall suffer the distrust of Austria and Germany, with no hope of acquiring the friendship of France. Moreover, even freeing ourselves from

Austria and Germany, we should be unable to follow an independent policy without strong armaments.

Posing the dilemma in this way we cannot free ourselves from the *Triplice* for the present. The lesser evil is to stay in it. In renewing it our interest is to improve the terms. It is necessary that the two allied powers associate themselves with us in all the questions in which we are opposed by France.

21. *Changing the helm: Tornielli to Rudinì, 13 March 1896* (DDI, iii, I, 13, extract)

Favoured by circumstances, by the errors of Germany, by the rivalry between the latter and England, France in the last year has composed many of her differences with England. . . . Consequently, the position that we long hoped to see England in – forced by necessity to side with the Triple Alliance – will not last much longer. . . .

On our part there is no reason to fear that France is inspired still by the ideas of 1849 or even those of Thiers or MacMahon. The papal question in the hands of the French government is no more than something which can be used to annoy us. Nobody in France thinks of unmaking Italy. . . .

You will remember, perhaps, what I wrote to you from London in 1891. At that time it seemed indispensable for our security that England should join the alliance of which we were a part.

Much has happened since then and everything indicates that the danger of being left isolated or in a state of great inferiority in the Mediterranean has been greatly augmented. The growth of British sea power then, as now, requires our help to be fully effective. England will have as many ships as she wants and the best ships in the world, but she has insufficient personnel and defended ports in the Mediterranean. The united forces of Italy and England would assure maritime supremacy for themselves and impose peace. . . .

I would never propose to bargain with the natural adversary [France] of our principal ally that we should abandon the alliance. But the continuation of the alliance without any assurance of British assistance seems to me to expose us to grave dangers and perhaps certain harm. Could we not stipulate the continuation for one year to give time not to us but to Germany to make certain of the accession of England? Do not the differences between the two nations give us good reason to look carefully at the future?

22. *Caetani to Nigra and Lanza, 26 April 1896* (DDI, iii, I, 87, extract)

The confidential exchange of views which has just taken place on the subject of the ministerial declarations of May 1882 concerning England, leads us to believe that the affirmations contained in these declarations is still in accordance with the common thinking of the three powers. Still today, the three governments agree in considering England as outside the combinations envisaged when the Triple Alliance was created and renewed.

As far as we are concerned, this statement is the only way of reconciling our obligations under the letter of the Treaty and the exigencies of our own situation. Italy would find herself in an impossible situation, if the Treaty arose; her geographical position would not permit her to join her allies in a struggle against the two strongest maritime powers in the world. No Minister in Italy could take the responsibility of leading the country into such a war. . . .

Our frankness must be the proof to the two governments Germany and Austria of our scrupulous fidelity towards the Triple Alliance, both as it exists and as we wish to see it maintained.

23. *Visconti Venosta to Tornielli, 30 August 1897* (DDI, iii, 2, 199, extract)

That something is changing in Europe is certain. An evolution is starting which is difficult to predict where and in what form it will finish. In this uncertainty about the future, I believe that today the best policy for us is to keep the present basis of our policy; but at the same time to make it our aim to improve relations with Russia and France. This improvement will be useful, whatever happens, both in the present and in the future. Such a programme is possible because of present circumstances, in which the *Triplice* and the Franco–Russian alliance appear to be two syndicates engaged in the same great game – the maintenance of European peace. But the *rapprochement* with France requires a certain reciprocity of intentions. The French government, without being exactly ill disposed towards us, seems to be so absorbed in the Russian alliance that it does not attach much importance to us and treats us as a *quantité negligéable*. The undertaking is made even more difficult by the disposition of French public opinion, always so susceptible, so partial. How can we always avoid every incident?

24. *Lanza to Visconti Venosta, 14 May 1900* (DDI, iii, 3, 397, extract)

It is unnecessary to tell you that ... I have tried many times to bring the conversation with Count Bülow around to a discussion of the Morocco–Tripoli question which is so important to us. His replies were always evasive and dilatory. . . . 'Until now', he suggested, 'all the information I have been able to gather induces me to believe that France does not contemplate advancing in Morocco at the moment; but the information is not too certain and I am waiting for more. Anyway, France would think twice before taking Morocco.' [Lanza thinks he will probably do something.]

In the end this ... might be enough, providing that in Italy they are really thinking of maintaining the *status quo* and not aspiring to the occupation of Tripoli in the near future. This is the difficulty. I think it is impossible, at least I don't feel capable of persuading Germany to say, 'If France goes into Morocco, then you take Tripoli: Germany will support you'. Here they know very well that once they said this the event would shortly follow, and Germany does not want to produce a state of affairs which, at the least, would lead to an armed clash between Italy and Turkey. That Turkey could be induced to let us take Tripoli from her, is an illusion that I do not share.

25. *Tittoni and the Balkans: Tittoni to Avarna, 7 November 1909* (F. Tommassini, *L'Italia alla viglia della guerra*, V, p. 549, extract)

In other terms, we both wish and believe that we are in agreement with Austria in wanting: first, the conservation of the *status quo* in the Ottoman Empire; second, when such conservation is no longer possible, the development of the Balkan states on the basis of the principle of nationality; third, when neither are possible and, despite everything, it comes to an Austrian occupation, then the assurance of adequate compensation for Italy. On the first two points there is not only Austrian and Italian agreement but also the full assent of Russia. . . . The third point concerns only Austria and Italy. . . . If this is right then my task does not seem in the least complicated, as it appears to Aehrenthal; instead it seems simple and clear. If, however, this is not the case, if the declarations of disinterest on somebody's part conceal ambitions for fresh territorial acquisitions, then certainly complications will arise: but not through my fault.

26. *The July Crisis: Di San Giuliano to Bollati, 14 July 1914*
    (DDI, iv, XII, no. 225, extract)

The belief that the principal cause of Italo–Austrian dissension in Albania is the attitude of Aliotti and Löwenthal at Durazzo is pretty superficial. . . .

Thanks to my efforts, seconded by Giolitti, Italian feelings towards Austria had become more friendly by last summer than they had ever been. All the friendly acts of Austria during the Libyan war were played up at my instigation; all the unfriendly ones . . . kept a close secret. During the Balkan wars Italo–Austrian relations were put to several severe tests, but we overcame them, and they emerged stronger than ever – until the Hohenlohe decrees came along. Although no Italian has yet suffered from them, these offended and deeply wounded the Italian Nation, which from this moment has shown itself always more hostile towards Austria and inclined to see in her an implacable enemy, sometimes hidden, sometimes open. The policy of close relations with Austria is seen as a *politique de dupe*, ingenuous, unworthy and dangerous. Once again the old *giri di walzer* has been raised, forgetting the dangers it led to, the humiliations we suffered: they are beginning to ask whether it suits us to remain in the Triple Alliance and whether it would not be more natural and convenient to join the Triple *Entente* – of which one power is similar to us in every respect and two are, like us, guided by liberal and modern principles. . . .

Unfortunately Albania is not the only reason for division between Italy and Austria, imperilling the Triple Alliance. . . .

We cannot allow Lovcen to pass into the hands of Austria, or see the latter gain territory, or see Albania become her southern frontier, unless we receive adequate territorial compensation, either in the Italian provinces of Austria or in the south of Albania. It is necessary that the German government be disillusioned on this score.

The same consideration applies to the possible Austro–Serb conflict in consequence of the assassination of the Archduke Ferdinand.

Our entire object in this case must be to prevent Austrian aggrandisement without corresponding territorial compensation on our part. And in this case the difficulty is aggravated by the fact that, as I explained to Flotow, we find it impossible to support Austria when she presents demands to Serbia that are incompatible with the liberal principles of our public law, demands inspired by the ideas of the Holy Alliance, legitimism and the divine right of kings. These ideas are not yet dead in Vienna or Berlin. . . .

In my view it is possible – perhaps even probable – that in the not-too-distant future we ought to leave the Triple Alliance, but it is certain that for the present we should remain in it. . . .

I do not think that leaving would improve our relations with Austria because the causes of discord would remain the same (Albania, Lovcen, etc.) whilst the means of attenuating the discord, that is the conciliatory work of Germany and the interest she has that Italy and Austria remain allies, would disappear.

27. *Di San Giuliano to Bollati and Avarna, 24 July 1914*
    (DDI, iv, 12, 468, extract)

I beg Y[our] E[xcellency] to declare at once to the Minister of Foreign Affairs that if Austria–Hungary should proceed to even temporary territorial occupations without our previous consent, then she will be in violation of Article VII of the Treaty of Alliance and we shall reserve our position. Besides, I think it opportune to observe that Austria–Hungary should not have taken the step she has, that may give rise to dangerous complications, without the previous consent of the allies. . . . It is our wish to follow a policy in concord with our allies but in Balkan affairs, except in the case of Albania for which there are special agreements, this will not be possible unless we are assured of agreement on the interpretation of Article VII. Without this our policy must be directed towards preventing the territorial aggrandisement of Austria–Hungary and must, therefore, proceed in agreement with those powers with the same interests. We are informing our allies of this through a sense of loyalty and with the hope of avoiding such a necessity.

28. *Salandra favours war: Martini–Salandra conversation, 17
    September 1914* (F. Martini, *Diario, 1914–1918,* pp. 102–4,
    extract)

Salandra: Our minister in Bucharest, Fasciotti, thinks that if we
          enter the war Romania will also.

Martini: And what does the king think?

Salandra: He understands the gravity of the situation. . . .

Martini: There is a rumour in Rome that the queen said . . . that the king would abdicate rather than go to war with Austria. . . .

Salandra: No, the king is not opposed nor does he hesitate: he does not want to decide himself: he will accept the decision of the government whatever it is. If it is for war, he told me that he will go to the war, as is the tradition of his house, just like his grandfather, his father and his uncle. . . .

Martini: But even if he does not want to decide himself, which way does he incline? Have you managed to discover this?

Salandra: I believe he inclines towards war. . . .

Martini: And you yourself, what have you decided?

Salandra: What you said in your letter is right. I think we must decide, re-open negotiations with England: I want to make another agreement. . . . Also I want an agreement with Romania binding ourselves reciprocally not to abandon neutrality without due warning to the other of the intention.

Martini: I agree completely: but I think we should not delay too long: I fear the speedy defeat of Austria. . . .

Salandra: No doubt about it: to gain time we should almost wish her a little victory. . . . Another thing. Do you think we should warn Giolitti of our decision? Call him to Rome? I am almost bound to him. . . .

Martini: I do not see any difficulty in warning Giolitti: but I can see very grave difficulty in asking his opinion. What if it is contrary to ours and he says so, what will we do then? Given that our decision is dictated by our conscience, by considerations pondered at length, we cannot change it to please Giolitti: he would have grounds for complaint if we asked him *pro forma* and took no notice of his views.

Salandra: Giolitti will probably say neither yes nor no and escape by the skin of his teeth, safe to condemn us if things go badly. . . . Now we must think of the military preparations. Amongst other things we must think of over-

> coats . . . of acquiring, if possible, a siege train and of
> talking about this to the Minister of the Treasury . . .
> even that is no small undertaking. . . .

The conversation continued on matters of minor importance and
closed with these words of Salandra:

> We cannot hesitate: if I were to think that I had the
> chance of restoring Trento and Trieste to Italy and I let
> it slip, then I would have no more peace of mind and I
> should ask myself what on earth I spent thirty years in
> parliament for.

29. *Italy and Romania: Sonnino to Fasciotti (Bucharest), 25 February*
    1915 (Sonnino Papers, 31/51, extract)

If in our enquiry we referred to 30 April as a terminal date this is
because the general situation is maturing rapidly and everything
leads us to believe that it will be difficult to postpone our own
definite decisions beyond the beginning of spring. . . .

We too have an interest in not precipitating events, so that we
can complete our preparations more fully and so that we can take
account as far as possible of the general progress of the war. But,
on the other hand, we must be careful not to miss opportunities,
and it is not always possible to leave our own decisions until the
last moment when we wish to co-ordinate our actions with those
of others.

It is exactly the close observation of the general situation and
the way it is always changing that has led us to put off a definite
decision still, but we wanted to indicate to this Romanian government – in conformity with the agreement of 23 September – our
present tendency so that it could estimate whether this is in agreement with its own intentions.

We shall certainly keep this government informed of every new
phase of the international situation and of every further decision on
our part, leaving the details to be discussed between us.

30. *Austria's final offer – Sonnino's comments* (S. Sonnino, *Diario,*
    1866–1916, pp. 144–7, 11 May 1915)

Prince Bülow. This morning (9 a.m.) sent me a letter in which he
enclosed a summary, signed by him and Baron Macchio, of the
concessions which Austria–Hungary is prepared to make to Italy,
enumerated as follows:

Les concessions que l'Autriche-Hongrie est prête à faire à l'Italie sont les suivantes:

1° - tout le Tyrol qui est de nationalité italienne,

2° - toute la rive occidentale de l'Isonzo, qui est de nationalité italienne avec Gradisca,

3° - pleine autonomie municipale, Université italienne et port franc pour Trieste, qui sera ville libre,

4° - Valona,

5° - désintéressement complet de l'Autriche en Albanie,

6° - sauvegarde pour les intérêts nationaux des sujets italiens en Autriche-Hongrie,

7° - examen bienveillant de voeux que l'Italie émettrait encore sur tout l'ensemble des questions qui forment l'objet des négociations (notamment Gorizia et les îles),

8° - l'Empire d'Allemagne assume toute garantie pour l'exécution fidèle et loyale de l'arrangement à conclure entre l'Italie et l'Autriche-Hongrie.

L'Ambassadeur d'Autriche-Hongrie et l'Ambassadeur d'Allemagne garantissent l'authenticité des propositions surmentionnées.

10 a.m. I observed to the prince that in the present situation, which was so difficult and delicate, every uncertainty of an expression of assurances is a reason for diffidence and suspicion. To refer the points enumerated to my colleagues in the government, therefore, and in time to parliament, it seemed to me necessary to elucidate various points in the offers listed.

1. Trentino. On 6 May Baron Macchio excluded from cession the east side of the Valle della Noce, not for reasons of nationality but for considerations of a military character. Was it instead included in the present offer? And for the Val di Fassa and the Ampezzano Burián and Macchio had given as their reason for excluding them that they were considered romansch rather than Italian. We consider them Italian. Does the formula used now include these valleys or not? Regarding the Trentino, Giolitti yesterday ... believed that Austria–Hungary was disposed to hand it over immediately. Is this in fact so? ... The question of the conscripts was an important point on which I had often laid stress in the past; this must be clarified.

2. On the frontier towards the Isonzo, I observed that the precise interpretation given to the phrase used in the note by Baron Macchio since 6 May ... was most imperfect from the

military viewpoint and would give rise to constant disputes and questions. . . .

6. I observed that the phrase used was so generic as to say little or nothing. It must be made much clearer and precise. . . .

7. I observed that the promise of a benevolent examination of our wishes on the other questions did not imply anything serious or concrete and was more inclined to inspire distrust than re-assurance. . . . To speak of two islands in general, without any precision, lacked serious intent when there were hundreds of islands, some miniscule, existing in the Adriatic. . . .

It was not possible to put vague assurances to parliament, precise and firm data were needed.

Bülow took note of all this saying that he would obtain clarification of the offers from Vienna and Berlin.

31. *Serbia and Croatian union opposed: Sonnino to Imperiali, 3 August 1915* (Sonnino Papers, 31/787, extract)

. . . we can in no way adhere to any sort of collective communication to Nish which . . . tends to prejudice the final solution to the questions interesting Fiume and Croatia beyond that stipulated in the Convention of London and that implies the adhesion of the Powers towards one rather than another settlement of these territories.

The only concession we can make . . . is to allow that Serbia should be notified unofficially that the four Powers are prepared to concede her access to the sea in the future through a stretch of the Dalmatian coast including the ports of Spalato [Split] and Ragusa [Dubrovnik], subject to their neutralisation. This to be made dependent upon Serbian helpfulness now in relation to the un-contested zone of Macedonia, and her [eventual] evacuation of Elbassan and Tirana and the Moslem territories of central Albania.

32. *Italy and Asia Minor: Sonnino to Imperiali, 6 July 1917* (Sonnino Papers 45/1119, extract)

Now it is a fact that at St Jean de Maurienne apart from the question of Asia Minor we examined the Greek question; and, as is well known to Y[our] E[xcellency] and to the British government, our conduct in the latest developments of the Greek question was subordinated to the decisions in our favour concerning Asia

Minor. . . . It would not be 'fair' [in original] that the British government, now that it has achieved what was proposed to us in Greece without any opposition on our part, should modify what was decided conjointly in our favour in Asia Minor. I am sure that this consideration will have a great effect upon the War Cabinet and in this way we shall avoid a renewal of the difficulties that the question of Asia Minor raised between Italy and her allies . . . as it involves the whole question of the Mediterranean equilibrium, which represents a vital and primeval interest for Italy.

33. *Italy at the Peace Conference: Colosimo (Minister of the Colonies) to Sonnino, 6 December 1918* (DDI, vi, I, 475, extract)

Balfour's speech of 29 October . . . with his explicit declaration that 'in no case . . . would the German colonies be restored' has significant importance for Italy. . . .

There is no doubt that, bearing in mind the enormous advantages that France and England propose obtaining in Africa and in Asia in the colonial field, what we ask is very little. As I told you in my letter of 4 January 1917 . . . what we need is something in reserve. . . . I said then and now confirm that the African territory that would really suit us, for a variety of reasons, would be Portuguese Angola; not as an occupied territory but as a region to be exploited through Italian capital and colonists. . . . I come to this conclusion not only on the grounds of equity, but also as a means of defence against the danger that France and England, under the guise of creating autonomous governments in the countries they wish to retain as a consequence of the war, should prepare formidable economic monopolies in their own favour. . . .

I have been shocked by the lack of reaction by our representatives in Paris and London to the dilatory replies by the British and French governments. . . . I should have thought that in the face of a vital national interest like this one could expect that our ambassadors would be not merely cold transmitters of messages but warm supporters of our just cause.

But, thinking . . . that Your Excellency has been one of the principal architects of our victory, I recovered my spirits quickly as you cannot allow the colonial question to become a great Italian delusion. I have complete faith that Your Excellency . . . will become also the architect of our colonial fortune, now so necessary for a great Italy at home and abroad.

34. *Sonnino to Sforza, 26 January 1919* (Sonnino Papers, 43/47, extract)

Following the entry of America into the war there has been a fundamental change in the international appearance of the interests of the Mediterranean Powers in Asiatic Turkey. Annexations and zones of administration are no longer spoken of; instead assistance to the native peoples, who must be free to choose a great power. To harmonise their aspirations with the principles of Wilson, we can expect France and England at an opportune moment to provoke appeals and petitions from notables, communities, tribes, municipalities and other bodies in favour of their respective help to the regions concerned. True, there exists a strong current amongst the Arabs for absolute independence, but it is likely that this current . . . will be more or less eliminated. . . .

There may derive from this a danger to Italian aspirations, which are connected with our vital interests in the Mediterranean. Our obvious competitors may oppose our claims, basing themselves on Wilson's principles, by saying that no people in Asiatic Turkey show themselves favourable to Italian assistance, or ask for it. We must see to this. [There follow detailed instructions on how to organise such appeals without making it too obvious.]

35. *Sonnino to Martino, 30 April 1919* (L. Aldrovandi-Marescotti, *La guerra diplomatica*, pp. 764–6, extract)

The declarations made by Premier Orlando to the Italian parliament which have led to such an unanimous vote on this order of the day are now well known:

> The Chamber, guardian of the dignity and interpreter of the will of the Italian people, declares complete solidarity with the Government and reaffirms full confidence that it will see prevail the supreme rights of Italy as an indispensable condition of a just and lasting peace.

After the vote it remains to the Government to examine the action to pursue. I draw Y[our] E[xcellency's] attention to the following point in Premier Orlando's speech . . .

> . . . until the entire disagreement between our allies and the Associated Power is resolved, the conclusion of peace is not possible as far as Italy is concerned; and we have already said that a peace which is not a general peace is not justice.

The possibility of reaching a compromise acceptable to Italy must be understood as subordinated to the following essentials:

Apart from the Brenner and the line of the Alps including Volosca to the border with Fiume, and apart from the islands of the Pact of London, Italy must have the right to the cities of Fiume, Zara and Sebenico.

The discussion can only concern the way of putting these rights into effect.

As far as our participation in the peace with Germany is concerned, it is subordinated to one of the following hypotheses:

(a) if President Wilson adheres to such an agreement with Italy we have no more to say;

(b) if President Wilson refuses, the consent of the Allied Powers will be enough, provided that they bind themselves from now on to recognise and guarantee the annexation of the above territories, an annexation by virtue of an act of public law.

Following such consent we can participate in the conclusion of peace with Germany.

36. *Collective telegram* to Sonnino, 5 May 1919*
(Aldrovandi-Marescotti, *Guerra diplomatica,* pp. 796–7)
From the conversations of the three ambassadors yesterday it emerges that the situation is worsening. There is now a serious danger that Great Britain and France will declare the Treaty of London lapsed if the Italian delegates remain absent from the opening of the conference with the Germans. The three ambassadors have formed the impression that it is not a case of empty threats. It is worth reflecting that, apart from contestability of the attitude of Lloyd George and Clemenceau, it is a fact that it is in the interests of Great Britain and France to seize this pretext to get out of the heavy obligations of the treaty, by employing the accusation of holding back the conclusion of peace. The jurists of one side or another can dispute *ad infinitum* but behind this lies the manifest interest of the two allies. We should remember the specious pretext used by Great Britain to get out of the August 1917 agreement.

It is evident that in the present situation the Treaty of London is our only means of salvation, whether we are reduced to claiming

* Signed: Crespi, Imperiali, Bonin, Cellere, Martino.

its execution pure and simple or whether we have to use it as a basis for a package deal.

In this state of affairs we must save the Treaty of London from any dispute, however artificial. The only way is for the Italian plenipotentaries to return for the opening conference with the Germans.

This involves a question of substance and a question of form. The question of substance lies in the previous settlement, if only in general, of the Adriatic problem. Today, confronted by the pre-arranged plan which blocks us and our isolation, that seems impossible.

The question of form consists of finding a means that allows the Italian delegation to return to Paris with the substantial point un-solved but saving the prestige of our country and the face of the delegation.

However, on this point we cannot express an opinion as the only judge is the R[oyal] Government bearing in mind the state of Italian public opinion. The dangers of the situation require a prompt decision.

37. *The Dodecanese: Curzon to Martino, 15 October 1922* (FO 371, C14136/1953/19)

... the question of the Dodecanese is one from which His Majesty's Government were, and still are, unable to disinterest themselves. ...

... the question of the Dodecanese formed the subject of repeated discussions between the two Governments; and since in entering upon such discussions M. Schanzer must be held to have admitted, contrary to his present contention, that the matter was not one which could be settled between Greece and Italy alone, His Majesty's Government were at that time prepared, as part of a general settlement, to use their good offices with the Greek Government to secure if possible some modification of the treaty of the 10th August; but they were not prepared to consider that the Dodecanese question was one which could be detached from the general settlement, or decided by unilateral action on the part of Italy. Such a solution of the question is not one which His Majesty's Government were then, or are now, willing either to recognise or to admit. ...

If the Italian Government now repudiate their undertaking to cede the islands to Greece, they cannot expect Great Britain to agree that Turkey should cede them to Italy under the treaty of peace for which negotiations are now about to reopen. His Majesty's Government have already manifested their readiness to recognise that the defeat of the Greek army in Asia Minor justifies Turkey in demanding important modifications in the territorial clauses of the Treaty of Sèvres. The three Allied Powers, Great Britain, France and Italy in agreement with Greece herself have consequently decided to allow Turkey's claim to the recovery of the territories in Anatolia and Eastern Thrace when the inhabitants of Turkish race constitute either a majority or at least a large compact body.

6. This consideration does not apply to the case of the islands, which are entirely peopled by Greeks. Moreover, Greece has always maintained as against Turkey the command of the sea; and, but for the fortuitous circumstance of the Italian occupation, she would no doubt have become possessed of the Dodecanese, as she became possessed of the other Aegean Islands in 1913, and would be holding them at the present moment in all security and with every prospect of permanency. . . .

. . . I would ask you also to indicate to them that, as was stated in the letter addressed by Lord Milner to M. Scialoja on the 13th April, 1920, the important concessions which His Majesty's Government were prepared to make to Italy in Africa could only become effective as part of the general settlement and of all the issues raised at the Peace Conference, which settlement included, among other matters, the cession to Greece, within the limits of the treaty of 1920, of the Dodecanese Islands. If the Italian Government now decide to repudiate this agreement regarding the Dodecanese, they should realise that such repudiation will logically and inevitably entail the cancellation of the other engagements into which, as part of the general settlement, His Majesty's Government had entered.

38. *M. Mussolini to Mr. MacDonald (received May 6), Rome, May 2 1924* (FO 371, C7363/160/19)

My dear Prime Minister,

YOUR personal letter was especially welcome to me for the reason that it shows me that our political motives are inspired by the same wish to improve and consolidate Anglo–Italian relations and tend to the same end of clearing the ground of all the causes of misunderstandings which arise as much from the complexity of the questions resulting from the war as from the spirit in which they have been approached, which perhaps was not always, as it should have been, that of an impartial estimate of reciprocal interests. . . .

It is no longer opportune to examine how and why the two questions of Jubaland and the Dodecanese have come to be treated together, since your Excellency proposes to give immediate effect to the agreement between England and Italy in regard to Jubaland. I note with the greatest satisfaction this friendly decision, and thank you for having been willing spontaneously to perform an act which will certainly have a happy repercussion on Italian opinion. As soon as I hear that you agree, I will make arrangements for the Italian experts to go to London to agree on the convention to regulate the migration of the nomad tribes.

In order to respond to the friendly and courteous attitude manifested by your Excellency, and wishing to take into account the interest of the British Government in an important Mediterranean question, I have no difficulty in informing you of my point of view and my intentions in regard to the Dodecanese. . . .

Italian possession of the Dodecanese constitutes consequently a kind of buffer which prevents friction between two nations – the Turkish and the Greek – divided by recent and ancient military and political animosities. . . .

I must also declare frankly to your Excellency that, so far as Rhodes and the islands which form part of the Rhodes group are concerned, together with those others in which Italy has paramount interests, I would not be able to take finally into consideration the possibility of renouncing Italian sovereignty over them. Only for such islands in which Italy has lesser interest could I eventually contemplate the possibility of a different settlement in regard to them. But such dispositions could only be justified by the interest of making an efficacious contribution to the final and pacific settlement of the Eastern Mediterranean, and these would accordingly demand adequate guarantees and compensation, which, moreover, should not be difficult to define. . . .

Documents

39. *Italo–Abyssinian Agreement, 2 August 1928* (RIIA, *Documents* 1928, p. 240)

ARTICLE I
There shall be durable peace and perpetual friendship between the kingdom of Italy and the Ethiopian Empire.

ARTICLE II
The two Governments mutually pledge themselves not to take, under any pretext, any action which might be detrimental to the independence of the other, and to safeguard the interests of their respective countries.

ARTICLE III
The two Governments undertake to develop and promote the trade existing between the two countries. ...

ARTICLE V
The two Governments agree to submit to a procedure of conciliation or arbitration any questions which may arise between them, and which it has not been possible to settle by the usual diplomatic means, without having recourse to the force of arms. By common agreement, notes shall be exchanged between the two Governments concerning the method of choosing arbitrators. ...

40. *Protocols signed by Austria, Hungary, and Italy, in Rome, 17 March 1934* (RIIA, *Documents* 1933, p. 396)

PROTOCOL NO. I
The Head of the Government of His Majesty the King of Italy, the Federal Chancellor of the Austrian Republic, and President of the Royal Council of Hungary, animated by a desire to co-operate in the maintenance of peace and in the economic restoration of Europe, on the basis of respect for the independence and rights of every state; persuaded that collaboration between the three Governments in this sense can establish real premises for wider co-operation with other States; undertake, for the achievement of the above-mentioned objects, to concert together, on all problems which particularly interest them and also on those of a general character, with the aim of developing in the spirit of the existing

Italo–Austrian, Italo–Hungarian, and Austro–Hungarian Treaties of Friendship based upon the recognition of the existence of their numerous common interests, a mutually agreed policy which shall be directed towards effective collaboration between European states and particularly between Italy, Austria, and Hungary.

To this end, the three Governments will proceed to common consultation each time that at least one of them may consider this course opportune.

41. *Extract from speech by Mussolini to the General Staff,* The Times, *28 August 1934* (RIIA, *Documents* 1934, p. 362)

It is, therefore, necessary to be prepared for war not to-morrow but to-day. We are becoming – and shall become so increasingly because this is our desire – a military nation. A militaristic nation, I will add, since we are not afraid of words. To complete the picture, war-like – that is to say, endowed ever to a higher degree with the virtues of obedience, sacrifice, and dedication to country. This means that the whole life of the nation, political, economic, and spiritual, must be systematically directed towards our military requirements. War has been described as the Court of Appeal but pursue the course dictated by their strength and by their historical dynamic nature, it falls that, in spite of all conferences, all protocols, and all the more or less highest and good intentions, the hard fact of war may be anticipated to accompany the human kind in the centuries to come just as it stands on record at the dawn of human history.

42. *Agreements adopted at the Stresa Conference, 11–14 April 1935* (RIIA, *Documents* 1935, 1, p. 80)

Joint Resolution of the Stresa Conference, April 14, 1935.

The Representatives of the Governments of Italy, France, and the United Kingdom have examined at Stresa the general European situation in the light of the results of the exchanges of views which have taken place in recent weeks, of the decision taken on March 16 by the German Government, and of the information obtained by British Ministers during the visits recently paid by them to several European capitals. Having considered the bearing of this situation on the policy defined in the arrangements reached respectively in Rome and in London, they found themselves in complete agreement on the various matters discussed. . . .

They confirmed the Anglo–Franco–Italian declarations of February 17 and September 27, 1934, in which the three Governments recognized that the necessity of maintaining the independence and integrity of Austria would continue to inspire their common policy.

Referring to the Franco–Italian protocol of January 7, 1935, and to the Anglo–French declarations of February 3, 1935, in which the decision was reaffirmed to consult together as to the measures to be taken in the case of threats to the integrity and independence of Austria, they agreed to recommend that representatives of all the Governments enumerated in the protocol of Rome should meet at a very early date with a view to concluding the Central European agreement. . . .

It was regretfully recognized that the method of unilateral repudiation adopted by the German Government, at a moment when steps were being taken to promote a freely-negotiated settlement of the question of armaments, had undermined public confidence in the security of a peaceful order. Moreover, the magnitude of the declared programme of German rearmament, already well in process of execution, had invalidated the quantitative assumptions upon which efforts for disarmament had hitherto been based and shaken the hopes by which those efforts were inspired. . . .

43. *Italy approaches Germany: The Ambassador in Italy to the Foreign Ministry, 21 June 1935* (DGFP, C, iv, no. 164)

. . . Precisely *what* is desired of Germany at the present juncture is not easy to define. What my above-mentioned confidant has to say on this point is, however, not without interest; he thinks that the *intesa* might, for instance, be developed along the following three lines:

1) Mutual *désinteressement* in questions which do not concern the other party: e.g. possibly Italy's *désinteressement* in the Eastern Pact, Germany's *désinteressement* in the Albanian question and in respect of Italy's Balkan policy – a point which would raise once again the question of a general German–Italian understanding regarding South East Europe. To this must, of course, be added benevolent neutrality in the Abyssinian question.

2) A common policy towards the League of Nations, proceeding from the assumption that Italy will withdraw in the autumn.

3) Common principles governing policy towards colonial ques-

tions, whereby Germany (besides adopting the attitude already mentioned to the Abyssinian question) would concentrate her desiderata on her own former colonies, thereby being assured of Italian goodwill. Italy's Abyssinian policy – as may be remarked in passing – is of advantage to us in that it introduces a dynamic element into the static situation of the colonial problem.

Behind all this there remains, of course, as a *pièce de résistance* or window-dressing, according to the way one looks at it, the Austrian problem. My confidant employed the following formula in this context: 'Postponement of the Austrian problem until such time as questions of territorial revision in South Eastern Europe become acute in any case.'

There is no need to emphasize that at the back of all cogitation as to how to achieve good and stable relations with Germany is the uncertain and difficult situation in which, to the discerning eye, Italy finds herself. So unfavourable is this situation that we cannot but wonder whether it would indeed be worth our while seriously to strive for friendly relations with a country like Italy in her present position. Understandable though this doubt may be, the question must, in my opinion, be answered in the affirmative. Neither the tactical nor the 'atmospheric' benefits of such relations with Italy should be rated too low even in future. To this extent the hints given by my confidant appear to me at least worthy of note. At all events it would in my opinion be advisable, as I have repeatedly stressed, to make use of every opportunity that offers to make the Italians feel that we fully consider them to be a Great Power and that we attach decisive importance to maintaining good relations with them. At the present moment I should have thought this could, for instance, be conveyed by our informing them in a friendly manner of our point of view and our aims over the London Naval Agreement.

... Attached to this report is the following handwritten minute (6001/E443085–86):

'1) The general idea is correct! 2) But why a *German initiative now*? 3) What good would it do us? 4) Italy's price will presumably come steadily down. 5) Gaining time means everything to us. 6) If commitments are unavoidable, then as late as possible. 7) If it were Cerruti who spoke and reported in this way I could understand it. K[opke].'

44. *Mussolini's demands in Abyssinia: Mussolini to Sir E. Drummond, 31 July 1935* (FO 371, J3472/1/1)

I HAVE in mind the substance of the conversations which I had on the 24th and the 25th June last with Mr. Eden, the United Kingdom Minister for League of Nations Affairs. . . .

The Italian Government themselves are also convinced that a system of collective security can alone ensure peace in Europe and it certainly has not been the Italian Government that has taken initiatives or concluded agreements which were not in harmony with the results of collective discussions. With these ideas in mind, and in pursuit of these aims, the Italian Government also consider that it is necessary to utilise the services of the League of Nations as far as may be possible and useful.

It thus being clearly established that Italy does not intend to withdraw her loyal and full collaboration from the League of Nations unless she is compelled to do so, I must with equal loyalty state that I do not consider that the prestige and strength of the League can be diminished if it adopts in regard to Abyssinia the only attitude which is suited to the conditions of that State, if, in short, the League of Nations were forced to choose between a colonial conflict in Africa and the contribution which Italy can make to the tranquillity of Europe.

The Italian Government do not dispute the good intentions behind the British Government's proposal to cede to Abyssinia the Port of Zeila with a corridor across British Somaliland, in return for the cession by Abyssinia to Italy of territory in the Ogaden country as part of a general arrangement including concessions in the economic sphere.

If this proposal was not accepted by the Italian Government, the reasons were fully explained to Mr. Eden and I regret that I do not find in your Excellency's note any arguments brought forward to meet these clear reasons, which I here repeat: namely, that the offer of the Port of Zeila would have resulted in making Abyssinia a maritime Power, with the consequent implication that the possibility would have been increased of that State becoming an ever greater menace to the safety not only of the Italian, but also of the French and British colonies.

It is not only as from to-day that the Italian Government have adopted this definite point of view; as long ago as 1931 the Emperor of Ethiopia offered to cede to the Italian Government the Ogaden territory provided that she secured a territorial outlet to the sea at a point in the colony of Eritrea near French Somaliland....

... How could the British Government think that the remedy for the existing state of affairs was to strengthen Abyssinia's position, to make the importation of arms easier for her and to withdraw all control over her maritime activities from the Italian Government by transferring elsewhere Ethiopia's maritime outlet to the sea? The British Government cannot certainly have had these considerations in mind, or they would have realised that, if the reasons for the Italo–Ethiopian conflict lie essentially in Italy's necessity to guarantee the security of her own colonies, it was no solution of this conflict to increase rather than diminish the Italian Government's reasons for apprehension. It is not a question, therefore, as your Excellency assumes in your note, that Italy has insufficiently appreciated the territorial sacrifice which Britain was prepared to make without asking for any compensation. It is rather a question of establishing whether this sacrifice of territory would serve the purpose of solving the controversy and of eliminating the reasons which are the fundamental cause of the existing conflict....

... From what is stated above two essential points emerge:—

(1) That the Italian Government have no intention of injuring in any way the prestige of the League of Nations or of lessening their own collaboration in the principle of collective security, since their action is directed against a State whose existence and activities have nothing to do with the principle of European collective security. To refuse to admit this standpoint of the Italian Government would be tantamount to a readiness to sacrifice deliberately the interests of a State such as Italy to the application of principles which in the case of Abyssinia cannot be applied. It would, moreover, be synonymous with granting impunity to the latter for her present action and with making it possible for her to become an ever-growing danger in the future, merely for the sake of defending principles of which Abyssinia avails herself to her own exclusive advantage, but to which she is unable to make any effective and responsible contribution in the comity of the civilised nations of Europe.

(2) That it is by no means the intention of Italy to violate

existing treaties, by which she considers herself to be strictly
bound especially towards England and France, but that it is
the firm determination of the Italian Government not to
allow these treaties to be given an interpretation which at
the present moment would only serve to mask the military
preparation of Ethiopia and to prevent Italy from attaining
that degree of security to which she, in common with other
States, is entitled in order to be in a position to bring to bear
on European collective security the whole weight and force
of her collaboration. . . .

45. *Mussolini abandons Austria: The Ambassador in Italy to the
Foreign Ministry, 7 January 1936* (DGFP, C, iv, no. 485)
Mussolini received me this afternoon, after I had let him know
that I would be in Berlin in the middle of next week. . . .

. . . As far as Germany was concerned, he fully appreciated her
neutrality, which he described as benevolent. This being so, he
thought it would now be possible to achieve a fundamental improvement in German–Italian relations and to dispose of the only
dispute, namely, the Austrian problem. Since we had always declared that we did not wish to infringe Austria's independence, the
simplest method would be for Berlin and Vienna themselves to
settle their relations on the basis of Austrian independence, e.g., in
the form of a treaty of friendship with a non-aggression pact, which
would in practice bring Austria into Germany's wake, so that she
could pursue no other foreign policy than one parallel with that of
Germany. If Austria, as a formally quite independent State, were
thus in practice to become a German satellite, he would have no
objection. He saw in this great advantages for Germany as well as
for Italy, in that Germany, as already stated, would acquire a
reliable satellite, while at the same time German–Italian mistrust
would be eliminated and all Danubian Pact machinations frustrated.
Should this not come about, then it was to be feared that Austria,
who was beginning to doubt Italy's ability to help her at the
decisive moment, would be driven to side with Czechoslovakia and
thus with France. I replied that these remarks were of very great
interest to me; had I rightly understood him to mean that Italy
would not oppose, either directly or indirectly, a settlement of
German–Austrian relations on the basis of formal independence

and close German–Austrian cooperation in foreign policy? Mussolini expressly confirmed this. . . .

46. *Speech by Mussolini, 9 May 1936, from* Corriere della Sera, *10 May 1936* (RIIA, *Documents* 1936, 2, p. 471)

. . . All knots were cut by our gleaming sword, and the African victory remains in the history of the fatherland entire and unsullied, a victory such as the legionaries that have fallen and those that survive dreamed of and willed. Italy has her empire at last: a fascist empire because it bears the indestructible tokens of the will and of the power of the Roman lictors, because this is the goal towards which, during fourteen years, were spurred on the exuberant and disciplined energies of the young and dashing generations of Italy. An empire of peace, because Italy desires peace, for herself and for all men, and she decides upon war only when it is forced upon her by imperious, irrepressible necessities of life. An empire of civilization and of humanity for all the populations of Abyssinia. That is in the tradition of Rome, who, after victory, associated the peoples with their own destiny.

47. *Conversation between the Duce and President Goering, in the presence of Count Ciano and Herr Schmidt, Rome (Palazzo Venezia), 23 January 1937* (Count Galeazzo Ciano, *Diplomatic Papers,* pp. 80–90.)

. . . The Duce replies that the relations of Italy with Austria are based on the principle of respect for the independence of that country with due regard to its sensibility. He (the Duce) is perfectly aware that the Austrian people, in large part, has no sympathy for Italy; should he wish to influence the Austrian Government he would therefore have to proceed with great caution so as not to expose himself to the danger of an unpleasant reply. In view of the fact, however, that Ministerpresident Goering expressed a desire to that effect, he will attempt to influence the Austrian Government in the manner suggested, adding that full execution of the Agreement of 11th July is also in the interest of Italy, particularly since at the time the Agreement was concluded at Italy's wish. He (the Duce) has both personally and by implication pointed out to Schuschnigg that, in view of the German character of Austria, it would be absurd to pursue an anti-German policy. Regular implementation of the Agreement of 11th July is, on the other hand, of the utmost importance from the international point of view. Any new conflict between Germany and Austria would, for example, be immediately exploited by France and there would once again be talk of the 'watch on the Brenner'. Italy does not intend to allow herself to be bound in any way on this point. . . .

Ministerpresident Goering said that this was one of the points on which there exists a certain divergence of views between Germany and Italy – the evaluation of the forces at work in Austria. Germany is of the opinion that the dominant tendencies in Austria are more internationally inclined than is apparently believed on the Italian side. For Germany's part, he can at all events give the assurance – and he believes that this is also true of Italy – that there will be no surprises as far as Austria is concerned. The Duce gave the same assurance, stressing that the guarantee is to be found in the very continuity of contracts between Italy and Germany. . . .

48. *Speech by Mussolini, 28 September 1937, Berlin* (RIIA, *Documents* 1937, p. 297)

. . . I have come not merely as Head of the Italian Government but above all in my capacity as the head of a national revolution, which thereby wishes to give proof of its close connexion with your revolution. The course of both revolutions may have been different; but the goal they have wished to reach and have reached is the same: the unity and greatness of the nation.

Fascism and National-Socialism are both expressions of the similarity in historical events in the life of our nations, which have reached unity in the same century and by the same event.

There are no secret intentions hidden behind my visit to Germany. Nothing will be planned here to divide a Europe which is already divided enough. The solemn confirmation of the fact and stability of the Rome–Berlin axis is not directed against other States. We National–Socialists and Fascists want peace which does not silently ignore, but solves, the questions arising from the life of the peoples.

To the whole world, which is asking tensely what the result of this meeting will be, war or peace, the *Fuhrer* and I can answer with a loud voice: Peace. . . .

49. *Ciano's Diary, 1937–1938, 6 November 1937*
We signed the Pact this morning. One was conscious of an

atmosphere definitely unlike that of the usual diplomatic ceremony. Three nations are embarking together upon a path which may perhaps lead them to war. A war necessary in order to break through the crust which is stifling the energy and the aspirations of the young nations. After the signature we went to see the Duce. I have seldom seen him so happy. The situation of 1935 has been transformed. Italy has broken out of her isolation: she is in the centre of the most formidable political and military combination which has ever existed. . . .

50. *Conversation with the Duce and Herr von Ribbentrop, Rome, 6 November 1937* (Count Galeazzo Ciano, *Diplomatic Papers*, pp. 142–6)

Finally, Ribbentrop discusses the Austrian question.

After stating that he is speaking in a purely personal capacity, he points out to the Duce that in the grand policy of Rome and Berlin, Austria now represents an element of secondary importance, and that he considers that at a certain moment it will be necessary to settle finally a question on which the enemies of the common Italo–German policy still speculate. The Duce replies that Austria is a German country by race, language and culture. The Austrian question must not be considered as a problem affecting Italy and Germany, but, on the contrary, as a problem of an international order. For his part he has stated, and repeats it now, that he is tired of mounting guard over Austrian independence, especially if the Austrians no longer want their independence. The Duce sees the situation thus: Austria is German state No. 2. It will never be able to do anything without Germany, far less against Germany. Italian interest today is no longer as lively as it was some years ago, for one thing because of Italy's imperialist development, which was now concentrating her interest on the Mediterranean and the Colonies. It must be added that the fact that the Austrians have not modified in the slightest their cold and negative attitude towards us has contributed to the decrease of Italian interest in Austria. According to the Duce, the best method is to let events take their natural course. One must not aggravate the situation, so as to avoid crises of an international nature. On the other hand, France knows that if a crisis should arise in Austria, Italy would do nothing. This was said to Schuschnigg, too, on the occasion of the Venice conversation. We cannot impose independence upon Austria which, by the very fact that it was imposed, would cease to be independence. On the Austrian question, therefore, it is necessary to abide by the formula enunciated during the conversation with Goering in the Karinhall: nothing will be done without previous exchange of information. . . .

51. *Ciano's Diary, 1937–1938, 8 November 1938*
It seems to me that there is not much hope of a *rapprochement* with France. The Duce, in my usual interview with him, traced the lines which our future policy will have to follow. 'Objectives: Jibuti, at least to the extent of a *condominium* and neutralization; Tunisia, with a more or less similar régime; Corsica, Italian and never gallicized, to be ruled directly; the frontier to be pushed back to the River Var. I am not interested in Savoy, which is neither historically nor geographically Italian. This is the general pattern of our claims. I do not specify one or five or ten years. The time will be settled by events. But we must never lose sight of this goal.' It is under these auspices that François-Poncet begins his mission. . . .

52. *Ciano's Diary, 1939–1943, 2 May 1939*
General Carboni, who has the reputation of being a deep student of military matters, today confirms the reports that our armament situation is disastrous. I have received this information from too many sources not to take it seriously. But what is the Duce doing? His attention seems to be spent mostly on matters of form; there is hell to pay if the 'Present Arms' is not done right or if an officer doesn't know how to lift his legs in the Roman step [Fascist equivalent of the goose step], but he seems to concern himself only up to a certain point about the real weaknesses which he certainly knows very well. In spite of my formal charges in connection with the results of Cavagnari's investigation of the efficiency of our aviation he has done nothing, absolutely nothing; and today in his conversation with Cavagnari he didn't even mention the matter. Why? Does he fear the truth so much that he is unwilling to listen? . . .

53. *Italy needs peace: Count Ciano to Foreign Minister Ribbentrop, 31 May 1939* (DGFP, D, vi, 459)
. . . I have entrusted General Cavallero with a confidential document drawn up by the Duce, which is of particular importance for

the development of military and economic collaboration between our two countries. The Duce wishes this document to be handed to the Führer, and I would ask you to be kind enough to arrange for it to be transmitted to the exalted recipient. . . .

ENCLOSURE

Now that the Alliance between Italy and Germany has been concluded and will be fully applied at all times according to the letter and spirit of the Treaty, I deem it appropriate to set down my views on the present situation and the way it will probably develop in future.

I

War between the plutocratic and therefore self-seeking conservative nations and the densely populated and poor nations is inevitable. In accordance with this situation appropriate preparations must be made.

II

Through the strategic positions secured in Bohemia and Albania the Axis Powers have a fundamental factor for success in their hands.

III

In a memorandum addressed to Herr von Ribbentrop at the time of the meeting in Milan I set out the reasons why Italy requires a period of preparation, which may extend until the end of 1942.

The reasons are as follows:

'The two European Axis Powers require a period of peace of not less than three years. Only from 1943 onwards will an effort by war have the greatest prospects of success.

Italy needs a period of peace for the following reasons:

(a) For the military organization of Libya and Albania, and also for the pacification of Ethiopia, from which latter region an army of half a million men must be formed.

(b) To complete the construction and reconditioning of the six battleships, which has already commenced.

(c) For the renewal of the whole of our medium and heavy calibre artillery.

(d) For the further development of plans for autarky, by which any attempt at a blockade by the satiated democracies must be thwarted.

(e) For carrying out the World Exhibition in 1942, which will not only document the twenty years' activity of the Fascist régime but could also bring in reserves of foreign exchange.

(f) For effecting the return home of Italians from France, which constitutes a very serious military and *moral* problem.

(g) For completing the transfer, already begun, of a large number of war industries from the plain of the Po to Southern Italy.

(h) For further intensifying relations not only between the Governments of the Axis Powers but also between both peoples. For this purpose, a *détente* in the relations between the Roman Catholic Church and National Socialism would doubtless be useful, and is also greatly desired by the Vatican.

For all these reasons, Fascist Italy does not wish to hasten a European war, although she is convinced of the inevitability of such a war. It may also be assumed that within three years Japan will have brought her war in China to a conclusion. . . .

. . . From the strategic point of view, the Western Powers should be regarded as 'walled in', that is practically unattackable by land forces. Consequently, a reciprocal defence position should be provided for on the Rhine, in the Alps and in Libya. On the other hand, the metropolitan and colonial forces in Ethiopia can start aggressive operations against the neighbouring French and British colonies.

The war in the West would thus assume the character of a predominantly air and naval struggle. Italy's naval problem has been made considerably easier by the conquest of Albania. The Adriatic has become an island sea which can be hermetically sealed.

VI

The war can only assume a dynamic character towards the East and South East. Poland and other guaranteed States will have to depend on themselves and can be paralysed before any real assistance is rendered them even from neighbouring Russia.

VII

The war for which the great democracies are preparing is a *war of attrition*. One must therefore proceed from the grimmest hypothesis, which is a hundred per cent probable. *The Axis will obtain nothing more from the rest of the world*. This prospect would be grave but the strategic positions secured by the Axis have considerably reduced the difficulty and danger of a war of attrition. To this end, the whole of the Danube and Balkan Basins (*sic*) must be seized in the first few hours of the war. We must not be satisfied with declarations of neutrality but must occupy the territories and exploit them for the provision of the necessary wartime food and industrial supplies. By this operation, which must be conducted with lightning speed and the utmost decision, not only would the 'guaranteed States', like Greece, Rumania and Turkey, be put *hors de combat,* but we would also safeguard our rear. In this game – as in chess – we can count on two favourable pawns: Hungary and Bulgaria.

VIII

Italy can mobilize a comparatively larger number of men than Germany. This abundance of men is balanced by modest means. Italy will, therefore, under the war plan, supply more men than material and Germany more material than men.

I am desirous of knowing whether the above observations meet with the Führer's approval. If so, the plans of the General Staff must be prepared on these lines.

54. *Ciano's Diary, 1939–1943, 13 August 1939*
. . . I return to Rome completely disgusted with the Germans, with their leader, with their way of doing things. They have betrayed us and lied to us. Now they are dragging us into an adventure which we have not wanted and which might compromise the régime and the country as a whole. The Italian people will boil over with horror when they know about the aggression against Poland and most probably will wish to fight the Germans. I don't know whether to wish Italy a victory or Germany a defeat. In any case, given the German attitude, I think that our hands are free, and I propose that we act accordingly, declaring that we have no intention of participating in a war which we have neither wanted nor provoked.

The Duce's reactions are varied. At first he agrees with me. Then he says that honor compels him to march with Germany. Finally, he states that he wants his part of the booty in Croatia and Dalmatia.

55. Ciano's Diary, 1939–1943, 26 August 1939

Berlin is showering us with requests for the list of our needs. We convene at the Palazzo Venezia at ten o'clock with the chiefs of staff of the three armies and with Benni. Before entering the Duce's room I remind these comrades of their responsibility. They must tell the whole truth on the extent of our stocks and not do what is usually done, be criminally optimistic. But they are all in precisely this state of mind, the most optimistic being Pariani.

Valle, on the other hand, is very much alive to his responsibility and is honest in his declarations.

We go over the list. It's enough to kill a bull – if a bull could read it. I remain alone with the Duce and we prepare a message to Hitler. We explain to him why it is that our needs are so vast, and we conclude by saying that Italy absolutely cannot enter the war without such provisions. The Duce makes some mention also of his political action to follow. In transmitting our request Attolico gets into trouble. (In a subsequent conference Attolico told me that this was not a mistake but that he had purposely done it in order to discourage the Germans from meeting our requests.) He asked for the immediate delivery of all the material, an impossible thing, since it involves seventeen million tons which require seventeen thousand cars for their transportation. I straightened things out. Soon Hitler's reply arrives. They can give us only iron, coal, and lumber. Only a few anti-aircraft batteries. He indicates that he understands our situation and urges us to be friendly. He proposes to annihilate Poland and beat France and England without help.

After Mackensen went away the Duce prepared the answer. He expressed regrets at not being able to intervene. He again proposed a political solution. The Duce is really out of his wits. His military instinct and his sense of honour were leading him to war. Reason has now stopped him. But this hurts him very much. In the military field he was badly served by his collaborators who, under the illusion of eternal peace, have lulled dangerous illusions in him. Now he has had to confront the hard truth. And this, for the Duce, is a great blow.

However, Italy is saved from a great tragedy, that very tragedy which is about to fall on the German people. Hitler is entering the war with an alarming scarcity of equipment and with a divided country.

The message is sent to the Führer at eight o'clock. He announces that he will reply.

56. Ciano's Diary, 1939–1943, 7 February 1940
Return of the Duce, with whom I have a long conversation. Meanwhile, he refuses to sell arms to Great Britain. He says that he does not want to reduce the means of making war that are at our disposal, and that he intends to keep the obligations recently confirmed with Germany. 'Governments, like individuals, must follow a line of morality and honour.' He is not concerned about the English reactions, which I prophesy will be inevitable and harsh. Neither does the lack of coal weigh on his mind. He repeats that it is good for the Italian people to be put to tests that cause them to shake off their century-old mental laziness. He is bitter toward the people. 'We must keep them disciplined and in uniform from morning till night. Beat them and beat them and beat them.' He does not discriminate between the classes, and calls 'the people' all those who wish to vegetate.

I inform Riccardi of the Duce's decision in the matter of commercial exchanges with England. He is very gloomy. . . .

57. Ciano's Diary, 1939–1943, 1 June 1940
An audience with the King. He approves the formula that I submit to him. He is now resigned, no, more than resigned, to the idea of war. He believes that in reality France and England have taken tremendously hard blows, but, with good reason, he attributes great importance to the eventual intervention of the United States. He feels that the country is going to war without enthusiasm. There is interventionist propaganda, but there is not in the least that enthusiasm we had in 1915. 'Those who talk of a short and easy war are fools. There are still many unknown factors, and the horizon is very different from that of May 1915.' Thus concludes the King. . . .

Bottai, who is one of the few who has not lost his head, proposed to me on the golf course today that in the face of so much official interventionism we form a new party: the 'Party of the Interventionists in Bad Faith.'

58. Ciano's Diary, 1939–1943, 13 October 1941
. . . The Duce received news that during his trip to the Russian

front a German is supposed to have said about him, 'There goes our Gauleiter for Italy'. An employee of the Embassy is supposed to have heard this remark. The Duce wrote to Alferi to ascertain the truth. Mussolini said, 'I believe it. In Germany there exist certain phonograph records. Hitler makes them; the others play them. The first record was the one about Italy being the loyal ally, on an equal footing with Germany, mistress of the Mediterranean as Germany was of the Baltic. Then came the second record, that of the victories, that Europe would be dominated by Germany. The conquered states will be colonies. The associated states will be confederated provinces of Germany. Among these the most important is Italy. We have to accept these conditions because any attempt to rebel would result in our being reduced from the position of a confederated province to the worse one of a colony. Even if they should ask for Trieste tomorrow, as part of the German Lebensraum, we would have to bow our heads. As a matter of fact, there is the possibility of a third phonograph record, the one which will be made if Anglo–American resistance makes our collaboration more useful to the Germans. But that is yet to come.'

I confined myself to saying that with such a prospect one can easily understand why Italian enthusiasm in this war is so slight. . . .

Notes

1 The Sixth Wheel

1 F. Chabod, *Storia della politica estera italiana dal 1870 al 1896* (Bari, 1952), p. 551.

2 Comparative figures are (million tons):

	Coal		Iron		Steel	
	1870	1914	1870	1914	1870	1914
Great Britain	112·0	292·0	6·0	11·0	0·7	6·5
Germany	34·0	277·0	1·3	14·7	0·3	14·0
France	13·3	40·0	1·2	4·6	0·3	3·5
Russia	0·75	36·2	0·4	3·6	0·01	4·1
Austria	8·6	47·0	0·4	2·0	0·01	2·7
Italy	0·05	0·75	0·05	0·5	0·0	0·9

3 R. Romeo, *Breve storia della grande industria in Italia* (3rd edn, Milan, 1967), pp. 195–201 and tables 1, 6, 8, 12.

4 Ibid., table 4.

5 *Atti Parlamentari*, 18 May 1893: England 802 francs, France 573, Germany 399, Italy 223.

6 Chabod, op cit., p. 492.

7 C. Seton-Watson, *Italy from Liberalism to Fascism* (London, 1967), p. 62.

8 1884–5, 81m. lire; 1886–7, 218m. lire; 1888–9, 485m. lire (25 lire = £1 = $5). Africa cost relatively little at first, it averaged 21m. lire 1888–91, but shot up to 140m. lire in 1895–6: hence its unpopularity.

9 Chabod, op. cit., p. 497.

10 It averaged 307m. lire 1861–5; 212m. lire 1871–5; 306m. lire 1881–6.

11 465m. lire 1887–8; 600m. lire 1888–9; 362m. lire 1893; 369m. lire 1904–5; 747m. lire 1913–14. Comparative figures (in £m sterling) are:

	Great Britain	France	Russia	Germany	Austria	Italy
1870	23·4	22·0	22·0	10·8	8·2	7·8
1914	76·8	57·4	88·2	110·8	36·4	28·2

12 An average of 35m. lire 1870–79; 85m. lire in 1889; 116m. lire in 1893; an average of 166m. lire 1907–14.

13 See Seton-Watson, op. cit., pp. 359–60. In 1914 Austria spent only one fifth of her defence budget on the navy: Italy spent one third.

14 Comparative figures are:

	Great Britain	France	Russia	Germany	Austria
Troops, 1888	280,000	523,000	885,000	470,000	250,000
Italian army budget,					
% age of (1) 1888	61·1	45·8	55·0	52·3	84·6
(2) 1914	62·0	46·1	28·1	20·4	64·3

15 Premier 1892–3, 1903–5, 1906–9, 1911–14.

16 Sidney Sonnino, *Diario 1866–1916* (Bari, 1972), II, p. 15. In 1915 there were few strategic railways in the Veneto: Giolitti thought it politically unwise to build them. For the parliamentary interest in the army 1906–8 see G. Volpe, *Italia moderna, 1910–14* (Florence, 1952), vol. III, pp. 37–47.

17 Chabod, op. cit., p. 689. Victor Emmanuel still had the aura of divine right and told politicians what to do: Umberto was strictly a constitutional monarch in the British sense. Ibid. pp. 660–69.

18 Domenico Farini, *Diario di fine secolo* (Rome, 1961), I, pp. 727, 733 (Farini was President of the Chamber of Deputies 1884–7, of the Senate 1887–98); *Atti Parlamentari,* 13 May 1894.

19 Ibid., 11 March 1887.

20 M. Vitale, *L'Italia in Africa, serie storico-militare: Africa settentrionale 1911–43* (Rome, 1964), p. 11.

21 Among others that Victor Emmanuel and his generals thought France would win: Chabod, op. cit., p. 655.

22 Chabod, op. cit., pp. 583–5.

23 The post of Secretary General roughly corresponded to that of the Permanent Under-Secretary in Britain or the Directeur Politique in France. From 1870 to 1883 and 1885 to 1887 it was held by Count Isaac Artom, the Marchese Carlo Alberto Maffei, Count Giuseppe Tornielli, Baron Alberto Blanc, and Marchese Raffaele Cappelli; all Piedmontese or Savoyard nobility. (The same is true of the diplomats, with minor exceptions, until at least 1900.) From 1883 to 1885, 1891 to 1892, and 1896 to 1907 it was held by Giacomo Malvano, also of the Right. Significantly, Crispi and Mussolini abolished the post. See L. Ferraris, *L'amministrazione centrale* . . . (Milan, 1954), pp. 32–41; S. Negri, *Direzione e controllo della politica estera in Italia* (Milan, 1967), p. 17 *et seq.* From 1900 to 1922 the Foreign Minister was to the political Right of the Premier.

24 Chabod, op. cit., pp. 38–48, 55–6, 61, 68, 75–7, 293, 472–3, 548.

25 Without armaments, Crispi said, and with two highly armed states – France and Austria – on her borders, Italy would become a battleground once more – as she had been for 300 years. *Atti Parlamentari,* 12 May, 22 December (2ª Fornata) 1888.

26 Alfredo Oriani, *Fino a Dogali* quoted in Chabod, op. cit., p. 301. See also pp. 183, 198. On Oriani see J. A. Thayer, *Italy and the Great War* (Wisconsin, 1964), pp. 134–40.

27 Chabod, op. cit., pp. 182–3.

28 G. Carocci, *Agostino Depretis e la politica interna italiana dal 1876 al 1886* (Turin, 1956), pp. 299–300, 589, 592–4. *Trasformismo* was basically

Depretis's method of keeping power by blurring the edges of political divisions and obtaining support – on different issues – from all parts of the political spectrum. Giolitti used the same methods. The effect was a decline in ideology and a rise of political 'bosses'. On the 'southern question' see Thayer, op. cit., pp. 173–191.

29 A simple illustration of Carocci's theory is the regional origin of the Premier and Minister of the Interior, the key political offices (usually in the same hands): 1870–87, north; 1887–98, south; 1898–1914, north; 1914–19, south.

30 Chabod, op. cit., pp. 460–63.

31 Carocci, op. cit.; F. Fonzi, *Crispi e lo stato di Milano* (Milan, 1965), pp. 5–37.

32 Chabod, op. cit., p. 361. See S. Halperin, *Italy and the Vatican at War* (Chicago, 1939).

33 AMEI, Tels 131 1775.

34 Chabod, op. cit., p. 461; DDI iii. 1, 13. Helped of course by the general decline by the end of the century of the belief in rationalism as opposed to superstition: on this see the brilliant pages of Chabod, op. cit., pp. 273–83.

2 From Independence to Alliance

1 Visconti Venosta to Robilant, 12 April 1872, G. Salvemini, *Opere* III, 4 (Milan, 1970), pp. 170–72.

2 Ibid., pp. 182–4; F. Chabod, *Storia della politica estera italiana dal 1870 al 1896* (Bari, 1952), pp. 563–6.

3 Salvemini, op. cit., pp. 158–9, 166.

4 Robilant called them 'those dreaming of a future which has no probability of eventual realisation'. To Visconti Venosta, 2 April 1874, ibid., p. 162.

5 Ibid., p. 164; Chabod, op. cit., pp. 665–6.

6 The term irredentism was coined by Imbriani in 1877: C. Seton-Watson, *Italy from Liberalism to Fascism* (London, 1967), p. 102.

7 Salvemini, op. cit., pp. 163, 179, 187, 190. Visconti wanted an exchange of views with Russia 'to let them know in what conditions they could count on Italy'. To Robilant, 15 September 1875.

8 Ibid., p. 214: Tornielli and Maffei di Boglio – both Piedmontese – were 'the real inspiration behind Depretis and Cairoli respectively of Italian international policy from 1876 to 1881'. Chabod, op. cit., pp. 529–30, 686.

9 Robilant to Melegari, 20 June 1876, Salvemini, op. cit., Doc. 1, p. 203. On Depretis see below p. 24.

10 Robilant to Melegari, 17 October 1876, 9 February 1877. Launay confirmed this. Bismarck's contempt for Italy was supreme: 'In official relations it is like dealing through a glass wall. Italy is no longer in a position to play a leading role. We are only the sixth wheel on the chariot.' To Robilant, 28 December 1876. Salvemini, op. cit., pp. 209–14.

11 Ibid.; Chabod, op. cit., pp. 461, 685.

12 Chabod, op. cit., pp. 55–6, 672–3, 680–3. Salisbury had found the court very bellicose the previous November: Salvemini, op. cit., pp. 209–14.

13 Melegari told Haymerle on 13 October: 'Il [Crispi] a fait des brioches

qu'un attaché n'aurait pas faites. Mais comment voulez-vous que nous désavouions un personnage de cette importance à l'interieur, un Président de la Chambre?' Salvemini, op. cit., pp. 220–34; Chabod, op. cit., pp. 686–8.

14 'Il y a un mois, le roi était bien décidé et convaincu de marcher avec Nicotera vers un regime plus conservateur; aujourd'hui il en est arrivé à Crispi et en arrivera peut-être à Cairoli malgré toute l'aversion qu'il professe pour cette eventualité.' Haymerle to Andrássy, 5 January 1878, Chabod, op. cit., p. 673.

15 Ibid., p. 666. For Victor Emmanuel's control of Depretis, see pp. 668–76.

16 Salvemini, op. cit., pp. 244–5.

17 Ibid., pp. 245–9, 254.

18 DDF, 1st series, III, p. 307. Robilant came to the same conclusion: 'the ideal of the Left is the system which flourishes in South America . . . and it won't be long before we reach that level'. Chabod, op. cit., pp. 640, 642; Salvemini, op. cit., pp. 259, 263–7.

19 L. Salvatorelli, *La triplice alleanza* (Milan, 1939), pp. 51–3. Chabod, op. cit., p. 646.

20 Estimates of numbers in 1881 vary from 9,000–30,000: Salvemini, op. cit., pp. 175–6. C. Morandi, *La politica estera dell'Italia* (Florence, 1968), p. 151, gives 11,000 Italians to 3,000 French in 1880. By contrast, French capital investment was much higher than Italian. Tunisian trade was over-whelmingly in Italian hands: 110 out of 186 steam-ships and 277 out of 327 sailing ships calling at Tunis in 1878 were Italian, only 2 of each were French. L. del Piano, *La penetrazione italiana in Tunisia 1861–1881* (Padua, 1964), p. 64.

21 Chabod, op. cit., pp. 543, 640; A. Torre, *La politica estera dell'Italia 1870–1896* (Bologna, 1959), pp. 164–78. As Salvemini points out, there is not the slightest reason to suppose that if Visconti had taken up Bismarck's suggestion in 1875 this would have stopped him giving Tunis to France in 1878, if it suited him: op. cit., pp. 265–7.

22 J. Ganiage, *Les origines du protectorat français à Tunisie 1861–1881* (Paris, 1959), pp. 540–633.

23 Torre, op. cit., pp. 189–95. For Salisbury's tergiversations see A. Marsden, *British Diplomacy and Tunis 1875–1902* (New York, 1971), pp. 50–66. Morandi (op. cit., p. 151) blames 'the uncertainties of Italian foreign policy'.

24 Torre, op. cit., pp. 202–8. This seems to be the origin of Gorrini's state-ment: 'We should have understood since 1878 that only by a military or diplomatic victory over the Republic that we could seize Tunis from her' (p. 47).

25 Salvatorelli, op. cit., pp. 54–8; Torre, op. cit., pp. 224–30; Morandi, op. cit., pp. 157–9; F. R. Bridge, *From Sadowa to Sarajevo* (London, 1972), p. 131. Maffei and Cairoli had wanted to try this in 1880 but Depretis refused. It is obvious that Bismarck would have opposed it anyway. Robilant consistently opposed any attempt to seek an alliance with the Central Powers from 1879 to 1882 for this very reason: Chabod, op. cit., pp. 634–5.

26 Ganiage, op. cit., pp. 612–15.

27 Marsden, op. cit., pp. 69–73.

28 A. Carocci, *Agostino Depretis e la politica interna italiana dal 1876 al 1886* (Turin, 1956), pp. 249–52; Morandi, op. cit., p. 154. Hence the king's remark to the Austrian ambassador on 24 June 1881: 'Monsieur Depretis est habile mais il ne vit que de compromis et de concessions et en le voyant je ne sais jamais quel nouveau mensonge il va me debiter.' Chabod, op. cit., p. 647.

29 On Egypt see below. For Depretis and France – Salvatorelli, op. cit., p. 59. King Umberto was similarly little affected by Tunis. On 24 June he told the Austrian ambassador 'qu'on peut ramener toutes les questions à des interêts personnels et surtout à des mobiles d'argent. Il n'en excepte aucunement l'affaire de Tunis et les agitations qui s'y rattachent. A son avis elles n'ont été que des pretextes pour les passions individuelles et au fond personne n'y pense plus sérieusement depuis que la question a été résolue par des faits accomplis qu'on peut regretter mais aux quels il n'y à plus rien à changer'.

30 Torre, op. cit., pp. 230–35; Carocci, op. cit., pp. 263–5. The sense of shock can best be judged by Blanc's pathetic statement to the Austrians on 30 September that Italy 'did not want to play the role of a Great Power' and preferred 'to return to the old conservative tradition of Piedmont'. Chabod, op. cit., p. 647. (Blanc replaced Maffei as Secretary-General in June.)

31 Salvatorelli, op. cit., p. 60; Chabod, op. cit., p. 680; Carocci, op. cit., pp. 267–72. As Carocci points out (p. 278), Minghetti's object was probably to keep out Crispi who, though now advocating an Austrian alliance, was 'a dangerous radical' at home. Nevertheless, Minghetti certainly wanted a strong foreign policy – see p. 32.

32 Salvatorelli, op. cit., pp. 60–70; Torre, op. cit., pp. 236–46; Morandi, op. cit., pp. 172–3.

33 'We want only respect for treaties and the simple maintenance of peace, renouncing any idea of an increase in our influence in the Mediterranean.' Launay to Bismarck, January 1882: Chabod, *Considerazioni sulla politica estera dell-Italia dal 1870 al 1915* (Amici della cultura n.i., n.d.).

34 For varying assessments of the treaty see Salvatorelli, op. cit., p. 71; Torre, op. cit., pp. 248–57; Salvemini, op. cit., pp. 317–18; Chabod, *Considerazioni*, pp. 31–7. It is printed in Bridge, op. cit., pp. 406–8.

35 Chabod, *Storia*, p. 552.

3 Mancini, Robilant and the Mediterranean, 1882–7

1 See L. E. Roberts, 'Italy and the Egyptian question, 1878–1882', in *JMH*, 1946; G. Talamo, 'Il mancato intervento in Egitto' in *RSR*, 1958; C. Morandi, *La politica estera dell'Italia* (Florence, 1968).

2 Mancini telegram to London and Paris, 18 September 1881, in *Affari di Egitto nel 1881–2* (Ministero dell'Estero, 1894), p. 1. Copy in ASC, Carte Pisani Dossi. (This is a summary of Italian and other correspondence printed in 35 pages, for internal use in the Italian Foreign Ministry.) For

P. S. Mancini, Foreign Minister May 1881 to June 1885, see C. Zaghi, *P. S. Mancini, L'Africa e il problema del Mediterraneo* (Rome, 1955).

3 'All our government sought was to initiate on the Nile a collective policy, which could become equally applicable to Tunis . . .', *Affari di Egitto*, p. 24.

4 Robilant to Mancini, 21 May 1882, *Affari di Egitto*, op. cit., p. 3. Advice from Launay, at Berlin, was similar: 'Let us keep our position at the side of the central powers . . .' (16 February).

5 *Affari di Egitto*, pp. 7, 12, 24.

6 Depretis to Mancini, 25 June 1882, quoted in Talamo, op. cit., p. 434.

7 'Prince Bismarck only intervened when it was necessary to help England overcome difficulties raised by Paris, Rome or St Petersburg . . .', *Affari di Egitto*, p. 13.

8 Robilant to Mancini, 15 July 1882, quoted in A. Torre, *La politica estera dell'Italia 1870–1896* (Bologna, 1959), p. 269.

9 Robilant to Mancini, 26 July 1882, ibid., p. 271.

10 Talamo, op. cit., p. 442. See also Doc. 2. p. 371 below.

11 C. Morandi, *La politica estera dell'Italia* (Florence, 1968), p. 190.

12 *Affari di Egitto*, pp. 10, 14.

13 Ibid., pp. 14, 30. The reason he gave Paget for rejecting Granville's proposal was that his public commitment to the concert prevented independent action: Salvatorelli, *La triplice alleanza* (Milan, 1939), p. 84.

14 *Affari di Egitto*, pp. 27–8. Salvatorelli (op. cit., p. 85) terms Crispi's view 'fantasy'.

15 C. Zaghi, op. cit., p. 45.

16 C. Morandi, op. cit., p. 190, termed Mancini's policy 'incomprensibile e ingiustificabile'. See also Talamo, op. cit., p. 446; Torre, op. cit., pp. 271–2; and F. Chabod, *Storia della politica estera italiana dal 1870 al 1896* (Bari, 1952), pp. 544–5.

17 Torre, op. cit., pp. 283–5: Salvatorelli, op. cit., pp. 79–80, 89.

18 Salvemini, *Opere* III, 4 (Milan, 1970), pp. 319–20.

19 Ibid.

20 Bismarck to Keudell, 6 April 1884, *GP*, III, no 678; Salvatorelli, op. cit., pp. 92–3.

21 Launay to Mancini, 10 June 1884, Zaghi, op. cit., p. 143.

22 Crispi once called it 'parliamentary incest'. See Chabod, op. cit., pp. 381–6; C. Seton-Watson, *Italy from Liberalism to Fascism* (London, 1967), pp. 52, 91–2; G. Carocci, *Agostino Depretis* . . . (Turin, 1956), pp. 303–9.

23 Zaghi, op. cit., pp. 15–16.

24 Ibid., pp. 18–19. Even Launay, who thought colonial adventures 'une grande folie', recognised that in these circumstances the seizure of Tripoli would be 'une nécessité politique'. Ibid., p. 69.

25 On this theme – new nations and dying nations – see Chabod, op. cit., pp. 58–65.

26 Zaghi, op. cit., pp. 22, 28.

27 DDF, i, v, no 251.

28 On the Egyptian conference see C. J. Lowe, *The Reluctant Imperialists* (London, 1967), pp. 57–9.

29 Telegram to Berlin, 23 Nov. 1884. As a colonialist critic pointed out, in fact Italy was represented by a professor of anthropology and a deaf geographer. Zaghi, op. cit., pp. 52, 54.

30 Launay to Mancini, 18 December 1884, ibid., p. 33.

31 Ibid., pp. 68–71.

32 Lord Tenterden, Permanent Under Secretary at the Foreign Office, told Maffei, First Secretary at the London Embassy, that 'Nothing was more likely to raise Parliament and the entire nation against Italy than the attempt to create an Italian possession in the Red Sea'. C. Giglio, *L'Italia in Africa*, vol. I: *Etiopa–Mar Rosso*, book I, 1857–1885 (Rome, 1956), p. 224.

33 Ibid., p. 189.

34 Ibid., pp. 231–4.

35 Giglio, op. cit., chapter X generally and pp. 336–77.

36 20 May 1884, quoted in Zaghi, op. cit., p. 48.

37 27 January 1885, ibid., p. 49.

38 The flour tax (*macinato*) was the means of balancing the budget: colonial adventures restored the deficit. See Carocci, op. cit., p. 599.

39 Speech in Chamber of Deputies, 30 June 1885, quoted in Giglio, op. cit., p. 342.

40 Mancini to Nigra, 29 October 1884, *L'Italia in Africa, Etiopia–Mar Rosso, Documenti 1883–5*, nos 344, 345.

41 Quoted in Zaghi, op. cit., p. 97.

42 *L'Italia in Africa*, Documenti nos 349, 352, 353.

43 '. . . des considerations parlementares nous indiqueraient l'opportunité de faire quelque chose pour donner satisfaction à l'esprit national . . .', ibid., no 371.

44 Ibid., no. 374. 'In other words, England neither pushed nor instigated Italy to occupy Massowa.' Giglio, op. cit., I, p. 353.

45 Giglio, op. cit., I, p. 421. Zaghi, op. cit., pp. 99–112.

46 *L'Italia in Africa*, Documenti, no 378. Sir Savile Lumley, British Ambassador at Rome, 1884–7.

47 Giglio, op. cit., I, pp. 426–36; Lowe, op. cit., pp. 71–2.

48 Ibid., 440–50; Zaghi, op. cit., pp. 120–36.

49 Salvemini, op. cit., p. 324.

50 Robilant to Corti, 12 May 1884: Chabod, op. cit., pp. 627, 632, 634.

51 'We don't have a foreign policy, we only have parliamentary alchemy.' To Corti, 16 October 1880, ibid., p. 639.

52 Salvemini, op. cit., p. 330.

53 To Corti, 28 February 1887, Chabod, op. cit., p. 631. 'What has happened proves that if we have made Italy we have not made the Italians. . . .'

54 'Il y a la France il est vrai: mais l'Italie monarchique ne saurait être l'allié de la République. Et si le peuple italien était assez insensé pour se rejeter dans ses bras . . . nous signerions en ce cas une bien mauvaise lettre de change.' To Robilant 26 August 1886, AMEI, Archivio Gabinetto, T.A. 230/1b. See also Doc. 5 below.

55 Chabod, op. cit., pp. 633–4.

56 Robilant to Launay 5 August 1886, AMEI, Archivio Gabinetto, T.A.

230/1b. See also A. Pribram, *The Secret Treaties of Austria–Hungary* (Cambridge, Mass., 1920), p. 48. See also Doc. 3 below.
57 For the general European situation see Lowe, op. cit., pp. 94, 99–104.
58 Pribram, op. cit., pp. 46, 52. Launay was quite specific in 1885 that in the event of a Franco–Italian diplomatic conflict, Bismarck would support France. See Zaghi, op. cit., p. 192.
59 Robilant to Launay, 5 August 1886, *supra*.
60 Robilant to Nigra, 2 October 1886, AMEI, Archivio Gabinetto, T.A. 230/1b. 'So far I have maintained the equilibrium with Russia made necessary by the possibility of an eventual *volte face* by Germany.' Ibid., 15 November. 'V. E. comprend combien serait grave pour nous un accord entre la Russie et l'Autriche sur ces bases.' Ibid., 24 December, Tels 113/1044.
61 'M. Freycinet m'en vient à dire en propres termes que c'est à une alliance entre la France et l'Italie qu'il faudra aboutir...'. Ressmann to Robilant, 9 October 1886, AMEI, Tels 75/1779.
62 Robilant to Launay, 13 October; Launay to Robilant, 17 October 1886, AMEI, Archivio Gabinetto, T.A. 230/1b. The dating of Bismarck's instructions to Vienna, in Pribram, op. cit., pp. 50–52, makes the influence of the French offer apparent.
63 Salvemini, op. cit., pp. 329–30. For the full text of the treaty see Pribram I, pp. 107–15. See also Doc. 6 below. Robilant in fact wanted to specify Italian gains in a successful war against France as Provence and Tunis but Bismarck refused lest (a) the emperor had scruples (b) they lost the war and the treaty was revealed. Launay to Robilant, 16 February 1887, Archivio Gabinetto, T.A. 230/1c.
64 Robilant to Catalani, 8 October 1886, AMEI, Seria politica Inghilterra, 1368/400.
65 Robilant minute on Catalani, 3 October, ibid., 1368/273.
66 Robilant to Catalani, 22 October 1886, ibid., 1368/459.
67 Launay to Robilant, 28 December 1886, AMEI, Carte Robilant, fasc. 28.
68 Iddesleigh to Salisbury, 25 and 27 September, Salisbury Papers.
69 Catalani to Robilant, 29 September, AMEI, Seria politica 1368/271, minuted by Robilant: 'notizie di massimo interesse per il governo del Re'.
70 Robilant to Corti, 9 December 1886, AMEI, Tels 113/1013. Corti succeeded Nigra at the London embassy in October 1885; recalled by Crispi October 1887.
71 Iddesleigh to Salisbury, 25 September, 4 October, Salisbury Papers.
72 See C. J. Lowe, *Salisbury and the Mediterranean* (London, 1965), pp. 12–13.
73 Ibid.
74 Lumley to Iddesleigh, 11 January 1887, FO, 45/574/8.
75 See GP, IV, no. 481; Launay to Robilant, 30 December 1886, AMEI, Archivio Gabinetto, T.A. 101/1c. See also Doc. 6 below.
76 Launay to Robilant, 22 January 1887, ibid., 119/1c.
77 For Salisbury's attitude see Lowe, *Salisbury and the Mediterranean*, pp. 13–17, and Lowe, *Reluctant Imperialists*, pp. 108–10.
78 Corti to Robilant, 1 and 3 February 1887, AMEI, Archivio Gabinetto, cassetta verde 6/1. See also Doc. 8 below.

79 Launay to Robilant, 17 February, ibid.

80 ASC, Carte Depretis, 119/33.

4 The Crispi Era

1 The people, 'who feel only the maladies of the stomach, not those of the spirit', hence had no share in a parliamentary state. F. Crispi, *Pensieri e profezie* (Rome, 1920), pp. 51–81. Depretis was too ill to preside over cabinet meetings so Crispi, Minister of the Interior since April, substituted for him until his death in July.

2 Kennedy to Salisbury, 21 February 1888, FO, 45/601/41.

3 F. Chabod, *Storia della politica estera italiana dal 1870 al 1896* (Bari, 1952), p. 612. Crispi, in contrast to most Italians of his day, believed that foreign policy *should* dominate internal considerations. Ibid., pp. 73–4. In February 1887 he refused Depretis's offer of the Ministry of Justice because it would bring no influence on foreign policy: *Diario,* 20 February 1887, in MRR, Carte Crispi, 667/8/3.

4 Chabod, op. cit., pp. 110, 555. Hence the comment of UxKull, the Russian Ambassador at Rome: 'Crispi is the greatest conspirator in Europe . . . : He says he is going only to Monza; no doubt he will come back from Hatfield with the Garter.' Kennedy to Salisbury, 4 October 1888, FO, 45/603/261.

5 Chabod, op. cit., pp. 21, 26, 37, 110, 548. See also his *Considerazioni sulla politica estera dell'Italia dal 1870 al 1915* in Amici della cultura, Quaderno 1.

6 Chabod, op. cit., pp. 52, 460–3. Crispi was unique in this respect, virtually all other Italian politicians retaining some affection for France.

7 Ibid., pp. 45, 477. A. C. Jemolo, *Crispi* (Florence, 1922), pp. 75–84, 112–20; E. Serra, *La questione tunisina* (Milan, 1967), pp. 31–4, 38.

8 For French knowledge of this see DDF, i, VII appendix I.

9 G. Salvemini, *Opere* III, 4 (Milan, 1970), p. 332. Similarly L. Salvatorelli *La triplice alleanza* (Milan, 1939), p. 146. Admiral Brin, Minister of Marine under Crispi, pointed this out to Billot in 1892: Crispi, he said, was affected with 'une défiance incurable'. DDF, IX, no. 3.

10 Text in DDI, ii, XXI, no. 622. The rationale is well explained in no. 346.

11 For a gross example of this see ibid., no. 531. It was obviously the purpose of the Friedrichsruhe invitation: as Salvemini observes, 'nothing was said at Friedrichsruhe which could not have been put on a postcard'. Salvemini, op. cit., p. 333.

12 Kennedy to Salisbury, 24 December 1888, FO, 45/603/338.

13 Salvemini, op. cit., pp. 110–11.

14 Kennedy to Salisbury, 21 February 1888, FO, 45/601/41.

15 Salvemini, op. cit., p. 333. It was originally Robilant who refused to renew on the 1881 basis: Robilant to Ressmann, 2 November 1886, AMEI, Tels 113/905.

16 DDI, XXI, no. 240. See also L. Luzzatti, *Memorie* (Bologna, 1935), II, pp. 249–55.

17 Flourens, even in February 1888, was willing to renew the 1881 treaty: it was Crispi who insisted on improvements. DDI, XXI, nos 621 628.

18 British, French and Austrian diplomats at Rome all concurred that Crispi's internal problems lay behind his string of incidents with France. C. J. Lowe, *Salisbury and the Mediterranean* (London, 1965), p. 29.

19 DDF, VII, no. 324; VIII, no. 185.

20 For the disastrous effects in Italy see G. Luzzatto, *L'economia italiana dal 1861 al 1914* (Turin, 1968), pp. 179–81. Widespread rural misery doubled the emigration rate in 1888 and led to revolt in 1893 in Sicily.

21 F. Crispi, *Questioni Internazionali* (Milan, 1913), pp. 129–30; *Chabod*, pp. 75–9; V. di Val Cismon, 'La scioglimento della Pro Patria di Trento nel carteggio Crispi-Nigra' in *RSR*, 1934, I. See also Salvatorelli, op. cit., pp. 150–8; Serra, op. cit., p. 122. Crispi's ideas in 1896 were essentially the same: see below p. 62.

22 See C. J. Lowe, *Reluctant Imperialists* (London, 1967), pp. 116–19. Crispi's object was twofold: (1) to turn the February agreement into a military alliance, (2) to make the Turks a fourth partner. Neither object was achieved. See especially DDI, XXI, nos 57, 86, 89, 148, 259. See also Docs 9, 10 below.

23 Photiades Pasha, Ottoman Ambassador at Rome, told Kennedy that although Blanc's reforms were well meant he was too inexperienced to be effective and had merely reinforced the Franco–Russian position at Constantinople. Kennedy to Salisbury, 13 November 1888, FO, 45/603/285.

24 To Salisbury, 4 May 1889, FO, 170/415/T17. Typical of Crispi's attitude was his telegram to Lanza on 7 August 1888: 'At Constantinople he who is feared is respected.' AMEI, Tels 129/1290.

25 Salisbury to Dufferin, 8 May 1889, FO, 170/415/94; Catalani to Crispi, 9 May, AMEI, Tel. Conf. 351/1179.

26 Dering to Salisbury, 1 October 1889, FO, 45/625/204.

27 Correspondence in ASC, *Crispi*, 161.7.1–4, copies of telegrams exchanged on 13, 14, 15, 16 January. See F. Crispi, *Triple Alliance* (London, 1913), p. 462. Nigra pointed out that Austria, England and Germany had considerable interest in Turkish feelings. For Crispi's attempts to obtain Tripoli in 1890 see Lowe, *Reluctant Imperialists,* pp. 155–8 and Lowe, *Salisbury and the Mediterranean*, pp. 68–70.

28 C. Giglio, *L'Italia in Africa,* vol. I, *Etiopia–Mar Rosso 1857–1885* (Rome, 1956), I, p. 408; C. Zaghi, *P. S. Mancini, L'Africa e il problema del Mediterraneo 1884–5* (Rome, 1955), p. 112; *L'Italia in Africa, Documenti 1885–6*, nos 158, 185, 178, 188 (information that Antonelli derived from Menelik); no 221, Genè to Robilant, 7 May 1886. His information on the negus' intentions came from Captain Smith, a British officer returned from an official mission to Abyssinia. Smith found Ras Alula extremely hostile to the Italians.

29 *L'Italia in Africa, Documenti 1885–6*, nos 190, 207.

30 Palamenghi Crispi, *L'Italia coloniale e Francesco Crispi* (Milan, 1928), p. 61.

31 Palamenghi Crispi, *La prima guerra d'Africa* (Milan, 1914), p. 30 maintains that mediation was Salisbury's idea. This is pure fiction: see DDI, ii, XXI, no 215. See also Doc. 9 below.

32 R. Battaglia, *La prima guerra d'Africa* (Turin, 1958), pp. 323–31, 355–8,

362–5; Salvatorelli, op. cit., p. 160. The Massowa-Zeila exchange is contained in Malet to Salisbury, Salisbury to Malet, 21 and 24 January 1888, Salisbury Papers.

33 DDI, XXI, nos 215, 631, 717, 722.

34 *Atti Parlamentari*, 12 May 1888.

35 Battaglia, op. cit., pp. 372–88, 396, 399; C. Zaghi (ed.) *Crispi e Menelich* ... (Bari, 1956), pp. 11–12. There were two disputed versions of Article XVII of the Treaty of Uccialli. The Italian said Menelik *would* use the king of Italy etc: the Amharic said he *could* do so. Salimbene maintained this was because Antonelli did not understand Amharic – supra p. xxiv.

36 *Atti Parlamentari*, 2 May, 19 July, 22 December, 2ª *tornata,* 1888. The other main cause of complaint was that it was a distraction from the sacred *terra irredenta*.

37 Lowe, *Salisbury and the Mediterranean*, p. 61. On this aspect generally see R. L. Hess, 'Germany and the Anglo-Italian Colonial Entente' in P. Gifford *et al.*, eds, *Britain and Germany in Africa: Imperial Rivalry and Colonial Rule* (Yale, 1967).

38 *L'Italia in Africa, Serie storica,* II, Book III; *Documenti relativi alla Somalia settentrionale 1884–91* (Rome, 1968), nos 4, 12, 14, 17, 19, 67, 82; Hess, pp. 161–3. See J. S. Galbraith, 'Italy, the British East Africa Company and the Benadir Coast, 1888–1893' in *JMH* (1970). The most important telegrams on the negotiations in 1888 are in AMEI, Tels 129/1327, 130/1851, 1912. See also Doc. 11 below.

39 *Zanzibar Trattative* (collection of documents printed by Ministero deali Esteri 1891, copy in ASC, Carte Pisani Dossi, 21) Part II, Memorandum, 7 August 1890; Crispi to Tornielli, 11 August 1890, AMEI, Tels. 150/516. See also Doc. 13 below.

40 Dufferin to Salisbury 8 November 1890, FO, 78/4325/192. Various cryptic references in the Italian Foreign Ministry telegrams to secret instructions give a strong impression that Crispi had ordered Gandolfi to use any raid as an excuse for a large scale operation to take Kassala. In particular AMEI, Tels 149/786, 871, 891; 150/224, 268; 154/274, 327. See also Battaglia, op. cit., pp. 361–6.

41 Lowe, *Reluctant Imperialists,* pp. 140–4; G. N. Sanderson, 'England, Italy and the Nile balance 1890–91' in *HJ* (1964), pp. 104–5; Crispi to Tornielli, 30 September 1890, AMEI, Tels 150/199.

42 Crispi to Massowa, 21 August 1890, 5 January 1891; Massowa to Crispi, 17 November, AMEI, Tels 149/893; 150/534; 154/338. See Zaghi (ed.), *Crispi e Menelich* ..., pp. 289–90.

43 Tornielli to Crispi, 17 October 1890, ASC, Carte Pisani Dossi, 18. See also Docs 19–22 below.

44 Crispi to Tornielli, 10/11 October, AMEI, Tels 150/208, ter., 208 quarta. Tornielli to Crispi, 12 November 1890, ASC, Carte Crispi, 154/9. To Dufferin, Salisbury was explicit: 'They imagine that their alliance is a pearl of great price. . . . To my mind the Italian alliance is an unprofitable and even slightly onerous corollary on the German alliance. . . .' Lowe, *Salisbury and the Mediterranean*, p. 72. C. Zaghi, 'Il problema di Cassala' in *NA* (1940), p. 235.

45 See F. Fonzi, *Crispi e lo stato di Milano* (Milan, 1965), pp. 5–37; S. F. Romano, *I Fasci Siciliani* (Bari, 1959); Volpe, *Italia Moderna, 1815–1914,* pp. 380–6; Farini, *Diario,* 6, 18, 19 December 1894. Nigra and Kálnoky both thought the republican opposition would bring down the monarchy: Monson to Kimberley, 15 June 1894, FO, 170/483/160.

46 Hence the attack on Rudinì in *The Times* of 18 January 1894. It was written by their Rome correspondent, Stillman, a blind admirer of Crispi. The editor apologised privately to Rudinì. For the internal crises of 1891–3 which brought down Crispi, Rudinì and Giolitti in turn see Seton-Watson, *Italy from Liberalism to Fascism* (London, 1967), pp. 141–57. For Rudinì's and Giolitti's foreign policy see also Lowe, *Reluctant Imperialists,* pp. 144–6, 158–62, 168–74.

47 Baron Alberto Blanc, Secretary-General at the Consulta 1870–71, 1881–3; Ambassador Madrid 1883–7; at Constantinople 1887–91; Foreign Minister 1893–96. See Chabod, op. cit., pp. 5–7; Serra, op. cit., pp. 66–104.

48 Eperjesy to Goluchowski, 16 November, SAW, XI, 112, 69A–C; GP, X, no 2504; Chabod, op. cit., p. 76. Blanc to Pansa and to Ferrero, 18 November, AMEI, Tels 217/2213, 2222.

49 See F. R. Bridge, *From Sadowa to Sarajevo* (London, 1972), pp. 216–18; Lowe, *Reluctant Imperialists,* pp. 198–9.

50 King Umberto was highly sceptical of the German belief that England was bound to come to the Triple Alliance sooner or later: 'We sought to obtain this, but it did not come about'. Pasetti to Goluchowski, 17 December, SAW, XI, 112, 76A–C. CP, X, nos 2552–6.

51 Pasetti to Goluchowski, 13, 25 January 1896, SAW, Geheimakten XXV, Karton Rot 463. 5A–E, 7A–G; Crispi, *Questioni internazionali,* pp. 280–81; MRR, Carte Crispi, 668/1/4, 5. Diary, 25 and 27 January 1896. See also Docs 19, 20 below.

52 GP, XI, no 2767, Crispi, *Questioni internazionali,* pp. 288–90; Salvemini, op. cit., p. 134.

53 Antonelli wrote a memorandum in March 1894 entitled *Africa Italiana* which still advocated working with Menelik. Silvestrelli urged on 11 May that it be suppressed as 'contrary to the views' of Blanc and Crispi. ASC, Carte Pisani Dossi, 17.

54 C. Conti-Rossini, *Italia ed Etiopia* ... (Rome, 1935), pp. 120–40; Farini, op. cit., 4 February 1895; *Atti Parlamentari,* 14 June, 25, 29 July 1895; E. Serra, 'Le questioni di Cassala e di Adua' *Storia e politica,* 1966, p. 532.

55 Farini, op. cit., 13, 26, 27 July 1895; E. Serra, 'Cassala ed Adua', pp. 535–8; Conti-Rossini, op. cit., pp. 143–8, 153. The king told Farini that Crispi was only waiting for the end of the session to resume the advance. Baratieri estimated Menelik had 30,000 rifles; in fact he had over 100,000.

56 On Crispi and the Zeila question see C. J. Lowe, 'Anglo–Italian Differences in East Africa, 1892–5' in *EHR* (1966), pp. 319–33.

57 See F. Salata, *Il nodo di Gibuti* (Milan, 1939), pp. 53–68, 83–105; Lowe, 'Anglo–Italian Differences ...', pp. 331–3. Bodio, a confidant of Crispi's, reported from Paris that Bourgeois and Berthelot told him privately that it was impossible to reach any agreement with Italy whilst she remained

in the Triple Alliance. MRR, Carte Crispi, 668/1/8. Diary, 4 February 1896. See also Doc. 18 below.

58 GP, XI, no 2767. Hohenlohe strongly disliked Crispi. In his memoirs he wrote, 'Crispi's government made Caprivi, Marschall and Holstein all uneasy as one could never be sure what that unbalanced man would do. Besides, he chose a restless character, Blanc, for his foreign minister. . . .' *Denkwurdigkeiten,* II, p. 507.

59 Serra, op. cit., pp. 540–41; Conti-Rossini, op. cit., pp. 314–24; Battaglia, pp. 727–37. Some 9,000 of the 16,500 Italian troops engaged escaped.

5 Back from Africa

1 D. Farini, *Diario di fine secolo* (Rome, 1961), II, 3–8 March 1896. On Caetani and Rudinì's entourage in general, E. Serra, *La questione tunisina,* (Milan, 1967), pp. 365–71.

2 Ibid., pp. 373–80.

3 Farini, op. cit., II, 4, 6, 25, 27 March, 18 April; DDI, iii, 1, nos 6, 13, 53, 104. See also Docs 21 and 22 below.

4 *Atti Parlamentari* (Deputati), 25 May, 1 July (2a *tornata*); E. Decleva, *Da Adua a Sarajevo* (Bari, 1971), p. 27; Serra, op. cit., p. 372.

5 Ibid. 408; Decleva, op. cit., pp. 23–6, 56–7. See also Doc. 23 below.

6 DDI, iii, 1, nos 116, 118, 122; Serra, op. cit., pp. 382, 393–401; Decleva, op. cit., pp. 30–31; A. Torre, *La politica estera dell'Italia 1896–1914* (Bologna, 1960), pp. 1–81.

7 For the political crisis see Farini, op. cit., II, 11, 20, July 1896.

8 To Luzzatti, 30 December 1898, Serra, op. cit., pp. 407–8, 448–9, 453. The essential study of Visconti Venosta is in F. Chabod, *Storia della politica estera italiana dal 1870 al 1896* (Bari, 1952), pp. 581–94.

9 Serra, op. cit., pp. 414–15. In fact on this occasion Italy had no cause for complaint: Salisbury settled with France in September 1897. See A. Marsden, *British Diplomacy and Tunis 1875–1902* (New York, 1972), pp. 200–205.

10 Serra, op. cit., pp. 416–27; Torre, op. cit., pp. 87–99.

11 DDI, iii, 2, no 90.

12 Decleva, op. cit., pp. 61–6.

13 E. Serra, *Camille Barrère e l'intesa italo-francese* (Milan, 1950), pp. 61–76. C. Andrew, *Théophile Delcassé* (London, 1968), pp. 82–3. For the fall of Rudinì see C. Seton-Watson, *Italy from Liberalism to Fascism* (London, 1967), pp. 191–2.

14 Decleva, op. cit., pp. 85–7.

15 Ibid., pp. 87–92. Torre, op. cit., pp. 122–3 takes Barrère's appreciation as fact, rather than wishful thinking.

16 Decleva, op. cit., pp. 94–105.

17 One of Crispi's supporters termed the March convention 'the most damaging act for us since the occupation of Tunis'. Ibid., pp. 102, 109.

18 Serra, *La questione tunisina,* pp. 381–2; Serra, *L'intesa mediterranea del 1902* (Milan, 1957), pp. 25–6.

19 Torre, op. cit., pp. 128–68; Serra, *Camille Barrère . . .*, pp. 80–2.

20 Infra.

21 Decleva, op. cit., pp. 116–17.

22 Serra, *Camille Barrère* . . ., pp. 83–6.

23 DDI, iii, 1, no 163; 3, nos 353, 357, 361, 397, 402; Decleva, op. cit., pp. 121–2; Torre, op. cit., pp. 150–51. See also Doc. 24 below.

24 Ibid., pp. 153–9; Andrew, op. cit., pp. 143–5. There was no mention of this in the French note.

25 For the divergence between Delcassé and Barrère see Andrew, op. cit., pp. 139–40.

26 Decleva, op. cit., pp. 84, 104.

27 For contrasting views see L. Salvatorelli, *La triplice alleanza* (Milan, 1939), p. 235; Seton-Watson, op. cit., p. 213; Serra, *Camille Barrère* . . ., pp. 98–100; Decleva, op. cit., pp. 122–4.

28 Barrère to Delcassé, 25 April 1903, Decleva, op. cit., p. 200.

29 Serra, *L'intesa* . . ., p. 70. For the political crisis which brought in Zanardelli see Seton-Watson, op. cit., pp. 192–98.

30 Decleva, op. cit., pp. 151–2, 166, 192. But F. Tommasini, *L'Italia alla viglia della guerra* (Bologna, 1934–41), I, pp. 82–3, says his supposed pro-Russian and Montenegrin orientation is pure myth.

31 Decleva, op. cit., pp. 131–5.

32 Ibid., pp. 134–9, 146–7.

33 Ibid., pp. 153–4, 171; Andrew, op. cit., pp. 187–8. Delcassé consented to publish since, in Barrère's words, 'L'Italie se liera publiquement les mains en ce qui concerne la Mediterranée.'

34 For Balkan policy see below. Vienna eventually made a new commercial treaty, but not until 1906. F. R. Bridge, *From Sadowa to Sarajevo* (London, 1972), pp. 250–51 points out that Bulow's speech was aimed at Austria as much as Italy.

35 Decleva, op. cit., pp. 165–73; Salvatorelli, op. cit., pp. 250–59; Serra, *L'intesa* . . ., p. 213.

36 Lansdowne to Currie, 12 December 1900; Currie to Lansdowne, 24 December 1901; Rodd to Lansdowne, 29 July 1902. Currie wrote Barrington on 27 November 1900 that Salisbury never replied when he tried to interest him in co-operation with Italy: FO, 800/132. Serra, *L'intesa* . . ., is the best survey of Anglo–Italian relations after 1896 but overestimates Italian importance to Britain.

37 G. Borsa, *Italia e Cina nel secolo XIX* (Milan, 1961), pp. 79–183. Delcassé, by contrast, actually supported Italy at Peking.

38 For this episode see Serra *L'intesa* . . ., pp. 82–3.

39 Ibid., pp. 117–18, 125. Tornielli observed that no doubt this spontaneous declaration would be drafted by the Consulta.

40 Ibid., pp. 134, 141, 150, 152–3. Text p. 180. Currie was allowed to copy the Visconti-Barrère exchange of 4 January 1901, thus discovering that Italy would not oppose France in Morocco.

41 Salvatorelli, op. cit., pp. 239–40, 257–8.

42 Decleva, op. cit., pp. 169–71.

43 Ibid., p. 173. This is what Prinetti told Francesco Rota in 1919.

44 Tornielli to Pansa, 18 January 1902, Serra, *L'intesa* . . ., p. 120.

45 Prinetti to Pansa, 3 January, Malvano to Pansa, 16 March, 1902: Serra, *L'intesa* . . ., pp. 131, 193–8. Decleva, op. cit., p. 172.

46 Rudinì to Barrère, 31 May 1903, Decleva, op. cit., pp. 202–3; Bertie to Lansdowne, 4 May 1904, FO, 800/133; W. C. Askew (ed.), *Power, Public Opinion and Diplomacy* (Duke, 1959), pp. 184–5.

47 Entered parliament 1886, follower of Rudinì; prefect of Perugia 1898, of Naples 1900–1903; Senator 1902; Foreign Minister November 1903–December 1905, May 1906–December 1909, June 1919–June 1920; Ambassador at London 1905–6, at Paris 1910–19.

48 Decleva, op. cit., pp. 204–9.

49 Ibid., pp. 200–1, 248–9; Tommasini, op. cit., I, pp. 329–31.

50 Decleva, op. cit., pp. 210–17, 224–6, 259–67; Torre, op. cit., pp. 227–30. For Italo–Austrian relations see below, p. 140.

51 Salvatorelli, op. cit., pp. 296–302.

52 Decleva, op. cit., pp. 280–9. There were similar articles by Luzzatti.

53 Ibid., pp. 291–3.

54 Salvatorelli, op. cit., pp. 303–21; Torre, op. cit., pp. 243–59; Bridge, op. cit., pp. 280–83.

55 Decleva, op. cit., pp. 303–20. Tittoni all but point-blank refused to stop over in Paris on his way from London to Rome.

56 Ibid., pp. 333–4; Grey to Rodd, 20 February 1911, FO, 800/64.

57 Torre, op. cit., pp. 253–4; Bridge, op. cit., p. 283; Salvatorelli, op. cit., pp. 321, 334–6.

58 Torre, op. cit., pp. 209–13, 229–34. For details of the demonstrations in 1903 and 1908–9 see Tommasini, op. cit., I, pp. 265–8 and IV, pp. 218–21, 639–43.

59 Ibid., V, p. 309; Decleva, op. cit., pp. 237–40; B. Vigezzi, *Da Giolitti a Salandra* (Florence, 1969), pp. 36–41. *Il Tempo* was at this time edited by Claudio Treves who took over *Avanti!* on Mussolini's resignation in October 1914.

60 Tommasini, op. cit., I, p. 393, IV, p. 643; Askew, op. cit., pp. 186, 212–14; Vigezzi, op. cit., pp. 30, 100–101; Decleva, op. cit., p. 183. For the nationalists see Ch. 6 below.

61 DDI, iii, 2, no 13.

62 Bridge, op. cit., pp. 226–7, 236, 258–9, 272; Askew, op. cit., pp. 199, 209.

63 Bridge, op. cit., p. 420; Askew, op. cit., pp. 200–205; Torre, op. cit., pp. 157–70.

64 Salvatorelli, op. cit., pp. 263–73; Decleva, op. cit., pp. 178–9.

65 Ibid., pp. 180, 186.

66 Tommasini, op. cit., I, pp. 253–4, 272; Decleva, op. cit., pp. 216, 264.

67 Bertie to Lansdowne, 30 January, 22 February 1904, FO, 800/133; Barrère to Delcassé, 10, 20 February 1904, Decleva, op. cit., p. 253; Salvatorelli, op. cit., p. 282.

68 Decleva, op. cit., pp. 218–19.

69 Tommasini, op. cit., I, pp. 354–5, 396, 400; Bridge, op. cit., pp. 266–7.

70 Isvolski revealed it to Tittoni at Racconigi in 1909 in this light: Torre, op. cit., p. 236, certainly accepts it as proof of Austrian trickery.

71 Di San Giuliano to Martini, 30 July 1905, Decleva, op. cit., pp. 263, 323; Tommasini, op. cit., I, p. 461; Bridge, op. cit., p. 268.

72 Askew, op. cit., pp. 186–9; Decleva, op. cit., p. 338.

73 Decleva, op. cit., pp. 341–2. On the Sanjak railway see Bridge, op. cit., pp. 297–9.

74 Tommasini, op. cit., IV, pp. 218–21, 275–81; Decleva, op. cit., pp. 339–42. There is no record of this meeting with Isvolski.

75 Tommasini, op. cit., IV, pp. 230–37, V, pp. 547–8; Torre, op. cit., pp. 288, 311–16.

76 Ibid., pp. 317–18, 324–8; Decleva, op. cit., p. 343; Tommasini, op. cit., IV, pp. 398, 639–41, 652–4.

77 Decleva, op. cit., pp. 343–7. Most of the armaments expenditure under Giolitti had gone on what Sonnino called 'parliamentary choreography', since the navy was more politically acceptable than the army to the Left. See Seton-Watson, op. cit., pp. 359–60.

78 Decleva, op. cit., pp. 349–52, 386, n. 48.

79 Ibid., p. 388 n. 67; Tommasini, op. cit., V, pp. 282–6; Rodd to Grey, 6 May 1909, FO' 800/64.

80 Decleva, op. cit., pp. 348, 354–5; Salvatorelli, op. cit., p. 357; Askew, op. cit., p. 193.

81 Tommasini, op. cit., V, pp. 487–90; Salvatorelli, op. cit., pp. 372–4.

82 Tittoni Memorandum, 12 December 1909, Decleva, op. cit., pp. 356–7. See also Tommasini, op. cit., V, pp. 496–7.

83 Ibid., V, pp. 537–49; Torre, op. cit., pp. 347–9. See also Doc. 25 below.

84 Guicciardini Memorandum, 23 December 1909, quoted in Tommasini, op. cit., V, pp. 563–4. Decleva, op. cit., p. 387 n. 61.

85 Rodd came to much the same conclusion as Lutzow but added, 'were she [Italy] convinced that the northern [Russia] and western powers were sufficiently strong and determined to hold the central combination in check, she would willingly free herself from the bonds which have become irksome and antipathetic to the national instinct'. To Grey, 23 August 1909, FO, 800/64.

86 Decleva, op. cit., p. 360.

6 The Revival of Italian Nationalism

1 L. Salvatorelli, *La triplice alleanza* (Milan, 1939), pp. 383–4. Aehrenthal thought him honest but optimistic.

2 E. Decleva, *Da Adua a Sarajevo* (Bari, 1971), pp. 247, 365, 376, 389; B. Vigezzi, *Da Giolitti a Salandra* (Florence, 1969), pp. 28–9. As Decleva points out, one important reason for the lack of any reference to Austria at this congress was the pressure exercised by the prefect of Florence, on government instructions.

3 J. A. Thayer, *Italy and the Great War* (Wisconsin, 1964), pp. 192–204. This contains much the best study of the literary antecedents of the Italian Nationalist movement.

4 Decleva, op. cit., pp. 361, 367, 398.

5 Ibid., pp. 337, 398–402; Thayer, op. cit., pp. 208–9.

6 Decleva, op. cit., pp. 402–6; Thayer, op. cit., pp. 240–1.

7 Decleva, op. cit., p. 382.

8 Ibid., op. cit., pp. 376, 407–8; A. Torre, *La politica esteva dell'Italia 1896–1914* (Bologna, 1960), p. 356.

9 Giovanni d'Amendola to Salvemini, 2 October 1911: 'I do not believe that at the moment we are up against nationalism: it is the government. Nor do I think that Giolitti has let the nationalists force his hand.' Decleva, op. cit., p. 454 n. 32. 'Giolitti, piuttosto, è convinto per ragioni di politica internazionale.' Vigezzi, op. cit., p. 69.

10 Decleva, op. cit., pp. 409–10; Thayer, op. cit., pp. 242–4, 252; C. Seton-Watson, *Italy from Liberalism to Fascism* (London, 1967), pp. 370–71, 383–7.

11 On the diplomacy of the Tripoli war see the excellent monograph by W. C. Askew, *Europe and Italy's Acquisition of Libya* (Duke, 1942).

12 Torre, op. cit., pp. 367, 370–6, 386, 389–91; F. R. Bridge, *From Sadowa to Sarajevo* (London, 1972), pp. 335–6, 342.

13 Churchill to Grey, 4 November 1911, FO, 800/86; BD, IX, nos 231, 399; Mensdorff to Berchtold, 29 March 1912, SAW, XII, 375/XXXX/4/19C.

14 BD, IX, nos 296, 308, 349; G. André, *L'Italia e il Mediterraneo* (Milan, 1967), pp. 13–16.

15 Ibid., pp. 18–21; Decleva, op. cit., p. 455.

16 Ibid., pp. 372, 412–16; André, op. cit., pp. 22–3, 101–5; E. Serra, *Camille Barrère el'intesa italo-francese* (Milan, 1950), pp. 248–9; BD, X(ii), no 396; Rodd to Grey, 16 November 1912, 29 January 1913, FO, 800/64.

17 André, op. cit., pp. 44, 55, 98–9. The basis of the Treaty of Ouchy was that Italy would relinquish the Dodecanese once the Turks withdrew from Libya, where Italian sovereignty was accepted against an indemnity. One of the major objects of British and French diplomacy over the next two years was to get Italy to fulfil this treaty but, since fighting continued in Libya, Rome kept the Dodecanese. See R. Bosworth, 'Britain and Italy's acquisition of the Dodecanese, 1912–15' in HJ (1970), pp. 683–705. R. Sertoli-Salis, *Le isole italiane dell'Egeo* (Rome, 1939), assumes as a matter of course that Italy had a right to the islands.

18 André, op. cit., pp. 108–24.

19 For good examples see Bosworth, op. cit., pp. 694, 697, 701. For Anglo-French naval problems in the Mediterranean in 1912 see C. J. Lowe and M. L. Dockrill, *The Mirage of Power*, (London 1972), I, pp. 52–8.

20 Rodd to Grey, 16 November *supra*. Similarly Laroche to Poincaré, 30 September, André, op. cit., p. 102.

21 Decleva, op. cit., pp. 421–5, 458, 462; B. Vigezzi, *Da Giolitti a Salandra* (Florence, 1969), p. 31.

22 André, op. cit., pp. 144–5; Decleva, op. cit., pp. 417–20; Torre, op. cit., pp. 401–6; Bridge, op. cit., pp. 347–8. For the negotiation of the naval convention see M. Gabriele, 'Origini della convenzione navale italo-austro-germanica del 1912' in RSR (July–December 1965).

23 Decleva, op. cit., pp. 426, 460; Torre, op. cit., pp. 412–17, 426. Rodd to Grey, 26 May 1913, FO, 800/64.

24 André, op. cit., pp. 148–57, 167–9; Decleva, op. cit., pp. 429–32.

25 To Avarna, 17 August 1913, *supra.*
26 Di San Giuliano to Avarna, 30 August, to Bollati, 1 October, André, op. cit., pp. 175–7, 189–90; Seton-Watson, op. cit., pp. 406–7; Vigezzi, *Da Giolitti* . . ., p. 30. For Austrian interests in Asia Minor see Bridge, op. cit., pp. 364–5.
27 André, op. cit., pp. 173–4, 190; Bridge, op. cit., p. 358; Decleva, op. cit., p. 445.
28 André, op. cit., pp. 184–5, 196–8.
29 Ibid., pp. 193–4, 209–12.
30 Ibid., pp. 215, 219–20.
31 Ibid., pp. 225–57; Bosworth, op. cit., pp. 702–5; Crowe Memo, 17 May 1914, BD, X(2), no 449.
32 Bridge, op. cit., pp. 356–60; Torre, op. cit., 424–6, 435–6.
33 Decleva, op. cit., pp. 444, 448; Seton-Watson, op. cit., p. 409 n. 1.
34 Decleva, op. cit., pp. 438–40.
35 Di San Giuliano to Bollati, 14 July 1914, Torre, op. cit., pp. 430–32. See also Doc. 26 below.

7 *Neutrality and War, 1914–15*

1 B. Vigezzi, 'I problemi della neutralità e della guerra nel carteggio Salandra-Sonnino, 1914–1917', *NRS* (1961), p. 397.
2 O. Malagodi, *Conversazioni della guerra* (Milan, 1960), I, 17. The ambassadors at Vienna and Berlin, Avarna and Bollati, held similar views: see B. Vigezzi, *L'Italia di fronte alla prima guerra mondiale* (Naples, 1966), I, pp. 50–51.
3 Ibid., p. 14. See also Doc. 27 below.
4 Rodd's assessment. C. J. Lowe, 'Britain and Italian Intervention, 1914–15', *Historical Journal* (1969), p. 539.
5 DDI, 4th series, XII, no 560.
6 'The only territorial compensation that interests us is the cession of part of Austria's Italian provinces . . .' (San Giuliano to Avarna, 27 July). 'Offers of French territory have not been made . . . but would not modify our intention to remain neutral' (To Fasciotti, at Bucharest, 3 August). Quoted in Vigezzi, *L'Italia* . . ., pp. 15, 39.
7 F. Martini, *Diario 1914–1918* (Milan, 1966), entry for 31 July. Martini was Minister for the Colonies, 1914–16.
8 A. Solmi, 'Carteggio tra Salandra e Sonnino . . . Agosto–Dicembre 1914' in *NA* (1935), p. 487.
9 'Our sword carries little weight', Malagodi, op. cit., I, p. 20 (12 September, 1914). See also A. Salandra, *La neutralita italiana* (Milan, 1928), p. 268.
10 G. Rochat, 'L'esercito italiano nell'estate 1914', *NRS* (1961), pp. 295–347.
11 Ibid., pp. 324–9, 332.
12 M. Toscano, 'Rivelazioni e nuovi documenti sul negoziato di Londra', *NA* (1965), p. 440. Giolitti was adamant that the army was never intended for and was incapable of fighting a European war: Malagodi, op. cit., I, pp. 56–7.
13 Vigezzi, *L'Italia* . . ., pp. 144, 177, 205, 220–25.

14 A. Monticone, cited in Lowe, op. cit., p. 548. For the press see B. Vigezzi, *Da Giolitti a Salandra* (Florence, 1969), p. 79.

15 Vigezzi, *L'Italia* . . ., p. 886; W. Rienzi, 'Italy's neutrality and entry into the Great War' in *AHR* (1968), p. 1431.

16 Malagodi, op. cit., I, p. 17.

17 Albertini owned the *Corriere della Sera*. His newspaper became the leading interventionist journal. Vigezzi, *L'Italia* . . ., p. 199.

18 Ibid., p. 22.

19 Malagodi, op. cit., I, p. 18; Martini, *Diario*, 4, 6, 9 August.

20 Lowe, op. cit., pp. 534–5; Vigezzi, *L'Italia* . . ., pp. 60, 67–70, 74–5, 88–90; Rochat, op. cit., pp. 331–2.

21 Malagodi, op. cit., I, p. 20; Martini, *Diario*, 12 September. See also Doc. 28 below.

22 Rochat, op. cit., pp. 345–7; Vigezzi, *Da Giolitti* . . ., pp. 80–81.

23 DDI, fifth series, I, nos 773, 796.

24 Vigezzi, *L'Italia* . . ., p. 109; Lowe, op. cit., pp. 536–7.

25 Ibid., Martini, *Diario*, 24 November.

26 Solmi, op. cit., p. 491; Sonnino, *Diario* (Bari, 1972), II, pp. 16–19. Sonnino's timetable was: January negotiate, February mobilise, March act.

27 Vigezzi, *L'Italia* . . ., pp. 714–15.

28 Ibid., pp. 433, 441. Rocco, a law professor at Padua, was the nationalist leader in the Veneto.

29 Martini, *Diario*, 16 September. Sonnino certainly believed Giolitti responsible: *Diario*, II, p. 15.

30 According to Spingardi, Giolitti's Minister of War, expenditure on the army and navy had doubled from 1904–13 (from L396m–L747m). Pollio, Cadorna's predecessor, had considered heavy artillery unnecessary for a defensive war, which was the only war Giolitti intended to fight, so the king told Salandra in 1916: Vigezzi, *L'Italia* . . ., pp. 739–47.

31 *Unita*, 28 August, ibid., pp. 413–14.

32 A Turin paper, which normally supported Giolitti, ibid., p. 477. Since the Consulta was paying out large subventions in this period to the press, this presumably means less than Martini assumed. The most recent review of this question is contained in W. A. Rienzi, 'Mussolini's sources of financial support, 1914–1915' in *History* (1971), pp. 189–206.

33 *Azione Socialista*, 8 August; *Avanti!*, 16 August; Vigezzi, *L'Italia* . . ., pp. 225, 246.

34 Ibid., pp. 339–41, 510, 542, 565, 578.

35 'It is doubtful if they want war in the South. Do they really want it anywhere else?' Martini, *Diario*, 26 September, 21 November.

36 Vigezzi, *L'Italia* . . ., pp. 550–59, 643, 677–90.

37 Solmi, op. cit., pp. 491–3. 'It might divert the attention of the public and calm the impatience of those who push us into war . . .', Martini, *Diario*, 11 September.

38 Ibid., 25 September, 14 November.

39 Vigezzi, *L'Italia* . . ., p. 115; Toscano, op. cit., pp. 448, 455; Lowe, op. cit., p. 538; DDI, 5th series, I, ff. nos 892, 932. Di San Giuliano's reluctance

was such that Sonnino advocated not telling him what was afoot at Saseno: Sonnino, *Diario* II, p. 19.

40 Solmi, op. cit., pp. 493, 500.

41 Ibid., 490, 496; Martini, *Diario*, 19 October. The speech was intended simply as an appeal to his staff to close their ranks. See C. Seton-Watson, *Italy from Liberalism to Fascism* (London, 1967), p. 426.

42 Martini, *Diario,* 16 September. Both Rodd and Malagodi made similar assessments: Lowe, op. cit., p. 539; Malagodi, op. cit., I, p. 30.

43 Rienzi, 'Italy and the Great War' p. 1245. An adequate biography of Sonnino is still lacking. A short character sketch is contained in F. D'Amoja, *La politica estera italiana da Caporetto alla conferenza per la pace di Parigi, le premesse* (Messina, 1970), pp. 9–13, and in the introduction by Giorgio Spini to Sonnino's Diary, pp. x–xxxiv.

44 Solmi, op. cit., p. 501. Both the ministers of War and the Treasury were replaced by men more sympathetic to intervention. For details see Seton-Watson.

45 Martini, *Diario,* 25 November.

46 Malagodi, op. cit., I, pp. 22–3.

47 Vigezzi, *L'Italia . . .*, p. 140.

48 Martini, *Diario,* 29 March, 24 April 1915; Rienzi, op. cit., p. 1425; Vigezzi, *Da Giolitti . . .*, pp. 59, 97.

49 Malagodi, op. cit., I, pp. 30–32.

50 Sonnino to Bollati, 20 December 1914, S(onnino) P(apers) (Reel) 28, (Frame) 4. He told Martini that 'since it is impossible that she [Austria] should concede as much as we are asking we shall then turn to the Triple Entente': Martini, *Diario,* 5 December 1914. Sonnino, *Diario,* II, pp. 25, 32, 36 makes it clear that his sympathies were with the *Entente*.

51 Malagodi, op. cit., I, p. 40. It is clear that Giolitti fully shared this view. Vigezzi, *Da Giolitti . . .*, pp. 89–90.

52 '. . . questi uomini di stato non brillino di intelligenza . . . prima di fare loro comprendere una cosa e indurli a prendere una decisione ci vuol tempo e poi tempo.' Avarna to Sonnino, 9 January 1915, SP, 7/6.

53 SP, 31/88. Salandra's supporters in Milan in February urged him to avoid war if Vienna would make concessions: Vigezzi, *Da Giolitti . . .*, p. 91.

54 Giolitti, prompted by Bülow, wrote an open letter printed in *La Tribuna* on 2 February claiming that 'much' could be obtained by negotiation with Vienna. Malagodi, the editor, altered 'much' to 'something' (*parecchio*). Malagodi, op. cit., I, p. 42.

55 SP, 7/19, 52, 54, 66. Avarna to Sonnino, 19 January, 10, 13, 22 February 1915. Sonnino announced his *intention* of breaking off negotiations on 13 February.

56 Vigezzi, *I problemi . . .*, p. 427: 'Io seguito a discutere e bi antineggiare a Vienna. . . .' Sonnino, *Diario,* II, pp. 55–97, is a clear exposition of this.

57 SP, 31/4, 24, 30, 44; 7/24, 29, 34, 35. See also Doc. 37 below.

58 SP, 31/85; *Diario,* II, p. 100.

59 SP, 7/67.

60 Vigezzi, *I problemi . . .*, pp. 429–30. Significantly, Martini noted in his

diary on 3 March the news from Athens that Greece was about to join the
Entente: Diario, 3 March.

61 Lowe, op. cit., pp. 541–4. 'Grey and Asquith, one must acknowledge, have
strenuously defended our interests . . .', Imperiali to Sonnino, 22 April
1915, quoted in Toscano, op. cit., p. 454.

62 Lowe, op. cit., p. 543; SP, 31/125. Salandra put it another way: 'the only
serious reason for siding with them [the *Entente*], bringing with us
Roumania, is the exclusion from the Adriatic of any military power.
Serbia is more dangerous than Austria because she is not decadent.' To
Sonnino, 2 April 1915, SP, 7/187 bis.

63 Lowe, op. cit., p. 545.

64 Sonnino told Malagodi on 6 April that he was far less sure of Bulgarian
action than he had been a month before, though he still counted on
Romania: Malagodi, op. cit., I, p. 50.

65 'Italy and the Great War', p. 1429. Sonnino's papers, in particular 7/111,
124; 31/67, 85, 86 make it quite clear that the initiative came from Vienna,
not Rome. Sonnino insisted on 10 March that negotiations must be
completed within two weeks. See also Doc. 38 below.

66 Vigezzi, *I problemi . . .*, pp. 431–2.

67 Malagodi, op. cit., I, pp. 51–2; Avarna to Sonnino, 25 April 1915, SP,
7/296; Sonnino, *Diario,* II, pp. 108–25.

68 Ibid., pp. 100, 101, 135; Vigezzi, *I problemi . . .*, p. 433. Sonnino was
highly suspicious of Austrian intentions. He rejected out of hand their
demand that he make an announcement in parliament that negotiations
with Vienna were in progress. Reports from Bucharest made it obvious
Burian was leaking the negotiations to Bratianu, no doubt to impress him:
Bratianu certainly feared Sonnino would close with Vienna, SP, 31/87,
7/125.

69 Martini, *Diario,* 10 September, 29 October, 1 December 1914.

70 Tittoni to Sonnino, 23, 24 March, SP, 7/148, 156.

71 SP, 7/67, 88, 129; 31/111. See also Toscano, 'Rivelazioni e nuovi documenti sul negoziato di Londra', *NA*, 1965, vol. 495, pp. 20–29. For
further detail see his 'Le origine diplomatiche dell'articolo 9 del Patto di
Londra' in *Storia e Politica* vol. 3, 1965.

72 SP, 7/143, 160; 31/136. For later amplifications of this see C. J. Lowe and
M. L. Dockrill, *The Mirage of Power* (London, 1972), II, pp. 223–7. The
financial convention, article 14, provided for a loan of £50 million, a
figure which bore no relation whatsoever to any anticipation of Italian
war expenses. Neither the ministry of war nor the Consulta gave it any
thought, the figure originating quite haphazardly. Clearly, it reflected
Sonnino's assumption that it would be a short war. See Toscano,
'Rivelazioni' vol. 495, pp. 30–35. See also Doc. 41 below.

73 Tittoni to Sonnino 23 March, 17 April, 9 July 1915, SP, 7/148, 246, 860.

74 SP, 31/787. See also Docs 40, 42 below.

75 SP, 7/337.

76 E.g. Imperiali to Grey, 22 March: 'Noi non siamo uno stato Balcanico.'
SP, 7/146.

77 Bratianu stated to Fasciotti: 'Rispondo che il Governo Romeno e deciso

nel caso di un'azione italiana ad intraprendere simultanamento e con ogni vigore anche la propria azione.' SP, 7/69.

78 SP, 31/232, 247, 480; Sonnino, *Diario,* II, pp. 157–8.

79 SP, 7/69, 208, 226, 582.

80 An idea which henceforth Sonnino accepted and pushed strongly in June.

81 SP, 7/256.

82 Giolitti later complained bitterly of Salandra, that he had been the victim of a 'confidence trick' ('E stato tutto un inganno da pugliese'). Malagodi, op. cit., I, pp. 63–5.

83 Martini, *Diario,* 29 April; Vigezzi, *I problemi . . .,* p. 435.

84 Seton-Watson, op. cit., p. 442; Sonnino *Diario,* II, p. 139; L. Valiani, *La dissoluzione dell'Austria-Ungheria* (Milan, 1966), pp. 115–19. Valiani suggests Vienna had no intention of keeping this bargain after the war. Grey warned Imperiali on 21 March that Kitchener had received information from secret sources in Berlin that this was the case. Since Jagow went to the trouble of denying similar French reports, maybe there was some truth in this. SP, 7/143, 402; Sonnino, *Diario,* II, pp. 144–50. See also Doc. 39 below.

85 Martini, *Diario,* 9 May.

86 Ibid., 12, 13 May. Vigezzi, 'Le Radiose Giornate del maggio 1915 nei rapporti dei prefetti' in *Da Giolitti . . .,* pp. 136–7.

87 Malagodi, op. cit., I, pp. 36–9.

88 Ibid., pp. 56–7; Martini, *Diario,* 11 May.

89 Malagodi, op. cit., I, 69. But see the interesting testimony of Senator Cefaly, ibid., p. 153.

90 Ibid., p. 60. Giolitti, of course, had a habit of evading responsibility. Martini censured him strongly for denouncing war everywhere except in the Chamber: 'This preaching in the corridors without assuming any responsibility is intolerable.' *Diario,* 21 March. For a partisan defence of Giolitti, see Thayer, *Italy and the Great War* (Wisconsin, 1964), pp. 326, 357–8.

91 Vigezzi, *I problemi . . .,* pp. 435–6; *Da Giolitti,* pp. 126, 131.

92 Ibid., pp. 141–62. Telegram from Castrovillari, Calabria, to Salandra, 13 May 1915.

93 Ibid., pp. 176–8; Rienzi, 'Mussolini's Sources . . .', pp. 192–5; R. de Felice, *Mussolini,* vol. I, *Il rivoluzionario 1883–1920* (Turin, 1965), pp. 270–90, 297, 303, 309–10. Vigezzi, *Da Giolitti . . .,* pp. 86–7, 98–101, is highly critical of the Marxist thesis.

94 D'Annunzio was tipped off by Martini: *Diario,* 13, 26 May 1915.

95 Malagodi, op. cit., I, 68, 79. The basic weakness was of course the inadequate technical foundation. Italian steel production in 1914 was one twelfth of French, one fortieth of German production. Rochat, op. cit., p. 309.

8 Italy at the Peace Conference

1 L. Salvatorelli and G. Mira, *Storia d'Italia nel periodo fascista* (Turin, 1956), pp. 73–4. Similarly P. Alatri, *Nitti, D'Annunzio e la questione adriatica*

(Milan, 1959), p. 16; R. Vivarelli, *Il dopoguerra in Italia* (Naples, 1967), p. 385; G. Rumi, *Alle origini della politica estera fascista* (Bari, 1968), p. 39; R. Albrecht-Carrié, *Italy at the Peace Conference* (New York, 1938), p. 17; I. Bonomi, *La politica italiana dopo Vittorio Veneto* (Turin, 1953), pp. 41–3.

2 Austrian census figures of 1910 in I. Lederer, *Yugoslavia at the Peace Conference* (Yale, 1963), pp. 105–6. Zara (Zadar) was the only town in Dalmatia with an Italian majority.

3 Ibid., pp. 135–6. In the Foreign Office the attempt to seize Fiume was seen as 'a flagrant violation both of the letter and the spirit of the treaty [of London]'. GT, 6515, 11 December 1918, Cab. 24/72.

4 The phrase was coined by D'Annunzio in a poem published in the *Corriere della Sera* on 24 October 1918.

5 Notes, 25 February 1919, BM add. mss, 49750 B.P.

6 Lederer, op. cit., p. 137.

7 Alatri, op. cit., p. 41.

8 Miller to House, 11 January 1919, quoted in Albrecht-Carrié, op cit., p. 91.

9 Albrecht-Carrié, op. cit., pp. 61–2.

10 Balfour denounced it in November: DDI, vi, I, 451.

11 Lederer, op. cit., pp. 146, 194.

12 The French attitude generally was one of contempt: 'They all say that the signal for an armistice was the signal for Italy to begin to fight.' Derby to Balfour, 15 November 1918, BM add. mss. 49744, Balfour Papers.

13 'Quelle nazionalità non sono una cosa seria; sono termi di propaganda.' Sonnino, quoted in F. Chabod, *L'Italia contemporanea* (Turin, 1961), p. 23.

14 O. Malagodi, *Conversazioni della guerra, 1914–1919* (Milan, 1960), II, pp. 464–5; DDI, vi. I, pp. 70, 134, 152.

15 E.g. Cadorna's verdict: 'ambitious and weak: therefore dishonest'. M. Silvestri, *Isonzo 1917* (Turin, 1965), p. 116.

16 Malagodi, op. cit., II, pp. 473–4; L. Valiani, 'Documenti francesi sull'Italia e il movimento Jugoslavo' in *RSI*, 1968, pp. 361–2.

17 G. Salvemini and C. Marinelli, *La Questione dell'Adriatico* (Rome, 1919), p. 7. Sonnino instructed Bonin Longare, Ambassador at Paris, on 9 November 1918 that he should not support any agitation for Fiume: D.D.I. vi. I, 70.

18 Albrecht-Carrié, op. cit., pp. 123, 171.

19 R. de Felice, *Mussolini, vol. I, Il rivoluzionario, 1883–1920* (Torino, 1966), p. 376; Salvemini and Marinelli, op. cit.; L. Bissolati, *La politica estera dell'Italia dal 1897 al 1920* (Milan, 1923), p. 335.

20 Vivarelli, op. cit., pp. 481–5, 489. See especially his speech at Venice on 25 April.

21 'Ora che siamo al Piave, voglio tutta la Dalmazia', De Felice, op. cit., pp. 380, 392.

22 Mussolini in *Popolo d'Italia,* 23 November 1918. Rumi, op. cit., pp. 9–11.

23 'Either Wilson or Lenin.' This was the theme of Mussolini's San Sepulcro programme of March 1919: Rumi, op. cit., p. 23; De Felice, op. cit., pp. 482–3. The socialist leader, Filippo Turati, though opposed to

Orlando, made exactly the same criticism of Wilsonian principles in April 1919: Vivarelli, op. cit., p. 491.

24 Rumi, op. cit., p. 28.

25 To the evident satisfaction of the leading industrialists, according to the Prefect of Milan: Ibid., p. 17.

26 Vivarelli, op. cit., pp. 485–7. By April 1919 the *Corriere della Sera* was the only liberal newspaper to oppose this popular current.

27 Rumi, op. cit., pp. 31–4; Malagodi, op. cit., II, 517.

28 Lederer, op. cit., pp. 63–73. Hence Bissolati's resignation on 28 December, followed by that of Nitti in January.

29 Ibid., pp. 166–70, 221–3; telegrams 42/14 (Sonnino to Paris, 4 January), 42/137 (Borsarelli to Comando Supremo, 29 January), 43/307 (Sonnino to Vienna, 21 March), 43/470 (De Martino to Rome, 30 April), SP.

30 Lederer, op. cit., p. 234; telegrams 43/50, 61 (Sonnino to Rome, 26, 30 January), 43/173 (Sonnino to Valona, 25 February), 43/174 (Sonnino to Washington, 25 February), 42/331 (Borsarelli to Belgrade, 8 April), 43/438 (Sonnino to Valona, 22 April), SP.

31 Lederer, op. cit., pp. 173–8; telegrams 41/54 (Bianchieri to Sonnino, 28 February), 43/259 (Sonnino to Budapest, 13 March), 43/665 (Sonnino to Budapest, 7 June), SP.

32 Lederer, op. cit., p. 103. Austria census figures of 1910 gave a Slav majority in Istria (58 per cent) but not for Trieste (43 per cent).

33 And for that matter, the succession states in general: Malagodi, op. cit., II, p. 474.

34 'We Italians went to the Conference knowing nothing of the true sentiments of Wilson', V. E. Orlando, *Memorie* (Milan, 1960), p. 388.

35 Albrecht-Carrié, op. cit., pp. 82–8. Lederer, op. cit., pp. 146–7.

36 BM add. mss. 49744, 49751, Balfour Papers.

37 Report of 12 April 1919, Lederer, op. cit., pp. 168–9.

38 Orlando thought Shantung the real explanation of Wilson's stand on Fiume: *Memorie*, p. 409.

39 Albrecht-Carrié, op. cit., p. 144. On the April negotiations see especially L. Aldrovandi-Marescotti, *La guerra diplomatica* (Milan, 1937), pp. 230–50. As Sonnino's *chef de cabinet* from 1914 to 1919 he was particularly well informed – as official Italian secretary he took minutes of the Council of Four, 19 April–24 June. The accuracy of the telegrams he prints is confirmed by the Sonnino Papers.

40 Memorandum of 23 April 1919 signed Clemenceau and Lloyd George, usually termed the Balfour Memorandum. Printed in Aldrovandi-Marescotti, op. cit., pp. 743–9.

41 Ibid., pp. 764–6, 796–7. See also Docs 45–7 below.

42 Aldrovandi-Marescotti, op. cit., p. 422. On the Tardieu Plan, see Lederer, op. cit., pp. 212–14.

43 Orlando, *Memorie*, p. 420.

44 DDI, vi, I, no 451. For the 1917 negotiations see C. J. Lowe and M. L Dockrill, *The Mirage of Power* (London, 1972), II, pp. 223–7.

45 'We have engaged to pay for Italian assistance and if they want payment I think we must pay it without bargaining.' Balfour in the Eastern

Committee, 5 December 1918, Cab. 27/24. (Repudiation was Lloyd George's idea.)

46 Tels 41/31, 65; 43/47, 96, 107, 167, 178, 271, SP. See also Doc. 34 below.

47 DDI, vi, I, nos 777, 788; tels 41/48, SP.

48 Lloyd George: 'You would not insist on having all of Anatolia if you had Fiume?' Orlando: 'Certainly not. If you give me Fiume it would be quite another thing.' Aldrovandi-Marescotti, op. cit., pp. 366–7. It should be remembered though that Sonnino and Orlando had different standpoints: Sonnino was concerned for the interests of Italy; Orlando for his majority.

49 DDI, vi, I, nos 393, 436, 475, 772, 853. Tel. 43/536, SP. Hardinge thought the claims 'somewhat ridiculous since their influence only extends to the range of their guns from the sea'. To Rodd, 6 December 1918, Hardinge Papers. See also Doc. 43 below.

50 Ibid., 43/532, 552, 578, 613, 622.

51 M. Toscano, *Pagine di Storia Contemporanea* (Milan, 1963), I, pp. 220–40.

52 Rodd to Curzon, 17 January 1919, FO, 371/3804. See also R. Albrecht-Carrié, 'Italian colonial policy, 1914–18' in *JMH* (1946). He concludes (p. 143) that in 1919 colonialist demands 'did not meet with a wide response among large sections of opinion, nor did they represent the official policy of the *Consulta*'.

53 Aldrovandi-Marescotti, op. cit., pp. 366–7; Albrecht-Carrié, *Italy at the Peace Conference*, pp. 217–23.

54 Alatri, op. cit., pp. 78–91.

55 'Una netta catastrofe, insomma, per la nostra politica estera in generale ed orientale in particolare.' R. Sertoli-Salis, *Le isole italiane dell'Egeo dall'occupazione alla sovranita* (Rome, 1939), p. 256. The Tittoni-Venizelos agreement was denounced by Sforza in 1920 and the Dodecanese recovered by Italy.

56 Vivarelli, op. cit., p. 266–7. By contrast, it would seem that the real wages of factory workers were maintained, a fact which accounts for the increasing middle-class resentment of the workers and political antagonism. Ibid., p. 398.

57 Imports from the USA alone were up 578 per cent by 1919: DDI, vi, I, p. 828.

58 R. Romeo, *Breve Storia della grande industria in Italia* (Capelli, 3rd ed. Milan, 1967), pp. 114–33. In 1914 it cost £0·5 per ton to ship coal from Britain to Italy; in 1918, £21 per ton. Taking 1913 as the base (= 100), in 1920 the price of cast iron reached 1,036 in Italy, as compared with 191 in Britain. Hydro-electric power doubled during the war but this was insufficient to compensate.

59 Alatri, op. cit., pp. 78–80, 319; C. Seton-Watson, *Italy from Liberalism to Fascism* (London, 1967), pp. 549–50.

60 Lloyd George liked Nitti as much as he had disliked Orlando: Hardinge to Graham, 10 April 1920, Hardinge Papers. For the San Remo conference and the Treaty of Sèvres see C. J. Lowe and M. L. Dockrill, op. cit., II, pp. 364–7.

61 Alatri, op. cit., pp. 78–87; C. Sforza, *Contemporary Italy* (New York, 1944), pp. 237–44, 270–72.
62 Alatri, op. cit., pp. 99–106; Seton-Watson, op. cit., pp. 537, 551.
63 Valiani, op. cit., pp. 361–2; Vivarelli, op. cit., p. 456.
64 Alatri, op. cit., p. 266.
65 C. Sforza, *Contemporary Italy* (New York, 1944), p. 263.
66 'La civiltà non è se non lo splendore della lotta incessante.' Vivarelli, op. cit., pp. 498–505.
67 For example the Augusteo demonstration in Rome on 29 June 1919, led by Corradini and Host Venturi, which marched on Nitti's residence in Piazza Barberini.
68 See the complaints of the Prefect of Bologna in July 1919, Vivarelli, op. cit., pp. 466–7.
69 Alatri, op. cit., pp. 107–9; Vivarelli, op. cit., pp. 461–5, 469. But compare De Felice, op. cit., pp. 547–8, who considers the plot a figment of Nitti's imagination. In fact Generals Diaz, Badoglio and Caviglia were loyal to the government, as Alatri acknowledges.
70 De Felice, op. cit., pp. 549–63.
71 Alatri, op. cit., p. 320.
72 Hence Mussolini's fears of a settlement with Yugoslavia and attacks on Nitti's 'secret diplomacy' in *Popolo d'Italia* during December. Rumi, op. cit., p. 69.
73 Basically the scheme proposed Fiume to Italy, Sušak to Yugoslavia, Zara a free state; Valona to Italy, the rest of Albania an Italian mandate; the islands divided and demilitarised. If Belgrade rejected this, then the Treaty of London was to be enforced.
74 For details see Lederer, op. cit., pp. 264–84.
75 Rumi, op. cit., pp. 90–91. In fact Nitti had supported a pro-German, anti-French line at the San Remo conference and suspected that France had contributed to his fall. See Seton-Watson, op. cit., pp. 558–9.
76 Giolitti had always opposed the Treaty of London: Malagodi, op. cit., II, 457. See also Sforza, op. cit., pp. 269–70.
77 Seton-Watson, op. cit., pp. 578–9.
78 See Lederer, op. cit., pp. 237–8, 302–6.
79 Rumi, op. cit., pp. 101, 104–5.
80 Mussolini's new-found realism probably owed a lot to the changing character of the fascist movement. Whereas up to 1919 it consisted largely of intellectuals, futurists, etc., in 1920–1 it absorbed the syndicalists amongst the urban workers and many landless peasants. These had little interest in either D'Annunzio's idealism or Dalmatia. See De Felice, *Mussolini*, vol. II, *Il fascista: la conquista del potere, 1921–1925*, pp. 7–15.
81 Letter to Luigi Albertini, 12 April 1919, printed in Vivarelli, op. cit., pp. 578–9.

9 Mussolini and the New Diplomacy

1 Sforza to Mussolini, 31 October 1922, DDI, vii, 1, no. 1.
2 Ennio di Nolfo, *Mussolini e la politica estera Italiana, 1919–1933* (Padua,

1960), chapter I passim; and Allan Cassels, *Mussolini's Early Diplomacy* (Princeton, 1970), pp. 3–21.

3 M. Donosti [M. Luccioli], *Mussolini e l'Europa* (Rome, 1945), p. 13.

4 B. Mussolini, *Opera Omnia* ed. E. and D. Susmel (36 vols, Florence, 1951–63), XVII, p. 124.

5 Curzon's note to De Martino on 10 February 1922, is printed as appendix V of 'Memorandum on the Dodecanese Question', 24 January 1928, FO 371, C976/976/22.

6 Buchanan's objectives are in his letter to Oliphant, 1 April, 1921, FO 371, E 3747/3568/16.

7 'Memorandum on the Dodecanese Question', op. cit.

8 Ibid.

9 Raffaele Guariglia, *Ricordi* (Naples, 1949), p. 19.

10 For the Turkish problem, 1919–22, see C. J. Lowe and M. L. Dockrill *Mirage of Power* (London, 1972), II, pp. 364–74.

11 Mussolini to Curzon, 3 November 1922, FO 371, C15283/1953/19.

12 Mussolini to della Torretta, 22 November 1922, DDI, vii, I, no 145.

13 Garroni to Mussolini, 4 December 1922, ibid., 200.

14 B. Mussolini, *Opera Omnia*, XIX, p. 38.

15 Memorandum to the inter-allied conference, 9 December 1922, DDI, vii, I, no 217.

16 Romano Avezzana to Mussolini, 20 December 1922, and 5 January 1923, ibid., 283 and 304.

17 Mussolini to Romano Avezzana, 10 January 1923, ibid., 324.

18 Della Torretta to Mussolini, 20 January 1923, ibid., 382.

19 Mussolini to Preziosi, 18 January 1923, ibid., 68, and Mussolini to Romano Avezzana, 18 January 1923, ibid., 373.

20 Della Torretta to Mussolini, 20 January 1923, ibid., 379. Avezzana to Mussolini, 20 January 1923, ibid., 377.

21 Curzon to Kennard, 14 March 1923, FO 371, C4877/1404/22; Graham to Curzon, 7 May 1923, FO 371, C8160/1404/22; Graham to Curzon, 7 June 1923, FO 371, C10142/1404/22.

22 SIM (Italian military intelligence) had infiltrated a delegation of Indian nationalists visiting Mussolini in February 1923. Following the visit a commercial institute was opened and some scholarships offered. Graham thought the whole scheme was got up by certain fascists to line their pockets, 31 May 1923, FO 371, C9802/1404/22.

23 Guariglia, op. cit., p. 27.

24 A. Foschini, *La verita sulle cannonate di Corfu* (Rome, 1953), pp. 25–8. See also E. Anchieri, 'L'affare di Corfu alla luce dei documenti diplomatici italiani', *Il Politico*, XX (1955), pp. 374–95; J. Barros, *The Corfu Incident of 1923* (Princeton, 1966).

25 Mussolini to Montagna, 29 August 1923, DDI, vii, 2, no 195.

26 Montagna to Mussolini, 31 August 1923, ibid., no 217.

27 Guariglia, op. cit., p. 29. According to Foschini, the island's military commander said he would oppose a peaceful occupation. He was warned at 1.45 p.m. on 31 July 1923 that the Italian ship would fire a salvo at military targets at 4 p.m., if there was no surrender. One of the shots hit

the Old Fortress killing seven and wounding ten Anatolian refugees, who apparently had not been warned of an impending attack on military installations. A. Foschini, *La verità*, pp. 39–44.

28 Kennard to Curzon, 2, 3, 4 September 1923, FO 371, C15166, 15171, 15263/15065/22; Kennard to Curzon, minute on, FO 371, C15171/15065 /22.

29 Graham to Curzon, 17 September 1923, FO 371, C16523/15065/62.

30 Minister of Marine to Mussolini, 13 September 1923, DDI, vii, 2, 347, 348. According to Foschini, the Italian navy had been mobilised to face the British threat: *La verità*, p. 58.

31 Graham to Curzon, 17 September 1923, FO 371, C16523/15065/62.

32 Curzon to Graham, 17 December 1923, FO 371, C21867/4/19, n. 1; Mussolini to Della Torretta, 27 December 1923, DDI, vii, 2, no 523, and minute on Della Torretta to Mussolini, 5 January 1924, ibid., no 534.

33 Mussolini to MacDonald, 2 May 1924, FO 361, C7363/160/19.

34 See B. Mussolini, *Opera Omnia*, XXI, p. 227, and Annual Report 1924, Rome Embassy, p. 12, FO 371, C3343/3343/22.

35 Statement of French president Doumergue, in Avezzana to Mussolini, 4 March 1925, DDI, vii, 3, no 743.

36 Mussolini's reply to the offer reaffirmed his faith in the peace treaties as presently formulated – a pledge he probably thought more solemn than any which might eventuate. See his messages to Della Torretta, Avezzana and De Bosdari, 14, 26, 29 March 1925; ibid., nos 761, 774, 780.

37 De Bosdari to Mussolini, 8 May 1923, ibid., no 846; the German accounts of the investigation do not put the same issue quite so strongly; see Cassels, op. cit., p. 275.

38 De Bosdari had reported as early as 24 March, that d'Abernon had suggested that Germany might annex Austria in compensation for concessions in the Rhineland. This news was confirmed by Avezzana, 3 June 1925, DDI, vii, 4, no 17. Mussolini's statement to the Senate is rendered faithfully in G. Salvemini, *Mussolini diplomatico, 1927–1932* (Bari, 1952), p. 97. *Gerarchia,* the party's official organ, used stronger language: 'In the meantime it is just as well to make this clear; either the Brenner is guaranteed or Italy does not sign the pact', 9 June 1925, quoted in di Nolfo, *Mussolini,* p. 130.

39 The best account is Cassels, op. cit., pp. 275–7.

40 Mussolini to De Bosdari, 30 May 1925, DDI, vii, 4, no 13.

41 The offers were made on 3 June, by Berthelot and on 9 June, 14 June and 27 August by Briand; DDI, vii, 4, nos 17, 27, 32, 111.

42 Mussolini to della Torretta, R. Avezzana and Scialoja, 8 June 1925, ibid., no. 21; and Mussolini to Avezzana, 14 September 1925, ibid., no. 120.

43 Conversation with Austen Chamberlain is in Scialoja to Mussolini, 10 June 1925, ibid., nos 28, 29. Mussolini's instructions to Avezzana are dated 23 June 1925, ibid., no. 42.

44 Mussolini to Avezzana, 14 September 1925, ibid., no. 120 n. 1.

45 Avezzana to Mussolini, 25 September 1925, ibid., no. 130.

46 Avezzana to Mussolini, 30 April 1925, DDI, vii, 3, no. 829.

47 See P. G. Edwards, 'The foreign office and fascism, 1924–29', and R. J. B.

Bosworth, 'The British press, the conservatives and Mussolini', in the *JCH* (1970), V, no. 2, pp. 153–61, 163–82.
48 On this see R. de Felice, *Mussolini* Vol. III, *Il fascista: l'organizzazione della stato fascista, 1925–1929* (Turin, 1968), *passim*.

10 Italo–French Relations after Locarno

1 *Gerarchia*, February 1927, quoted in E. di Nolfo, *Mussolini e la politica estera Italiana, 1919–1933* (Padua, 1960), p. 217.
2 One of the principal problems was Italy's claim to representation in the administration of Tangier on a footing of equality with the three signatory powers of the Tangier Statute of 1924. A conference between Great Britain, France, Spain and Italy met in March 1928, and on 25 July 1928, an agreement satisfying nearly all Italy's demands was signed by the four powers.
3 'Memorandum respecting Franco–Italian Relations', 18 January 1930, FO 371, C576/29/22.
4 DDI, vii, 6, nos 68, 77; French version in Robert de Dampierre, 'Dix annécs de politique française à Rome (1925–1935), *La revue des deux mondes* (November–December 1953), pp. 25ff.
5 Mussolini to Manzoni, 13 April 1928, DDI, vii, 6, no. 248.
6 'The question of Libya's southern frontier', 30 March 1928, ibid., no. 208.
7 Quoted in Foreign Office 'Memorandum respecting Franco–Italian relations', op. cit.
8 DDI, vii, 6, no. 248.
9 Manzoni to Mussolini, 19 April 1928, ibid., nos 264, 278.
10 DDI, vii, 7, no. 182.
11 Ibid.
12 R. Guariglia, *Ricardi, 1922–1946* (Naples, 1949), pp. 144–63.
13 Ibid.
14 Graham to Simon, 15 June 1932, FO 371, C4890/2863/22.
15 R. Cantalupo, *Fu la Spagna: ambasciata presso Franco febbraio–aprile 1937* (Milan, 1948), p. 42.
16 B. Mussolini, *Opera Omnia*, XXV, pp. 141–4.

11 The Watch on the Brenner

1 See R. Guariglia, *Ricordi, 1922–1946* (Naples, 1949), p. 150, and P. Aloisi, *Journal* (Paris, 1957), 29 July 1932. The French side of the negotiations is summarised in DDF, i, 2, no. 182. Theodoli was Under-Secretary at the Italian Ministry of Colonies.
2 Aloisi, op. cit., 4 October 1932.
3 On Italo–French relations in the early 1930s see E. Robertson, 'Mussolini and Ethiopia: The Prehistory of the Rome Agreement', in M. S. Anderson and R. Hatton (eds), *Essays in Diplomatic History in Memory of D. B. Horn* (London, 1970), pp. 339–56. See also 'Memorandum on Italo–French relations', FO 371, C7646/175/22.

4 Ibid.

5 The Franco–Yugoslav pact of 1927 had been renewed on 2 December 1932. An announcement of its renewal had been put off in the hope of obtaining, as in 1926, a tripartite arrangement with Italy, still the technique preferred by Paris to both propitiate and contain Italy's aspirations in Yugoslavia.

6 For Jouvenel's offer see DDF, i, 2, no. 386; Paul Boncour's acceptance, no. 400.

7 Ibid., no. 478.

8 DDF, i, 4, no. 293.

9 Foreign Office Memorandum on Franco–Italian relations, R 1177/1/67.

10 Ibid.

11 On this subject see F. G. Stambrook, 'The German–Austrian customs union project of 1931', in H. Gatzke, *European Diplomacy between two Wars, 1919–1939* (Chicago, 1972).

12 Guariglia (who accompanied Grandi), op. cit., pp. 130–40.

13 Prince Ernst Starhemberg, *Between Hitler and Mussolini* (London, 1943), pp. 26–7.

14 Starhemberg, op. cit., p. 90.

15 D'Amoja, op. cit., p. 142; Aloisi, op. cit., 17 February 1933.

16 Kopke's memorandum of 23 March 1933, on Hitler's conversation with Cerutti in DGFP, C, 1, no. 112.

17 Based on Paul R. Sweet, 'Mussolini and Dollfuss: an episode in fascist diplomacy', in J. Braunthal, *The Tragedy of Austria* (London, 1948). See Mussolini to Dollfuss, 1 July 1923, cited p. 185.

18 Kopke's memorandum, 14 July 1933, DGFP, C, 1, no. 363; and Braunthal, op. cit., p. 192.

19 Aloisi, op. cit., 27 July 1933; DGFP, c, 1, nos 377–9, 382, 388, 392.

20 Memorandum by Bülow, 31 July 1935, ibid., no. 383.

21 Memorandum by Bülow, 5 August 1933, ibid., no. 395.

22 On this see Vansittart, 28 August 1933, DBFP, ii, 5, no. 371.

23 DGFP, c, 1, no. 402.

24 Braunthal, op. cit., p. 194. Hadow to Foreign Office, 23 August 1933, FO 371, C7529/3311/3.

25 Vansittart's memorandum on present and future conditions of Europe, 28 August 1933, DBFP, ii, 5, no. 371.

26 See Campbell to Simon, 1 September 1933, ibid., no. 379; Vansittart to Campbell, 12 September 1933, ibid., no. 387; an outline of the French plan is in no. 383.

27 Austrian note of 17 January 1934, DGFP, c, 2, no. 188, enclosure; DBFP, ii, 6, appendix to no. 201.

28 This is the interpretation advanced by J. Gehl, *Austria, Germany, and the Anschluss, 1931–1938* (London, 1963), p. 81.

29 On this see, DGFP, c, 2, no. 29; and Mackensen's report of 26 February 1934, no. 279.

30 Georgy Ranki, 'Il patto tripartito di Roma e la politica estera dell' Italia', in *Studi Storia,* III, no. 2, April–June 1962, p. 364.

31 Drummond's report of 20 March 1934, DBFP, ii, 6, no. 358.

32 Neurath's memorandum of 15 June 1934, DGFP, c, 3, no. 5, and unsigned memorandum approved by Hitler, no. 7.
33 Erbach's report of 31 July 1934, ibid., no. 137.
34 Clerk to Simon, 31 July 1934, DBFP, ii, 6, no. 548. Simon to Clerk, 3 August 1934, no. 560.

12 The Abyssinian War

1 Quoted in S. Rumi, 'Il fascismo delle origini', *Movimento di Liberazione Nazionale,* no. 75, April 1964, p. 11.
2 For a thorough discussion see G. Carocci, *La politica estera dell' Italia fascista 1925–1929* (Bari, 1969), ch. 1, *passim.*
3 Salvatore Saladino, 'Italy', in H. Rogger and E. Weber, eds, *The European Right: a Historical Profile* (Berkeley, 1965), pp. 233–4.
4 'Atto di nascita del fascismo', B. Mussolini, *Opera Omnia,* XII, p. 323.
5 *Impero,* quoted in Rumi, op. cit., p. 16.
6 G. W. Baer, *The Coming of the Italo–Ethiopean War* (Cambridge, Mass., 1967), for the most scholarly statement of this view.
7 Quoted in Rumi, op. cit., p. 27.
8 Memorandum of a conversation between Sperling and Baccari, 19 March 1920, FO 371, A1757/12/60.
9 Russell to Curzon, 2 February 1923, FO 371, A1129 and A1130/25/1.
10 H. Goodwin, *Historical Summary,* 2 September 1935, FO 371/19175.
11 Giuseppe Vedoto, *Gli accordi Italo–Etiopici dell' Agosto 1928* (Florence, 1956), p. 41.
12 The text of the treaty and the convention are in Vedovato, op. cit., pp. 102–5. For the rearguard action of the Africanists, see ibid., pp. 59–93.
13 Guariglia remarked to the British chargé d'affaires in Rome in July 1930, that the main importance of Abyssinia to France was as a means of causing difficulties to Italy and Great Britain. Barton, the British Minister in Addis Ababa, agreed. 'There is no doubt that the French are making every effort at the present moment to pursue a forward policy in this country largely at Italy's expense', Barton to Henderson, 2 September 1930, FO 371, J 3267/1994/1.
14 Quoted in Vedovato, op. cit., p. 210.
15 Memorandum of 27 August 1932, Guariglia, *Ricordi, 1922–1946* (Naples, 1949), pp. 763–73.
16 B. Mussolini, 'The Doctrine of Fascism', *Enciclopedia Italiana di scienze, lettere ed arti* (Milano, 1932), XIV, pp. 846–51.
17 '*Direttive per l'oltre confino*', circular letter no. 400, 1 August 1932, quoted in Robert Hess, *Italian Colonialism in Somalia* (Chicago, 1966), p. 172.
18 E. de Bono, *La preparazione e le prime operazioni* (Rome 1937), pp. 5–8.
19 P. Aloisi, *Journal* (Paris, 1957), 3 January 1933.
20 Minutes of a meeting between Mussolini, De Bono, Badoglio, Suvich, 31 May 1934, quoted in Hess, op. cit., p. 172–3. See also P. Badoglio, *La guerra d' Etiopia* (Milan, 1936).
21 E. de Bono, *Anno XIII, the Conquest of an Empire* (London, 1937), p. 16.

22 Nino d' Aroma, *Vent' anni insieme; Vittorio Emanuele e Benito Mussolini* (Rome, 1957), pp. 229–30.
23 FRUS 1934, II, p. 754.
24 Minute by G. A. Wallinger on Murray to FO, 18 September 1934, FO 371, J2190/2082/1.
25 Minute on FO 371, J2043/1352/1. British nervousness was increased by the fact that the British firm, Vickers, was selling arms to Abyssinia illegally. Memorandum 30 July 1934, FO 371, J1820/1820/1.
26 Memorandum by G. H. Thompson, 'Diplomatic Action taken by His Majesty's Government as from November 23, 1934 . . .', 14 October 1935, FO 371, J6295/1/1, para. 1.
27 Loc. cit.
28 Loc. cit., and Drummond to FO, 29 August 1935, FO 371, J4204/1/1.
29 H. Goodwin, op. cit.
30 This was the first time the claim was made explicitly and the Italian government appeared to base its justification on the grounds that the wells were in the territory of the Sultanate of Obbia, a tribe towards the coast, within the meaning of Article IV of the 1906 treaty.
31 Thompson, op. cit., para. 6.
32 Loc. cit.
33 Loc. cit.
34 Text in A. Lessona, *Memorie* (Roma, 1963), pp. 165–71.
35 Guariglia, op. cit., p. 144. De Caix, 'Notes sur les conversations avec le Marquis Theodoli', DDF, i, 2, no. 182. appendix 1.
36 Guariglia, op. cit., p. 165; 'Memorandum on Franco–Italian relations, August 1933–January 1935', FO 371, R1177/1/67.
37 E. Robertson, 'Mussolini and Ethiopia: the Prehistory of the Rome Agreement' in *Essays in Diplomatic History in Memory of D. B. Horn,* ed. M. S. Anderson and R. Hatton (London, 1970), p. 346.
38 Loc. cit. and Guariglia, op. cit., p. 141.
39 Haute Court de Justice, *Procès du Marechal Pétain* (Paris, 1945), p. 183.
40 'Memorandum on Franco–Italian relations', op. cit. Robert de Dampierre, 'Dix anneés de politique Francais à Rome', part II, *La Revue des Deux Mondes* (15 November 1953), p. 279; G. Warner, *Pierre Laval and the Eclipse of France* (London, 1968), pp. 65–6.
41 Aloisi, op. cit., 29 December 1934.
42 The public agreements are in *British Foreign and State Papers,* CXXXIX, pp. 946–51. The texts of the secret agreements are in D. C. Watt, 'The secret Laval–Mussolini agreement of 1935', *The Middle East Journal* (Winter 1961), pp. 69–78.
43 Mussolini's letter to Laval of 25 December 1935, in reply to Laval's letter to Mussolini of 22 December 1935, in Hubert Lagardelle, *Mission à Rome: Mussolini* (Paris, 1955), pp. 278–9. In this letter Mussolini exonerated Laval from a formal acknowledgment of the possibility of war. See also Laval's speech of 28 December 1935, in *Journal Officiel,* pp. 2863–6. Laval's interpretation of the January Accords is in his letter to Mussolini of 23 January 1936, DDF, ii, I, pp. 145–7.
44 *Les Evènements survenus en france, 1936–40* (Paris, 1947), *Rapport,* I, p. 136,

p. 488 ff., M. Gamelin, *Servir* (Paris, 1947), ii, pp. 165–9; Mario Roalta, *Il Processo Roalta* (Rome, 1945), pp. 30–1, 200–1.

45 Record of conversation, 29 January 1935, FO 371, J380/97/1.

46 Record of conversation between Vitetti and Thompson, 28 January 1935, FO 371 J609/97/1.

47 Wallinger's minute on Barton to FO, 4 January 1935, FO 371, J52/52/1.

48 Thompson's minute on Barton to FO, op. cit., and on Barton to FO, 18 January 1935, FO 371, J223/52/1.

49 Simon to Barton, 22 January 1935, FO 371, J223/52/1. Barton to FO, 23 January 1935, FO 371, J306/52/1, and Simon to Barton, 31 January 1935, FO 371, J306/52/1.

50 Memorandum by Thompson, op. cit., para. 29.

51 De Bono, *La preparazione,* pp. 80–1.

52 In a letter to George V, quoted in Harold Nicolson, *King George the Fifth,* (London, 1952), p. 528.

53 Memorandum by Thompson, op. cit., para. 35. A message from Thompson dated 12 April 1935 went further: '... What I did endeavour to do, however, was to make it quite clear to Signor Guarnaschelli (Signor Vitetti is under no illusions on this point), that it would be useless to expect, as he tentatively suggested, that we could in any way actively assist Italy to attain her Ethiopian objectives.' FO 371, J1490/1/1.

54 Guariglia, op. cit., pp. 231–2.

55 De Bono, *Anno XIII ...,* p. 161.

56 Memorandum by Simon, filed on 21 May 1935, FO 371, J1850/1/1.

57 Drummond to Simon, 21 May 1935, FO 371, J2016/1/1.

58 Lord Avon, *Facing the Dictators* (London, 1962), p. 205.

59 Aloisi, op. cit., p. 275.

60 Flandin, *Politique française, 1919–1940* (Paris, 1947), pp. 172–3. Apparently because of Laval's reluctance to create the impression of an anti-German Italo–French alliance, the agreement was initialled but not formally signed. Internal evidence suggests that it was none the less operative. See also *Les Evènements ...,* vol. II, p. 388; Gamelin's testimony, vol. I, p. 134, and Flandin's testimony, vol. IX, pp. 2560–71.

61 DGFP, c, 4, no. 230, to Neurath, 30 May 1935.

62 The report was published in the *Giornale d' Italia,* on 19 February 1936; a translation into English from the Italian appeared in the London *Times* and the *New York Times,* on 20 February 1936; the original is dated 18 June 1935, FO 371, J238/97/1.

63 Winston Churchill, *The Gathering Storm* (London, 1949), p. 132.

64 Drummond to Simon, 1 June 1935, FO 371, J2205/1/1.

65 Vansittart to Drummond, 17 June 1935, FO 371, J2380/1/1.

66 The Italian record of this conversation (substantially the same), has been published in M. Toscano, *Pagine di Storia Diplomatica,* vol. II (Milan, 1963), pp. 142–51.

67 Drummond to Hoare, 18 June 1935, FO 371, J2402/1/1.

68 Aloisi, op. cit., 24–26 June 1935. Conversation between Strang and Aloisi, 28 June 1935, FO 371, J2535/1/1.

69 Eden to Hoare, 27 June 1935, FO 371, J2510/1/1. Eden's account in his memoirs leaves a different impression: Avon, op. cit., p. 232.

70 Minutes on FO 371, J2535/1/1.

71 Drummond to Mussolini, 24 July 1935, FO 371, J3213/1/1.

72 Mussolini to Drummond, 31 July 1935, FO 371, J3472/1/1.

73 Hoare to Clerk, 29 July 1935, FO 371, J3204/1/1.

74 Aloisi, op. cit., 31 July 1935.

75 Avon, op. cit., pp. 251–2.

76 Quoted in Stephen Heald, *Documents on International Affairs, 1935,* vol. II (London, 1937), p. 297.

77 Text of British reply in Heald, op. cit., pp. 300–301. See also A. Toynbee, *Survey of International Affairs, 1935* (London, 1936), vol. II, pp. 258–62. Flandin, op. cit., pp. 182–3. Avon, op. cit., pp. 268–9. Flandin's testimony, *Les Evènements . . .*, I, pp. 148–9.

78 Aloisi, op. cit., 9 August 1935.

79 Ibid., 17 August 1935.

80 Mussolini to de Bono 25 August 1935, de Bono, *Anno XIII,* p. 130.

81 *Corriere d'Informazione,* 14–17 January 1946, for the relevant documents.

82 Conclusions from papers by the Board of Trade, the Treasury and the FO, 30 August 1935, FO 371, J4223/1/1.

83 Sir Samuel Hoare (Viscount Templewood), *Nine Troubled Years* (London, 1954), pp. 168–9.

84 Laval's speech of 28 December 1935, *Journal Officiel* (Paris, 1936), p. 2863.

85 Report of the Committee of Imperial Defence, August 1935, FO 371, J5104/1/1.

86 *Official Journal, League of Nations* (Geneva, 1935), November 1935, pp. 1620–27. Aloisi, op. cit., 21–25 September 1935. Guariglia, op. cit., pp. 265–9.

87 B. Mussolini, *Opera Omnia,* XXVII, pp. 728–36.

88 Avon, op. cit., p. 269.

89 Letter cited in F. Rossi, *Mussolini e lo Stato Maggiore* (Rome, 1951), pp. 24–6.

90 Drummond to FO, 20 September 1935, FO 371, J5026/1/1.

91 Guariglia, op. cit., p. 278. These terms are also in Clerk to Hoare, 24 October 1935, FO 371, J6790/1/1.

92 Minutes on Clerk to FO, 18 October 1935, FO 371, J6452/1/1.

93 Lord Ernle Chatfield, *The Navy and Defence,* vol. II: *It Might Happen Again* (London, 1947), p. 87.

94 Report of the Admiralty, 3 October 1935, FO 371, J5570/5499/1.

95 Minutes of the fifteenth meeting of the Sub-committee on Defence Policy and Requirements, 6 December 1935, FO 371, J9156/J861/1.

96 Loc. cit.

97 Hoare to Drummond, 17 October 1935, FO 371, J6430/1/1.

98 Minute by Thompson on Drummond to FO, 24 January 1936, FO 371, J812/89/1.

99 Clerk to Hoare, 15 December 1935, FO 371, J9493/1/1.

100 Clerk to Hoare, 10 December 1935, FO 371, J9108/1/1.

101 Hoare to Clerk, 10 December 1935, FO 371, J9083/1/1.

102 Communication of the governments of the United Kingdom and France to the League of Nations, 13 December 1935, FO 371, J9382/1/1.
103 Hoare to Barton, 10 December 1935, FO 371, J9154/1/1.
104 In *Il Conflitto Italo–Etiopico: Documenti,* vol. II (Milan, 1936), pp. 264–5.
105 Vansittart to Lindsey, 21 December 1935, FO 371, C9652/1/1.
106 Several fruitless conversations took place between Grandi and Eden and Mussolini and De Chambrun. Britain remained adamant while the best suggestion the French government could make was to internationalise the problem by subsuming it into a general Mediterranean agreement. Drummond to FO, 24 January 1936, FO 371, J812/89/1.
107 *Official Journal, League of Nations, Special Supplement* no. 148 (Geneva, 1936), pp. 64–7.

13 The Brenner Abandoned

1 G. Ciano, *L'Europa verso la catastrofe* (Milan, 1948), pp. 90–1.
2 In late 1935, Italy had under consideration a sweeping friendship pact with Yugoslavia. See Pompeo Aloisi, *La mia attività al servizio della pace* (Rome, 1946), pp. 34–7.
3 The conversations between Ciano and the Yugoslav minister, 18–28 December 1936, do not mention threats but they were conveyed to Campbell. G. Ciano, *Diplomatic Papers* (London, 1948), pp. 70–1.
4 Eden to Campbell, 4 February 1937, FO 371, R889/224/92.
5 Vansittart to Campbell, 26 February 1937, FO 371, R1340/224/92.
6 It was at once an indication of Yugoslavia's disaffection with Paris and of the impact of the occupation of the Rhineland on Germany's eastern neighbours that France was hardly consulted during the negotiations with Italy. The cautionings of the French Minister in Belgrade were by and large embedded; see Belgrade to Paris, 20 January 1937, DDF, ii, 4, no. 326.
7 Campbell to FO, 10 March 1937, FO 371, R1687/224/92.
8 Information from Campbell to Eden, 27 March 1937, FO 371, R2193/224/92.
9 In justifying his country's re-orientation Stoyadinović regretfully explained to the French chargé on 9 April 1937, that, 'France particularly could not do a great deal for the little entente as she has no means of communication, since, by definition, Italy would be at war against her'; DDF, ii, 5, no. 235.
10 G. Ciano, *Diplomatic Papers,* pp. 98–105.
11 Ibid.
12 Kurt von Schuschnigg, *Austrian Requiem* (London, 1946), p. 123.
13 DGFP, D, I, no. 207. See also Hassel to Göring, 30 January 1937, enclosure in no. 208; Ciano's minute, 23 January 1937, *Diplomatic Papers,* pp. 88–91.
14 Dante Maria Tuninetti, *La mia missione segreta in Austria 1937–8* (Milan, 1946), pp. 52–63.
15 Ibid., pp. 69–70. The Chancellor admitted he had made the agreement reluctantly and Ciano revealed he had leaked the proposal, pp. 77, 87–9.

16 Ciano, *Diplomatic Papers*, p. 112.
17 Cited in A. Magistrati, *L'Italia a Berlino, 1937–9* (Milan, 1956), p. 30. During the course of Schuschnigg's visit to Venice, a German ship, bedecked in swastikas, was anchored near his hotel. Mussolini made a point of visiting it.
18 Magistrati, op. cit., pp. 58–9.
19 Ibid., pp. 63–4.
20 During the visit, Ciano confirmed to Neurath the Duce's irrevocable decision not to deviate from the Rome–Berlin alignment; Neurath–Ciano talk, 25 September 1937, M. Tournier and J. R. Wieland, *Les archives secrets de la Wilhelmstrasse* (Paris, 1950–4), III, pp. 19–21, no. 2.
21 Ciano, *Diplomatic Papers*, p. 146.
22 Ibid.
23 Ciano, *Diary 1937–8* (London, 1952), 24 November 1937.
24 Ciano, *Diary*, 17 December 1937.
25 Ibid., 10–12 January 1938.
26 DGFP, D, I, no. 296.
27 Ciano, *Diplomatic Papers*, p. 163, 18 February 1938.
28 DGFP, D, I, no. 329.
29 J. Gehl, *Austria, Germany, and the Anschluss, 1931–1938* (London, 1963), p. 184; Ciano, *Diary*, 10, 11 March 1938; Halifax to Palairet, 11 March 1938, DBFP, iii, I, no. 25.
30 Ciano, *Diary*, 11 March 1938; DGFP, D, I, nos 349, 350, 361.
31 Ciano, *Diary*, 12 March 1938. Gehl (op. cit., p. 195) concludes that events forced Hitler's hand and the *Anschluss* took place almost against his will.
32 Hitler to Mussolini, DGFP, D, I, no. 352.
33 Ciano, *Diary*, 12 March 1938.
34 Ribbentrop to Hitler, 17 March 1938, DGFP, D, I, no. 396; and Attolico to Ribbentrop, no. 397.
35 Ciano, *Diary*, 24 April 1938.
36 D. C. Watt, 'An earlier model for the Pact of Steel. The draft treaties exchanged between Italy and Germany during Hitler's visit to Rome in May 1938', *International Affairs*, April 1957, p. 196.
37 M. Toscano, *Storio diplomatica della questione dell' Alto Adige* (Bari, 1967), p. 154.
38 See Hitler's remarks to his adjutant, Colonel Schmundt, in DGFP, D, 2, no. 132.
39 Watt, op. cit., pp. 186–9, 193–6.
40 Drummond to FO, 26 March 1936, FO 371, R1851/226/22.
41 Conversation with Japanese Ambassador, 18 November 1936, Ciano, *Diplomatic Papers*, pp. 68–9.
42 Conversation with Japanese Ambassador, 31 July 1937, ibid., pp. 130–1.
43 M. Toscano, *Le origini del patto d'acciaio* (Florence, 1948), pp. 11–12.
44 Conversation with Japanese Ambassador, 20 September 1937, Ciano, *Diplomatic Papers*, pp. 138–9.
45 Conversation with Japanese Ambassador, 6 November 1937, ibid., pp. 141–2.
46 Secret protocol in DGFP, D, I, no. 463.

47 Ciano, *Diary*, 1, 6 November 1937.
48 B. Mussolini, *Opera Omnia* (Florence, 1951–63), XXIX, pp. 96–7.
49 Ciano, *Diary*, 10 May 1938.
50 DGFP, D, I, nos 740, 741, 746.
51 Ciano, *Diary*, 20–22 April 1938; G. Bonnet, *De Washington au Quai d'Orsay* (Paris, 1946), p. 145; J. Blondel, *Au Fil de la carrière* (Paris, 1960), p. 380.
52 See FRUS, 1938, I, 446.
53 Ibid., and Bulletin to Secretary of State, 9 March, FRUS, 1938, I, 193.
54 Ciano, *Diary*, 11 May 1938.
55 Blondel, op. cit., p. 380.
56 Mussolini, *Opera Omnia*, XXIX, pp. 99–102.
57 Bonnet, op. cit., p. 110.
58 FRUS, 1938, I, 40, 44, 48; DBFP, iii, I, nos 168–94, 265–82; Ciano, *Diary*, 21 May 1938; Ciano, *Diplomatic Papers*, pp. 209–10.
59 Ciano, *Diplomatic Papers*, 3 June 1938, p. 212; Ciano, *Diary*, 3 June 1938.
60 Ciano, *Diplomatic Papers*, pp. 216–18; DBFP, iii, 3, no. 326, annex 1.
61 Italian memorandum in reply to British note of 20 June 1938, dated 1 July 1938; Ciano, *Diplomatic Papers*, pp. 220–21; conversation with Perth, 2 July, ibid., pp. 221–2.
62 Conversations with Perth, 11 July 1938, Ciano, *Diplomatic Papers* pp. 224–6 (original italics).

14 *Munich and After*

1 Mussolini's report to Fascist Grand Council, 4 February 1939, quoted in F. W. Deakin, *The Brutal Friendship: Mussolini, Hitler, and the Fall of Italian Fascism* (New York and London, 1962), pp. 5–6.
2 Ibid., p. 7.
3 Attolico to Ciano, 23 June 1938, quoted in M. Toscano, *The Origins of the Pact of Steel* (Baltimore, 1968), p. 29.
4 See M. Toscano (ed.) *La politica estera italiana dal 1914 al 1943* (Turin, 1963), pp. 222–3, quoting Attolico of 19 June 1938.
5 G. Ciano, *Diplomatic Papers* (London, 1948), p. 228.
6 Ribbentrop's assurances to Attolico, DGFP, D, 2, no. 384; Hitler's message, no. 415. See also Ciano, *Diary*, 6–7 September 1938.
7 Ibid., 25 October 1938.
8 Toscano, *La politica estera*, p. 224.
9 Ibid., p. 221.
10 Ciano, *Diary*, 30 September 1938.
11 Ibid., 27 October 1938.
12 Ibid., 28 October 1938.
13 Mussolini–Ribbentrop conversation, 28 October 1938; Ciano, *Diplomatic Papers*, pp. 242–6, and *Diary*, 29 October 1938.
14 To Attolico, 24 November 1938, quoted in M. Toscano, *The Origins . . .*, p. 92.
15 Ciano, *Diary*, 23 October 1938.
16 Ciano to Ribbentrop, 2 January 1939, Ciano, *Diplomatic Papers*, pp. 258–9.

17 Ciano, *Diary,* 9 January 1939.
18 Ibid., 6, 8 February 1939.
19 Attolico to Ciano, 9 March 1939, in Toscano, *The Origins . . .*, p. 162.
20 F. Anfuso, *Da Palazzo Venezia al Lago di Garda* (Bologna, 1957), pp. 111–12; A. Magistrati, *L'Italia a Berlino 1937–9* (Milan, 1956), pp. 317–21; M. Donosti, *Mussolini e l'Europa* (Rome, 1945), pp. 151–5.
21 Ciano, *Diary,* 14, 15 March 1939.
22 Ibid., 9 March 1939.
23 Ibid., 16 March 1939.
24 Ibid.
25 Perth to Halifax, 21 March, DBFP, iii, 4, nos 375, 376; 24 March, no. 505.
26 André François Poncet, *Au Palais Farnèse* (Paris, 1961), pp. 96–7; G. Bonnet, *Fin d'une Europe* (Paris, 1946), pp. 70–2.
27 Lane to Hull, FRUS, 1940, I, 82; Campbell to Halifax, 23 March 1939, DBFP, iii, 4, no. 379.
28 Ribbentrop to Ciano, 20 March 1939, Ciano, *Diplomatic Papers,* pp. 278–9; DGFP, D, 6, no. 55. But see also political report from Heeren, 7 March 1939 (ibid., 5, no. 310), suggesting that the fall of Stoyadinović had given Germany freedom to cultivate the Croatian separatists.
29 Ciano, *Diary,* 20 March 1939.
30 Circular letter, DGFP, D, 6, no. 94.
31 G. Bottai, *Vent' anni e un giorno* (Milan, 1949), p. 126.
32 Ciano, *Diary,* 10, 11 February 1939.
33 Ibid., 13, 26 March 1938.
34 Ciano, *Diplomatic Papers,* p. 203.
35 Ciano to Guariglia and Grandi, 4 April 1939, in Toscano, *The Origins . . .*, p. 232. See also R. Guariglia, *Ricordi, 1922–1946* (Naples, 1949), pp. 388–9.
36 Perth to Halifax, 7 April 1939, DBFP, iii, 5, no. 82; Halifax to Perth, no. 83; Halifax to Campbell, 7 April, no. 87.
37 Ciano, *Diary,* 29 March 1939.
38 Halifax to Waterlow, 9 April 1939, DBFP, iii, 5, no. 111, footnotes 2, 3; Halifax to Perth, no. 109.
39 Halifax to Phipps, 9 April 1939, ibid., no. 100; Phipps to Halifax, nos 103, 106.
40 Metaxas to legation in Rome, 10 April 1939, Greece, Ministère des affaires étrangères, 1942, *Greek White Book: Diplomatic Documents relating to Italy's Aggression against Greece* (London, 1942), no. 27; Metaxas to Rome, 11 April 1939, no. 28.
41 Weizsacker Memorandum, 14 April 1939, DGFP, D, 6, no. 197; Weizsacker to Mackensen, 15 April 1939, no. 203.
42 Unsigned Memorandum in DGFP, D, 6, nos 205, 211; Mackensen to Weizsacker, 12 April 1939, no. 252; Ciano, *Diary,* 14–17 April 1939.
43 Mussolini to Ciano, 4 May 1939; Toscano, *The Origins . . .*, pp. 289–91.
44 DGFP, D, 6, pp. 444–9.
45 Ribbentrop–Ciano talks, 6–7 May 1939. Ciano, *Diplomatic Papers,* pp. 283–286; German record in DGFP. D. 6, no. 341.
46 Attolico to Ciano, 12 May 1939, in Toscano, *The Origins . . .*, pp. 344–5.
47 Ciano, *Diary,* 13 May 1939.

48 Cavallero Memorandum, DDI, viii, 12, no. 59.

15 *War, 1940*

1 Ciano, *Diary*, 9 August 1939. The meeting had come about as a result of Attolico's efforts to open Ciano's and Mussolini's minds to the true German intentions in Poland and Danzig. See E. Anchieri, 'Dal patto d'acciaio al convegno di Salisburgo', *Il Politico*, no. 1, 1953; and M. Magistrati, 'Salisburgo 1939', *Rivista di Studi Politici Internazionali*, no. 4, 1949.

2 Record of conversation between Ciano and Ribbentrop, 12 August 1939, DDI, viii, 13, no. 1; G. Ciano, *Diplomatic Papers* (London, 1948), pp. 297–9; G. Ciano, *The Ciano Diaries, 1939–1943*, New York, 1946, 11 August 1939.

3 Record of Ciano–Hitler talks, 12, 13 August 1939, DDI, viii, 12, nos 4, 21; Ciano, *Diplomatic Papers*, pp. 299–304; DGFP, D, 7, nos 43, 47.

4 Anfuso to Ciano, minute, 14 August 1939, DDI, viii, 12, no. 28.

5 Ciano, *Diary*, 13 August 1939.

6 M. Donosti, *Mussolini e l'Europa* (Rome, 1945), p. 206.

7 Ciano, *Diary*, 15 August 1939.

8 Consul in Munich, Pittalis to Ciano, 19 August 1939, DDI, viii, 13, no. 100; record of conversation, Ribbentrop–Attolico, 19 August 1939, no. 102; Donosti, op. cit., p. 207.

9 Loraine to Ciano, 20 August 1939, DDI, viii, 13, no. 117.

10 Ciano, *Diary*, 21 August 1939.

11 Chronology in appendix of DDI, viii, 13; see also nos 129, 130.

12 M. Toscano, 'Le conversationi militari Italo–Tedesche alla vigilia della 2a guerra mondiale', *RSI*, 1952, pp. 349–59; DDI, viii, 13, appendix III.

13 DDI, viii, 12, nos 59, 130, Attolico to Ciano, 6 June 1939. As late as 28 August, the Reich Foreign Minister, having once again confirmed the 'absolute obligation' to consult and agree with Italy, had asserted to Attolico his and the Führer's decision 'to avoid a general conflagration' without consultation between the two heads of state. Attolico to Ciano, 28 August 1939, DDI, viii, 12, no. 717.

14 Mussolini to Hitler, 21 August 1939, DDI, viii, 13, no. 136 (not sent).

15 Ciano, *Diary*, 21 August 1939.

16 Ibid.; Badoglio to Mussolini, 22 August 1939, DDI, viii, 13, no. 162.

17 Ciano, *Diary*, 23 August 1939.

18 Ciano to Attolico, 25 August 1939, DDI, viii, 13, no. 232.

19 Hitler to Mussolini, 25 August 1939, ibid., no. 245.

20 Mussolini to Hitler, 25 August 1939, ibid., no. 250.

21 Hitler to Mussolini, 25 August 1939, ibid., no. 262.

22 Hitler to Mussolini, 26 August 1939, ibid., no. 298.

23 Mussolini to Hitler, 26 August 1939, ibid., no. 304.

24 Hitler readily granted Mussolini's request for a message expressly freeing Italy from any obligation to support Germany. The message was displayed prominently in all Italian newspapers. Hitler thanked Mussolini for his political support, asserted the conviction that Germany's armed forces

were equal to the present task and concluded, therefore, that there was no need for Italian military help. Hitler to Mussolini, 1 September 1939, ibid. no. 530.

25 Ciano–Hitler conversation, 1 October 1939, DGFP, D, 8, no. 176.

26 Speech in *Relazioni Internazionali, 1939* (Milan 1939), 51, p. 1065.

27 Mussolini to Hitler, 5 January 1940, DDI, ix, 3, no. 33; DGFP, D, 8, no. 504.

28 Ciano, *Diary*, 26 December 1939 and 2 January 1940. The repercussion of the warning caused Hitler to postpone the invasion scheduled for 17 January 1940. See F. Marzari, 'Prospects for an Italian-led Balkan bloc of neutrals September–December 1939', in *Historical Journal*, XIII, no. 4 (1970), pp. 767–88.

29 Ibid.

30 Ciano, *Diary*, 15 September 1939; Ghigi to Ciano, 21 September 1939; Ciano to Attolico, 23 September 1939, DDI, ix, 1, nos 370, 394.

31 Ciano, *Diary*, 24 September 1939.

32 Memorandum by Weizsacker, 27 September 1939, DGFP, D, 8, no. 145.

33 Ciano to Cerruti, 29 September 1939, DDI, ix, 1, no. 505; Cerruti replied it was unlikely Japan would join because of the bloc's obvious anti-British and anti-American aspect. Cerruti to Ciano, 4 October 1939, no. 559. Further sounding confirmed this view. Cerruti to Ciano, 6 and 9 October 1939, nos 625, 627.

34 Ciano, *Diary*, 29 September 1939; Mussolini to Victor Emmanuel, DDI, ix, 1, no. 523.

35 Ciano to Mussolini, 1 October 1939, ibid., no. 552; Ciano, *Diplomatic Papers*, pp. 309–16; Ciano, *Diary*, 1 October 1939; German record, DGFP, D, 8, no. 176.

36 Mackensen to Foreign Ministry, 17 October 1939, ibid., no. 266.

37 Gafencu's project consisted of six points. Text is in Schulenburg to Foreign Minister, 14 November 1939, ibid., no. 358 and enclosure.

38 DDI, ix, 2, no. 121.

39 R. Massigli, *La Turquie devant la guerre: mission à Ankara 1939–40* (Paris, 1964), pp. 322–3.

40 Molotov pointedly asked why Italy's 'patronage' was sought. Although there is not much evidence on which to elaborate the point, it is clear that the USSR regarded Italy as unwelcome competition in the Balkans and there are indications that at one time the Soviet government contemplated placing a bloc of Balkan neutrals under its leadership. Leaflets distributed by the Bulgarian communist party advanced this view. Talamo to Ciano, 23 October 1939, DDI, ix, 1, no. 865.

41 Ibid., no. 248; DGFP, D, 8, nos 359, 362.

42 François Poncet to Ciano, 5 September 1939; Guariglia to Ciano, 15 September 1939; Ciano to Mussolini, 16 September 1939; DDI, ix, 1, nos 46, 214, 230.

43 Halifax to Ciano, 8 September 1939, ibid., no. 110; W. N. Medlicott, *The Economic Blockade* (London, 1952), p. 280 ff.

44 I. S. Playfair, *The Mediterranean and the Middle East* (London, 1954), pp. 23–4, 39, 41.

45 Ibid., pp. 90–91.
46 Loraine to Ciano, 24 October 1939, DDI, ix, 1, no. 877; Medlicott, op. cit., p. 280.
47 Attolico to Ciano, 27 November 1939, DDI, ix, 2, no. 358; Ciano, *Diary*, 24 November 1939, 2 December 1939; Mackensen to Foreign Minister, 2 December 1939, DGFP, D, 8, no. 410.
48 DDI, ix, 2, nos 639, 706.
49 Ciano, *Diary*, 24, 29 December 1939; E. L. Woodward, *British Foreign Policy in the Second World War* (London, 1962), p. 15.
50 Attolico to Ciano, 10, 12, 13 January 1940; Magistrati to Ciano, 15 January 1940; DDI, ix, 3, nos 78, 95, 111, 126; DGFP, D, 8, no. 518.
51 Ibid.
52 Ciano, *Diary*, 8, 10 February 1940.
53 Ibid., 20 February 1940; Clodeus and Mackensen to Foreign Ministry, 22 February 1940, DGFP, D, 8, no. 627.
54 Sumner Wells, US Under-Secretary of State, had just paid a visit to Rome. The pope had also received a special envoy from the USA.
55 Handwritten note, 10 March 1940, DDI, ix, 3, no. 511.
56 No Italian records were kept; two weeks later Rome was supplied with copies of the German transcripts. The first Mussolini–Ribbentrop conversation is in DGFP, D, 8, no. 665, the second in ibid., no. 669; Ribbentrop's impressions are in nos 667 and 670.
57 No Italian record; German record, 17 March 1940, ibid., 9, no. 1.
58 DDI, ix, 3, no. 669 (italics in the original). The inevitability of a war with Germany if Italy changed sides was one of the constant refrains from the time of the *Anschluss* onwards.
59 Ibid., no. 669.
60 See his talks with the Chiefs of Staff, 29 May 1940, in DDI, ix, 4, no. 642.
61 Ibid., and Ciano, *Diary*, 21 April 1940.
62 Ibid., 13 May 1940.
63 Mackensen to Foreign Ministry, 29 May 1940, DGFP, D, 9, no. 243.
64 Badoglio to Mussolini, 6 April 1940, E. Faldella, *L'Italia nella seconda guerra mondiale: revisione di guidizi* (Bologna, 1959), pp. 145–6.
65 Record of Chiefs of Staff meeting, 9 April 1940, text in Faldella, op. cit., pp. 728–38.
66 Text in R. Bernotti, *La guerra sui mari* (Rome, 1950), 1, pp. 166–7.
67 Badoglio to Mussolini, 11–13 April 1940, Faldella, op. cit., pp. 150–3.
68 F. Rossi, *Mussolini e lo stato maggiore* (Rome, 1951), p. 21.
69 V. Zincone (ed.), *Hitler: Mussolini, lettere e documenti* (Milan, 1946), pp. 43–7.
70 Lothian to Roosevelt, 26 May, FRUS, 1940, II, pp. 709–10; Hull to Phillips, 26 May 1940, ibid.; Phillips to Hull, 27 May 1940, ibid., pp. 711–13; Hull to Phillips, 30 May 1940, ibid., pp. 713–14; Phillips to Hull, 1 June 1940, ibid., p. 715.
71 Faldella, op. cit., pp. 739–42, reporting meeting of 30 May 1940.
72 M. Toscano, *Una mancata intesa italo-sovietica nel 1940 e 1941* (Florence, 1953), pp. 28–9.
73 J. Benoist Mechin, *Procès Benoist Mechin* (Paris, 1948), II, p. 293.
74 W. L. Langer and S. E. Gleason, *The Challenge to Isolation, 1937–40*

(London 1952), pp. 548–9, on the basis of unpublished general staff documents, say Mussolini wanted hard terms; an incomplete record of Hitler–Mussolini talks on 18 June 1940, in Zinconi, op. cit., pp. 51–4; Ciano's record of conversation with Ribbentrop, 18–19 June 1940, in Ciano, *L'Europa*, pp. 562–5; conversation, Hitler, Mussolini, Ribbentrop, Ciano, Von Keitel, Roatta, in DGFP, D, 9, no. 479; also Ciano, *Diary*, 18 June 1940. On Mussolini's decision not to seize French territories as he had hoped to do in March, see Langer and Gleason, op. cit., pp. 577–8; Donosti, op. cit., p. 233; Faldella, op. cit., pp. 182–8; Mussolini's letter to Hitler of 22 June 1940, is in DGFP, D, 9, no. 526. Text of armistice in *Relazioni Internazionali*, 1940 (Milan 1940), 26, pp. 907–8.

Bibliography

Archive sources

(a) *Official papers*
Foreign Office correspondence, Public Record Office, London
    Series FO 45 Italy
          FO 170 Rome Embassy
          FO 371 political
          FO 800 private
Ministero degli Affari Esteri, Rome
    Archivo del Gabinetto, 1886–7
    Seria politica Inghilterra, 1886–96
    Telegrammi, 1886–96
Haus-, Hof-, und Staatsarchiv, Vienna
    Politisches Archiv, 1886–96

(b) *Private papers*

Balfour Papers,	British Museum
Crispi Papers,	Archivio di Stato Centrale (ASC), Rome
	Museo del Risorgimento, Rome
Depretis Papers,	ASC
Hardinge Papers,	Cambridge University Library
Pisani Dossi Papers,	ASC
Salisbury Papers,	Christ Church, Oxford
Sonnino Papers (SP),	Microfilm, University of Alberta

Official publications of documents

British Documents on the Origins of the War, 1898–1914, eds Gooch, G. P., and Temperley, H. W. V. (11 vols), London, 1926–38 (BD).
Documents on British Foreign Policy, 1919–1939, eds Woodward, E. L., and Butler, R., London, 1947– (DBFP).
Documents diplomatiques français, 1870–1914, Ministère des Affaires Étrangères, Paris, 1929–55 (DDF).
Documents diplomatiques français, 1932–1939, Ministère des Affaires Étrangères, Paris, 1964– (DDF).

Bibliography

Documenti diplomatici italiani, 1870–1939, Ministero degli Affari Esteri, Rome, 1952– (DDI).

Die Grosse Politik der europaischen Kabinette, 1870–1914, (40 vols), eds. Lepsius, J., Mendelssohn-Bartholdy, A., and Thimme, F., 1922–7 (GP).

Documents on German Foreign Policy, 1933–1939, Series C, D, London, 1957–1964 (DGFP).

Documents on International Affairs, 1928–39, Royal Institute of International Affairs, London, 1929–54 (RIIA).

L'Italia in Africa, seria storica, documenti, vol. I, *Etiopia–Mare Rosso, 1883–5, 1885–6*; vol. II, *Somalia settentrionale, 1884–91*, ed. C. Giglio, Ministero degli Affari Esteri, Rome, 1968.

Papers relating to the Foreign Relations of the United States, 1919–1940, U.S. Department of State, Washington, 1935–61 (FRUS).

Official Journal 1935, League of Nations, Geneva, 1935.

Published books

ALATRI, P., *Nitti, D'Annunzio e la questione adriatica* (Milan, 1959).
ALBERTINI, A., *Vita di Luigi Albertini* (Milan, 1945).
ALBERTINI, A., *Venti anni di vita politica* (Bologna, 1951–3).
ALBERTINI, L., *The Origins of the War of 1914*, 3 vols (London, 1952).
ALBERTINI, L., *Epistolario, 1911–1926*, 4 vols (Milan, 1968).
ALBRECHT-CARRIÉ, R., *Italy at the Paris Peace Conference* (New York, 1938).
ALDROVANDI-MARESCOTTI, L., *La guerra diplomatica* (Milan, 1937).
ALDROVANDI-MARESCOTTI, L., *Nuovi ricordi* (Milan, 1938).
ALFIERI, D., *Due dittatori di fronte* (Milan, 1948).
ALOISI, P., *La mia attività al servizio della pace* (Rome, 1946).
ALOISI, P., *Journal 25 juillet 1932–14 juin 1936* (Paris, 1957).
ANDRÉ, G., *L'Italia ed il Mediterraneo* (Milan, 1967).
ANDREW, C., *Théophile Delcassé* (London, 1968).
ANFUSO, F., *Da Palazzo Venezia al Lago di Garda* (Bologna, 1957).
AROMA, N., *Vent'anni insieme; Vittorio Emanuele e Benito Mussolini* (Rome, 1957).
ASKEW, W. C., *Europe and Italy's Acquisition of Libya* (Duke, 1942).
BADOGLIO, P., *La guerra d'Etiopia* (Milan, 1936).
BAER, G. W., *The Coming of the Italian–Ethiopian War* (Cambridge, Mass., 1967).
BARROS, J., *The Corfu Incident of 1923* (Princeton, 1965).
BASTIANINI, G., *Uomini, cose, fatti: memorie di un ambasciatore* (Milan, 1959).
BATTAGLIA, R., *La prima guerra d'Africa* (Turin, 1958).
BENOIST MECHIN, J., *Procès Benoist Mechin* (Paris, 1948).

BERNOTTI, R., *La guerra sui mari* (Rome, 1950).

BILLOT, A., *La France et l'Italie* (Paris, 1905).

BISSOLATI, L., *La politica estera dell'Italia dal 1897 al 1920* (Milan, 1923).

BLONDEL, J., *Au Fil de la carrière* (Paris, 1960).

BONNET, G., *De Washington au Quai d'Orsay* (Paris, 1946).

BONNET, G., *Fin d'une Europe* (Paris, 1948).

BONO, EMILIO DE, *Anno XIII; the conquest of an empire* (London, 1937).

BONO, EMILIO DE, *La Preparazione e le prime operazioni* (Rome, 1937).

BONOMI, I., *La politica italiana da Porta Pia a Vittorio Veneto, 1870–1918* (Rome, 1946).

BONOMI, I., *La politica italiana dopo Vittorio Veneto* (Turin, 1953).

BORSA, G., *Italia e Cina nel secolo XIX* (Milan, 1961).

BOTTAI, G., *Vent'anni e un giorno* (Milan, 1949).

BRAUNTHAL, J., *The Tragedy of Austria* (London, 1948).

BRIDGE, F. R., *From Sadowa to Sarajevo* (London, 1972).

CANTALUPO, R., *Fu la Spagna: ambasciata presso Franco febbraio–aprile 1937* (Milan, 1948).

CAROCCI, G., *Agostino Depretis e la politica interna italiana dal 1876 al 1886* (Turin, 1956).

CAROCCI, G., *Giolitti e l'età giolittiana* (Turin, 1961).

CAROCCI, G., *La politica estera dell'Italia fascista, 1925–1928* (Bari, 1969).

CASSELS, A., *Mussolini's Early Diplomacy* (Princeton, 1970).

CATTALUCCIO, F., *Antonio di San Giuliano e la politica estera italiana dal 1900 al 1914* (Florence, 1935).

CAVALLERO, U., *Commando Supremo. Diario 1940–43 del Capo di Stato Maggiore* (Bologna, 1948).

CERVI, M., *Storia della guerra di Grecia* (Milan, 1965).

CHABOD, F., *Storia della politica estera italiana dal 1870 al 1896* (Bari, 1952).

CHABOD, F., *L'Italia contemporanea* (Turin, 1961).

CHABOD, F., *Considerazioni sulla politica estera dell'Italia dal 1870 al 1915* (Amici della cultura n.i., n.d.).

CHARLES-ROUX, F., *Souvenirs diplomatiques, Rome-Quirinal fevrier 1916–fevrier 1919* (Paris, 1958).

CIANO, GALEAZZO, COUNT, *The Ciano Diaries, 1939–1943* (New York, 1946).

CIANO, GALEAZZO, COUNT, *L'Europa verso la catastrofe* (Milan, 1948).

CIANO, GALEAZZO, COUNT, *Diario 1937–8* (Bologna, 1948).

CIANO, GALEAZZO, COUNT, *Ciano's Diplomatic Papers*, ed. Malcolm Muggeridge (London, 1948).

CIANO, GALEAZZO, COUNT, *Diario, I 1939–40, II 1941–3* (Milan, 1950).

CIASCA, R., *Storia coloniale dell'Italia contemporanea* (Milan, 1938).

COLLOTTI, E., *L'Italia nell'Europa danubiana durante la 2a guerra mondiale* (Monza, 1968).

Bibliography

CONTI-ROSSINI, C., *Italia ed Etiopia* (Rome, 1935).

COSTELLANO, G., *Come firmai l'Armistizio di Cassibile* (Rome, 1945).

CRESPI, S., *Alla difensa d'Italia in guerra e a Versailles* (Milan, 1937).

CRISPI, F., *Triple Alliance* (London, 1913).

CRISPI, F., *Questione internationali* (Milan, 1913).

CRISPI, F., *Pensieri profezie* (Rome, 1920).

CRISPI, P., *La prima guerra d'Africa* (Milan, 1914).

CRISPI, P., *L'Italia coloniale e Francesco Crispi* (Milan, 1928).

CURATO, F., *La questione marocchina*, 2 vols (Milan, 1961-4).

D'AMOJA, F., *La politica estera italiana da Caporetto alla conferenza per la pace di Parigi. Le premesse* (Messina, 1970).

DEAKIN, F. W., *The Brutal Friendship: Mussolini, Hitler, and the Fall of Italian Fascism* (New York and London, 1962).

DECLEVA, E., *Da Adua a Sarajevo* (Bari, 1971).

DEL PIANO, L., *La penetrazione italiana in Tunisia 1861-1881* (Padua, 1964).

DONOSTI, M. (pseudonym LUCCIOLI, M.), *Mussolini e l'Europa* (Rome, 1945).

DUKOBOVITCH, N., *Les relations italo-yougoslaves de 1914 à 1920* (Lausanne, 1938).

EDEN, ANTHONY, EARL OF AVON, *The Eden Memoirs; Facing the Dictators* (London, 1962).

EDMONDS, SIR J. E. and DAVIES, H. R., *Military Operations: Italy 1915-1919* (London, 1949).

FALDELLA, E., *L'Italia nella seconda guerra mondiale; revisione di giudizi* (Bologna, 1959).

FALDELLA, E., *La grande guerra. Vol. I: Le battaglie dell'Isonzo, 1915-1917* (Milano, 1965).

FARINI, D., *Diario di fine secolo*, 2 vols, ed. E. Morelli (Rome, 1961).

FEILING, K., *The Life of Neville Chamberlain* (London, 1947).

FELICE, R. DE, *Mussolini*, vol. I, *Il rivoluzionario, 1883-1920* (Turin, 1966).

FELICE, R. DE, *Mussolini*, vol. II, *Il fascista: la conquista del potere, 1921-1925* (Turin, 1966).

FELICE, R. DE, *Mussolini*, vol. III, *Il fascista: l'organizzazione della stato fascista, 1925-1929* (Turin, 1968).

FERRARIS, L., *L'amministrazione centrale del Ministero degli Esteri* (Milan, 1954).

FLANDIN, P., *Discours; le ministère Flandin, novembre 1934 - mai 1935* (Paris, 1937).

FLANDIN, P., *Politique française, 1919-1940* (Paris, 1947).

FLANDIN, P., *Le procès Flandin devant la Haute Cour de Justice, 23-26 juillet 1946* (Paris, 1947).

FONZI, F., *Crispi e lo stato di Milano* (Milan, 1965).

FOSCHINI, A., *La verità sulle cannonate di Corfu* (Rome, 1953).

FRANCHETTI, L., *Mezzogiorno e colonie* (Florence, 1950).

FRASSATI, A., *Giolitti* (Florence, 1959).

GAMELIN, M., *Servir* (Paris, 1947).

GANIAGE, J., *Les origines du protectorat français à Tunisie 1861–1881* (Paris, 1959).

GARLAND, A. and MCGRAW SMYTH, H. (eds), *The U.S. Army in World War II: The Mediterranean Theater of Operations – Sicily and the Surrender of Italy* (Washington, 1965).

GATTI, A., *Caporetto, dal diario di guerra inedito maggio–dicembre 1917* (Bologna, 1965).

GEHL, J., *Austria, Germany, and the Anschluss, 1931–1938* (London, 1963).

GIANNINI, A., *Documenti per la storia dei rapporti fra l'Italia e Yugoslavia* (Rome, 1924).

GIFFORD, P., *et al.* (eds), *Britain and Germany in Africa: Imperial Rivalry and Colonial Rule* (New Haven, 1967).

GIGLIO, C., *L'Italia in Africa*, vol. I, *Etiopia – Mar Rosso 1857–1885* (Rome, 1956).

GORRINI, G., *Tunisi e Biserta: leggenda e storia* (Milan, 1940).

GREGOR, A., *The Ideology of Fascism* (New York, 1969).

GUARIGLIA, R., *Ricordi, 1922–1946* (Naples, 1949).

HALPERIN, S., *Italy and the Vatican at War* (Chicago, 1939).

HEALD, S. (ed.), *Documents on International Affairs* (London, 1937).

HERBER, H. (ed.), *Hitler's Logebespreckungen* (Stuttgart, 1962).

HESS, R., 'Germany and the Anglo–Italian Colonial Entente' in Gifford *et al.*, *Britain and Germany in Africa* (New Haven, 1967).

HESS, R., *Italian Colonialism in Somalia* (Chicago, 1966).

ISSELIN, H., *La Battaglia della Marna* (Florence, 1967).

JEMOLO, A. C., *Crispi* (Florence, 1922).

LAGARDELLE, H., *Mission à Rome: Mussolini* (Paris, 1955).

LANGER, W. L. and GLEASON, S. E., *The Challenge to Isolation 1937–40* (London, 1952).

LEDERER, I., *Yugoslavia at the Peace Conference* (Yale, 1963).

LESSONA, A., *Memorie* (Rome, 1963).

LOWE, C. J., *Salisbury and the Mediterranean* (London, 1965).

LOWE, C. J., *The Reluctant Imperialists* (London, 1967).

LOWE, C. J., and DOCKRILL, M. L., *The Mirage of Power* (London, 1972).

LUZZATI, L., *Memorie*, 2 vols (Bologna, 1935).

LUZZATTO, G., *L'economia italiana dal 1861 al 1914* (Turin, 1968).

MACARTNEY, C. A., *October Fifteenth; a history of modern Hungary, 1929–1945*, 2 vols (Edinburgh, 1956).

MAGISTRATI, A. *L'Italia a Berlino 1937–9* (Milan, 1956).

MALAGODI, O., *Conversazioni della guerra, 1914–1919*, 2 vols (Milan, 1960).

Bibliography

MALAPARTE, C., *L'Europa vivente e altri saggi politici (1921–1931)* (Florence, 1961).

MARINELLI, C. and SALVEMINI, G., *La questione dell'Adriatico* (Rome, 1919).

MARSDEN, A., *British Diplomacy and Tunis 1875–1902* (New York, 1971).

MARTEL, A., *Les confins saharo – tripolitains de la Tunisie* (1881–1911), 2 vols (Paris, 1965).

MARTINI, F., *Diario 1914–1918* (Milan, 1966).

MASSIGLI, R., *La Turquie devant la guerre: mission à Ankara 1939–40* (Paris, 1964).

MATURI, W., *Interpretazioni del Risorgimento: lezioni di storia della storiografia* (Turin, 1962).

MEDLICOTT, W. N., *The Economic Blockade* (London, 1952).

MELOGRANI, P., *Storia politica della grande guerra, 1915–1918* (Bari, 1969).

MONTICONE, A., *Nitti e la grande guerra, 1914–1918* (Milan, 1961).

MOODIE, A. E., *The Italo–Yugoslav boundary, a Study in Political Geography* (London, 1945).

MORANDI, C., *La politica estera dell'Italia* (Florence, 1968).

MUSSOLINI, B., 'The Doctrine of Fascism', *Enciclopedia Italiana di Scienza, Lettere ed Arti* (Milan, 1932).

MUSSOLINI, B., *Memoirs, 1942–1943, with documents relating to the period* (London, 1949).

MUSSOLINI, B., *Opera Omnia*, eds E. and D. Susmel, 36 vols (Florence, 1951–63).

NATALE, G., *Giolitti e gli Italiani* (Milan, 1949).

NEGRI, S., *La direzione e il controllo democratico della politica estera in Italia* (Milan, 1967).

NOLFO, ENNIO, DI, *Mussolini e la politica estera Italiana, 1919–1933* (Padua, 1960).

OMODÈO, A., *Momenti della vita di guerra. Dai diari e dalle lettere dei caduti, 1915–1918* (Turin, 1968).

ORLANDO, V. E., *Memorie, 1915–1919* (Milan, 1960).

PASTORELLI, P., *L'Albania nella politica estera italiana 1914–26* (Bari, 1970).

PAVONE, C., *Dalle carte di Giovanni Giolitti*, 3 vols (Milan, 1962).

PLAYFAIR, I. S., *The Mediterranean and the Middle East* (London, 1954).

PLEHWE, FRIEDRICH-KARL VON, *The End of an Alliance; Rome's Defection from the Axis in 1943* (London, 1971).

PONCET, A. FRANÇOIS, *Au Palais Farnèse* (Paris, 1961).

PRIBRAM, A. F., *The Secret Treaties of Austria–Hungary*, 2 vols (Cambridge, Mass., 1920).

ROATTA, M., *Il processo Roatta* (Rome, 1945).

ROATTA, M., *Otto milioni di baionetti* (Milan, 1946).

ROBERTSON, E., 'Mussolini and Ethiopia: The Prehistory of the Rome Agreement.' in *Essays in Diplomatic History in Memory of D. B. Horn* ed. M. S. Anderson and R. Hatton, pp. 339–56 (London, 1970).

ROCHAT, G., *L'esercito italiano da Vittorio Veneto a Mussolini, 1919–1925* (Bari, 1967).

ROMANO, S. F., *I fasci Siciliani* (Bari, 1959).

ROMEO, R., *Breve storia della grande industria in Italia* (3rd ed. Milan, 1967).

ROMOLOTTI, G., *1914 suicidio d'Europa* (Milan, 1964).

ROSENGARTEN, F., *The Italian Anti-Fascist Press (1919–1945); from the Legal Opposition Press to the Underground Newspapers of World War II* (Cleveland, 1968).

ROSSI, F., *Mussolini e la stato Maggiore* (Rome, 1951).

RUMI, S., *Alle origini della politica estera fascista, 1918–1923* (Bari, 1968).

RUSINOW, D. I., *Italy's Austrian Heritage, 1919–1946* (Oxford, 1969).

SALADINO, S., 'Italy', in *The European Right; a Historical Profile,* eds Hans Rogger and Eugen Weber (Berkeley, 1965).

SALAMONE, A. W., *Italy in the Giolittian Era* (Philadelphia, 1960).

SALANDRA, A., *I discorsi della guerra con alcune note* (Milan, 1922).

SALANDRA, A., *La neutralità italiana* (Milan, 1928).

SALATA, F., *Per la storia diplomatica della questione romana* (Milan, 1929).

SALATA, F., *Il nodo di Gibuti* (Milan, 1939).

SALVATORELLI, L., *La triplice alleanza* (Milan, 1939).

SALVATORELLI, L. and MIRA, G., *Storia d'Italia nel periodo fascista* (Turin, 1956).

SALVEMINI, G., *Dal Patto di Londra alla pace di Roma* (Turin, 1925).

SALVEMINI, G., *La politica estera dell'Italia dal 1871 al 1915* in *Opere* III, vol. 4 (Milan, 1970).

SALVERIN, G., *Mussolini diplomatico, 1927–1932* (Bari, 1952).

SCHRAMM, P. E. (ed.), *Kriegstagebuch des Oberkommandos der Wehrmacht, 1940–1945,* vol. III (Frankfurt, 1963).

SCHUSCHNIGG, KURT VON, *Austrian Requiem* (London, 1946).

SCOPPA, R. B., *Colloqui con due dittatore* (Rome, 1949).

SERRA, E., *Camille Barrère e l'intesa italo-francese* (Milan, 1950).

SERRA, E., *L'intesa mediterranea del 1902* (Milan, 1957).

SERRA, E., *La questione tunisina* (Milan, 1967).

SERTOLI-SALIS, R., *L'isole italiane dell'Egeo dall'occupazione alla sovranità* (Rome, 1939).

SETON-WATSON, C., *Italy from Liberalism to Fascism* (London, 1967).

SFORZA, C., *Pensiero e azione di una politica estera italiana* (Bari, 1924).

SFORZA, C., *Fifty Years of War and Diplomacy in the Balkans; Pashich and the Union of the Yugoslavs* (New York, 1940).

SFORZA, C., *Contemporary Italy* (New York, 1944).

SILVESTRI, M., *Isonzo, 1917* (Turin, 1965).

Bibliography

SIMONI, L., *Berlino, ambasciata d'Italia 1939–43* (Rome, 1946).

SONNINO, S., *Discorsi per la guerra, raccolti a cura di Amadia Giovannini* (Foligno, 1922).

SONNINO, S., *Discorsi parlamentari*, 3 vols (Rome, 1925).

SONNINO, S., *Diario 1866–1916*, 2 vols (Bari, 1972).

STAMBROOK, F. G., 'The German–Austrian Customs Union Project of 1931', in *European Diplomacy between two Wars, 1919–1939*, ed. H. Gatzke (Chicago, 1972).

STARHEMBERG, PRINCE ERNST, *Between Hitler and Mussolini* (London, 1943).

SWEET, P. R., 'Mussolini and Dollfuss: an episode in Fascist Diplomacy', in *The Tragedy of Austria*, ed. J. Braunthal (London, 1948).

SWIRE, J., *Albania; the Rise of a Kingdom* (New York, 1930).

TAMARO, A., *Due anni di storia 1943–5* (Rome, 1948).

TEMPLEWOOD, VISCOUNT, *Nine Troubled Years* (London, 1954).

THAYER, J. A., *Italy and the Great War* (Wisconsin, 1964).

TOMMASSINI, F., *L'Italia alla viglia della guerra*, 5 vols (Bologna, 1934–41).

TORRE, A., *La politica estera dell'Italia dal 1870 al 1896* (Bologna, 1959).

TORRE, A., *La politica estera dell'Italia dal 1896 al 1914* (Bologna, 1960).

TOSCANO, M., *Il patto di Londra* (Milan, 1934).

TOSCANO, M., *Gli accord di San Giovanni di Moriana* (Milan, 1936).

TOSCANO, M., *La Serbia e l'intervento in guerra dell'Italia* (Milan, 1939).

TOSCANO, M., *Le origine del patto d'acciaio* (Florence, 1948).

TOSCANO, M., *Una mancata intesa italo–sovietica nel 1940 e 1941* (Florence, 1953).

TOSCANO, M., *Pagine di storia diplomatica contemporanea* (Milan, 1963).

TOSCANO, M. (ed.), *La politica estera italiana dal 1914 al 1943* (Turin, 1963).

TOSCANO, M., *Dal 25 luglio all' 8 settembre* (Florence, 1966).

TOSCANO, M., *Storia diplomatica della questione dell' Alto Adige* (Bari, 1967).

TOSCANO, M., *The Origins of the Pact of Steel* (Baltimore, 1968).

TOURNIER, M. and WIELAND, J. R., *Les archives secrets de la Wilhelmstrasse*, 5 vols (Paris, 1950–4).

TOYNBEE, A., *Survey of International Affairs, 1935,* vol. II (London, 1936).

TOYNBEE, A. and V. M. (eds), *Hitler's Europe: Survey of International Affairs, 1939–1946* (London, 1962).

VALERI, N., *La lotta politica in Italia dall'unità al 1925; idee e documenti* (Florence, 1966).

VALIANI, L., *La dissoluzione dell' Austria–Ungeria* (Milan, 1966).

VALIANI, L., *L'historiographie de L'Italie contemporaine* (Geneva, 1968).

VEDOVATO, G., *Gli accordi Italo Etiopici dell'agosto 1928* (Florence, 1956).

VIGEZZI, B., *I problemi della neutralità della guerra nel carteggio Salandra-Sonnino, 1914–1917* (Milan, 1962).

VIGEZZI, B., *L'Italia di fronte alla prima guerra mondiale*, vol. I: *l'Italia neutrale* (Naples, 1966).

Bibliography

VIGEZZI, B., *Da Giolitti a Salandra* (Florence, 1969).

VITALE, M., *L'Italia in Africa, serie storico-militare: Africa settentrionale 1911–43* (Rome, 1964).

VIVARELLI, R., *Il dopoguerra in Italia e l'avento del fascismo (1918–1922), I: Dalla fine della guerra all'impresa di Fiume* (Naples, 1967).

VOLPE, G., *Italia moderna, 1815–1914*, 3 vols (Florence, 1949–1952).

WANDYCZ, P., *France and her East European Allies, 1919–1925: French–Czechoslovak–Polish Relations from the Paris Peace Conference to Locarno* (Minneapolis, 1962).

WARNER, G., *Pierre Laval and the Eclipse of France* (London, 1968).

WHEELER-BENNETT, J., *Disarmament and Security Since Locarno, 1925–1931* (London, 1932).

WOODWARD, E. L., *British Foreign Policy in the Second World War*, vol. I (London, 1970).

ZAGHI, C., *P. S. Mancini, L'Africa e il problema del Mediterraneo 1884–5* (Rome, 1955).

ZAGHI, C. (ed.), *Crispi e Menelich* (Bari, 1956).

ZAMBONI, G., *Mussolinis Expansionspolitik auf dem Balkan* (Hamburg, 1970).

ZINCONI, V. (ed.), *Hitler: Mussolini, lettere e documenti* (Milan, 1946).

Periodicals

ALBRECHT-CARRIÉ, R., 'Fiume: nationalism versus economics', *JCEA* (1942).

ALBRECHT-CARRIÉ, R., 'Italian colonial problems in 1919', *Political Science Quarterly* (1943).

ALBRECHT-CARRIÉ, R., 'Italian colonial policy, 1914–1918', *JMH* (1946).

ALBRECHT-CARRIÉ, R., 'Italian foreign policy, 1914–1922', *JMH* (1948).

ANCHIERI, E., 'Dal patto d'acciaio al convegno di Salisburgo', *Il Politico* (1953).

ANCHIERI, E., 'L'affare di Corfu alla luce dei documenti diplomatici italiani', *Il Politico*, XX (1955), pp. 374–95.

BOSWORTH, R. J., 'Britain and Italy's acquisition of the Dodecanese, 1912–15', *HJ* (1970).

BOSWORTH, R. J., 'The British press, conservatives, and Mussolini', *JCH*, vol. V, no. 2 (1970).

BOSWORTH, R. J., 'Sir Rennell Rodd e l'Italia', *NRS* (1970).

CUNSOLO, S., 'Libya, Italian nationalism, and the revolt against Giolitti', *JMH* (1965).

DAMPIERRE, ROBERT DE, 'Dix années de politique française à Rome (1925–1935)', *La revue des deux mondes* (November–December 1953).

EDWARDS, P. G., 'The foreign office and fascism, 1924–29', *JCH* (1970).

Bibliography

GABRIELE, M., 'Origini della convenzione navale italo–austro–germanica del 1912', *RSR* (1965).

GALBRAITH, J. S., 'Italy, the British East Africa Company and the Benadir Coast, 1888–1893', *JMH* (1970).

GALLI, C., 'Yugoslava tragica 1928–1934', *NA* (1953).

JEDLICKA, L., 'The Austrian Heimwehr', *JCH* (1966).

LOWE, C. J., 'Anglo–Italian differences over East Africa, 1892–5', *EHR* (1966).

LOWE, C. J., 'Britain and Italian intervention, 1914–15', *HJ* (1969).

MAGISTRATI, M., 'Salisburgo 1939', *RSPI* (1949).

MANUEL, F. E., 'The Palestine question in Italian diplomacy, 1917–1920', *JMH* (1955).

MARZARI, F., 'Projects for an Italian-led Balkan bloc of neutrals, September–December 1939', *HJ*, XIII, no. 4 (1970), pp. 767–88.

PAVLOVIČ, K., '*La Yugoslavie et l'Italie entre les deux guerres; les conversations Marinkovitch-Grandi (1930–1931)*', *Revue d'histoire diplomatique* (July–September 1967), pp. 259–61.

RAUKI, G., 'Il patto triparto di Roma e la politica estera dell'Italia', *Studi Storia,* vol. 3, no. 2 (April–June 1962).

RIENZI, W. A., 'Italy's neutrality and entrance into the Great War: a re-examination,' *AHR* (1968).

RIENZI, W. A., 'Mussolini's sources of financial support, 1914–1915', *History* (June 1971), pp. 189–206.

ROBERTS, L. E., 'Italy and the Egyptian question, 1878–1882', *JMH* (1946).

ROCHAT, G., 'L'esercito italiano nell'estate 1914', *NRS* (1961).

ROSEN, E. R., 'Giovanni Giolitti und die italienische politik im ersten Weltkrieg', *HZ* (1962).

ROSEN, E. R., 'Italiens Kriegseintritt im Jahre 1915 als innenpolitisches Problem der Giolitti-Ara. Ein Beitrag zur Vorgeschichte des Faschismus', *HZ* (1959).

RUMI, S., 'Il fascismo delle origine', *Movimento di Liberazione Nazionale,* no. 75 (April 1964).

SANDERSON, G. N., 'England, Italy and the Nile balance 1890–91', *HJ* (1964).

SCHMITT, B. E., 'The Italian documents for July 1914', *JMH* (1965).

SERRA, E., 'Le questioni di Cassala e di Adua', *Storia e Politica* (1966).

SFORZA, C., 'Sonnino and his foreign policy', *Contemporary Review* (1929).

SIEBERT, F., 'Adua, eine Wende italienischer und europäischer Politik', *HZ* (1956).

SOLMI, A., 'Carteggio tra Salandra e Sonnino ... Agosto–Dicembre 1914', *NA* (1935).

TALAMO, G., 'Il mancato intervento in Egitto', *RSR* (1958).

TORREY, G., 'The Rumanian–Italian agreement of 23 September 1914', *SR* (1966).

TOSCANO, M., 'Le conversationi militari Italo-Tedesche alla vigilia della 2a guerra mondiale', *RSI* (1952), pp. 349–59.

TOSCANO, M., 'Rivelazioni e nuovi documenti sul negoziato di Londra', *NA*, vol. 494 (1965), pp. 20–9.

TOSCANO, M., 'Le origine diplomatiche dell'articolo 9 del Patto di Londra', *Storia e Politica,* vol. 3 (1965).

VALIANI, L., 'La dissoluzione dell'Austria–Ungheria', *RSI* (1961, 1962).

VALIANI, L., 'I documenti diplomatici italiani', *RSI* (1966).

VALIANI, L., 'Italian–Austro–Hungarian negotiations 1914–1915', *JCH* (1966).

VALIANI, L., 'Documenti francesi sull'Italia e il movimento jugoslavo', *RSI* (1968).

VIGEZZI, B., 'Le "Radiose giornate" del maggio 1915 nei rapporti dei Prefetti', *NRS* (1959, 1960).

VIGEZZI, B., 'Le "Rivelazioni" di Giolitti del 5 dicembre 1914, e i rapporti con Salandra', *NRS* (1961).

WATT, D. C., 'An earlier model for the Pact of Steel: the draft treaties exchanged between Germany and Italy during Hitler's visit to Rome in May 1938', *International Affairs* (1957).

WATT, D. F., 'The secret Laval-Mussolini agreement of 1935', *Middle East Journal* (1961).

ZAGHI, C., 'Il problema di Cassala', *NA* (1940).

Index

Index

Barzilai, Salvatore, republican politician, 76, 97, 115, 120, 122

Bertolè-Viale, General Ettore, Minister of War (1887–91), 56

Bismarck, Prince Otto von, 4, 7, 8, 23–5, 29–32, 41, 56–8

Bissolati, Leonida: editor of *Avanti!* (1896–1911), 97, 101, 103, 116, 123; minister in Boselli and Orlando governments (1917–18), 162

Blanc, Baron Alberto: Secretary-General, Foreign Ministry, 3, 420 n.30; Italian Ambassador in Constantinople (1887), 53, 376; Foreign Minister (1893–6), 62–3, 382–3

Bollati, Riccardo, diplomatist, 127, 131

Bosnia: revolts in (1875–6), 15; annexation of (1908–9), 105–11, 114

Briand, Aristide, 206, 215, 216

Bulgaria: and Italy, 40–4, 52, 165, 295, 297–8, 303, 354; and Germany, 303

Cadorna, General Luigi, Commander-in-Chief (1914–17), 135, 138, 140, 145, 158–9

Caetani, Duke of Sermoneta, Foreign Minister (March–July 1896), 69, 72–3

Cairoli, Benedetto, Premier (1878, 1879–81), 8, 11, 15–16, 19, 35

Canevaro, Admiral Felice Napoleone, Foreign Minister (1898–9), 76–9, 85–6

Cavalotti, Felice, radical politician, 11, 24, 49, 71, 89, 97

Cerrutti, Vittorio: Italian Ambassador in Berlin (1932), 234; Italian Ambassador in Paris (1934–6), 283–4

Chamberlain, Austen, British Foreign Secretary (1924–9), 202, 205, 207–8, 214

Chamberlain, Neville, British Prime Minister (1937–40), 308, 310, 311, 313, 318, 320, 329–30

Cialdini, General Enrico, Italian Ambassador in Paris (1870–81), 22–3

Ciano, Galeazzo, Count, Foreign Minister (1936–43), 293, 296–7, 302, 305–9, 310–12, 320–1, 322–5, 331–2, 333–8, 345–6, 349–50, 363–4, 367–70; and *Anschluss*, 299–300, 302, 303, 310; sees Britain as Italy's main enemy, 308; offends Ribbentrop irreparably, 309; and Albanian invasion, 327–31; and Hitler and Ribbentrop in Salzburg (August 1939), 337–9; is disgusted with Germany, 339–40; advises Mussolini to 'rip up' Pact of Steel, 342; and Nazi-Soviet Pact (1939), 340, 344; and 'neutralist bloc' (1940), 353–62

Contarini, Salvatore, Secretary-General of the Consulta (1922–6), 184, 209

Corfu Incident (1923), 194–8

Corradini, Enrico, intellectual and nationalist, 112–14, 116

Corridoni, Filippo, syndicalist leader, 141, 157

Corti, Count Luigi: Foreign Minister (1878), 19–21; Italian Ambassador in London (1886–7), 44–6

Crispi, Francesco: urges large armaments, 5, 7, 9, 417 n.25; and the Roman Question, 12; Minister of Interior (1878), urges German alliance, 17–19; President of the Council, Minister of the Interior and of Foreign Affairs (1887–91), attitude towards Risorgimento, 47; and France, 48–51; and irrendentism, 51–2; and the Ottoman Empire, 52–4; and colonial expansion, 9–10, 54–68, 416 n.8, 426 n.40; second administration of (1893–6), 61–8

Curzon, George N., British Foreign Secretary (1919–24), 187, 189–90, 191, 194, 197, 199

470

Index

E3